McGRAW-HILL'S
Interest Amortization Tables

McGRAW-HILL'S
Interest Amortization Tables

Third Edition

Jack C. Estes

Dennis R. Kelley

Charles Freedenberg

McGraw-Hill, Inc.

New York   Chicago   San Francisco   Lisbon

London   Madrid   Mexico City   Milan   New Delhi

San Juan   Seoul   Singapore   Sydney   Toronto

10 11 12 13 DOC/DOC 1 4 3

ISBN 0-07-146811-0

Printed and bound by RR Donnelley.

McGraw-Hill books are available at special quantity discounts to use as premiums and sales promotions, or for use in corporate training programs. For more information, please write to the Director of Special Sales, Professional Publishing, McGraw-Hill, Two Penn Plaza, New York, NY 10121-2298. Or contact your local bookstore.

 This book is printed on recycled, acid-free paper containing a minimum of 50% recycled, de-inked fiber.

Contents

Foreword

Anyone involved with mortgages, either once or on an on-going basis, will find this book invaluable—especially if they prefer their numbers on paper rather than on a screen.

For example, you can easily find the monthly payment on the mortgage you are contemplating. You can check on how much interest you need to pay at closing to cover the period from closing to the first day of the following month, when the contractual term of the loan begins. The way in which your loan will amortize if you make only the required payment is laid out, along with several options for making additional payments.

For example, you can determine how much interest you will save and how much sooner you will pay off the loan if you increase the payment by a specified percent. The same information is available if you shift to a biweekly payment program. There are also tables that show the breakdown of payments into principal and interest, and show cumulative payments of both since the loan began.

Charles Freedenberg has filled gaps in the previous edition, and brought the coverage abreast of the current market. Loan amounts now go to $900,000, from $250,000 in the previous edition, and interest rates now start at 3% rather than 5%.

Readers can be assured that the numbers in this book are correct. Charles programmed all the calculators that appear on my web site (www.mtgprofessor.com), and I can assure you that he is a diligent and careful craftsman of numbers.

Jack Guttentag

Preface

This power-packed guide fills the need for quick, reliable data on today's complex mortgage loans. It was the intent of the late Jack C. Estes to provide a stockpile of mortgage information in a convenient form for mortgage and appraisal professionals, home buyers, educators, and students. This third edition has been completely updated to cover a broader range of mortgage data, retaining the strengths of the perennially popular second edition.

Its tables provide mortgage payments on loans from $10 to $900,000, at interest rates from 3 percent to 18 percent. The tables also show the remaining balance on a loan at the end of any year, and how to figure the interest on loans. Differing loan types include standard 30-year loans, 15-year loans, adjustable rate mortgages (ARMs) and biweekly payment loans, and answer such questions as

- What is the payment on a $150,000 loan for 30 years at 6 percent interest?
- What are the payments on a biweekly loan? How much shorter will the loan term be?
- My loan has a balloon payment after seven years. How much will it be?
- If my ARM can rise up to 3 percent, what payments are needed to keep the same payoff schedule?
- If I make regular additional payments to principal, how much loan interest would I save and how much shorter would the loan term be?
- What is my loan balance after four years?

Practical examples are fully worked out for each use of the tables, to show you how to apply the tables to your specific case.

In the office, at closings, or in the classroom, *McGraw-Hill's Interest Amortization Tables*, 31e, will furnish the real estate mortgage information you need.

What the Tables Show

Mortgage loans in the United States run for a period of ten to thirty or forty years, and typically call for monthly payments with a fixed rate of interest. The payments are calculated to pay the interest for the preceding month, plus a small amount of principal that reduces the balance of the loan. These standard loans are covered in Tables 1, 2, and 7.

Table 1 gives the monthly payment on $1000 for a wider variety of interest rates and amortization periods.

Table 2 gives the remaining balance of a loan at the end of each year. Balloon payment loans, where a lump sum payment of the entire balance comes due, are also covered in Table 2.

The interest on a loan for any number of days is shown in Table 3.

Loans with fixed rates are standard in the U.S., but adjustable rate mortgages (ARMs) continue to grow in popularity. With an ARM, the interest rate moves up or down, usually once a year, according to an index. ARMs are covered in Table 4.

To build equity in real estate, nothing beats making extra principal payments. Regular additional payments slash interest and shorten the loan term. Structuring a savings plan with regular additional payments is shown in Table 5.

Biweekly payments suit the convenience of many households, and offer a built-in prepayment feature to save interest and shorten the loan term. Table 6 gives the payments and shows the savings in both interest and loan duration.

Table 7 contains a wealth of pre-calculated monthly payments on loan amounts from $10 to $900,000 at interest rates from 3 percent to 18 percent at ¼ percent intervals.

About the Author

Mr. Freedenberg was formerly an IRS attorney in the 1970's.

He was a commercial investment real estate broker from 1978–1996 and a senior intructor in the national CCIM (Certified Commercial Investment Member–www.ccim.com) instructor cadre for 16 years teaching financial mathematics and investment analysis.

Mr. Freedenberg is a co-author of the 4th edition of *Real Estate Investment & Taxation* published by Prentice Hall in 1990—a textbook on commercial real estate investing.

He has been programming financial applications for over 30 years. Since 1999, Mr. Freedenberg has been programming interactive applications for the Internet. He currently has 39 specialized mortgage calculators running on his website www.compareloans.com, that he developed in collaboration with Jack Guttentag, The Mortgage Professor (www.mtgprofessor.com) a nationally syndicated columnist and retired finance Professor Emeritus from The Wharton School of Business.

Mr. Freedenberg is currently retired, and lives in Newcastle, WA.

Table 1
Monthly Loan Factors on $1000

Table 1 contains amortization periods from 1 to 40 years, at interest rates from 3 percent to 18 percent.

Table 1 uses a divide and then multiply approach to arriving at monthly payment amounts.

Example 1.   Monthly Payment on a Loan

Bill will take back a purchase money mortgage of $537,500 for a term of 25 years at 6.25 percent.

To find the payment, enter Table 1 at the page for 25 years. On the 6.25 percent line under 25 years, read $6.5967. Divide the loan amount by 1000 and multiply by this payment per $1000 of loan to arrive at

$$\frac{\$537,500}{1000} \times \$6.5967 = \$3,545.73, \text{ the monthly}$$
payment for a loan with these terms.

Example 2.   Loan Balance Not Given in Table 2

Table 1 may also be used to find the mortgage loan balance on a loan. For the balance at the end of any year, divide the factor in Table 1 for the *original* term of the loan by the factor for the number of years remaining.

For a 6.5 percent loan that has 22 of 30 years remaining, this will be the original 30-year payment divided by the payment for a 22-year loan. Using a loan of $100,000 will give

$$\frac{\$6.3207}{7.1294} = .886568 \times \$100,000 = \$88,656.80,$$
the remaining balance on the loan.

This case could have been solved more quickly using Table 2. The terms were selected, though, to let you confirm that the method gives the same answer as

Table 2. The difference in this case is $0.37. Table 2 gives more accurate results by a few cents.

Example 3. The Annual Mortgage Constant

Real estate professionals prefer the annual mortgage constant to the actual monthly payment. Annual mortgage constants express the *rate* of mortgage payment as a percentage of the loan represented by one year's payments. Comparison of loan plans is simplified using the "constant."

Sara has offers for a mortgage loan, one at 6 percent for 20 years, another at 6.25 percent amortized over 25 years.

Enter Table 1 on the pages containing loan factors for 20 and 25 years. On the 6 percent line, take the factor under 20 years; it is 7.1643 per $1000. Multiply this by 1.2 to get 8.597160 percent, the annual mortgage constant on a 6 percent 20-year loan.

On the 6.25 percent line, take the factor under 25 years; it is 6.5967 per $1000. Multiply this also by 1.2, to get 7.916040 percent, the annual mortgage constant for a 6.25 percent, 25-year loan.

Even though the interest rate is higher, many people would prefer the loan with the lower annual constant, since it will have lower monthly payments.

Monthly Payment Factors

Payment per $1000

Amortization Period in Years

Interest Rate	1	2	3	4	5
3.00%	84.6937	42.9812	29.0812	22.1343	17.9687
3.25%	84.8076	43.0919	29.1915	22.2450	18.0800
3.50%	84.9216	43.2027	29.3021	22.3560	18.1917
3.75%	85.0357	43.3137	29.4129	22.4674	18.3039
4.00%	85.1499	43.4249	29.5240	22.5791	18.4165
4.25%	85.2642	43.5363	29.6353	22.6911	18.5296
4.50%	85.3785	43.6478	29.7469	22.8035	18.6430
4.75%	85.4930	43.7595	29.8588	22.9162	18.7569
5.00%	85.6075	43.8714	29.9709	23.0293	18.8712
5.25%	85.7221	43.9834	30.0833	23.1427	18.9860
5.50%	85.8368	44.0957	30.1959	23.2565	19.1012
5.75%	85.9516	44.2080	30.3088	23.3706	19.2168
6.00%	86.0664	44.3206	30.4219	23.4850	19.3328
6.25%	86.1814	44.4333	30.5353	23.5998	19.4493
6.50%	86.2964	44.5463	30.6490	23.7150	19.5661
6.75%	86.4115	44.6593	30.7629	23.8304	19.6835
7.00%	86.5267	44.7726	30.8771	23.9462	19.8012
7.25%	86.6420	44.8860	30.9915	24.0624	19.9194
7.50%	86.7574	44.9996	31.1062	24.1789	20.0379
7.75%	86.8729	45.1134	31.2212	24.2957	20.1570
8.00%	86.9884	45.2273	31.3364	24.4129	20.2764
8.25%	87.1041	45.3414	31.4518	24.5304	20.3963
8.50%	87.2198	45.4557	31.5675	24.6483	20.5165
8.75%	87.3356	45.5701	31.6835	24.7665	20.6372
9.00%	87.4515	45.6847	31.7997	24.8850	20.7584
9.25%	87.5675	45.7995	31.9162	25.0039	20.8799
9.50%	87.6835	45.9145	32.0329	25.1231	21.0019
9.75%	87.7997	46.0296	32.1499	25.2427	21.1242
10.00%	87.9159	46.1449	32.2672	25.3626	21.2470
10.25%	88.0322	46.2604	32.3847	25.4828	21.3703
10.50%	88.1486	46.3760	32.5024	25.6034	21.4939
10.75%	88.2651	46.4919	32.6205	25.7243	21.6180
11.00%	88.3817	46.6078	32.7387	25.8455	21.7424
11.25%	88.4983	46.7240	32.8572	25.9671	21.8673
11.50%	88.6151	46.8403	32.9760	26.0890	21.9926
11.75%	88.7319	46.9568	33.0950	26.2113	22.1183
12.00%	88.8408	47.0735	33.2143	26.3338	22.2444
12.25%	88.9658	47.1903	33.3338	26.4568	22.3710
12.50%	89.0829	47.3073	33.4536	26.5800	22.4979
12.75%	89.2000	47.4245	33.5737	26.7036	22.6253
13.00%	89.3173	47.5418	33.6940	26.8275	22.7531
13.25%	89.4346	47.6593	33.8145	26.9517	22.8813
13.50%	89.5520	47.7770	33.9353	27.0763	23.0098
13.75%	89.6695	47.8949	34.0563	27.2012	23.1388
14.00%	89.7871	48.0129	34.1776	27.3265	23.2683
14.25%	89.9048	48.1311	34.2992	27.4520	23.3981
14.50%	90.0225	48.2494	34.4210	27.5780	23.5283
14.75%	90.1404	48.3680	34.5430	27.7042	23.6589
15.00%	90.2583	48.4866	34.6653	27.8307	23.7899
15.25%	90.3763	48.6055	34.7879	27.9576	23.9214
15.50%	90.4944	48.7245	34.9107	28.0849	24.0532
15.75%	90.6126	48.8437	35.0337	28.2124	24.1854
16.00%	90.7309	48.9631	35.1570	28.3403	24.3181
16.25%	90.8492	49.0826	35.2806	28.4685	24.4511
16.50%	90.9676	49.2024	35.4044	28.5970	24.5845
16.75%	91.0862	49.3222	35.5284	28.7259	24.7184
17.00%	91.2048	49.4423	35.6527	28.8550	24.8526
17.25%	91.3234	49.5625	35.7773	28.9845	24.9872
17.50%	91.4422	49.6828	35.9021	29.1144	25.1222
17.75%	91.5611	49.8034	36.0271	29.2445	25.2576
18.00%	91.6800	49.9241	36.1524	29.3750	25.3934

Table 1   3

Monthly Payment Factors

Payment per $1000

Interest Rate	Amortization Period in Years				
	6	7	8	9	10
3.00%	15.1937	13.2133	11.7296	10.5769	9.6561
3.25%	15.3058	13.3263	11.8435	10.6918	9.7719
3.50%	15.4184	13.4399	11.9581	10.8074	9.8886
3.75%	15.5315	13.5540	12.0733	10.9238	10.0061
4.00%	15.6452	13.6688	12.1893	11.0410	10.1245
4.25%	15.7593	13.7842	12.3059	11.1589	10.2438
4.50%	15.8740	13.9002	12.4232	11.2776	10.3638
4.75%	15.9892	14.0167	12.5412	11.3971	10.4848
5.00%	16.1049	14.1339	12.6599	11.5173	10.6066
5.25%	16.2212	14.2517	12.7793	11.6383	10.7292
5.50%	16.3379	14.3700	12.8993	11.7600	10.8526
5.75%	16.4551	14.4890	13.0200	11.8825	10.9769
6.00%	16.5729	14.6086	13.1414	12.0057	11.1021
6.25%	16.6912	14.7287	13.2635	12.1298	11.2280
6.50%	16.8099	14.8494	13.3862	12.2545	11.3548
6.75%	16.9292	14.9708	13.5096	12.3800	11.4824
7.00%	17.0490	15.0927	13.6337	12.5063	11.6108
7.25%	17.1693	15.2152	13.7585	12.6333	11.7401
7.50%	17.2901	15.3383	13.8839	12.7610	11.8702
7.75%	17.4114	15.4620	14.0099	12.8895	12.0011
8.00%	17.5332	15.5862	14.1367	13.0187	12.1328
8.25%	17.6556	15.7111	14.2641	13.1487	12.2653
8.50%	17.7784	15.8365	14.3921	13.2794	12.3986
8.75%	17.9017	15.9625	14.5208	13.4108	12.5327
9.00%	18.0255	16.0891	14.6502	13.5429	12.6676
9.25%	18.1499	16.2162	14.7802	13.6758	12.8033
9.50%	18.2747	16.3440	14.9109	13.8094	12.9398
9.75%	18.4000	16.4723	15.0422	13.9437	13.0770
10.00%	18.5258	16.6012	15.1742	14.0787	13.2151
10.25%	18.6522	16.7306	15.3068	14.2144	13.3539
10.50%	18.7790	16.8607	15.4400	14.3509	13.4935
10.75%	18.9063	16.9913	15.5739	14.4880	13.6339
11.00%	19.0341	17.1224	15.7084	14.6259	13.7750
11.25%	19.1624	17.2542	15.8436	14.7644	13.9169
11.50%	19.2912	17.3865	15.9794	14.9037	14.0595
11.75%	19.4204	17.5193	16.1158	15.0436	14.2029
12.00%	19.5502	17.6527	16.2528	15.1842	14.3471
12.25%	19.6804	17.7867	16.3905	15.3256	14.4920
12.50%	19.8112	17.9212	16.5288	15.4676	14.6376
12.75%	19.9424	18.0563	16.6677	15.6102	14.7840
13.00%	20.0741	18.1920	16.8073	15.7536	14.9311
13.25%	20.2063	18.3282	16.9474	15.8976	15.0789
13.50%	20.3390	18.4649	17.0882	16.0423	15.2274
13.75%	20.4721	18.6022	17.2295	16.1877	15.3767
14.00%	20.6057	18.7400	17.3715	16.3337	15.5266
14.25%	20.7398	18.8784	17.5141	16.4804	15.6773
14.50%	20.8744	19.0173	17.6573	16.6277	15.8287
14.75%	21.0095	19.1568	17.8010	16.7757	15.9807
15.00%	21.1450	19.2968	17.9454	16.9243	16.1335
15.25%	21.2810	19.4373	18.0904	17.0736	16.2869
15.50%	21.4175	19.5783	18.2359	17.2235	16.4411
15.75%	21.5544	19.7199	18.3821	17.3741	16.5958
16.00%	21.6918	19.8621	18.5288	17.5253	16.7513
16.25%	21.8297	20.0047	18.6761	17.6771	16.9074
16.50%	21.9681	20.1479	18.8240	17.8295	17.0642
16.75%	22.1069	20.2916	18.9724	17.9825	17.2217
17.00%	22.2461	20.4358	19.1215	18.1362	17.3798
17.25%	22.3859	20.5805	19.2710	18.2905	17.5385
17.50%	22.5260	20.7258	19.4212	18.4453	17.6979
17.75%	22.6667	20.8716	19.5719	18.6008	17.8579
18.00%	22.8078	21.0178	19.7232	18.7569	18.0185

Monthly Payment Factors

Payment per $1000

Interest Rate	\multicolumn{5}{c}{Amortization Period in Years}
	11	12	13	14	15
3.00%	8.9038	8.2779	7.7492	7.2970	6.9058
3.25%	9.0206	8.3957	7.8680	7.4168	7.0267
3.50%	9.1383	8.5145	7.9880	7.5378	7.1488
3.75%	9.2570	8.6344	8.1090	7.6601	7.2722
4.00%	9.3767	8.7553	8.2312	7.7835	7.3969
4.25%	9.4972	8.8772	8.3544	7.9080	7.5228
4.50%	9.6187	9.0001	8.4787	8.0338	7.6499
4.75%	9.7411	9.1240	8.6041	8.1607	7.7783
5.00%	9.8645	9.2489	8.7306	8.2887	7.9079
5.25%	9.9888	9.3748	8.8582	8.4179	8.0388
5.50%	10.1139	9.5017	8.9868	8.5483	8.1708
5.75%	10.2400	9.6296	9.1165	8.6797	8.3041
6.00%	10.3670	9.7585	9.2472	8.8124	8.4386
6.25%	10.4949	9.8884	9.3790	8.9461	8.5742
6.50%	10.6238	10.0192	9.5119	9.0810	8.7111
6.75%	10.7535	10.1510	9.6458	9.2169	8.8491
7.00%	10.8841	10.2838	9.7807	9.3540	8.9883
7.25%	11.0156	10.4176	9.9167	9.4922	9.1286
7.50%	11.1480	10.5523	10.0537	9.6314	9.2701
7.75%	11.2813	10.6879	10.1917	9.7718	9.4128
8.00%	11.4154	10.8245	10.3307	9.9132	9.5565
8.25%	11.5505	10.9621	10.4708	10.0557	9.7014
8.50%	11.6864	11.1006	10.6118	10.1992	9.8474
8.75%	11.8232	11.2400	10.7538	10.3438	9.9945
9.00%	11.9608	11.3803	10.8968	10.4894	10.1427
9.25%	12.0993	11.5216	11.0408	10.6360	10.2919
9.50%	12.2386	11.6637	11.1857	10.7837	10.4422
9.75%	12.3788	11.8068	11.3316	10.9324	10.5936
10.00%	12.5199	11.9508	11.4785	11.0820	10.7461
10.25%	12.6618	12.0957	11.6263	11.2327	10.8995
10.50%	12.8045	12.2414	11.7750	11.3843	11.0540
10.75%	12.9480	12.3880	11.9247	11.5370	11.2095
11.00%	13.0923	12.5356	12.0753	11.6905	11.3660
11.25%	13.2375	12.6839	12.2268	11.8451	11.5234
11.50%	13.3835	12.8332	12.3792	12.0006	11.6819
11.75%	13.5303	12.9833	12.5325	12.1570	11.8413
12.00%	13.6779	13.1342	12.6867	12.3143	12.0017
12.25%	13.8263	13.2860	12.8417	12.4725	12.1630
12.50%	13.9754	13.4386	12.9977	12.6317	12.3252
12.75%	14.1254	13.5920	13.1545	12.7917	12.4884
13.00%	14.2761	13.7463	13.3121	12.9526	12.6524
13.25%	14.4276	13.9013	13.4706	13.1144	12.8174
13.50%	14.5799	14.0572	13.6299	13.2771	12.9832
13.75%	14.7329	14.2138	13.7901	13.4406	13.1499
14.00%	14.8867	14.3713	13.9510	13.6049	13.3174
14.25%	15.0412	14.5295	14.1128	13.7701	13.4858
14.50%	15.1964	14.6885	14.2754	13.9360	13.6550
14.75%	15.3524	14.8483	14.4387	14.1028	13.8250
15.00%	15.5091	15.0088	14.6029	14.2704	13.9959
15.25%	15.6666	15.1700	14.7678	14.4388	14.1675
15.50%	15.8247	15.3320	14.9335	14.6079	14.3399
15.75%	15.9836	15.4948	15.0999	14.7778	14.5131
16.00%	16.1432	15.6583	15.2670	14.9485	14.6870
16.25%	16.3034	15.8224	15.4349	15.1199	14.8617
16.50%	16.4644	15.9873	15.6036	15.2920	15.0371
16.75%	16.6260	16.1529	15.7729	15.4648	15.2132
17.00%	16.7883	16.3192	15.9430	15.6384	15.3900
17.25%	16.9513	16.4862	16.1137	15.8126	15.5676
17.50%	17.1149	16.6539	16.2851	15.9876	15.7458
17.75%	17.2792	16.8222	16.4572	16.1632	15.9247
18.00%	17.4442	16.9912	16.6300	16.3395	16.1042

Table 1   5

Monthly Payment Factors

Payment per $1000

Interest Rate	16	17	18	19	20
3.00%	6.5643	6.2637	5.9972	5.7594	5.5460
3.25%	6.6862	6.3867	6.1212	5.8844	5.6720
3.50%	6.8095	6.5110	6.2466	6.0109	5.7996
3.75%	6.9340	6.6368	6.3736	6.1390	5.9289
4.00%	7.0600	6.7639	6.5020	6.2687	6.0598
4.25%	7.1872	6.8925	6.6319	6.3999	6.1923
4.50%	7.3158	7.0225	6.7632	6.5327	6.3265
4.75%	7.4456	7.1538	6.8961	6.6670	6.4622
5.00%	7.5768	7.2866	7.0303	6.8028	6.5996
5.25%	7.7093	7.4206	7.1660	6.9401	6.7384
5.50%	7.8430	7.5561	7.3032	7.0789	6.8789
5.75%	7.9781	7.6929	7.4417	7.2191	7.0208
6.00%	8.1144	7.8310	7.5816	7.3608	7.1643
6.25%	8.2519	7.9705	7.7229	7.5040	7.3093
6.50%	8.3908	8.1112	7.8656	7.6486	7.4557
6.75%	8.5308	8.2533	8.0096	7.7945	7.6036
7.00%	8.6721	8.3966	8.1550	7.9419	7.7530
7.25%	8.8146	8.5412	8.3017	8.0907	7.9038
7.50%	8.9583	8.6871	8.4497	8.2408	8.0559
7.75%	9.1032	8.8342	8.5990	8.3922	8.2095
8.00%	9.2493	8.9826	8.7496	8.5450	8.3644
8.25%	9.3965	9.1321	8.9015	8.6991	8.5207
8.50%	9.5449	9.2829	9.0546	8.8545	8.6782
8.75%	9.6945	9.4349	9.2089	9.0111	8.8371
9.00%	9.8452	9.5880	9.3644	9.1690	8.9973
9.25%	9.9970	9.7423	9.5212	9.3281	9.1587
9.50%	10.1499	9.8978	9.6791	9.4884	9.3213
9.75%	10.3039	10.0544	9.8382	9.6499	9.4852
10.00%	10.4590	10.2121	9.9984	9.8126	9.6502
10.25%	10.6152	10.3709	10.1598	9.9764	9.8164
10.50%	10.7724	10.5308	10.3223	10.1414	9.9838
10.75%	10.9307	10.6918	10.4858	10.3075	10.1523
11.00%	11.0900	10.8538	10.6505	10.4746	10.3219
11.25%	11.2503	11.0169	10.8162	10.6429	10.4926
11.50%	11.4116	11.1810	10.9830	10.8122	10.6643
11.75%	11.5740	11.3461	11.1507	10.9825	10.8371
12.00%	11.7373	11.5122	11.3195	11.1539	11.0109
12.25%	11.9015	11.6792	11.4893	11.3262	11.1856
12.50%	12.0667	11.8473	11.6600	11.4995	11.3614
12.75%	12.2328	12.0162	11.8317	11.6738	11.5381
13.00%	12.3999	12.1861	12.0043	11.8490	11.7158
13.25%	12.5678	12.3570	12.1779	12.0251	11.8943
13.50%	12.7367	12.5287	12.3523	12.2021	12.0737
13.75%	12.9064	12.7013	12.5276	12.3800	12.2541
14.00%	13.0770	12.8748	12.7038	12.5588	12.4352
14.25%	13.2484	13.0491	12.8809	12.7384	12.6172
14.50%	13.4207	13.2242	13.0587	12.9188	12.8000
14.75%	13.5938	13.4002	13.2374	13.1000	12.9836
15.00%	13.7677	13.5770	13.4169	13.2820	13.1679
15.25%	13.9424	13.7546	13.5972	13.4647	13.3530
15.50%	14.1179	13.9329	13.7782	13.6483	13.5388
15.75%	14.2941	14.1120	13.9600	13.8325	13.7253
16.00%	14.4711	14.2919	14.1425	14.0175	13.9126
16.25%	14.6488	14.4725	14.3257	14.2031	14.1005
16.50%	14.8273	14.6538	14.5096	14.3894	14.2890
16.75%	15.0065	14.8358	14.6942	14.5764	14.4782
17.00%	15.1863	15.0184	14.8795	14.7641	14.6680
17.25%	15.3669	15.2018	15.0654	14.9524	14.8584
17.50%	15.5481	15.3858	15.2519	15.1412	15.0494
17.75%	15.7300	15.5704	15.4391	15.3307	15.2410
18.00%	15.9126	15.7557	15.6269	15.5208	15.4331

Monthly Payment Factors

Payment per $1000

Interest Rate	Amortization Period in Years				
	21	22	23	24	25
3.00%	5.3534	5.1790	5.0202	4.8751	4.7421
3.25%	5.4804	5.3070	5.1492	5.0051	4.8732
3.50%	5.6092	5.4368	5.2801	5.1371	5.0062
3.75%	5.7396	5.5684	5.4129	5.2711	5.1413
4.00%	5.8718	5.7018	5.5475	5.4069	5.2784
4.25%	6.0056	5.8370	5.6840	5.5446	5.4174
4.50%	6.1412	5.9739	5.8222	5.6842	5.5583
4.75%	6.2784	6.1125	5.9623	5.8257	5.7012
5.00%	6.4172	6.2528	6.1041	5.9690	5.8459
5.25%	6.5576	6.3948	6.2476	6.1140	5.9925
5.50%	6.6997	6.5385	6.3929	6.2609	6.1409
5.75%	6.8434	6.6838	6.5398	6.4095	6.2911
6.00%	6.9886	6.8307	6.6885	6.5598	6.4430
6.25%	7.1353	6.9793	6.8387	6.7118	6.5967
6.50%	7.2836	7.1294	6.9906	6.8654	6.7521
6.75%	7.4334	7.2811	7.1441	7.0207	6.9091
7.00%	7.5847	7.4342	7.2992	7.1776	7.0678
7.25%	7.7375	7.5889	7.4558	7.3361	7.2281
7.50%	7.8917	7.7451	7.6139	7.4960	7.3899
7.75%	8.0473	7.9027	7.7735	7.6576	7.5533
8.00%	8.2043	8.0618	7.9345	7.8205	7.7182
8.25%	8.3627	8.2222	8.0970	7.9850	7.8845
8.50%	8.5224	8.3841	8.2609	8.1508	8.0523
8.75%	8.6834	8.5472	8.4261	8.3181	8.2214
9.00%	8.8458	8.7117	8.5927	8.4866	8.3920
9.25%	9.0094	8.8775	8.7606	8.6566	8.5638
9.50%	9.1743	9.0446	8.9297	8.8277	8.7370
9.75%	9.3405	9.2129	9.1002	9.0002	8.9114
10.00%	9.5078	9.3825	9.2718	9.1739	9.0870
10.25%	9.6763	9.5532	9.4447	9.3488	9.2638
10.50%	9.8460	9.7251	9.6187	9.5248	9.4418
10.75%	10.0168	9.8981	9.7938	9.7020	9.6209
11.00%	10.1887	10.0722	9.9701	9.8803	9.8011
11.25%	10.3617	10.2475	10.1474	10.0596	9.9824
11.50%	10.5358	10.4237	10.3258	10.2400	10.1647
11.75%	10.7109	10.6011	10.5052	10.4214	10.3480
12.00%	10.8870	10.7794	10.6856	10.6038	10.5322
12.25%	11.0641	10.9587	10.8670	10.7872	10.7174
12.50%	11.2422	11.1390	11.0494	10.9714	10.9035
12.75%	11.4212	11.3202	11.2326	11.1566	11.0905
13.00%	11.6011	11.5023	11.4168	11.3427	11.2784
13.25%	11.7820	11.6853	11.6018	11.5296	11.4670
13.50%	11.9637	11.8691	11.7876	11.7173	11.6564
13.75%	12.1463	12.0538	11.9743	11.9058	11.8467
14.00%	12.3297	12.2393	12.1617	12.0950	12.0376
14.25%	12.5139	12.4256	12.3500	12.2851	12.2293
14.50%	12.6989	12.6126	12.5389	12.4758	12.4216
14.75%	12.8847	12.8004	12.7286	12.6672	12.6146
15.00%	13.0712	12.9890	12.9190	12.8593	12.8083
15.25%	13.2584	13.1782	13.1100	13.0520	13.0026
15.50%	13.4464	13.3681	13.3018	13.2454	13.1975
15.75%	13.6350	13.5587	13.4941	13.4394	13.3929
16.00%	13.8243	13.7499	13.6871	13.6339	13.5889
16.25%	14.0143	13.9417	13.8806	13.8290	13.7854
16.50%	14.2048	14.1342	14.0747	14.0247	13.9824
16.75%	14.3960	14.3272	14.2694	14.2208	14.1800
17.00%	14.5878	14.5208	14.4646	14.4175	14.3780
17.25%	14.7802	14.7149	14.6603	14.6147	14.5764
17.50%	14.9731	14.9095	14.8565	14.8123	14.7753
17.75%	15.1666	15.1047	15.0532	15.0104	14.9746
18.00%	15.3605	15.3004	15.2504	15.2089	15.1743

Table 1   7

Monthly Payment Factors

Payment per $1000

Rate	26	27	28	29	30
3.00%	4.6198	4.5070	4.4027	4.3059	4.2160
3.25%	4.7519	4.6401	4.5367	4.4410	4.3521
3.50%	4.8860	4.7753	4.6730	4.5783	4.4904
3.75%	5.0222	4.9126	4.8115	4.7179	4.6312
4.00%	5.1605	5.0521	4.9521	4.8597	4.7742
4.25%	5.3008	5.1936	5.0949	5.0038	4.9194
4.50%	5.4430	5.3372	5.2398	5.1499	5.0669
4.75%	5.5873	5.4828	5.3868	5.2982	5.2165
5.00%	5.7334	5.6304	5.5357	5.4486	5.3682
5.25%	5.8815	5.7799	5.6867	5.6010	5.5220
5.50%	6.0314	5.9314	5.8397	5.7554	5.6779
5.75%	6.1832	6.0847	5.9945	5.9118	5.8357
6.00%	6.3368	6.2399	6.1512	6.0700	5.9955
6.25%	6.4921	6.3968	6.3098	6.2302	6.1572
6.50%	6.6492	6.5555	6.4702	6.3921	6.3207
6.75%	6.8079	6.7160	6.6323	6.5558	6.4860
7.00%	6.9684	6.8781	6.7961	6.7213	6.6530
7.25%	7.1304	7.0419	6.9616	6.8884	6.8218
7.50%	7.2941	7.2073	7.1287	7.0572	6.9921
7.75%	7.4593	7.3743	7.2974	7.2276	7.1641
8.00%	7.6260	7.5428	7.4676	7.3995	7.3376
8.25%	7.7942	7.7128	7.6393	7.5729	7.5127
8.50%	7.9638	7.8842	7.8125	7.7477	7.6891
8.75%	8.1348	8.0570	7.9871	7.9240	7.8670
9.00%	8.3072	8.2313	8.1630	8.1016	8.0462
9.25%	8.4810	8.4068	8.3403	8.2805	8.2268
9.50%	8.6560	8.5836	8.5188	8.4607	8.4085
9.75%	8.8323	8.7617	8.6986	8.6421	8.5915
10.00%	9.0098	8.9410	8.8796	8.8248	8.7757
10.25%	9.1885	9.1214	9.0618	9.0085	8.9610
10.50%	9.3683	9.3030	9.2450	9.1934	9.1474
10.75%	9.5492	9.4857	9.4294	9.3793	9.3348
11.00%	9.7313	9.6695	9.6148	9.5663	9.5232
11.25%	9.9143	9.8543	9.8012	9.7542	9.7126
11.50%	10.0984	10.0401	9.9886	9.9431	9.9029
11.75%	10.2835	10.2268	10.1769	10.1329	10.0941
12.00%	10.4695	10.4145	10.3661	10.3236	10.2861
12.25%	10.6565	10.6030	10.5562	10.5151	10.4790
12.50%	10.8443	10.7925	10.7471	10.7074	10.6726
12.75%	11.0329	10.9827	10.9388	10.9005	10.8669
13.00%	11.2224	11.1738	11.1313	11.0943	11.0620
13.25%	11.4127	11.3656	11.3246	11.2888	11.2577
13.50%	11.6038	11.5581	11.5185	11.4841	11.4541
13.75%	11.7956	11.7514	11.7131	11.6799	11.6511
14.00%	11.9881	11.9453	11.9084	11.8764	11.8487
14.25%	12.1813	12.1399	12.1043	12.0735	12.0469
14.50%	12.3751	12.3351	12.3007	12.2711	12.2456
14.75%	12.5696	12.5310	12.4978	12.4693	12.4448
15.00%	12.7647	12.7274	12.6954	12.6680	12.6444
15.25%	12.9604	12.9243	12.8935	12.8672	12.8446
15.50%	13.1566	13.1218	13.0922	13.0668	13.0452
15.75%	13.3534	13.3198	13.2913	13.2669	13.2462
16.00%	13.5507	13.5183	13.4908	13.4674	13.4476
16.25%	13.7485	13.7173	13.6908	13.6684	13.6493
16.50%	13.9468	13.9167	13.8912	13.8697	13.8515
16.75%	14.1456	14.1165	14.0921	14.0714	14.0540
17.00%	14.3447	14.3168	14.2933	14.2734	14.2568
17.25%	14.5443	14.5174	14.4948	14.4758	14.4599
17.50%	14.7443	14.7184	14.6967	14.6785	14.6633
17.75%	14.9447	14.9198	14.8989	14.8815	14.8669
18.00%	15.1455	15.1215	15.1015	15.0848	15.0709

Monthly Payment Factors

Payment per $1000

Interest Rate	Amortization Period in Years				
	31	32	33	34	35
3.00%	4.1323	4.0542	3.9811	3.9127	3.8485
3.25%	4.2693	4.1922	4.1201	4.0526	3.9894
3.50%	4.4087	4.3326	4.2616	4.1951	4.1329
3.75%	4.5506	4.4755	4.4056	4.3402	4.2791
4.00%	4.6947	4.6208	4.5520	4.4878	4.4277
4.25%	4.8412	4.7685	4.7009	4.6378	4.5789
4.50%	4.9899	4.9185	4.8521	4.7902	4.7326
4.75%	5.1408	5.0707	5.0056	4.9450	4.8886
5.00%	5.2939	5.2251	5.1613	5.1020	5.0469
5.25%	5.4491	5.3817	5.3192	5.2613	5.2074
5.50%	5.6064	5.5404	5.4793	5.4227	5.3702
5.75%	5.7657	5.7011	5.6414	5.5862	5.5350
6.00%	5.9269	5.8638	5.8055	5.7517	5.7019
6.25%	6.0901	6.0284	5.9716	5.9192	5.8708
6.50%	6.2552	6.1950	6.1396	6.0886	6.0415
6.75%	6.4220	6.3633	6.3094	6.2598	6.2142
7.00%	6.5906	6.5334	6.4810	6.4328	6.3886
7.25%	6.7609	6.7052	6.6543	6.6075	6.5647
7.50%	6.9328	6.8787	6.8292	6.7839	6.7424
7.75%	7.1064	7.0538	7.0057	6.9619	6.9218
8.00%	7.2815	7.2304	7.1838	7.1414	7.1026
8.25%	7.4581	7.4085	7.3634	7.3223	7.2849
8.50%	7.6361	7.5880	7.5444	7.5047	7.4686
8.75%	7.8155	7.7689	7.7267	7.6884	7.6536
9.00%	7.9963	7.9512	7.9103	7.8734	7.8399
9.25%	8.1783	8.1347	8.0953	8.0596	8.0274
9.50%	8.3616	8.3194	8.2814	8.2471	8.2161
9.75%	8.5461	8.5053	8.4687	8.4356	8.4059
10.00%	8.7318	8.6924	8.6570	8.6253	8.5967
10.25%	8.9185	8.8805	8.8465	8.8159	8.7886
10.50%	9.1063	9.0697	9.0369	9.0076	8.9813
10.75%	9.2952	9.2598	9.2283	9.2002	9.1750
11.00%	9.4850	9.4509	9.4206	9.3936	9.3696
11.25%	9.6757	9.6429	9.6138	9.5880	9.5649
11.50%	9.8673	9.8358	9.8079	9.7831	9.7611
11.75%	10.0598	10.0295	10.0027	9.9790	9.9579
12.00%	10.2531	10.2240	10.1983	10.1756	10.1555
12.25%	10.4472	10.4192	10.3946	10.3729	10.3537
12.50%	10.6420	10.6152	10.5916	10.5708	10.5525
12.75%	10.8375	10.8118	10.7892	10.7694	10.7520
13.00%	11.0337	11.0090	10.9874	10.9685	10.9519
13.25%	11.2306	11.2069	11.1863	11.1682	11.1524
13.50%	11.4281	11.4054	11.3856	11.3684	11.3534
13.75%	11.6261	11.6044	11.5855	11.5691	11.5549
14.00%	11.8247	11.8040	11.7859	11.7703	11.7567
14.25%	12.0239	12.0040	11.9868	11.9719	11.9590
14.50%	12.2235	12.2045	12.1881	12.1739	12.1617
14.75%	12.4237	12.4055	12.3898	12.3764	12.3647
15.00%	12.6242	12.6069	12.5920	12.5792	12.5681
15.25%	12.8252	12.8087	12.7945	12.7823	12.7718
15.50%	13.0267	13.0109	12.9973	12.9858	12.9758
15.75%	13.2285	13.2134	13.2005	13.1895	13.1801
16.00%	13.4307	13.4163	13.4040	13.3936	13.3847
16.25%	13.6332	13.6195	13.6078	13.5979	13.5895
16.50%	13.8360	13.8230	13.8119	13.8025	13.7945
16.75%	14.0392	14.0268	14.0162	14.0073	13.9998
17.00%	14.2427	14.2308	14.2208	14.2124	14.2053
17.25%	14.4464	14.4351	14.4256	14.4176	14.4109
17.50%	14.6504	14.6397	14.6307	14.6231	14.6168
17.75%	14.8547	14.8445	14.8359	14.8288	14.8228
18.00%	15.0592	15.0495	15.0414	15.0346	15.0289

Table 1   9

Monthly Payment Factors

Payment per $1000

Interest Rate	36	37	38	39	40
			Amortization Period in Years		
3.00%	3.7882	3.7314	3.6780	3.6275	3.5798
3.25%	3.9300	3.8742	3.8217	3.7721	3.7254
3.50%	4.0746	4.0197	3.9682	3.9197	3.8739
3.75%	4.2218	4.1680	4.1175	4.0700	4.0253
4.00%	4.3716	4.3189	4.2695	4.2231	4.1794
4.25%	4.5239	4.4724	4.4241	4.3788	4.3362
4.50%	4.6787	4.6284	4.5812	4.5371	4.4956
4.75%	4.8359	4.7868	4.7409	4.6979	4.6576
5.00%	4.9955	4.9476	4.9029	4.8611	4.8220
5.25%	5.1573	5.1107	5.0672	5.0266	4.9887
5.50%	5.3214	5.2760	5.2338	5.1944	5.1577
5.75%	5.4875	5.4435	5.4025	5.3644	5.3289
6.00%	5.6558	5.6130	5.5733	5.5364	5.5021
6.25%	5.8260	5.7845	5.7461	5.7105	5.6774
6.50%	5.9981	5.9580	5.9208	5.8864	5.8546
6.75%	6.1721	6.1333	6.0974	6.0642	6.0336
7.00%	6.3478	6.3103	6.2757	6.2438	6.2143
7.25%	6.5253	6.4891	6.4557	6.4250	6.3967
7.50%	6.7044	6.6694	6.6374	6.6079	6.5807
7.75%	6.8850	6.8514	6.8205	6.7922	6.7662
8.00%	7.0672	7.0348	7.0052	6.9780	6.9531
8.25%	7.2508	7.2196	7.1912	7.1652	7.1414
8.50%	7.4358	7.4058	7.3786	7.3537	7.3309
8.75%	7.6220	7.5933	7.5672	7.5434	7.5217
9.00%	7.8096	7.7820	7.7570	7.7343	7.7136
9.25%	7.9983	7.9719	7.9480	7.9263	7.9066
9.50%	8.1882	8.1629	8.1400	8.1193	8.1006
9.75%	8.3791	8.3549	8.3331	8.3134	8.2956
10.00%	8.5710	8.5479	8.5271	8.5084	8.4915
10.25%	8.7640	8.7419	8.7221	8.7042	8.6882
10.50%	8.9578	8.9368	8.9179	8.9009	8.8857
10.75%	9.1526	9.1325	9.1145	9.0984	9.0840
11.00%	9.3481	9.3290	9.3119	9.2966	9.2829
11.25%	9.5445	9.5262	9.5100	9.4955	9.4826
11.50%	9.7415	9.7242	9.7087	9.6950	9.6828
11.75%	9.9393	9.9228	9.9082	9.8952	9.8836
12.00%	10.1378	10.1221	10.1082	10.0959	10.0850
12.25%	10.3368	10.3219	10.3088	10.2971	10.2869
12.50%	10.5365	10.5223	10.5099	10.4989	10.4892
12.75%	10.7367	10.7233	10.7115	10.7011	10.6920
13.00%	10.9374	10.9247	10.9135	10.9037	10.8951
13.25%	11.1386	11.1266	11.1160	11.1068	11.0987
13.50%	11.3403	11.3289	11.3189	11.3102	11.3026
13.75%	11.5424	11.5316	11.5222	11.5140	11.5069
14.00%	11.7450	11.7347	11.7258	11.7181	11.7114
14.25%	11.9479	11.9382	11.9298	11.9225	11.9162
14.50%	12.1511	12.1420	12.1341	12.1272	12.1213
14.75%	12.3547	12.3461	12.3386	12.3322	12.3267
15.00%	12.5587	12.5505	12.5435	12.5374	12.5322
15.25%	12.7629	12.7552	12.7486	12.7429	12.7380
15.50%	12.9674	12.9601	12.9539	12.9486	12.9440
15.75%	13.1721	13.1653	13.1594	13.1544	13.1502
16.00%	13.3771	13.3707	13.3652	13.3605	13.3565
16.25%	13.5823	13.5763	13.5711	13.5667	13.5630
16.50%	13.7878	13.7821	13.7772	13.7731	13.7696
16.75%	13.9934	13.9880	13.9835	13.9796	13.9764
17.00%	14.1993	14.1942	14.1899	14.1863	14.1832
17.25%	14.4053	14.4005	14.3965	14.3931	14.3902
17.50%	14.6114	14.6069	14.6032	14.6000	14.5973
17.75%	14.8177	14.8135	14.8100	14.8070	14.8045
18.00%	15.0242	15.0202	15.0169	15.0141	15.0118

Table 2
Remaining Loan Balance

Table 2 shows the remaining balance on a loan at the end of each year, and allows you to figure the interest or principal paid during each year. Balloon payments of the balance remaining are given as well.

Example 4.   Remaining Balance on a Loan

Betty's loan, taken out four years ago, had an original amount of $225,000 and a loan term of 30 years and bears interest at 5 percent. She is considering refinancing at a lower interest rate and wishes to know the current balance.

Enter Table 2 in the section marked 30 years. On the line for 5 percent under 4 years, read the percent remaining; it is 93.6296, the percentage balance on the loan. Multiply the original loan amount by the percentage balance to get

$$\$225,000 \times 93.6296 = \$210,666.60,$$
the balance on the loan after four years.

Example 5.   Amount of a Balloon Payment

Steve has a proposal for a loan at 6.5 percent interest. The amortization period of the loan will be 25 years, but there will be a balloon payment at the end of 7 years.

A balloon payment is the same as the balance due. Enter Table 2 in the section marked 25 years. On the line for 6.5 percent, read the figure under percent remaining for 7 years. The answer, 85.8426 is the percentage of the original loan that will be due as a balloon payment after 7 years.

Example 6.   Interest or Principal Paid in a Year

The Cabots are considering the effect of income tax deductions for interest on their home mortgage loan. The loan they plan is for $350,000, calls for 30-year amortization and a rate of 6.5 percent. From Table 7 they find that the payments will be $2,212.24 per month, or $26,546.88 per year. They want to calculate the principal and interest for the first year.

Principal: Enter Table 2 at the section for 30 years. On the line for 6.5 percent, read under year 1 the percentage, 98.8823. Multiply the original loan amount by this percentage to get

$350,000 × 98.8823 = $346,088.05,
the remaining balance after 1 year.

Subtracting this amount from $350,000 give $3,911.95 principal paid in the first year.

Interest: Subtract the principal paid from the payments in one year to get

$26,546.88 − $3,911.95 = $22,634.93,
the interest paid in the first year.

The procedure for the second and succeeding years is similar: Subtract the percent remaining at the end of the year in question from the percent remaining the previous year. Multiply that percentage by the original loan amount to get the principal paid for that year. Subtract the principal paid from the total payments for the year to get the interest paid.

Example 7.   Principal, Interest since Loan Began

Charles took out a 7 percent loan on a 15 year amortization schedule nine years ago in the original amount of $125,000. He is making payments of $1,123.54 per month.

Principal: To find the principal pay down, enter Table 2 at the section for 15-year amortization. On the line for 7 percent, find the percent remaining under 9 years; it is 52.7200 percent. Subtract this from 100 percent and multiply it by the original loan amount to get

$$\$125,000 \times 0.472800 = \$59,100.00,$$
the principal paid off over 9 years.

Interest: Take the total loan payments made and subtract the total principal paid. Since Charles has made 108 payments of $1,123.54, his total payments have been

$$\$1,123.54 \times 108 = \$121,342.32$$

Subtracting the $59,100.00 of principal payments gives $62,242.32 total interest paid from the start of the loan through the end of the ninth year.

Table 2   13

10 Years

Remaining Loan Balance

Percent remaining at end of year

Interest Rate	1	2	3	4	5
3.00%	91.2936	82.3224	73.0784	63.5531	53.7382
3.25%	91.3962	82.5086	73.3277	63.8440	54.0475
3.50%	91.4982	82.6939	73.5766	64.1349	54.3575
3.75%	91.5991	82.8778	73.8237	64.4242	54.6661
4.00%	91.6994	83.0606	74.0699	64.7128	54.9746
4.25%	91.7989	83.2424	74.3151	65.0009	55.2830
4.50%	91.8976	83.4229	74.5589	65.2877	55.5906
4.75%	91.9955	83.6023	74.8017	65.5739	55.8980
5.00%	92.0925	83.7804	75.0431	65.8588	56.2045
5.25%	92.1888	83.9575	75.2834	66.1429	56.5108
5.50%	92.2842	84.1331	75.5223	66.4258	56.8161
5.75%	92.3788	84.3077	75.7601	66.7078	57.1210
6.00%	92.4727	84.4812	75.9967	66.9890	57.4256
6.25%	92.5657	84.6532	76.2318	67.2687	57.7291
6.50%	92.6581	84.8244	76.4662	67.5481	58.0329
6.75%	92.7494	84.9940	76.6986	67.8255	58.3347
7.00%	92.8401	85.1626	76.9301	68.1025	58.6367
7.25%	92.9299	85.3298	77.1601	68.3779	58.9375
7.50%	93.0190	85.4961	77.3892	68.6528	59.2383
7.75%	93.1073	85.6609	77.6166	68.9262	59.5378
8.00%	93.1947	85.8246	77.8427	69.1984	59.8366
8.25%	93.2814	85.9870	78.0675	69.4695	60.1346
8.50%	93.3672	86.1482	78.2910	69.7394	60.4319
8.75%	93.4523	86.3081	78.5132	70.0081	60.7283
9.00%	93.5366	86.4668	78.7339	70.2756	61.0238
9.25%	93.6201	86.6243	78.9533	70.5418	61.3184
9.50%	93.7027	86.7805	79.1712	70.8067	61.6121
9.75%	93.7846	86.9354	79.3877	71.0703	61.9047
10.00%	93.8658	87.0892	79.6031	71.3330	62.1970
10.25%	93.9460	87.2415	79.8166	71.5938	62.4875
10.50%	94.0257	87.3930	80.0294	71.8543	62.7783
10.75%	94.1045	87.5430	80.2403	72.1127	63.0671
11.00%	94.1824	87.6915	80.4496	72.3696	63.3546
11.25%	94.2597	87.8393	80.6581	72.6261	63.6424
11.50%	94.3361	87.9854	80.8647	72.8804	63.9281
11.75%	94.4118	88.1305	81.0700	73.1337	64.2131
12.00%	94.4868	88.2744	81.2741	73.3859	64.4974
12.25%	94.5609	88.4169	81.4764	73.6364	64.7802
12.50%	94.6342	88.5580	81.6771	73.8851	65.0613
12.75%	94.7070	88.6982	81.8769	74.1333	65.3425
13.00%	94.7788	88.8370	82.0750	74.3796	65.6220
13.25%	94.8500	88.9746	82.2717	74.6247	65.9006
13.50%	94.9203	89.1108	82.4666	74.8678	66.1773
13.75%	94.9900	89.2460	82.6606	75.1103	66.4538
14.00%	95.0589	89.3798	82.8527	75.3507	66.7284
14.25%	95.1270	89.5124	83.0433	75.5897	67.0018
14.50%	95.1945	89.6440	83.2329	75.8280	67.2749
14.75%	95.2612	89.7741	83.4206	76.0640	67.5459
15.00%	95.3272	89.9032	83.6073	76.2993	67.8165
15.25%	95.3924	90.0308	83.7919	76.5323	68.0847
15.50%	95.4569	90.1574	83.9755	76.7643	68.3525
15.75%	95.5207	90.2827	84.1575	76.9947	68.6187
16.00%	95.5838	90.4067	84.3378	77.2234	68.8835
16.25%	95.6462	90.5297	64.5170	77.4511	69.1475
16.50%	95.7078	90.6514	84.6946	77.6770	69.4098
16.75%	95.7689	90.7720	84.8709	77.9017	69.6714
17.00%	95.8292	90.8913	85.0455	78.1247	69.9311
17.25%	95.8887	91.0093	85.2184	78.3457	70.1890
17.50%	95.9477	91.1265	85.3905	78.5661	70.4469
17.75%	96.0059	91.2423	85.5608	78.7846	70.7028
18.00%	96.0634	91.3567	85.7293	79.0010	70.9566

Remaining Loan Balance   **10 Years**

Interest Rate	Percent remaining at end of year			
	6	7	8	9
3.00%	43.6247	33.2036	22.4655	11.4009
3.25%	43.9278	33.4742	22.6758	11.5212
3.50%	44.2323	33.7469	22.8887	11.6442
3.75%	44.5357	34.0188	23.1007	11.7660
4.00%	44.8396	34.2917	23.3140	11.8891
4.25%	45.1440	34.5656	23.5287	12.0135
4.50%	45.4480	34.8395	23.7436	12.1379
4.75%	45.7524	35.1143	23.9597	12.2636
5.00%	46.0564	35.3890	24.1759	12.3891
5.25%	46.3606	35.6646	24.3933	12.5158
5.50%	46.6644	35.9400	24.6107	12.6423
5.75%	46.9683	36.2162	24.8292	12.7700
6.00%	47.2725	36.4930	25.0488	12.8987
6.25%	47.5759	36.7696	25.2682	13.0270
6.50%	47.8803	37.0478	25.4899	13.1579
6.75%	48.1830	37.3245	25.7100	13.2867
7.00%	48.4867	37.6029	25.9323	13.4180
7.25%	48.7894	37.8806	26.1541	13.5487
7.50%	49.0929	38.1599	26.3781	13.6817
7.75%	49.3954	38.4385	26.6015	13.8139
8.00%	49.6977	38.7174	26.8256	13.9469
8.25%	49.9998	38.9966	27.0504	14.0806
8.50%	50.3016	39.2760	27.2757	14.2148
8.75%	50.6031	39.5555	27.5016	14.3496
9.00%	50.9042	39.8352	27.7279	14.4849
9.25%	51.2048	40.1149	27.9546	14.6206
9.50%	51.5049	40.3946	28.1817	14.7566
9.75%	51.8045	40.6742	28.4089	14.8929
10.00%	52.1043	40.9548	28.6378	15.0310
10.25%	52.4026	41.2340	28.8653	15.1676
10.50%	52.7020	41.5153	29.0958	15.3077
10.75%	52.9997	41.7951	29.3248	15.4459
11.00%	53.2964	42.0743	29.5536	15.5840
11.25%	53.5943	42.3556	29.7852	15.7255
11.50%	53.8901	42.6350	30.0150	15.8648
11.75%	54.1859	42.9149	30.2460	16.0056
12.00%	54.4815	43.1955	30.4780	16.1477
12.25%	54.7760	43.4751	30.7095	16.2891
12.50%	55.0692	43.7538	30.9402	16.4298
12.75%	55.3631	44.0342	31.1734	16.5736
13.00%	55.6556	44.3135	31.4058	16.7164
13.25%	55.9476	44.5929	31.6388	16.8601
13.50%	56.2381	44.8710	31.8707	17.0025
13.75%	56.5291	45.1505	32.1047	17.1478
14.00%	56.8184	45.4285	32.3375	17.2915
14.25%	57.1070	45.7063	32.5705	17.4358
14.50%	57.3959	45.9853	32.8056	17.5826
14.75%	57.6828	46.2625	33.0389	17.7274
15.00%	57.9700	46.5407	33.2740	17.8747
15.25%	58.2550	46.8169	33.5072	18.0197
15.50%	58.5401	47.0939	33.7420	18.1670
15.75%	58.8240	47.3703	33.9764	18.3139
16.00%	59.1067	47.6458	34.2104	18.4605
16.25%	59.3893	47.9219	34.4457	18.6090
16.50%	59.6705	48.1970	34.6804	18.7569
16.75%	59.9515	48.4725	34.9161	18.9063
17.00%	60.2309	48.7468	35.1509	19.0549
17.25%	60.5086	49.0198	35.3846	19.2023
17.50%	60.7871	49.2945	35.6212	19.3535
17.75%	61.0638	49.5676	35.8564	19.5034
18.00%	61.3386	49.8391	36.0901	19.6516

Table 2   15

15 Years   **Remaining Loan Balance**

Interest
Percent remaining at end of year

Rate	1	2	3	4	5
3.00%	94.6396	89.1162	83.4248	77.5602	71.5173
3.25%	94.7401	89.3066	83.6939	77.8961	71.9070
3.50%	94.8391	89.4945	83.9600	78.2285	72.2932
3.75%	94.9368	89.6804	84.2235	78.5585	72.6772
4.00%	95.0333	89.8643	84.4847	78.8859	73.0590
4.25%	95.1285	90.0458	84.7429	79.2102	73.4377
4.50%	95.2223	90.2250	84.9982	79.5313	73.8132
4.75%	95.3148	90.4021	85.2510	79.8497	74.1863
5.00%	95.4061	90.5771	85.5011	80.1654	74.5567
5.25%	95.4961	90.7500	85.7486	80.4782	74.9243
5.50%	95.5847	90.9204	85.9929	80.7876	75.2885
5.75%	95.6721	91.0886	86.2346	81.0940	75.6499
6.00%	95.7583	91.2550	86.4739	81.3979	76.0089
6.25%	95.8431	91.4188	86.7100	81.6982	76.3641
6.50%	95.9268	91.5807	86.9436	81.9959	76.7169
6.75%	96.0091	91.7403	87.1744	82.2904	77.0665
7.00%	96.0902	91.8977	87.4022	82.5817	77.4127
7.25%	96.1700	92.0528	87.6271	82.8695	77.7554
7.50%	96.2485	92.2059	87.8493	83.1546	78.0954
7.75%	96.3260	92.3568	88.0689	83.4367	78.4324
8.00%	96.4021	92.5055	88.2855	83.7153	78.7657
8.25%	96.4770	92.6520	88.4993	83.9908	79.0959
8.50%	96.5508	92.7967	88.7108	84.2638	79.4236
8.75%	96.6233	92.9390	88.9191	84.5330	79.7473
9.00%	96.6946	93.0792	89.1246	84.7990	80.0677
9.25%	96.7647	93.2172	89.3272	85.0617	80.3845
9.50%	96.8337	93.3532	89.5273	85.3216	80.6985
9.75%	96.9015	93.4871	89.7244	85.5781	81.0089
10.00%	96.9682	93.6190	89.9190	85.8316	81.3162
10.25%	97.0337	93.7486	90.1106	86.0816	81.6197
10.50%	97.0982	93.8766	90.2999	86.3292	81.9208
10.75%	97.1614	94.0023	90.4862	86.5730	82.2177
11.00%	97.2236	94.1259	90.6697	86.8136	82.5113
11.25%	97.2846	94.2475	90.8505	87.0511	82.8014
11.50%	97.3447	94.3673	91.0290	87.2858	83.0887
11.75%	97.4034	94.4848	91.2041	87.5165	83.3715
12.00%	97.4613	94.6007	91.3773	87.7451	83.6522
12.25%	97.5181	94.7145	91.5476	87.9701	83.9289
12.50%	97.5738	94.8262	91.7149	88.1916	84.2017
12.75%	97.6285	94.9363	91.8801	88.4107	84.4721
13.00%	97.6821	95.0443	92.0424	88.6261	84.7382
13.25%	97.7348	95.1506	92.2024	88.8389	85.0017
13.50%	97.7865	95.2550	92.3598	89.0486	85.2617
13.75%	97.8372	95.3575	92.5145	89.2551	85.5180
14.00%	97.8868	95.4580	92.6665	89.4582	85.7706
14.25%	97.9357	95.5572	92.8167	89.6591	86.0211
14.50%	97.9833	95.6540	92.9636	89.8560	86.2667
14.75%	98.0302	95.7495	93.1086	90.0507	86.5101
15.00%	98.0762	95.8432	93.2512	90.2425	86.7501
15.25%	98.1213	95.9351	93.3913	90.4313	86.9869
15.50%	98.1653	96.0251	93.5285	90.6163	87.2192
15.75%	98.2086	96.1138	93.6642	90.7996	87.4498
16.00%	98.2509	96.2005	93.7968	90.9791	87.6759
16.25%	98.2925	96.2859	93.9278	91.1566	87.9001
16.50%	98.3332	96.3695	94.0562	91.3309	88.1204
16.75%	98.3729	96.4513	94.1819	91.5019	88.3368
17.00%	98.4119	96.5318	94.3059	91.6707	88.5510
17.25%	98.4501	96.6107	94.4277	91.8368	88.7620
17.50%	98.4875	96.6881	94.5472	92.0001	88.9697
17.75%	98.5241	96.7638	94.6644	92.1605	89.1741
18.00%	98.5599	96.8380	94.7793	92.3179	89.3750

Remaining Loan Balance   **15 Years**

Percent remaining at end of year

Interest Rate	6	7	8	9	10
3.00%	65.2906	58.8745	52.2632	45.4509	38.4313
3.25%	65.7203	59.3295	52.7279	45.9086	38.8642
3.50%	66.1468	59.7818	53.1904	46.3646	39.2960
3.75%	66.5716	60.2331	53.6528	46.8214	39.7293
4.00%	66.9947	60.6833	54.1148	47.2787	40.1641
4.25%	67.4150	61.1313	54.5753	47.7352	40.5986
4.50%	67.8325	61.5770	55.0341	48.1906	41.0328
4.75%	68.2478	62.0211	55.4921	48.6462	41.4678
5.00%	68.6610	62.4637	55.9493	49.1017	41.9037
5.25%	69.0718	62.9045	56.4056	49.5571	42.3402
5.50%	69.4793	63.3425	56.8594	50.0107	42.7756
5.75%	69.8843	63.7704	57.3119	50.4637	43.2112
6.00%	70.2875	64.2131	57.7642	50.9175	43.6484
6.25%	70.6869	64.6446	58.2135	51.3689	44.0839
6.50%	71.0844	65.0746	58.6623	51.8206	44.5207
6.75%	71.4788	65.5020	59.1091	52.2711	44.9569
7.00%	71.8700	65.9267	59.5537	52.7200	45.3923
7.25%	72.2580	66.3484	59.9959	53.1672	45.8267
7.50%	72.6434	66.7682	60.4368	53.6140	46.2615
7.75%	73.0262	67.1858	60.8763	54.0602	46.6965
8.00%	73.4053	67.6000	61.3129	54.5039	47.1298
8.25%	73.7815	68.0118	61.7476	54.9466	47.5629
8.50%	74.1556	68.4220	62.1816	55.3898	47.9973
8.75%	74.5257	68.8284	62.6121	55.8296	48.4291
9.00%	74.8925	69.2319	63.0402	56.2677	48.8600
9.25%	75.2559	69.6322	63.4657	56.7039	49.2895
9.50%	75.6166	70.0304	63.8897	57.1396	49.7195
9.75%	75.9738	70.4252	64.3107	57.5727	50.1477
10.00%	76.3280	70.8175	64.7299	58.0049	50.5757
10.25%	76.6783	71.2060	65.1456	58.4341	51.0013
10.50%	77.0266	71.5930	65.5606	58.8635	51.4283
10.75%	77.3705	71.9758	65.9717	59.2894	51.8522
11.00%	77.7111	72.3555	66.3801	59.7132	52.2749
11.25%	78.0482	72.7319	66.7856	60.1348	52.6960
11.50%	78.3827	73.1061	67.1896	60.5557	53.1173
11.75%	78.7124	73.4753	67.5887	60.9718	53.5343
12.00%	79.0402	73.8433	67.9874	61.3887	53.9532
12.25%	79.3640	74.2073	68.3822	61.8022	54.3692
12.50%	79.6835	74.5671	68.7731	62.2119	54.7819
12.75%	80.0009	74.9251	89.1629	62.6216	55.1958
13.00%	80.3137	75.2785	69.5482	63.0270	55.6056
13.25%	80.6241	75.6298	69.9321	63.4318	56.0160
13.50%	80.9307	75.9775	70.3126	63.8338	56.4241
13.75%	81.2335	76.3213	70.6895	64.2325	56.8296
14.00%	81.5324	76.6612	71.0626	64.6278	57.2320
14.25%	81.8293	76.9997	71.4350	65.0235	57.6363
14.50%	82.1209	77.3324	71.8014	65.4130	58.0341
14.75%	82.4104	77.6633	72.1668	65.8024	58.4331
15.00%	82.6964	77.9910	72.5291	66.1893	58.8303
15.25%	82.9789	78.3151	72.8882	66.5733	59.2252
15.50%	83.2565	78.6340	73.2419	66.9519	59.6147
15.75%	83.5327	78.9520	73.5955	67.3317	60.0069
16.00%	83.8037	79.2645	73.9432	67.7053	60.3928
16.25%	84.0731	79.5757	74.2905	68.0796	60.7807
16.50%	84.3382	79.8824	74.6333	68.4494	61.1644
16.75%	84.5989	80.1845	74.9712	68.8145	61.5435
17.00%	84.8575	80.4848	75.3081	69.1793	61.9236
17.25%	85.1127	80.7817	75.6416	69.5412	62.3013
17.50%	85.3644	81.0749	75.9716	69.8999	62.6762
17.75%	85.6123	81.3643	76.2977	70.2549	63.0470
18.00%	85.8564	81.6496	76.6197	70.6060	63.4158

Table 2   17

15 Years   Remaining Loan Balance

Interest Rate	Percent remaining at end of year			
	11	12	13	14
3.00%	31.1983	23.7452	16.0655	8.1521
3.25%	31.5875	24.0708	16.3061	8.2852
3.50%	31.9760	24.3957	16.5457	8.4165
3.75%	32.3667	24.7232	16.7881	8.5503
4.00%	32.7596	25.0534	17.0333	8.6864
4.25%	33.1528	25.3842	17.2790	8.8225
4.50%	33.5461	25.7154	17.5251	8.9585
4.75%	33.9410	26.0488	17.7734	9.0963
5.00%	34.3375	26.3841	18.0239	9.2359
5.25%	34.7353	26.7213	18.2763	9.3772
5.50%	35.1324	27.0581	18.5283	9.5174
5.75%	35.5305	27.3963	18.7818	9.6588
6.00%	35.9311	27.7378	19.0391	9.8039
6.25%	36.3304	28.0782	19.2951	9.9471
6.50%	36.7319	28.4215	19.5545	10.0936
6.75%	37.1335	28.7653	19.8145	10.2405
7.00%	37.5349	29.1095	20.0750	10.3874
7.25%	37.9359	29.4536	20.3355	10.5340
7.50%	38.3382	29.7997	20.5985	10.6828
7.75%	38.7415	30.1476	20.8635	10.8338
8.00%	39.1437	30.4947	21.1278	10.9835
8.25%	39.5464	30.8429	21.3937	11.1347
8.50%	39.9515	31.1946	21.6636	11.2902
8.75%	40.3546	31.5444	21.9317	11.4433
9.00%	40.7573	31.8946	22.2004	11.5969
9.25%	41.1595	32.2447	22.4694	11.7505
9.50%	41.5630	32.5970	22.7412	11.9072
9.75%	41.9654	32.9487	23.0125	12.0631
10.00%	42.3685	33.3020	23.2861	12.2213
10.25%	42.7698	33.6538	23.5583	12.3779
10.50%	43.1737	34.0094	23.8352	12.5398
10.75%	43.5750	34.3628	24.1100	12.6990
11.00%	43.9758	34.7163	24.3853	12.8589
11.25%	44.3757	35.0696	24.6609	13.0189
11.50%	44.7770	35.4254	24.9398	13.1827
11.75%	45.1741	35.7770	25.2143	13.3414
12.00%	45.5746	36.1334	25.4949	13.5071
12.25%	45.9727	36.4880	25.7738	13.6710
12.50%	46.3681	36.8401	26.0505	13.8321
12.75%	46.7658	37.1959	26.3320	13.9990
13.00%	47.1599	37.5483	26.6101	14.1620
13.25%	47.5557	37.9037	26.8922	14.3298
13.50%	47.9499	38.2581	27.1739	14.4972
13.75%	48.3421	38.6111	27.4545	14.6634
14.00%	48.7318	38.9621	27.7334	14.8278
14.25%	49.1248	39.3180	28.0187	14.9999
14.50%	49.5113	39.6671	28.2967	15.1635
14.75%	49.9003	40.0202	28.5801	15.3338
15.00%	50.2883	40.3731	28.8640	15.5048
15.25%	50.6748	40.7253	29.1478	15.6760
15.50%	51.0559	41.0720	29.4258	15.8405
15.75%	51.4414	41.4251	29.7121	16.0153
16.00%	51.8205	41.7715	29.9913	16.1817
16.25%	52.2033	42.1234	30.2779	16.3574
16.50%	52.5822	42.4718	30.5610	16.5292
16.75%	52.9566	42.8158	30.8396	16.6961
17.00%	53.3335	43.1639	31.1241	16.8703
17.25%	53.7088	43.5111	31.4083	17.0446
17.50%	54.0818	43.8567	31.6916	17.2181
17.75%	54.4521	44.2002	31.9730	17.3899
18.00%	54.8192	44.5408	32.2519	17.5590

Remaining Loan Balance   ## 20 Years

Percent remaining at end of year

Interest Rate	1	2	3	4	5
3.00%	96.2941	92.4755	88.5408	84.4864	80.3086
3.25%	96.3901	92.6612	88.8093	84.8302	80.7199
3.50%	96.4844	92.8438	89.0738	85.1696	81.1266
3.75%	96.5769	93.0232	89.3339	85.5038	81.5277
4.00%	96.6675	93.1992	89.5895	85.8329	81.9231
4.25%	96.7564	93.3723	89.8415	86.1576	82.3142
4.50%	96.8436	93.5423	90.0892	86.4775	82.6999
4.75%	96.9290	93.7088	90.3323	86.7920	83.0797
5.00%	97.0126	93.8724	90.5716	87.1018	83.4546
5.25%	97.0945	94.0328	90.8065	87.4066	83.8238
5.50%	97.1748	94.1903	91.0373	87.7066	84.1879
5.75%	97.2533	94.3444	91.2638	88.0013	84.5462
6.00%	97.3301	94.4955	91.4861	88.2911	84.8990
6.25%	97.4054	94.6438	91.7046	88.5764	85.2470
6.50%	97.4788	94.7888	91.9186	88.8562	85.5886
6.75%	97.5507	94.9309	92.1286	89.1313	85.9252
7.00%	97.6210	95.0701	92.3348	89.4017	86.2565
7.25%	97.6897	95.2062	92.5365	89.6667	86.5818
7.50%	97.7567	95.3393	92.7342	89.9269	86.9016
7.75%	97.8223	95.4698	92.9282	90.1826	87.2165
8.00%	97.8862	95.5970	93.1177	90.4327	87.5249
8.25%	97.9487	95.7217	93.3039	90.6788	87.8288
8.50%	98.0097	95.8434	93.4857	90.9196	88.1267
8.75%	98.0691	95.9624	93.6637	91.1557	88.4191
9.00%	98.1272	96.0788	93.8382	91.3874	88.7067
9.25%	98.1838	96.1924	94.0087	91.6142	88.9887
9.50%	98.2390	96.3031	94.1752	91.8360	89.2647
9.75%	98.2928	96.4115	94.3384	92.0538	89.5363
10.00%	98.3452	96.5170	94.4975	92.2664	89.8018
10.25%	98.3962	96.6202	94.6532	92.4749	90.0626
10.50%	98.4461	96.7209	94.8056	92.6792	90.3185
10.75%	98.4945	96.8189	94.9541	92.8786	90.5687
11.00%	98.5416	96.9145	95.0991	93.0737	90.8138
11.25%	98.5875	97.0077	95.2407	93.2643	91.0537
11.50%	98.6322	97.0986	95.3790	93.4509	91.2890
11.75%	98.6757	97.1871	95.5138	93.6330	91.5189
12.00%	98.7179	97.2733	95.6454	93.8110	91.7440
12.25%	98.7590	97.3572	95.7736	93.9848	91.9642
12.50%	98.7989	97.4308	95.8986	94.1545	92.1794
12.75%	98.8378	97.5184	96.0207	94.3204	92.3902
13.00%	98.8756	97.5960	96.1398	94.4826	92.5966
13.25%	98.9122	97.6713	96.2555	94.6403	92.7976
13.50%	98.9479	97.7447	96.3686	94.7947	92.9948
13.75%	98.9825	97.8160	96.4786	94.9452	93.1872
14.00%	99.0161	97.8852	96.5855	95.0917	93.3748
14.25%	99.0488	97.9529	96.6902	95.2353	93.5590
14.50%	99.0805	98.0184	96.7917	95.3747	93.7381
14.75%	99.1112	98.0820	96.8904	95.5106	93.9129
15.00%	99.1411	98.1440	96.9867	95.6434	94.0841
15.25%	99.1700	98.2041	97.0803	95.7725	94.2507
15.50%	99.1979	98.2623	97.1709	95.8978	94.4127
15.75%	99.2252	98.3191	97.2595	96.0205	94.5716
16.00%	99.2516	98.3742	97.3457	96.1400	94.7266
16.25%	99.2771	98.4276	97.4293	96.2562	94.8775
16.50%	99.3018	98.4794	97.5104	96.3690	95.0242
16.75%	99.3260	98.5300	97.5899	96.4797	95.1685
17.00%	99.3491	98.5785	97.6662	96.5862	95.3075
17.25%	99.3717	98.6259	97.7409	96.6905	95.4439
17.50%	99.3935	98.6719	97.8133	96.7919	95.5767
17.75%	99.4147	98.7166	97.8840	96.8910	95.7067
18.00%	99.4351	98.7596	97.9520	96.9864	95.8320

Table 2   19

20 Years   Remaining Loan Balance

Percent remaining at end of year

Interest Rate	6	7	8	9	10
3.00%	76.0038	71.5681	66.9974	62.2877	57.4348
3.25%	76.4741	72.0881	67.5575	62.8774	58.0429
3.50%	76.9397	72.6040	68.1140	63.4644	58.6494
3.75%	77.3998	73.1145	68.6656	64.0471	59.2523
4.00%	77.8541	73.6193	69.2120	64.6251	59.8514
4.25%	78.3041	74.1203	69.7551	65.2008	60.4491
4.50%	78.7488	74.6162	70.2937	65.7726	61.0438
4.75%	79.1872	75.1057	70.8261	66.3387	61.6335
5.00%	79.6207	75.5907	71.3545	66.9016	62.2209
5.25%	80.0484	76.0699	71.8774	67.4595	62.8040
5.50%	80.4708	76.5440	72.3957	68.0135	63.3840
5.75%	80.8870	77.0119	72.9080	68.5617	63.9589
6.00%	81.2977	77.4742	73.4150	69.1054	64.5300
6.25%	81.7034	77.9319	73.9178	69.6455	65.0983
6.50%	82.1023	78.3825	74.4135	70.1787	65.6604
6.75%	82.4959	78.8278	74.9044	70.7077	66.2189
7.00%	82.8841	79.2678	75.3901	71.2321	66.7735
7.25%	83.2657	79.7010	75.8691	71.7499	67.3220
7.50%	83.6415	80.1282	76.3423	72.2624	67.8658
7.75%	84.0121	80.5504	76.8107	72.7706	68.4061
8.00%	84.3756	80.9650	77.2713	73.2711	68.9388
8.25%	84.7346	81.3752	77.7279	73.7681	69.4690
8.50%	85.0869	81.7784	78.1774	74.2582	69.9925
8.75%	85.4333	82.1755	78.6209	74.7425	70.5108
9.00%	85.7746	82.5674	79.0593	75.2222	71.0251
9.25%	86.1096	82.9527	79.4911	75.6953	71.5332
9.50%	86.4382	83.3312	79.9158	76.1614	72.0345
9.75%	86.7621	83.7049	80.3360	76.6235	72.5324
10.00%	87.0791	84.0712	80.7484	77.0777	73.0226
10.25%	87.3910	84.4323	81.1557	77.5271	73.5085
10.50%	87.6976	84.7879	81.5576	77.9712	73.9897
10.75%	87.9979	85.1366	81.9522	78.4080	74.4635
11.00%	88.2924	85.4793	82.3408	78.8388	74.9317
11.25%	88.5812	85.8158	82.7226	79.2630	75.3935
11.50%	88.8650	86.1470	83.0994	79.6823	75.8509
11.75%	89.1426	86.4715	83.4691	80.0943	76.3009
12.00%	89.4149	86.7903	83.8329	80.5005	76.7454
12.25%	89.6816	87.1032	84.1906	80.9004	77.1838
12.50%	89.9427	87.4099	84.5417	81.2937	77.6156
12.75%	90.1990	87.7115	84.8876	81.6819	78.0427
13.00%	90.4503	88.0077	85.2280	82.0646	78.4646
13.25%	90.6954	88.2971	85.5609	82.4394	78.8782
13.50%	90.9363	88.5820	85.8894	82.8100	79.2881
13.75%	91.1717	88.8608	86.2114	83.1738	79.6913
14.00%	91.4014	89.1334	86.5266	83.5306	80.0871
14.25%	91.6276	89.4023	86.8383	83.8841	80.4803
14.50%	91.8478	89.6644	87.1425	84.2296	80.8651
14.75%	92.0630	89.9210	87.4408	84.5690	81.2437
15.00%	92.2742	90.1733	87.7346	84.9040	81.6183
15.25%	92.4800	90.4195	88.0219	85.2319	81.9855
15.50%	92.6803	90.6595	88.3022	85.5525	82.3449
15.75%	92.8773	90.8961	88.5792	85.8699	82.7016
16.00%	93.0697	91.1274	88.8505	86.1813	83.0524
16.25%	93.2574	91.3534	89.1159	86.4866	83.3966
16.50%	93.4401	91.5738	89.3752	86.7851	83.7338
16.75%	93.6201	91.7915	89.6319	87.0815	84.0695
17.00%	93.7937	92.0016	89.8798	87.3679	84.3941
17.25%	93.9644	92.2086	90.1247	87.6515	84.7163
17.50%	94.1309	92.4108	90.3642	87.9294	85.0326
17.75%	94.2942	92.6095	90.6002	88.2038	85.3457
18.00%	94.4517	92.8014	90.8283	88.4692	85.6486

Remaining Loan Balance   **20 Years**

Interest Rate	Percent remaining at end of year				
	11	12	13	14	15
3.00%	52.4342	47.2816	41.9722	36.5014	30.8641
3.25%	53.0490	47.8903	42.5614	37.0567	31.3705
3.50%	53.6631	48.4995	43.1522	37.6147	31.8803
3.75%	54.2746	49.1070	43.7423	38.1728	32.3909
4.00%	54.8831	49.7124	44.3311	38.7305	32.9018
4.25%	55.4915	50.3190	44.9224	39.2919	33.4174
4.50%	56.0978	50.9246	45.5137	39.8542	33.9348
4.75%	56.6998	51.5267	46.1023	40.4147	34.4509
5.00%	57.3006	52.1287	46.6921	40.9775	34.9704
5.25%	57.8980	52.7283	47.2804	41.5396	35.4901
5.50%	58.4933	53.3269	47.8689	42.1031	36.0121
5.75%	59.0843	53.9220	48.4548	42.6649	36.5331
6.00%	59.6723	54.5151	49.0398	43.2268	37.0552
6.25%	60.2588	55.1079	49.6257	43.7909	37.5807
6.50%	60.8394	55.6955	50.2072	44.3513	38.1032
6.75%	61.4175	56.2817	50.7884	44.9126	38.6277
7.00%	61.9926	56.8661	51.3689	45.4744	39.1538
7.25%	62.5622	57.4456	51.9455	46.0331	39.6775
7.50%	63.1278	58.0221	52.5200	46.5907	40.2011
7.75%	63.6910	58.5972	53.0944	47.1496	40.7273
8.00%	64.2470	59.1657	53.6627	47.7029	41.2485
8.25%	64.8015	59.7340	54.2323	48.2591	41.7741
8.50%	65.3499	60.2968	54.7971	48.8112	42.2963
8.75%	65.8936	60.8558	55.3590	49.3616	42.8177
9.00%	66.4343	61.4128	55.9203	49.9126	43.3413
9.25%	66.9693	61.9649	56.4774	50.4603	43.8623
9.50%	67.4979	62.5111	57.0294	51.0036	44.3798
9.75%	68.0242	63.0562	57.5816	51.5487	44.9005
10.00%	68.5429	63.5941	58.1270	52.0875	45.4156
10.25%	69.0581	64.1295	58.6712	52.6265	45.9322
10.50%	69.5693	64.6618	59.2135	53.1647	46.4494
10.75%	70.0735	65.1875	59.7497	53.6976	46.9618
11.00%	70.5724	65.7087	60.2822	54.2278	47.4727
11.25%	71.0655	66.2247	60.8103	54.7544	47.9810
11.50%	71.5548	66.7378	61.3367	55.2806	48.4902
11.75%	72.0370	67.2441	61.8568	55.8012	48.9945
12.00%	72.5140	67.7461	62.3734	56.3193	49.4974
12.25%	72.9854	68.2429	62.8857	56.8340	49.9980
12.50%	73.4505	68.7339	63.3927	57.3442	50.4948
12.75%	73.9114	69.2215	63.8974	57.8533	50.9920
13.00%	74.3676	69.7051	64.3990	58.3605	51.4885
13.25%	74.8155	70.1804	64.8926	58.8599	51.9776
13.50%	75.2603	70.6537	65.3853	59.3600	52.4690
13.75%	75.6985	71.1207	65.8723	59.8550	52.9561
14.00%	76.1294	71.5806	66.3524	60.3435	53.4372
14.25%	76.5585	72.0399	66.8336	60.8349	53.9234
14.50%	76.9790	72.4905	67.3060	61.3177	54.4011
14.75%	77.3934	72.9352	67.7731	61.7959	54.8750
15.00%	77.8044	73.3774	68.2387	62.2740	55.3504
15.25%	78.2079	73.8121	68.6972	62.7452	55.8194
15.50%	78.6033	74.2387	69.1473	63.2083	56.2804
15.75%	78.9968	74.6644	69.5981	63.6738	56.7459
16.00%	79.3843	75.0844	70.0438	64.1348	57.2078
16.25%	79.7654	75.4981	70.4833	64.5901	57.6646
16.50%	80.1391	75.9044	70.9156	65.0384	58.1147
16.75%	80.5124	76.3116	71.3505	65.4916	58.5723
17.00%	80.8734	76.7053	71.7707	65.9287	59.0123
17.25%	81.2328	77.0984	72.1918	66.3685	59.4573
17.50%	81.5861	77.4857	72.6073	66.8032	59.8979
17.75%	81.9368	77.8712	73.0222	67.2309	60.3413
18.00%	82.2763	78.2442	73.4235	67.6597	60.7683

Table 2   21

20 Years   Remaining Loan Balance

Interest
Rate	Percent remaining at end of year		
	16	17	18	19
3.00%	25.0554	19.0700	12.9026	6.5475
3.25%	25.4966	19.4290	13.1612	6.6867
3.50%	25.9419	19.7924	13.4241	6.8293
3.75%	26.3884	20.1569	13.6877	6.9717
4.00%	26.8356	20.5222	13.9516	7.1133
4.25%	27.2882	20.8935	14.2216	7.2606
4.50%	27.7434	21.2675	14.4942	7.4097
4.75%	28.1976	21.6407	14.7654	7.5564
5.00%	28.6560	22.0185	15.0415	7.7075
5.25%	29.1152	22.3974	15.3183	7.8585
5.50%	29.5775	22.7799	15.5989	8.0128
5.75%	30.0393	23.1621	15.8789	8.1657
6.00%	30.5030	23.5467	16.1613	8.3204
6.25%	30.9712	23.9365	16.4493	8.4805
6.50%	31.4366	24.3236	16.7343	8.6366
6.75%	31.9052	24.7146	17.0234	8.7966
7.00%	32.3763	25.1088	17.3159	8.9597
7.25%	32.8455	25.5014	17.6067	9.1204
7.50%	33.3155	25.8953	17.8991	9.2822
7.75%	33.7893	26.2940	18.1968	9.4493
8.00%	34.2583	26.6880	18.4894	9.6102
8.25%	34.7333	27.0892	18.7901	9.7798
8.50%	35.2055	27.4879	19.0882	9.9460
8.75%	35.6778	27.8875	19.3875	10.1132
9.00%	36.1536	28.2916	19.6921	10.2859
9.25%	36.6275	28.6944	19.9956	10.4570
9.50%	37.0986	29.0947	20.2965	10.6250
9.75%	37.5745	29.5013	20.6048	10.8011
10.00%	38.0451	29.9028	20.9078	10.9710
10.25%	38.5186	30.3083	21.2159	11.1463
10.50%	38.9940	30.7170	21.5279	11.3260
10.75%	39.4653	31.1219	21.8360	11.5013
11.00%	39.9360	31.5271	22.1452	11.6775
11.25%	40.4050	31.9314	22.4537	11.8531
11.50%	40.8764	32.3393	22.7671	12.0341
11.75%	41.3435	32.7434	23.0766	12.2108
12.00%	41.8104	33.1484	23.3879	12.3895
12.25%	42.2758	33.5528	23.6991	12.5682
12.50%	42.7385	33.9551	24.0086	12.7450
12.75%	43.2029	34.3605	24.3225	12.9271
13.00%	43.6680	34.7679	24.6394	13.1128
13.25%	44.1258	35.1682	24.9488	13.2901
13.50%	44.5880	35.5746	25.2662	13.4768
13.75%	45.0464	35.9780	25.5810	13.6608
14.00%	45.4996	36.3765	25.8909	13.8394
14.25%	45.9601	36.7848	26.2132	14.0327
14.50%	46.4121	37.1846	26.5265	14.2160
14.75%	46.8613	37.5824	26.8383	14.3979
15.00%	47.3139	37.9854	27.1573	14.5886
15.25%	47.7604	38.3828	27.4707	14.7731
15.50%	48.1990	38.7721	27.7756	14.9482
15.75%	48.6446	39.1711	28.0930	15.1384
16.00%	49.0875	39.5684	28.4094	15.3279
16.25%	49.5260	39.9618	28.7223	15.5139
16.50%	49.9581	40.3491	29.0290	15.6931
16.75%	50.4008	40.7505	29.3537	15.8943
17.00%	50.8242	41.1302	29.6537	16.0667
17.25%	51.2551	41.5205	29.9674	16.2561
17.50%	51.6823	41.9079	30.2789	16.4434
17.75%	52.1146	42.3030	30.6008	16.6439
18.00%	52.5290	42.6778	30.8996	16.8174

Remaining Loan Balance   <u>25 Years</u>

Interest Rate	Percent remaining at end of year				
	1	2	3	4	5
3.00%	97.2721	94.4611	91.5647	88.5802	85.5049
3.25%	97.3631	94.6392	91.8255	88.9190	85.9165
3.50%	97.4518	94.8130	92.0803	89.2505	86.3200
3.75%	97.5383	94.9827	92.3296	89.5752	86.7158
4.00%	97.6226	95.1484	92.5734	89.8935	87.1044
4.25%	97.7048	95.3100	92.8115	90.2048	87.4850
4.50%	97.7846	95.4674	93.0438	90.5088	87.8574
4.75%	97.8624	95.6211	93.2709	90.8066	88.2227
5.00%	97.9380	95.7704	93.4920	91.0970	88.5795
5.25%	98.0116	95.9163	93.7083	91.3815	88.9296
5.50%	98.0831	96.0580	93.9187	91.6588	89.2714
5.75%	98.1525	96.1959	94.1238	91.9294	89.6054
6.00%	98.2199	96.3299	94.3234	92.1931	89.9315
6.25%	98.2854	96.4605	94.5182	92.4510	90.2509
6.50%	98.3489	96.5872	94.7075	92.7019	90.5620
6.75%	98.4104	96.7101	94.8914	92.9461	90.8653
7.00%	98.4702	96.8298	95.0708	93.1846	91.1621
7.25%	98.5280	96.9457	95.2447	93.4163	91.4508
7.50%	98.5840	97.0580	95.4136	93.6416	91.7319
7.75%	98.6383	97.1673	95.5782	93.8614	92.0067
8.00%	98.6908	97.2730	95.7376	94.0746	92.2737
8.25%	98.7416	97.3754	95.8921	94.2817	92.5332
8.50%	98.7909	97.4748	96.0425	94.4835	92.7868
8.75%	98.8383	97.5709	96.1879	94.6790	93.0326
9.00%	98.8843	97.6640	96.3292	94.8692	93.2722
9.25%	98.9287	97.7539	96.4658	95.0533	93.5044
9.50%	98.9716	97.8411	96.5984	95.2324	93.7308
9.75%	99.0130	97.9253	96.7267	95.4059	93.9504
10.00%	99.0528	98.0065	96.8506	95.5737	94.1631
10.25%	99.0914	98.0852	96.9709	95.7368	94.3701
10.50%	99.1286	98.1611	97.0870	95.8946	94.5707
10.75%	99.1644	98.2345	97.1995	96.0475	94.7655
11.00%	99.1990	98.3053	97.3081	96.1956	94.9543
11.25%	99.2323	98.3737	97.4134	96.3392	95.1378
11.50%	99.2644	98.4396	97.5147	96.4778	95.3151
11.75%	99.2952	98.5031	97.6126	96.6118	95.4867
12.00%	99.3249	98.5642	97.7070	96.7411	95.6527
12.25%	99.3535	98.6232	97.7982	96.8664	95.8117
12.50%	99.3810	98.6801	97.8863	96.9874	95.9695
12.75%	99.4074	98.7348	97.9711	97.1042	96.1201
13.00%	99.4329	98.7876	98.0531	97.2173	96.2661
13.25%	99.4573	98.8382	98.1318	97.3260	96.4067
13.50%	99.4809	98.8871	98.2081	97.4315	96.5433
13.75%	99.5034	98.9341	98.2814	97.5331	96.6751
14.00%	99.5250	98.9792	98.3518	97.6307	96.8019
14.25%	99.5459	99.0228	98.4200	97.7255	96.9253
14.50%	99.5659	99.0644	98.4852	97.8162	97.0435
14.75%	99.5850	99.1046	98.5483	97.9041	97.1582
15.00%	99.6034	99.1430	98.6086	97.9884	97.2684
15.25%	99.6211	99.1803	98.6672	98.0703	97.3757
15.50%	99.6380	99.2157	98.7231	98.1485	97.4783
15.75%	99.6543	99.2500	98.7772	98.2243	97.5779
16.00%	99.6698	99.2827	98.8289	98.2970	97.6734
16.25%	99.6846	99.3139	98.8784	98.3665	97.7649
16.50%	99.6989	99.3442	98.9263	98.4340	97.8541
16.75%	99.7126	99.3732	98.9723	98.4990	97.9399
17.00%	99.7257	99.4009	99.0164	98.5612	98.0223
17.25%	99.7381	99.4274	99.0585	98.6208	98.1012
17.50%	99.7502	99.4531	99.0995	98.6789	98.1785
17.75%	99.7617	99.4775	99.1385	98.7343	98.2521
18.00%	99.7727	99.5009	99.1760	98.7875	98.3230

Table 2   23

25 Years — Remaining Loan Balance

Percent remaining at end of year

Interest Rate	6	7	8	9	10
3.00%	82.3361	79.0709	75.7063	72.2395	68.6672
3.25%	82.8150	79.6112	76.3018	72.8831	69.3517
3.50%	83.2852	80.1426	76.8881	73.5179	70.0279
3.75%	83.7473	80.6655	77.4662	74.1448	70.6966
4.00%	84.2017	81.1807	78.0366	74.7644	71.3589
4.25%	84.6474	81.6868	78.5979	75.3751	72.0127
4.50%	85.0842	82.1835	79.1496	75.9764	72.6573
4.75%	85.5134	82.6725	79.6937	76.5703	73.2953
5.00%	85.9332	83.1515	80.2274	77.1538	73.9229
5.25%	86.3458	83.6230	80.7539	77.7304	74.5443
5.50%	86.7492	84.0849	81.2702	78.2968	75.1556
5.75%	87.1442	84.5377	81.7773	78.8539	75.7579
6.00%	87.5303	84.9811	82.2746	79.4012	76.3506
6.25%	87.9092	85.4169	82.7643	79.9410	76.9362
6.50%	88.2787	85.8426	83.2433	80.4700	77.5109
6.75%	88.6396	86.2590	83.7126	80.9890	78.0756
7.00%	88.9934	86.6679	84.1743	81.5004	78.6333
7.25%	89.3380	87.0668	84.6253	82.0009	79.1797
7.50%	89.6740	87.4564	85.0666	82.4912	79.7159
7.75%	90.0031	87.8386	85.5002	82.9741	80.2450
8.00%	90.3232	88.2109	85.9233	83.4458	80.7626
8.25%	90.6350	88.5741	86.3366	83.9073	81.2699
8.50%	90.9400	88.9301	86.7425	84.3615	81.7700
8.75%	91.2363	89.2763	87.1378	84.8044	82.2585
9.00%	91.5254	89.6147	87.5248	85.2389	82.7385
9.25%	91.8061	89.9439	87.9019	85.6628	83.2075
9.50%	92.0802	90.2658	88.2713	86.0788	83.6687
9.75%	92.3465	90.5790	88.6312	86.4849	84.1196
10.00%	92.6047	90.8832	88.9814	86.8804	84.5595
10.25%	92.8566	91.1804	89.3241	87.2684	84.9917
10.50%	93.1010	91.4693	89.6577	87.6465	85.4137
10.75%	93.3387	91.7506	89.9832	88.0162	85.8269
11.00%	93.5694	92.0242	90.3003	88.3768	86.2307
11.25%	93.7940	92.2911	90.6100	88.7298	86.6267
11.50%	94.0114	92.5496	90.9105	89.0727	87.0121
11.75%	94.2222	92.8007	91.2030	89.4071	87.3884
12.00%	94.4263	93.0443	91.4871	89.7323	87.7550
12.25%	94.6246	93.2813	91.7640	90.0499	88.1137
12.50%	94.8168	93.5115	92.0333	90.3594	88.4639
12.75%	95.0029	93.7346	92.2949	90.6604	88.8049
13.00%	95.1837	93.9518	92.5498	90.9544	89.1387
13.25%	95.3579	94.1613	92.7963	91.2389	89.4622
13.50%	95.5275	94.3658	93.0372	91.5177	89.7798
13.75%	95.6914	94.5636	93.2706	91.7881	90.0885
14.00%	95.8493	94.7545	93.4962	92.0499	90.3877
14.25%	96.0033	94.9410	93.7171	92.3068	90.6820
14.50%	96.1510	95.1202	93.9295	92.5542	90.9657
14.75%	96.2946	95.2946	94.1367	92.7959	91.2435
15.00%	96.4326	95.4625	94.3365	93.0295	91.5123
15.25%	96.5674	95.6269	94.5324	93.2589	91.7770
15.50%	96.6964	95.7843	94.7204	93.4794	92.0317
15.75%	96.8218	95.9378	94.9040	93.6951	92.2814
16.00%	96.9424	96.0855	95.0810	93.9033	92.5229
16.25%	97.0580	96.2273	95.2510	94.1037	92.7555
16.50%	97.1709	96.3660	95.4178	94.3007	92.9848
16.75%	97.2797	96.5000	95.5791	94.4917	93.2074
17.00%	97.3843	96.6290	95.7348	94.6761	93.4228
17.25%	97.4847	96.7529	95.8844	94.8537	93.6305
17.50%	97.5831	96.8748	96.0320	95.0293	93.8364
17.75%	97.6770	96.9912	96.1732	95.1975	94.0339
18.00%	97.7676	97.1036	96.3097	95.3605	94.2256

Remaining Loan Balance   <u>25 Years</u>

Interest Rate	Percent remaining at end of year				
	11	12	13	14	15
3.00%	64.9862	61.1933	57.2850	53.2578	49.1082
3.25%	65.7037	61.9355	58.0429	54.0219	49.8682
3.50%	66.4137	62.6709	58.7951	54.7814	50.6249
3.75%	67.1170	63.4007	59.5427	55.5375	51.3795
4.00%	67.8147	64.1261	60.2872	56.2918	52.1338
4.25%	68.5045	64.8444	61.0255	57.0412	52.8843
4.50%	69.1858	65.5548	61.7570	57.7847	53.6300
4.75%	69.8613	66.2605	62.4850	58.5261	54.3750
5.00%	70.5267	66.9568	63.2042	59.2597	55.1133
5.25%	71.1868	67.6488	63.9205	59.9917	55.8516
5.50%	71.8373	68.3318	64.6285	60.7164	56.5835
5.75%	72.4792	69.0069	65.3295	61.4351	57.3107
6.00%	73.1118	69.6732	66.0226	62.1468	58.0320
6.25%	73.7381	70.3343	66.7115	62.8557	58.7519
6.50%	74.3536	70.9849	67.3906	63.5555	59.4636
6.75%	74.9595	71.6263	68.0611	64.2476	60.1687
7.00%	75.5588	72.2622	68.7272	64.9366	60.8721
7.25%	76.1470	72.8870	69.3827	65.6157	61.5663
7.50%	76.7252	73.5023	70.0292	66.2865	62.2532
7.75%	77.2968	74.1117	70.6709	66.9538	62.9381
8.00%	77.8568	74.7097	71.3015	67.6104	63.6129
8.25%	78.4065	75.2977	71.9225	68.2581	64.2797
8.50%	78.9495	75.8797	72.5385	68.9020	64.9441
8.75%	79.4807	76.4498	73.1428	69.5346	65.5977
9.00%	80.0036	77.0121	73.7400	70.1610	66.2462
9.25%	80.5153	77.5632	74.3262	70.7767	66.8846
9.50%	81.0195	78.1073	74.9061	71.3872	67.5190
9.75%	81.5132	78.6409	75.4758	71.9878	68.1442
10.00%	81.9955	79.1630	76.0340	72.5773	68.7586
10.25%	82.4704	79.6782	76.5859	73.1614	69.3689
10.50%	82.9348	80.1828	77.1274	73.7354	69.9695
10.75%	83.3904	80.6786	77.6606	74.3016	70.5631
11.00%	83.8364	81.1649	78.1843	74.8588	71.1484
11.25%	84.2745	81.6436	78.7010	75.4097	71.7284
11.50%	84.7016	82.1109	79.2060	75.9490	72.2969
11.75%	85.1193	82.5688	79.7019	76.4793	72.8571
12.00%	85.5270	83.0164	80.1873	76.9995	73.4073
12.25%	85.9266	83.4559	80.6650	77.5123	73.9511
12.50%	86.3173	83.8866	81.1339	78.0167	74.4868
12.75%	86.6986	84.3074	81.5929	78.5113	75.0130
13.00%	87.0724	84.7209	82.0449	78.9994	75.5335
13.25%	87.4353	85.1229	82.4847	79.4750	76.0413
13.50%	87.7923	85.5192	82.9196	79.9464	76.5461
13.75%	88.1399	85.9057	83.3443	80.4076	77.0406
14.00%	88.4772	86.2814	83.7577	80.8571	77.5233
14.25%	88.8069	86.6528	84.1675	81.3040	78.0047
14.50%	89.1309	87.0117	84.5639	81.7366	78.4710
14.75%	89.4460	87.3646	84.9547	82.1642	78.9331
15.00%	89.7513	87.7071	85.3344	82.5802	79.3833
15.25%	90.0527	88.0462	85.7114	82.9946	79.8332
15.50%	90.3430	88.3731	86.0752	83.3948	80.2680
15.75%	90.6283	88.6952	86.4346	83.7911	80.6999
16.00%	90.9046	89.0075	86.7836	84.1766	81.1205
16.25%	91.1711	89.3092	87.1211	84.5497	81.5280
16.50%	91.4345	89.6082	87.4566	84.9220	81.9359
16.75%	91.6907	89.8995	87.7841	85.2859	82.3356
17.00%	91.9389	90.1822	88.1025	85.6403	82.7254
17.25%	92.1787	90.4557	88.4108	85.9840	83.1037
17.50%	92.4172	90.7287	88.7197	86.3296	83.4860
17.75%	92.6461	90.9909	89.0167	86.6622	83.8541
18.00%	92.8688	91.2465	89.3068	86.9877	84.2150

Table 2   25

<u>25 Years</u>   **Remaining Loan Balance**

Percent remaining at end of year

Rate	16	17	18	19	20
3.00%	44.8323	40.4264	35.8865	31.2084	26.3881
3.25%	45.5776	41.1454	36.5670	31.8375	26.9521
3.50%	46.3206	41.8632	37.2473	32.4672	27.5170
3.75%	47.0629	42.5816	37.9293	33.0995	28.0854
4.00%	47.8063	43.3025	38.6152	33.7369	28.6599
4.25%	48.5471	44.0220	39.3008	34.3750	29.2357
4.50%	49.2843	44.7391	39.9850	35.0125	29.8116
4.75%	50.0225	45.4586	40.6731	35.6554	30.3940
5.00%	50.7548	46.1732	41.3573	36.2950	30.9737
5.25%	51.4888	46.8914	42.0467	36.9415	31.5617
5.50%	52.2176	47.6053	42.7329	37.5857	32.1481
5.75%	52.9428	48.3171	43.4182	38.2301	32.7358
6.00%	53.6633	49.0252	44.1011	38.8732	33.3229
6.25%	54.3842	49.7355	44.7878	39.5218	33.9172
6.50%	55.0977	50.4394	45.4691	40.1659	34.5076
6.75%	55.8057	51.1389	46.1472	40.8079	35.0968
7.00%	56.5137	51.8402	46.8289	41.4554	35.6933
7.25%	57.2134	52.5342	47.5042	42.0973	36.2850
7.50%	57.9068	53.2230	48.1755	42.7362	36.8747
7.75%	58.5999	53.9132	48.8502	43.3806	37.4716
8.00%	59.2837	54.5951	49.5173	44.0182	38.0625
8.25%	59.9603	55.2709	50.1795	44.6519	38.6506
8.50%	60.6363	55.9478	50.8448	45.2908	39.2459
8.75%	61.3021	56.6152	51.5014	45.9217	39.8338
9.00%	61.9642	57.2805	52.1574	46.5538	40.4245
9.25%	62.6168	57.9371	52.8056	47.1789	41.0090
9.50%	63.2669	58.5929	53.4549	47.8070	41.5985
9.75%	63.9087	59.2411	54.0977	48.4296	42.1836
10.00%	64.5401	59.8798	54.7315	49.0442	42.7613
10.25%	65.1688	60.5175	55.3663	49.6616	43.3439
10.50%	65.7886	61.1469	55.9938	50.2727	43.9212
10.75%	66.4024	61.7718	56.6180	50.8821	44.4982
11.00%	67.0087	62.3900	57.2368	51.4872	45.0724
11.25%	67.6110	63.0056	57.8547	52.0934	45.6495
11.50%	68.2021	63.6107	58.4625	52.6901	46.2177
11.75%	68.7856	64.2090	59.0648	53.2825	46.7829
12.00%	69.3596	64.7986	59.6591	53.8678	47.3419
12.25%	69.9282	65.3838	60.2505	54.4517	47.9014
12.50%	70.4895	65.9628	60.8367	55.0319	48.4584
12.75%	71.0417	66.5334	61.4154	55.6054	49.0098
13.00%	71.5893	67.1006	61.9923	56.1790	49.5632
13.25%	72.1241	67.6550	62.5565	56.7399	50.1041
13.50%	72.6572	68.2096	63.1230	57.3056	50.6523
13.75%	73.1804	68.7546	63.6805	57.8629	51.1931
14.00%	73.6916	69.2878	64.2262	58.4087	51.7224
14.25%	74.2032	69.8233	64.7768	58.9623	52.2629
14.50%	74.6991	70.3424	65.3102	59.4980	52.7846
14.75%	75.1919	70.8599	65.8440	60.0361	53.3112
15.00%	75.6724	71.3650	66.3652	60.5616	53.8251
15.25%	76.1546	71.8740	66.8930	61.0971	54.3527
15.50%	76.6206	72.3659	67.4029	61.6135	54.8601
15.75%	77.0851	72.8580	67.9149	62.1345	55.3751
16.00%	77.5379	73.3382	68.4149	62.6435	55.8779
16.25%	77.9769	73.8038	68.8997	63.1366	56.3639
16.50%	78.4182	74.2741	69.3920	63.6406	56.8651
16.75%	78.8513	74.7365	69.8770	64.1381	57.3605
17.00%	79.2744	75.1888	70.3519	64.6256	57.8462
17.25%	79.6854	75.6285	70.8137	65.0995	58.3177
17.50%	80.1029	76.0778	71.2890	65.5915	58.8130
17.75%	80.5048	76.5103	71.7461	66.0639	59.2869
18.00%	80.8998	76.9362	72.1972	66.5311	59.7567

Remaining Loan Balance   25 Years

Interest Rate	Percent remaining at end of year			
	21	22	23	24
3.00%	21.4212	16.3032	11.0295	5.5955
3.25%	21.9054	16.6923	11.3072	5.7445
3.50%	22.3909	17.0824	11.5851	5.8922
3.75%	22.8801	17.4762	11.8661	6.0420
4.00%	23.3760	17.8769	12.1537	6.1974
4.25%	23.8737	18.2793	12.4425	6.3527
4.50%	24.3717	18.6820	12.7309	6.5063
4.75%	24.8772	19.0926	13.0271	6.6672
5.00%	25.3802	19.5005	13.3199	6.8232
5.25%	25.8925	19.9185	13.6232	6.9893
5.50%	26.4038	20.3355	13.9249	7.1526
5.75%	26.9170	20.7547	14.2285	7.3171
6.00%	27.4302	21.1741	14.5322	7.4806
6.25%	27.9520	21.6031	14.8459	7.6540
6.50%	28.4703	22.0287	15.1556	7.8223
6.75%	28.9881	22.4541	15.4651	7.9895
7.00%	29.5148	22.8896	15.7854	8.1677
7.25%	30.0370	23.3207	16.1010	8.3400
7.50%	30.5581	23.7511	16.4157	8.5108
7.75%	31.0882	24.1920	16.7420	8.6936
8.00%	31.6126	24.6273	17.0623	8.8694
8.25%	32.1351	25.0612	17.3811	9.0429
8.50%	32.6666	25.5058	17.7121	9.2294
8.75%	33.1912	25.9436	18.0357	9.4074
9.00%	33.7202	26.3870	18.3660	9.5925
9.25%	34.2436	26.8252	18.6907	9.7711
9.50%	34.7739	27.2720	19.0255	9.9605
9.75%	35.3007	27.7158	19.3574	10.1467
10.00%	35.8205	28.1529	19.6825	10.3250
10.25%	36.3473	28.5990	20.0180	10.5149
10.50%	36.8697	29.0411	20.3497	10.7005
10.75%	37.3933	29.4858	20.6851	10.8903
11.00%	37.9152	29.9298	21.0203	11.0799
11.25%	38.4420	30.3806	21.3640	11.2791
11.50%	38.9605	30.8233	21.6993	11.4690
11.75%	39.4772	31.2652	22.0347	11.6592
12.00%	39.9885	31.7024	22.3655	11.8444
12.25%	40.5020	32.1435	22.7017	12.0360
12.50%	41.0145	32.5849	23.0391	12.2292
12.75%	41.5223	33.0223	23.3729	12.4188
13.00%	42.0342	33.4659	23.7150	12.6181
13.25%	42.5335	33.8966	24.0433	12.8020
13.50%	43.0432	34.3408	24.3881	13.0054
13.75%	43.5461	34.7787	24.7269	13.2025
14.00%	44.0376	35.2051	25.0535	13.3859
14.25%	44.5439	35.6502	25.4031	13.5965
14.50%	45.0304	36.0740	25.7291	13.7803
14.75%	45.5245	36.5083	26.0685	13.9804
15.00%	46.0057	36.9293	26.3937	14.1646
15.25%	46.5049	37.3729	26.7468	14.3819
15.50%	46.9823	37.7929	27.0735	14.5692
15.75%	47.4707	38.2274	27.4186	14.7788
16.00%	47.9468	38.6493	27.7502	14.9734
16.25%	48.4050	39.0518	28.0604	15.1436
16.50%	48.8830	39.4796	28.4018	15.3513
16.75%	49.3563	39.9036	28.7402	15.5564
17.00%	49.8201	40.3182	29.0688	15.7509
17.25%	50.2691	40.7168	29.3800	15.9254
17.50%	50.7484	41.1535	29.7381	16.1568
17.75%	51.2042	41.5641	30.0666	16.3537
18.00%	51.6570	41.9730	30.3945	16.5511

Table 2   27

30 Years   **Remaining Loan Balance**

Percent remaining at end of year

Interest Rate	1	2	3	4	5
3.00%	97.9121	95.7607	93.5439	91.2597	88.9060
3.25%	97.9978	95.9296	93.7932	91.5862	89.3065
3.50%	98.0808	96.0934	94.0352	91.9039	89.6967
3.75%	98.1612	96.2522	94.2704	92.2129	90.0770
4.00%	98.2389	96.4061	94.4985	92.5133	90.4472
4.25%	98.3141	96.5552	94.7200	92.8054	90.8077
4.50%	98.3867	96.6993	94.9344	93.0884	91.1576
4.75%	98.4569	96.8389	95.1423	93.3634	91.4981
5.00%	98.5245	96.9736	95.3433	93.6296	91.8282
5.25%	98.5899	97.1039	95.5380	93.8879	92.1491
5.50%	98.6529	97.2298	95.7264	94.1383	92.4605
5.75%	98.7135	97.3510	95.9081	94.3800	92.7617
6.00%	98.7719	97.4680	96.0837	94.6140	93.0537
6.25%	98.8282	97.5810	96.2535	94.8407	93.3370
6.50%	98.8823	97.6896	96.4172	95.0595	93.6108
6.75%	98.9342	97.7942	96.5749	95.2706	93.8756
7.00%	98.9841	97.8948	96.7267	95.4741	94.1311
7.25%	99.0321	97.9916	96.8732	95.6709	94.3785
7.50%	99.0781	98.0846	97.0140	95.8603	94.6170
7.75%	99.1222	98.1739	97.1495	96.0428	94.8472
8.00%	99.1646	98.2598	97.2799	96.2187	95.0695
8.25%	99.2052	98.3422	97.4053	96.3881	95.2837
8.50%	99.2440	98.4211	97.5255	96.5507	95.4898
8.75%	99.2811	98.4967	97.6409	96.7071	95.6882
9.00%	99.3167	98.5693	97.7518	96.8576	95.8796
9.25%	99.3508	98.6389	97.8583	97.0023	96.0637
9.50%	99.3833	98.7054	97.9602	97.1410	96.2405
9.75%	99.4144	98.7690	98.0579	97.2742	96.4106
10.00%	99.4440	98.8298	98.1513	97.4017	96.5737
10.25%	99.4723	98.8880	98.2409	97.5242	96.7305
10.50%	99.4995	98.9438	98.3269	97.6420	96.8816
10.75%	99.5252	98.9967	98.4086	97.7540	97.0255
11.00%	99.5498	99.0475	98.4871	97.8618	97.1641
11.25%	99.5732	99.0958	98.5619	97.9647	97.2967
11.50%	99.5955	99.1420	98.6335	98.0633	97.4240
11.75%	99.6169	99.1862	98.7022	98.1581	97.5465
12.00%	99.6370	99.2280	98.7671	98.2478	97.6626
12.25%	99.6563	99.2681	98.8296	98.3342	97.7746
12.50%	99.6747	99.3062	98.8890	98.4166	97.8816
12.75%	99.6920	99.3424	98.9455	98.4949	97.9834
13.00%	99.7086	99.3771	98.9997	98.5703	98.0816
13.25%	99.7243	99.4098	99.0509	98.6415	98.1745
13.50%	99.7392	99.4410	99.0999	98.7097	98.2636
13.75%	99.7534	99.4707	99.1465	98.7749	98.3488
14.00%	99.7669	99.4989	99.1909	98.8369	98.4301
14.25%	99.7797	99.5259	99.2334	98.8965	98.5082
14.50%	99.7918	99.5513	99.2736	98.9528	98.5822
14.75%	99.8033	99.5755	99.3118	99.0064	98.6529
15.00%	99.8142	99.5985	99.3481	99.0574	98.7201
15.25%	99.8246	99.6204	99.3828	99.1064	98.7847
15.50%	99.8343	99.6410	99.4156	99.1526	98.8458
15.75%	99.8436	99.6607	99.4468	99.1967	98.9042
16.00%	99.8524	99.6793	99.4764	99.2386	98.9598
16.25%	99.8606	99.6969	99.5044	99.2783	99.0125
16.50%	99.8686	99.7137	99.5313	99.3164	99.0632
16.75%	99.8760	99.7295	99.5565	99.3522	99.1109
17.00%	99.8830	99.7445	99.5805	99.3864	99.1565
17.25%	99.8897	99.7587	99.6033	99.4189	99.2000
17.50%	99.8960	99.7722	99.6249	99.4497	99.2412
17.75%	99.9019	99.7848	99.6452	99.4788	99.2802
18.00%	99.9075	99.7970	99.6648	99.5068	99.3178

Remaining Loan Balance　　**30 Years**

Interest Rate	Percent remaining at end of year				
	6	7	8	9	10
3.00%	86.4807	83.9816	81.4065	78.7531	76.0190
3.25%	86.9516	84.5190	82.0061	79.4103	76.7290
3.50%	87.4111	85.0441	82.5930	80.0547	77.4261
3.75%	87.8596	85.5576	83.1678	80.6868	78.1111
4.00%	88.2969	86.0590	83.7299	81.3060	78.7833
4.25%	88.7234	86.5489	84.2801	81.9129	79.4432
4.50%	89.1381	87.0258	84.8165	82.5057	80.0887
4.75%	89.5422	87.4914	85.3410	83.0862	80.7220
5.00%	89.9346	87.9442	85.8519	83.6526	81.3408
5.25%	90.3167	88.3858	86.3510	84.2068	81.9473
5.50%	90.6881	88.8158	86.8378	84.7483	82.5408
5.75%	91.0478	89.2328	87.3106	85.2749	83.1190
6.00%	91.3971	89.6384	87.7712	85.7888	83.6842
6.25%	91.7366	90.0333	88.2204	86.2909	84.2372
6.50%	92.0652	90.4160	88.6564	86.7790	84.7758
6.75%	92.3834	90.7873	89.0800	87.2539	85.3007
7.00%	92.6909	91.1466	89.4907	87.7151	85.8111
7.25%	92.9892	91.4958	89.8904	88.1648	86.3097
7.50%	93.2772	91.8334	90.2775	88.6009	86.7940
7.75%	93.5555	92.1602	90.6528	89.0243	87.2650
8.00%	93.8248	92.4768	91.0170	89.4360	87.7237
8.25%	94.0847	92.7830	91.3697	89.8353	88.1694
8.50%	94.3351	93.0783	91.7104	90.2217	88.6013
8.75%	94.5765	93.3636	92.0401	90.5961	89.0206
9.00%	94.8098	93.6396	92.3597	90.9597	89.4283
9.25%	95.0346	93.9061	92.6686	91.3117	89.8239
9.50%	95.2507	94.1626	92.9666	91.6518	90.2066
9.75%	95.4589	94.4102	93.2545	91.9810	90.5776
10.00%	95.6589	94.6483	93.5320	92.2987	90.9363
10.25%	95.8515	94.8781	93.8000	92.6062	91.2840
10.50%	96.0375	95.1003	94.0598	92.9047	91.6222
10.75%	96.2146	95.3122	94.3079	93.1901	91.9460
11.00%	96.3857	95.5173	94.5484	93.4673	92.2611
11.25%	96.5496	95.7140	94.7794	93.7340	92.5648
11.50%	96.7071	95.9034	95.0021	93.9916	92.8585
11.75%	96.8591	96.0863	95.2178	94.2415	93.1441
12.00%	97.0032	96.2602	95.4229	94.4794	93.4163
12.25%	97.1425	96.4284	95.6218	94.7107	93.6814
12.50%	97.2757	96.5896	95.8127	94.9329	93.9366
12.75%	97.4027	96.7435	95.9952	95.1457	94.1813
13.00%	97.5255	96.8925	96.1723	95.3525	94.4197
13.25%	97.6417	97.0338	96.3403	95.5491	94.6465
13.50%	97.7533	97.1697	96.5023	95.7390	94.8660
13.75%	97.8603	97.3002	96.6581	95.9219	95.0779
14.00%	97.9625	97.4251	96.8074	96.0975	95.2815
14.25%	98.0609	97.5455	96.9516	96.2674	95.4791
14.50%	98.1542	97.6598	97.0888	96.4293	95.6675
14.75%	98.2434	97.7694	97.2205	96.5849	95.8490
15.00%	98.3285	97.8740	97.3464	96.7340	96.0231
15.25%	98.4105	97.9749	97.4681	96.8784	96.1922
15.50%	98.4880	98.0706	97.5836	97.0156	96.3530
15.75%	98.5622	98.1622	97.6945	97.1476	96.5081
16.00%	98.6329	98.2498	97.8006	97.2741	96.6569
16.25%	98.7001	98.3331	97.9017	97.3948	96.7992
16.50%	98.7649	98.4135	97.9996	97.5119	96.9374
16.75%	98.8260	98.4895	98.0920	97.6227	97.0684
17.00%	98.8844	98.5623	98.1809	97.7294	97.1948
17.25%	98.9402	98.6319	98.2659	97.8317	97.3163
17.50%	98.9932	98.6981	98.3471	97.9294	97.4325
17.75%	99.0434	98.7609	98.4241	98.0223	97.5431
18.00%	99.0919	98.8218	98.4989	98.1128	97.6512

Table 2　　29

30 Years　　**Remaining Loan Balance**

Interest

Percent remaining at end of year

Rate	11	12	13	14	15
3.00%	73.2017	70.2987	67.3075	64.2252	61.0492
3.25%	73.9591	71.0979	68.1423	65.0892	61.9353
3.50%	74.7040	71.8851	68.9660	65.9430	62.8125
3.75%	75.4372	72.6613	69.7794	66.7877	63.6817
4.00%	76.1578	73.4253	70.5815	67.6219	64.5416
4.25%	76.8665	74.1780	71.3731	68.4466	65.3933
4.50%	77.5607	74.9166	72.1510	69.2583	66.2328
4.75%	78.2430	75.6436	72.9181	70.0602	67.0636
5.00%	78.9107	76.3562	73.6711	70.8486	67.8817
5.25%	79.5662	77.0572	74.4131	71.6269	68.6908
5.50%	80.2089	77.7454	75.1430	72.3938	69.4894
5.75%	80.8358	78.4179	75.8571	73.1452	70.2732
6.00%	81.4497	79.0774	76.5589	73.8849	71.0461
6.25%	82.0515	79.7252	77.2493	74.6141	71.8094
6.50%	82.6385	80.3580	77.9248	75.3286	72.5585
6.75%	83.2114	80.9767	78.5864	76.0296	73.2948
7.00%	83.7695	81.5803	79.2328	76.7156	74.0165
7.25%	84.3156	82.1720	79.8678	77.3908	74.7281
7.50%	84.8469	82.7486	80.4874	78.0507	75.4248
7.75%	85.3644	83.3112	81.0931	78.6969	76.1081
8.00%	85.8694	83.8611	81.6861	79.3307	76.7797
8.25%	86.3608	84.3971	82.2653	79.9507	77.4378
8.50%	86.8377	84.9183	82.8291	80.5553	78.0806
8.75%	87.3015	85.4258	83.3793	81.1463	78.7099
9.00%	87.7533	85.9212	83.9172	81.7253	79.3277
9.25%	88.1924	86.4035	84.4419	82.2909	79.9323
9.50%	88.6179	86.8715	84.9518	82.8416	80.5220
9.75%	89.0311	87.3269	85.4489	83.3794	81.0988
10.00%	89.4312	87.7685	85.9318	83.9027	81.6611
10.25%	89.8198	88.1982	86.4024	84.4136	82.2111
10.50%	90.1984	88.6178	86.8629	84.9146	82.7517
10.75%	90.5614	89.0205	87.3054	85.3966	83.2722
11.00%	90.9154	89.4139	87.7387	85.8696	83.7843
11.25%	91.2570	89.7943	88.1582	86.3284	84.2817
11.50%	91.5881	90.1636	88.5664	86.7754	84.7674
11.75%	91.9106	90.5241	88.9655	87.2137	85.2446
12.00%	92.2183	90.8685	89.3474	87.6334	85.7020
12.25%	92.5187	91.2054	89.7218	88.0458	86.1527
12.50%	92.8084	91.5307	90.0839	88.4455	86.5902
12.75%	93.0865	91.8436	90.4327	88.8310	87.0128
13.00%	93.3581	92.1499	90.7750	89.2103	87.4296
13.25%	93.6167	92.4419	91.1017	89.5727	87.8283
13.50%	93.8676	92.7258	91.4199	89.9263	88.2182
13.75%	94.1101	93.0007	91.7286	90.2702	88.5982
14.00%	94.3437	93.2658	92.0270	90.6031	88.9666
14.25%	94.5707	93.5242	92.3184	90.9290	89.3283
14.50%	94.7876	93.7713	92.5975	91.2416	89.6756
14.75%	94.9969	94.0102	92.8678	91.5450	90.0133
15.00%	95.1980	94.2402	93.1285	91.8380	90.3401
15.25%	95.3937	94.4645	93.3834	92.1253	90.6613
15.50%	95.5801	94.6785	93.6268	92.4000	90.9689
15.75%	95.7602	94.8856	93.8629	92.6670	91.2685
16.00%	95.9333	95.0851	94.0908	92.9252	91.5588
16.25%	96.0991	95.2765	94.3097	93.1736	91.8385
16.50%	96.2607	95.4634	94.5241	93.4175	92.1140
16.75%	96.4139	95.6408	94.7279	93.6497	92.3764
17.00%	96.5620	95.8127	94.9257	93.8756	92.6324
17.25%	96.7046	95.9786	95.1170	94.0945	92.8809
17.50%	96.8413	96.1379	95.3010	94.3054	93.1208
17.75%	96.9716	96.2900	95.4770	94.5074	93.3510
18.00%	97.0992	96.4393	95.6503	94.7070	93.5791

Remaining Loan Balance   <u>**30 Years**</u>

Interest Rate	\multicolumn{5}{c}{Percent remaining at end of year}

Interest Rate	16	17	18	19	20
3.00%	57.7766	54.4045	50.9298	47.3494	43.6601
3.25%	58.6775	55.3121	51.8358	48.2448	44.5353
3.50%	59.5707	56.2135	52.7370	49.1368	45.4086
3.75%	60.4573	57.1099	53.6347	50.0270	46.2816
4.00%	61.3359	57.9996	54.5273	50.9136	47.1527
4.25%	62.2077	58.8840	55.4162	51.7982	48.0234
4.50%	63.0682	59.7583	56.2963	52.6753	48.8879
4.75%	63.9215	60.6268	57.1722	53.5499	49.7518
5.00%	64.7630	61.4847	58.0387	54.4164	50.6088
5.25%	65.5968	62.3364	58.9006	55.2801	51.4648
5.50%	66.4213	63.1801	59.7561	56.1389	52.3177
5.75%	67.2316	64.0105	60.5992	56.9864	53.1604
6.00%	68.0321	64.8323	61.4351	57.8284	53.9992
6.25%	68.8243	65.6472	62.2657	58.6667	54.8363
6.50%	69.6030	66.4495	63.0848	59.4948	55.6643
6.75%	70.3696	67.2408	63.8940	60.3143	56.4853
7.00%	71.1222	68.0188	64.6909	61.1225	57.2962
7.25%	71.8659	68.7891	65.4817	61.9263	58.1045
7.50%	72.5951	69.5457	66.2595	62.7183	58.9021
7.75%	73.3115	70.2903	67.0265	63.5005	59.6913
8.00%	74.0170	71.0250	67.7846	64.2753	60.4748
8.25%	74.7095	71.7475	68.5316	65.0401	61.2495
8.50%	75.3870	72.4554	69.2647	65.7919	62.0122
8.75%	76.0516	73.1511	69.9863	66.5333	62.7657
9.00%	76.7052	73.8367	70.6991	67.2672	63.5133
9.25%	77.3461	74.5102	71.4006	67.9908	64.2519
9.50%	77.9721	75.1692	72.0881	68.7012	64.9781
9.75%	78.5857	75.8163	72.7645	69.4014	65.6954
10.00%	79.1848	76.4491	73.4271	70.0886	66.4005
10.25%	79.7720	77.0707	74.0792	70.7662	67.0973
10.50%	80.3503	77.6843	74.7246	71.4386	67.7905
10.75%	80.9079	78.2764	75.3478	72.0883	68.4606
11.00%	81.4576	78.8617	75.9653	72.7339	69.1285
11.25%	81.9925	79.4320	76.5682	73.3651	69.7824
11.50%	82.5158	79.9912	77.1605	73.9865	70.4276
11.75%	83.0313	80.5433	77.7468	74.6035	71.0702
12.00%	83.5257	81.0734	78.3100	75.1962	71.6875
12.25%	84.0142	81.5985	78.8696	75.7871	72.3050
12.50%	84.4892	82.1100	79.4157	76.3647	72.9096
12.75%	84.9486	82.6054	79.9453	76.9255	73.4973
13.00%	85.4031	83.0969	80.4724	77.4856	74.0865
13.25%	85.8382	83.5678	80.9776	78.0225	74.6513
13.50%	86.2647	84.0305	81.4753	78.5530	75.2108
13.75%	86.6811	84.4833	81.9634	79.0743	75.7620
14.00%	87.0857	84.9239	82.4393	79.5836	76.3014
14.25%	87.4839	85.3588	82.9103	80.0892	76.8388
14.50%	87.8667	85.7774	83.3642	80.5769	77.3574
14.75%	88.2398	86.1862	83.8084	81.0552	77.8673
15.00%	88.6014	86.5832	84.2405	81.5213	78.3649
15.25%	88.9578	86.9756	84.6691	81.9851	78.8620
15.50%	89.2996	87.3523	85.0808	82.4310	79.3401
15.75%	89.6331	87.7208	85.4845	82.8694	79.8113
16.00%	89.9570	88.0792	85.8780	83.2975	80.2725
16.25%	90.2695	88.4257	86.2589	83.7126	80.7202
16.50%	90.5783	88.7691	86.6378	84.1270	81.1691
16.75%	90.8727	89.0968	86.9996	84.5227	81.5977
17.00%	91.1606	89.4181	87.3552	84.9129	82.0215
17.25%	91.4407	89.7313	87.7027	85.2950	82.4376
17.50%	91.7115	90.0348	88.0400	85.6666	82.8429
17.75%	91.9717	90.3268	88.3648	86.0249	83.2341
18.00%	92.2306	90.6183	88.6906	86.3859	83.6302

Table 2   31

30 Years

Remaining Loan Balance

Interest

Percent remaining at end of year

Rate	21	22	23	24	25
3.00%	39.8586	35.9415	31.9052	27.7461	23.4606
3.25%	40.7034	36.7451	32.6563	28.4325	24.0694
3.50%	41.5477	37.5496	33.4092	29.1216	24.6814
3.75%	42.3934	38.3568	34.1662	29.8157	25.2993
4.00%	43.2385	39.1648	34.9252	30.5129	25.9208
4.25%	44.0849	39.9758	35.6887	31.2157	26.5489
4.50%	44.9265	40.7832	36.4495	31.9167	27.1757
4.75%	45.7692	41.5933	37.2147	32.6235	27.8094
5.00%	46.6064	42.3992	37.9768	33.3281	28.4416
5.25%	47.4444	43.2077	38.7432	34.0386	29.0809
5.50%	48.2809	44.0165	39.5114	34.7523	29.7247
5.75%	49.1085	44.8174	40.2729	35.4601	30.3631
6.00%	49.9339	45.6178	41.0354	36.1705	31.0055
6.25%	50.7594	46.4204	41.8022	36.8870	31.6556
6.50%	51.5773	47.2166	42.5639	37.5995	32.3027
6.75%	52.3897	48.0089	43.3231	38.3110	32.9499
7.00%	53.1932	48.7936	44.0760	39.0174	33.5930
7.25%	53.9962	49.5799	44.8326	39.7294	34.2438
7.50%	54.7897	50.3580	45.5822	40.4357	34.8897
7.75%	55.5762	51.1306	46.3280	41.1396	35.5346
8.00%	56.3588	51.9011	47.0735	41.8452	36.1830
8.25%	57.1340	52.6659	47.8149	42.5482	36.8302
8.50%	57.8984	53.4210	48.5478	43.2438	37.4710
8.75%	58.6550	54.1697	49.2759	43.9362	38.1101
9.00%	59.4074	54.9162	50.0037	44.6304	38.7531
9.25%	60.1522	55.6567	50.7272	45.3220	39.3950
9.50%	60.8856	56.3868	51.4416	46.0056	40.0301
9.75%	61.6115	57.1111	52.1518	46.6868	40.6644
10.00%	62.3262	57.8252	52.8530	47.3601	41.2920
10.25%	63.0340	58.5342	53.5508	48.0320	41.9201
10.50%	63.7404	59.2440	54.2520	48.7099	42.5571
10.75%	64.4231	59.9296	54.9285	49.3625	43.1678
11.00%	65.1058	60.6177	55.6102	50.0233	43.7898
11.25%	65.7752	61.2933	56.2803	50.6733	44.4020
11.50%	66.4372	61.9629	56.9461	51.3209	45.0136
11.75%	67.0987	62.6345	57.6166	51.9763	45.6363
12.00%	67.7338	63.2787	58.2585	52.6017	46.2274
12.25%	68.3716	63.9284	58.9092	53.2394	46.8348
12.50%	68.9971	64.5665	59.5491	53.8675	47.4334
12.75%	69.6056	65.1877	60.1724	54.4788	48.0154
13.00%	70.2183	65.8161	60.8062	55.1049	48.6165
13.25%	70.8052	66.4116	61.4116	55.7007	49.1855
13.50%	71.3885	67.0169	62.0173	56.2994	49.7600
13.75%	71.9644	67.6105	62.6186	56.8955	50.3339
14.00%	72.5291	68.1934	63.2102	57.4828	50.9000
14.25%	73.0937	68.7786	63.8069	58.0786	51.4784
14.50%	73.6388	69.3437	64.3827	58.6526	52.0341
14.75%	74.1760	69.9019	64.9529	59.2226	52.5875
15.00%	74.7011	70.4484	65.5120	59.7820	53.1310
15.25%	75.2279	70.9992	66.0785	60.3527	53.6900
15.50%	75.7346	71.5287	66.6226	60.8996	54.2237
15.75%	76.2353	72.0536	67.1636	61.4453	54.7584
16.00%	76.7264	72.5694	67.6963	61.9837	55.2870
16.25%	77.2037	73.0712	68.2148	62.5077	55.8010
16.50%	77.6844	73.5793	68.7431	63.0458	56.3340
16.75%	78.1433	74.0637	69.2458	63.5559	56.8364
17.00%	78.5984	74.5458	69.7480	64.0679	57.3433
17.25%	79.0464	75.0216	70.2450	64.5760	57.8480
17.50%	79.4835	75.4866	70.7313	65.0738	58.3428
17.75%	79.9055	75.9356	71.2009	65.5538	58.8187
18.00%	80.3355	76.3963	71.6866	66.0555	59.3229

Remaining Loan Balance   **30 Years**

Percent remaining at end of year

Interest Rate	26	27	28	29
3.00%	19.0447	14.4945	9.8059	4.9747
3.25%	19.5624	14.9068	10.0975	5.1296
3.50%	20.0834	15.3218	10.3909	5.2846
3.75%	20.6105	15.7429	10.6895	5.4434
4.00%	21.1416	16.1677	10.9911	5.6037
4.25%	21.6798	16.5997	11.2995	5.7695
4.50%	22.2169	17.0302	11.6053	5.9312
4.75%	22.7616	17.4687	11.9189	6.0997
5.00%	23.3050	17.9057	12.2301	6.2642
5.25%	23.8566	18.3514	12.5500	6.4367
5.50%	24.4135	18.8028	12.8755	6.6139
5.75%	24.9653	19.2487	13.1947	6.7832
6.00%	25.5220	19.7002	13.5193	6.9573
6.25%	26.0877	20.1617	13.8546	7.1417
6.50%	26.6511	20.6211	14.1872	7.3224
6.75%	27.2156	21.0820	14.5213	7.5039
7.00%	27.7766	21.5396	14.8518	7.6805
7.25%	28.3469	22.0080	15.1939	7.8691
7.50%	28.9131	22.4726	15.5320	8.0526
7.75%	29.4794	22.9379	15.8710	8.2366
8.00%	30.0507	23.4096	16.2172	8.4278
8.25%	30.6222	23.8822	16.5647	8.6201
8.50%	31.1880	24.3496	16.9067	8.8060
8.75%	31.7533	24.8174	17.2497	8.9926
9.00%	32.3244	25.2927	17.6014	9.1885
9.25%	32.8959	25.7695	17.9553	9.3868
9.50%	33.4615	26.2410	18.3039	9.5790
9.75%	34.0279	26.7146	18.6555	9.7746
10.00%	34.5886	27.1832	19.0023	9.9648
10.25%	35.1515	27.6555	19.3541	10.1606
10.50%	35.7261	28.1424	19.7230	10.3756
10.75%	36.2733	28.6001	20.0600	10.5554
11.00%	36.8350	29.0755	20.4179	10.7586
11.25%	37.3876	29.5421	20.7670	10.9522
11.50%	37.9416	30.0119	21.1207	11.1514
11.75%	38.5100	30.4997	21.4959	11.3752
12.00%	39.0447	30.9511	21.8310	11.5542
12.25%	39.5999	31.4274	22.1955	11.7670
12.50%	40.1474	31.8966	22.5533	11.9728
12.75%	40.6780	32.3485	22.8926	12.1580
13.00%	41.2326	32.8294	23.2663	12.3832
13.25%	41.7525	33.2726	23.5984	12.5615
13.50%	42.2810	33.7274	23.9450	12.7570
13.75%	42.8109	34.1859	24.2972	12.9597
14.00%	43.3342	34.6384	24.6441	13.1571
14.25%	43.8738	35.1119	25.0166	13.3849
14.50%	44.3895	35.5597	25.3610	13.5811
14.75%	44.9047	36.0089	25.7086	13.7819
15.00%	45.4108	36.4495	26.0476	13.9736
15.25%	45.9371	36.9157	26.4181	14.2029
15.50%	46.4363	37.3522	26.7557	14.3949
15.75%	48.9389	37.7949	27.1021	14.5980
16.00%	47.4366	38.2338	27.4456	14.7990
16.25%	47.9195	38.6574	27.7728	14.9817
16.50%	48.4271	39.1121	28.1385	15.2108
16.75%	48.9007	39.5289	28.4610	15.3901
17.00%	49.3820	39.9568	28.7984	15.5880
17.25%	49.8631	40.3865	29.1396	15.7916
17.50%	50.3347	40.8070	29.4716	15.9854
17.75%	50.7859	41.2054	29.7789	16.1509
18.00%	51.2732	41.6489	30.1419	16.3840

Table 2   33

40 Years

Remaining Loan Balance

Percent remaining at end of year

Interest Rate	1	2	3	4	5
3.00%	98.6862	97.3323	95.9374	94.4999	93.0188
3.25%	98.7611	97.4812	96.1592	94.7935	93.3828
3.50%	98.8326	97.6237	96.3717	95.0753	93.7327
3.75%	98.9009	97.7598	96.5752	95.3454	94.0687
4.00%	98.9659	97.8897	96.7696	95.6039	94.3907
4.25%	99.0276	98.0131	96.9547	95.8504	94.6982
4.50%	99.0865	98.1310	97.1316	96.0863	94.9930
4.75%	99.1424	98.2431	97.3002	96.3115	95.2748
5.00%	99.1953	98.3495	97.4604	96.5258	95.5433
5.25%	99.2455	98.4503	97.6124	96.7295	95.7991
5.50%	99.2930	98.5461	97.7571	96.9236	96.0430
5.75%	99.3381	98.6370	97.8946	97.1084	96.2757
6.00%	99.3805	98.7228	98.0245	97.2832	96.4961
6.25%	99.4207	98.8042	98.1480	97.4495	96.7062
6.50%	99.4585	98.8808	98.2644	97.6067	96.9050
6.75%	99.4942	98.9532	98.3746	97.7556	97.0936
7.00%	99.5278	99.0214	98.4784	97.8962	97.2718
7.25%	99.5594	99.0858	98.5766	98.0293	97.4410
7.50%	99.5891	99.1463	98.6691	98.1549	97.6008
7.75%	99.6172	99.2036	98.7567	98.2740	97.7526
8.00%	99.6433	99.2569	98.8385	98.3854	97.8946
8.25%	99.6680	99.3074	98.9161	98.4911	98.0298
8.50%	99.6909	99.3546	98.9885	98.5900	98.1563
8.75%	99.7125	99.3988	99.0565	98.6831	98.2756
9.00%	99.7327	99.4404	99.1206	98.7708	98.3882
9.25%	99.7516	99.4792	99.1806	98.8531	98.4940
9.50%	99.7693	99.5157	99.2369	98.9304	98.5936
9.75%	99.7859	99.5499	99.2899	99.0034	98.6876
10.00%	99.8013	99.5817	99.3392	99.0712	98.7752
10.25%	99.8157	99.6115	99.3854	99.1350	98.8578
10.50%	99.8290	99.6391	99.4283	99.1942	98.9344
10.75%	99.8415	99.6652	99.4689	99.2505	99.0073
11.00%	99.8531	99.6893	99.5065	99.3025	99.0749
11.25%	99.8640	99.7119	99.5418	99.3515	99.1387
11.50%	99.8740	99.7328	99.5744	99.3968	99.1976
11.75%	99.8834	99.7524	99.6051	99.4395	99.2534
12.00%	99.8922	99.7707	99.6338	99.4796	99.3058
12.25%	99.9002	99.7876	99.6603	99.5165	99.3540
12.50%	99.9078	99.8034	99.6851	99.5512	99.3996
12.75%	99.9147	99.8179	99.7080	99.5833	99.4417
13.00%	99.9212	99.8315	99.7294	99.6132	99.4810
13.25%	99.9272	99.8442	99.7496	99.6415	99.5183
13.50%	99.9327	99.8557	99.7677	99.6670	99.5519
13.75%	99.9379	99.8667	99.7851	99.6915	99.5842
14.00%	99.9426	99.8766	99.8008	99.7137	99.6136
14.25%	99.9471	99.8861	99.8158	99.7349	99.6416
14.50%	99.9512	99.8947	99.8296	99.7543	99.6674
14.75%	99.9550	99.9029	99.8426	99.7727	99.6918
15.00%	99.9585	99.9102	99.8543	99.7893	99.7139
15.25%	99.9617	99.9171	99.8652	99.8048	99.7345
15.50%	99.9648	99.9237	99.8757	99.8198	99.7546
15.75%	99.9675	99.9294	99.8850	99.8330	99.7722
16.00%	99.9701	99.9350	99.8938	99.8456	99.7891
16.25%	99.9724	99.9400	99.9019	99.8571	99.8045
16.50%	99.9746	99.9447	99.9095	99.8680	99.8191
16.75%	99.9766	99.9489	99.9162	99.8777	99.8321
17.00%	99.9784	99.9528	99.9226	99.8868	99.8443
17.25%	99.9801	99.9565	99.9285	99.8953	99.8558
17.50%	99.9817	99.9599	99.9340	99.9032	99.8665
17.75%	99.9832	99.9631	99.9391	99.9105	99.8764
18.00%	99.9845	99.9659	99.9437	99.9172	99.8855

Remaining Loan Balance   **40 Years**

Interest Rate	Percent remaining at end of year				
	6	7	8	9	10
3.00%	91.4926	89.9200	88.2996	86.6298	84.9093
3.25%	91.9256	90.4203	88.8653	87.2591	85.5998
3.50%	92.3424	90.9026	89.4117	87.8676	86.2687
3.75%	92.7433	91.3674	89.9389	88.4559	86.9164
4.00%	93.1280	91.8140	90.4463	89.0230	87.5417
4.25%	93.4960	92.2418	90.9332	89.5680	88.1435
4.50%	93.8494	92.6533	91.4023	90.0938	88.7252
4.75%	94.1877	93.0479	91.8528	90.5996	89.2856
5.00%	94.5104	93.4251	92.2841	91.0846	89.8238
5.25%	94.8186	93.7854	92.6966	91.5492	90.3402
5.50%	95.1128	94.1301	93.0920	91.9954	90.8368
5.75%	95.3939	94.4600	93.4710	92.4235	91.3143
6.00%	95.6605	94.7734	93.8316	92.8316	91.7700
6.25%	95.9151	95.0730	94.1768	93.2230	92.2078
6.50%	96.1562	95.3573	94.5049	93.5955	92.6251
6.75%	96.3854	95.6280	94.8178	93.9512	93.0242
7.00%	96.6024	95.8845	95.1148	94.2894	93.4043
7.25%	96.8085	96.1287	95.3979	94.6123	93.7679
7.50%	97.0037	96.3601	95.6667	94.9194	94.1141
7.75%	97.1892	96.5806	95.9232	95.2129	94.4456
8.00%	97.3632	96.7876	96.1642	95.4891	94.7580
8.25%	97.5289	96.9851	96.3947	95.7537	95.0578
8.50%	97.6843	97.1705	96.6114	96.0028	95.3404
8.75%	97.8310	97.3459	96.8166	96.2391	95.6090
9.00%	97.9697	97.5120	97.0113	96.4636	95.8646
9.25%	98.1002	97.6684	97.1950	96.6759	96.1066
9.50%	98.2233	97.8162	97.3688	96.8769	96.3363
9.75%	98.3397	97.9562	97.5337	97.0681	96.5549
10.00%	98.4482	98.0870	97.6879	97.2471	96.7600
10.25%	98.5507	98.2106	97.8340	97.4169	96.9550
10.50%	98.6459	98.3257	97.9701	97.5754	97.1371
10.75%	98.7368	98.4356	98.1004	97.7274	97.3123
11.00%	98.8210	98.5377	98.2217	97.8690	97.4756
11.25%	98.9006	98.6344	98.3366	98.0035	97.6309
11.50%	98.9744	98.7240	98.4433	98.1286	97.7756
11.75%	99.0442	98.8090	98.5447	98.2476	97.9137
12.00%	99.1100	98.8893	98.6406	98.3604	98.0447
12.25%	99.1705	98.9633	98.7291	98.4647	98.1659
12.50%	99.2279	99.0335	98.8133	98.5639	98.2816
12.75%	99.2809	99.0984	98.8912	98.6560	98.3890
13.00%	99.3305	99.1593	98.9644	98.7426	98.4902
13.25%	99.3777	99.2173	99.0343	98.8255	98.5873
13.50%	99.4202	99.2696	99.0973	98.9003	98.6750
13.75%	99.4612	99.3202	99.1585	98.9731	98.7605
14.00%	99.4985	99.3662	99.2141	99.0394	98.8385
14.25%	99.5341	99.4103	99.2676	99.1032	98.9138
14.50%	99.5670	99.4510	99.3171	99.1623	98.9836
14.75%	99.5981	99.4897	99.3641	99.2187	99.0503
15.00%	99.6264	99.5248	99.4068	99.2699	99.1110
15.25%	99.6528	99.5576	99.4469	99.3181	99.1682
15.50%	99.6785	99.5897	99.4861	99.3654	99.2245
15.75%	99.7010	99.6179	99.5206	99.4069	99.2740
16.00%	99.7228	99.6452	99.5541	99.4473	99.3222
16.25%	99.7426	99.6699	99.5845	99.4841	99.3662
16.50%	99.7615	99.6936	99.6137	99.5195	99.4086
16.75%	99.7783	99.7147	99.6397	99.5510	99.4464
17.00%	99.7941	99.7347	99.6643	99.5810	99.4823
17.25%	99.8090	99.7534	99.6875	99.6092	99.5164
17.50%	99.8229	99.7710	99.7092	99.6358	99.5484
17.75%	99.8358	99.7873	99.7294	99.6605	99.5782
18.00%	99.8476	99.8023	99.7481	99.6832	99.6058

Table 2   35

<u>40 Years</u>   **Remaining Loan Balance**

Percent remaining at end of year

Interest Rate	11	12	13	14	15
3.00%	83.1365	81.3097	79.4274	77.4878	75.4892
3.25%	83.8858	82.1153	80.2864	78.3971	76.4455
3.50%	84.6129	82.8983	81.1226	79.2838	77.3796
3.75%	85.3181	83.6588	81.9363	80.1480	78.2915
4.00%	86.0000	84.3955	82.7257	80.9878	79.1791
4.25%	86.6573	85.1067	83.4889	81.8010	80.0399
4.50%	87.2937	85.7964	84.2304	82.5924	80.8792
4.75%	87.9078	86.4632	84.9483	83.3600	81.6945
5.00%	88.4985	87.1054	85.6410	84.1017	82.4837
5.25%	89.0661	87.7235	86.3088	84.8179	83.2468
5.50%	89.6129	88.3200	86.9542	85.5113	83.9870
5.75%	90.1395	88.8954	87.5779	86.1825	84.7048
6.00%	90.6429	89.4463	88.1758	86.8271	85.3951
6.25%	91.1273	89.9773	88.7533	87.4506	86.0641
6.50%	91.5897	90.4850	89.3063	88.0486	86.7068
6.75%	92.0327	90.9722	89.8379	88.6245	87.3267
7.00%	92.4553	91.4376	90.3464	89.1763	87.9216
7.25%	92.8601	91.8843	90.8354	89.7078	88.4957
7.50%	93.2462	92.3110	91.3032	90.2172	89.0468
7.75%	93.6166	92.7211	91.7537	90.7085	89.5795
8.00%	93.9662	93.1086	92.1799	91.1741	90.0849
8.25%	94.3022	93.4819	92.5913	91.6244	90.5746
8.50%	94.6195	93.8349	92.9809	92.0514	91.0398
8.75%	94.9215	94.1713	93.3529	92.4598	91.4854
9.00%	95.2094	94.4927	93.7088	92.8513	91.9135
9.25%	95.4824	94.7979	94.0474	93.2245	92.3221
9.50%	95.7419	95.0886	94.3704	93.5810	92.7132
9.75%	95.9895	95.3664	94.6798	93.9231	93.0893
10.00%	96.2220	95.6277	94.9711	94.2458	93.4445
10.25%	96.4434	95.8769	95.2495	94.5547	93.7853
10.50%	96.6506	96.1105	95.5108	94.8450	94.1059
10.75%	96.8502	96.3359	95.7636	95.1266	94.4177
11.00%	97.0366	96.5468	96.0004	95.3907	94.7104
11.25%	97.2143	96.7482	96.2269	95.6439	94.9917
11.50%	97.3799	96.9363	96.4388	95.8809	95.2555
11.75%	97.5383	97.1164	96.6421	96.1090	95.5098
12.00%	97.6889	97.2880	96.8362	96.3272	95.7536
12.25%	97.8284	97.4472	97.0165	96.5301	95.9805
12.50%	97.9618	97.5997	97.1897	96.7254	96.1996
12.75%	98.0859	97.7418	97.3512	96.9078	96.4044
13.00%	96.2030	97.8761	97.5041	97.0808	96.5990
13.25%	98.3156	98.0056	97.6519	97.2484	96.7881
13.50%	98.4174	98.1227	97.7856	97.4002	96.9594
13.75%	98.5168	98.2375	97.9171	97.5499	97.1288
14.00%	98.6077	98.3423	98.0374	97.6869	97.2841
14.25%	98.6956	98.4441	98.1544	97.8206	97.4361
14.50%	98.7772	98.5388	98.2634	97.9453	97.5780
14.75%	98.8554	98.6297	98.3683	98.0657	97.7153
15.00%	98.9266	98.7125	98.4640	98.1756	97.8407
15.25%	98.9938	98.7908	98.5546	98.2798	97.9600
15.50%	99.0601	98.8684	98.6447	98.3838	98.0795
15.75%	99.1185	98.9366	98.7240	98.4753	98.1845
16.00%	99.1755	99.0035	98.8020	98.5656	98.2886
16.25%	99.2275	99.0646	98.8732	98.6482	98.3839
16.50%	99.2779	99.1240	98.9426	98.7289	98.4772
16.75%	99.3228	99.1768	99.0044	98.8007	98.5603
17.00%	99.3655	99.2273	99.0636	98.8698	98.6404
17.25%	99.4061	99.2753	99.1200	98.9358	98.7171
17.50%	99.4444	99.3206	99.1734	98.9983	98.7899
17.75%	99.4801	99.3631	99.2235	99.0570	98.8585
18.00%	99.5131	99.4024	99.2699	99.1116	98.9223

Remaining Loan Balance   **40 Years**

Interest Rate	16	17	18	19	20
3.00%	73.4299	71.3078	69.1213	66.8682	64.5467
3.25%	74.4295	72.3470	70.1959	67.9737	65.6783
3.50%	75.4076	73.3655	71.2508	69.0609	66.7930
3.75%	76.3642	74.3633	72.2861	70.1297	67.8910
4.00%	77.2967	75.3377	73.2988	71.1768	68.9684
4.25%	78.2026	76.2856	74.2855	72.1987	70.0215
4.50%	79.0872	77.2130	75.2526	73.2022	71.0576
4.75%	79.9482	78.1171	76.1971	74.1839	72.0729
5.00%	80.7828	78.9950	77.1156	75.1401	73.0636
5.25%	81.5912	79.8466	78.0082	76.0709	74.0294
5.50%	82.3767	80.6756	78.8786	76.9802	74.9747
5.75%	83.1398	81.4825	79.7273	77.8684	75.8998
6.00%	83.8748	82.2607	80.5471	78.7278	76.7963
6.25%	84.5885	83.0179	81.3463	79.5671	77.6736
6.50%	85.2750	83.7474	82.1175	80.3784	78.5228
6.75%	85.9385	84.4536	82.8654	81.1666	79.3495
7.00%	86.5762	85.1336	83.5867	81.9279	80.1492
7.25%	87.1927	85.7921	84.2865	82.6681	80.9283
7.50%	87.7856	86.4265	84.9618	83.3835	81.6826
7.75%	88.3597	87.0420	85.6185	84.0806	82.4192
8.00%	88.9052	87.6276	86.2439	84.7455	83.1226
8.25%	89.4349	88.1975	86.8540	85.3955	83.8119
8.50%	89.9387	88.7403	87.4360	86.0164	84.4713
8.75%	90.4223	89.2623	87.9966	86.6157	85.1089
9.00%	90.8876	89.7655	88.5382	87.1957	85.7273
9.25%	91.3325	90.2475	89.0578	87.7532	86.3227
9.50%	91.7593	90.7107	89.5581	88.2910	86.8982
9.75%	92.1704	91.1579	90.0420	88.8124	87.4574
10.00%	92.5593	91.5814	90.5011	89.3077	87.9893
10.25%	92.9331	91.9894	90.9443	89.7869	88.5051
10.50%	93.2853	92.3743	91.3628	90.2400	88.9933
10.75%	93.6286	92.7505	91.7731	90.6854	89.4748
11.00%	93.9515	93.1047	92.1599	91.1058	89.9297
11.25%	94.2623	93.4465	92.5340	91.5134	90.3719
11.50%	94.5542	93.7678	92.8862	91.8976	90.7891
11.75%	94.8362	94.0792	93.2282	92.2716	91.1964
12.00%	95.1072	94.3789	93.5582	92.6334	91.5913
12.25%	95.3598	94.6586	93.8665	92.9717	91.9610
12.50%	95.6041	94.9298	94.1663	93.3016	92.3224
12.75%	95.8329	95.1841	94.4477	93.6116	92.6625
13.00%	96.0508	95.4268	94.7167	93.9086	92.9890
13.25%	96.2630	95.6639	94.9804	94.2006	93.3110
13.50%	96.4552	95.8786	95.2191	94.4650	93.6024
13.75%	96.6461	98.0927	95.4581	94.7306	93.8965
14.00%	96.8211	96.2889	95.6773	94.9744	94.1664
14.25%	96.9929	96.4824	95.8941	95.2163	94.4354
14.50%	97.1536	96.6635	96.0974	95.4435	94.6882
14.75%	97.3095	96.8397	96.2957	95.6659	94.9365
15.00%	97.4521	97.0009	96.4773	95.8695	95.1639
15.25%	97.5879	97.1549	96.6511	96.0648	95.3825
15.50%	97.7245	97.3104	96.8273	96.2639	95.6066
15.75%	97.8445	97.4469	96.9819	96.4382	95.8024
16.00%	97.9639	97.5832	97.1369	96.6137	96.0004
16.25%	98.0732	97.7081	97.2790	96.7748	96.1822
16.50%	98.1806	97.8313	97.4197	96.9349	96.3637
16.75%	98.2763	97.9409	97.5449	97.0771	96.5247
17.00%	98.3688	98.0472	97.6665	97.2158	96.6822
17.25%	98.4575	98.1495	97.7839	97.3500	96.8350
17.50%	98.5420	98.2471	97.8962	97.4787	96.9820
17.75%	98.6217	98.3393	98.0025	97.6007	97.1216
18.00%	98.6960	98.4254	98.1018	97.7150	97.2525

Table 2   37

40 Years   **Remaining Loan Balance**

Interest

Percent remaining at end of year

Rate	21	22	23	24	25
3.00%	62.1545	59.6895	57.1496	54.5324	51.8356
3.25%	63.3071	60.8577	58.3275	55.7139	53.0140
3.50%	64.4446	62.0126	59.4941	56.8860	54.1851
3.75%	65.5668	63.1540	60.6492	58.0488	55.3492
4.00%	66.6700	64.2780	61.7886	59.1977	56.5012
4.25%	67.7500	65.3800	62.9072	60.3274	57.6357
4.50%	68.8144	66.4682	64.0143	61.4476	58.7629
4.75%	69.8595	67.5386	65.1050	62.5533	59.8778
5.00%	70.8808	68.5863	66.1745	63.6392	60.9743
5.25%	71.8781	69.6111	67.2222	64.7048	62.0520
5.50%	72.8560	70.6179	68.2535	65.7557	63.1171
5.75%	73.8150	71.6071	69.2689	66.7926	64.1700
6.00%	74.7457	72.5685	70.2571	67.8032	65.1978
6.25%	75.6582	73.5132	71.2303	68.8004	66.2143
6.50%	76.5430	74.4306	72.1767	69.7718	67.2060
6.75%	77.4058	75.3269	73.1031	70.7246	68.1804
7.00%	78.2420	76.1968	74.0039	71.6524	69.1309
7.25%	79.0581	77.0477	74.8866	72.5636	70.0664
7.50%	79.8497	77.8744	75.7459	73.4521	70.9802
7.75%	80.6244	78.6854	76.5907	74.3278	71.8831
8.00%	81.3651	79.4616	77.4002	75.1677	72.7499
8.25%	82.0927	80.2261	78.1996	75.9994	73.6107
8.50%	82.7897	80.9594	78.9673	76.7992	74.4394
8.75%	83.4649	81.6711	79.7139	77.5784	75.2484
9.00%	84.1211	82.3643	80.4426	78.3407	76.0416
9.25%	84.7541	83.0341	81.1481	79.0801	76.8124
9.50%	85.3672	83.6842	81.8342	79.8006	77.5651
9.75%	85.9643	84.3188	82.5056	80.5074	78.3055
10.00%	86.5329	84.9240	83.1466	81.1830	79.0139
10.25%	87.0856	85.5135	83.7725	81.8444	79.7092
10.50%	87.6093	86.0728	84.3669	82.4731	80.3705
10.75%	88.1274	86.6278	84.9589	83.1014	81.0341
11.00%	88.6176	87.1535	85.5201	83.6977	81.6643
11.25%	89.0951	87.6670	86.0698	84.2832	82.2850
11.50%	89.5462	88.1526	86.5900	84.8379	82.8734
11.75%	89.9878	88.6293	87.1023	85.3859	83.4566
12.00%	90.4171	89.0939	87.6030	85.9229	84.0298
12.25%	90.8192	89.5294	88.0725	86.4268	84.5677
12.50%	91.2136	89.9579	88.5359	86.9257	85.1023
12.75%	91.5850	90.3619	88.9733	87.3970	85.6076
13.00%	91.9424	90.7514	89.3960	87.8534	86.0980
13.25%	92.2961	91.1382	89.8173	88.3103	86.5910
13.50%	92.6159	91.4877	90.1974	88.7217	87.0340
13.75%	92.9402	91.8438	90.5868	89.1457	87.4933
14.00%	93.2379	92.1706	90.9439	89.5341	87.9137
14.25%	93.5356	92.4989	91.3044	89.9281	88.3424
14.50%	93.8158	92.8082	91.6444	90.3002	88.7475
14.75%	94.0921	93.1143	91.9820	90.6711	89.1531
15.00%	94.3450	93.3943	92.2909	91.0101	89.5234
15.25%	94.5887	93.6649	92.5900	91.3393	89.8838
15.50%	94.8398	93.9454	92.9021	91.6851	90.2654
15.75%	95.0588	94.1894	93.1726	91.9837	90.5933
16.00%	95.2815	94.4387	93.4507	92.2925	90.9348
16.25%	95.4859	94.6676	93.7059	92.5758	91.2477
16.50%	95.6908	94.8981	93.9642	92.8640	91.5680
16.75%	95.8724	95.1019	94.1921	93.1175	91.8485
17.00%	96.0505	95.3026	94.4172	93.3690	92.1281
17.25%	96.2239	95.4986	94.6378	93.6162	92.4037
17.50%	96.3910	95.6879	94.8514	93.8563	92.6722
17.75%	96.5502	95.8686	95.0557	94.0862	92.9299
18.00%	96.6995	96.0383	95.2478	94.3027	93.1727

Remaining Loan Balance ___40 Years___

Interest Rate	Percent remaining at end of year				
	26	27	28	29	30
3.00%	49.0568	46.1935	43.2430	40.2029	37.0702
3.25%	50.2250	47.3441	44.3681	41.2940	38.1184
3.50%	51.3882	48.4918	45.4924	42.3864	39.1698
3.75%	52.5466	49.6370	46.6165	43.4807	40.2253
4.00%	53.6949	50.7743	47.7346	44.5712	41.2788
4.25%	54.8274	51.8973	48.8403	45.6508	42.3231
4.50%	55.9550	53.0180	49.9462	46.7332	43.3726
4.75%	57.0723	54.1306	51.0461	47.8119	44.4206
5.00%	58.1730	55.2283	52.1331	48.8794	45.4593
5.25%	59.2566	56.3108	53.2065	49.9353	46.4882
5.50%	60.3296	57.3849	54.2740	50.9877	47.5160
5.75%	61.3927	58.4514	55.3364	52.0376	48.5439
6.00%	62.4318	59.4952	56.3775	53.0674	49.5533
6.25%	63.4619	60.5324	57.4145	54.0960	50.5641
6.50%	64.4682	61.5471	58.4304	55.1049	51.5568
6.75%	65.4591	62.5483	59.4349	56.1046	52.5425
7.00%	66.4271	63.5279	80.4191	57.0855	53.5110
7.25%	67.3820	64.4964	61.3945	58.0601	54.4757
7.50%	68.3164	65.4459	62.3524	59.0189	55.4265
7.75%	69.2422	66.3890	63.3068	59.9770	56.3798
8.00%	70.1314	67.2956	64.2245	60.8984	57.2962
8.25%	71.0173	68.2017	65.1448	61.8259	58.2226
8.50%	71.8710	69.0756	66.0331	62.7216	59.1175
8.75%	72.7061	69.9322	66.9056	63.6034	60.0003
9.00%	73.5269	70.7762	67.7675	64.4766	60.8770
9.25%	74.3258	71.5992	68.6095	65.3311	61.7364
9.50%	75.1078	72.4066	69.4373	66.1733	62.5854
9.75%	75.8790	73.2051	70.2585	67.0115	63.4333
10.00%	76.6177	73.9705	71.0461	67.8155	64.2466
10.25%	77.3445	74.7257	71.8255	68.6137	65.0567
10.50%	78.0363	75.4447	72.5676	69.3735	65.8273
10.75%	78.7333	76.1726	73.3227	70.1508	66.6207
11.00%	79.3957	76.8645	74.0404	70.8896	67.3741
11.25%	80.0501	77.5503	74.7543	71.6271	68.1293
11.50%	80.6706	78.2008	75.4314	72.3263	68.8446
11.75%	81.2880	78.8504	76.1104	73.0306	69.5688
12.00%	81.8966	79.4928	76.7842	73.7320	70.2928
12.25%	82.4676	80.0954	77.4156	74.3885	70.9691
12.50%	83.0374	80.6990	78.0511	75.0525	71.6568
12.75%	83.5761	81.2700	78.6521	75.6801	72.3063
13.00%	84.1002	81.8267	79.2394	76.2949	72.9440
13.25%	84.6296	82.3920	79.8391	76.9267	73.6041
13.50%	85.1039	82.8964	80.3717	77.4843	74.1821
13.75%	85.5990	83.4270	80.9369	78.0820	74.8088
14.00%	86.0513	83.9108	81.4506	78.6230	75.3732
14.25%	86.5154	84.4103	81.9848	79.1902	75.9703
14.50%	86.9541	84.8827	82.4902	79.7267	76.5348
14.75%	87.3955	85.3603	83.0039	80.2753	77.1159
15.00%	87.7977	85.7946	83.4695	80.7706	77.6378
15.25%	88.1903	86.2196	83.9265	81.2581	78.1532
15.50%	88.6094	86.6776	84.4242	81.7956	78.7293
15.75%	88.9675	87.0663	84.8430	82.2432	79.2029
16.00%	89.3432	87.4774	85.2902	82.7262	79.7205
16.25%	89.6870	87.8529	85.6976	83.1647	80.1881
16.50%	90.0411	88.2423	86.1233	83.6269	80.6860
16.75%	90.3499	88.5800	86.4899	84.0214	81.1062
17.00%	90.6589	88.9195	86.8604	84.4225	81.5363
17.25%	90.9647	89.2569	87.2301	84.8246	81.9698
17.50%	91.2635	89.5876	87.5936	85.2213	82.3988
17.75%	91.5509	89.9061	87.9443	85.6047	82.8142
18.00%	91.8216	90.2062	88.2749	85.9657	83.2048

Table 2   39

40 Years

Remaining Loan Balance

Interest Rate

Percent remaining at end of year

Interest Rate	31	32	33	34	35
3.00%	33.8423	30.5162	27.0890	23.5575	19.9185
3.25%	34.8381	31.4495	27.9492	24.3334	20.5983
3.50%	35.8389	32.3894	28.8173	25.1182	21.2874
3.75%	36.8457	33.3372	29.6948	25.9134	21.9878
4.00%	37.8523	34.2862	30.5748	26.7122	22.6923
4.25%	38.8512	35.2287	31.4494	27.5062	23.3921
4.50%	39.8576	36.1811	32.3358	28.3138	24.1070
4.75%	40.8647	37.1362	33.2266	29.1273	24.8290
5.00%	41.8642	38.0852	34.1129	29.9373	25.5481
5.25%	42.8557	39.0278	34.9941	30.7434	26.2641
5.50%	43.8485	39.9741	35.8812	31.5574	26.9897
5.75%	44.8440	40.9257	36.7760	32.3813	27.7272
6.00%	45.8223	41.8613	37.6559	33.1912	28.4510
6.25%	46.8050	42.8042	38.5459	34.0138	29.2102
6.50%	47.7710	43.7316	39.4218	34.8233	29.9168
6.75%	48.7324	44.6569	40.2977	35.6350	30.6476
7.00%	49.6780	45.5680	41.1609	36.4352	31.3678
7.25%	50.6227	46.4808	42.0285	37.2424	32.0976
7.50%	51.5553	47.3835	42.8878	38.0432	32.8224
7.75%	52.4937	48.2955	43.7601	38.8604	33.5673
8.00%	53.3951	49.1702	44.5946	39.6393	34.2726
8.25%	54.3106	50.0633	45.4521	40.4457	35.0103
8.50%	55.1948	50.9254	46.2786	41.2211	35.7165
8.75%	56.0690	51.7795	47.0993	41.9928	36.4211
9.00%	56.9397	52.6331	47.9224	42.7699	37.1341
9.25%	57.7946	53.4724	48.7329	43.5360	37.8375
9.50%	58.6414	54.3059	49.5401	44.3014	38.5428
9.75%	59.4902	55.1450	50.3566	45.0800	39.2653
10.00%	60.3040	55.9486	51.1371	45.8218	39.9498
10.25%	61.1175	56.7551	51.9239	46.5735	40.6482
10.50%	61.8903	57.5194	52.6669	47.2796	41.2986
10.75%	62.6917	58.3190	53.4523	48.0360	42.0078
11.00%	63.4518	59.0756	54.1930	48.7455	42.6675
11.25%	64.2170	59.8413	54.9470	49.4729	43.3502
11.50%	64.9408	60.5635	55.6555	50.1523	43.9818
11.75%	65.6775	61.3036	56.3872	50.8609	44.6492
12.00%	66.4174	62.0505	57.1297	51.5849	45.3368
12.25%	67.1064	62.7431	57.8142	52.2464	45.9569
12.50%	67.8115	63.4570	58.5260	52.9419	46.6185
12.75%	68.4762	64.1283	59.1924	53.5891	47.2281
13.00%	69.1306	64.7908	59.8520	54.2314	47.8350
13.25%	69.8134	65.4889	60.5552	54.9267	48.5053
13.50%	70.4054	66.0861	61.1462	55.4966	49.0354
13.75%	71.0560	66.7535	61.8206	56.1651	49.6809
14.00%	71.6380	67.3449	62.4108	56.7397	50.2218
14.25%	72.2604	67.9860	63.0610	57.3865	50.8484
14.50%	72.8480	68.5896	63.6711	57.9900	51.4281
14.75%	73.4577	69.2219	64.3173	58.6383	52.0626
15.00%	74.0014	69.7805	64.8811	59.1940	52.5927
15.25%	74.5402	70.3360	65.4440	59.7515	53.1275
15.50%	75.1525	70.9802	66.1132	60.4358	53.8132
15.75%	75.6478	71.4904	66.6289	60.9439	54.2960
16.00%	76.1970	72.0665	67.2244	61.5482	54.8941
16.25%	76.6902	72.5795	67.7487	62.0718	55.4005
16.50%	77.2214	73.1399	68.3316	62.6671	55.9939
16.75%	77.6635	73.5977	68.7960	63.1254	56.4286
17.00%	78.1194	74.0742	69.2850	63.6152	56.9027
17.25%	78.5816	74.5605	69.7882	64.1243	57.4024
17.50%	79.0409	75.0457	70.2926	64.6375	57.9095
17.75%	79.4860	75.5166	70.7824	65.1360	58.4016
18.00%	79.9039	75.9572	71.2385	65.5967	58.8512

Remaining Loan Balance — **40 Years**

Rate	Percent remaining at end of year			
	36	37	38	39
3.00%	16.1689	12.3053	8.3241	4.2219
3.25%	16.7400	12.7544	8.6374	4.3845
3.50%	17.3205	13.2124	8.9582	4.5527
3.75%	17.9124	13.6815	9.2892	4.7294
4.00%	18.5085	14.1543	9.6228	4.9065
4.25%	19.0997	14.6213	9.9489	5.0739
4.50%	19.7069	15.1048	10.2912	5.2564
4.75%	20.3219	15.5961	10.6408	5.4450
5.00%	20.9343	16.0845	10.9865	5.6278
5.25%	21.5439	16.5698	11.3283	5.8048
5.50%	22.1643	17.0668	11.6817	5.9928
5.75%	22.7983	17.5783	12.0502	6.1957
6.00%	23.4186	18.0757	12.4033	6.3810
6.25%	24.0563	18.5921	12.7765	6.5869
6.50%	24.6818	19.0961	13.1363	6.7775
6.75%	25.3130	19.6069	13.5035	6.9752
7.00%	25.9341	20.1077	13.8600	7.1607
7.25%	26.5672	20.6222	14.2315	7.3619
7.50%	27.1963	21.1335	14.6000	7.5593
7.75%	27.8490	21.6715	14.9978	7.7882
8.00%	28.4605	22.1661	15.3492	7.9665
8.25%	29.1092	22.7024	15.7465	8.1946
8.50%	29.7253	23.2046	16.1076	8.3832
8.75%	30.3418	23.7087	16.4714	8.5748
9.00%	30.9695	24.2267	16.8514	8.7841
9.25%	31.5889	24.7372	17.2241	8.9859
9.50%	32.2126	25.2541	17.6050	9.1968
9.75%	32.8577	25.7965	18.0154	9.4407
10.00%	33.4631	26.2970	18.3806	9.6353
10.25%	34.0862	26.8191	18.7711	9.8583
10.50%	34.6584	27.2865	19.1022	10.0160
10.75%	35.2986	27.8316	19.5212	10.2720
11.00%	35.8862	28.3201	19.8786	10.4602
11.25%	36.5020	28.8424	20.2752	10.6929
11.50%	37.0631	29.3055	20.6071	10.8540
11.75%	37.6669	29.8186	20.9968	11.0807
12.00%	38.2964	30.3630	21.4235	11.3502
12.25%	38.8523	30.8267	21.7609	11.5200
12.50%	39.4577	31.3487	22.1660	11.7673
12.75%	40.0070	31.8094	22.5033	11.9388
13.00%	40.5557	32.2717	22.8441	12.1153
13.25%	41.1796	32.8219	23.2871	12.4093
13.50%	41.6457	33.1944	23.5289	12.4746
13.75%	42.2468	33.7236	23.9517	12.7481
14.00%	42.7304	34.1202	24.2242	12.8503
14.25%	43.3153	34.6357	24.6353	13.1130
14.50%	43.8489	35.0947	24.9832	13.3041
14.75%	44.4487	35.6326	25.4246	13.6047
15.00%	44.9302	36.0360	25.7119	13.7283
15.25%	45.4197	36.4508	26.0143	13.8701
15.50%	46.0879	37.0763	26.5643	14.3020
15.75%	46.5221	37.4313	26.8008	14.3697
16.00%	47.0938	37.9496	27.2302	14.6642
16.25%	47.5605	38.3473	27.5203	14.7967
16.50%	48.1324	38.8711	27.9606	15.1072
16.75%	48.5197	39.1796	28.1491	15.1223
17.00%	48.9559	39.5478	28.4095	15.2230
17.25%	49.4247	39.9566	28.7199	15.3839
17.50%	49.9049	40.3814	29.0510	15.5707
17.75%	50.3698	40.7903	29.3652	15.7386
18.00%	50.7863	41.1436	29.6147	15.8306

Table 2   41

Table 3
Daily Interest on $1000

Interest for a day, a week, a month, or fractions of a month is calculated on $1000 in Table 3. Two bases for interest are shown, a 360-day year, called ordinary interest, and a 365-day year, called exact interest. A 360-day year is used in mortgage loans. The 365-day year is used for prorations at closing and for other loans, unless specified differently.

Example 8. Interest on Loan for Given Period

Coronado Manor will be sold subject to a loan of $299,600 at 10 percent. At the closing, the buyer will receive credit for 10 days of interest.

Enter Table 3 on the page for 360-day years. On the line for 10 percent, read the factor under 10 days, $2.77778 per $1000 of loan. Multiply this by the number of thousands in the loan to get

$$\$2.77778 \times 299.6 = \$832.22,$$
the proration credit for 10 days interest.

Example 9. Short-term Rental of a House

The seller agrees the Fords may move into their new $350,000 home 5 days before closing, if they will pay rent at 6 percent, the fair market rate.

Enter Table 3 at the page for 365-day years. On the 6 percent line under 5 days, find $0.82192 per $1000. Multiply it by the thousands of value to get

$$\$0.82192 \times 350 = \$287.67,$$
the fair rental by reference to interest rate tables.

360 Days Daily Interest on $1000

Number of days in a 360-day year

Interest Rate	1	5	7	10	15	30
3.00%	0.08333	0.41667	0.58333	0.83333	1.25000	2.50000
3.25%	0.09028	0.45139	0.63194	0.90278	1.35417	2.70833
3.50%	0.09722	0.48611	0.68056	0.97222	1.45833	2.91667
3.75%	0.10417	0.52083	0.72917	1.04167	1.56250	3.12500
4.00%	0.11111	0.55556	0.77778	1.11111	1.66667	3.33333
4.25%	0.11806	0.59028	0.82639	1.18056	1.77083	3.54167
4.50%	0.12500	0.62500	0.87500	1.25000	1.87500	3.75000
4.75%	0.13194	0.65972	0.92361	1.31944	1.97917	3.95833
5.00%	0.13889	0.69444	0.97222	1.38889	2.08333	4.16667
5.25%	0.14583	0.72917	1.02083	1.45833	2.18750	4.37500
5.50%	0.15278	0.76389	1.06944	1.52778	2.29167	4.58333
5.75%	0.15972	0.79861	1.11806	1.59722	2.39583	4.79167
6.00%	0.16667	0.83333	1.16667	1.66667	2.50000	5.00000
6.25%	0.17361	0.86806	1.21528	1.73611	2.60417	5.20833
6.50%	0.18056	0.90278	1.26389	1.80556	2.70833	5.41667
6.75%	0.18750	0.93750	1.31250	1.87500	2.81250	5.62500
7.00%	0.19444	0.97222	1.36111	1.94444	2.91667	5.83333
7.25%	0.20139	1.00694	1.40972	2.01389	3.02083	6.04167
7.50%	0.20833	1.04167	1.45833	2.08333	3.12500	6.25000
7.75%	0.21528	1.07639	1.50694	2.15278	3.22917	6.45833
8.00%	0.22222	1.11111	1.55556	2.22222	3.33333	6.66667
8.25%	0.22917	1.14583	1.60417	2.29167	3.43750	6.87500
8.50%	0.23611	1.18056	1.65278	2.36111	3.54167	7.08333
8.75%	0.24306	1.21528	1.70139	2.43056	3.64583	7.29167
9.00%	0.25000	1.25000	1.75000	2.50000	3.75000	7.50000
9.25%	0.25694	1.28472	1.79861	2.56944	3.85417	7.70833
9.50%	0.26389	1.31944	1.84722	2.63889	3.95833	7.91667
9.75%	0.27083	1.35417	1.89583	2.70833	4.06250	8.12500
10.00%	0.27778	1.38889	1.94444	2.77778	4.16667	8.33333
10.25%	0.28472	1.42361	1.99306	2.84722	4.27083	8.54167
10.50%	0.29167	1.45833	2.04167	2.91667	4.37500	8.75000
10.75%	0.29861	1.49306	2.09028	2.98611	4.47917	8.95833
11.00%	0.30556	1.52778	2.13889	3.05556	4.58333	9.16667
11.25%	0.31250	1.56250	2.18750	3.12500	4.68750	9.37500
11.50%	0.31944	1.59722	2.23611	3.19444	4.79167	9.58333
11.75%	0.32639	1.63194	2.28472	3.26389	4.89583	9.79167
12.00%	0.33333	1.66667	2.33333	3.33333	5.00000	10.00000
12.25%	0.34028	1.70139	2.38194	3.40278	5.10417	10.20833
12.50%	0.34722	1.73611	2.43056	3.47222	5.20833	10.41667
12.75%	0.35417	1.77083	2.47917	3.54167	5.31250	10.62500
13.00%	0.36111	1.80556	2.52778	3.61111	5.41667	10.83333
13.25%	0.36806	1.84028	2.57639	3.68056	5.52083	11.04167
13.50%	0.37500	1.87500	2.62500	3.75000	5.62500	11.25000
13.75%	0.38194	1.90972	2.67361	3.81944	5.72917	11.45833
14.00%	0.38889	1.94444	2.72222	3.88889	5.83333	11.66667
14.25%	0.39583	1.97917	2.77083	3.95833	5.93750	11.87500
14.50%	0.40278	2.01389	2.81944	4.02778	6.04167	12.08333
14.75%	0.40972	2.04861	2.86806	4.09722	6.14583	12.29167
15.00%	0.41667	2.08333	2.91667	4.16667	6.25000	12.50000
15.25%	0.42361	2.11806	2.96528	4.23611	6.35417	12.70833
15.50%	0.43056	2.15278	3.01389	4.30556	6.45833	12.91667
15.75%	0.43750	2.18750	3.06250	4.37500	6.56250	13.12500
16.00%	0.44444	2.22222	3.11111	4.44444	6.66667	13.33333
16.25%	0.45139	2.25694	3.15972	4.51389	6.77083	13.54167
16.50%	0.45833	2.29167	3.20833	4.58333	6.87500	13.75000
16.75%	0.46528	2.32639	3.25694	4.65278	6.97917	13.95833
17.00%	0.47222	2.36111	3.30556	4.72222	7.08333	14.16667
17.25%	0.47917	2.39583	3.35417	4.79167	7.18750	14.37500
17.50%	0.48611	2.43056	3.40278	4.86111	7.29167	14.58333
17.75%	0.49306	2.46528	3.45139	4.93056	7.39583	14.79167
18.00%	0.50000	2.50000	3.50000	5.00000	7.50000	15.00000

Daily Interest on $1000   **365 Days**

Interest Rate	Number of days in a 365-day year					
	1	5	7	10	15	30
3.00%	0.08219	0.41096	0.57534	0.82192	1.23288	2.46575
3.25%	0.08904	0.44521	0.62329	0.89041	1.33562	2.67123
3.50%	0.09589	0.47945	0.67123	0.95890	1.43836	2.87671
3.75%	0.10274	0.51370	0.71918	1.02740	1.54110	3.08219
4.00%	0.10959	0.54795	0.76712	1.09589	1.64384	3.28767
4.25%	0.11644	0.58219	0.81507	1.16438	1.74658	3.49315
4.50%	0.12329	0.61644	0.86301	1.23288	1.84932	3.69863
4.75%	0.13014	0.65068	0.91096	1.30137	1.95205	3.90411
5.00%	0.13699	0.68493	0.95890	1.36986	2.05479	4.10959
5.25%	0.14384	0.71918	1.00685	1.43836	2.15753	4.31507
5.50%	0.15068	0.75342	1.05479	1.50685	2.26027	4.52055
5.75%	0.15753	0.78767	1.10274	1.57534	2.36301	4.72603
6.00%	0.16438	0.82192	1.15068	1.64384	2.46575	4.93151
6.25%	0.17123	0.85616	1.19863	1.71233	2.56849	5.13699
6.50%	0.17808	0.89041	1.24658	1.78082	2.67123	5.34247
6.75%	0.18493	0.92466	1.29452	1.84932	2.77397	5.54795
7.00%	0.19178	0.95890	1.34247	1.91781	2.87671	5.75342
7.25%	0.19863	0.99315	1.39041	1.98630	2.97945	5.95890
7.50%	0.20548	1.02740	1.43836	2.05479	3.08219	6.16438
7.75%	0.21233	1.06164	1.48630	2.12329	3.18493	6.36986
8.00%	0.21918	1.09589	1.53425	2.19178	3.28767	6.57534
8.25%	0.22603	1.13014	1.58219	2.26027	3.39041	6.78082
8.50%	0.23288	1.16438	1.63014	2.32877	3.49315	6.98630
8.75%	0.23973	1.19863	1.67808	2.39726	3.59589	7.19178
9.00%	0.24658	1.23288	1.72603	2.46575	3.69863	7.39726
9.25%	0.25342	1.26712	1.77397	2.53425	3.80137	7.60274
9.50%	0.26027	1.30137	1.82192	2.60274	3.90411	7.80822
9.75%	0.26712	1.33562	1.86986	2.67123	4.00685	8.01370
10.00%	0.27397	1.36986	1.91781	2.73973	4.10959	8.21918
10.25%	0.28082	1.40411	1.96575	2.80822	4.21233	8.42466
10.50%	0.28767	1.43836	2.01370	2.87671	4.31507	8.63014
10.75%	0.29452	1.47260	2.06164	2.94521	4.41781	8.83562
11.00%	0.30137	1.50685	2.10959	3.01370	4.52055	9.04110
11.25%	0.30822	1.54110	2.15753	3.08219	4.62329	9.24658
11.50%	0.31507	1.57534	2.20548	3.15068	4.72603	9.45205
11.75%	0.32192	1.60959	2.25342	3.21918	4.82877	9.65753
12.00%	0.32877	1.64384	2.30137	3.28767	4.93151	9.86301
12.25%	0.33562	1.67808	2.34932	3.35616	5.03425	10.06849
12.50%	0.34247	1.71233	2.39726	3.42466	5.13699	10.27397
12.75%	0.34932	1.74658	2.44521	3.49315	5.23973	10.47945
13.00%	0.35616	1.78082	2.49315	3.56164	5.34247	10.68493
13.25%	0.36301	1.81507	2.54110	3.63014	5.44521	10.89041
13.50%	0.36986	1.84932	2.58904	3.69863	5.54795	11.09589
13.75%	0.37671	1.88356	2.63699	3.76712	5.65068	11.30137
14.00%	0.38356	1.91781	2.68493	3.83562	5.75342	11.50685
14.25%	0.39041	1.95205	2.73288	3.90411	5.85616	11.71233
14.50%	0.39726	1.98630	2.78082	3.97260	5.95890	11.91781
14.75%	0.40411	2.02055	2.82877	4.04110	6.06164	12.12329
15.00%	0.41096	2.05479	2.87671	4.10959	6.16438	12.32877
15.25%	0.41781	2.08904	2.92466	4.17808	6.26712	12.53425
15.50%	0.42466	2.12329	2.97260	4.24658	6.36986	12.73973
15.75%	0.43151	2.15753	3.02055	4.31507	6.47260	12.94521
16.00%	0.43836	2.19178	3.06849	4.38356	6.57534	13.15068
16.25%	0.44521	2.22603	3.11644	4.45205	6.67808	13.35616
16.50%	0.45205	2.26027	3.16438	4.52055	6.78082	13.56164
16.75%	0.45890	2.29452	3.21233	4.58904	6.88356	13.76712
17.00%	0.46575	2.32877	3.26027	4.65753	6.98630	13.97260
17.25%	0.47260	2.38301	3.30822	4.72603	7.08904	14.17808
17.50%	0.47945	2.39726	3.35616	4.79452	7.19178	14.38356
17.75%	0.48630	2.43151	3.40411	4.86301	7.29452	14.58904
18.00%	0.49315	2.46575	3.45205	4.93151	7.39726	14.79452

Table 3   45

Table 4
Benefits of Regular Additional Payments

Prepaying a mortgage loan regularly cuts interest expense and builds equity. Even $50 per month added to $1000 of loan payment can cut five years or more from the loan term. Table 4 gives the particulars of the shortened loan life and the interest savings that regular additional payments bring.

The secret to substantial savings that come from small additional payments lies in interest compounding. Principal payments reduce future interest expense at the compounded mortgage rate.

Table 4, of necessity, must be based on additional payments as a percent of the original loan payment. Using dollar amounts, while perhaps, a more useful approach, would result in fixed payments having vastly different impacts on a loan of $200,000 versus a loan of $500,000. Using a percent of the original loan payment eliminates this problem.

Example 10. Benefits of Regular Additional Payments

Jeff has taken out a 30 year loan at 6.50 percent interest. He can put an additional $100 per month, or 10 percent of the total, toward the mortgage.

To find the benefits of such a program, enter Table 4 at 6.50 percent interest; in the section for added pay of 10 percent, read across on the line for an original term of 30 years. Under 6.50 percent, the loan is shown to have been shortened by 80 months.

Next to the number of months, read under interest savings, 33.21 percent. The additional payments will save interest equal to 33.21 percent of the original loan amount, compared to what the interest would be without additional payments.

To find what the interest would be without additional payments simply multiply the original loan payment by the number of months the loan was originally scheduled to run

$$\$1,000 \times 360 \text{ months} = \$360,000$$

Then subtract the original loan amount from this number to arrive at how much interest would have been paid without making additional payments.

$$\$360,000 - 158,210.82 = \$201,789.18$$

By making additional payments of $100 Jeff will save 33.21 percent of the original loan amount in interest.

$$\$158,210.82 \times 33.21\% = \$52,542 \text{ in saved interest.}$$

The loan amount used in this example had to be "fudged" in order to make the additional payment of $100 be 10 percent of the original payment. In this case a loan payment of $1000, on which $100 would be an additional 10 percent, would translate into a loan amount of $158,210.82 at 6.50 percent over a 30-year term.

Benefits of Additional Payments

Term Reduction and Interest Savings

Additional Payment	Original Term	3.00% Interest		3.50% Interest		4.00% Interest	
		Increased Payment Will Shorten Loan By:	Interest Savings as % of Original Loan Amt	Increased Payment Will Shorten Loan By:	Interest Savings as % of Original Loan Amt	Increased Payment Will Shorten Loan By:	Interest Savings as % of Original Loan Amt
2.50%	15 yrs	6 mos	0.79%	6 mos	0.98%	6 mos	1.19%
	20 yrs	8 mos	1.19%	8 mos	1.50%	9 mos	1.85%
	25 yrs	11 mos	1.67%	12 mos	2.15%	12 mos	2.70%
	30 yrs	14 mos	2.25%	15 mos	2.95%	17 mos	3.78%
4.00%	15 yrs	9 mos	1.24%	9 mos	1.53%	9 mos	1.86%
	20 yrs	12 mos	1.86%	13 mos	2.34%	14 mos	2.89%
	25 yrs	17 mos	2.61%	18 mos	3.34%	19 mos	4.20%
	30 yrs	22 mos	3.51%	24 mos	4.58%	26 mos	5.85%
5.00%	15 yrs	11 mos	1.53%	11 mos	1.89%	12 mos	2.29%
	20 yrs	15 mos	2.29%	16 mos	2.88%	17 mos	3.55%
	25 yrs	21 mos	3.21%	22 mos	4.11%	24 mos	5.15%
	30 yrs	27 mos	4.31%	29 mos	5.61%	31 mos	7.15%
6.00%	15 yrs	13 mos	1.81%	13 mos	2.24%	14 mos	2.71%
	20 yrs	18 mos	2.71%	19 mos	3.40%	20 mos	4.19%
	25 yrs	25 mos	3.79%	26 mos	4.85%	28 mos	6.07%
	30 yrs	32 mos	5.08%	34 mos	6.61%	37 mos	8.41%
7.50%	15 yrs	16 mos	2.22%	16 mos	2.74%	17 mos	3.31%
	20 yrs	22 mos	3.31%	23 mos	4.16%	25 mos	5.12%
	25 yrs	30 mos	4.63%	32 mos	5.91%	34 mos	7.38%
	30 yrs	39 mos	6.19%	42 mos	8.03%	45 mos	10.19%
10.00%	15 yrs	20 mos	2.87%	21 mos	3.54%	22 mos	4.27%
	20 yrs	29 mos	4.27%	30 mos	5.35%	32 mos	6.57%
	25 yrs	39 mos	5.95%	41 mos	7.57%	44 mos	9.43%
	30 yrs	50 mos	7.93%	53 mos	10.25%	57 mos	12.94%
12.50%	15 yrs	24 mos	3.49%	25 mos	4.29%	26 mos	5.17%
	20 yrs	35 mos	5.17%	37 mos	6.47%	38 mos	7.92%
	25 yrs	47 mos	7.18%	50 mos	9.11%	52 mos	11.31%
	30 yrs	60 mos	9.53%	64 mos	12.28%	69 mos	15.44%
15.00%	15 yrs	29 mos	4.07%	30 mos	5.00%	31 mos	6.01%
	20 yrs	41 mos	6.01%	43 mos	7.51%	44 mos	9.17%
	25 yrs	54 mos	8.32%	57 mos	10.54%	61 mos	13.05%
	30 yrs	70 mos	11.02%	74 mos	14.14%	79 mos	17.73%
20.00%	15 yrs	36 mos	5.13%	37 mos	6.29%	39 mos	7.55%
	20 yrs	51 mos	7.55%	54 mos	9.40%	56 mos	11.44%
	25 yrs	68 mos	10.40%	72 mos	13.11%	76 mos	16.15%
	30 yrs	87 mos	13.69%	92 mos	17.48%	98 mos	21.77%
25.00%	15 yrs	43 mos	6.09%	44 mos	7.45%	46 mos	8.92%
	20 yrs	61 mos	8.93%	63 mos	11.07%	66 mos	13.44%
	25 yrs	81 mos	12.23%	85 mos	15.36%	89 mos	18.85%
	30 yrs	102 mos	16.03%	108 mos	20.35%	114 mos	25.23%
33.33%	15 yrs	53 mos	7.49%	55 mos	9.13%	56 mos	10.90%
	20 yrs	75 mos	10.91%	77 mos	13.47%	80 mos	16.28%
	25 yrs	98 mos	14.85%	103 mos	18.54%	107 mos	22.63%
	30 yrs	124 mos	19.33%	131 mos	24.38%	137 mos	30.01%

Table 4   49

Benefits of Additional Payments

Term Reduction and Interest Savings

Additional Payment	Original Term	4.50% Interest — Increased Payment Will Shorten Loan By:	4.50% Interest — Interest Savings as % of Original Loan Amt	5.00% Interest — Increased Payment Will Shorten Loan By:	5.00% Interest — Interest Savings as % of Original Loan Amt	5.50% Interest — Increased Payment Will Shorten Loan By:	5.50% Interest — Interest Savings as % of Original Loan Amt
2.50%	15 yrs	6 mos	1.42%	6 mos	1.67%	7 mos	1.95%
	20 yrs	9 mos	2.25%	10 mos	2.70%	10 mos	3.21%
	25 yrs	13 mos	3.35%	14 mos	4.09%	15 mos	4.94%
	30 yrs	18 mos	4.76%	20 mos	5.92%	21 mos	7.27%
4.00%	15 yrs	10 mos	2.21%	10 mos	2.60%	10 mos	3.03%
	20 yrs	15 mos	3.50%	15 mos	4.20%	16 mos	4.97%
	25 yrs	21 mos	5.19%	22 mos	6.32%	23 mos	7.61%
	30 yrs	28 mos	7.34%	30 mos	9.09%	33 mos	11.11%
5.00%	15 yrs	12 mos	2.73%	12 mos	3.20%	13 mos	3.73%
	20 yrs	18 mos	4.30%	19 mos	5.15%	20 mos	6.09%
	25 yrs	25 mos	6.35%	27 mos	7.73%	29 mos	9.28%
	30 yrs	34 mos	8.96%	37 mos	11.06%	40 mos	13.49%
6.00%	15 yrs	14 mos	3.22%	15 mos	3.79%	15 mos	4.40%
	20 yrs	21 mos	5.07%	22 mos	6.07%	23 mos	7.17%
	25 yrs	30 mos	7.47%	32 mos	9.07%	34 mos	10.88%
	30 yrs	40 mos	10.51%	43 mos	12.94%	47 mos	15.73%
7.50%	15 yrs	17 mos	3.94%	18 mos	4.63%	19 mos	5.37%
	20 yrs	26 mos	6.19%	27 mos	7.38%	29 mos	8.71%
	25 yrs	36 mos	9.07%	38 mos	10.98%	41 mos	13.14%
	30 yrs	48 mos	12.70%	52 mos	15.59%	56 mos	18.88%
10.00%	15 yrs	22 mos	5.07%	23 mos	5.94%	24 mos	6.89%
	20 yrs	33 mos	7.92%	35 mos	9.43%	36 mos	11.09%
	25 yrs	46 mos	11.54%	49 mos	13.93%	52 mos	16.60%
	30 yrs	62 mos	16.04%	66 mos	19.60%	71 mos	23.62%
12.50%	15 yrs	27 mos	6.13%	28 mos	7.17%	29 mos	8.30%
	20 yrs	40 mos	9.53%	42 mos	11.31%	44 mos	13.27%
	25 yrs	55 mos	13.80%	59 mos	16.60%	62 mos	19.71%
	30 yrs	73 mos	19.07%	78 mos	23.19%	84 mos	27.82%
15.00%	15 yrs	32 mos	7.12%	33 mos	8.32%	34 mos	9.61%
	20 yrs	46 mos	11.01%	48 mos	13.05%	51 mos	15.28%
	25 yrs	64 mos	15.88%	67 mos	19.03%	71 mos	22.54%
	30 yrs	84 mos	21.81%	90 mos	26.42%	95 mos	31.57%
20.00%	15 yrs	40 mos	8.92%	41 mos	10.39%	42 mos	11.98%
	20 yrs	58 mos	13.69%	60 mos	16.15%	63 mos	18.84%
	25 yrs	79 mos	19.55%	83 mos	23.32%	87 mos	27.47%
	30 yrs	104 mos	26.61%	110 mos	32.02%	116 mos	38.00%
25.00%	15 yrs	47 mos	10.51%	48 mos	12.22%	50 mos	14.06%
	20 yrs	68 mos	16.02%	71 mos	18.84%	73 mos	21.91%
	25 yrs	93 mos	22.72%	97 mos	26.98%	101 mos	31.63%
	30 yrs	120 mos	30.68%	127 mos	36.71%	133 mos	43.33%
33.33%	15 yrs	58 mos	12.81%	59 mos	14.84%	61 mos	17.01%
	20 yrs	83 mos	19.32%	86 mos	22.62%	89 mos	26.18%
	25 yrs	112 mos	27.12%	116 mos	32.02%	121 mos	37.32%
	30 yrs	144 mos	36.23%	150 mos	43.05%	157 mos	50.45%

Benefits of Additional Payments

Term Reduction and Interest Savings

Additional Payment	Original Term	6.00% Interest Increased Payment Will Shorten Loan By:	6.00% Interest Savings as % of Original Loan Amt	6.50% Interest Increased Payment Will Shorten Loan By:	6.50% Interest Savings as % of Original Loan Amt	7.00% Interest Increased Payment Will Shorten Loan By:	7.00% Interest Savings as % of Original Loan Amt
2.50%	15 yrs	7 mos	2.25%	7 mos	2.58%	8 mos	2.94%
	20 yrs	11 mos	3.78%	12 mos	4.41%	12 mos	5.12%
	25 yrs	16 mos	5.92%	17 mos	7.03%	19 mos	8.29%
	30 yrs	23 mos	8.85%	25 mos	10.68%	28 mos	12.79%
4.00%	15 yrs	11 mos	3.50%	11 mos	4.01%	12 mos	4.57%
	20 yrs	17 mos	5.84%	18 mos	6.81%	19 mos	7.88%
	25 yrs	25 mos	9.08%	27 mos	10.75%	29 mos	12.63%
	30 yrs	35 mos	13.46%	38 mos	16.14%	42 mos	19.21%
5.00%	15 yrs	13 mos	4.30%	14 mos	4.92%	15 mos	5.60%
	20 yrs	21 mos	7.15%	22 mos	8.32%	23 mos	9.61%
	25 yrs	31 mos	11.06%	33 mos	13.05%	35 mos	15.29%
	30 yrs	43 mos	16.28%	46 mos	19.47%	50 mos	23.08%
6.00%	15 yrs	16 mos	5.07%	16 mos	5.80%	17 mos	6.60%
	20 yrs	25 mos	8.40%	26 mos	9.76%	27 mos	11.26%
	25 yrs	36 mos	12.93%	38 mos	15.23%	41 mos	17.81%
	30 yrs	50 mos	18.94%	54 mos	22.57%	58 mos	26.68%
7.50%	15 yrs	19 mos	6.18%	20 mos	7.07%	21 mos	8.02%
	20 yrs	30 mos	10.18%	31 mos	11.81%	33 mos	13.60%
	25 yrs	43 mos	15.58%	46 mos	18.30%	49 mos	21.32%
	30 yrs	60 mos	22.64%	65 mos	26.87%	69 mos	31.61%
10.00%	15 yrs	25 mos	7.92%	26 mos	9.03%	27 mos	10.23%
	20 yrs	38 mos	12.93%	40 mos	14.95%	42 mos	17.16%
	25 yrs	55 mos	19.59%	58 mos	22.91%	61 mos	26.57%
	30 yrs	75 mos	28.16%	80 mos	33.21%	86 mos	38.84%
12.50%	15 yrs	30 mos	9.52%	31 mos	10.84%	32 mos	12.26%
	20 yrs	46 mos	15.43%	48 mos	17.79%	50 mos	20.37%
	25 yrs	65 mos	23.18%	69 mos	27.00%	73 mos	31.19%
	30 yrs	89 mos	33.00%	94 mos	38.73%	100 mos	45.04%
15.00%	15 yrs	35 mos	11.01%	36 mos	12.51%	37 mos	14.13%
	20 yrs	53 mos	17.72%	55 mos	20.38%	57 mos	23.27%
	25 yrs	75 mos	26.41%	79 mos	30.66%	83 mos	35.30%
	30 yrs	101 mos	37.29%	107 mos	43.58%	113 mos	50.45%
20.00%	15 yrs	44 mos	13.68%	45 mos	15.51%	46 mos	17.46%
	20 yrs	65 mos	21.76%	68 mos	24.92%	70 mos	28.33%
	25 yrs	91 mos	32.01%	96 mos	36.95%	100 mos	42.29%
	30 yrs	122 mos	44.57%	128 mos	51.72%	134 mos	59.46%
25.00%	15 yrs	51 mos	16.02%	53 mos	18.11%	54 mos	20.33%
	20 yrs	76 mos	25.22%	79 mos	28.78%	82 mos	32.60%
	25 yrs	106 mos	36.70%	110 mos	42.17%	114 mos	48.05%
	30 yrs	139 mos	50.54%	146 mos	58.32%	152 mos	66.68%
33.33%	15 yrs	62 mos	19.32%	64 mos	21.77%	65 mos	24.36%
	20 yrs	91 mos	30.00%	94 mos	34.08%	97 mos	38.41%
	25 yrs	125 mos	43.04%	130 mos	49.16%	134 mos	55.69%
	30 yrs	163 mos	58.43%	169 mos	66.97%	176 mos	76.05%

Table 4   51

Benefits of Additional Payments

Term Reduction and Interest Savings

Additional Payment	Original Term	7.50% Interest		8.00% Interest		8.50% Interest	
		Increased Payment Will Shorten Loan By:	Interest Savings as % of Original Loan Amt	Increased Payment Will Shorten Loan By:	Interest Savings as % of Original Loan Amt	Increased Payment Will Shorten Loan By:	Interest Savings as % of Original Loan Amt
	15 yrs	8 mos	3.34%	8 mos	3.77%	9 mos	4.24%
2.50%	20 yrs	13 mos	5.91%	14 mos	6.79%	15 mos	7.76%
	25 yrs	20 mos	9.73%	22 mos	11.34%	23 mos	13.15%
	30 yrs	30 mos	15.21%	33 mos	17.97%	36 mos	21.11%
	15 yrs	12 mos	5.18%	13 mos	5.84%	13 mos	6.55%
4.00%	20 yrs	20 mos	9.08%	21 mos	10.39%	22 mos	11.84%
	25 yrs	31 mos	14.75%	33 mos	17.11%	35 mos	19.74%
	30 yrs	45 mos	22.69%	49 mos	26.62%	53 mos	31.01%
	15 yrs	15 mos	6.34%	16 mos	7.14%	16 mos	8.00%
5.00%	20 yrs	24 mos	11.05%	26 mos	12.63%	27 mos	14.36%
	25 yrs	37 mos	17.82%	40 mos	20.61%	42 mos	23.71%
	30 yrs	54 mos	27.16%	58 mos	31.72%	63 mos	36.80%
	15 yrs	18 mos	7.46%	18 mos	8.39%	19 mos	9.40%
6.00%	20 yrs	29 mos	12.92%	30 mos	14.74%	32 mos	16.73%
	25 yrs	43 mos	20.69%	46 mos	23.87%	49 mos	27.39%
	30 yrs	63 mos	31.28%	67 mos	36.39%	72 mos	42.05%
	15 yrs	22 mos	9.06%	22 mos	10.18%	23 mos	11.38%
7.50%	20 yrs	35 mos	15.57%	36 mos	17.72%	38 mos	20.06%
	25 yrs	52 mos	24.68%	55 mos	28.37%	58 mos	32.43%
	30 yrs	74 mos	36.89%	79 mos	42.71%	85 mos	49.10%
	15 yrs	28 mos	11.53%	29 mos	12.92%	30 mos	14.41%
10.00%	20 yrs	44 mos	19.58%	46 mos	22.20%	48 mos	25.04%
	25 yrs	65 mos	30.60%	69 mos	35.00%	72 mos	39.79%
	30 yrs	91 mos	45.01%	97 mos	51.77%	103 mos	59.10%
	15 yrs	33 mos	13.79%	34 mos	15.42%	35 mos	17.17%
12.50%	20 yrs	52 mos	23.16%	54 mos	26.19%	57 mos	29.45%
	25 yrs	76 mos	35.77%	80 mos	40.74%	84 mos	46.12%
	30 yrs	106 mos	51.93%	112 mos	59.40%	118 mos	67.44%
	15 yrs	38 mos	15.86%	40 mos	17.71%	41 mos	19.68%
15.00%	20 yrs	60 mos	26.40%	62 mos	29.76%	65 mos	33.38%
	25 yrs	87 mos	40.34%	91 mos	45.78%	95 mos	51.62%
	30 yrs	119 mos	57.91%	125 mos	65.94%	131 mos	74.53%
	15 yrs	48 mos	19.54%	49 mos	21.75%	50 mos	24.09%
20.00%	20 yrs	73 mos	31.99%	76 mos	35.91%	78 mos	40.09%
	25 yrs	104 mos	48.05%	109 mos	54.21%	113 mos	60.77%
	30 yrs	141 mos	67.76%	147 mos	76.62%	153 mos	86.01%
	15 yrs	56 mos	22.70%	57 mos	25.20%	59 mos	27.85%
25.00%	20 yrs	84 mos	36.68%	87 mos	41.02%	90 mos	45.62%
	25 yrs	119 mos	54.34%	123 mos	61.02%	128 mos	68.09%
	30 yrs	158 mos	75.59%	165 mos	85.02%	171 mos	94.96%
	15 yrs	67 mos	27.10%	69 mos	29.98%	70 mos	33.01%
33.33%	20 yrs	100 mos	43.02%	103 mos	47.88%	106 mos	53.00%
	25 yrs	139 mos	62.61%	143 mos	69.91%	147 mos	77.58%
	30 yrs	182 mos	85.65%	188 mos	95.73%	194 mos	106.27%

Benefits of Additional Payments

Term Reduction and Interest Savings

Additional Payment	Original Term	9.00% Interest		9.50% Interest		10.00% Interest	
		Increased Payment Will Shorten Loan By:	Interest Savings as % of Original Loan Amt	Increased Payment Will Shorten Loan By:	Interest Savings as % of Original Loan Amt	Increased Payment Will Shorten Loan By:	Interest Savings as % of Original Loan Amt
2.50%	15 yrs	9 mos	4.75%	9 mos	5.30%	10 mos	5.90%
	20 yrs	15 mos	8.83%	16 mos	10.02%	17 mos	11.33%
	25 yrs	25 mos	15.19%	27 mos	17.46%	29 mos	19.99%
	30 yrs	39 mos	24.66%	42 mos	28.64%	46 mos	33.09%
4.00%	15 yrs	14 mos	7.33%	14 mos	8.16%	15 mos	9.06%
	20 yrs	24 mos	13.43%	25 mos	15.18%	26 mos	17.09%
	25 yrs	38 mos	22.66%	40 mos	25.90%	43 mos	29.46%
	30 yrs	57 mos	35.91%	61 mos	41.34%	66 mos	47.31%
5.00%	15 yrs	17 mos	8.94%	18 mos	9.95%	18 mos	11.03%
	20 yrs	29 mos	16.25%	30 mos	18.33%	32 mos	20.59%
	25 yrs	45 mos	27.13%	48 mos	30.89%	51 mos	35.01%
	30 yrs	67 mos	42.42%	72 mos	48.58%	77 mos	55.31%
6.00%	15 yrs	20 mos	10.48%	21 mos	11.65%	22 mos	12.91%
	20 yrs	33 mos	18.91%	35 mos	21.28%	37 mos	23.85%
	25 yrs	52 mos	31.25%	55 mos	35.47%	59 mos	40.07%
	30 yrs	77 mos	48.27%	82 mos	55.05%	87 mos	62.41%
7.50%	15 yrs	24 mos	12.67%	25 mos	14.06%	26 mos	15.55%
	20 yrs	40 mos	22.60%	42 mos	25.37%	44 mos	28.35%
	25 yrs	62 mos	36.86%	65 mos	41.66%	69 mos	46.87%
	30 yrs	90 mos	56.06%	95 mos	63.60%	101 mos	71.70%
10.00%	15 yrs	31 mos	16.02%	32 mos	17.73%	33 mos	19.56%
	20 yrs	50 mos	28.12%	52 mos	31.42%	55 mos	34.97%
	25 yrs	76 mos	44.98%	80 mos	50.56%	84 mos	56.55%
	30 yrs	108 mos	67.01%	114 mos	75.47%	120 mos	84.49%
12.50%	15 yrs	37 mos	19.04%	38 mos	21.03%	39 mos	23.14%
	20 yrs	59 mos	32.95%	62 mos	36.71%	64 mos	40.71%
	25 yrs	88 mos	51.89%	92 mos	58.07%	97 mos	64.64%
	30 yrs	124 mos	76.04%	130 mos	85.18%	136 mos	94.85%
15.00%	15 yrs	42 mos	21.78%	43 mos	24.01%	45 mos	26.37%
	20 yrs	67 mos	37.24%	70 mos	41.36%	73 mos	45.74%
	25 yrs	99 mos	57.87%	103 mos	64.51%	108 mos	71.55%
	30 yrs	137 mos	83.66%	143 mos	93.31%	149 mos	103.46%
20.00%	15 yrs	52 mos	26.58%	53 mos	29.20%	55 mos	31.97%
	20 yrs	81 mos	44.52%	84 mos	49.22%	87 mos	54.17%
	25 yrs	117 mos	67.72%	122 mos	75.06%	126 mos	82.77%
	30 yrs	159 mos	95.90%	165 mos	106.27%	171 mos	117.09%
25.00%	15 yrs	60 mos	30.64%	62 mos	33.57%	63 mos	36.65%
	20 yrs	93 mos	50.49%	96 mos	55.61%	99 mos	60.98%
	25 yrs	132 mos	75.55%	136 mos	83.37%	141 mos	91.54%
	30 yrs	177 mos	105.37%	183 mos	116.21%	188 mos	127.47%
33.33%	15 yrs	72 mos	36.19%	73 mos	39.52%	75 mos	42.99%
	20 yrs	109 mos	58.38%	111 mos	64.01%	114 mos	69.87%
	25 yrs	152 mos	85.61%	156 mos	93.97%	160 mos	102.66%
	30 yrs	199 mos	117.24%	205 mos	128.60%	210 mos	140.32%

Table 4   53

Benefits of Additional Payments

Term Reduction and Interest Savings

		10.50% Interest		11.00% Interest		11.50% Interest	
Additional Payment	Original Term	Increased Payment Will Shorten Loan By:	Interest Savings as % of Original Loan Amt	Increased Payment Will Shorten Loan By:	Interest Savings as % of Original Loan Amt	Increased Payment Will Shorten Loan By:	Interest Savings as % of Original Loan Amt
	15 yrs	10 mos	6.55%	11 mos	7.25%	11 mos	8.00%
2.50%	20 yrs	18 mos	12.75%	19 mos	14.32%	21 mos	16.04%
	25 yrs	31 mos	22.80%	33 mos	25.90%	35 mos	29.30%
	30 yrs	49 mos	38.03%	53 mos	43.51%	58 mos	49.53%
	15 yrs	16 mos	10.03%	16 mos	11.08%	17 mos	12.20%
4.00%	20 yrs	28 mos	19.16%	29 mos	21.43%	31 mos	23.88%
	25 yrs	46 mos	33.36%	48 mos	37.62%	51 mos	42.23%
	30 yrs	70 mos	53.82%	75 mos	60.93%	80 mos	68.59%
	15 yrs	19 mos	12.20%	20 mos	13.45%	21 mos	14.79%
5.00%	20 yrs	33 mos	23.03%	35 mos	25.69%	37 mos	28.55%
	25 yrs	54 mos	39.49%	57 mos	44.35%	61 mos	49.60%
	30 yrs	82 mos	62.60%	88 mos	70.47%	93 mos	78.90%
	15 yrs	22 mos	14.25%	23 mos	15.69%	24 mos	17.23%
6.00%	20 yrs	39 mos	26.62%	41 mos	29.62%	43 mos	32.85%
	25 yrs	62 mos	45.05%	66 mos	50.41%	69 mos	56.16%
	30 yrs	93 mos	70.32%	98 mos	78.80%	104 mos	87.83%
	15 yrs	27 mos	17.14%	28 mos	18.84%	29 mos	20.65%
7.50%	20 yrs	46 mos	31.55%	48 mos	35.00%	50 mos	38.68%
	25 yrs	73 mos	52.46%	76 mos	58.45%	80 mos	64.83%
	30 yrs	107 mos	80.35%	113 mos	89.56%	118 mos	99.28%
	15 yrs	34 mos	21.50%	35 mos	23.57%	36 mos	25.76%
10.00%	20 yrs	57 mos	38.76%	60 mos	42.81%	62 mos	47.11%
	25 yrs	88 mos	62.93%	92 mos	69.70%	96 mos	76.86%
	30 yrs	126 mos	94.03%	132 mos	104.07%	138 mos	114.59%
	15 yrs	40 mos	25.38%	42 mos	27.76%	43 mos	30.26%
12.50%	20 yrs	67 mos	44.97%	69 mos	49.48%	72 mos	54.26%
	25 yrs	101 mos	71.61%	105 mos	78.96%	109 mos	86.68%
	30 yrs	142 mos	105.00%	148 mos	115.63%	154 mos	126.69%
	15 yrs	46 mos	28.87%	48 mos	31.50%	49 mos	34.28%
15.00%	20 yrs	75 mos	50.37%	78 mos	55.27%	81 mos	60.42%
	25 yrs	112 mos	78.97%	116 mos	86.75%	120 mos	94.89%
	30 yrs	155 mos	114.07%	161 mos	125.12%	167 mos	136.57%
	15 yrs	56 mos	34.87%	58 mos	37.93%	59 mos	41.13%
20.00%	20 yrs	90 mos	59.38%	92 mos	64.84%	95 mos	70.55%
	25 yrs	130 mos	90.83%	134 mos	99.24%	139 mos	107.96%
	30 yrs	177 mos	128.32%	182 mos	139.94%	188 mos	151.91%
	15 yrs	65 mos	39.88%	66 mos	43.25%	68 mos	46.77%
25.00%	20 yrs	101 mos	66.60%	104 mos	72.47%	107 mos	78.57%
	25 yrs	145 mos	100.05%	149 mos	108.87%	153 mos	117.98%
	30 yrs	194 mos	139.10%	199 mos	151.09%	204 mos	163.39%
	15 yrs	77 mos	46.61%	78 mos	50.37%	80 mos	54.28%
33.33%	20 yrs	117 mos	75.97%	120 mos	82.30%	122 mos	88.85%
	25 yrs	164 mos	111.64%	168 mos	120.91%	171 mos	130.45%
	30 yrs	215 mos	152.38%	220 mos	164.74%	224 mos	177.38%

Benefits of Additional Payments

Term Reduction and Interest Savings

Additional Payment	Original Term	12.00% Interest		12.50% Interest		13.00% Interest	
		Increased Payment Will Shorten Loan By:	Interest Savings as % of Original Loan Amt	Increased Payment Will Shorten Loan By:	Interest Savings as % of Original Loan Amt	Increased Payment Will Shorten Loan By:	Interest Savings as % of Original Loan Amt
2.50%	15 yrs	12 mos	8.82%	12 mos	9.70%	13 mos	10.64%
	20 yrs	22 mos	17.91%	23 mos	19.96%	24 mos	22.17%
	25 yrs	38 mos	33.05%	41 mos	37.12%	43 mos	41.56%
	30 yrs	62 mos	56.09%	67 mos	63.20%	71 mos	70.87%
4.00%	15 yrs	18 mos	13.41%	18 mos	14.70%	19 mos	16.08%
	20 yrs	32 mos	26.54%	34 mos	29.41%	36 mos	32.49%
	25 yrs	55 mos	47.24%	58 mos	52.63%	61 mos	58.41%
	30 yrs	86 mos	76.80%	91 mos	85.56%	96 mos	94.85%
5.00%	15 yrs	21 mos	16.23%	22 mos	17.76%	23 mos	19.40%
	20 yrs	39 mos	31.64%	41 mos	34.96%	43 mos	38.50%
	25 yrs	64 mos	55.24%	68 mos	61.26%	71 mos	67.69%
	30 yrs	99 mos	87.87%	104 mos	97.36%	110 mos	107.35%
6.00%	15 yrs	25 mos	18.88%	26 mos	20.63%	27 mos	22.50%
	20 yrs	45 mos	36.31%	47 mos	40.01%	49 mos	43.95%
	25 yrs	73 mos	62.33%	77 mos	68.88%	80 mos	75.82%
	30 yrs	110 mos	97.38%	115 mos	107.43%	121 mos	117.95%
7.50%	15 yrs	30 mos	22.57%	31 mos	24.62%	32 mos	26.79%
	20 yrs	53 mos	42.62%	55 mos	46.80%	57 mos	51.23%
	25 yrs	84 mos	71.62%	88 mos	78.78%	92 mos	86.32%
	30 yrs	124 mos	109.48%	130 mos	120.15%	135 mos	131.25%
10.00%	15 yrs	38 mos	28.08%	39 mos	30.53%	40 mos	33.12%
	20 yrs	64 mos	51.66%	67 mos	56.48%	70 mos	61.54%
	25 yrs	100 mos	84.40%	104 mos	92.31%	108 mos	100.56%
	30 yrs	144 mos	125.55%	149 mos	136.91%	155 mos	148.66%
12.50%	15 yrs	44 mos	32.91%	46 mos	35.70%	47 mos	38.62%
	20 yrs	75 mos	59.29%	77 mos	64.57%	80 mos	70.10%
	25 yrs	113 mos	94.76%	117 mos	103.18%	122 mos	111.93%
	30 yrs	159 mos	130.15%	165 mos	149.97%	170 mos	162.14%
15.00%	15 yrs	50 mos	37.20%	52 mos	40.26%	53 mos	43.46%
	20 yrs	83 mos	65.82%	86 mos	71.48%	89 mos	77.37%
	25 yrs	124 mos	103.38%	129 mos	112.18%	133 mos	121.28%
	30 yrs	172 mos	148.39%	178 mos	160.53%	183 mos	173.00%
20.00%	15 yrs	61 mos	44.47%	62 mos	47.96%	64 mos	51.60%
	20 yrs	98 mos	76.50%	101 mos	82.69%	103 mos	89.10%
	25 yrs	143 mos	117.00%	147 mos	126.33%	150 mos	135.92%
	30 yrs	193 mos	164.19%	198 mos	176.77%	203 mos	189.62%
25.00%	15 yrs	70 mos	50.44%	71 mos	54.25%	73 mos	58.20%
	20 yrs	110 mos	84.91%	112 mos	91.46%	115 mos	98.23%
	25 yrs	157 mos	127.38%	161 mos	137.05%	164 mos	146.95%
	30 yrs	209 mos	175.97%	214 mos	188.81%	218 mos	201.89%
33.33%	15 yrs	81 mos	58.33%	83 mos	62.52%	85 mos	66.84%
	20 yrs	125 mos	95.61%	128 mos	102.58%	130 mos	109.73%
	25 yrs	175 mos	140.24%	178 mos	150.26%	182 mos	160.49%
	30 yrs	229 mos	190.27%	233 mos	203.38%	237 mos	216.70%

Table 4   55

Benefits of Additional Payments

Term Reduction and Interest Savings

Additional Payment	Original Term	13.50% Interest		14.00% Interest		14.50% Interest	
		Increased Payment Will Shorten Loan By:	Interest Savings as % of Original Loan Amt	Increased Payment Will Shorten Loan By:	Interest Savings as % of Original Loan Amt	Increased Payment Will Shorten Loan By:	Interest Savings as % of Original Loan Amt
2.50%	15 yrs	13 mos	11.64%	14 mos	12.73%	14 mos	13.89%
	20 yrs	26 mos	24.57%	27 mos	27.16%	29 mos	29.96%
	25 yrs	46 mos	46.37%	49 mos	51.56%	52 mos	57.12%
	30 yrs	76 mos	79.13%	81 mos	87.92%	86 mos	97.22%
4.00%	15 yrs	20 mos	17.55%	21 mos	19.13%	22 mos	20.81%
	20 yrs	38 mos	35.80%	40 mos	39.35%	42 mos	43.12%
	25 yrs	65 mos	64.58%	68 mos	71.15%	72 mos	78.09%
	30 yrs	102 mos	104.67%	107 mos	114.97%	113 mos	125.73%
5.00%	15 yrs	24 mos	21.14%	25 mos	22.99%	26 mos	24.96%
	20 yrs	45 mos	42.29%	47 mos	46.32%	49 mos	50.60%
	25 yrs	75 mos	74.51%	79 mos	81.70%	83 mos	89.27%
	30 yrs	115 mos	117.84%	121 mos	128.76%	126 mos	140.09%
6.00%	15 yrs	28 mos	24.47%	29 mos	26.58%	30 mos	28.80%
	20 yrs	51 mos	48.14%	53 mos	52.58%	56 mos	57.27%
	25 yrs	84 mos	83.13%	88 mos	90.83%	92 mos	98.88%
	30 yrs	127 mos	128.93%	132 mos	140.31%	138 mos	152.07%
7.50%	15 yrs	33 mos	29.08%	35 mos	31.50%	36 mos	34.05%
	20 yrs	60 mos	55.92%	62 mos	60.86%	65 mos	66.06%
	25 yrs	96 mos	94.23%	100 mos	102.49%	104 mos	111.08%
	30 yrs	141 mos	142.77%	147 mos	154.64%	152 mos	166.86%
10.00%	15 yrs	41 mos	35.84%	43 mos	38.70%	44 mos	41.71%
	20 yrs	72 mos	66.85%	75 mos	72.42%	77 mos	78.23%
	25 yrs	112 mos	109.15%	116 mos	118.06%	120 mos	127.27%
	30 yrs	160 mos	160.77%	166 mos	173.18%	171 mos	185.88%
12.50%	15 yrs	49 mos	41.69%	50 mos	44.90%	51 mos	48.25%
	20 yrs	83 mos	75.88%	85 mos	81.90%	88 mos	88.15%
	25 yrs	126 mos	120.98%	130 mos	130.33%	133 mos	139.95%
	30 yrs	176 mos	174.62%	181 mos	187.38%	185 mos	200.38%
15.00%	15 yrs	55 mos	46.81%	56 mos	50.30%	58 mos	53.94%
	20 yrs	91 mos	83.50%	94 mos	89.86%	97 mos	96.45%
	25 yrs	137 mos	130.68%	141 mos	140.34%	144 mos	150.25%
	30 yrs	188 mos	185.74%	193 mos	198.74%	197 mos	211.95%
20.00%	15 yrs	66 mos	55.38%	67 mos	59.30%	69 mos	63.37%
	20 yrs	106 mos	95.74%	109 mos	102.58%	111 mos	109.63%
	25 yrs	154 mos	145.76%	158 mos	155.84%	161 mos	166.13%
	30 yrs	207 mos	202.70%	212 mos	216.00%	216 mos	229.48%
25.00%	15 yrs	74 mos	62.29%	76 mos	66.52%	78 mos	70.89%
	20 yrs	118 mos	105.20%	120 mos	112.37%	123 mos	119.73%
	25 yrs	168 mos	157.08%	171 mos	167.43%	175 mos	177.96%
	30 yrs	222 mos	215.19%	226 mos	228.67%	230 mos	242.31%
33.33%	15 yrs	86 mos	71.30%	88 mos	75.89%	89 mos	80.61%
	20 yrs	133 mos	117.08%	135 mos	124.60%	138 mos	132.28%
	25 yrs	185 mos	170.92%	188 mos	181.54%	191 mos	192.32%
	30 yrs	241 mos	230.21%	244 mos	243.88%	248 mos	257.69%

Benefits of Additional Payments

Term Reduction and Interest Savings

Additional Payment	Original Term	15.00% Interest		15.50% Interest		16.00% Interest	
		Increased Payment Will Shorten Loan By:	Interest Savings as % of Original Loan Amt	Increased Payment Will Shorten Loan By:	Interest Savings as % of Original Loan Amt	Increased Payment Will Shorten Loan By:	Interest Savings as % of Original Loan Amt
2.50%	15 yrs	15 mos	15.12%	16 mos	16.46%	16 mos	17.87%
	20 yrs	30 mos	32.95%	32 mos	36.19%	34 mos	39.64%
	25 yrs	55 mos	63.09%	59 mos	69.42%	62 mos	76.15%
	30 yrs	91 mos	107.05%	97 mos	117.35%	102 mos	128.11%
4.00%	15 yrs	22 mos	22.58%	23 mos	24.48%	24 mos	26.48%
	20 yrs	44 mos	47.14%	46 mos	51.41%	48 mos	55.93%
	25 yrs	76 mos	85.42%	79 mos	93.11%	83 mos	101.16%
	30 yrs	118 mos	136.91%	123 mos	148.50%	129 mos	160.45%
5.00%	15 yrs	27 mos	27.03%	28 mos	29.24%	29 mos	31.57%
	20 yrs	51 mos	55.12%	54 mos	59.91%	56 mos	64.94%
	25 yrs	87 mos	97.21%	90 mos	105.48%	94 mos	114.10%
	30 yrs	131 mos	151.82%	137 mos	163.89%	142 mos	176.29%
6.00%	15 yrs	31 mos	31.14%	32 mos	33.62%	33 mos	36.23%
	20 yrs	58 mos	62.21%	61 mos	67.41%	63 mos	72.85%
	25 yrs	96 mos	107.28%	100 mos	116.00%	104 mos	125.03%
	30 yrs	143 mos	164.18%	148 mos	176.61%	153 mos	189.32%
7.50%	15 yrs	37 mos	36.74%	38 mos	39.57%	39 mos	42.53%
	20 yrs	67 mos	71.49%	70 mos	77.19%	72 mos	83.12%
	25 yrs	108 mos	120.00%	112 mos	129.20%	116 mos	138.69%
	30 yrs	157 mos	179.38%	162 mos	192.18%	167 mos	205.23%
10.00%	15 yrs	45 mos	44.85%	47 mos	48.14%	48 mos	51.57%
	20 yrs	80 mos	84.27%	83 mos	90.56%	85 mos	97.06%
	25 yrs	124 mos	136.76%	128 mos	146.51%	132 mos	156.50%
	30 yrs	176 mos	198.84%	180 mos	212.03%	185 mos	225.43%
12.50%	15 yrs	53 mos	51.75%	54 mos	55.40%	56 mos	59.18%
	20 yrs	91 mos	94.63%	93 mos	101.33%	96 mos	108.23%
	25 yrs	137 mos	149.82%	141 mos	159.92%	145 mos	170.25%
	30 yrs	190 mos	213.62%	195 mos	227.05%	199 mos	240.66%
15.00%	15 yrs	59 mos	57.72%	61 mos	61.65%	62 mos	65.71%
	20 yrs	99 mos	103.24%	102 mos	110.25%	105 mos	117.45%
	25 yrs	148 mos	160.39%	152 mos	170.74%	155 mos	181.29%
	30 yrs	202 mos	225.37%	206 mos	238.97%	210 mos	252.73%
20.00%	15 yrs	70 mos	67.57%	72 mos	71.91%	73 mos	76.39%
	20 yrs	114 mos	116.87%	117 mos	124.30%	119 mos	131.90%
	25 yrs	165 mos	176.63%	168 mos	187.30%	172 mos	198.14%
	30 yrs	220 mos	243.14%	224 mos	256.94%	228 mos	270.89%
25.00%	15 yrs	79 mos	75.39%	81 mos	80.03%	82 mos	84.79%
	20 yrs	125 mos	127.26%	128 mos	134.96%	130 mos	142.81%
	25 yrs	178 mos	188.68%	181 mos	199.55%	184 mos	210.57%
	30 yrs	234 mos	256.12%	238 mos	270.05%	241 mos	284.10%
33.33%	15 yrs	91 mos	85.45%	92 mos	90.42%	94 mos	95.50%
	20 yrs	140 mos	140.11%	142 mos	148.11%	144 mos	156.23%
	25 yrs	194 mos	203.26%	197 mos	214.33%	199 mos	225.54%
	30 yrs	251 mos	271.63%	254 mos	285.69%	257 mos	299.85%

Table 4   57

Benefits of Additional Payments

Term Reduction and Interest Savings

		16.50% Interest		17.00% Interest		17.50% Interest	
Additional Payment	Original Term	Increased Payment Will Shorten Loan By:	Interest Savings as % of Original Loan Amt	Increased Payment Will Shorten Loan By:	Interest Savings as % of Original Loan Amt	Increased Payment Will Shorten Loan By:	Interest Savings as % of Original Loan Amt
2.50%	15 yrs	17 mos	19.37%	18 mos	20.98%	18 mos	22.68%
	20 yrs	35 mos	43.33%	37 mos	47.25%	39 mos	51.41%
	25 yrs	65 mos	83.26%	69 mos	90.74%	72 mos	98.58%
	30 yrs	107 mos	139.30%	112 mos	150.91%	117 mos	162.85%
4.00%	15 yrs	25 mos	28.59%	26 mos	30.84%	27 mos	33.20%
	20 yrs	50 mos	60.69%	52 mos	65.71%	55 mos	70.97%
	25 yrs	87 mos	109.57%	91 mos	118.29%	94 mos	127.32%
	30 yrs	134 mos	172.72%	139 mos	185.31%	144 mos	198.17%
5.00%	15 yrs	30 mos	34.02%	31 mos	36.61%	32 mos	39.32%
	20 yrs	58 mos	70.22%	61 mos	75.75%	63 mos	81.52%
	25 yrs	98 mos	123.04%	102 mos	132.27%	106 mos	141.78%
	30 yrs	147 mos	188.98%	152 mos	201.94%	157 mos	215.13%
6.00%	15 yrs	35 mos	38.96%	36 mos	41.84%	37 mos	44.85%
	20 yrs	65 mos	78.55%	68 mos	84.47%	70 mos	90.64%
	25 yrs	108 mos	134.36%	111 mos	143.96%	115 mos	153.82%
	30 yrs	158 mos	202.30%	163 mos	215.52%	168 mos	228.92%
7.50%	15 yrs	41 mos	45.63%	42 mos	48.87%	43 mos	52.25%
	20 yrs	75 mos	89.28%	77 mos	95.68%	80 mos	102.30%
	25 yrs	120 mos	148.45%	123 mos	158.46%	127 mos	168.68%
	30 yrs	172 mos	218.50%	176 mos	231.98%	181 mos	245.63%
10.00%	15 yrs	50 mos	55.13%	51 mos	58.85%	53 mos	62.70%
	20 yrs	88 mos	103.80%	90 mos	110.73%	93 mos	117.86%
	25 yrs	136 mos	166.73%	139 mos	177.17%	143 mos	187.79%
	30 yrs	190 mos	239.01%	194 mos	252.76%	198 mos	266.65%
12.50%	15 yrs	57 mos	63.10%	59 mos	67.17%	60 mos	71.38%
	20 yrs	98 mos	115.35%	101 mos	122.65%	104 mos	130.13%
	25 yrs	148 mos	180.77%	152 mos	191.48%	155 mos	202.35%
	30 yrs	203 mos	254.44%	207 mos	268.36%	211 mos	282.40%
15.00%	15 yrs	64 mos	69.91%	65 mos	74.26%	67 mos	78.73%
	20 yrs	107 mos	124.84%	110 mos	132.41%	112 mos	140.14%
	25 yrs	159 mos	192.02%	162 mos	202.91%	165 mos	213.96%
	30 yrs	214 mos	266.63%	218 mos	280.66%	222 mos	294.80%
20.00%	15 yrs	75 mos	80.99%	76 mos	85.73%	78 mos	90.59%
	20 yrs	121 mos	139.66%	124 mos	147.59%	126 mos	155.65%
	25 yrs	175 mos	209.14%	178 mos	220.28%	181 mos	231.54%
	30 yrs	231 mos	284.95%	235 mos	299.12%	238 mos	313.39%
25.00%	15 yrs	84 mos	89.67%	85 mos	94.68%	87 mos	99.80%
	20 yrs	132 mos	150.82%	135 mos	158.97%	137 mos	167.24%
	25 yrs	187 mos	221.73%	190 mos	233.02%	192 mos	244.41%
	30 yrs	244 mos	298.26%	247 mos	312.52%	250 mos	326.86%
33.33%	15 yrs	95 mos	100.69%	97 mos	106.00%	98 mos	111.41%
	20 yrs	146 mos	164.49%	148 mos	172.87%	150 mos	181.36%
	25 yrs	202 mos	236.86%	205 mos	248.29%	207 mos	259.82%
	30 yrs	260 mos	314.11%	263 mos	328.45%	265 mos	342.86%

Table 5
Adjustable Rate Mortgages

Adjustable Rate Mortgages (ARMs) have benefits for borrowers and lenders. Borrowers get a lower rate of interest at the start and qualify for a larger loan than with a fixed-rate plan. Lenders avoid the interest rate risk they face with fixed-rate loans.

The payment in the first year of an ARM is the same as in the customary 30-year case. Each year after that, the rate is adjusted according to one of the several indexes. Rate increases are limited in any one year and in total over the life of the loan.

If the interest rate goes up and the lender permits the loan payment to remain constant, the result is negative amortization: The loan balance goes up. To avoid negative amortization, the payment can be increased. Table 6 shows the payments that will keep the loan amortizing on its original 30-year schedule, if the interest rate rises at any of four rates of increase, $\frac{1}{4}$, $\frac{1}{2}$, $\frac{3}{4}$, or 1 percent per year.

Example 11.   Finding the Payments on an ARM

Jan is looking at a $240,000 ARM with an initial interest rate of 4 percent per year. The rate may rise by 1 percent in any year and by a maximum of 4 percent over the loan term.

Jan wants to know what payments would be needed to keep the loan on the original schedule and avoid negative amortization.

Enter Table 5 on the page for rate increases of 1 percent per year. Under the column for year 1 on the 4 percent line, read 4.7742 per $1000, the payment on the usual 30-year loan. Multiply this by the number of thousands to get

$$4.7742 \times 240 = \$1,145.81,$$
the payment in the first year.

Repeat the process, using the figure from the column for year 2, 5.3527, for the second year, then from the column for year 3, 5.9478, for the third year and so on, always staying on the line for 4 percent interest. The interest rates built into these columns is 1 percent higher in each column.

Example 12.   Maximum Payment on an ARM

Y is offered a $275,000 loan that could rise ½ percent per year or a maximum of 2 percent over the life of the loan, starting from a 4.50 percent rate.

To find the maximum payment, enter Table 5 on the page for rate increases of ½ percent per year. On the line for 4.50 percent interest, read the payment under the column for year 4, 5.9491, which contains a rate 2 percent higher than at the start. This will be the maximum payment on a $1000 loan with this data.

Next, multiply the payment by the number of thousands to get

$$5.9491 \times 275 = \$1,636.01,$$

the maximum payment on $275,000 that begins at 4.50 percent and rises ½ percent per year, with a maximum 2 percent increase.

Adjustable Rate Mortgages   **30 Year Loan**

Rate increases ¼% per year

Interest Rate	1	2	3	4	5
		Payment per $1000			
3.00%	4.2160	4.3483	4.4789	4.6077	4.7345
3.25%	4.3521	4.4866	4.6196	4.7507	4.8799
3.50%	4.4904	4.6274	4.7626	4.8961	5.0275
3.75%	4.6312	4.7704	4.9079	5.0436	5.1773
4.00%	4.7742	4.9156	5.0554	5.1933	5.3292
4.25%	4.9194	5.0631	5.2051	5.3452	5.4833
4.50%	5.0669	5.2128	5.3569	5.4992	5.6394
4.75%	5.2165	5.3645	5.5108	5.6552	5.7975
5.00%	5.3602	5.5184	5.6668	5.8133	5.9577
5.25%	5.5220	5.6743	5.8247	5.9733	6.1197
5.50%	5.6779	5.8321	5.9846	6.1352	6.2836
5.75%	5.8357	5.9920	6.1464	6.2989	6.4493
6.00%	5.9955	6.1537	6.3101	6.4645	6.6168
6.25%	6.1572	6.3172	6.4755	6.6318	6.7861
6.50%	6.3207	6.4826	6.6427	6.8009	6.9570
6.75%	6.4860	6.6497	6.8116	6.9716	7.1295
7.00%	6.6530	6.8185	6.9821	7.1439	7.3035
7.25%	6.8218	6.9889	7.1543	7.3177	7.4791
7.50%	6.9921	7.1609	7.3280	7.4931	7.6562
7.75%	7.1641	7.3345	7.5032	7.6699	7.8347
8.00%	7.3376	7.5096	7.6798	7.8482	8.0145
8.25%	7.5127	7.6861	7.8579	8.0278	8.1957
8.50%	7.6891	7.8641	8.0373	8.2087	8.3781
8.75%	7.8670	8.0433	8.2180	8.3909	8.5617
9.00%	8.0462	8.2239	8.4000	8.5743	8.7466
9.25%	8.2268	8.4058	8.5832	8.7588	8.9325
9.50%	8.4085	8.5889	8.7676	8.9445	9.1196
9.75%	8.5915	8.7731	8.9531	9.1313	9.3077
10.00%	8.7757	8.9585	9.1396	9.3191	9.4968
10.25%	8.9610	9.1449	9.3273	9.5080	9.6868
10.50%	9.1474	9.3324	9.5159	9.6977	9.8778
10.75%	9.3348	9.5209	9.7055	9.8885	10.0697
11.00%	9.5232	9.7103	9.8960	10.0800	10.2624
11.25%	9.7126	9.9007	10.0874	10.2725	10.4559
11.50%	9.9029	10.0919	10.2796	10.4657	10.6502
11.75%	10.0941	10.2840	10.4726	10.6597	10.8452
12.00%	10.2861	10.4769	10.6664	10.8544	11.0409
12.25%	10.4790	10.6706	10.8610	11.0499	11.2373
12.50%	10.6726	10.8650	11.0562	11.2460	11.4343
12.75%	10.8669	11.0602	11.2521	11.4428	11.6319
13.00%	11.0620	11.2560	11.4487	11.6401	11.8301
13.25%	11.2577	11.4524	11.6459	11.8381	12.0289
13.50%	11.4541	11.6495	11.8437	12.0366	12.2282
13.75%	11.6511	11.8471	12.0420	12.2356	12.4279
14.00%	11.8487	12.0453	12.2409	12.4352	12.6282
14.25%	12.0469	12.2441	12.4402	12.6352	12.8289
14.50%	12.2456	12.4433	12.6401	12.8357	13.0300
14.75%	12.4448	12.6431	12.8404	13.0366	13.2316
15.00%	12.6444	12.8433	13.0411	13.2379	13.4335
15.25%	12.8446	13.0439	13.2423	13.4396	13.6358
15.50%	13.0452	13.2449	13.4438	13.6417	13.8384
15.75%	13.2462	13.4464	13.6457	13.8441	14.0414
16.00%	13.4476	13.6482	13.8480	14.0469	14.2446
16.25%	13.6493	13.8504	14.0506	14.2499	14.4482
16.50%	13.8515	14.0529	14.2535	14.4533	14.6521
16.75%	14.0540	14.2557	14.4568	14.6569	14.8562
17.00%	14.2568	14.4589	14.6603	14.8609	15.0605
17.25%	14.4599	14.6623	14.8641	15.0650	15.2651
17.50%	14.6633	14.8660	15.0681	15.2695	15.4699
17.75%	14.8669	15.0700	15.2724	15.4741	15.6749
18.00%	15.0709	15.2742	15.4769	15.6790	15.8801

Table 5   61

30 Year Loan Adjustable Rate Mortgages

Rate increases ½% per year

Payment per $1000

Interest Rate	1	2	3	4	5
3.00%	4.2160	4.4827	4.7505	5.0186	5.2863
3.25%	4.3521	4.6234	4.8958	5.1684	5.4406
3.50%	4.4904	4.7665	5.0434	5.3204	5.5969
3.75%	4.6312	4.9117	5.1931	5.4745	5.7553
4.00%	4.7742	5.0592	5.3450	5.6307	5.9158
4.25%	4.9194	5.2089	5.4990	5.7889	6.0781
4.50%	5.0669	5.3607	5.6550	5.9491	6.2424
4.75%	5.2165	5.5146	5.8131	6.1113	6.4086
5.00%	5.3682	5.6705	5.9731	6.2753	6.5765
5.25%	5.5220	5.8284	6.1350	6.4411	6.7462
5.50%	5.6779	5.9883	6.2987	6.6087	6.9176
5.75%	5.8357	6.1500	6.4643	6.7781	7.0906
6.00%	5.9955	6.3136	6.6317	6.9491	7.2653
6.25%	6.1512	6.4790	6.8007	7.1217	7.4414
6.50%	6.3207	6.6462	6.9714	7.2959	7.6191
6.75%	6.4860	6.8150	7.1437	7.4716	7.7982
7.00%	6.6530	6.9855	7.3176	7.6488	7.9787
7.25%	6.8218	7.1576	7.4930	7.8275	8.1605
7.50%	6.9921	7.3312	7.6698	8.0074	8.3436
7.75%	7.1641	7.5064	7.8481	8.1888	8.5280
8.00%	7.3376	7.6830	8.0277	8.3713	8.7135
8.25%	7.5127	7.8610	8.2086	8.5552	8.9002
8.50%	7.6891	8.0403	8.3908	8.7401	9.0879
8.75%	7.8670	8.2210	8.5742	8.9263	9.2768
9.00%	8.0462	8.4029	8.7588	9.1135	9.4666
9.25%	8.2268	8.5860	8.9445	9.3017	9.6574
9.50%	8.4085	8.7704	9.1313	9.4910	9.8491
9.75%	8.5915	8.9558	9.3191	9.6812	10.0417
10.00%	8.7757	9.1423	9.5080	9.8723	10.2351
10.25%	8.9610	9.3299	9.6977	10.0644	10.4294
10.50%	9.1474	9.5184	9.8885	10.2572	10.6244
10.75%	9.3348	9.7079	10.0801	10.4509	10.8201
11.00%	9.5232	9.8984	10.2725	10.6453	11.0165
11.25%	9.7126	10.0897	10.4657	10.8405	11.2136
11.50%	9.9029	10.2818	10.6597	11.0363	11.4114
11.75%	10.0941	10.4748	10.8545	11.2329	11.6097
12.00%	10.2861	10.6686	11.0499	11.4301	11.8086
12.25%	10.4790	10.8630	11.2461	11.6278	12.0080
12.50%	10.6726	11.0582	11.4428	11.8262	12.2080
12.75%	10.8669	11.2541	11.6402	12.0251	12.4084
13.00%	11.0620	11.4506	11.8382	12.2245	12.6093
13.25%	11.2577	11.6477	12.0367	12.4244	12.8107
13.50%	11.4541	11.8454	12.2357	12.6248	13.0124
13.75%	11.6511	12.0437	12.4353	12.8256	13.2146
14.00%	11.8487	12.2425	12.6353	13.0269	13.4171
14.25%	12.0469	12.4418	12.8358	13.2286	13.6200
14.50%	12.2456	12.6416	13.0367	13.4306	13.8232
14.75%	12.4448	12.8419	13.2380	13.6330	14.0267
15.00%	12.6444	13.0425	13.4397	13.8358	14.2305
15.25%	12.8446	13.2436	13.6418	14.0388	14.4346
15.50%	13.0452	13.4451	13.8442	14.2422	14.6390
15.75%	13.2462	13.6470	14.0470	14.4459	14.8436
16.00%	13.4476	13.8492	14.2500	14.6498	15.0484
16.25%	13.6493	14.0518	14.4534	14.8540	15.2535
16.50%	13.8515	14.2547	14.6571	15.0585	15.4587
16.75%	14.0540	14.4579	14.8610	15.2631	15.6642
17.00%	14.2568	14.6614	15.0652	15.4680	15.8698
17.25%	14.4599	14.8651	15.2696	15.6731	16.0756
17.50%	14.6633	15.0691	15.4742	15.8784	16.2816
17.75%	14.8669	16.2734	15.6791	16.0839	16.4878
18.00%	15.0709	15.4778	15.8841	16.2896	16.6940

Adjustable Rate Mortgages   **30 Year Loan**

Rate increases ¾% per year

Interest Rate	Payment per $1000				
	1	2	3	4	5
3.00%	4.2160	4.6194	5.0306	5.4479	5.8696
3.25%	4.3521	4.7624	5.1804	5.6042	6.0323
3.50%	4.4904	4.9077	5.3324	5.7626	6.1969
3.75%	4.6312	5.0552	5.4864	5.9230	6.3634
4.00%	4.7742	5.2049	5.6425	6.0853	6.5318
4.25%	4.9194	5.3567	5.8007	6.2496	6.7019
4.50%	5.0669	5.5107	5.9608	6.4157	6.8738
4.75%	5.2165	5.6666	6.1228	6.5835	7.0473
5.00%	5.3682	5.8246	6.2867	6.7532	7.2225
5.25%	5.5220	5.9845	6.4524	6.9245	7.3992
5.50%	5.6779	6.1463	6.6199	7.0975	7.5775
5.75%	5.8357	6.3099	6.7891	7.2720	7.7572
6.00%	5.9955	6.4753	6.9600	7.4481	7.9384
6.25%	6.1572	6.6425	7.1325	7.6257	8.1209
6.50%	6.3207	6.8114	7.3065	7.8047	8.3047
6.75%	6.4860	6.9820	7.4821	7.9851	8.4898
7.00%	6.6530	7.1541	7.6591	8.1668	8.6760
7.25%	6.8218	7.3278	7.8376	8.3498	8.8634
7.50%	6.9921	7.5030	8.0174	8.5341	9.0520
7.75%	7.1641	7.6797	8.1985	8.7195	9.2416
8.00%	7.3376	7.8578	8.3809	8.9060	9.4322
8.25%	7.5127	8.0372	8.5645	9.0937	9.6238
8.50%	7.6891	8.2179	8.7493	9.2824	9.8163
8.75%	7.8670	8.3999	8.9353	9.4721	10.0097
9.00%	8.0462	8.5831	9.1223	9.6628	10.2039
9.25%	8.2268	8.7675	9.3103	9.8544	10.3990
9.50%	8.4085	8.9530	9.4994	10.0469	10.5948
9.75%	8.5915	9.1396	9.6894	10.2402	10.7913
10.00%	8.7757	9.3272	9.8803	10.4344	10.9885
10.25%	8.9610	9.5158	10.0722	10.6292	11.1864
10.50%	9.1474	9.7054	10.2648	10.8249	11.3849
10.75%	9.3348	9.8959	10.4583	11.0212	11.5841
11.00%	9.5232	10.0873	10.6525	11.2182	11.7837
11.25%	9.7126	10.2795	10.8475	11.4158	11.9839
11.50%	9.9029	10.4726	11.0431	11.6140	12.1846
11.75%	10.0941	10.6664	11.2395	11.8128	12.3858
12.00%	10.2861	10.8609	11.4365	12.0121	12.5875
12.25%	10.4790	11.0562	11.6340	12.2120	12.7895
12.50%	10.6726	11.2521	11.8322	12.4123	12.9920
12.75%	10.8669	11.4487	12.0309	12.6131	13.1948
13.00%	11.0620	11.6459	12.2301	12.8143	13.3980
13.25%	11.2577	11.8437	12.4299	13.0160	13.6016
13.50%	11.4541	12.0420	12.6301	13.2180	13.8054
13.75%	11.6511	12.2409	12.8308	13.4204	14.0096
14.00%	11.8487	12.4402	13.0318	13.6232	14.2140
14.25%	12.0469	12.6401	13.2333	13.8263	14.4187
14.50%	12.2456	12.8404	13.4352	14.0297	14.6236
14.75%	12.4448	13.0411	13.6375	14.2335	14.8288
15.00%	12.6444	13.2423	13.8400	14.4375	15.0342
15.25%	12.8446	13.4438	14.0430	14.6417	15.2398
15.50%	13.0452	13.6457	14.2462	14.8462	15.4456
15.75%	13.2462	13.8480	14.4497	15.0510	15.6516
16.00%	13.4476	14.0506	14.6535	15.2560	15.8577
16.25%	13.6493	14.2536	14.8576	15.4611	16.0640
16.50%	13.8515	14.4568	15.0619	15.6665	16.2705
16.75%	14.0540	14.6603	15.2664	15.8721	16.4771
17.00%	14.2568	14.8641	15.4712	16.0778	16.6838
17.25%	14.4599	15.0682	15.6762	16.2837	16.8906
17.50%	14.6633	15.2724	15.8814	16.4898	17.0976
17.75%	14.8669	15.4770	16.0867	16.6960	17.3046
18.00%	15.0709	15.6817	16.2923	16.9023	17.5118

Table 5   63

30 Year Loan   Adjustable Rate Mortgages

Rate increases 1% per year

Payment per $1000

Interest Rate	1	2	3	4	5
3.00%	4.2160	4.7583	5.3190	5.8948	6.4824
3.25%	4.3521	4.9036	5.4732	6.0573	6.6529
3.50%	4.4904	5.0511	5.6294	6.2218	6.8252
3.75%	4.6312	5.2008	5.7876	6.3881	6.9992
4.00%	4.7742	5.3527	5.9478	6.5562	7.1749
4.25%	4.9194	5.5066	6.1099	6.7261	7.3522
4.50%	5.0669	5.6626	6.2740	6.8977	7.5311
4.75%	5.2165	5.8206	6.4398	7.0710	7.7114
5.00%	5.3682	5.9805	6.6074	7.2459	7.8932
5.25%	5.5220	6.1423	6.7768	7.4224	8.0764
5.50%	5.6779	6.3060	6.9478	7.6003	8.2609
5.75%	5.8357	6.4715	7.1205	7.7797	8.4467
6.00%	5.9955	6.6388	7.2947	7.9605	8.6337
6.25%	6.1572	6.8077	7.4705	8.1427	8.8219
6.50%	6.3207	6.9783	7.6477	8.3261	9.0113
6.75%	6.4860	7.1505	7.8263	8.5108	9.2017
7.00%	6.6530	7.3243	8.0064	8.6967	9.3931
7.25%	6.8218	7.4996	8.1877	8.8837	9.5855
7.50%	6.9921	7.6763	8.3703	9.0719	9.7789
7.75%	7.1641	7.8544	8.5542	9.2611	9.9732
8.00%	7.3376	8.0339	8.7392	9.4513	10.1683
8.25%	7.5127	8.2147	8.9253	9.6424	10.3642
8.50%	7.6891	8.3968	9.1126	9.8345	10.5609
8.75%	7.8670	8.5800	9.3009	10.0275	10.7583
9.00%	8.0462	8.7645	9.4901	10.2213	10.9564
9.25%	8.2268	8.9501	9.6804	10.4159	11.1551
9.50%	8.4085	9.1367	9.8716	10.6113	11.3545
9.75%	8.5915	9.3244	10.0636	10.8074	11.5545
10.00%	8.7757	9.5131	10.2565	11.0043	11.7550
10.25%	8.9610	9.7028	10.4502	11.2017	11.9561
10.50%	9.1474	9.8934	10.6447	11.3998	12.1576
10.75%	9.3348	10.0848	10.8399	11.5985	12.3596
11.00%	9.5232	10.2771	11.0358	11.7978	12.5621
11.25%	9.7126	10.4702	11.2323	11.9976	12.7649
11.50%	9.9029	10.6641	11.4295	12.1979	12.9682
11.75%	10.0941	10.8587	11.6273	12.3987	13.1718
12.00%	10.2861	11.0541	11.8257	12.5999	13.3758
12.25%	10.4790	11.2501	12.0246	12.8016	13.5801
12.50%	10.6726	11.4467	12.2241	13.0037	13.7847
12.75%	10.8669	11.6440	12.4240	13.2061	13.9895
13.00%	11.0620	11.8418	12.6244	13.4090	14.1947
13.25%	11.2577	12.0402	12.8253	13.6122	14.4001
13.50%	11.4541	12.2391	13.0266	13.8157	14.6057
13.75%	11.6511	12.4385	13.2282	14.0195	14.8115
14.00%	11.8487	12.6385	13.4303	14.2236	15.0176
14.25%	12.0469	12.8388	13.6327	14.4279	15.2238
14.50%	12.2456	13.0396	13.8355	14.6326	15.4302
14.75%	12.4448	13.2408	14.0386	14.8374	15.6368
15.00%	12.6444	13.4424	14.2420	15.0425	15.8435
15.25%	12.8446	13.6444	14.4457	15.2478	16.0503
15.50%	13.0452	13.8467	14.6496	15.4533	16.2573
15.75%	13.2462	14.0494	14.8538	15.6590	16.4644
16.00%	13.4476	14.2524	15.0583	15.8649	16.6717
16.25%	13.6493	14.4557	15.2630	16.0709	16.8790
16.50%	13.8515	14.6592	15.4679	16.2771	17.0864
16.75%	14.0540	14.8631	15.6730	16.4834	17.2939
17.00%	14.2568	15.0672	15.8783	16.6899	17.5015
17.25%	14.4599	15.2715	16.0838	16.8965	17.7092
17.50%	14.6633	15.4760	16.2895	17.1032	17.9169
17.75%	14.8669	15.6808	16.4953	17.3100	18.1247
18.00%	15.0709	15.8858	16.7013	17.5170	18.3326

Table 6
Biweekly Payment Loans

Biweekly loans combine convenience with thrift. Every two weeks, biweekly borrowers pay one-half the payment on a normal 30-year loan. This works out to 13 months of payments yearly, prepaying the loan a full month every year and bringing important interest savings as well.

Studies show that biweekly loans are particularly convenient for households with weekly or biweekly paychecks. But smoothing out household bills also suits the convenience of many families with monthly pay, or that receive commission income.

Example 13. Biweekly Payments and Savings

Fred needs a $325,000 loan at the current loan rate of 6.25 percent interest. He wants to check the features of a biweekly payment loan.

To find the payment, enter Table 6 on the page for 30-year loans. On the line for 6.25 percent, the biweekly payment is $3.0786 per $1000. For a loan of $325,000, this will be $1,000.55 every two weeks.

On the same line, the savings (in months) achieved by making biweekly payments is 68 months. By making biweekly payments Fred has cut 68 months off of the original loan term.

Still on the 6.25 percent line under total interest are the figures $949 per $1000 interest paid. This seems to be a large amount, until it is considered that this is a savings, shown in the next column, of 26.76 percent of the original loan amount compared to what would be paid on an ordinary 30-year loan.

Example 14. Biweekly versus Other Loans

The Williams have the possibility to take a loan with a 20-year amortization plan, or a biweekly payment on a 25 year amortization term. Either way, the loan would be for $350,000 at an interest rate of 6.25 percent.

In Table 6, on the page for a 25 year loan term, on the line for 6.25 percent interest, find the reduction in loan term of the biweekly. Subtract this amount from 25 years (300 months).

300 months − 49 months = 251 months

The biweekly requires about 11 months longer to full payoff than the 20-year loan.

The payment on the 20-year loan is found in Table 7. It is found to be $2,558.25 per month or $30,699.00 per year. The biweekly payment, on the 6.25 percent line for a 25 year loan is $3.2983 per $1000 every two weeks, a total of $30,014.53, or $684.47 per year less.

For total interest, Table 6 shows the total interest on this biweekly to be $278,250 ($795 × 350) over its life.

For the 20-year loan, multiply $30,699.00 times 20 and subtract $350,000, to get $263,980. The plans are fairly similar in total interest cost. The advantage of the biweekly plan is its lower payment. Both save a great deal of interest compared to a 30-year loan, the 20-year plan having an edge over the biweekly.

Biweekly Payment Loans   **10 Year Loan**

Payment Per $1000 on a 10 Year Loan

Interest Rate	Biweekly Payment	Ordinary Payment	Biweekly Payments Shorten Term by	Total Interest Paid per $1000 of Loan with Biweekly Payments	Interest Saved as % of Original Loan Amount
3.00%	4.8280	9.6561	11 mos	144	1.45%
3.25%	4.8860	9.7719	11 mos	157	1.61%
3.50%	4.9443	9.8886	11 mos	169	1.76%
3.75%	5.0031	10.0061	11 mos	182	1.92%
4.00%	5.0623	10.1245	11 mos	194	2.09%
4.25%	5.1219	10.2438	11 mos	207	2.26%
4.50%	5.1819	10.3638	11 mos	219	2.44%
4.75%	5.2424	10.4848	12 mos	232	2.63%
5.00%	5.3033	10.6066	12 mos	245	2.82%
5.25%	5.3646	10.7292	12 mos	257	3.01%
5.50%	5.4263	10.8526	12 mos	270	3.21%
5.75%	5.4885	10.9769	12 mos	283	3.42%
6.00%	5.5510	11.1021	12 mos	296	3.64%
6.25%	5.6140	11.2280	12 mos	309	3.86%
6.50%	5.6774	11.3548	13 mos	322	4.09%
6.75%	5.7412	11.4824	13 mos	335	4.32%
7.00%	5.8054	11.6108	13 mos	348	4.56%
7.25%	5.8701	11.7401	13 mos	361	4.81%
7.50%	5.9351	11.8702	13 mos	374	5.07%
7.75%	6.0005	12.0011	13 mos	387	5.33%
8.00%	6.0664	12.1328	13 mos	400	5.61%
8.25%	6.1326	12.2653	14 mos	413	5.89%
8.50%	6.1993	12.3986	14 mos	426	6.17%
8.75%	6.2663	12.5327	14 mos	439	6.47%
9.00%	6.3338	12.6676	14 mos	452	6.77%
9.25%	6.4016	12.8033	14 mos	466	7.08%
9.50%	6.4699	12.9398	15 mos	479	7.40%
9.75%	6.5385	13.0770	15 mos	492	7.73%
10.00%	6.6075	13.2151	15 mos	505	8.07%
10.25%	6.6770	13.3539	15 mos	518	8.42%
10.50%	6.7467	13.4935	15 mos	532	8.77%
10.75%	6.8169	13.6339	15 mos	545	9.14%
11.00%	6.8875	13.7750	16 mos	558	9.51%
11.25%	6.9584	13.9169	16 mos	571	9.89%
11.50%	7.0298	14.0595	16 mos	584	10.29%
11.75%	7.1015	14.2029	16 mos	597	10.69%
12.00%	7.1735	14.3471	16 mos	611	11.10%
12.25%	7.2460	14.4920	17 mos	624	11.53%
12.50%	7.3188	14.6376	17 mos	637	11.96%
12.75%	7.3920	14.7840	17 mos	650	12.40%
13.00%	7.4655	14.9311	17 mos	663	12.86%
13.25%	7.5394	15.0789	17 mos	676	13.32%
13.50%	7.6137	15.2274	18 mos	689	13.80%
13.75%	7.6883	15.3767	18 mos	702	14.29%
14.00%	7.7633	15.5266	18 mos	715	14.79%
14.25%	7.8387	15.6773	18 mos	728	15.30%
14.50%	7.9143	15.8287	18 mos	741	15.82%
14.75%	7.9904	15.9807	19 mos	754	16.35%
15.00%	8.0667	16.1335	19 mos	767	16.90%
15.25%	8.1435	16.2869	19 mos	780	17.46%
15.50%	8.2205	16.4411	19 mos	793	18.03%
15.75%	8.2979	16.5958	20 mos	805	18.61%
16.00%	8.3757	16.7513	20 mos	818	19.20%
16.25%	8.4537	16.9074	20 mos	831	19.81%
16.50%	8.5321	17.0642	20 mos	843	20.43%
16.75%	8.6108	17.2217	21 mos	856	21.06%
17.00%	8.6899	17.3798	21 mos	868	21.71%
17.25%	8.7693	17.5385	21 mos	881	22.37%
17.50%	8.8489	17.6979	21 mos	893	23.04%
17.75%	8.9289	17.8579	21 mos	906	23.72%
18.00%	9.0093	18.0185	22 mos	918	24.42%

Table 6   67

15 Year Loan   Biweekly Payment Loans

Payment Per $1000 on a 15 Year Loan

Interest Rate	Biweekly Payment	Ordinary Payment	Biweekly Payments Shorten Term by	Total Interest Paid per $1000 of Loan with Biweekly Payments	Interest Saved as % of Original Loan Amount
3.00%	3.4529	6.9058	17 mos	219	2.44%
3.25%	3.5133	7.0267	17 mos	238	2.72%
3.50%	3.5744	7.1488	18 mos	257	3.01%
3.75%	3.6361	7.2722	18 mos	276	3.32%
4.00%	3.6984	7.3969	18 mos	295	3.64%
4.25%	3.7614	7.5228	19 mos	314	3.97%
4.50%	3.8250	7.6499	19 mos	334	4.32%
4.75%	3.8892	7.7783	19 mos	353	4.69%
5.00%	3.9540	7.9079	20 mos	373	5.07%
5.25%	4.0194	8.0388	20 mos	392	5.47%
5.50%	4.0854	8.1708	20 mos	412	5.89%
5.75%	4.1521	8.3041	21 mos	432	6.32%
6.00%	4.2193	8.4386	21 mos	451	6.78%
6.25%	4.2871	8.5742	22 mos	471	7.25%
6.50%	4.3555	8.7111	22 mos	491	7.74%
6.75%	4.4245	8.8491	22 mos	510	8.25%
7.00%	4.4941	8.9883	23 mos	530	8.78%
7.25%	4.5643	9.1286	23 mos	550	9.33%
7.50%	4.6351	9.2701	24 mos	570	9.90%
7.75%	4.7064	9.4128	24 mos	589	10.50%
8.00%	4.7783	9.5565	25 mos	609	11.12%
8.25%	4.8507	9.7014	25 mos	629	11.76%
8.50%	4.9237	9.8474	25 mos	648	12.42%
8.75%	4.9972	9.9945	26 mos	668	13.11%
9.00%	5.0713	10.1427	26 mos	687	13.82%
9.25%	5.1460	10.2919	27 mos	707	14.56%
9.50%	5.2211	10.4422	27 mos	726	15.33%
9.75%	5.2968	10.5936	28 mos	746	16.12%
10.00%	5.3730	10.7461	28 mos	765	16.93%
10.25%	5.4498	10.8995	29 mos	784	17.78%
10.50%	5.5270	11.0540	29 mos	803	18.65%
10.75%	5.6047	11.2095	30 mos	822	19.55%
11.00%	5.6830	11.3660	30 mos	841	20.48%
11.25%	5.7617	11.5234	31 mos	860	21.44%
11.50%	5.8409	11.6819	32 mos	879	22.42%
11.75%	5.9207	11.8413	32 mos	897	23.44%
12.00%	6.0008	12.0017	33 mos	915	24.49%
12.25%	6.0815	12.1630	33 mos	934	25.57%
12.50%	6.1626	12.3252	34 mos	952	26.68%
12.75%	6.2442	12.4884	34 mos	970	27.82%
13.00%	6.3262	12.6524	35 mos	987	29.00%
13.25%	6.4087	12.8174	36 mos	1,005	30.20%
13.50%	6.4916	12.9832	36 mos	1,023	31.44%
13.75%	6.5749	13.1499	37 mos	1,040	32.72%
14.00%	6.6587	13.3174	37 mos	1,057	34.02%
14.25%	6.7429	13.4858	38 mos	1,074	35.37%
14.50%	6.8275	13.6550	39 mos	1,090	36.74%
14.75%	6.9125	13.8250	39 mos	1,107	38.15%
15.00%	6.9979	13.9959	40 mos	1,123	39.59%
15.25%	7.0837	14.1675	41 mos	1,139	41.07%
15.50%	7.1700	14.3399	41 mos	1,155	42.59%
15.75%	7.2565	14.5131	42 mos	1,171	44.14%
16.00%	7.3435	14.6870	43 mos	1,186	45.72%
16.25%	7.4308	14.8817	43 mos	1,202	47.34%
16.50%	7.5185	15.0371	44 mos	1,217	48.99%
16.75%	7.6066	15.2132	45 mos	1,232	50.68%
17.00%	7.6950	15.3900	45 mos	1,246	52.41%
17.25%	7.7838	15.5676	48 mos	1,260	54.17%
17.50%	7.8729	15.7458	47 mos	1,275	55.97%
17.75%	7.9623	15.9247	47 mos	1,288	57.80%
18.00%	8.0521	16.1042	48 mos	1,302	59.67%

Biweekly Payment Loans   # 20 Year Loan

Payment Per $1000 on a 20 Year Loan

Interest Rate	Biweekly Payment	Ordinary Payment	Biweekly Payments Shorten Term by	Total Interest Paid per $1000 of Loan with Biweekly Payments	Interest Saved as % of Original Loan Amount
3.00%	2.7730	5.5460	25 mos	295	3.64%
3.25%	2.8360	5.6720	25 mos	320	4.09%
3.50%	2.8998	5.7996	26 mos	346	4.57%
3.75%	2.9644	5.9289	26 mos	372	5.07%
4.00%	3.0299	6.0598	27 mos	398	5.61%
4.25%	3.0962	6.1923	28 mos	424	6.18%
4.50%	3.1632	6.3265	28 mos	451	6.78%
4.75%	3.2311	6.4622	29 mos	477	7.41%
5.00%	3.2998	6.5996	30 mos	503	8.08%
5.25%	3.3692	6.7384	30 mos	529	8.78%
5.50%	3.4394	6.8789	31 mos	556	9.53%
5.75%	3.5104	7.0208	32 mos	582	10.31%
6.00%	3.5822	7.1643	33 mos	608	11.13%
6.25%	3.6546	7.3093	34 mos	634	11.99%
6.50%	3.7279	7.4557	34 mos	660	12.89%
6.75%	3.8018	7.6036	35 mos	687	13.84%
7.00%	3.8765	7.7530	36 mos	712	14.83%
7.25%	3.9519	7.9038	37 mos	738	15.86%
7.50%	4.0280	8.0559	38 mos	764	16.95%
7.75%	4.1047	8.2095	39 mos	789	18.08%
8.00%	4.1822	8.3644	40 mos	815	19.27%
8.25%	4.2603	8.5207	41 mos	840	20.50%
8.50%	4.3391	8.6782	42 mos	865	21.79%
8.75%	4.4186	8.8371	43 mos	890	23.13%
9.00%	4.4986	8.9973	44 mos	914	24.52%
9.25%	4.5793	9.1587	45 mos	938	25.97%
9.50%	4.6607	9.3213	46 mos	962	27.48%
9.75%	4.7426	9.4852	47 mos	986	29.04%
10.00%	4.8251	9.6502	48 mos	1,009	30.66%
10.25%	4.9082	9.8164	49 mos	1,033	32.34%
10.50%	4.9919	9.9838	50 mos	1,055	34.08%
10.75%	5.0761	10.1523	51 mos	1,078	35.88%
11.00%	5.1609	10.3219	52 mos	1,100	37.75%
11.25%	5.2463	10.4926	53 mos	1,122	39.67%
11.50%	5.3321	10.6643	55 mos	1,143	41.65%
11.75%	5.4185	10.8371	56 mos	1,164	43.70%
12.00%	5.5054	11.0109	57 mos	1,184	45.81%
12.25%	5.5928	11.1856	58 mos	1,205	47.99%
12.50%	5.6807	11.3614	59 mos	1,224	50.23%
12.75%	5.7691	11.5381	60 mos	1,244	52.53%
13.00%	5.8579	11.7158	62 mos	1,263	54.89%
13.25%	5.9472	11.8943	63 mos	1,281	57.32%
13.50%	6.0369	12.0737	64 mos	1,300	59.81%
13.75%	6.1270	12.2541	65 mos	1,317	62.37%
14.00%	6.2176	12.4352	67 mos	1,335	64.99%
14.25%	6.3086	12.6172	68 mos	1,351	67.67%
14.50%	6.4000	12.8000	69 mos	1,368	70.41%
14.75%	6.4918	12.9836	71 mos	1,384	73.21%
15.00%	6.5839	13.1679	72 mos	1,400	76.08%
15.25%	6.6765	13.3530	73 mos	1,415	79.01%
15.50%	6.7694	13.5388	74 mos	1,429	81.99%
15.75%	6.8627	13.7253	76 mos	1,444	85.04%
16.00%	6.9563	13.9126	77 mos	1,458	88.14%
16.25%	7.0502	14.1005	78 mos	1,471	91.30%
16.50%	7.1445	14.2890	80 mos	1,484	94.52%
16.75%	7.2391	14.4782	81 mos	1,497	97.79%
17.00%	7.3340	14.6680	82 mos	1,509	101.12%
17.25%	7.4292	14.8584	83 mos	1,521	104.50%
17.50%	7.5247	15.0494	85 mos	1,533	107.94%
17.75%	7.6205	15.2410	86 mos	1,544	111.42%
18.00%	7.7166	15.4331	87 mos	1,554	114.96%

Table 6   69

<u>25 Year Loan</u>　　**Biweekly Payment Loans**

Payment Per $1000 on a 25 Year Loan

Interest Rate	Biweekly Payment	Ordinary Payment	Biweekly Payments Shorten Term by	Total Interest Paid per $1000 of Loan with Biweekly Payments	Interest Saved as % of Original Loan Amount
3.00%	2.3711	4.7421	33 mos	372	5.08%
3.25%	2.4366	4.8732	34 mos	404	5.75%
3.50%	2.5031	5.0062	35 mos	437	6.48%
3.75%	2.5707	5.1413	36 mos	470	7.25%
4.00%	2.6392	5.2784	37 mos	503	8.08%
4.25%	2.7087	5.4174	38 mos	536	8.97%
4.50%	2.7792	5.5583	40 mos	568	9.91%
4.75%	2.8506	5.7012	41 mos	601	10.92%
5.00%	2.9230	5.8459	42 mos	634	11.99%
5.25%	2.9962	5.9925	43 mos	666	13.13%
5.50%	3.0704	6.1409	45 mos	699	14.33%
5.75%	3.1455	6.2911	46 mos	731	15.61%
6.00%	3.2215	6.4430	47 mos	763	16.96%
6.25%	3.2983	6.5967	49 mos	795	18.39%
6.50%	3.3760	6.7521	50 mos	827	19.89%
6.75%	3.4546	6.9091	52 mos	858	21.48%
7.00%	3.5339	7.0678	53 mos	889	23.15%
7.25%	3.6140	7.2281	55 mos	919	24.90%
7.50%	3.6950	7.3899	56 mos	950	26.74%
7.75%	3.7766	7.5533	58 mos	979	28.67%
8.00%	3.8591	7.7182	60 mos	1,009	30.69%
8.25%	3.9423	7.8845	61 mos	1,037	32.81%
8.50%	4.0261	8.0523	63 mos	1,066	35.01%
8.75%	4.1107	8.2214	65 mos	1,093	37.31%
9.00%	4.1960	8.3920	67 mos	1,120	39.71%
9.25%	4.2819	8.5638	69 mos	1,147	42.21%
9.50%	4.3685	8.7370	70 mos	1,173	44.81%
9.75%	4.4557	8.9114	72 mos	1,198	47.50%
10.00%	4.5435	9.0870	74 mos	1,223	50.29%
10.25%	4.6319	9.2638	76 mos	1,247	53.18%
10.50%	4.7209	9.4418	78 mos	1,271	56.18%
10.75%	4.8105	9.6209	80 mos	1,294	59.27%
11.00%	4.9006	9.8011	82 mos	1,316	62.46%
11.25%	4.9912	9.9824	84 mos	1,337	65.75%
11.50%	5.0823	10.1647	86 mos	1,358	69.14%
11.75%	5.1740	10.3480	88 mos	1,378	72.62%
12.00%	5.2661	10.5322	90 mos	1,398	76.20%
12.25%	5.3587	10.7174	92 mos	1,416	79.88%
12.50%	5.4518	10.9035	94 mos	1,435	83.65%
12.75%	5.5453	11.0905	96 mos	1,452	87.51%
13.00%	5.6392	11.2784	98 mos	1,469	91.46%
13.25%	5.7335	11.4670	100 mos	1,485	95.50%
13.50%	5.8282	11.6564	102 mos	1,501	99.62%
13.75%	5.9233	11.8467	104 mos	1,516	103.84%
14.00%	6.0188	12.0376	106 mos	1,530	108.13%
14.25%	6.1146	12.2293	108 mos	1,544	112.51%
14.50%	6.2108	12.4216	110 mos	1,557	116.96%
14.75%	6.3073	12.6146	112 mos	1,569	121.49%
15.00%	6.4042	12.8083	114 mos	1,582	126.09%
15.25%	6.5013	13.0026	116 mos	1,593	130.77%
15.50%	6.5987	13.1975	118 mos	1,604	135.51%
15.75%	6.6964	13.3929	120 mos	1,615	140.33%
16.00%	6.7944	13.5889	122 mos	1,625	145.20%
16.25%	6.8927	13.7854	124 mos	1,634	150.14%
16.50%	6.9912	13.9824	125 mos	1,643	155.14%
16.75%	7.0900	14.1800	127 mos	1,652	160.20%
17.00%	7.1890	14.3780	129 mos	1,660	165.32%
17.25%	7.2882	14.5764	131 mos	1,668	170.48%
17.50%	7.3876	14.7753	133 mos	1,676	175.70%
17.75%	7.4873	14.9746	135 mos	1,683	180.97%
18.00%	7.5871	15.1743	136 mos	1,689	186.29%

Biweekly Payment Loans   **30 Year Loan**

Payment Per $1000 on a 30 Year Loan

Interest Rate	Biweekly Payment	Ordinary Payment	Biweekly Payments Shorten Term by	Total Interest Paid per $1000 of Loan with Biweekly Payments	Interest Saved as % of Original Loan Amount
3.00%	2.1080	4.2160	43 mos	450	6.78%
3.25%	2.1760	4.3521	44 mos	489	7.75%
3.50%	2.2452	4.4904	46 mos	529	8.79%
3.75%	2.3156	4.6312	47 mos	568	9.92%
4.00%	2.3871	4.7742	49 mos	607	11.13%
4.25%	2.4597	4.9194	51 mos	647	12.44%
4.50%	2.5334	5.0669	53 mos	686	13.85%
4.75%	2.6082	5.2165	55 mos	724	15.35%
5.00%	2.6841	5.3682	57 mos	763	16.97%
5.25%	2.7610	5.5220	59 mos	801	18.69%
5.50%	2.8389	5.6779	61 mos	839	20.53%
5.75%	2.9179	5.8357	63 mos	876	22.48%
6.00%	2.9978	5.9955	65 mos	913	24.56%
6.25%	3.0786	6.1572	68 mos	949	26.76%
6.50%	3.1603	6.3207	70 mos	985	29.09%
6.75%	3.2430	6.4860	73 mos	1,019	31.55%
7.00%	3.3265	6.6530	75 mos	1,054	34.14%
7.25%	3.4109	6.8218	78 mos	1,087	36.87%
7.50%	3.4961	6.9921	80 mos	1,120	39.74%
7.75%	3.5821	7.1641	83 mos	1,152	42.76%
8.00%	3.6688	7.3376	85 mos	1,182	45.91%
8.25%	3.7563	7.5127	88 mos	1,213	49.20%
8.50%	3.8446	7.6891	91 mos	1,242	52.64%
8.75%	3.9335	7.8670	94 mos	1,270	56.23%
9.00%	4.0231	8.0462	96 mos	1,297	59.96%
9.25%	4.1134	8.2268	99 mos	1,323	63.83%
9.50%	4.2043	8.4085	102 mos	1,349	67.84%
9.75%	4.2958	8.5915	105 mos	1,373	71.99%
10.00%	4.3879	8.7757	108 mos	1,396	76.28%
10.25%	4.4805	8.9610	111 mos	1,419	80.71%
10.50%	4.5737	9.1474	114 mos	1,440	85.27%
10.75%	4.6674	9.3348	117 mos	1,461	89.97%
11.00%	4.7616	9.5232	120 mos	1,480	94.79%
11.25%	4.8563	9.7126	122 mos	1,499	99.74%
11.50%	4.9515	9.9029	125 mos	1,517	104.81%
11.75%	5.0470	10.0941	128 mos	1,634	110.00%
12.00%	5.1431	10.2861	131 mos	1,550	115.31%
12.25%	5.2395	10.4790	134 mos	1,565	120.73%
12.50%	5.3363	10.6726	137 mos	1,580	126.25%
12.75%	5.4335	10.8669	140 mos	1,593	131.88%
13.00%	5.5310	11.0620	143 mos	1,606	137.61%
13.25%	5.6289	11.2577	145 mos	1,618	143.43%
13.50%	5.7271	11.4541	148 mos	1,630	149.34%
13.75%	5.8256	11.6511	151 mos	1,641	155.35%
14.00%	5.9244	11.8487	153 mos	1,651	161.43%
14.25%	6.0234	12.0469	156 mos	1,661	167.60%
14.50%	6.1228	12.2456	159 mos	1,670	173.84%
14.75%	6.2224	12.4448	161 mos	1,679	180.15%
15.00%	6.3222	12.6444	164 mos	1,687	186.53%
15.25%	6.4223	12.8446	166 mos	1,694	192.98%
15.50%	6.5226	13.0452	169 mos	1,701	199.49%
15.75%	6.6231	13.2462	171 mos	1,708	206.05%
16.00%	6.7238	13.4476	174 mos	1,714	212.67%
16.25%	6.8247	13.6493	176 mos	1,720	219.35%
16.50%	6.9257	13.8515	178 mos	1,726	226.07%
16.75%	7.0270	14.0540	181 mos	1,731	232.84%
17.00%	7.1284	14.2568	183 mos	1,736	239.66%
17.25%	7.2299	14.4599	185 mos	1,740	246.51%
17.50%	7.3316	14.6633	187 mos	1,745	253.40%
17.75%	7.4335	14.8669	189 mos	1,749	260.33%
18.00%	7.5354	15.0709	191 mos	1,753	267.30%

Table 6   71

40 Year Loan   Biweekly Payment Loans

Payment Per $1000 on a 40 Year Loan

Interest Rate	Biweekly Payment	Ordinary Payment	Biweekly Payments Shorten Term by	Total Interest Paid per $1000 of Loan with Biweekly Payments	Interest Saved as % of Original Loan Amount
3.00%	1.7899	3.5798	66 mos	607	11.14%
3.25%	1.8627	3.7254	69 mos	659	12.90%
3.50%	1.9370	3.8739	72 mos	711	14.85%
3.75%	2.0126	4.0253	76 mos	762	16.98%
4.00%	2.0897	4.1794	80 mos	813	19.30%
4.25%	2.1681	4.3362	83 mos	863	21.83%
4.50%	2.2478	4.4956	87 mos	912	24.57%
4.75%	2.3288	4.6576	92 mos	960	27.54%
5.00%	2.4110	4.8220	96 mos	1,007	30.74%
5.25%	2.4944	4.9887	100 mos	1,053	34.17%
5.50%	2.5789	5.1577	105 mos	1,097	37.85%
5.75%	2.6644	5.3289	109 mos	1,140	41.78%
6.00%	2.7511	5.5021	114 mos	1,181	45.96%
6.25%	2.8387	5.6774	119 mos	1,221	50.39%
6.50%	2.9273	5.8546	124 mos	1,259	55.08%
6.75%	3.0168	6.0336	129 mos	1,296	60.03%
7.00%	3.1072	6.2143	134 mos	1,131	65.23%
7.25%	3.1984	6.3967	139 mos	1,364	70.68%
7.50%	3.2904	6.5807	144 mos	1,395	76.38%
7.75%	3.3831	6.7662	149 mos	1,424	82.33%
8.00%	3.4766	6.9531	154 mos	1,452	88.51%
8.25%	3.5707	7.1414	160 mos	1,479	94.93%
8.50%	3.6655	7.3309	165 mos	1,503	101.57%
8.75%	3.7609	7.5217	170 mos	1,526	108.42%
9.00%	3.8568	7.7136	175 mos	1,548	115.49%
9.25%	3.9533	7.9066	180 mos	1,568	122.75%
9.50%	4.0503	8.1006	185 mos	1,586	130.20%
9.75%	4.1478	8.2956	190 mos	1,604	137.83%
10.00%	4.2457	8.4915	195 mos	1,620	145.63%
10.25%	4.3441	8.6882	200 mos	1,634	153.59%
10.50%	4.4429	8.8857	205 mos	1,648	161.70%
10.75%	4.5420	9.0840	210 mos	1,661	169.95%
11.00%	4.6415	9.2829	214 mos	1,672	178.33%
11.25%	4.7413	9.4826	219 mos	1,683	186.84%
11.50%	4.8414	9.6828	223 mos	1,693	195.47%
11.75%	4.9418	9.8836	228 mos	1,702	204.20%
12.00%	5.0425	10.0850	232 mos	1,711	213.03%
12.25%	5.1434	10.2869	236 mos	1,718	221.95%
12.50%	5.2446	10.4892	240 mos	1,725	230.96%
12.75%	5.3460	10.6920	244 mos	1,732	240.05%
13.00%	5.4476	10.8951	248 mos	1,738	249.22%
13.25%	5.5493	11.0987	252 mos	1,743	258.45%
13.50%	5.6513	11.3026	256 mos	1,748	267.74%
13.75%	5.7534	11.5069	259 mos	1,752	277.09%
14.00%	5.8557	11.7114	263 mos	1,757	286.49%
14.25%	5.9581	11.9162	266 mos	1,760	295.94%
14.50%	6.0607	12.1213	270 mos	1,764	305.44%
14.75%	6.1633	12.3267	273 mos	1,767	314.97%
15.00%	6.2661	12.5322	276 mos	1,770	324.55%
15.25%	6.3690	12.7380	279 mos	1,773	334.15%
15.50%	6.4720	12.9440	282 mos	1,775	343.79%
15.75%	6.5751	13.1502	285 mos	1,777	353.46%
16.00%	6.6782	13.3565	288 mos	1,780	363.16%
16.25%	6.7815	13.5630	291 mos	1,781	372.88%
16.50%	6.8848	13.7696	293 mos	1,783	382.62%
16.75%	6.9882	13.9764	296 mos	1,785	392.38%
17.00%	7.0916	14.1832	299 mos	1,786	402.16%
17.25%	7.1951	14.3902	301 mos	1,788	411.95%
17.50%	7.2987	14.5973	304 mos	1,789	421.76%
17.75%	7.4023	14.8045	306 mos	1,790	431.59%
18.00%	7.5059	15.0118	308 mos	1,791	441.43%

Table 7
Monthly Payment Loans

By far the most common mortgage loan in the United States calls for equal monthly payments beginning one month after the loan closing.

Today's loans most often have an amortization period of 30 years, but loans amortized in 15 years are increasing in popularity. By amortization period is meant that, if the payments are continued for the entire amortization period, the loan will be fully paid. Many loans are only offered for a shorter term than the amortization period. This results in a balloon payment, meaning that the entire balance remaining on the loan falls due in one payment.

When using the tables, be sure to look up the payment according to the amortization period, not the term. For example, if a lender quotes a loan that has a term of 7 years, but an amortization period of 30 years, use the column for 30 years.

These tables cannot cover every imaginable loan amount. To compensate for this the table entries can be added together to reach any result desired. You are not limited to two entries. You may add as many individual items together as necessary to reach the desired loan amount. An example of how to do this is shown below.

When there is a balloon payment, the borrower takes the risk of higher interest rates at the end of the term. To compensate, many lenders offer a lower interest rate on balloons than on loans that will be fully amortized.

Example 15.   Finding the Monthly Payment

The Jones' are seeking a $360,000 loan at the current 6.25 percent interest rate. The loan documents will call for monthly payments and will have a 30-year amortization period.

To find the monthly payment, turn to the page of Table 7 for 6.25 percent interest and 30 years. Read down the left-hand column to $350,000 and across on that line to the column headed 30 years. The entry there is $2,155.02. Repeat this procedure using the same table and 30 year column but this time locate the entry corresponding to the left-hand column amount of $10,000. This entry is $61.58. Add the two entries together to get the payment needed to amortize a $360,000 loan over a 30 year term. The result is $2,216.60. Payments derived by combining more than one entry may result in rounding errors of a few cents.

Note that the monthly payment will be the same, even if the loan has a balloon payment earlier than 30 years.

Example 16.   Amount Not Shown in Table

There are several ways to approach finding the payment on a loan amount that is not shown in the table. We will discuss these ways in order of increasing accuracy.

First way: Divide the loan amount by 1000. Then look up the payment on $1000 of loan for the applicable interest rate and amortization period. Next, multiply the payment shown in the table by the number arrived at by dividing the loan by 1000.

Here's an example: Loan Amount $87,000 — interest rate 6.50 percent — term 25 years. The payment on $1,000 = $6.76. Next, multiply the size of the loan in thousands by the payment amount per $1,000 of loan

$$\$6.76 \times 87 = \$588.12$$

Second way: Find entries in the table that add up to the loan amount and add up the payments on those entries. Using the same example as used above:

$50,000	$337.61
$30,000	$202.57
$ 5,000	$ 33.77
$ 2,000	$ 13.51
$87,000	$587.46

The actual payment is $587.44. Both of the examples shown above suffer from rounding errors.

Third way: Use Table 1. Table 1 may be more accurate because the factors in Table 1 have been carried out to more decimal places. Using the approach above but using the factor from Table 1 we get

$$6.7521 \times 87 = \$587.4327$$

Payment amounts are always rounded to the next highest penny to avoid having a final payment that is greater than the regular monthly payment amount. In this case the payment would be rounded up to $587.44 — an amount that corresponds to the actual payment required on an $87,000 loan at 6.5 percent amortized over 25 years.

When adding several payment amounts rounding can cause the total payment amount to be "off" by as much as one cent for each item added. In the example above, adding four items could have been "off" by as much as four cents. In this case it was only two cents "off".

Example 17.   Total Interest over the Life of a Loan

Jim has offers of two different loan plans for the $400,000 loan he seeks. The first calls for amortization over 15 years and an interest rate of 6 percent. The second requires interest of 6.5 percent, but allows payment over a 30-year period. Obviously, 15-year amortization will mean higher payments than a 30-year plan, but he suspects the interest saved over time may be worth it.

To find the total interest cost, begin by finding the payments for each loan. On the page for 6 percent interest and 15-year amortization period, read on the $400,000 line under 15 years, $3,375.43. Multiply this payment by 180 months, the number of payments in the loan, to get

$$\$3,375.43 \times 180 = \$607,577.40,$$
the total cost of the loan.

Subtract the original loan amount from it to get $207,577.40, the total interest paid on the 15-year loan over its life.

Using the same procedure, on the 6.5 percent page, read across on the $400,000 line to 30 years, and find $2,528.28, the payment on the 30-year loan.

Multiply this payment by 360 for the thirty year term, to get

$$\$2,528.28 \times 360 = \$910,180.80,$$
the total cost of a 30-year plan.

Subtracting the original principal gives $510,180.80, the total interest paid in 30 years.

Jim concludes that not only does the lower interest rate save money, but more rapid amortization brings tremendous savings. In this example, $19,620 of the $302,603.40 savings comes from the lower interest rate. The other $282,983.40 is saved by paying the loan off in 15 rather than 30 years. The $19,620 is derived by calculating what the payments on a 15-year loan at 6.50 percent interest would have been and subtracting the total payments on the loan at 6 percent interest.

Monthly Payment Loans   **3.00%**

Amortization Period in Years

Loan Amount	5	7	8	10	12
10	0.18	0.14	0.12	0.10	0.09
20	0.36	0.27	0.24	0.20	0.17
30	0.54	0.40	0.36	0.29	0.25
40	0.72	0.53	0.47	0.39	0.34
50	0.90	0.67	0.59	0.49	0.42
100	1.80	1.33	1.18	0.97	0.83
200	3.60	2.65	2.35	1.94	1.66
300	5.40	3.97	3.52	2.90	2.49
400	7.19	5.29	4.70	3.87	3.32
500	8.99	6.61	5.87	4.83	4.14
1,000	17.97	13.22	11.73	9.66	8.28
2,000	35.94	26.43	23.46	19.32	16.56
3,000	53.91	39.64	35.19	28.97	24.84
4,000	71.88	52.86	46.92	38.63	33.12
5,000	89.85	66.07	58.65	48.29	41.39
10,000	179.69	132.14	117.30	96.57	82.78
20,000	359.38	264.27	234.60	193.13	165.56
30,000	539.07	396.40	351.89	289.69	248.34
40,000	718.75	528.54	469.19	386.25	331.12
50,000	898.44	660.67	586.48	482.81	413.90
100,000	1796.87	1321.34	1172.96	965.61	827.79
125,000	2246.09	1651.67	1466.20	1207.01	1034.74
150,000	2695.31	1982.00	1759.44	1448.42	1241.69
175,000	3144.53	2312.33	2052.68	1689.82	1448.63
200,000	3593.74	2642.67	2345.92	1931.22	1655.58
225,000	4042.96	2973.00	2639.16	2172.62	1862.53
250,000	4492.18	3303.33	2932.40	2414.02	2069.47
275,000	4941.39	3633.66	3225.64	2655.43	2276.42
300,000	5390.61	3964.00	3518.88	2896.83	2483.37
325,000	5839.83	4294.33	3812.12	3138.23	2690.31
350,000	6289.05	4624.66	4105.36	3379.63	2897.26
375,000	6738.26	4954.99	4398.59	3621.03	3104.21
400,000	7187.48	5285.33	4691.83	3862.43	3311.15
425,000	7636.70	5615.66	4985.07	4103.84	3518.10
450,000	8085.92	5945.99	5278.31	4345.24	3725.05
475,000	8535.13	6276.32	5571.55	4586.64	3931.99
500,000	8984.35	6606.66	5864.79	4828.04	4138.94
525,000	9433.57	6936.99	6158.03	5069.44	4345.89
550,000	9882.78	7267.32	6451.27	5310.85	4552.83
575,000	10332.00	7597.65	6744.51	5552.25	4759.78
600,000	10781.22	7927.99	7037.75	5793.65	4966.73
625,000	11230.44	8258.32	7330.99	6035.05	5173.67
650,000	11679.65	8588.65	7624.23	6276.45	5380.62
675,000	12128.87	8918.98	7917.47	6517.86	5587.57
700,000	12578.09	9249.32	8210.71	6759.26	5794.51
725,000	13027.31	9579.65	8503.94	7000.66	6001.46
750,000	13476.52	9909.98	8797.18	7242.06	6208.41
775,000	13925.74	10240.31	9090.42	7483.46	6415.35
800,000	14374.96	10570.65	9383.66	7724.86	6622.30
825,000	14824.17	10900.98	9676.90	7966.27	6829.25
850,000	15273.39	11231.31	9970.14	8207.67	7036.19
875,000	15722.61	11561.64	10263.38	8449.07	7243.14
900,000	16171.83	11891.98	10556.62	8690.47	7450.09

Table 7   77

3.00%   Monthly Payment Loans

Loan

Amount			Amortization Period in Years		
	15	16	17	18	20
10	0.07	0.07	0.07	0.06	0.06
20	0.14	0.14	0.13	0.12	0.12
30	0.21	0.20	0.19	0.18	0.17
40	0.28	0.27	0.26	0.24	0.23
50	0.35	0.33	0.32	0.30	0.28
100	0.70	0.66	0.63	0.60	0.56
200	1.39	1.32	1.26	1.20	1.11
300	2.08	1.97	1.88	1.80	1.67
400	2.77	2.63	2.51	2.40	2.22
500	3.46	3.29	3.14	3.00	2.78
1,000	6.91	6.57	6.27	6.00	5.55
2,000	13.82	13.13	12.53	12.00	11.10
3,000	20.72	19.70	18.80	18.00	16.64
4,000	27.63	26.26	25.06	23.99	22.19
5,000	34.53	32.83	31.32	29.99	27.73
10,000	69.06	65.65	62.64	59.98	55.46
20,000	138.12	131.29	125.28	119.95	110.92
30,000	207.18	196.94	187.92	179.92	166.38
40,000	276.24	262.58	250.55	239.89	221.84
50,000	345.30	328.22	313.19	299.87	277.30
100,000	690.59	656.44	626.38	599.73	554.60
125,000	863.23	820.55	782.97	749.66	693.25
150,000	1035.88	984.66	939.57	899.59	831.90
175,000	1208.52	1148.76	1096.16	1049.52	970.55
200,000	1381.17	1312.87	1252.75	1199.45	1109.20
225,000	1553.81	1476.98	1409.35	1349.38	1247.85
250,000	1726.46	1641.09	1565.94	1499.31	1386.50
275,000	1899.10	1805.20	1722.54	1649.24	1525.15
300,000	2071.75	1969.31	1879.13	1799.17	1663.80
325,000	2244.40	2133.41	2035.72	1949.11	1802.45
350,000	2417.04	2297.52	2192.32	2099.04	1941.10
375,000	2589.69	2461.63	2348.91	2248.97	2079.75
400,000	2762.33	2625.74	2505.50	2398.90	2218.40
425,000	2934.98	2789.85	2662.10	2548.83	2357.04
450,000	3107.62	2953.96	2818.69	2698.76	2495.69
475,000	3280.27	3118.06	2975.28	2848.69	2634.34
500,000	3452.91	3282.17	3131.88	2998.62	2772.99
525,000	3625.56	3446.28	3288.47	3148.55	2911.64
550,000	3798.20	3610.39	3445.07	3298.48	3050.29
575,000	3970.85	3774.50	3601.66	3448.41	3188.94
600,000	4143.49	3938.61	3758.25	3598.34	3327.59
625,000	4316.14	4102.71	3914.85	3748.28	3466.24
650,000	4488.79	4266.82	4071.44	3898.21	3604.89
675,000	4661.43	4430.93	4228.03	4048.14	3743.54
700,000	4834.08	4595.04	4384.63	4198.07	3882.19
725,000	5006.72	4759.15	4541.22	4348.00	4020.84
750,000	5179.37	4923.26	4697.82	4497.93	4159.49
775,000	5352.01	5087.37	4854.41	4647.86	4298.14
800,000	5524.66	5251.47	5011.00	4797.79	4436.79
825,000	5697.30	5415.58	5167.60	4947.72	4575.44
850,000	5869.95	5579.69	5324.19	5097.65	4714.08
875,000	6042.59	5743.80	5480.78	5247.58	4852.73
900,000	6215.24	5907.91	5637.38	5397.51	4991.38

Monthly Payment Loans **3.00%**

Loan Amount	Amortization Period in Years				
	21	22	23	24	25
10	0.06	0.06	0.06	0.05	0.05
20	0.11	0.11	0.11	0.10	0.10
30	0.17	0.16	0.16	0.15	0.15
40	0.22	0.21	0.21	0.20	0.19
50	0.27	0.26	0.26	0.25	0.24
100	0.54	0.52	0.51	0.49	0.48
200	1.08	1.04	1.01	0.98	0.95
300	1.61	1.56	1.51	1.47	1.43
400	2.15	2.08	2.01	1.96	1.90
500	2.68	2.59	2.52	2.44	2.38
1,000	5.36	5.18	5.03	4.88	4.75
2,000	10.71	10.36	10.05	9.76	9.49
3,000	16.07	15.54	15.07	14.63	14.23
4,000	21.42	20.72	20.09	19.51	18.97
5,000	26.77	25.90	25.11	24.38	23.72
10,000	53.54	51.79	50.21	48.76	47.43
20,000	107.07	103.58	100.41	97.51	94.85
30,000	160.61	155.37	150.61	146.26	142.27
40,000	214.14	207.16	200.81	195.01	189.69
50,000	267.68	258.95	251.01	243.76	237.11
100,000	535.35	517.90	502.02	487.51	474.22
125,000	669.19	647.37	627.53	609.39	592.77
150,000	803.02	776.85	753.03	731.27	711.32
175,000	936.86	906.32	878.53	853.15	829.87
200,000	1070.69	1035.80	1004.04	975.02	948.43
225,000	1204.53	1165.27	1129.54	1096.90	1066.98
250,000	1338.37	1294.74	1255.05	1218.78	1185.53
275,000	1472.20	1424.22	1380.55	1340.66	1304.09
300,000	1606.04	1553.69	1506.05	1462.53	1422.64
325,000	1739.87	1683.17	1631.56	1584.41	1541.19
350,000	1873.71	1812.64	1757.06	1706.29	1659.74
375,000	2007.55	1942.11	1882.57	1828.17	1778.30
400,000	2141.38	2071.59	2008.07	1950.04	1896.85
425,000	2275.22	2201.06	2133.57	2071.92	2015.40
450,000	2409.05	2330.54	2259.08	2193.80	2133.96
475,000	2542.89	2460.01	2384.58	2315.68	2252.51
500,000	2676.73	2589.48	2510.09	2437.55	2371.06
525,000	2810.56	2718.96	2635.59	2559.43	2489.61
550,000	2944.40	2848.43	2761.09	2681.31	2608.17
575,000	3078.23	2977.90	2886.60	2803.19	2726.72
600,000	3212.07	3107.38	3012.10	2925.06	2845.27
625,000	3345.91	3236.85	3137.61	3046.94	2963.83
650,000	3479.74	3366.33	3263.11	3168.82	3082.38
675,000	3613.58	3495.80	3388.61	3290.70	3200.93
700,000	3747.41	3625.27	3514.12	3412.57	3319.48
725,000	3881.25	3754.75	3639.62	3534.45	3438.04
750,000	4015.09	3884.22	3765.13	3656.33	3556.59
775,000	4148.92	4013.70	3890.63	3778.21	3675.14
800,000	4282.76	4143.17	4016.13	3900.08	3793.70
825,000	4416.59	4272.64	4141.64	4021.96	3912.25
850,000	4550.43	4402.12	4267.14	4143.84	4030.80
875,000	4684.27	4531.59	4392.65	4265.72	4149.35
900,000	4818.10	4661.07	4518.15	4387.59	4267.91

Table 7   79

Monthly Payment Loans

Amortization Period in Years

Loan Amount	26	27	28	29	30
10	0.05	0.05	0.05	0.05	0.05
20	0.10	0.10	0.09	0.09	0.09
30	0.14	0.14	0.14	0.13	0.13
40	0.19	0.19	0.18	0.18	0.17
50	0.24	0.23	0.23	0.22	0.22
100	0.47	0.46	0.45	0.44	0.43
200	0.93	0.91	0.89	0.87	0.85
300	1.39	1.36	1.33	1.30	1.27
400	1.85	1.81	1.77	1.73	1.69
500	2.31	2.26	2.21	2.16	2.11
1,000	4.62	4.51	4.41	4.31	4.22
2,000	9.24	9.02	8.81	8.62	8.44
3,000	13.86	13.53	13.21	12.92	12.65
4,000	18.48	18.03	17.62	17.23	16.87
5,000	23.10	22.54	22.02	21.53	21.09
10,000	46.20	45.08	44.03	43.06	42.17
20,000	92.40	90.15	88.06	86.12	84.33
30,000	138.60	135.22	132.09	129.18	126.49
40,000	184.80	180.29	176.11	172.24	168.65
50,000	231.00	225.36	220.14	215.30	210.81
100,000	461.99	450.71	440.27	430.60	421.61
125,000	577.48	563.38	550.34	538.25	527.01
150,000	692.98	676.06	660.41	645.90	632.41
175,000	808.47	788.73	770.47	753.54	737.81
200,000	923.97	901.41	880.54	861.19	843.21
225,000	1039.46	1014.08	990.61	968.84	948.61
250,000	1154.96	1126.76	1100.67	1076.49	1054.02
275,000	1270.45	1239.43	1210.74	1184.14	1159.42
300,000	1385.95	1352.11	1320.81	1291.79	1264.82
325,000	1501.44	1464.78	1430.87	1399.44	1370.22
350,000	1616.94	1577.46	1540.94	1507.08	1475.62
375,000	1732.43	1690.13	1651.01	1614.73	1581.02
400,000	1847.93	1802.81	1761.07	1722.38	1686.42
425,000	1963.43	1915.48	1871.14	1830.03	1791.82
450,000	2078.92	2028.16	1981.21	1937.68	1897.22
475,000	2194.42	2140.83	2091.28	2045.33	2002.62
500,000	2309.91	2253.51	2201.34	2152.97	2108.03
525,000	2425.41	2366.18	2311.41	2260.62	2213.43
550,000	2540.90	2478.86	2421.48	2368.27	2318.83
575,000	2656.40	2591.53	2531.54	2475.92	2424.23
600,000	2771.89	2704.21	2641.61	2583.57	2529.63
625,000	2887.39	2816.88	2751.68	2691.22	2635.03
650,000	3002.88	2929.56	2861.74	2798.87	2740.43
675,000	3118.38	3042.23	2971.81	2906.51	2845.83
700,000	3233.87	3154.91	3081.88	3014.16	2951.23
725,000	3349.37	3267.58	3191.94	3121.81	3056.63
750,000	3464.86	3380.26	3302.01	3229.46	3162.04
775,000	3580.36	3492.93	3412.08	3337.11	3267.44
800,000	3695.85	3605.61	3522.14	3444.76	3372.84
825,000	3811.35	3718.28	3632.21	3552.41	3478.24
850,000	3926.85	3830.96	3742.28	3660.05	3583.64
875,000	4042.34	3943.63	3852.34	3767.70	3689.04
900,000	4157.84	4056.31	3962.41	3875.35	3794.44

Monthly Payment Loans   **3.25%**

Loan Amount	Amortization Period in Years				
	5	7	8	10	12
10	0.19	0.14	0.12	0.10	0.09
20	0.37	0.27	0.24	0.20	0.17
30	0.55	0.40	0.36	0.30	0.26
40	0.73	0.54	0.48	0.40	0.34
50	0.91	0.67	0.60	0.49	0.42
100	1.81	1.34	1.19	0.98	0.84
200	3.62	2.67	2.37	1.96	1.68
300	5.43	4.00	3.56	2.94	2.52
400	7.24	5.34	4.74	3.91	3.36
500	9.05	6.67	5.93	4.89	4.20
1,000	18.09	13.33	11.85	9.78	8.40
2,000	36.17	26.66	23.69	19.55	16.80
3,000	54.25	39.98	35.54	29.32	25.19
4,000	72.33	53.31	47.38	39.09	33.59
5,000	90.41	66.64	59.22	48.86	41.98
10,000	180.81	133.27	118.44	97.72	83.96
20,000	361.61	266.53	236.87	195.44	167.92
30,000	542.41	399.79	355.31	293.16	251.88
40,000	723.21	533.06	473.74	390.88	335.83
50,000	904.01	666.32	592.18	488.60	419.79
100,000	1808.01	1332.63	1184.35	977.20	839.57
125,000	2260.01	1665.79	1480.44	1221.49	1049.47
150,000	2712.01	1998.95	1776.53	1465.79	1259.36
175,000	3164.01	2332.10	2072.61	1710.09	1469.25
200,000	3616.01	2665.26	2368.70	1954.39	1679.14
225,000	4068.01	2998.42	2664.79	2198.68	1889.04
250,000	4520.01	3331.57	2960.87	2442.98	2098.93
275,000	4972.01	3664.73	3256.96	2687.28	2308.82
300,000	5424.01	3997.89	3553.05	2931.58	2518.71
325,000	5876.01	4331.04	3849.13	3175.87	2728.60
350,000	6328.01	4664.20	4145.22	3420.17	2938.50
375,000	6780.01	4997.36	4441.31	3664.47	3148.39
400,000	7232.01	5330.51	4737.39	3908.77	3358.28
425,000	7684.01	5663.67	5033.48	4153.06	3568.17
450,000	8136.01	5996.83	5329.57	4397.36	3778.07
475,000	8588.01	6329.99	5625.65	4641.66	3987.96
500,000	9040.01	6663.14	5921.74	4885.96	4197.85
525,000	9492.01	6996.30	6217.83	5130.25	4407.74
550,000	9944.01	7329.46	6513.91	5374.55	4617.64
575,000	10396.01	7662.61	6810.00	5618.85	4827.53
600,000	10848.01	7995.77	7106.09	5863.15	5037.42
625,000	11300.01	8328.93	7402.17	6107.44	5247.31
650,000	11752.01	8662.08	7698.26	6351.74	5457.20
675,000	12204.01	8995.24	7994.35	6596.04	5667.10
700,000	12656.01	9328.40	8290.43	6840.34	5876.99
725,000	13108.01	9661.55	8586.52	7084.63	6086.88
750,000	13560.01	9994.71	8882.61	7328.93	6296.77
775,000	14012.01	10327.87	9178.69	7573.23	6506.67
800,000	14464.01	10661.02	9474.78	7817.53	6716.56
825,000	14916.01	10994.18	9770.87	8061.82	6926.45
850,000	15368.01	11327.34	10066.95	8306.12	7136.34
875,000	15820.01	11660.50	10363.04	8550.42	7346.23
900,000	16272.01	11993.65	10659.13	8794.72	7556.13

Table 7   81

3.25%   Monthly Payment Loans

Loan Amount	Amortization Period in Years				
	15	16	17	18	20
10	0.08	0.07	0.07	0.07	0.06
20	0.15	0.14	0.13	0.13	0.12
30	0.22	0.21	0.20	0.19	0.18
40	0.29	0.27	0.26	0.25	0.23
50	0.36	0.34	0.32	0.31	0.29
100	0.71	0.67	0.64	0.62	0.57
200	1.41	1.34	1.28	1.23	1.14
300	2.11	2.01	1.92	1.84	1.71
400	2.82	2.68	2.56	2.45	2.27
500	3.52	3.35	3.20	3.07	2.84
1,000	7.03	6.69	6.39	6.13	5.68
2,000	14.06	13.38	12.78	12.25	11.35
3,000	21.09	20.06	19.16	18.37	17.02
4,000	28.11	26.75	25.55	24.49	22.69
5,000	35.14	33.44	31.94	30.61	28.36
10,000	70.27	66.87	63.87	61.22	56.72
20,000	140.54	133.73	127.74	122.43	113.44
30,000	210.81	200.59	191.60	183.64	170.16
40,000	281.07	267.45	255.47	244.85	226.88
50,000	351.34	334.32	319.34	306.06	283.60
100,000	702.67	668.63	638.67	612.12	567.20
125,000	878.34	835.78	798.34	765.15	709.00
150,000	1054.01	1002.94	958.00	918.18	850.80
175,000	1229.68	1170.10	1117.67	1071.21	992.60
200,000	1405.34	1337.25	1277.34	1224.24	1134.40
225,000	1581.01	1504.41	1437.00	1377.27	1276.20
250,000	1756.68	1671.56	1596.67	1530.30	1417.99
275,000	1932.34	1838.72	1756.34	1683.33	1559.79
300,000	2108.01	2005.87	1916.00	1836.36	1701.59
325,000	2283.68	2173.03	2075.67	1989.39	1843.39
350,000	2459.35	2340.19	2235.34	2142.42	1985.19
375,000	2635.01	2507.34	2395.00	2295.44	2126.99
400,000	2810.68	2674.50	2554.67	2448.47	2268.79
425,000	2986.35	2841.65	2714.34	2601.50	2410.59
450,000	3162.01	3008.81	2874.00	2754.53	2552.39
475,000	3337.68	3175.96	3033.67	2907.56	2694.18
500,000	3513.35	3343.12	3193.34	3060.59	2835.98
525,000	3689.02	3510.28	3353.00	3213.62	2977.78
550,000	3864.68	3677.43	3512.67	3366.65	3119.58
575,000	4040.35	3844.59	3672.34	3519.68	3261.38
600,000	4216.02	4011.74	3832.00	3672.71	3403.18
625,000	4391.68	4178.90	3991.67	3825.74	3544.98
650,000	4567.35	4346.05	4151.34	3978.77	3686.78
675,000	4743.02	4513.21	4311.00	4131.80	3828.58
700,000	4918.69	4680.37	4470.67	4284.83	3970.38
725,000	5094.35	4847.52	4630.34	4437.85	4112.17
750,000	5270.02	5014.68	4790.00	4590.88	4253.97
775,000	5445.69	5181.83	4949.67	4743.91	4395.77
800,000	5621.36	5348.99	5109.34	4896.94	4537.57
825,000	5797.02	5516.14	5269.00	5049.97	4679.37
850,000	5972.69	5683.30	5428.67	5203.00	4821.17
875,000	6148.36	5850.46	5588.34	5356.03	4962.97
900,000	6324.02	6017.61	5748.00	5509.06	5104.77

Monthly Payment Loans   **3.25%**

Loan Amount	Amortization Period in Years				
	21	22	23	24	25
10	0.06	0.06	0.06	0.06	0.05
20	0.11	0.11	0.11	0.11	0.10
30	0.17	0.16	0.16	0.16	0.15
40	0.22	0.22	0.21	0.21	0.20
50	0.28	0.27	0.26	0.26	0.25
100	0.55	0.54	0.52	0.51	0.49
200	1.10	1.07	1.03	1.01	0.98
300	1.65	1.60	1.55	1.51	1.47
400	2.20	2.13	2.06	2.01	1.95
500	2.75	2.66	2.58	2.51	2.44
1,000	5.49	5.31	5.15	5.01	4.88
2,000	10.97	10.62	10.30	10.02	9.75
3,000	16.45	15.93	15.45	15.02	14.62
4,000	21.93	21.23	20.60	20.03	19.50
5,000	27.41	26.54	25.75	25.03	24.37
10,000	54.81	53.07	51.50	50.06	48.74
20,000	109.61	106.14	102.99	100.11	97.47
30,000	164.42	159.21	154.48	150.16	146.20
40,000	219.22	212.28	205.97	200.21	194.93
50,000	274.03	265.35	257.46	250.26	243.66
100,000	548.05	530.70	514.92	500.52	487.32
125,000	685.06	663.38	643.65	625.65	609.15
150,000	822.07	796.05	772.38	750.78	730.98
175,000	959.08	928.73	901.11	875.90	852.81
200,000	1096.09	1061.40	1029.84	1001.03	974.64
225,000	1233.10	1194.07	1158.57	1126.16	1096.47
250,000	1370.12	1326.75	1287.30	1251.29	1218.30
275,000	1507.13	1459.42	1416.03	1376.42	1340.12
300,000	1644.14	1592.10	1544.76	1501.55	1461.95
325,000	1781.15	1724.77	1673.49	1626.68	1583.78
350,000	1918.16	1857.45	1802.22	1751.80	1705.61
375,000	2055.17	1990.12	1930.95	1876.93	1827.44
400,000	2192.18	2122.79	2059.68	2002.06	1949.27
425,000	2329.19	2255.47	2188.41	2127.19	2071.10
450,000	2466.20	2388.14	2317.14	2252.32	2192.93
475,000	2603.22	2520.82	2445.87	2377.45	2314.76
500,000	2740.23	2653.49	2574.60	2502.57	2436.59
525,000	2877.24	2786.17	2703.33	2627.70	2558.42
550,000	3014.25	2918.84	2832.06	2752.83	2680.24
575,000	3151.26	3051.51	2960.79	2877.96	2802.07
600,000	3288.27	3184.19	3089.52	3003.09	2923.90
625,000	3425.28	3316.86	3218.25	3128.22	3045.73
650,000	3562.29	3449.54	3346.98	3253.35	3167.56
675,000	3699.30	3582.21	3475.71	3378.47	3289.39
700,000	3836.31	3714.89	3604.44	3503.60	3411.22
725,000	3973.33	3847.56	3733.17	3628.73	3533.05
750,000	4110.34	3980.23	3861.90	3753.86	3654.88
775,000	4247.35	4112.91	3990.63	3878.99	3776.71
800,000	4384.36	4245.58	4119.36	4004.12	3898.53
825,000	4521.37	4378.26	4248.09	4129.25	4020.36
850,000	4658.38	4510.93	4376.82	4254.37	4142.19
875,000	4795.39	4643.61	4505.55	4379.50	4264.02
900,000	4932.40	4776.28	4634.28	4504.63	4385.85

Table 7   83

<u>3.25%</u>   **Monthly Payment Loans**

Amortization Period in Years

Loan Amount	26	27	28	29	30
10	0.05	0.05	0.05	0.05	0.05
20	0.10	0.10	0.10	0.09	0.09
30	0.15	0.14	0.14	0.14	0.14
40	0.20	0.19	0.19	0.18	0.18
50	0.24	0.24	0.23	0.23	0.22
100	0.48	0.47	0.46	0.45	0.44
200	0.96	0.93	0.91	0.89	0.88
300	1.43	1.40	1.37	1.34	1.31
400	1.91	1.86	1.82	1.78	1.75
500	2.38	2.33	2.27	2.23	2.18
1,000	4.76	4.65	4.54	4.45	4.36
2,000	9.51	9.29	9.08	8.89	8.71
3,000	14.26	13.93	13.62	13.33	13.06
4,000	19.01	18.57	18.15	17.77	17.41
5,000	23.76	23.21	22.69	22.21	21.77
10,000	47.52	46.41	45.37	44.41	43.53
20,000	95.04	92.81	90.74	88.82	87.05
30,000	142.56	139.21	136.11	133.23	130.57
40,000	190.08	185.61	181.47	177.64	174.09
50,000	237.60	232.01	226.84	222.05	217.61
100,000	475.19	464.01	453.68	444.10	435.21
125,000	593.99	580.01	567.10	555.13	544.01
150,000	712.78	696.01	680.51	666.15	652.81
175,000	831.58	812.02	793.93	777.18	761.62
200,000	950.38	928.02	907.35	888.20	870.42
225,000	1069.17	1044.02	1020.77	999.22	979.22
250,000	1187.97	1160.02	1134.19	1110.25	1088.02
275,000	1306.77	1276.02	1247.60	1221.27	1196.82
300,000	1425.56	1392.02	1361.02	1332.30	1305.62
325,000	1544.36	1508.02	1474.44	1443.32	1414.43
350,000	1663.16	1624.03	1587.86	1554.35	1523.23
375,000	1781.95	1740.03	1701.28	1665.37	1632.03
400,000	1900.75	1856.03	1814.69	1776.40	1740.83
425,000	2019.55	1972.03	1928.11	1887.42	1849.63
450,000	2138.34	2088.03	2041.53	1998.44	1958.43
475,000	2257.14	2204.03	2154.95	2109.47	2067.24
500,000	2375.94	2320.03	2268.37	2220.49	2176.04
525,000	2494.73	2436.04	2381.78	2331.52	2284.84
550,000	2613.53	2552.04	2495.20	2442.54	2393.64
575,000	2732.33	2668.04	2608.62	2553.57	2502.44
600,000	2851.12	2784.04	2722.04	2664.59	2611.24
625,000	2969.92	2900.04	2835.46	2775.62	2720.04
650,000	3088.72	3016.04	2948.87	2886.64	2828.85
675,000	3207.51	3132.04	3062.29	2997.66	2937.65
700,000	3326.31	3248.05	3175.71	3108.69	3046.45
725,000	3445.11	3364.05	3289.13	3219.71	3155.25
750,000	3563.90	3480.05	3402.55	3330.74	3264.05
775,000	3682.70	3596.05	3515.96	3441.76	3372.85
800,000	3801.50	3712.05	3629.38	3552.79	3481.66
825,000	3920.29	3828.05	3742.80	3663.81	3590.46
850,000	4039.09	3944.05	3856.22	3774.84	3699.26
875,000	4157.89	4060.06	3969.64	3885.86	3808.06
900,000	4276.68	4176.06	4083.05	3996.88	3916.86

Monthly Payment Loans   **3.50%**

Loan Amount	Amortization Period in Years				
	5	7	8	10	12
10	0.19	0.14	0.12	0.10	0.09
20	0.37	0.27	0.24	0.20	0.18
30	0.55	0.41	0.36	0.30	0.26
40	0.73	0.54	0.48	0.40	0.35
50	0.91	0.68	0.60	0.50	0.43
100	1.82	1.35	1.20	0.99	0.86
200	3.64	2.69	2.40	1.98	1.71
300	5.46	4.04	3.59	2.97	2.56
400	7.28	5.38	4.79	3.96	3.41
500	9.10	6.72	5.98	4.95	4.26
1,000	18.20	13.44	11.96	9.89	8.52
2,000	36.39	26.88	23.92	19.78	17.03
3,000	54.58	40.32	35.88	29.67	25.55
4,000	72.77	53.76	47.84	39.56	34.06
5,000	90.96	67.20	59.80	49.45	42.58
10,000	181.92	134.40	119.59	98.89	85.15
20,000	363.84	268.80	239.17	197.78	170.30
30,000	545.76	403.20	358.75	296.66	255.44
40,000	727.67	537.60	478.33	395.55	340.59
50,000	909.59	672.00	597.91	494.43	425.73
100,000	1819.18	1343.99	1195.81	988.86	851.46
125,000	2273.97	1679.99	1494.76	1236.08	1064.32
150,000	2728.77	2015.98	1793.71	1483.29	1277.19
175,000	3183.56	2351.98	2092.66	1730.51	1490.05
200,000	3638.35	2687.98	2391.62	1977.72	1702.91
225,000	4093.15	3023.97	2690.57	2224.94	1915.78
250,000	4547.94	3359.97	2989.52	2472.15	2128.64
275,000	5002.73	3695.96	3288.47	2719.37	2341.50
300,000	5457.53	4031.96	3587.42	2966.58	2554.37
325,000	5912.32	4367.96	3886.37	3213.80	2767.23
350,000	6367.12	4703.95	4185.32	3461.01	2980.09
375,000	6821.91	5039.95	4484.27	3708.23	3192.96
400,000	7276.70	5375.95	4783.23	3955.44	3405.82
425,000	7731.50	5711.94	5082.18	4202.65	3618.68
450,000	8186.29	6047.94	5381.13	4449.87	3831.55
475,000	8641.08	6383.93	5680.08	4697.08	4044.41
500,000	9095.88	6719.93	5979.03	4944.30	4257.27
525,000	9550.67	7055.93	6277.98	5191.51	4470.14
550,000	10005.46	7391.92	6576.93	5438.73	4683.00
575,000	10460.26	7727.92	6875.88	5685.94	4895.86
600,000	10915.05	8063.92	7174.84	5933.16	5108.73
625,000	11369.85	8399.91	7473.79	6180.37	5321.59
650,000	11824.64	8735.91	7772.74	6427.59	5534.45
675,000	12279.43	9071.90	8071.69	6674.80	5747.32
700,000	12734.23	9407.90	8370.64	6922.02	5960.18
725,000	13189.02	9743.90	8669.59	7169.23	6173.04
750,000	13643.81	10079.89	8968.54	7416.45	6385.91
775,000	14098.61	10415.89	9267.50	7663.66	6598.77
800,000	14553.40	10751.89	9566.45	7910.87	6811.63
825,000	15008.19	11087.88	9865.40	8158.09	7024.50
850,000	15462.99	11423.88	10164.35	8405.30	7237.36
875,000	15917.78	11759.87	10463.30	8652.52	7450.23
900,000	16372.58	12095.87	10762.25	8899.73	7663.09

Table 7   85

3.50%   Monthly Payment Loans

Amortization Period in Years

Loan Amount	15	16	17	18	20
10	0.08	0.07	0.07	0.07	0.06
20	0.15	0.14	0.14	0.13	0.12
30	0.22	0.21	0.20	0.19	0.18
40	0.29	0.28	0.27	0.25	0.24
50	0.36	0.35	0.33	0.32	0.29
100	0.72	0.69	0.66	0.63	0.58
200	1.43	1.37	1.31	1.25	1.16
300	2.15	2.05	1.96	1.88	1.74
400	2.86	2.73	2.61	2.50	2.32
500	3.58	3.41	3.26	3.13	2.90
1,000	7.15	6.81	6.52	6.25	5.80
2,000	14.30	13.62	13.03	12.50	11.60
3,000	21.45	20.43	19.54	18.74	17.40
4,000	28.60	27.24	26.05	24.99	23.20
5,000	35.75	34.05	32.56	31.24	29.00
10,000	71.49	68.10	65.12	62.47	58.00
20,000	142.98	136.19	130.23	124.94	116.00
30,000	214.47	204.29	195.34	187.40	173.99
40,000	285.96	272.38	260.45	249.87	231.99
50,000	357.45	340.48	325.56	312.34	289.98
100,000	714.89	680.95	651.11	624.67	579.96
125,000	893.61	851.19	813.88	780.83	724.95
150,000	1072.33	1021.43	976.66	937.00	869.94
175,000	1251.05	1191.66	1139.43	1093.16	1014.93
200,000	1429.77	1361.90	1302.21	1249.33	1159.92
225,000	1608.49	1532.14	1464.98	1405.49	1304.91
250,000	1787.21	1702.37	1627.76	1561.66	1449.90
275,000	1965.93	1872.61	1790.53	1717.82	1594.89
300,000	2144.65	2042.85	1953.31	1873.99	1739.88
325,000	2323.37	2213.08	2116.08	2030.15	1884.87
350,000	2502.09	2383.32	2278.86	2186.32	2029.86
375,000	2680.81	2553.56	2441.63	2342.49	2174.85
400,000	2859.54	2723.79	2604.41	2498.65	2319.84
425,000	3038.26	2894.03	2767.18	2654.82	2464.83
450,000	3216.98	3064.27	2929.96	2810.98	2609.82
475,000	3395.70	3234.50	3092.73	2967.15	2754.81
500,000	3574.42	3404.74	3255.51	3123.31	2899.80
525,000	3753.14	3574.98	3418.28	3279.48	3044.79
550,000	3931.86	3745.21	3581.06	3435.64	3189.78
575,000	4110.58	3915.45	3743.83	3591.81	3334.77
600,000	4289.30	4085.69	3906.61	3747.97	3479.76
625,000	4468.02	4255.92	4069.38	3904.14	3624.75
650,000	4646.74	4426.16	4232.16	4060.30	3769.74
675,000	4825.46	4596.40	4394.93	4216.47	3914.73
700,000	5004.18	4766.63	4557.71	4372.63	4059.72
725,000	5182.90	4936.87	4720.48	4528.80	4204.71
750,000	5361.62	5107.11	4883.26	4684.97	4349.70
775,000	5540.34	5277.34	5046.03	4841.13	4494.69
800,000	5719.07	5447.58	5208.81	4997.30	4639.68
825,000	5897.79	5617.82	5371.58	5153.46	4784.67
850,000	6076.51	5788.05	5534.36	5309.63	4929.66
875,000	6255.23	5958.29	5697.13	5465.79	5074.65
900,000	6433.95	6128.53	5859.91	5621.96	5219.64

Monthly Payment Loans   3.50%

Loan Amount	Amortization Period in Years				
	21	22	23	24	25
10	0.06	0.06	0.06	0.06	0.06
20	0.12	0.11	0.11	0.11	0.11
30	0.17	0.17	0.16	0.16	0.16
40	0.23	0.22	0.22	0.21	0.21
50	0.29	0.28	0.27	0.26	0.26
100	0.57	0.55	0.53	0.52	0.51
200	1.13	1.09	1.06	1.03	1.01
300	1.69	1.64	1.59	1.55	1.51
400	2.25	2.18	2.12	2.06	2.01
500	2.81	2.72	2.65	2.57	2.51
1,000	5.61	5.44	5.29	5.14	5.01
2,000	11.22	10.88	10.57	10.28	10.02
3,000	16.83	16.32	15.85	15.42	15.02
4,000	22.44	21.75	21.13	20.55	20.03
5,000	28.05	27.19	26.41	25.69	25.04
10,000	56.10	54.37	52.81	51.38	50.07
20,000	112.19	108.74	105.61	102.75	100.13
30,000	168.28	163.11	158.41	154.12	150.19
40,000	224.37	217.48	211.21	205.49	200.25
50,000	280.46	271.84	264.01	256.86	250.32
100,000	560.92	543.68	528.02	513.72	500.63
125,000	701.15	679.60	660.02	642.15	625.78
150,000	841.38	815.52	792.02	770.58	750.94
175,000	981.61	951.44	924.02	899.00	876.10
200,000	1121.84	1087.36	1056.03	1027.43	1001.25
225,000	1262.07	1223.28	1188.03	1155.86	1126.41
250,000	1402.30	1359.20	1320.03	1284.29	1251.56
275,000	1542.53	1495.12	1452.03	1412.72	1376.72
300,000	1682.76	1631.04	1584.04	1541.15	1501.88
325,000	1822.99	1766.96	1716.04	1669.57	1627.03
350,000	1963.22	1902.88	1848.04	1798.00	1752.19
375,000	2103.45	2038.80	1980.04	1926.43	1877.34
400,000	2243.68	2174.72	2112.05	2054.86	2002.50
425,000	2383.90	2310.64	2244.05	2183.29	2127.66
450,000	2524.13	2446.56	2376.05	2311.72	2252.81
475,000	2664.36	2582.48	2508.06	2440.14	2377.97
500,000	2804.59	2718.40	2640.06	2568.57	2503.12
525,000	2944.82	2854.32	2772.06	2697.00	2628.28
550,000	3085.05	2990.24	2904.06	2825.43	2753.43
575,000	3225.28	3126.16	3036.07	2953.86	2878.59
600,000	3365.51	3262.08	3168.07	3082.29	3003.75
625,000	3505.74	3398.00	3300.07	3210.71	3128.90
650,000	3645.97	3533.92	3432.07	3339.14	3254.06
675,000	3786.20	3669.84	3564.08	3467.57	3379.21
700,000	3926.43	3805.76	3696.08	3596.00	3504.37
725,000	4066.66	3941.68	3828.08	3724.43	3629.53
750,000	4206.89	4077.60	3960.08	3852.86	3754.68
775,000	4347.12	4213.52	4092.09	3981.28	3879.84
800,000	4487.35	4349.44	4224.09	4109.71	4004.99
825,000	4627.58	4485.36	4356.09	4238.14	4130.15
850,000	4767.80	4621.28	4480.09	4366.57	4255.31
875,000	4908.03	4757.20	4620.10	4495.00	4380.46
900,000	5048.26	4893.12	4752.10	4623.43	4505.62

Table 7   87

3.50%   Monthly Payment Loans

Amortization Period in Years

Loan Amount	26	27	28	29	30
10	0.05	0.05	0.05	0.05	0.05
20	0.10	0.10	0.10	0.10	0.09
30	0.15	0.15	0.15	0.14	0.14
40	0.20	0.20	0.19	0.19	0.18
50	0.25	0.24	0.24	0.23	0.23
100	0.49	0.48	0.47	0.46	0.45
200	0.98	0.96	0.94	0.92	0.90
300	1.47	1.44	1.41	1.38	1.35
400	1.96	1.92	1.87	1.84	1.80
500	2.45	2.39	2.34	2.29	2.25
1,000	4.89	4.78	4.68	4.58	4.50
2,000	9.78	9.56	9.35	9.16	8.99
3,000	14.66	14.33	14.02	13.74	13.48
4,000	19.55	19.11	18.70	18.32	17.97
5,000	24.44	23.88	23.37	22.90	22.46
10,000	48.87	47.76	46.73	45.79	44.91
20,000	97.73	95.51	93.46	91.57	89.81
30,000	146.59	143.26	140.19	137.35	134.72
40,000	195.45	191.02	186.92	183.14	179.62
50,000	244.31	238.77	233.65	228.92	224.53
100,000	488.61	477.53	467.30	457.84	449.05
125,000	610.76	596.91	584.13	572.29	561.31
150,000	732.91	716.30	700.95	686.75	673.57
175,000	855.06	835.68	817.78	801.21	785.83
200,000	977.21	955.06	934.60	915.67	898.09
225,000	1099.36	1074.44	1051.43	1030.12	1010.36
250,000	1221.51	1193.82	1168.25	1144.58	1122.62
275,000	1343.66	1313.20	1285.08	1259.04	1234.88
300,000	1465.81	1432.59	1401.90	1373.50	1347.14
325,000	1587.96	1551.97	1518.73	1487.96	1459.40
350,000	1710.11	1671.35	1635.55	1602.41	1571.66
375,000	1832.26	1790.73	1752.38	1716.87	1683.92
400,000	1954.41	1910.11	1869.20	1831.33	1796.18
425,000	2076.56	2029.50	1986.03	1945.79	1908.44
450,000	2198.71	2148.88	2102.85	2060.24	2020.71
475,000	2320.86	2268.26	2219.68	2174.70	2132.97
500,000	2443.01	2387.64	2336.50	2289.16	2245.23
525,000	2565.16	2507.02	2453.33	2403.62	2357.49
550,000	2687.31	2626.40	2570.15	2518.08	2469.75
575,000	2809.46	2745.79	2686.98	2632.53	2582.01
600,000	2931.61	2865.17	2803.80	2746.99	2694.27
625,000	3053.76	2984.55	2920.63	2861.45	2806.53
650,000	3175.91	3103.93	3037.45	2975.91	2918.80
675,000	3298.06	3223.31	3154.28	3090.36	3031.06
700,000	3420.21	3342.70	3271.10	3204.82	3143.32
725,000	3542.36	3462.08	3387.93	3319.28	3255.58
750,000	3664.51	3581.46	3504.75	3433.74	3367.84
775,000	3786.66	3700.84	3621.58	3548.20	3480.10
800,000	3908.81	3820.22	3738.40	3662.65	3592.36
825,000	4030.96	3939.60	3855.23	3777.11	3704.62
850,000	4153.11	4058.99	3972.05	3891.57	3816.88
875,000	4275.26	4178.37	4088.88	4006.03	3929.15
900.000	4397.42	4297.75	4205.70	4120.48	4041.41

Monthly Payment Loans   3.75%

Loan Amount	Amortization Period in Years				
	5	7	8	10	12
10	0.19	0.14	0.13	0.11	0.09
20	0.37	0.28	0.25	0.21	0.18
30	0.55	0.41	0.37	0.31	0.26
40	0.74	0.55	0.49	0.41	0.35
50	0.92	0.68	0.61	0.51	0.44
100	1.84	1.36	1.21	1.01	0.87
200	3.67	2.72	2.42	2.01	1.73
300	5.50	4.07	3.63	3.01	2.60
400	7.33	5.43	4.83	4.01	3.46
500	9.16	6.78	6.04	5.01	4.32
1,000	18.31	13.56	12.08	10.01	8.64
2,000	36.61	27.11	24.15	20.02	17.27
3,000	54.92	40.67	36.22	30.02	25.91
4,000	73.22	54.22	48.30	40.03	34.54
5,000	91.52	67.78	60.37	50.04	43.18
10,000	183.04	135.55	120.74	100.07	86.35
20,000	366.08	271.09	241.47	200.13	172.69
30,000	549.12	406.63	362.20	300.19	259.04
40,000	732.16	542.17	482.94	400.25	345.38
50,000	915.20	677.71	603.67	500.31	431.73
100,000	1830.40	1355.41	1207.34	1000.62	863.45
125,000	2287.99	1694.26	1509.17	1250.77	1079.31
150,000	2745.59	2033.11	1811.00	1500.92	1295.17
175,000	3203.19	2371.96	2112.84	1751.08	1511.03
200,000	3660.79	2710.81	2414.67	2001.23	1726.89
225,000	4118.39	3049.66	2716.50	2251.38	1942.75
250,000	4575.98	3388.51	3018.34	2501.54	2158.61
275,000	5033.58	3727.36	3320.17	2751.69	2374.47
300,000	5491.18	4066.21	3622.00	3001.84	2590.33
325,000	5948.78	4405.06	3923.83	3252.00	2806.19
350,000	6406.38	4743.91	4225.67	3502.15	3022.05
375,000	6863.97	5082.77	4527.50	3752.30	3237.91
400,000	7321.57	5421.62	4829.33	4002.45	3453.77
425,000	7779.17	5760.47	5131.17	4252.61	3669.63
450,000	8236.77	6099.32	5433.00	4502.76	3885.49
475,000	8694.37	6438.17	5734.83	4752.91	4101.35
500,000	9151.96	6777.02	6036.67	5003.07	4317.21
525,000	9609.56	7115.87	6338.50	5253.22	4533.07
550,000	10067.16	7454.72	6640.33	5503.37	4748.93
575,000	10524.76	7793.57	6942.16	5753.53	4964.79
600,000	10982.36	8132.42	7244.00	6003.68	5180.65
625,000	11439.95	8471.27	7545.83	6253.83	5396.51
650,000	11897.55	8810.12	7847.66	6503.99	5612.37
675,000	12355.15	9148.97	8149.50	6754.14	5828.23
700,000	12812.75	9487.82	8451.33	7004.29	6044.09
725,000	13270.35	9826.68	8753.16	7254.45	6259.95
750,000	13727.94	10165.53	9055.00	7504.60	6475.81
775,000	14185.54	10504.38	9356.83	7754.75	6691.67
800,000	14643.14	10843.23	9658.66	8004.90	6907.53
825,000	15100.74	11182.08	9960.49	8255.06	7123.39
850,000	15558.34	11520.93	10262.33	8505.21	7339.25
875,000	16015.93	11859.78	10564.16	8755.36	7555.11
900,000	16473.53	12198.63	10865.99	9005.52	7770.97

Table 7   89

3.75%   Monthly Payment Loans

Amortization Period in Years

Loan Amount	15	16	17	18	20
10	0.08	0.07	0.07	0.07	0.06
20	0.15	0.14	0.14	0.13	0.12
30	0.22	0.21	0.20	0.20	0.18
40	0.30	0.28	0.27	0.26	0.24
50	0.37	0.35	0.34	0.32	0.30
100	0.73	0.70	0.67	0.64	0.60
200	1.46	1.39	1.33	1.28	1.19
300	2.19	2.09	2.00	1.92	1.78
400	2.91	2.78	2.66	2.55	2.38
500	3.64	3.47	3.32	3.19	2.97
1,000	7.28	6.94	6.64	6.38	5.93
2,000	14.55	13.87	13.28	12.75	11.86
3,000	21.82	20.81	19.92	19.13	17.79
4,000	29.09	27.74	26.55	25.50	23.72
5,000	36.37	34.68	33.19	31.87	29.65
10,000	72.73	69.35	66.37	63.74	59.29
20,000	145.45	138.69	132.74	127.48	118.58
30,000	218.17	208.03	199.11	191.21	177.87
40,000	290.89	277.37	265.48	254.95	237.16
50,000	363.62	346.71	331.84	318.68	296.45
100,000	727.23	693.41	663.68	637.36	592.89
125,000	909.03	866.76	829.60	796.70	741.12
150,000	1090.84	1040.11	995.52	956.04	889.34
175,000	1272.64	1213.46	1161.44	1115.38	1037.56
200,000	1454.45	1386.81	1327.36	1274.72	1185.78
225,000	1636.26	1560.17	1493.28	1434.05	1334.00
250,000	1818.06	1733.52	1659.20	1593.39	1482.23
275,000	1999.87	1906.87	1825.12	1752.73	1630.45
300,000	2181.67	2080.22	1991.03	1912.07	1778.67
325,000	2363.48	2253.57	2156.95	2071.41	1926.89
350,000	2545.28	2426.92	2322.87	2230.75	2075.11
375,000	2727.09	2600.27	2488.79	2390.09	2223.34
400,000	2908.89	2773.62	2654.71	2549.43	2371.56
425,000	3090.70	2946.98	2820.63	2708.76	2519.78
450,000	3272.51	3120.33	2986.55	2868.10	2668.00
475,000	3454.31	3293.68	3152.47	3027.44	2816.22
500,000	3636.12	3467.03	3318.39	3186.78	2964.45
525,000	3817.92	3640.38	3484.31	3346.12	3112.67
550,000	3999.73	3813.73	3650.23	3505.46	3260.89
575,000	4181.53	3987.08	3816.14	3664.80	3409.11
600,000	4363.34	4160.43	3982.06	3824.14	3557.33
625,000	4545.15	4333.79	4147.98	3983.48	3705.56
650,000	4726.95	4507.14	4313.90	4142.81	3853.78
675,000	4908.76	4680.49	4479.82	4302.15	4002.00
700,000	5090.56	4853.84	4645.74	4461.49	4150.22
725,000	5272.37	5027.19	4811.66	4620.83	4298.45
750,000	5454.17	5200.54	4977.58	4780.17	4446.67
775,000	5635.98	5373.89	5143.50	4939.51	4594.89
800,000	5817.78	5547.24	5309.42	5098.85	4743.11
825,000	5999.59	5720.59	5475.34	5258.19	4891.33
850,000	6181.40	5893.95	5641.25	5417.52	5039.56
875,000	6363.20	6067.30	5807.17	5576.86	5187.78
900,000	6545.01	6240.65	5973.09	5736.20	5336.00

Monthly Payment Loans   **3.75%**

Table 7   91

Loan Amount	Amortization Period in Years				
	21	22	23	24	25
10	0.06	0.06	0.06	0.06	0.06
20	0.12	0.12	0.11	0.11	0.11
30	0.18	0.17	0.17	0.16	0.16
40	0.23	0.23	0.22	0.22	0.21
50	0.29	0.28	0.28	0.27	0.26
100	0.58	0.56	0.55	0.53	0.52
200	1.15	1.12	1.09	1.06	1.03
300	1.73	1.68	1.63	1.59	1.55
400	2.30	2.23	2.17	2.11	2.06
500	2.87	2.79	2.71	2.64	2.58
1,000	5.74	5.57	5.42	5.28	5.15
2,000	11.48	11.14	10.83	10.55	10.29
3,000	17.22	16.71	16.24	15.82	15.43
4,000	22.96	22.28	21.66	21.09	20.57
5,000	28.70	27.85	27.07	26.36	25.71
10,000	57.40	55.69	54.13	52.72	51.42
20,000	114.80	111.37	108.26	105.43	102.83
30,000	172.19	167.06	162.39	158.14	154.24
40,000	229.59	222.74	216.52	210.85	205.66
50,000	286.99	278.43	270.65	263.56	257.07
100,000	573.97	556.85	541.29	527.11	514.14
125,000	717.46	696.06	676.62	658.89	642.67
150,000	860.95	835.27	811.94	790.66	771.20
175,000	1004.44	974.48	947.26	922.44	899.73
200,000	1147.93	1113.69	1082.58	1054.22	1028.27
225,000	1291.42	1252.90	1217.90	1185.99	1156.80
250,000	1434.91	1392.11	1353.23	1317.77	1285.33
275,000	1578.40	1531.32	1488.55	1449.55	1413.87
300,000	1721.89	1670.53	1623.87	1581.32	1542.40
325,000	1865.38	1809.74	1759.19	1713.10	1670.93
350,000	2008.88	1948.95	1894.51	1844.88	1799.46
375,000	2152.37	2088.16	2029.84	1976.65	1928.00
400,000	2295.86	2227.37	2165.16	2108.43	2056.53
425,000	2439.35	2366.58	2300.48	2240.21	2185.06
450,000	2582.84	2505.79	2435.80	2371.98	2313.60
475,000	2726.33	2645.00	2571.12	2503.76	2442.13
500,000	2869.82	2784.21	2706.45	2635.54	2570.66
525,000	3013.31	2923.42	2841.77	2767.31	2699.19
550,000	3156.80	3062.63	2977.09	2899.09	2827.73
575,000	3300.29	3201.84	3112.41	3030.87	2956.26
600,000	3443.78	3341.05	3247.73	3162.64	3084.79
625,000	3587.27	3480.26	3383.06	3294.42	3213.32
650,000	3730.76	3619.48	3518.38	3426.20	3341.86
675,000	3874.26	3758.69	3653.70	3557.97	3470.39
700,000	4017.75	3897.90	3789.02	3689.75	3598.92
725,000	4161.24	4037.11	3924.34	3821.53	3727.46
750,000	4304.73	4176.32	4059.67	3953.30	3855.99
775,000	4448.22	4315.53	4194.99	4085.08	3984.52
800,000	4591.71	4454.74	4330.31	4216.86	4113.05
825,000	4735.20	4593.95	4465.63	4348.63	4241.59
850,000	4878.69	4733.16	4600.95	4480.41	4370.12
875,000	5022.18	4872.37	4736.28	4612.19	4498.65
900,000	5165.67	5011.58	4871.60	4743.96	4627.19

3.75%   **Monthly Payment Loans**

Amortization Period in Years

Loan Amount	26	27	28	29	30
10	0.06	0.05	0.05	0.05	0.05
20	0.11	0.10	0.10	0.10	0.10
30	0.16	0.15	0.15	0.15	0.14
40	0.21	0.20	0.20	0.19	0.19
50	0.26	0.25	0.25	0.24	0.24
100	0.51	0.50	0.49	0.48	0.47
200	1.01	0.99	0.97	0.95	0.93
300	1.51	1.48	1.45	1.42	1.39
400	2.01	1.97	1.93	1.89	1.86
500	2.52	2.46	2.41	2.36	2.32
1,000	5.03	4.92	4.82	4.72	4.64
2,000	10.05	9.83	9.63	9.44	9.27
3,000	15.07	14.74	14.44	14.16	13.90
4,000	20.09	19.66	19.25	18.88	18.53
5,000	25.12	24.57	24.06	23.59	23.16
10,000	50.23	49.13	48.12	47.18	46.32
20,000	100.45	98.26	96.23	94.36	92.63
30,000	150.67	147.38	144.35	141.54	138.94
40,000	200.89	196.51	192.46	188.72	185.25
50,000	251.12	245.64	240.58	235.90	231.56
100,000	502.23	491.27	481.15	471.80	463.12
125,000	627.78	614.08	601.44	589.74	578.90
150,000	753.34	736.90	721.73	707.69	694.68
175,000	878.89	859.71	842.01	825.64	810.46
200,000	1004.45	982.53	962.30	943.59	926.24
225,000	1130.01	1105.35	1082.59	1061.53	1042.02
250,000	1255.56	1228.16	1202.87	1179.48	1157.79
275,000	1381.12	1350.98	1323.16	1297.43	1273.57
300,000	1506.67	1473.79	1443.45	1415.38	1389.35
325,000	1632.23	1596.61	1563.73	1533.33	1505.13
350,000	1757.78	1719.42	1684.02	1651.27	1620.91
375,000	1883.34	1842.24	1804.31	1769.22	1736.69
400,000	2008.90	1965.05	1924.60	1887.17	1852.47
425,000	2134.45	2087.87	2044.88	2005.12	1968.25
450,000	2260.01	2210.69	2165.17	2123.06	2084.03
475,000	2385.56	2333.50	2285.46	2241.01	2199.80
500,000	2511.12	2456.32	2405.74	2358.96	2315.58
525,000	2636.67	2579.13	2526.03	2476.91	2431.36
550,000	2762.23	2701.95	2646.32	2594.85	2547.14
575,000	2887.79	2824.76	2766.60	2712.80	2662.92
600,000	3013.34	2947.58	2886.89	2830.75	2778.70
625,000	3138.90	3070.39	3007.18	2948.70	2894.48
650,000	3264.45	3193.21	3127.46	3066.65	3010.26
675,000	3390.01	3316.03	3247.75	3184.59	3126.04
700,000	3515.56	3438.84	3368.04	3302.54	3241.81
725,000	3641.12	3561.66	3488.33	3420.49	3357.59
750,000	3766.68	3684.47	3608.61	3538.44	3473.37
775,000	3892.23	3807.29	3728.90	3656.38	3589.15
800,000	4017.79	3930.10	3849.19	3774.33	3704.93
825,000	4143.34	4052.92	3969.47	3892.28	3820.71
850,000	4268.90	4175.73	4089.76	4010.23	3936.49
875,000	4394.45	4298.55	4210.05	4128.17	4052.27
900,000	4520.01	4421.37	4330.33	4246.12	4168.05

Monthly Payment Loans   **4.00%**

Loan Amount	\multicolumn{5}{c}{Amortization Period in Years}				
	5	7	8	10	12
10	0.19	0.14	0.13	0.11	0.09
20	0.37	0.28	0.25	0.21	0.18
30	0.56	0.42	0.37	0.31	0.27
40	0.74	0.55	0.49	0.41	0.36
50	0.93	0.69	0.61	0.51	0.44
100	1.85	1.37	1.22	1.02	0.88
200	3.69	2.74	2.44	2.03	1.76
300	5.53	4.11	3.66	3.04	2.63
400	7.37	5.47	4.88	4.05	3.51
500	9.21	6.84	6.10	5.07	4.38
1,000	18.42	13.67	12.19	10.13	8.76
2,000	36.84	27.34	24.38	20.25	17.52
3,000	55.25	41.01	36.57	30.38	26.27
4,000	73.67	54.68	48.76	40.50	35.03
5,000	92.09	68.35	60.95	50.63	43.78
10,000	184.17	136.69	121.90	101.25	87.56
20,000	368.34	273.38	243.79	202.50	175.11
30,000	552.50	410.07	365.68	303.74	262.66
40,000	736.67	546.76	487.58	404.99	350.22
50,000	920.83	683.45	609.47	506.23	437.77
100,000	1841.66	1366.89	1218.93	1012.46	875.53
125,000	2302.07	1708.61	1523.66	1265.57	1094.42
150,000	2762.48	2050.33	1828.40	1518.68	1313.30
175,000	3222.90	2392.05	2133.13	1771.79	1532.18
200,000	3683.31	2733.77	2437.86	2024.91	1751.06
225,000	4143.72	3075.49	2742.59	2278.02	1969.94
250,000	4604.14	3417.21	3047.32	2531.13	2188.83
275,000	5064.55	3758.93	3352.06	2784.25	2407.71
300,000	5524.96	4100.65	3656.79	3037.36	2626.59
325,000	5985.37	4442.37	3961.52	3290.47	2845.47
350,000	6445.79	4784.09	4266.25	3543.58	3064.35
375,000	6906.20	5125.81	4570.98	3796.70	3283.24
400,000	7366.61	5467.53	4875.72	4049.81	3502.12
425,000	7827.03	5809.25	5180.45	4302.92	3721.00
450,000	8287.44	6150.97	5485.18	4556.04	3939.88
475,000	8747.85	6492.69	5789.91	4809.15	4158.76
500,000	9208.27	6834.41	6094.64	5062.26	4377.65
525,000	9668.68	7176.13	6399.37	5315.37	4596.53
550,000	10129.09	7517.85	6704.11	5568.49	4815.41
575,000	10589.51	7859.57	7008.84	5821.60	5034.29
600,000	11049.92	8201.29	7313.57	6074.71	5253.18
625,000	11510.33	8543.01	7618.30	6327.83	5472.06
650,000	11970.74	8884.73	7923.03	6580.94	5690.94
675,000	12431.16	9226.45	8227.77	6834.05	5909.82
700,000	12891.57	9568.17	8532.50	7087.16	6128.70
725,000	13351.98	9909.89	8837.23	7340.28	6347.59
750,000	13812.40	10251.61	9141.96	7593.39	6566.47
775,000	14272.81	10593.33	9446.69	7846.50	6785.35
800,000	14733.22	10935.05	9751.43	8099.62	7004.23
825,000	15193.64	11276.77	10056.16	8352.73	7223.11
850,000	15654.05	11618.49	10360.89	8605.84	7442.00
875,000	16114.46	11960.21	10665.62	8858.95	7660.88
900,000	16574.87	12301.93	10970.35	9112.07	7879.76

Table 7   93

4.00%   Monthly Payment Loans

Amortization Period in Years

Loan Amount	15	16	17	18	20
10	0.08	0.08	0.07	0.07	0.07
20	0.15	0.15	0.14	0.14	0.13
30	0.23	0.22	0.21	0.20	0.19
40	0.30	0.29	0.28	0.27	0.25
50	0.37	0.36	0.34	0.33	0.31
100	0.74	0.71	0.68	0.66	0.61
200	1.48	1.42	1.36	1.31	1.22
300	2.22	2.12	2.03	1.96	1.82
400	2.96	2.83	2.71	2.61	2.43
500	3.70	3.53	3.39	3.26	3.03
1,000	7.40	7.06	6.77	6.51	6.06
2,000	14.80	14.12	13.53	13.01	12.12
3,000	22.20	21.18	20.30	19.51	18.18
4,000	29.59	28.24	27.06	26.01	24.24
5,000	36.99	35.30	33.82	32.51	30.30
10,000	73.97	70.60	67.64	65.02	60.60
20,000	147.94	141.20	135.28	130.04	121.20
30,000	221.91	211.80	202.92	195.06	181.80
40,000	295.88	282.40	270.56	260.08	242.40
50,000	369.85	353.00	338.20	325.10	303.00
100,000	739.69	706.00	676.40	650.20	605.99
125,000	924.61	882.50	845.50	812.75	757.48
150,000	1109.54	1059.00	1014.60	975.30	908.98
175,000	1294.46	1235.50	1183.69	1137.85	1060.47
200,000	1479.38	1412.00	1352.79	1300.40	1211.97
225,000	1664.30	1588.50	1521.89	1462.95	1363.46
250,000	1849.22	1765.00	1690.99	1625.50	1514.96
275,000	2034.15	1941.49	1860.09	1788.05	1666.45
300,000	2219.07	2117.99	2029.19	1950.60	1817.95
325,000	2403.99	2294.49	2198.28	2113.15	1969.44
350,000	2588.91	2470.99	2367.38	2275.70	2120.94
375,000	2773.83	2647.49	2536.48	2438.25	2272.43
400,000	2958.76	2823.99	2705.58	2600.80	2423.93
425,000	3143.68	3000.49	2874.68	2763.35	2575.42
450,000	3328.60	3176.99	3043.78	2925.89	2726.92
475,000	3513.52	3353.49	3212.87	3088.44	2878.41
500,000	3698.44	3529.99	3381.97	3250.99	3029.91
525,000	3883.37	3706.49	3551.07	3413.54	3181.40
550,000	4068.29	3882.98	3720.17	3576.09	3332.90
575,000	4253.21	4059.48	3889.27	3738.64	3484.39
600,000	4438.13	4235.98	4058.37	3901.19	3635.89
625,000	4623.05	4412.48	4227.46	4063.74	3787.38
650,000	4807.98	4588.98	4396.56	4226.29	3938.88
675,000	4992.90	4765.48	4565.66	4388.84	4090.37
700,000	5177.82	4941.98	4734.76	4551.39	4241.87
725,000	5362.74	5118.48	4903.86	4713.94	4393.36
750,000	5547.66	5294.98	5072.96	4876.49	4544.86
775,000	5732.59	5471.48	5242.05	5039.04	4696.35
800,000	5917.51	5647.97	5411.15	5201.59	4847.85
825,000	6102.43	5824.47	5580.25	5364.14	4999.34
850,000	6287.35	6000.97	5749.35	5526.69	5150.84
875,000	6472.27	6177.47	5918.45	5689.23	5302.33
900,000	6657.20	6353.97	6087.55	5851.78	5453.83

Monthly Payment Loans   **4.00%**

Loan Amount	Amortization Period in Years				
	21	22	23	24	25
10	0.06	0.06	0.06	0.06	0.06
20	0.12	0.12	0.12	0.11	0.11
30	0.18	0.18	0.17	0.17	0.16
40	0.24	0.23	0.23	0.22	0.22
50	0.30	0.29	0.28	0.28	0.27
100	0.59	0.58	0.56	0.55	0.53
200	1.18	1.15	1.11	1.09	1.06
300	1.77	1.72	1.67	1.63	1.59
400	2.35	2.29	2.22	2.17	2.12
500	2.94	2.86	2.78	2.71	2.64
1,000	5.88	5.71	5.55	5.41	5.28
2,000	11.75	11.41	11.10	10.82	10.56
3,000	17.62	17.11	16.65	16.23	15.84
4,000	23.49	22.81	22.20	21.63	21.12
5,000	29.36	28.51	27.74	27.04	26.40
10,000	58.72	57.02	55.48	54.07	52.79
20,000	117.44	114.04	110.96	108.14	105.57
30,000	176.16	171.06	166.43	162.21	158.36
40,000	234.88	228.08	221.91	216.28	211.14
50,000	293.59	285.10	277.38	270.35	263.92
100,000	587.18	570.19	554.76	540.70	527.84
125,000	733.98	712.73	693.44	675.87	659.80
150,000	880.77	855.28	832.13	811.04	791.76
175,000	1027.57	997.82	970.82	946.21	923.72
200,000	1174.36	1140.37	1109.51	1081.39	1055.68
225,000	1321.16	1282.91	1248.19	1216.56	1187.64
250,000	1467.95	1425.46	1386.88	1351.73	1319.60
275,000	1614.75	1568.00	1525.57	1486.90	1451.56
300,000	1761.54	1710.55	1664.26	1622.08	1583.52
325,000	1908.34	1853.09	1802.94	1757.25	1715.47
350,000	2055.13	1995.64	1941.63	1892.42	1847.43
375,000	2201.93	2138.18	2080.32	2027.60	1979.39
400,000	2348.72	2280.73	2219.01	2162.77	2111.35
425,000	2495.52	2423.27	2357.69	2297.94	2243.31
450,000	2642.31	2565.82	2496.38	2433.11	2375.27
475,000	2789.11	2708.36	2635.07	2568.29	2507.23
500,000	2935.90	2850.91	2773.76	2703.46	2639.19
525,000	3082.70	2993.46	2912.44	2838.63	2771.15
550,000	3229.49	3136.00	3051.13	2973.80	2903.11
575,000	3376.28	3278.55	3189.82	3108.98	3035.07
600,000	3523.08	3421.09	3328.51	3244.15	3167.03
625,000	3669.87	3563.64	3467.20	3379.32	3298.99
650,000	3816.67	3706.18	3605.88	3514.49	3430.94
675,000	3963.46	3848.73	3744.57	3649.67	3562.90
700,000	4110.26	3991.27	3883.26	3784.84	3694.86
725,000	4257.05	4133.82	4021.95	3920.01	3826.82
750,000	4403.85	4276.36	4160.63	4055.19	3958.78
775,000	4550.64	4418.91	4299.32	4190.36	4090.74
800,000	4697.44	4561.45	4438.01	4325.53	4222.70
825,000	4844.23	4704.00	4576.70	4460.70	4354.66
850,000	4991.03	4846.54	4715.38	4595.88	4486.62
875,000	5137.82	4989.09	4854.07	4731.05	4618.58
900,000	5284.62	5131.63	4992.76	4866.22	4750.54

Table 7   95

Monthly Payment Loans

Amortization Period in Years

Loan Amount	26	27	28	29	30
10	0.06	0.06	0.05	0.05	0.05
20	0.11	0.11	0.10	0.10	0.10
30	0.16	0.16	0.15	0.15	0.15
40	0.21	0.21	0.20	0.20	0.20
50	0.26	0.26	0.25	0.25	0.24
100	0.52	0.51	0.50	0.49	0.48
200	1.04	1.02	1.00	0.98	0.96
300	1.55	1.52	1.49	1.46	1.44
400	2.07	2.03	1.99	1.95	1.91
500	2.59	2.53	2.48	2.43	2.39
1,000	5.17	5.06	4.96	4.86	4.78
2,000	10.33	10.11	9.91	9.72	9.55
3,000	15.49	15.16	14.86	14.58	14.33
4,000	20.65	20.21	19.81	19.44	19.10
5,000	25.81	25.27	24.77	24.30	23.88
10,000	51.61	50.53	49.53	48.60	47.75
20,000	103.21	101.05	99.05	97.20	95.49
30,000	154.82	151.57	148.57	145.80	143.23
40,000	206.42	202.09	198.09	194.39	190.97
50,000	258.03	252.61	247.61	242.99	238.71
100,000	516.05	505.21	495.22	485.98	477.42
125,000	645.07	631.52	619.02	607.47	596.77
150,000	774.08	757.82	742.82	728.97	716.13
175,000	903.09	884.12	866.63	850.46	835.48
200,000	1032.10	1010.42	990.43	971.95	954.84
225,000	1161.12	1136.72	1114.23	1093.45	1074.19
250,000	1290.13	1263.03	1238.04	1214.94	1193.54
275,000	1419.14	1389.33	1361.84	1336.43	1312.90
300,000	1548.15	1515.63	1485.64	1457.93	1432.25
325,000	1677.16	1641.93	1609.45	1579.42	1551.60
350,000	1806.18	1768.23	1733.25	1700.91	1670.96
375,000	1935.19	1894.54	1857.05	1822.41	1790.31
400,000	2064.20	2020.84	1980.85	1943.90	1909.67
425,000	2193.21	2147.14	2104.66	2065.39	2029.02
450,000	2322.23	2273.44	2228.46	2186.89	2148.37
475,000	2451.24	2399.74	2352.26	2308.38	2267.73
500,000	2580.25	2526.05	2476.07	2429.87	2387.08
525,000	2709.26	2652.35	2599.87	2551.37	2506.44
550,000	2838.27	2778.65	2723.67	2672.86	2625.79
575,000	2967.29	2904.95	2847.48	2794.35	2745.14
600,000	3096.30	3031.25	2971.28	2915.85	2864.50
625,000	3225.31	3157.56	3095.08	3037.34	2983.85
650,000	3354.32	3283.86	3218.89	3158.83	3103.20
675,000	3483.34	3410.16	3342.69	3280.33	3222.56
700,000	3612.35	3536.46	3466.49	3401.82	3341.91
725,000	3741.36	3662.76	3590.29	3523.31	3461.27
750,000	3870.37	3789.07	3714.10	3644.81	3580.62
775,000	3999.38	3915.37	3837.90	3766.30	3699.97
800,000	4128.40	4041.67	3961.70	3887.79	3819.33
825,000	4257.41	4167.97	4085.51	4009.29	3938.68
850,000	4386.42	4294.27	4209.31	4130.78	4058.04
875,000	4515.43	4420.58	4333.11	4252.27	4177.39
900,000	4644.45	4546.88	4456.92	4373.77	4296.74

Monthly Payment Loans   **4.25%**

Loan Amount	Amortization Period in Years				
	5	7	8	10	12
10	0.19	0.14	0.13	0.11	0.09
20	0.38	0.28	0.25	0.21	0.18
30	0.56	0.42	0.37	0.31	0.27
40	0.75	0.56	0.50	0.41	0.36
50	0.93	0.69	0.62	0.52	0.45
100	1.86	1.38	1.24	1.03	0.89
200	3.71	2.76	2.47	2.05	1.78
300	5.56	4.14	3.70	3.08	2.67
400	7.42	5.52	4.93	4.10	3.56
500	9.27	6.90	6.16	5.13	4.44
1,000	18.53	13.79	12.31	10.25	8.88
2,000	37.06	27.57	24.62	20.49	17.76
3,000	55.59	41.36	36.92	30.74	26.64
4,000	74.12	55.14	49.23	40.98	35.51
5,000	92.65	68.93	61.53	51.22	44.39
10,000	185.30	137.85	123.06	102.44	88.78
20,000	370.60	275.69	246.12	204.88	177.55
30,000	555.89	413.53	369.18	307.32	266.32
40,000	741.19	551.37	492.24	409.76	355.09
50,000	926.48	689.21	615.30	512.19	443.86
100,000	1852.96	1378.42	1230.60	1024.38	887.72
125,000	2316.20	1723.03	1538.24	1280.47	1109.65
150,000	2779.44	2067.63	1845.89	1536.57	1331.58
175,000	3242.68	2412.24	2153.54	1792.66	1553.51
200,000	3705.92	2756.84	2461.19	2048.76	1775.44
225,000	4169.16	3101.45	2768.84	2304.85	1997.37
250,000	4632.39	3446.05	3076.48	2560.94	2219.30
275,000	5095.63	3790.66	3384.13	2817.04	2441.23
300,000	5558.87	4135.26	3691.78	3073.13	2663.16
325,000	6022.11	4479.86	3999.43	3329.22	2885.09
350,000	6485.35	4824.47	4307.07	3585.32	3107.02
375,000	6948.59	5169.07	4614.72	3841.41	3328.95
400,000	7411.83	5513.68	4922.37	4097.51	3550.88
425,000	7875.07	5858.28	5230.02	4353.60	3772.81
450,000	8338.31	6202.89	5537.67	4609.69	3994.74
475,000	8801.54	6547.49	5845.31	4865.79	4216.66
500,000	9264.78	6892.10	6152.96	5121.88	4438.59
525,000	9728.02	7236.70	6460.61	5377.98	4660.52
550,000	10191.26	7581.31	6768.26	5634.07	4882.45
575,000	10654.50	7925.91	7075.91	5890.16	5104.38
600,000	11117.74	8270.52	7383.55	6146.26	5326.31
625,000	11580.98	8615.12	7691.20	6402.35	5548.24
650,000	12044.22	8959.72	7998.85	6658.44	5770.17
675,000	12507.46	9304.33	8306.50	6914.54	5992.10
700,000	12970.69	9648.93	8614.14	7170.63	6214.03
725,000	13433.93	9993.54	8921.79	7426.73	6435.96
750,000	13897.17	10338.14	9229.44	7682.82	6657.89
775,000	14360.41	10682.75	9537.09	7938.91	6879.82
800,000	14823.65	11027.35	9844.74	8195.01	7101.75
825,000	15286.89	11371.96	10152.38	8451.10	7323.68
850,000	15750.13	11716.56	10460.03	8707.20	7545.61
875,000	16213.37	12061.17	10767.68	8963.29	7767.54
900,000	16676.61	12405.77	11075.33	9219.38	7989.47

Table 7   97

4.25%   **Monthly Payment Loans**

Amortization Period in Years

Loan Amount	15	16	17	18	20
10	0.08	0.08	0.07	0.07	0.07
20	0.16	0.15	0.14	0.14	0.13
30	0.23	0.22	0.21	0.20	0.19
40	0.31	0.29	0.28	0.27	0.25
50	0.38	0.36	0.35	0.34	0.31
100	0.76	0.72	0.69	0.67	0.62
200	1.51	1.44	1.38	1.33	1.24
300	2.26	2.16	2.07	1.99	1.86
400	3.01	2.88	2.76	2.66	2.48
500	3.77	3.60	3.45	3.32	3.10
1,000	7.53	7.19	6.90	6.64	6.20
2,000	15.05	14.38	13.79	13.27	12.39
3,000	22.57	21.57	20.68	19.90	18.58
4,000	30.10	28.75	27.58	26.53	24.77
5,000	37.62	35.94	34.47	33.16	30.97
10,000	75.23	71.88	68.93	66.32	61.93
20,000	150.46	143.75	137.86	132.64	123.85
30,000	225.69	215.62	206.78	198.96	185.78
40,000	300.92	287.49	275.71	265.28	247.70
50,000	376.14	359.37	344.63	331.60	309.62
100,000	752.28	718.73	689.26	663.19	619.24
125,000	940.35	898.41	861.57	828.99	774.05
150,000	1128.42	1078.09	1033.88	994.79	928.86
175,000	1316.49	1257.77	1206.19	1160.58	1083.67
200,000	1504.56	1437.45	1378.51	1326.38	1238.47
225,000	1692.63	1617.13	1550.82	1492.18	1393.28
250,000	1880.70	1796.81	1723.13	1657.97	1548.09
275,000	2068.77	1976.49	1895.44	1823.77	1702.90
300,000	2256.84	2156.17	2067.76	1989.57	1857.71
325,000	2444.91	2335.85	2240.07	2155.37	2012.52
350,000	2632.98	2515.53	2412.38	2321.16	2167.33
375,000	2821.05	2695.21	2584.70	2486.96	2322.13
400,000	3009.12	2874.89	2757.01	2652.76	2476.94
425,000	3197.19	3054.57	2929.32	2818.55	2631.75
450,000	3385.26	3234.25	3101.63	2984.35	2786.56
475,000	3573.33	3413.93	3273.95	3150.15	2941.37
500,000	3761.40	3593.61	3446.26	3315.94	3096.18
525,000	3949.47	3773.29	3618.57	3481.74	3250.99
550,000	4137.54	3952.97	3790.88	3647.54	3405.79
575,000	4325.61	4132.65	3963.20	3813.33	3560.60
600,000	4513.68	4312.33	4135.51	3979.13	3715.41
625,000	4701.75	4492.01	4307.82	4144.93	3870.22
650,000	4889.81	4671.69	4480.14	4310.73	4025.03
675,000	5077.88	4851.37	4652.45	4476.52	4179.84
700,000	5265.95	5031.05	4824.76	4642.32	4334.65
725,000	5454.02	5210.73	4997.07	4808.12	4489.45
750,000	5642.09	5390.41	5169.39	4973.91	4644.26
775,000	5830.16	5570.09	5341.70	5139.71	4799.07
800,000	6018.23	5749.77	5514.01	5305.51	4953.88
825,000	6206.30	5929.45	5686.32	5471.30	5108.69
850,000	6394.37	6109.13	5858.64	5637.10	5263.50
875,000	6582.44	6288.81	6030.95	5802.90	5418.31
900,000	6770.51	6468.49	6203.26	5968.70	5573.12

Monthly Payment Loans **4.25%**

Loan Amount	Amortization Period in Years				
	21	22	23	24	25
10	0.07	0.06	0.06	0.06	0.06
20	0.13	0.12	0.12	0.12	0.11
30	0.19	0.18	0.18	0.17	0.17
40	0.25	0.24	0.23	0.23	0.22
50	0.31	0.30	0.29	0.28	0.28
100	0.61	0.59	0.57	0.56	0.55
200	1.21	1.17	1.14	1.11	1.09
300	1.81	1.76	1.71	1.67	1.63
400	2.41	2.34	2.28	2.22	2.17
500	3.01	2.92	2.85	2.78	2.71
1,000	6.01	5.84	5.69	5.55	5.42
2,000	12.02	11.68	11.37	11.09	10.84
3,000	18.02	17.52	17.06	16.64	16.26
4,000	24.03	23.35	22.74	22.18	21.67
5,000	30.03	29.19	28.42	27.73	27.09
10,000	60.06	58.37	56.84	55.45	54.18
20,000	120.12	116.74	113.68	110.90	108.35
30,000	180.17	175.11	170.52	166.34	162.53
40,000	240.23	233.48	227.36	221.79	216.70
50,000	300.29	291.85	284.20	277.24	270.87
100,000	600.57	583.70	568.40	554.47	541.74
125,000	750.71	729.63	710.50	693.09	677.18
150,000	900.85	875.55	852.60	831.70	812.61
175,000	1050.99	1021.47	994.70	970.32	948.05
200,000	1201.13	1167.40	1136.80	1108.93	1083.48
225,000	1351.27	1313.32	1278.89	1247.55	1218.92
250,000	1501.42	1459.25	1420.99	1386.17	1354.35
275,000	1651.56	1605.17	1563.09	1524.78	1489.78
300,000	1801.70	1751.09	1705.19	1663.40	1625.22
325,000	1951.84	1897.02	1847.29	1802.01	1760.65
350,000	2101.98	2042.94	1989.39	1940.63	1896.09
375,000	2252.12	2188.87	2131.49	2079.25	2031.52
400,000	2402.26	2334.79	2273.59	2217.86	2166.96
425,000	2552.40	2480.72	2415.69	2356.48	2302.39
450,000	2702.54	2626.64	2557.78	2495.09	2437.83
475,000	2852.69	2772.56	2699.88	2633.71	2573.26
500,000	3002.83	2918.49	2841.98	2772.33	2708.70
525,000	3152.97	3064.41	2984.08	2910.94	2844.13
550,000	3303.11	3210.34	3126.18	3049.56	2979.56
575,000	3453.25	3356.26	3268.28	3188.17	3115.00
600,000	3603.39	3502.18	3410.38	3326.79	3250.43
625,000	3753.53	3648.11	3552.48	3465.41	3385.87
650,000	3903.67	3794.03	3694.57	3604.02	3521.30
675,000	4053.81	3939.96	3836.67	3742.64	3656.74
700,000	4203.95	4085.88	3978.77	3881.26	3792.17
725,000	4354.10	4231.80	4120.87	4019.87	3927.61
750,000	4504.24	4377.73	4262.97	4158.49	4063.04
775,000	4654.38	4523.65	4405.07	4297.10	4198.48
800,000	4804.52	4669.58	4547.17	4435.72	4333.91
825,000	4954.66	4815.50	4689.27	4574.34	4469.34
850,000	5104.80	4961.43	4831.37	4712.95	4604.78
875,000	5254.94	5107.35	4973.46	4851.57	4740.21
900,000	5405.08	5253.27	5115.56	4990.18	4875.65

Table 7   99

4.25% Monthly Payment Loans

Table 7

Loan Amount	Amortization Period in Years				
	26	27	28	29	30
10	0.06	0.06	0.06	0.06	0.05
20	0.11	0.11	0.11	0.11	0.10
30	0.16	0.16	0.16	0.16	0.15
40	0.22	0.21	0.21	0.21	0.20
50	0.27	0.26	0.26	0.26	0.25
100	0.54	0.52	0.51	0.51	0.50
200	1.07	1.04	1.02	1.01	0.99
300	1.60	1.56	1.53	1.51	1.48
400	2.13	2.08	2.04	2.01	1.97
500	2.66	2.60	2.55	2.51	2.46
1,000	5.31	5.20	5.10	5.01	4.92
2,000	10.61	10.39	10.19	10.01	9.84
3,000	15.91	15.59	15.29	15.02	14.76
4,000	21.21	20.78	20.38	20.02	19.68
5,000	26.51	25.97	25.48	25.02	24.60
10,000	53.01	51.94	50.95	50.04	49.20
20,000	106.02	103.88	101.90	100.08	98.39
30,000	159.03	155.81	152.85	150.12	147.59
40,000	212.04	207.75	203.80	200.16	196.78
50,000	265.04	259.69	254.75	250.19	245.97
100,000	530.08	519.37	509.50	500.38	491.94
125,000	662.60	649.21	636.87	625.47	614.93
150,000	795.12	779.05	764.24	750.57	737.91
175,000	927.64	908.89	891.61	875.66	860.90
200,000	1060.16	1038.73	1018.99	1000.76	983.88
225,000	1192.68	1168.57	1146.36	1125.85	1106.87
250,000	1325.20	1298.41	1273.73	1250.94	1229.85
275,000	1457.72	1428.25	1401.10	1376.04	1352.84
300,000	1590.24	1558.09	1528.48	1501.13	1475.82
325,000	1722.76	1687.93	1655.85	1626.23	1598.81
350,000	1855.27	1817.77	1783.22	1751.32	1721.79
375,000	1987.79	1947.61	1910.60	1876.41	1844.78
400,000	2120.31	2077.45	2037.97	2001.51	1967.76
425,000	2252.83	2207.29	2165.34	2126.60	2090.75
450,000	2385.35	2337.13	2292.71	2251.69	2213.73
475,000	2517.87	2466.97	2420.09	2376.79	2336.72
500,000	2650.39	2596.81	2547.46	2501.88	2459.70
525,000	2782.91	2726.66	2674.83	2626.98	2582.69
550,000	2915.43	2856.50	2802.20	2752.07	2705.67
575,000	3047.95	2986.34	2929.58	2877.16	2828.66
600,000	3180.47	3116.18	3056.95	3002.26	2951.64
625,000	3312.99	3246.02	3184.32	3127.35	3074.63
650,000	3445.51	3375.86	3311.70	3252.45	3197.61
675,000	3578.02	3505.70	3439.07	3377.54	3320.60
700,000	3710.54	3635.54	3566.44	3502.63	3443.58
725,000	3843.06	3765.38	3693.81	3627.73	3566.57
750,000	3975.58	3895.22	3821.19	3752.82	3689.55
775,000	4108.10	4025.06	3948.56	3877.92	3812.54
800,000	4240.62	4154.90	4075.93	4003.01	3935.52
825,000	4373.14	4284.74	4203.30	4128.10	4058.51
850,000	4505.66	4414.58	4330.68	4253.20	4181.49
875,000	4638.18	4544.42	4458.05	4378.29	4304.48
900,000	4770.70	4674.26	4585.42	4503.38	4427.46

Monthly Payment Loans   **4.50%**

Loan Amount	Amortization Period in Years				
	5	7	8	10	12
10	0.19	0.14	0.13	0.11	0.10
20	0.38	0.28	0.25	0.21	0.19
30	0.56	0.42	0.38	0.32	0.28
40	0.75	0.56	0.50	0.42	0.37
50	0.94	0.70	0.63	0.52	0.46
100	1.87	1.40	1.25	1.04	0.91
200	3.73	2.79	2.49	2.08	1.81
300	5.60	4.18	3.73	3.11	2.71
400	7.46	5.57	4.97	4.15	3.61
500	9.33	6.96	6.22	5.19	4.51
1,000	18.65	13.91	12.43	10.37	9.01
2,000	37.29	27.81	24.85	20.73	18.01
3,000	55.93	41.71	37.27	31.10	27.01
4,000	74.58	55.61	49.70	41.46	36.01
5,000	93.22	69.51	62.12	51.82	45.01
10,000	186.44	139.01	124.24	103.64	90.01
20,000	372.87	278.01	248.47	207.28	180.01
30,000	559.30	417.01	372.70	310.92	270.01
40,000	745.73	556.01	496.93	414.56	360.01
50,000	932.16	695.01	621.17	518.20	450.01
100,000	1864.31	1390.02	1242.33	1036.39	900.01
125,000	2330.38	1737.53	1552.91	1295.49	1125.02
150,000	2796.46	2085.03	1863.49	1554.58	1350.02
175,000	3262.53	2432.53	2174.07	1813.68	1575.02
200,000	3728.61	2780.04	2484.65	2072.77	1800.02
225,000	4194.68	3127.54	2795.23	2331.87	2025.02
250,000	4660.76	3475.05	3105.81	2590.97	2250.03
275,000	5126.84	3822.55	3416.39	2850.06	2475.03
300,000	5592.91	4170.05	3726.98	3109.16	2700.03
325,000	6058.99	4517.56	4037.56	3368.25	2925.03
350,000	6525.06	4865.06	4348.14	3627.35	3150.03
375,000	6991.14	5212.57	4658.72	3886.45	3375.04
400,000	7457.21	5560.07	4969.30	4145.54	3600.04
425,000	7923.29	5907.57	5279.88	4404.64	3825.04
450,000	8389.36	6255.08	5590.46	4663.73	4050.04
475,000	8855.44	6602.58	5901.04	4922.83	4275.04
500,000	9321.51	6950.09	6211.62	5181.93	4500.05
525,000	9787.59	7297.59	6522.20	5441.02	4725.05
550,000	10253.67	7645.09	6832.78	5700.12	4950.05
575,000	10719.74	7992.60	7143.36	5959.21	5175.05
600,000	11185.82	8340.10	7453.95	6218.31	5400.05
625,000	11651.89	8687.61	7764.53	6477.41	5625.06
650,000	12117.97	9035.11	8075.11	6736.50	5850.06
675,000	12584.04	9382.61	8385.69	6995.60	6075.06
700,000	13050.12	9730.12	8696.27	7254.69	6300.06
725,000	13516.19	10077.62	9006.85	7513.79	6525.06
750,000	13982.27	10425.13	9317.43	7772.89	6750.07
775,000	14448.34	10772.63	9628.01	8031.98	6975.07
800,000	14914.42	11120.13	9938.59	8291.08	7200.07
825,000	15380.50	11467.64	10249.17	8550.17	7425.07
850,000	15846.57	11815.14	10559.75	8809.27	7650.07
875,000	16312.65	12162.65	10870.34	9068.37	7875.08
900,000	16778.72	12510.15	11180.92	9327.46	8100.08

Table 7   101

4.50%   **Monthly Payment Loans**

Amortization Period in Years

Loan Amount	15	16	17	18	20
10	0.08	0.08	0.08	0.07	0.07
20	0.16	0.15	0.15	0.14	0.13
30	0.23	0.22	0.22	0.21	0.19
40	0.31	0.30	0.29	0.28	0.26
50	0.39	0.37	0.36	0.34	0.32
100	0.77	0.74	0.71	0.68	0.64
200	1.53	1.47	1.41	1.36	1.27
300	2.30	2.20	2.11	2.03	1.90
400	3.06	2.93	2.81	2.71	2.54
500	3.83	3.66	3.52	3.39	3.17
1,000	7.65	7.32	7.03	6.77	6.33
2,000	15.30	14.64	14.05	13.53	12.66
3,000	22.95	21.95	21.07	20.29	18.98
4,000	30.60	29.27	28.09	27.06	25.31
5,000	38.25	36.58	35.12	33.82	31.64
10,000	76.50	73.16	70.23	67.64	63.27
20,000	153.00	146.32	140.45	135.27	126.53
30,000	229.50	219.48	210.68	202.90	189.80
40,000	306.00	292.64	280.90	270.53	253.06
50,000	382.50	365.79	351.13	338.17	316.33
100,000	765.00	731.58	702.25	676.33	632.65
125,000	956.25	914.48	877.81	845.41	790.82
150,000	1147.49	1097.37	1053.38	1014.49	948.98
175,000	1338.74	1280.26	1228.94	1183.57	1107.14
200,000	1529.99	1463.16	1404.50	1352.65	1265.30
225,000	1721.24	1646.05	1580.06	1521.74	1423.47
250,000	1912.49	1828.95	1755.62	1690.82	1581.63
275,000	2103.74	2011.84	1931.19	1859.90	1739.79
300,000	2294.98	2194.73	2106.75	2028.98	1897.95
325,000	2486.23	2377.63	2282.31	2198.06	2056.12
350,000	2677.48	2560.52	2457.87	2367.14	2214.28
375,000	2868.73	2743.42	2633.43	2536.22	2372.44
400,000	3059.98	2926.31	2808.99	2705.30	2530.60
425,000	3251.23	3109.20	2984.56	2874.38	2688.76
450,000	3442.47	3292.10	3160.12	3043.47	2846.93
475,000	3633.72	3474.99	3335.68	3212.55	3005.09
500,000	3824.97	3657.89	3511.24	3381.63	3163.25
525,000	4016.22	3840.78	3686.80	3550.71	3321.41
550,000	4207.47	4023.67	3862.37	3719.79	3479.58
575,000	4398.72	4206.57	4037.93	3888.87	3637.74
600,000	4589.96	4389.46	4213.49	4057.95	3795.90
625,000	4781.21	4572.36	4389.05	4227.03	3954.06
650,000	4972.46	4755.25	4564.61	4396.11	4112.23
675,000	5163.71	4938.14	4740.18	4565.20	4270.39
700,000	5354.96	5121.04	4915.74	4734.28	4428.55
725,000	5546.21	5303.93	5091.30	4903.36	4586.71
750,000	5737.45	5486.83	5266.86	5072.44	4744.88
775,000	5928.70	5669.72	5442.42	5241.52	4903.04
800,000	6119.95	5852.61	5617.98	5410.60	5061.20
825,000	6311.20	6035.51	5793.55	5579.68	5219.36
850,000	6502.45	6218.40	5969.11	5748.76	5377.52
875,000	6693.70	6401.30	6144.67	5917.85	5535.69
900,000	6884.94	6584.19	6320.23	6086.93	5693.85

Monthly Payment Loans   **4.50%**

Amortization Period in Years

Loan Amount	21	22	23	24	25
10	0.07	0.06	0.06	0.06	0.06
20	0.13	0.12	0.12	0.12	0.12
30	0.19	0.18	0.18	0.18	0.17
40	0.25	0.24	0.24	0.23	0.23
50	0.31	0.30	0.30	0.29	0.28
100	0.62	0.60	0.59	0.57	0.56
200	1.23	1.20	1.17	1.14	1.12
300	1.85	1.80	1.75	1.71	1.67
400	2.46	2.39	2.33	2.28	2.23
500	3.08	2.99	2.92	2.85	2.78
1,000	6.15	5.98	5.83	5.69	5.56
2,000	12.29	11.95	11.65	11.37	11.12
3,000	18.43	17.93	17.47	17.06	16.68
4,000	24.57	23.90	23.29	22.74	22.24
5,000	30.71	29.87	29.12	28.43	27.80
10,000	61.42	59.74	58.23	56.85	55.59
20,000	122.83	119.48	116.45	113.69	111.17
30,000	184.24	179.22	174.67	170.53	166.75
40,000	245.65	238.96	232.89	227.37	222.34
50,000	307.06	298.70	291.12	284.22	277.92
100,000	614.12	597.39	582.23	568.43	555.84
125,000	767.65	746.74	727.78	710.54	694.80
150,000	921.18	896.08	873.34	852.64	833.75
175,000	1074.71	1045.43	1018.89	994.75	972.71
200,000	1228.24	1194.78	1164.45	1136.85	1111.67
225,000	1381.77	1344.12	1310.00	1278.96	1250.63
250,000	1535.30	1493.47	1455.56	1421.07	1389.59
275,000	1688.83	1642.82	1601.12	1563.17	1528.54
300,000	1842.36	1792.16	1746.67	1705.28	1667.50
325,000	1995.89	1941.51	1892.22	1847.39	1806.46
350,000	2149.41	2090.86	2037.78	1989.49	1945.42
375,000	2302.94	2240.20	2183.33	2131.60	2084.38
400,000	2456.47	2389.55	2328.89	2273.70	2223.33
425,000	2610.00	2538.90	2474.44	2415.81	2362.29
450,000	2763.53	2688.24	2620.00	2557.92	2501.25
475,000	2917.06	2837.59	2765.55	2700.02	2640.21
500,000	3070.59	2986.94	2911.11	2842.13	2779.17
525,000	3224.12	3136.28	3056.67	2984.24	2918.13
550,000	3377.65	3285.63	3202.22	3126.34	3057.08
575,000	3531.18	3434.98	3347.78	3268.45	3196.04
600,000	3684.71	3584.32	3493.33	3410.55	3335.00
625,000	3838.24	3733.67	3638.89	3552.66	3473.96
650,000	3991.77	3883.02	3784.44	3694.77	3612.92
675,000	4145.29	4032.36	3930.00	3836.87	3751.87
700,000	4298.82	4181.71	4075.55	3978.98	3890.83
725,000	4452.35	4331.05	4221.11	4121.09	4029.79
750,000	4605.88	4480.40	4366.66	4263.19	4168.75
775,000	4759.41	4629.75	4512.22	4405.30	4307.71
800,000	4912.94	4779.09	4657.77	4547.40	4446.66
825,000	5066.47	4928.44	4803.33	4689.51	4585.62
850,000	5220.00	5077.79	4948.88	4831.62	4724.58
875,000	5373.53	5227.13	5094.44	4973.72	4863.54
900,000	5527.06	5376.48	5239.99	5115.83	5002.50

Table 7   103

4.50%　　　Monthly Payment Loans

Loan Amount	Amortization Period in Years				
	26	27	28	29	30
10	0.06	0.06	0.06	0.06	0.06
20	0.11	0.11	0.11	0.11	0.11
30	0.17	0.17	0.16	0.16	0.16
40	0.22	0.22	0.21	0.21	0.21
50	0.28	0.27	0.27	0.26	0.26
100	0.55	0.54	0.53	0.52	0.51
200	1.09	1.07	1.05	1.03	1.02
300	1.64	1.61	1.58	1.55	1.53
400	2.18	2.14	2.10	2.06	2.03
500	2.73	2.67	2.62	2.58	2.54
1,000	5.45	5.34	5.24	5.15	5.07
2,000	10.89	10.68	10.48	10.30	10.14
3,000	16.33	16.02	15.72	15.45	15.21
4,000	21.78	21.35	20.96	20.60	20.27
5,000	27.22	26.69	26.20	25.75	25.34
10,000	54.44	53.38	52.40	51.50	50.67
20,000	108.87	106.75	104.80	103.00	101.34
30,000	163.30	160.12	157.20	154.50	152.01
40,000	217.73	213.49	209.60	206.00	202.68
50,000	272.16	266.87	261.99	257.50	253.35
100,000	544.31	533.73	523.98	515.00	506.69
125,000	680.39	667.16	654.98	643.75	633.36
150,000	816.46	800.59	785.97	772.49	760.03
175,000	952.54	934.02	916.97	901.24	886.70
200,000	1088.61	1067.45	1047.96	1029.99	1013.38
225,000	1224.69	1200.88	1178.96	1158.74	1140.05
250,000	1360.77	1334.31	1309.95	1287.49	1266.72
275,000	1496.84	1467.74	1440.95	1416.24	1393.39
300,000	1632.92	1601.17	1571.94	1544.98	1520.06
325,000	1768.99	1734.60	1702.94	1673.73	1646.73
350,000	1905.07	1868.03	1833.93	1802.48	1773.40
375,000	2041.15	2001.46	1964.93	1931.23	1900.07
400,000	2177.22	2134.89	2095.92	2059.98	2026.75
425,000	2313.30	2268.32	2226.92	2188.73	2153.42
450,000	2449.37	2401.75	2357.91	2317.47	2280.09
475,000	2585.45	2535.18	2488.91	2446.22	2406.76
500,000	2721.53	2668.61	2619.90	2574.97	2533.43
525,000	2857.60	2802.04	2750.90	2703.72	2660.10
550,000	2993.68	2935.47	2881.89	2832.47	2786.77
575,000	3129.75	3068.90	3012.89	2961.22	2913.45
600,000	3265.83	3202.33	3143.88	3089.96	3040.12
625,000	3401.91	3335.76	3274.88	3218.71	3166.79
650,000	3537.98	3469.19	3405.87	3347.46	3293.46
675,000	3674.06	3602.62	3536.87	3476.21	3420.13
700,000	3810.13	3736.05	3667.86	3604.96	3546.80
725,000	3946.21	3869.48	3798.86	3733.71	3673.47
750,000	4082.29	4002.91	3929.85	3862.45	3800.14
775,000	4218.36	4136.34	4060.85	3991.20	3926.82
800,000	4354.44	4269.77	4191.84	4119.95	4053.49
825,000	4490.51	4403.20	4322.84	4248.70	4180.16
850,000	4626.59	4536.63	4453.83	4377.45	4306.83
875,000	4762.67	4670.06	4584.83	4506.20	4433.50
900,000	4898.74	4803.49	4715.82	4634.94	4560.17

Monthly Payment Loans   **4.75%**

Loan Amount	Amortization Period in Years				
	5	7	8	10	12
10	0.19	0.15	0.13	0.11	0.10
20	0.38	0.29	0.26	0.21	0.19
30	0.57	0.43	0.38	0.32	0.28
40	0.76	0.57	0.51	0.42	0.37
50	0.94	0.71	0.63	0.53	0.46
100	1.88	1.41	1.26	1.05	0.92
200	3.76	2.81	2.51	2.10	1.83
300	5.63	4.21	3.77	3.15	2.74
400	7.51	5.61	5.02	4.20	3.65
500	9.38	7.01	6.28	5.25	4.57
1,000	18.76	14.02	12.55	10.49	9.13
2,000	37.52	28.04	25.09	20.97	18.25
3,000	56.28	42.06	37.63	31.46	27.38
4,000	75.03	56.07	50.17	41.94	36.50
5,000	93.79	70.09	62.71	52.43	45.62
10,000	187.57	140.17	125.42	104.85	91.24
20,000	375.14	280.34	250.83	209.70	182.48
30,000	562.71	420.51	376.24	314.55	273.72
40,000	750.28	560.67	501.65	419.40	364.96
50,000	937.85	700.84	627.07	524.24	456.20
100,000	1875.70	1401.68	1254.13	1048.48	912.40
125,000	2344.62	1752.10	1567.66	1310.60	1140.50
150,000	2813.54	2102.52	1881.19	1572.72	1368.60
175,000	3282.46	2452.93	2194.72	1834.84	1596.70
200,000	3751.39	2803.35	2508.25	2096.96	1824.80
225,000	4220.31	3153.77	2821.78	2359.08	2052.90
250,000	4689.23	3504.19	3135.31	2621.20	2281.00
275,000	5158.16	3854.61	3448.85	2883.32	2509.10
300,000	5627.08	4205.03	3762.38	3145.44	2737.20
325,000	6096.00	4555.44	4075.91	3407.56	2965.30
350,000	6564.92	4905.86	4389.44	3669.68	3193.40
375,000	7033.85	5256.28	4702.97	3931.80	3421.50
400,000	7502.77	5606.70	5016.50	4193.91	3649.60
425,000	7971.69	5957.12	5330.03	4456.03	3877.70
450,000	8440.62	6307.54	5643.56	4718.15	4105.80
475,000	8909.54	6657.95	5957.09	4980.27	4333.90
500,000	9378.46	7008.37	6270.62	5242.39	4562.00
525,000	9847.38	7358.79	6584.15	5504.51	4790.10
550,000	10316.31	7709.21	6897.69	5766.63	5018.20
575,000	10785.23	8059.63	7211.22	6028.75	5246.30
600,000	11254.15	8410.05	7524.75	6290.87	5474.40
625,000	11723.07	8760.47	7838.28	6552.99	5702.50
650,000	12192.00	9110.88	8151.81	6815.11	5930.60
675,000	12660.92	9461.30	8465.34	7077.23	6158.70
700,000	13129.84	9811.72	8778.87	7339.35	6386.80
725,000	13598.77	10162.14	9092.40	7601.47	6614.90
750,000	14067.59	10512.56	9405.93	7863.59	6843.00
775,000	14536.61	10862.98	9719.46	8125.71	7071.10
800,000	15005.53	11213.39	10032.99	8387.82	7299.20
825,000	15474.46	11563.81	10346.53	8649.94	7527.30
850,000	15943.38	11914.23	10660.06	8912.06	7755.40
875,000	16412.30	12264.65	10973.59	9174.18	7983.50
900,000	16881.23	12615.07	11287.12	9436.30	8211.60

Table 7   105

4.75%   Monthly Payment Loans

Amortization Period in Years

Loan Amount	15	16	17	18	20
10	0.08	0.08	0.08	0.07	0.07
20	0.16	0.15	0.15	0.14	0.13
30	0.24	0.23	0.22	0.21	0.20
40	0.32	0.30	0.29	0.28	0.26
50	0.39	0.38	0.36	0.35	0.33
100	0.78	0.75	0.72	0.69	0.65
200	1.56	1.49	1.44	1.38	1.30
300	2.34	2.24	2.15	2.07	1.94
400	3.12	2.98	2.87	2.76	2.59
500	3.89	3.73	3.58	3.45	3.24
1,000	7.78	7.45	7.16	6.90	6.47
2,000	15.56	14.90	14.31	13.80	12.93
3,000	23.34	22.34	21.47	20.69	19.39
4,000	31.12	29.79	28.62	27.59	25.85
5,000	38.90	37.23	35.77	34.49	32.32
10,000	77.79	74.46	71.54	68.97	64.63
20,000	155.57	148.92	143.08	137.93	129.25
30,000	233.35	223.37	214.62	206.89	193.87
40,000	311.14	297.83	286.16	275.85	258.49
50,000	388.92	372.29	357.70	344.81	323.12
100,000	777.84	744.57	715.39	689.61	646.23
125,000	972.29	930.71	894.23	862.01	807.78
150,000	1166.75	1116.85	1073.08	1034.42	969.34
175,000	1361.21	1302.99	1251.92	1206.82	1130.90
200,000	1555.67	1489.13	1430.77	1379.22	1292.45
225,000	1750.13	1675.27	1609.62	1551.62	1454.01
250,000	1944.58	1861.41	1788.46	1724.02	1615.56
275,000	2139.04	2047.55	1967.31	1896.42	1777.12
300,000	2333.50	2233.70	2146.15	2068.83	1938.68
325,000	2527.96	2419.84	2325.00	2241.23	2100.23
350,000	2722.42	2605.98	2503.84	2413.63	2261.79
375,000	2916.87	2792.12	2682.69	2586.03	2423.34
400,000	3111.33	2978.26	2861.54	2758.43	2584.90
425,000	3305.79	3164.40	3040.38	2930.83	2746.46
450,000	3500.25	3350.54	3219.23	3103.24	2908.01
475,000	3694.71	3536.68	3398.07	3275.64	3069.57
500,000	3889.16	3722.82	3576.92	3448.04	3231.12
525,000	4083.62	3908.96	3755.76	3620.44	3392.68
550,000	4278.08	4095.10	3934.61	3792.84	3554.23
575,000	4472.54	4281.24	4113.46	3965.25	3715.79
600,000	4667.00	4467.39	4292.30	4137.65	3877.35
625,000	4861.45	4653.53	4471.15	4310.05	4038.90
650,000	5055.91	4839.67	4649.99	4482.45	4200.46
675,000	5250.37	5025.81	4828.84	4654.85	4362.01
700,000	5444.83	5211.95	5007.68	4827.25	4523.57
725,000	5639.29	5398.09	5186.53	4999.66	4685.13
750,000	5833.74	5584.23	5365.37	5172.06	4846.68
775,000	6028.20	5770.37	5544.22	5344.46	5008.24
800,000	6222.66	5956.51	5723.07	5516.86	5169.79
825,000	6417.12	6142.65	5901.91	5689.26	5331.35
850,000	6611.58	6328.79	6080.76	5861.66	5492.91
875,000	6806.03	6514.93	6259.60	6034.07	5654.46
900,000	7000.49	6701.08	6438.45	6206.47	5816.02

Monthly Payment Loans   **4.75%**

Loan Amount	Amortization Period in Years				
	21	22	23	24	25
10	0.07	0.07	0.06	0.06	0.06
20	0.13	0.13	0.12	0.12	0.12
30	0.19	0.19	0.18	0.18	0.18
40	0.26	0.25	0.24	0.24	0.23
50	0.32	0.31	0.30	0.30	0.29
100	0.63	0.62	0.60	0.59	0.58
200	1.26	1.23	1.20	1.17	1.15
300	1.89	1.84	1.79	1.75	1.72
400	2.52	2.45	2.39	2.34	2.29
500	3.14	3.06	2.99	2.92	2.86
1,000	6.28	6.12	5.97	5.83	5.71
2,000	12.56	12.23	11.93	11.66	11.41
3,000	18.84	18.34	17.89	17.48	17.11
4,000	25.12	24.45	23.85	23.31	22.81
5,000	31.40	30.57	29.82	29.13	28.51
10,000	62.79	61.13	59.63	58.26	57.02
20,000	125.57	122.25	119.25	116.52	114.03
30,000	188.36	183.38	178.87	174.78	171.04
40,000	251.14	244.50	238.50	233.03	228.05
50,000	313.92	305.63	298.12	291.29	285.06
100,000	627.84	611.25	596.23	582.58	570.12
125,000	784.80	764.07	745.29	728.22	712.65
150,000	941.76	916.88	894.34	873.86	855.18
175,000	1098.72	1069.69	1043.40	1019.50	997.71
200,000	1255.68	1222.50	1192.46	1165.15	1140.24
225,000	1412.64	1375.31	1341.51	1310.79	1282.77
250,000	1569.59	1528.13	1490.57	1456.43	1425.30
275,000	1726.55	1680.94	1639.62	1602.07	1567.83
300,000	1883.51	1833.75	1788.68	1747.72	1710.36
325,000	2040.47	1986.56	1937.74	1893.36	1852.89
350,000	2197.43	2139.37	2086.79	2039.00	1995.42
375,000	2354.39	2292.19	2235.85	2184.64	2137.95
400,000	2511.35	2445.00	2384.91	2330.29	2280.47
425,000	2668.31	2597.81	2533.96	2475.93	2423.00
450,000	2825.27	2750.62	2683.02	2621.57	2565.53
475,000	2982.22	2903.43	2832.08	2767.21	2708.06
500,000	3139.18	3056.25	2981.13	2912.86	2850.59
525,000	3296.14	3209.06	3130.19	3058.50	2993.12
550,000	3453.10	3361.87	3279.24	3204.14	3135.65
575,000	3610.06	3514.68	3428.30	3349.78	3278.18
600,000	3767.02	3667.49	3577.36	3495.43	3420.71
625,000	3923.98	3820.31	3726.41	3641.07	3563.24
650,000	4080.94	3973.12	3875.47	3786.71	3705.77
675,000	4237.90	4125.93	4024.53	3932.35	3848.30
700,000	4394.85	4278.74	4173.58	4078.00	3990.83
725,000	4551.81	4431.55	4322.64	4223.64	4133.36
750,000	4708.77	4584.37	4471.69	4369.28	4275.89
775,000	4865.73	4737.18	4620.75	4514.92	4418.41
800,000	5022.69	4889.99	4769.81	4660.57	4560.94
825,000	5179.65	5042.80	4918.86	4806.21	4703.47
850,000	5336.61	5195.61	5067.92	4951.85	4846.00
875,000	5493.57	5348.43	5216.98	5097.49	4988.53
900,000	5650.53	5501.24	5366.03	5243.14	5131.06

Table 7   107

Monthly Payment Loans

Loan Amount	Amortization Period in Years				
	26	27	28	29	30
10	0.06	0.06	0.06	0.06	0.06
20	0.12	0.11	0.11	0.11	0.11
30	0.17	0.17	0.17	0.16	0.16
40	0.23	0.22	0.22	0.22	0.21
50	0.28	0.28	0.27	0.27	0.27
100	0.56	0.55	0.54	0.53	0.53
200	1.12	1.10	1.08	1.06	1.05
300	1.68	1.65	1.62	1.59	1.57
400	2.24	2.20	2.16	2.12	2.09
500	2.80	2.75	2.70	2.65	2.61
1,000	5.59	5.49	5.39	5.30	5.22
2,000	11.18	10.97	10.78	10.60	10.44
3,000	16.77	16.45	16.17	15.90	15.65
4,000	22.35	21.94	21.55	21.20	20.87
5,000	27.94	27.42	26.94	26.50	26.09
10,000	55.88	54.83	53.87	52.99	52.17
20,000	111.75	109.66	107.74	105.97	104.33
30,000	167.62	164.49	161.61	158.95	156.50
40,000	223.50	219.32	215.48	211.93	208.66
50,000	279.37	274.15	269.34	264.92	260.83
100,000	558.73	548.29	538.68	529.83	521.65
125,000	698.41	685.36	673.35	662.28	652.06
150,000	838.10	822.43	808.02	794.74	782.48
175,000	977.78	959.50	942.69	927.20	912.89
200,000	1117.46	1096.57	1077.36	1059.65	1043.30
225,000	1257.14	1233.64	1212.02	1192.11	1173.71
250,000	1396.82	1370.71	1346.69	1324.56	1304.12
275,000	1536.50	1507.78	1481.36	1457.02	1434.54
300,000	1676.19	1644.85	1616.03	1589.47	1564.95
325,000	1815.87	1781.92	1750.70	1721.93	1695.36
350,000	1955.55	1918.99	1885.37	1854.39	1825.77
375,000	2095.23	2056.06	2020.04	1986.84	1956.18
400,000	2234.91	2193.13	2154.71	2119.30	2086.59
425,000	2374.60	2330.20	2289.37	2251.75	2217.01
450,000	2514.28	2467.27	2424.04	2384.21	2347.42
475,000	2653.96	2604.34	2558.71	2516.66	2477.83
500,000	2793.64	2741.41	2693.38	2649.12	2608.24
525,000	2933.32	2878.48	2828.05	2781.58	2738.65
550,000	3073.00	3015.55	2962.72	2914.03	2869.07
575,000	3212.69	3152.62	3097.39	3046.49	2999.48
600,000	3352.37	3289.69	3232.06	3178.94	3129.89
625,000	3492.05	3426.76	3366.72	3311.40	3260.30
650,000	3631.73	3563.83	3501.39	3443.85	3390.71
675,000	3771.41	3700.90	3636.06	3576.31	3521.12
700,000	3911.10	3837.97	3770.73	3708.77	3651.54
725,000	4050.78	3975.04	3905.40	3841.22	3781.95
750,000	4190.46	4112.11	4040.07	3973.68	3912.36
775,000	4330.14	4249.18	4174.74	4106.13	4042.77
800,000	4469.82	4386.25	4309.41	4238.59	4173.18
825,000	4609.50	4523.32	4444.08	4371.04	4303.60
850,000	4749.19	4660.39	4578.74	4503.50	4434.01
875,000	4888.87	4797.46	4713.41	4635.96	4564.42
900,000	5028.55	4934.53	4848.08	4768.41	4694.83

Monthly Payment Loans   **5.00%**

Loan Amount	\multicolumn{5}{c}{Amortization Period in Years}				
	5	7	8	10	12
10	0.19	0.15	0.13	0.11	0.10
20	0.38	0.29	0.26	0.22	0.19
30	0.57	0.43	0.38	0.32	0.28
40	0.76	0.57	0.51	0.43	0.37
50	0.95	0.71	0.64	0.54	0.47
100	1.89	1.42	1.27	1.07	0.93
200	3.78	2.83	2.54	2.13	1.85
300	5.67	4.25	3.80	3.19	2.78
400	7.55	5.66	5.07	4.25	3.70
500	9.44	7.07	6.33	5.31	4.63
1,000	18.88	14.14	12.66	10.61	9.25
2,000	37.75	28.27	25.32	21.22	18.50
3,000	56.62	42.41	37.98	31.82	27.75
4,000	75.49	56.54	50.64	42.43	37.00
5,000	94.36	70.67	63.30	53.04	46.25
10,000	188.72	141.34	126.60	106.07	92.49
20,000	377.43	282.68	253.20	212.14	184.98
30,000	566.14	424.02	379.80	318.20	277.47
40,000	754.85	565.36	506.40	424.27	369.96
50,000	943.57	706.70	633.00	530.33	462.45
100,000	1887.13	1413.40	1266.00	1060.66	924.90
125,000	2358.91	1766.74	1582.50	1325.82	1156.12
150,000	2830.69	2120.09	1898.99	1590.99	1387.34
175,000	3302.47	2473.44	2215.49	1856.15	1618.56
200,000	3774.25	2826.79	2531.99	2121.32	1849.79
225,000	4246.03	3180.13	2848.49	2386.48	2081.01
250,000	4717.81	3533.48	3164.99	2651.64	2312.23
275,000	5189.59	3886.83	3481.48	2916.81	2543.45
300,000	5661.38	4240.18	3797.98	3181.97	2774.68
325,000	6133.16	4593.53	4114.48	3447.13	3005.90
350,000	6604.94	4946.87	4430.98	3712.30	3237.12
375,000	7076.72	5300.22	4747.48	3977.46	3468.34
400,000	7548.50	5653.57	5063.97	4242.63	3699.57
425,000	8020.28	6006.92	5380.47	4507.79	3930.79
450,000	8492.06	6360.26	5696.97	4772.95	4162.01
475,000	8963.84	6713.61	6013.47	5038.12	4393.23
500,000	9435.62	7066.96	6329.97	5303.28	4624.46
525,000	9907.40	7420.31	6646.46	5568.44	4855.68
550,000	10379.18	7773.65	6962.96	5833.61	5086.90
575,000	10850.96	8127.00	7279.46	6098.77	5318.12
600,000	11322.75	8480.35	7595.96	6363.94	5549.35
625,000	11794.53	8833.70	7912.46	6629.10	5780.57
650,000	12266.31	9187.05	8228.95	6894.26	6011.79
675,000	12738.09	9540.39	8545.45	7159.43	6243.02
700,000	13209.87	9893.74	8861.95	7424.59	6474.24
725,000	13681.65	10247.09	9178.45	7689.75	6705.46
750,000	14153.43	10600.44	9494.95	7954.92	6936.68
775,000	14625.21	10953.78	9811.44	8220.08	7167.91
800,000	15096.99	11307.13	10127.94	8485.25	7399.13
825,000	15568.77	11660.48	10444.44	8750.41	7630.35
850,000	16040.55	12013.83	10760.94	9015.57	7861.57
875,000	16512.33	12367.18	11077.44	9280.74	8092.80
900,000	16984.12	12720.52	11393.93	9545.90	8324.02

5.00%　　　Monthly Payment Loans

Loan Amount	\multicolumn{5}{c}{Amortization Period in Years}
	15	16	17	18	20
10	0.08	0.08	0.08	0.08	0.07
20	0.16	0.16	0.15	0.15	0.14
30	0.24	0.23	0.22	0.22	0.20
40	0.32	0.31	0.30	0.29	0.27
50	0.40	0.38	0.37	0.36	0.33
100	0.80	0.76	0.73	0.71	0.66
200	1.59	1.52	1.46	1.41	1.32
300	2.38	2.28	2.19	2.11	1.98
400	3.17	3.04	2.92	2.82	2.64
500	3.96	3.79	3.65	3.52	3.30
1,000	7.91	7.58	7.29	7.04	6.60
2,000	15.82	15.16	14.58	14.07	13.20
3,000	23.73	22.74	21.86	21.10	19.80
4,000	31.64	30.31	29.15	28.13	26.40
5,000	39.54	37.89	36.44	35.16	33.00
10,000	79.08	75.77	72.87	70.31	66.00
20,000	158.16	151.54	145.74	140.61	132.00
30,000	237.24	227.31	218.60	210.92	197.99
40,000	316.32	303.08	291.47	281.22	263.99
50,000	395.40	378.85	364.33	351.52	329.98
100,000	790.80	757.69	728.66	703.04	659.96
125,000	988.50	947.11	910.82	878.80	824.95
150,000	1186.20	1136.53	1092.99	1054.56	989.94
175,000	1383.89	1325.95	1275.15	1230.31	1154.93
200,000	1581.59	1515.37	1457.32	1406.07	1319.92
225,000	1779.29	1704.79	1639.48	1581.83	1484.91
250,000	1976.99	1894.21	1821.64	1757.59	1649.89
275,000	2174.69	2083.63	2003.81	1933.35	1814.88
300,000	2372.39	2273.05	2185.97	2109.11	1979.87
325,000	2570.08	2462.47	2368.13	2284.87	2144.86
350,000	2767.78	2651.89	2550.30	2460.62	2309.85
375,000	2965.48	2841.31	2732.46	2636.38	2474.84
400,000	3163.18	3030.73	2914.63	2812.14	2639.83
425,000	3360.88	3220.15	3096.79	2987.90	2804.82
450,000	3558.58	3409.57	3278.95	3163.66	2969.81
475,000	3756.27	3598.99	3461.12	3339.42	3134.79
500,000	3953.97	3788.41	3643.28	3515.17	3299.78
525,000	4151.67	3977.83	3825.45	3690.93	3464.77
550,000	4349.37	4167.25	4007.61	3866.69	3629.76
575,000	4547.07	4356.67	4189.77	4042.45	3794.75
600,000	4744.77	4546.09	4371.94	4218.21	3959.74
625,000	4942.47	4735.51	4554.10	4393.97	4124.73
650,000	5140.16	4924.93	4736.26	4569.73	4289.72
675,000	5337.86	5114.35	4918.43	4745.48	4454.71
700,000	5535.56	5303.77	5100.59	4921.24	4619.70
725,000	5733.26	5493.19	5282.76	5097.00	4784.68
750,000	5930.96	5682.61	5464.92	5272.76	4949.67
775,000	6128.66	5872.03	5647.08	5448.52	5114.66
800,000	6326.35	6061.45	5829.25	5624.28	5279.65
825,000	6524.05	6250.87	6011.41	5800.03	5444.64
850,000	6721.75	6440.29	6193.57	5975.79	5609.63
875,000	6919.45	6629.71	6375.74	6151.55	5774.62
900,000	7117.15	6819.13	6557.90	6327.31	5939.61

Monthly Payment Loans   **5.00%**

Amortization Period in Years

Loan Amount	21	22	23	24	25
10	0.07	0.07	0.07	0.06	0.06
20	0.13	0.13	0.13	0.12	0.12
30	0.20	0.19	0.19	0.18	0.18
40	0.26	0.26	0.25	0.24	0.24
50	0.33	0.32	0.31	0.30	0.30
100	0.65	0.63	0.62	0.60	0.59
200	1.29	1.26	1.23	1.20	1.17
300	1.93	1.88	1.84	1.80	1.76
400	2.57	2.51	2.45	2.39	2.34
500	3.21	3.13	3.06	2.99	2.93
1,000	6.42	6.26	6.11	5.97	5.85
2,000	12.84	12.51	12.21	11.94	11.70
3,000	19.26	18.76	18.32	17.91	17.54
4,000	25.67	25.02	24.42	23.88	23.39
5,000	32.09	31.27	30.53	29.85	29.23
10,000	64.18	62.53	61.05	59.69	58.46
20,000	128.35	125.06	122.09	119.38	116.92
30,000	192.52	187.59	183.13	179.07	175.38
40,000	256.69	250.12	244.17	238.76	233.84
50,000	320.86	312.65	305.21	298.45	292.30
100,000	641.72	625.29	610.41	596.90	584.60
125,000	802.15	781.61	763.01	746.13	730.74
150,000	962.58	937.93	915.61	895.35	876.89
175,000	1123.01	1094.25	1068.22	1044.58	1023.04
200,000	1283.44	1250.57	1220.82	1193.80	1169.19
225,000	1443.87	1406.89	1373.42	1343.02	1315.33
250,000	1604.30	1563.21	1526.02	1492.25	1461.48
275,000	1764.73	1719.53	1678.62	1641.47	1607.63
300,000	1925.16	1875.85	1831.22	1790.70	1753.78
325,000	2085.59	2032.17	1983.82	1939.92	1899.92
350,000	2246.02	2188.49	2136.43	2089.15	2046.07
375,000	2406.45	2344.81	2289.03	2238.37	2192.22
400,000	2566.88	2501.13	2441.63	2387.60	2338.37
425,000	2727.31	2657.45	2594.23	2536.82	2484.51
450,000	2887.74	2813.77	2746.83	2686.04	2630.66
475,000	3048.17	2970.09	2899.43	2835.27	2776.81
500,000	3208.60	3126.41	3052.03	2984.49	2922.96
525,000	3369.03	3282.73	3204.64	3133.72	3069.10
550,000	3529.46	3439.05	3357.24	3282.94	3215.25
575,000	3689.89	3595.37	3509.84	3432.17	3361.40
600,000	3850.32	3751.69	3662.44	3581.39	3507.55
625,000	4010.75	3908.01	3815.04	3730.61	3653.69
650,000	4171.18	4064.33	3967.64	3879.84	3799.84
675,000	4331.61	4220.65	4120.25	4029.06	3945.99
700,000	4492.04	4376.97	4272.85	4178.29	4092.14
725,000	4652.47	4533.29	4425.45	4327.51	4238.28
750,000	4812.89	4689.61	4578.05	4476.74	4384.43
775,000	4973.32	4845.93	4730.65	4625.96	4530.58
800,000	5133.75	5002.25	4883.25	4775.19	4676.73
825,000	5294.18	5158.57	5035.85	4924.41	4822.87
850,000	5454.61	5314.89	5188.46	5073.63	4969.02
875,000	5615.04	5471.21	5341.06	5222.86	5115.17
900,000	5775.47	5627.53	5493.66	5372.08	5261.32

Table 7   111

5.00%   Monthly Payment Loans

Loan Amount	26	27	28	29	30
10	0.06	0.06	0.06	0.06	0.06
20	0.12	0.12	0.12	0.11	0.11
30	0.18	0.17	0.17	0.17	0.17
40	0.23	0.23	0.23	0.22	0.22
50	0.29	0.29	0.28	0.28	0.27
100	0.58	0.57	0.56	0.55	0.54
200	1.15	1.13	1.11	1.09	1.08
300	1.73	1.69	1.67	1.64	1.62
400	2.30	2.26	2.22	2.18	2.15
500	2.87	2.82	2.77	2.73	2.69
1,000	5.74	5.64	5.54	5.45	5.37
2,000	11.47	11.27	11.08	10.90	10.74
3,000	17.21	16.90	16.61	16.35	16.11
4,000	22.94	22.53	22.15	21.80	21.48
5,000	28.67	28.16	27.68	27.25	26.85
10,000	57.34	56.31	55.36	54.49	53.69
20,000	114.67	112.61	110.72	108.98	107.37
30,000	172.01	168.92	166.08	163.46	161.05
40,000	229.34	225.22	221.43	217.95	214.73
50,000	286.68	281.52	276.79	272.44	268.42
100,000	573.35	563.04	553.58	544.87	536.83
125,000	716.68	703.80	691.97	681.08	671.03
150,000	860.02	844.56	830.37	817.30	805.24
175,000	1003.36	985.32	968.76	953.51	939.44
200,000	1146.69	1126.08	1107.15	1089.73	1073.65
225,000	1290.03	1266.84	1245.55	1225.94	1207.85
250,000	1433.36	1407.60	1383.94	1362.16	1342.06
275,000	1576.70	1548.36	1522.33	1498.37	1476.26
300,000	1720.04	1689.12	1660.73	1634.59	1610.47
325,000	1863.37	1829.88	1799.12	1770.80	1744.68
350,000	2006.71	1970.64	1937.51	1907.02	1878.88
375,000	2150.04	2111.40	2075.91	2043.23	2013.09
400,000	2293.38	2252.16	2214.30	2179.45	2147.29
425,000	2436.72	2392.92	2352.69	2315.66	2281.50
450,000	2580.05	2533.68	2491.09	2451.88	2415.70
475,000	2723.39	2674.44	2629.48	2588.09	2549.91
500,000	2866.72	2815.20	2767.87	2724.31	2684.11
525,000	3010.06	2955.96	2906.27	2860.52	2818.32
550,000	3153.39	3096.72	3044.66	2996.74	2952.52
575,000	3296.73	3237.48	3183.06	3132.95	3086.73
600,000	3440.07	3378.24	3321.45	3269.17	3220.93
625,000	3583.40	3519.00	3459.84	3405.38	3355.14
650,000	3726.74	3659.76	3598.24	3541.60	3489.35
675,000	3870.07	3800.52	3736.63	3677.81	3623.55
700,000	4013.41	3941.28	3875.02	3814.03	3757.76
725,000	4156.75	4082.04	4013.42	3950.24	3891.96
750,000	4300.08	4222.80	4151.81	4086.46	4026.17
775,000	4443.42	4363.56	4290.20	4222.67	4160.37
800,000	4586.75	4504.32	4428.60	4358.89	4294.58
825,000	4730.09	4645.08	4566.99	4495.10	4428.78
850,000	4873.43	4785.84	4705.38	4631.32	4562.99
875,000	5016.76	4926.60	4843.78	4767.53	4697.19
900,000	5160.10	5067.36	4982.17	4903.75	4831.40

Monthly Payment Loans $\qquad$ 5.25%

Loan Amount	Amortization Period in Years				
	5	7	8	10	12
10	0.19	0.15	0.13	0.11	0.10
20	0.38	0.29	0.26	0.22	0.19
30	0.57	0.43	0.39	0.33	0.29
40	0.76	0.58	0.52	0.43	0.38
50	0.95	0.72	0.64	0.54	0.47
100	1.90	1.43	1.28	1.08	0.94
200	3.80	2.86	2.56	2.15	1.88
300	5.70	4.28	3.84	3.22	2.82
400	7.60	5.71	5.12	4.30	3.75
500	9.50	7.13	6.39	5.37	4.69
1,000	18.99	14.26	12.78	10.73	9.38
2,000	37.98	28.51	25.56	21.46	18.75
3,000	56.96	42.76	38.34	32.19	28.13
4,000	75.95	57.01	51.12	42.92	37.50
5,000	94.93	71.26	63.90	53.65	46.88
10,000	189.86	142.52	127.80	107.30	93.75
20,000	379.72	285.04	255.59	214.59	187.50
30,000	569.58	427.56	383.38	321.88	281.25
40,000	759.44	570.07	511.18	429.17	375.00
50,000	949.30	712.59	638.97	536.46	468.75
100,000	1898.60	1425.17	1277.93	1072.92	937.49
125,000	2373.25	1781.46	1597.42	1341.15	1171.86
150,000	2847.90	2137.76	1916.90	1609.38	1406.23
175,000	3322.55	2494.05	2236.38	1877.61	1640.60
200,000	3797.20	2850.34	2555.86	2145.84	1874.97
225,000	4271.85	3206.63	2875.34	2414.07	2109.34
250,000	4746.50	3562.92	3194.83	2682.30	2343.71
275,000	5221.15	3919.22	3514.31	2950.53	2578.08
300,000	5695.80	4275.51	3833.79	3218.76	2812.45
325,000	6170.45	4631.80	4153.27	3486.99	3046.82
350,000	6645.10	4988.09	4472.75	3755.21	3281.19
375,000	7119.75	5344.38	4792.24	4023.44	3515.56
400,000	7594.40	5700.68	5111.72	4291.67	3749.93
425,000	8069.05	6056.97	5431.20	4559.90	3984.30
450,000	8543.70	6413.26	5750.68	4828.13	4218.67
475,000	9018.35	6769.55	6070.16	5096.36	4453.04
500,000	9493.00	7125.84	6389.65	5364.59	4687.41
525,000	9967.65	7482.14	6709.13	5632.82	4921.78
550,000	10442.30	7838.43	7028.61	5901.05	5156.15
575,000	10916.95	8194.72	7348.09	6169.28	5390.52
600,000	11391.60	8551.01	7667.57	6437.51	5624.89
625,000	11866.24	8907.30	7987.06	6705.74	5859.26
650,000	12340.89	9263.60	8306.54	6973.97	6093.64
675,000	12815.54	9619.89	8626.02	7242.19	6328.01
700,000	13290.19	9976.18	8945.50	7510.42	6562.38
725,000	13764.84	10332.47	9264.98	7778.65	6796.75
750,000	14239.49	10688.76	9584.47	8046.88	7031.12
775,000	14714.14	11045.06	9903.95	8315.11	7265.49
800,000	15188.79	11401.35	10223.43	8583.34	7499.86
825,000	15663.44	11757.64	10542.91	8851.57	7734.23
850,000	16138.09	12113.93	10862.39	9119.80	7968.60
875,000	16612.74	12470.22	11181.88	9388.03	8202.97
900,000	17087.39	12826.52	11501.36	9656.26	8437.34

Table 7   113

5.25%   Monthly Payment Loans

Loan Amount	Amortization Period in Years				
	15	16	17	18	20
10	0.09	0.08	0.08	0.08	0.07
20	0.17	0.16	0.15	0.15	0.14
30	0.25	0.24	0.23	0.22	0.21
40	0.33	0.31	0.30	0.29	0.27
50	0.41	0.39	0.38	0.36	0.34
100	0.81	0.78	0.75	0.72	0.68
200	1.61	1.55	1.49	1.44	1.35
300	2.42	2.32	2.23	2.15	2.03
400	3.22	3.09	2.97	2.87	2.70
500	4.02	3.86	3.72	3.59	3.37
1,000	8.04	7.71	7.43	7.17	6.74
2,000	16.08	15.42	14.85	14.34	13.48
3,000	24.12	23.13	22.27	21.50	20.22
4,000	32.16	30.84	29.69	28.67	26.96
5,000	40.20	38.55	37.11	35.84	33.70
10,000	80.39	77.10	74.21	71.67	67.39
20,000	160.78	154.19	148.42	143.33	134.77
30,000	241.17	231.28	222.62	214.99	202.16
40,000	321.56	308.38	296.83	286.65	269.54
50,000	401.94	385.47	371.04	358.31	336.93
100,000	803.88	770.93	742.07	716.61	673.85
125,000	1004.85	963.67	927.59	895.76	842.31
150,000	1205.82	1156.40	1113.10	1074.91	1010.77
175,000	1406.79	1349.13	1298.62	1254.06	1179.23
200,000	1607.76	1541.86	1484.13	1433.21	1347.69
225,000	1808.73	1734.59	1669.65	1612.36	1516.15
250,000	2009.70	1927.33	1855.17	1791.52	1684.62
275,000	2210.67	2120.06	2040.68	1970.67	1853.08
300,000	2411.64	2312.79	2226.20	2149.82	2021.54
325,000	2612.61	2505.52	2411.71	2328.97	2190.00
350,000	2813.58	2698.25	2597.23	2508.12	2358.46
375,000	3014.55	2890.99	2782.75	2687.27	2526.92
400,000	3215.52	3083.72	2968.26	2866.42	2695.38
425,000	3416.49	3276.45	3153.78	3045.57	2863.84
450,000	3617.45	3469.18	3339.30	3224.72	3032.30
475,000	3818.42	3661.91	3524.81	3403.87	3200.76
500,000	4019.39	3854.65	3710.33	3583.03	3369.23
525,000	4220.36	4047.38	3895.84	3762.18	3537.69
550,000	4421.33	4240.11	4081.36	3941.33	3706.15
575,000	4622.30	4432.84	4266.88	4120.48	3874.61
600,000	4823.27	4625.57	4452.39	4299.63	4043.07
625,000	5024.24	4818.31	4637.91	4478.78	4211.53
650,000	5225.21	5011.04	4823.42	4657.93	4379.99
675,000	5426.18	5203.77	5008.94	4837.08	4548.45
700,000	5627.15	5396.50	5194.46	5016.23	4716.91
725,000	5828.12	5589.23	5379.97	5195.38	4885.38
750,000	6029.09	5781.97	5565.49	5374.54	5053.84
775,000	6230.06	5974.70	5751.00	5553.69	5222.30
800,000	6431.03	6167.43	5936.52	5732.84	5390.76
825,000	6632.00	6360.16	6122.04	5911.99	5559.22
850,000	6832.97	6552.89	6307.55	6091.14	5727.68
875,000	7033.94	6745.63	6493.07	6270.29	5896.14
900,000	7234.90	6938.36	6678.59	6449.44	6064.60

Monthly Payment Loans 5.25%

Loan Amount	Amortization Period in Years				
	21	22	23	24	25
10	0.07	0.07	0.07	0.07	0.06
20	0.14	0.13	0.13	0.13	0.12
30	0.20	0.20	0.19	0.19	0.18
40	0.27	0.26	0.25	0.25	0.24
50	0.33	0.32	0.32	0.31	0.30
100	0.66	0.64	0.63	0.62	0.60
200	1.32	1.28	1.25	1.23	1.20
300	1.97	1.92	1.88	1.84	1.80
400	2.63	2.56	2.50	2.45	2.40
500	3.28	3.20	3.13	3.06	3.00
1,000	6.56	6.40	6.25	6.12	6.00
2,000	13.12	12.79	12.50	12.23	11.99
3,000	19.68	19.19	18.75	18.35	17.98
4,000	26.24	25.58	25.00	24.46	23.97
5,000	32.79	31.98	31.24	30.58	29.97
10,000	65.58	63.95	62.48	61.15	59.93
20,000	131.16	127.90	124.96	122.29	119.85
30,000	196.73	191.85	187.43	183.43	179.78
40,000	262.31	255.80	249.91	244.57	239.70
50,000	327.89	319.75	312.39	305.71	299.63
100,000	655.77	639.49	624.77	611.41	599.25
125,000	819.71	799.36	780.96	764.26	749.06
150,000	983.65	959.23	937.15	917.11	898.88
175,000	1147.59	1119.10	1093.34	1069.96	1048.69
200,000	1311.53	1278.97	1249.53	1222.81	1198.50
225,000	1475.47	1438.84	1405.72	1375.67	1348.31
250,000	1639.42	1598.71	1561.91	1528.52	1498.12
275,000	1803.36	1758.58	1718.10	1681.37	1647.94
300,000	1967.30	1918.45	1874.09	1834.22	1797.75
325,000	2131.24	2078.32	2030.48	1987.07	1947.56
350,000	2295.18	2238.19	2186.67	2139.92	2097.37
375,000	2459.12	2398.06	2342.86	2292.77	2247.18
400,000	2623.06	2557.93	2499.05	2445.62	2397.00
425,000	2787.00	2717.80	2655.24	2598.47	2546.81
450,000	2950.94	2877.67	2811.43	2751.33	2696.62
475,000	3114.88	3037.54	2967.62	2904.18	2846.43
500,000	3278.83	3197.41	3123.81	3057.03	2996.24
525,000	3442.77	3357.28	3280.00	3209.88	3146.06
550,000	3606.71	3517.15	3436.19	3362.73	3295.87
575,000	3770.65	3677.02	3592.38	3515.58	3445.68
600,000	3934.59	3836.90	3748.57	3668.43	3595.49
625,000	4098.53	3996.77	3904.76	3821.28	3745.30
650,000	4262.47	4156.64	4060.95	3974.14	3895.12
675,000	4426.41	4316.51	4217.14	4126.99	4044.93
700,000	4590.35	4476.38	4373.33	4279.84	4194.74
725,000	4754.29	4636.25	4529.52	4432.69	4344.55
750,000	4918.24	4796.12	4685.71	4585.54	4494.36
775,000	5082.18	4955.99	4841.90	4738.39	4644.17
800,000	5246.12	5115.86	4998.09	4891.24	4793.99
825,000	5410.06	5275.73	5154.28	5044.09	4943.80
850,000	5574.00	5435.60	5310.47	5196.94	5093.61
875,000	5737.94	5595.47	5466.66	5349.80	5243.42
900,000	5901.88	5755.34	5622.85	5502.65	5393.23

Table 7   115

5.25%   **Monthly Payment Loans**

Amortization Period in Years

Loan Amount	26	27	28	29	30
10	0.06	0.06	0.06	0.06	0.06
20	0.12	0.12	0.12	0.12	0.12
30	0.18	0.18	0.18	0.17	0.17
40	0.24	0.24	0.23	0.23	0.23
50	0.30	0.29	0.29	0.29	0.28
100	0.59	0.58	0.57	0.57	0.56
200	1.18	1.16	1.14	1.13	1.11
300	1.77	1.74	1.71	1.69	1.66
400	2.36	2.32	2.28	2.25	2.21
500	2.95	2.89	2.85	2.81	2.77
1,000	5.89	5.78	5.69	5.61	5.53
2,000	11.77	11.56	11.38	11.21	11.05
3,000	17.65	17.34	17.07	16.81	16.57
4,000	23.53	23.12	22.75	22.41	22.09
5,000	29.41	28.90	28.44	28.01	27.62
10,000	58.82	57.80	56.87	56.02	55.23
20,000	117.64	115.60	113.74	112.03	110.45
30,000	176.45	173.40	170.61	168.04	165.67
40,000	235.27	231.20	227.47	224.05	220.89
50,000	294.08	289.00	284.34	280.06	276.11
100,000	588.16	578.00	568.68	560.11	552.21
125,000	735.19	722.50	710.85	700.13	690.26
150,000	882.23	866.99	853.01	840.16	828.31
175,000	1029.27	1011.49	995.18	980.18	966.36
200,000	1176.31	1155.99	1137.35	1120.21	1104.41
225,000	1323.34	1300.49	1279.52	1260.23	1242.46
250,000	1470.38	1444.99	1421.69	1400.26	1380.51
275,000	1617.42	1589.48	1563.85	1540.28	1518.57
300,000	1764.46	1733.98	1706.02	1680.31	1656.62
325,000	1911.49	1878.48	1848.19	1820.33	1794.67
350,000	2058.53	2022.98	1990.36	1960.36	1932.72
375,000	2205.57	2167.48	2132.53	2100.39	2070.77
400,000	2352.61	2311.97	2274.69	2240.41	2208.82
425,000	2499.64	2456.47	2416.86	2380.44	2346.87
450,000	2646.68	2600.97	2559.03	2520.46	2484.92
475,000	2793.72	2745.47	2701.20	2660.49	2622.97
500,000	2940.76	2889.97	2843.37	2800.51	2761.02
525,000	3087.79	3034.46	2985.53	2940.54	2899.07
550,000	3234.83	3178.96	3127.70	3080.56	3037.13
575,000	3381.87	3323.46	3269.87	3220.59	3175.18
600,000	3528.91	3467.96	3412.04	3360.61	3313.23
625,000	3675.94	3612.46	3554.21	3500.64	3451.28
650,000	3822.98	3756.95	3696.37	3640.66	3589.33
675,000	3970.02	3901.45	3838.54	3780.69	3727.38
700,000	4117.06	4045.95	3980.71	3920.72	3865.43
725,000	4264.09	4190.45	4122.88	4060.74	4003.48
750,000	4411.13	4334.95	4265.05	4200.77	4141.53
775,000	4558.17	4479.44	4407.21	4340.79	4279.58
800,000	4705.21	4623.94	4549.38	4480.82	4417.63
825,000	4852.24	4768.44	4691.55	4620.84	4555.69
850,000	4999.28	4912.94	4833.72	4760.87	4693.74
875,000	5146.32	5057.44	4975.89	4900.89	4831.79
900,000	5293.36	5201.94	5118.05	5040.92	4969.84

Monthly Payment Loans 5.50%

Loan Amount	Amortization Period in Years				
	5	7	8	10	12
10	0.20	0.15	0.13	0.11	0.10
20	0.39	0.29	0.26	0.22	0.20
30	0.58	0.44	0.39	0.33	0.29
40	0.77	0.58	0.52	0.44	0.39
50	0.96	0.72	0.65	0.55	0.48
100	1.92	1.44	1.29	1.09	0.96
200	3.83	2.88	2.58	2.18	1.91
300	5.74	4.32	3.87	3.26	2.86
400	7.65	5.75	5.16	4.35	3.81
500	9.56	7.19	6.45	5.43	4.76
1,000	19.11	14.38	12.90	10.86	9.51
2,000	38.21	28.75	25.80	21.71	19.01
3,000	57.31	43.12	38.70	32.56	28.51
4,000	76.41	57.49	51.60	43.42	38.01
5,000	95.51	71.86	64.50	54.27	47.51
10,000	191.02	143.71	129.00	108.53	95.02
20,000	382.03	287.41	257.99	217.06	190.04
30,000	573.04	431.11	386.98	325.58	285.06
40,000	764.05	574.81	515.98	434.11	380.07
50,000	955.06	718.51	644.97	542.64	475.09
100,000	1910.12	1437.01	1289.94	1085.27	950.18
125,000	2387.65	1796.26	1612.42	1356.58	1187.72
150,000	2865.18	2155.51	1934.90	1627.90	1425.26
175,000	3342.71	2514.76	2257.39	1899.21	1662.81
200,000	3820.24	2874.01	2579.87	2170.53	1900.35
225,000	4297.77	3233.26	2902.35	2441.85	2137.89
250,000	4775.30	3592.52	3224.84	2713.16	2375.44
275,000	5252.82	3951.77	3547.32	2984.48	2612.98
300,000	5730.35	4311.02	3869.80	3255.79	2850.52
325,000	6207.88	4670.27	4192.28	3527.11	3088.06
350,000	6685.41	5029.52	4514.77	3798.42	3325.61
375,000	7162.94	5388.77	4837.25	4069.74	3563.15
400,000	7640.47	5748.02	5159.73	4341.06	3800.69
425,000	8118.00	6107.27	5482.22	4612.37	4038.24
450,000	8595.53	6466.52	5804.70	4883.69	4275.78
475,000	9073.06	6825.78	6127.18	5155.00	4513.32
500,000	9550.59	7185.03	6449.67	5426.32	4750.87
525,000	10028.12	7544.28	6772.15	5697.63	4988.41
550,000	10505.64	7903.53	7094.63	5968.95	5225.95
575,000	10983.17	8262.78	7417.12	6240.27	5463.49
600,000	11460.70	8622.03	7739.60	6511.58	5701.04
625,000	11938.23	8981.28	8062.08	6782.90	5938.58
650,000	12415.76	9340.53	8384.56	7054.21	6176.12
675,000	12893.29	9699.78	8707.05	7325.53	6413.67
700,000	13370.82	10059.03	9029.53	7596.84	6651.21
725,000	13848.35	10418.29	9352.01	7868.16	6888.75
750,000	14325.88	10777.54	9674.50	8139.48	7126.30
775,000	14803.41	11136.79	9996.98	8410.79	7363.84
800,000	15280.93	11496.04	10319.46	8682.11	7601.38
825,000	15758.46	11855.29	10641.95	8953.42	7838.93
850,000	16235.99	12214.54	10964.43	9224.74	8076.47
875,000	16713.52	12573.79	11286.91	9496.05	8314.01
900,000	17191.05	12933.04	11609.39	9767.37	8551.55

Table 7   117

5.50%   **Monthly Payment Loans**

Amortization Period in Years

Loan Amount	15	16	17	18	20
10	0.09	0.08	0.08	0.08	0.07
20	0.17	0.16	0.16	0.15	0.14
30	0.25	0.24	0.23	0.22	0.21
40	0.33	0.32	0.31	0.30	0.28
50	0.41	0.40	0.38	0.37	0.35
100	0.82	0.79	0.76	0.74	0.69
200	1.64	1.57	1.52	1.47	1.38
300	2.46	2.36	2.27	2.20	2.07
400	3.27	3.14	3.03	2.93	2.76
500	4.09	3.93	3.78	3.66	3.44
1,000	8.18	7.85	7.56	7.31	6.88
2,000	16.35	15.69	15.12	14.61	13.76
3,000	24.52	23.53	22.67	21.91	20.64
4,000	32.69	31.38	30.23	29.22	27.52
5,000	40.86	39.22	37.79	36.52	34.40
10,000	81.71	78.44	75.57	73.04	68.79
20,000	163.42	156.87	151.13	146.07	137.58
30,000	245.13	235.30	226.69	219.10	206.37
40,000	326.84	313.73	302.25	292.13	275.16
50,000	408.55	392.16	377.81	365.16	343.95
100,000	817.09	784.31	755.61	730.32	687.89
125,000	1021.36	980.38	944.52	912.90	859.86
150,000	1225.63	1176.46	1133.42	1095.48	1031.84
175,000	1429.90	1372.54	1322.32	1278.06	1203.81
200,000	1634.17	1568.61	1511.22	1460.64	1375.78
225,000	1838.44	1764.69	1700.13	1643.22	1547.75
250,000	2042.71	1960.76	1889.03	1825.80	1719.72
275,000	2246.98	2156.84	2077.93	2008.37	1891.70
300,000	2451.26	2352.92	2266.83	2190.95	2063.67
325,000	2655.53	2548.99	2455.73	2373.53	2235.64
350,000	2859.80	2745.07	2644.64	2556.11	2407.61
375,000	3064.07	2941.14	2833.54	2738.69	2579.58
400,000	3268.34	3137.22	3022.44	2921.27	2751.55
425,000	3472.61	3333.30	3211.34	3103.85	2923.53
450,000	3676.88	3529.37	3400.25	3286.43	3095.50
475,000	3881.15	3725.45	3589.15	3469.01	3267.47
500,000	4085.42	3921.52	3778.05	3651.59	3439.44
525,000	4289.69	4117.60	3966.95	3834.17	3611.41
550,000	4493.96	4313.68	4155.86	4016.74	3783.39
575,000	4698.23	4509.75	4344.76	4199.32	3955.36
600,000	4902.51	4705.83	4533.66	4381.90	4127.33
625,000	5106.78	4901.90	4722.56	4564.48	4299.30
650,000	5311.05	5097.98	4911.46	4747.06	4471.27
675,000	5515.32	5294.06	5100.37	4929.64	4643.24
700,000	5719.59	5490.13	5289.27	5112.22	4815.22
725,000	5923.86	5686.21	5478.17	5294.80	4987.19
750,000	6128.13	5882.28	5667.07	5477.38	5159.16
775,000	6332.40	6078.36	5855.98	5659.96	5331.13
800,000	6536.67	6274.44	6044.88	5842.54	5503.10
825,000	6740.94	6470.51	6233.78	6025.11	5675.08
850,000	6945.21	6666.59	6422.68	6207.69	5847.05
875,000	7149.49	6862.66	6611.59	6390.27	6019.02
900,000	7353.76	7058.74	6800.49	6572.85	6190.99

Monthly Payment Loans   <u>5.50%</u>

Loan Amount	\multicolumn{5}{c}{Amortization Period in Years}				
	21	22	23	24	25
10	0.07	0.07	0.07	0.07	0.07
20	0.14	0.14	0.13	0.13	0.13
30	0.21	0.20	0.20	0.19	0.19
40	0.27	0.27	0.26	0.26	0.25
50	0.34	0.33	0.32	0.32	0.31
100	0.67	0.66	0.64	0.63	0.62
200	1.34	1.31	1.28	1.26	1.23
300	2.01	1.97	1.92	1.88	1.85
400	2.68	2.62	2.56	2.51	2.46
500	3.35	3.27	3.20	3.14	3.08
1,000	6.70	6.54	6.40	6.27	6.15
2,000	13.40	13.08	12.79	12.53	12.29
3,000	20.10	19.62	19.18	18.79	18.43
4,000	26.80	26.16	25.58	25.05	24.57
5,000	33.50	32.70	31.97	31.31	30.71
10,000	67.00	65.39	63.93	62.61	61.41
20,000	134.00	130.77	127.86	125.22	122.82
30,000	201.00	196.16	191.79	187.83	184.23
40,000	267.99	261.54	255.72	250.44	245.64
50,000	334.99	326.93	319.65	313.05	307.05
100,000	669.98	653.85	639.29	626.09	614.09
125,000	837.47	817.32	799.11	782.62	767.61
150,000	1004.96	980.78	958.94	939.14	921.14
175,000	1172.45	1144.24	1118.76	1095.66	1074.66
200,000	1339.95	1307.70	1278.58	1252.18	1228.18
225,000	1507.44	1471.17	1438.40	1408.71	1381.70
250,000	1674.93	1634.63	1598.22	1565.23	1535.22
275,000	1842.42	1798.09	1758.05	1721.75	1688.75
300,000	2009.92	1961.55	1917.87	1878.27	1842.27
325,000	2177.41	2125.01	2077.69	2034.79	1995.79
350,000	2344.90	2288.48	2237.51	2191.32	2149.31
375,000	2512.39	2451.94	2397.33	2347.84	2302.83
400,000	2679.89	2615.40	2557.16	2504.36	2456.35
425,000	2847.38	2778.86	2716.98	2660.88	2609.88
450,000	3014.87	2942.33	2876.80	2817.41	2763.40
475,000	3182.36	3105.79	3036.62	2973.93	2916.92
500,000	3349.86	3269.25	3196.44	3130.45	3070.44
525,000	3517.35	3432.71	3356.27	3286.97	3223.96
550,000	3684.84	3596.18	3516.09	3443.49	3377.49
575,000	3852.33	3759.64	3675.91	3600.02	3531.01
600,000	4019.83	3923.10	3835.73	3756.54	3684.53
625,000	4187.32	4086.56	3995.55	3913.06	3838.05
650,000	4354.81	4250.02	4155.37	4069.58	3991.57
675,000	4522.30	4413.49	4315.20	4226.11	4145.10
700,000	4689.80	4576.95	4475.02	4382.63	4298.62
725,000	4857.29	4740.41	4634.84	4539.15	4452.14
750,000	5024.78	4903.87	4794.66	4695.67	4605.66
775,000	5192.27	5067.34	4954.48	4852.19	4759.18
800,000	5359.77	5230.80	5114.31	5008.72	4912.70
825,000	5527.26	5394.26	5274.13	5165.24	5066.23
850,000	5694.75	5557.72	5433.95	5321.76	5219.75
875,000	5862.24	5721.18	5593.77	5478.28	5373.27
900,000	6029.74	5884.65	5753.59	5634.81	5526.79

Table 7   119

5.50%   Monthly Payment Loans

Amortization Period in Years

Loan Amount	26	27	28	29	30
10	0.07	0.06	0.06	0.06	0.06
20	0.13	0.12	0.12	0.12	0.12
30	0.19	0.18	0.18	0.18	0.18
40	0.25	0.24	0.24	0.24	0.23
50	0.31	0.30	0.30	0.29	0.29
100	0.61	0.60	0.59	0.58	0.57
200	1.21	1.19	1.17	1.16	1.14
300	1.81	1.78	1.76	1.73	1.71
400	2.42	2.38	2.34	2.31	2.28
500	3.02	2.97	2.92	2.88	2.84
1,000	6.04	5.94	5.84	5.76	5.68
2,000	12.07	11.87	11.68	11.52	11.36
3,000	18.10	17.80	17.52	17.27	17.04
4,000	24.13	23.73	23.36	23.03	22.72
5,000	30.16	29.66	29.20	28.78	28.39
10,000	60.32	59.32	58.40	57.56	56.78
20,000	120.63	118.63	116.80	115.11	113.56
30,000	180.95	177.95	175.19	172.67	170.34
40,000	241.26	237.26	233.59	230.22	227.12
50,000	301.58	296.57	291.99	287.78	283.90
100,000	603.15	593.14	583.97	575.55	567.79
125,000	753.93	741.43	729.96	719.43	709.74
150,000	904.72	889.71	875.95	863.32	851.69
175,000	1055.51	1037.99	1021.95	1007.20	993.64
200,000	1206.29	1186.28	1167.94	1151.09	1135.58
225,000	1357.08	1334.56	1313.93	1294.97	1277.53
250,000	1507.86	1482.85	1459.92	1438.86	1419.48
275,000	1658.65	1631.13	1605.91	1582.75	1561.42
300,000	1809.43	1779.42	1751.90	1726.63	1703.37
325,000	1960.22	1927.70	1897.89	1870.52	1845.32
350,000	2111.01	2075.98	2043.89	2014.40	1987.27
375,000	2261.79	2224.27	2189.88	2158.29	2129.21
400,000	2412.58	2372.55	2335.87	2302.17	2271.16
425,000	2563.36	2520.84	2481.86	2446.06	2413.11
450,000	2714.15	2669.12	2627.85	2589.94	2555.06
475,000	2864.94	2817.40	2773.84	2733.83	2697.00
500,000	3015.72	2965.69	2919.83	2877.72	2838.95
525,000	3166.51	3113.97	3065.83	3021.60	2980.90
550,000	3317.29	3262.26	3211.82	3165.49	3122.84
575,000	3468.08	3410.54	3357.81	3309.37	3264.79
600,000	3618.86	3558.83	3503.80	3453.26	3406.74
625,000	3769.65	3707.11	3649.79	3597.14	3548.69
650,000	3920.44	3855.39	3795.78	3741.03	3690.63
675,000	4071.22	4003.68	3941.77	3884.91	3832.58
700,000	4222.01	4151.96	4087.77	4028.80	3974.53
725,000	4372.79	4300.25	4233.76	4172.68	4116.48
750,000	4523.58	4448.53	4379.75	4316.57	4258.42
775,000	4674.36	4596.82	4525.74	4460.46	4400.37
800,000	4825.15	4745.10	4671.73	4604.34	4542.32
825,000	4975.94	4893.38	4817.72	4748.23	4684.26
850,000	5126.72	5041.67	4963.71	4892.11	4826.21
875,000	5277.51	5189.95	5109.71	5036.00	4968.16
900,000	5428.29	5338.24	5255.70	5179.88	5110.11

Monthly Payment Loans   **5.75%**

Loan Amount	Amortization Period in Years				
	5	7	8	10	12
10	0.20	0.15	0.14	0.11	0.10
20	0.39	0.29	0.27	0.22	0.20
30	0.58	0.44	0.40	0.33	0.29
40	0.77	0.58	0.53	0.44	0.39
50	0.97	0.73	0.66	0.55	0.49
100	1.93	1.45	1.31	1.10	0.97
200	3.85	2.90	2.61	2.20	1.93
300	5.77	4.35	3.91	3.30	2.89
400	7.69	5.80	5.21	4.40	3.86
500	9.61	7.25	6.52	5.49	4.82
1,000	19.22	14.49	13.03	10.98	9.63
2,000	38.44	28.98	26.05	21.96	19.26
3,000	57.66	43.47	39.07	32.94	28.89
4,000	76.87	57.96	52.09	43.91	38.52
5,000	96.09	72.45	65.11	54.89	48.15
10,000	192.17	144.90	130.21	109.77	96.30
20,000	384.34	289.79	260.41	219.54	192.60
30,000	576.51	434.68	390.61	329.31	288.89
40,000	768.68	579.57	520.81	439.08	385.19
50,000	960.84	724.46	651.01	548.85	481.49
100,000	1921.68	1448.91	1302.01	1097.70	962.97
125,000	2402.10	1811.13	1627.51	1372.12	1203.71
150,000	2882.52	2173.36	1953.01	1646.54	1444.45
175,000	3362.94	2535.58	2278.51	1920.97	1685.19
200,000	3843.36	2897.81	2604.01	2195.39	1925.93
225,000	4323.78	3260.03	2929.51	2469.81	2166.67
250,000	4804.20	3622.26	3255.01	2744.24	2407.41
275,000	5284.62	3984.48	3580.52	3018.66	2648.15
300,000	5765.04	4346.71	3906.02	3293.08	2888.89
325,000	6245.45	4708.93	4231.52	3567.50	3129.63
350,000	6725.87	5071.16	4557.02	3841.93	3370.37
375,000	7206.29	5433.38	4882.52	4116.35	3611.11
400,000	7686.71	5795.61	5208.02	4390.77	3851.85
425,000	8167.13	6157.83	5533.52	4665.20	4092.59
450,000	8647.55	6520.06	5859.02	4939.62	4333.33
475,000	9127.97	6882.28	6184.52	5214.04	4574.07
500,000	9608.39	7244.51	6510.02	5488.47	4814.81
525,000	10088.81	7606.73	6835.53	5762.89	5055.55
550,000	10569.23	7968.96	7161.03	6037.31	5296.30
575,000	11049.65	8331.18	7486.53	6311.74	5537.04
600,000	11530.07	8693.41	7812.03	6586.16	5777.78
625,000	12010.49	9055.63	8137.53	6860.58	6018.52
650,000	12490.90	9417.86	8463.03	7135.00	6259.26
675,000	12971.32	9780.08	8788.53	7409.43	6500.00
700,000	13451.74	10142.31	9114.03	7683.85	6740.74
725,000	13932.16	10504.53	9439.53	7958.27	6961.48
750,000	14412.58	10866.76	9765.03	8232.70	7222.22
775,000	14893.00	11228.98	10090.53	8507.12	7462.96
800,000	15373.42	11591.21	10416.04	8781.54	7703.70
825,000	15853.84	11953.43	10741.54	9055.97	7944.44
850,000	16334.26	12315.66	11067.04	9330.39	8185.18
875,000	16814.68	12677.88	11392.54	9604.81	8425.92
900,000	17295.10	13040.11	11718.04	9879.23	8666.66

Table 7   121

5.75%   **Monthly Payment Loans**

Amortization Period in Years

Loan Amount	15	16	17	18	20
10	0.09	0.08	0.08	0.08	0.08
20	0.17	0.16	0.16	0.15	0.15
30	0.25	0.24	0.24	0.23	0.22
40	0.34	0.32	0.31	0.30	0.29
50	0.42	0.40	0.39	0.38	0.36
100	0.84	0.80	0.77	0.75	0.71
200	1.67	1.60	1.54	1.49	1.41
300	2.50	2.40	2.31	2.24	2.11
400	3.33	3.20	3.08	2.98	2.81
500	4.16	3.99	3.85	3.73	3.52
1,000	8.31	7.98	7.70	7.45	7.03
2,000	16.61	15.96	15.39	14.89	14.05
3,000	24.92	23.94	23.08	22.33	21.07
4,000	33.22	31.92	30.78	29.77	28.09
5,000	41.53	39.90	38.47	37.21	35.11
10,000	83.05	79.79	76.93	74.42	70.21
20,000	166.09	159.57	153.86	148.84	140.42
30,000	249.13	239.35	230.79	223.26	210.63
40,000	332.17	319.13	307.72	297.67	280.84
50,000	415.21	398.91	384.65	372.09	351.05
100,000	830.42	797.81	769.29	744.17	702.09
125,000	1038.02	997.26	961.62	930.22	877.61
150,000	1245.62	1196.72	1153.94	1116.26	1053.13
175,000	1453.22	1396.17	1346.26	1302.30	1228.65
200,000	1660.83	1595.62	1538.58	1488.34	1404.17
225,000	1868.43	1795.07	1730.90	1674.39	1579.69
250,000	2076.03	1994.52	1923.23	1860.43	1755.21
275,000	2283.63	2193.98	2115.55	2046.47	1930.73
300,000	2491.24	2393.43	2307.87	2232.51	2106.26
325,000	2698.84	2592.88	2500.19	2418.56	2281.78
350,000	2906.44	2792.33	2692.51	2604.60	2457.30
375,000	3114.04	2991.78	2884.84	2790.64	2632.82
400,000	3321.65	3191.23	3077.16	2976.68	2808.34
425,000	3529.25	3390.69	3269.48	3162.73	2983.86
450,000	3736.85	3590.14	3461.80	3348.77	3159.38
475,000	3944.45	3789.59	3654.12	3534.81	3334.90
500,000	4152.06	3989.04	3846.45	3720.85	3510.42
525,000	4359.66	4188.49	4038.77	3906.90	3685.94
550,000	4567.26	4387.95	4231.09	4092.94	3861.46
575,000	4774.86	4587.40	4423.41	4278.98	4036.99
600,000	4982.47	4786.85	4615.73	4465.02	4212.51
625,000	5190.07	4986.30	4808.06	4651.06	4388.03
650,000	5397.67	5185.75	5000.38	4837.11	4563.55
675,000	5605.27	5385.21	5192.70	5023.15	4739.07
700,000	5812.88	5584.66	5385.02	5209.19	4914.59
725,000	6020.48	5784.11	5577.35	5395.23	5090.11
750,000	6228.08	5983.56	5769.67	5581.28	5265.63
775,000	6435.68	6183.01	5961.99	5767.32	5441.15
800,000	6643.29	6382.46	6154.31	5953.36	5616.67
825,000	6850.89	6581.92	6346.63	6139.40	5792.19
850,000	7058.49	6781.37	6538.96	6325.45	5967.71
875,000	7266.09	6980.82	6731.28	6511.49	6143.24
900,000	7473.70	7180.27	6923.60	6697.53	6318.76

Monthly Payment Loans   5.75%

Loan Amount	Amortization Period in Years				
	21	22	23	24	25
10	0.07	0.07	0.07	0.07	0.07
20	0.14	0.14	0.14	0.13	0.13
30	0.21	0.21	0.20	0.20	0.19
40	0.28	0.27	0.27	0.26	0.26
50	0.35	0.34	0.33	0.33	0.32
100	0.69	0.67	0.66	0.65	0.63
200	1.37	1.34	1.31	1.29	1.26
300	2.06	2.01	1.97	1.93	1.89
400	2.74	2.68	2.62	2.57	2.52
500	3.43	3.35	3.27	3.21	3.15
1,000	6.85	6.69	6.54	6.41	6.30
2,000	13.69	13.37	13.08	12.82	12.59
3,000	20.54	20.06	19.62	19.23	18.88
4,000	27.38	26.74	26.16	25.64	25.17
5,000	34.22	33.42	32.70	32.05	31.46
10,000	68.44	66.84	65.40	64.10	62.92
20,000	136.87	133.68	130.80	128.19	125.83
30,000	205.31	200.52	196.20	192.29	188.74
40,000	273.74	267.36	261.60	256.38	251.65
50,000	342.17	334.20	327.00	320.48	314.56
100,000	684.34	668.39	653.99	640.95	629.11
125,000	855.42	835.48	817.48	801.19	786.39
150,000	1026.51	1002.58	980.98	961.43	943.66
175,000	1197.59	1169.67	1144.48	1121.66	1100.94
200,000	1368.68	1336.77	1307.97	1281.90	1258.22
225,000	1539.76	1503.86	1471.47	1442.14	1415.49
250,000	1710.84	1670.96	1634.96	1602.37	1572.77
275,000	1881.93	1838.05	1798.46	1762.61	1730.05
300,000	2053.01	2005.15	1961.96	1922.85	1887.32
325,000	2224.09	2172.24	2125.45	2083.08	2044.60
350,000	2395.18	2339.34	2288.95	2243.32	2201.88
375,000	2566.26	2506.43	2452.44	2403.56	2359.15
400,000	2737.35	2673.53	2615.94	2563.80	2516.43
425,000	2908.43	2840.62	2779.44	2724.03	2673.71
450,000	3079.51	3007.72	2942.93	2884.27	2830.98
475,000	3250.60	3174.81	3106.43	3044.51	2988.26
500,000	3421.68	3341.91	3269.92	3204.74	3145.54
525,000	3592.76	3509.00	3433.42	3364.98	3302.81
550,000	3763.85	3676.10	3596.92	3525.22	3460.09
575,000	3934.93	3843.19	3760.41	3685.45	3617.37
600,000	4106.02	4010.29	3923.91	3845.69	3774.64
625,000	4277.10	4177.38	4087.40	4005.93	3931.92
650,000	4448.18	4344.48	4250.90	4166.16	4089.20
675,000	4619.27	4511.58	4414.40	4326.40	4246.47
700,000	4790.35	4678.67	4577.89	4486.64	4403.75
725,000	4961.43	4845.77	4741.39	4646.88	4561.03
750,000	5132.52	5012.86	4904.88	4807.11	4718.30
775,000	5303.60	5179.96	5068.38	4967.35	4875.58
800,000	5474.69	5347.05	5231.88	5127.59	5032.86
825,000	5645.77	5514.15	5395.37	5287.82	5190.13
850,000	5816.85	5681.24	5558.87	5448.06	5347.41
875,000	5987.94	5848.34	5722.36	5608.30	5504.69
900,000	6159.02	6015.43	5885.86	5768.53	5661.96

Table 7   123

5.75%   Monthly Payment Loans

Amortization Period in Years

Loan Amount	26	27	28	29	30
10	0.07	0.07	0.06	0.06	0.06
20	0.13	0.13	0.12	0.12	0.12
30	0.19	0.19	0.18	0.18	0.18
40	0.25	0.25	0.24	0.24	0.24
50	0.31	0.31	0.30	0.30	0.30
100	0.62	0.61	0.60	0.60	0.59
200	1.24	1.22	1.20	1.19	1.17
300	1.86	1.83	1.80	1.78	1.76
400	2.48	2.44	2.40	2.37	2.34
500	3.10	3.05	3.00	2.96	2.92
1,000	6.19	6.09	6.00	5.92	5.84
2,000	12.37	12.17	11.99	11.83	11.68
3,000	18.55	18.26	17.99	17.74	17.51
4,000	24.74	24.34	23.98	23.65	23.35
5,000	30.92	30.43	29.98	29.56	29.18
10,000	61.84	60.85	59.95	59.12	58.36
20,000	123.67	121.70	119.90	118.24	116.72
30,000	185.50	182.55	179.84	177.36	175.08
40,000	247.33	243.39	239.79	236.48	233.43
50,000	309.17	304.24	299.73	295.59	291.79
100,000	618.33	608.47	599.46	591.18	583.58
125,000	772.91	760.59	749.32	738.98	729.47
150,000	927.49	912.71	899.18	886.77	875.36
175,000	1082.07	1064.83	1049.04	1034.57	1021.26
200,000	1236.65	1216.94	1198.91	1182.36	1167.15
225,000	1391.23	1369.06	1348.77	1330.16	1313.04
250,000	1545.81	1521.18	1498.63	1477.95	1458.94
275,000	1700.39	1673.29	1648.50	1625.74	1604.83
300,000	1854.97	1825.41	1798.36	1773.54	1750.72
325,000	2009.55	1977.53	1948.22	1921.33	1896.62
350,000	2164.13	2129.65	2098.08	2069.13	2042.51
375,000	2318.71	2281.76	2247.95	2216.92	2188.40
400,000	2473.29	2433.88	2397.81	2364.72	2334.30
425,000	2627.87	2586.00	2547.67	2512.51	2480.19
450,000	2782.45	2738.12	2697.54	2660.31	2626.08
475,000	2937.03	2890.23	2847.40	2808.10	2771.98
500,000	3091.61	3042.35	2997.26	2955.89	2917.87
525,000	3246.19	3194.47	3147.12	3103.69	3063.76
550,000	3400.77	3346.58	3296.99	3251.48	3209.66
575,000	3555.35	3498.70	3446.85	3399.28	3355.55
600,000	3709.93	3650.82	3596.71	3547.07	3501.44
625,000	3864.51	3802.94	3746.57	3694.87	3647.34
650,000	4019.09	3955.05	3896.44	3842.66	3793.23
675,000	4173.67	4107.17	4046.30	3990.46	3939.12
700,000	4328.25	4259.29	4196.16	4138.25	4085.01
725,000	4482.83	4411.41	4346.03	4286.04	4230.91
750,000	4637.41	4563.52	4495.89	4433.84	4376.80
775,000	4791.99	4715.64	4645.75	4581.63	4522.69
800,000	4946.57	4867.76	4795.61	4729.43	4668.59
825,000	5101.15	5019.87	4945.48	4877.22	4814.48
850,000	5255.73	5171.99	5095.34	5025.02	4960.37
875,000	5410.31	5324.11	5245.20	5172.81	5106.27
900,000	5564.89	5476.23	5395.07	5320.61	5252.16

124   Table 7

Monthly Payment Loans $\qquad$ **6.00%**

Table 7   125

Loan Amount	Amortization Period in Years				
	5	7	8	10	12
10	0.20	0.15	0.14	0.12	0.10
20	0.39	0.30	0.27	0.23	0.20
30	0.58	0.44	0.40	0.34	0.30
40	0.78	0.59	0.53	0.45	0.40
50	0.97	0.74	0.66	0.56	0.49
100	1.94	1.47	1.32	1.12	0.98
200	3.87	2.93	2.63	2.23	1.96
300	5.80	4.39	3.95	3.34	2.93
400	7.74	5.85	5.26	4.45	3.91
500	9.67	7.31	6.58	5.56	4.88
1,000	19.34	14.61	13.15	11.11	9.76
2,000	38.67	29.22	26.29	22.21	19.52
3,000	58.00	43.83	39.43	33.31	29.28
4,000	77.34	58.44	52.57	44.41	39.04
5,000	96.67	73.05	65.71	55.52	48.80
10,000	193.33	146.09	131.42	111.03	97.59
20,000	386.66	292.18	262.83	222.05	195.18
30,000	579.99	438.26	394.25	333.07	292.76
40,000	773.32	584.35	525.66	444.09	390.35
50,000	966.65	730.43	657.08	555.11	487.93
100,000	1933.29	1460.86	1314.15	1110.21	975.86
125,000	2416.61	1826.07	1642.68	1387.76	1219.82
150,000	2899.93	2191.29	1971.22	1665.31	1463.78
175,000	3383.25	2556.50	2299.76	1942.86	1707.74
200,000	3866.57	2921.72	2628.29	2220.42	1951.71
225,000	4349.89	3286.93	2956.83	2497.97	2195.67
250,000	4833.21	3652.14	3285.36	2775.52	2439.63
275,000	5316.53	4017.36	3613.90	3053.07	2683.59
300,000	5799.85	4382.57	3942.43	3330.62	2927.56
325,000	6283.17	4747.79	4270.97	3608.17	3171.52
350,000	6766.49	5113.00	4599.51	3885.72	3415.48
375,000	7249.81	5478.21	4928.04	4163.27	3659.44
400,000	7733.13	5843.43	5256.58	4440.83	3903.41
425,000	8216.45	6208.64	5585.11	4718.38	4147.37
450,000	8699.77	6573.85	5913.65	4995.93	4391.33
475,000	9183.09	6939.07	6242.18	5273.48	4635.29
500,000	9666.41	7304.28	6570.72	5551.03	4879.26
525,000	10149.73	7669.50	6899.26	5828.58	5123.22
550,000	10633.05	8034.71	7227.79	6106.13	5367.18
575,000	11116.37	8399.92	7556.33	6383.68	5611.14
600,000	11599.69	8765.14	7884.86	6661.24	5855.11
625,000	12083.01	9130.35	8213.40	6938.79	6099.07
650,000	12566.33	9495.57	8541.93	7216.34	6343.03
675,000	13049.65	9860.78	8870.47	7493.89	6586.99
700,000	13532.97	10225.99	9199.01	7771.44	6830.96
725,000	14016.29	10591.21	9527.54	8048.99	7074.92
750,000	14499.61	10956.42	9856.08	8326.54	7318.88
775,000	14982.93	11321.63	10184.61	8604.09	7562.84
800,000	15466.25	11686.85	10513.15	8881.65	7806.81
825,000	15949.57	12052.06	10841.68	9159.20	8050.77
850,000	16432.89	12417.28	11170.22	9436.75	8294.73
875,000	16916.21	12782.49	11498.76	9714.30	8538.69
900,000	17399.53	13147.70	11827.29	9991.85	8782.66

Monthly Payment Loans

Amortization Period in Years

Loan Amount	15	16	17	18	20
10	0.09	0.09	0.08	0.08	0.08
20	0.17	0.17	0.16	0.16	0.15
30	0.26	0.25	0.24	0.23	0.22
40	0.34	0.33	0.32	0.31	0.29
50	0.43	0.41	0.40	0.38	0.36
100	0.85	0.82	0.79	0.76	0.72
200	1.69	1.63	1.57	1.52	1.44
300	2.54	2.44	2.35	2.28	2.15
400	3.38	3.25	3.14	3.04	2.87
500	4.22	4.06	3.92	3.80	3.59
1,000	8.44	8.12	7.84	7.59	7.17
2,000	16.88	16.23	15.67	15.17	14.33
3,000	25.32	24.35	23.50	22.75	21.50
4,000	33.76	32.46	31.33	30.33	28.66
5,000	42.20	40.58	39.16	37.91	35.83
10,000	84.39	81.15	78.32	75.82	71.65
20,000	168.78	162.29	156.63	151.64	143.29
30,000	253.16	243.44	234.94	227.45	214.93
40,000	337.55	324.58	313.25	303.27	286.58
50,000	421.93	405.72	391.56	379.09	358.22
100,000	843.86	811.44	783.11	758.17	716.44
125,000	1054.83	1014.30	978.88	947.71	895.54
150,000	1265.79	1217.16	1174.66	1137.25	1074.65
175,000	1476.75	1420.02	1370.43	1326.79	1253.76
200,000	1687.72	1622.88	1566.21	1516.33	1432.87
225,000	1898.68	1825.74	1761.98	1705.87	1611.97
250,000	2109.65	2028.60	1957.76	1895.41	1791.08
275,000	2320.61	2231.46	2153.53	2084.95	1970.19
300,000	2531.58	2434.32	2349.31	2274.49	2149.30
325,000	2742.54	2637.18	2545.08	2464.03	2328.41
350,000	2953.50	2840.04	2740.86	2653.57	2507.51
375,000	3164.47	3042.90	2936.83	2843.11	2686.62
400,000	3375.43	3245.76	3132.41	3032.65	2865.73
425,000	3586.40	3448.62	3328.18	3222.19	3044.84
450,000	3797.36	3651.48	3523.96	3411.74	3223.94
475,000	4008.32	3854.33	3719.73	3601.28	3403.05
500,000	4219.29	4057.19	3915.51	3790.82	3582.16
525,000	4430.25	4260.05	4111.28	3980.36	3761.27
550,000	4641.22	4462.91	4307.06	4169.90	3940.38
575,000	4852.18	4665.77	4502.83	4359.44	4119.48
600,000	5063.15	4868.63	4698.61	4548.98	4298.59
625,000	5274.11	5071.49	4894.38	4738.52	4477.70
650,000	5485.07	5274.35	5090.16	4928.06	4656.81
675,000	5696.04	5477.21	5285.94	5117.60	4835.91
700,000	5907.00	5680.07	5481.71	5307.14	5015.02
725,000	6117.97	5882.93	5677.49	5496.68	5194.13
750,000	6328.93	6085.79	5873.26	5686.22	5373.24
775,000	6539.90	6288.65	6069.04	5875.76	5552.35
800,000	6750.86	6491.51	6264.81	6065.30	5731.45
825,000	6961.82	6694.37	6460.59	6254.84	5910.56
850,000	7172.79	6897.23	6656.36	6444.38	6089.67
875,000	7383.75	7100.09	6852.14	6633.93	6268.78
900,000	7594.72	7302.95	7047.91	6823.47	6447.88

Monthly Payment Loans   **6.00%**

Loan Amount	Amortization Period in Years				
	21	22	23	24	25
10	0.07	0.07	0.07	0.07	0.07
20	0.14	0.14	0.14	0.14	0.13
30	0.21	0.21	0.21	0.20	0.20
40	0.28	0.28	0.27	0.27	0.26
50	0.35	0.35	0.34	0.33	0.33
100	0.70	0.69	0.67	0.66	0.65
200	1.40	1.37	1.34	1.32	1.29
300	2.10	2.05	2.01	1.97	1.94
400	2.80	2.74	2.68	2.63	2.58
500	3.50	3.42	3.35	3.28	3.23
1,000	6.99	6.84	6.69	6.56	6.45
2,000	13.98	13.67	13.38	13.12	12.89
3,000	20.97	20.50	20.07	19.68	19.33
4,000	27.96	27.33	26.76	26.24	25.78
5,000	34.95	34.16	33.45	32.80	32.22
10,000	69.89	68.31	66.89	65.60	64.44
20,000	139.78	136.62	133.77	131.20	128.87
30,000	209.66	204.93	200.66	196.80	193.30
40,000	279.55	273.23	267.54	262.40	257.73
50,000	349.43	341.54	334.43	327.99	322.16
100,000	698.86	683.08	668.85	655.98	644.31
125,000	873.58	853.85	836.06	819.98	805.38
150,000	1048.29	1024.62	1003.28	983.97	966.48
175,000	1223.00	1195.39	1170.49	1147.97	1127.53
200,000	1397.72	1366.15	1337.70	1311.96	1288.61
225,000	1572.43	1536.92	1504.91	1475.96	1449.68
250,000	1747.15	1707.69	1672.12	1639.95	1610.76
275,000	1921.86	1878.46	1839.33	1803.94	1771.83
300,000	2096.58	2049.23	2006.55	1967.94	1932.91
325,000	2271.29	2220.00	2173.76	2131.93	2093.98
350,000	2446.00	2390.77	2340.97	2295.93	2255.06
375,000	2620.72	2561.53	2508.18	2459.92	2416.14
400,000	2795.43	2732.30	2675.39	2623.92	2577.21
425,000	2970.15	2903.07	2842.61	2787.91	2738.29
450,000	3144.86	3073.84	3009.82	2951.91	2899.36
475,000	3319.58	3244.61	3177.03	3115.90	3060.44
500,000	3494.29	3415.38	3344.24	3279.90	3221.51
525,000	3669.00	3586.15	3511.45	3443.89	3382.59
550,000	3843.72	3756.91	3678.66	3607.88	3543.66
575,000	4018.43	3927.68	3845.88	3771.88	3704.74
600,000	4193.15	4098.45	4013.09	3935.87	3865.81
625,000	4367.86	4269.22	4180.30	4099.87	4026.89
650,000	4542.57	4439.99	4347.51	4263.86	4187.96
675,000	4717.29	4610.76	4514.72	4427.86	4349.04
700,000	4892.00	4781.53	4681.94	4591.85	4510.11
725,000	5066.72	4952.29	4849.15	4755.85	4671.19
750,000	5241.43	5123.06	5016.36	4919.84	4832.27
775,000	5416.15	5293.83	5183.57	5083.84	4993.34
800,000	5590.86	5464.60	5350.78	5247.83	5154.42
825,000	5765.57	5635.37	5517.99	5411.82	5315.49
850,000	5940.29	5806.14	5685.21	5575.82	5476.57
875,000	6115.00	5976.91	5852.42	5739.81	5637.64
900,000	6289.72	6147.68	6019.63	5903.81	5798.72

Table 7   127

6.00%   Monthly Payment Loans

Amortization Period in Years

Loan Amount	26	27	28	29	30
10	0.07	0.07	0.07	0.07	0.06
20	0.13	0.13	0.13	0.13	0.12
30	0.20	0.19	0.19	0.19	0.18
40	0.26	0.25	0.25	0.25	0.24
50	0.32	0.32	0.31	0.31	0.30
100	0.64	0.63	0.62	0.61	0.60
200	1.27	1.25	1.24	1.22	1.20
300	1.91	1.88	1.85	1.83	1.80
400	2.54	2.50	2.47	2.43	2.40
500	3.17	3.12	3.08	3.04	3.00
1,000	6.34	6.24	6.16	6.08	6.00
2,000	12.68	12.48	12.31	12.15	12.00
3,000	19.02	18.72	18.46	18.22	17.99
4,000	25.35	24.96	24.61	24.29	23.99
5,000	31.69	31.20	30.76	30.36	29.98
10,000	63.37	62.40	61.52	60.71	59.96
20,000	126.74	124.80	123.03	121.41	119.92
30,000	190.11	187.20	184.54	182.11	179.87
40,000	253.48	249.60	246.05	242.81	239.83
50,000	316.84	312.00	307.57	303.51	299.78
100,000	633.68	623.99	615.13	607.01	599.56
125,000	792.10	779.99	768.91	758.76	749.44
150,000	950.52	935.98	922.69	910.51	899.33
175,000	1108.94	1091.98	1076.47	1062.26	1049.22
200,000	1267.36	1247.98	1230.25	1214.01	1199.11
225,000	1425.78	1403.97	1384.03	1365.77	1348.99
250,000	1584.20	1559.97	1537.82	1517.52	1498.88
275,000	1742.62	1715.96	1691.60	1669.27	1648.77
300,000	1901.04	1871.96	1845.38	1821.02	1798.66
325,000	2059.46	2027.96	1999.16	1972.77	1948.54
350,000	2217.87	2183.95	2152.94	2124.52	2098.43
375,000	2376.29	2339.95	2306.72	2276.27	2248.32
400,000	2534.71	2495.95	2460.50	2428.02	2398.21
425,000	2693.13	2651.94	2614.28	2579.77	2548.09
450,000	2851.55	2807.94	2768.06	2731.53	2697.98
475,000	3009.97	2963.94	2921.84	2883.28	2847.87
500,000	3168.39	3119.93	3075.63	3035.03	2997.76
525,000	3326.81	3275.93	3229.41	3186.78	3147.65
550,000	3485.23	3431.92	3383.19	3338.53	3297.53
575,000	3643.65	3587.92	3536.97	3490.28	3447.42
600,000	3802.07	3743.92	3690.75	3642.03	3597.31
625,000	3960.49	3899.91	3844.53	3793.78	3747.20
650,000	4118.91	4055.91	3998.31	3945.53	3897.08
675,000	4277.32	4211.91	4152.09	4097.29	4046.97
700,000	4435.74	4367.90	4305.87	4249.04	4196.86
725,000	4594.16	4523.90	4459.65	4400.79	4346.75
750,000	4752.58	4679.90	4613.44	4552.54	4496.63
775,000	4911.00	4835.89	4767.22	4704.29	4646.52
800,000	5069.42	4991.89	4921.00	4856.04	4796.41
825,000	5227.84	5147.88	5074.78	5007.79	4946.30
850,000	5386.26	5303.88	5228.56	5159.54	5096.18
875,000	5544.68	5459.88	5382.34	5311.30	5246.07
900,000	5703.10	5615.87	5536.12	5463.05	5395.96

Monthly Payment Loans   **6.25%**

Loan Amount	Amortization Period in Years				
	5	7	8	10	12
10	0.20	0.15	0.14	0.12	0.10
20	0.39	0.30	0.27	0.23	0.20
30	0.59	0.45	0.40	0.34	0.30
40	0.78	0.59	0.54	0.45	0.40
50	0.98	0.74	0.67	0.57	0.50
100	1.95	1.48	1.33	1.13	0.99
200	3.89	2.95	2.66	2.25	1.98
300	5.84	4.42	3.98	3.37	2.97
400	7.78	5.90	5.31	4.50	3.96
500	9.73	7.37	6.64	5.62	4.95
1,000	19.45	14.73	13.27	11.23	9.89
2,000	38.90	29.46	26.53	22.46	19.78
3,000	58.35	44.19	39.80	33.69	29.67
4,000	77.80	58.92	53.06	44.92	39.56
5,000	97.25	73.65	66.32	56.15	49.45
10,000	194.50	147.29	132.64	112.29	98.89
20,000	388.99	294.58	265.27	224.57	197.77
30,000	583.48	441.87	397.91	336.85	296.66
40,000	777.98	589.15	530.54	449.13	395.54
50,000	972.47	736.44	663.18	561.41	494.42
100,000	1944.93	1472.87	1326.35	1122.81	988.84
125,000	2431.16	1841.09	1657.94	1403.51	1236.05
150,000	2917.39	2209.31	1989.53	1684.21	1483.26
175,000	3403.63	2577.53	2321.12	1964.91	1730.47
200,000	3889.86	2945.74	2652.70	2245.61	1977.68
225,000	4376.09	3313.96	2984.29	2526.31	2224.89
250,000	4862.32	3682.18	3315.88	2807.01	2472.10
275,000	5348.55	4050.40	3647.47	3087.71	2719.31
300,000	5834.78	4418.61	3979.05	3368.41	2966.52
325,000	6321.02	4786.83	4310.64	3649.11	3213.72
350,000	6807.25	5155.05	4642.23	3929.81	3460.93
375,000	7293.48	5523.27	4973.82	4210.51	3708.14
400,000	7779.71	5091.48	5305.40	4491.21	3955.35
425,000	8265.94	6259.70	5636.99	4771.91	4202.56
450,000	8752.17	6627.92	5968.58	5052.61	4449.77
475,000	9238.40	6996.14	6300.17	5333.31	4696.98
500,000	9724.64	7364.35	6631.75	5614.01	4944.19
525,000	10210.87	7732.57	6963.34	5894.71	5191.40
550,000	10697.10	8100.79	7294.93	6175.41	5438.61
575,000	11183.33	8469.01	7626.51	6456.11	5685.82
600,000	11669.56	8837.22	7958.10	6736.81	5933.03
625,000	12155.79	9205.44	8289.69	7017.51	6180.23
650,000	12642.03	9573.66	8621.28	7298.21	6427.44
675,000	13128.26	9941.88	8952.86	7578.91	6674.65
700,000	13614.49	10310.09	9284.45	7859.61	6921.86
725,000	14100.72	10678.31	9616.04	8140.31	7169.07
750,000	14586.95	11046.53	9947.63	8421.01	7416.28
775,000	15073.18	11414.75	10279.21	8701.71	7663.49
800,000	15559.41	11782.96	10610.80	8982.41	7910.70
825,000	16045.65	12151.18	10942.39	9263.11	8157.91
850,000	16531.88	12519.40	11273.98	9543.81	8405.12
875,000	17018.11	12887.62	11605.56	9824.51	8652.33
900,000	17504.34	13255.83	11937.15	10105.21	8899.54

Table 7   129

Monthly Payment Loans

Amortization Period in Years

Loan Amount	15	16	17	18	20
10	0.09	0.09	0.08	0.08	0.08
20	0.18	0.17	0.16	0.16	0.15
30	0.26	0.25	0.24	0.24	0.22
40	0.35	0.34	0.32	0.31	0.30
50	0.43	0.42	0.40	0.39	0.37
100	0.86	0.83	0.80	0.78	0.74
200	1.72	1.66	1.60	1.55	1.47
300	2.58	2.48	2.40	2.32	2.20
400	3.43	3.31	3.19	3.09	2.93
500	4.29	4.13	3.99	3.87	3.66
1,000	8.58	8.26	7.98	7.73	7.31
2,000	17.15	16.51	15.95	15.45	14.62
3,000	25.73	24.76	23.92	23.17	21.93
4,000	34.30	33.01	31.89	30.90	29.24
5,000	42.88	41.26	39.86	38.62	36.55
10,000	85.75	82.52	79.71	77.23	73.10
20,000	171.49	165.04	159.41	154.46	146.19
30,000	257.23	247.56	239.12	231.69	219.28
40,000	342.97	330.08	318.82	308.92	292.38
50,000	428.72	412.60	398.53	386.15	365.47
100,000	857.43	825.20	797.05	772.30	730.93
125,000	1071.78	1031.50	996.31	965.37	913.67
150,000	1286.14	1237.80	1195.57	1158.45	1096.40
175,000	1500.50	1444.09	1394.83	1351.52	1279.13
200,000	1714.85	1650.39	1594.10	1544.59	1461.86
225,000	1929.21	1856.69	1793.36	1737.67	1644.59
250,000	2143.56	2062.99	1992.62	1930.74	1827.33
275,000	2357.92	2269.29	2191.88	2123.81	2010.06
300,000	2572.27	2475.59	2391.14	2316.89	2192.79
325,000	2786.63	2681.89	2590.40	2509.96	2375.52
350,000	3000.99	2888.18	2789.66	2703.03	2558.25
375,000	3215.34	3094.48	2988.93	2896.11	2740.99
400,000	3429.70	3300.78	3188.19	3089.18	2923.72
425,000	3644.05	3507.08	3387.45	3282.25	3106.45
450,000	3858.41	3713.38	3586.71	3475.33	3289.18
475,000	4072.76	3919.68	3785.97	3668.40	3471.91
500,000	4287.12	4125.98	3985.23	3861.47	3654.65
525,000	4501.48	4332.27	4184.49	4054.55	3837.38
550,000	4715.83	4538.57	4383.75	4247.62	4020.11
575,000	4930.19	4744.87	4583.02	4440.69	4202.84
600,000	5144.54	4951.17	4782.28	4633.77	4385.57
625,000	5358.90	5157.47	4981.54	4826.84	4568.31
650,000	5573.25	5363.77	5180.80	5019.91	4751.04
675,000	5787.61	5570.07	5380.06	5212.99	4933.77
700,000	6001.97	5776.36	5579.32	5406.06	5116.50
725,000	6216.32	5982.66	5778.58	5599.13	5299.23
750,000	6430.68	6188.96	5977.85	5792.21	5481.97
775,000	6645.03	6395.26	6177.11	5985.28	5664.70
800,000	6859.39	6601.56	6376.37	6178.35	5847.43
825,000	7073.74	6807.86	6575.63	6371.43	6030.16
850,000	7288.10	7014.16	6774.89	6564.50	6212.89
875,000	7502.46	7220.45	6974.15	6757.57	6395.63
900,000	7716.81	7426.75	7173.41	6950.65	6578.36

Monthly Payment Loans   6.25%

Loan Amount	Amortization Period in Years				
	21	22	23	24	25
10	0.08	0.07	0.07	0.07	0.07
20	0.15	0.14	0.14	0.14	0.14
30	0.22	0.21	0.21	0.21	0.20
40	0.29	0.28	0.28	0.27	0.27
50	0.36	0.35	0.35	0.34	0.33
100	0.72	0.70	0.69	0.68	0.66
200	1.43	1.40	1.37	1.35	1.32
300	2.15	2.10	2.06	2.02	1.98
400	2.86	2.80	2.74	2.69	2.64
500	3.57	3.49	3.42	3.36	3.30
1,000	7.14	6.98	6.84	6.72	6.60
2,000	14.28	13.96	13.68	13.43	13.20
3,000	21.41	20.94	20.52	20.14	19.80
4,000	28.55	27.92	27.36	26.85	26.39
5,000	35.68	34.90	34.20	33.56	32.99
10,000	71.36	69.80	68.39	67.12	65.97
20,000	142.71	139.59	136.78	134.24	131.94
30,000	214.07	209.38	205.17	201.36	197.91
40,000	285.42	279.18	273.55	268.48	263.87
50,000	356.77	348.97	341.94	335.59	329.84
100,000	713.54	697.93	683.88	671.18	659.67
125,000	891.92	872.41	854.85	838.98	824.59
150,000	1070.31	1046.90	1025.82	1006.77	989.51
175,000	1248.69	1221.38	1196.79	1174.57	1154.43
200,000	1427.07	1395.86	1367.75	1342.36	1319.34
225,000	1605.46	1570.34	1538.72	1510.15	1484.26
250,000	1783.84	1744.82	1709.69	1677.95	1649.18
275,000	1962.22	1919.31	1880.66	1845.74	1814.10
300,000	2140.61	2093.79	2051.63	2013.54	1979.01
325,000	2318.99	2268.27	2222.60	2181.33	2143.93
350,000	2497.37	2442.75	2393.57	2349.13	2308.85
375,000	2675.76	2617.23	2564.54	2516.92	2473.77
400,000	2854.14	2791.72	2735.50	2684.71	2638.68
425,000	3032.52	2966.20	2906.47	2852.51	2803.60
450,000	3210.91	3140.68	3077.44	3020.30	2968.52
475,000	3389.29	3315.16	3248.41	3188.10	3133.43
500,000	3567.67	3489.64	3419.38	3355.89	3298.35
525,000	3746.06	3664.13	3590.35	3523.69	3463.27
550,000	3924.44	3838.61	3761.32	3691.48	3628.19
575,000	4102.82	4013.09	3932.29	3859.27	3793.10
600,000	4281.21	4187.57	4103.25	4027.07	3958.02
625,000	4459.59	4362.05	4274.22	4194.86	4122.94
650,000	4637.97	4536.54	4445.19	4362.66	4287.86
675,000	4816.36	4711.02	4616.16	4530.45	4452.77
700,000	4994.74	4885.50	4787.13	4698.25	4617.69
725,000	5173.12	5059.98	4958.10	4866.04	4782.61
750,000	5351.51	5234.46	5129.07	5033.84	4947.53
775,000	5529.89	5408.95	5300.04	5201.63	5112.44
800,000	5708.27	5583.43	5471.00	5369.42	5277.36
825,000	5886.66	5757.91	5641.97	5537.22	5442.28
850,000	6065.04	5932.39	5812.94	5705.01	5607.19
875,000	6243.42	6106.87	5983.91	5872.81	5772.11
900,000	6421.81	6281.36	6154.88	6040.60	5937.03

Table 7   131

6.25%   Monthly Payment Loans

Amortization Period in Years

Loan Amount	26	27	28	29	30
10	0.07	0.07	0.07	0.07	0.07
20	0.13	0.13	0.13	0.13	0.13
30	0.20	0.20	0.19	0.19	0.19
40	0.26	0.26	0.26	0.25	0.25
50	0.33	0.32	0.32	0.32	0.31
100	0.65	0.64	0.64	0.63	0.62
200	1.30	1.28	1.27	1.25	1.24
300	1.95	1.92	1.90	1.87	1.85
400	2.60	2.56	2.53	2.50	2.47
500	3.25	3.20	3.16	3.12	3.08
1,000	6.50	6.40	6.31	6.24	6.16
2,000	12.99	12.80	12.62	12.47	12.32
3,000	19.48	19.20	18.93	18.70	18.48
4,000	25.97	25.59	25.24	24.93	24.63
5,000	32.47	31.99	31.55	31.16	30.79
10,000	64.93	63.97	63.10	62.31	61.58
20,000	129.85	127.94	126.20	124.61	123.15
30,000	194.77	191.91	189.30	186.91	184.72
40,000	259.69	255.88	252.40	249.21	246.29
50,000	324.61	319.85	315.50	311.51	307.86
100,000	649.22	639.69	630.99	623.02	615.72
125,000	811.52	799.61	788.73	778.78	769.65
150,000	973.82	959.53	946.48	934.53	923.58
175,000	1136.12	1119.45	1104.22	1090.29	1077.51
200,000	1298.43	1279.37	1261.97	1246.04	1231.44
225,000	1460.73	1439.29	1419.71	1401.79	1385.37
250,000	1623.03	1599.21	1577.46	1557.55	1539.30
275,000	1785.33	1759.13	1735.20	1713.30	1693.23
300,000	1947.64	1919.05	1892.95	1869.06	1847.16
325,000	2109.94	2078.97	2050.69	2024.81	2001.09
350,000	2272.24	2238.89	2208.44	2180.57	2155.02
375,000	2434.55	2398.81	2366.18	2336.32	2308.94
400,000	2596.85	2558.73	2523.93	2492.08	2462.87
425,000	2759.15	2718.65	2681.67	2647.83	2616.80
450,000	2921.45	2878.57	2839.42	2803.58	2770.73
475,000	3083.76	3038.49	2997.16	2959.34	2924.66
500,000	3246.06	3198.41	3154.91	3115.09	3078.59
525,000	3408.36	3358.34	3312.65	3270.85	3232.52
550,000	3570.66	3518.26	3470.40	3426.60	3386.45
575,000	3732.97	3678.18	3628.14	3582.36	3540.38
600,000	3895.27	3838.10	3785.89	3738.11	3694.31
625,000	4057.57	3998.02	3943.63	3893.87	3848.24
650,000	4219.87	4157.94	4101.38	4049.62	4002.17
675,000	4382.18	4317.86	4259.12	4205.37	4156.10
700,000	4544.48	4477.78	4416.87	4361.13	4310.03
725,000	4706.78	4637.70	4574.61	4516.88	4463.95
750,000	4869.09	4797.62	4732.36	4672.64	4617.88
775,000	5031.39	4957.54	4890.10	4828.39	4771.81
800,000	5193.69	5117.46	5047.85	4984.15	4925.74
825,000	5355.99	5277.38	5205.59	5139.90	5079.67
850,000	5518.30	5437.30	5363.34	5295.66	5233.60
875,000	5680.60	5597.22	5521.08	5451.41	5387.53
900,000	5842.90	5757.14	5678.83	5607.16	5541.46

Monthly Payment Loans   **6.50%**

Loan Amount	Amortization Period in Years				
	5	7	8	10	12
10	0.20	0.15	0.14	0.12	0.11
20	0.40	0.30	0.27	0.23	0.21
30	0.59	0.45	0.41	0.35	0.31
40	0.79	0.60	0.54	0.46	0.41
50	0.98	0.75	0.67	0.57	0.51
100	1.96	1.49	1.34	1.14	1.01
200	3.92	2.97	2.68	2.28	2.01
300	5.87	4.46	4.02	3.41	3.01
400	7.83	5.94	5.36	4.55	4.01
500	9.79	7.43	6.70	5.68	5.01
1,000	19.57	14.85	13.39	11.36	10.02
2,000	39.14	29.70	26.78	22.71	20.04
3,000	58.70	44.55	40.16	34.07	30.06
4,000	78.27	59.40	53.55	45.42	40.08
5,000	97.84	74.25	66.94	56.78	50.10
10,000	195.67	148.50	133.87	113.55	100.20
20,000	391.33	296.99	267.73	227.10	200.39
30,000	586.99	445.49	401.59	340.65	300.58
40,000	782.65	593.98	535.45	454.20	400.77
50,000	978.31	742.48	669.32	567.74	500.97
100,000	1956.62	1484.95	1338.63	1135.48	1001.93
125,000	2445.77	1856.18	1673.28	1419.35	1252.41
150,000	2934.93	2227.42	2007.94	1703.22	1502.89
175,000	3424.08	2598.66	2342.60	1987.09	1753.37
200,000	3913.23	2969.89	2677.25	2270.96	2003.85
225,000	4402.39	3341.13	3011.91	2554.83	2254.33
250,000	4891.54	3712.36	3346.56	2838.70	2504.81
275,000	5380.70	4083.60	3681.22	3122.57	2755.29
300,000	5869.85	4454.84	4015.87	3406.44	3005.77
325,000	6359.00	4826.07	4350.53	3690.31	3256.25
350,000	6848.16	5197.31	4685.19	3974.18	3506.73
375,000	7337.31	5568.54	5019.84	4258.05	3757.21
400,000	7826.46	5939.78	5354.50	4541.92	4007.69
425,000	8315.62	6311.02	5689.15	4825.79	4258.17
450,000	8804.77	6682.25	6023.81	5109.66	4508.65
475,000	9293.93	7053.49	6358.47	5393.53	4759.13
500,000	9783.08	7424.72	6693.12	5677.40	5009.61
525,000	10272.23	7795.96	7027.78	5961.27	5260.09
550,000	10761.39	8167.20	7362.43	6245.14	5510.57
575,000	11250.54	8538.43	7697.09	6529.01	5761.05
600,000	11739.69	8909.67	8031.74	6812.88	6011.53
625,000	12228.85	9280.90	8366.40	7096.75	6262.01
650,000	12718.00	9652.14	8701.06	7380.62	6512.49
675,000	13207.16	10023.37	9035.71	7664.49	6762.97
700,000	13696.31	10394.61	9370.37	7948.36	7013.45
725,000	14185.46	10765.85	9705.02	8232.23	7263.93
750,000	14674.62	11137.08	10039.68	8516.10	7514.41
775,000	15163.77	11508.32	10374.34	8799.97	7764.89
800,000	15652.92	11879.55	10708.99	9083.84	8015.37
825,000	16142.08	12250.79	11043.65	9367.71	8265.85
850,000	16631.23	12622.03	11378.30	9651.58	8516.33
875,000	17120.38	12993.26	11712.96	9935.45	8766.81
900,000	17609.54	13364.50	12047.61	10219.32	9017.29

Table 7   133

6.50%   Monthly Payment Loans

Loan Amount	15	16	17	18	20
10	0.09	0.09	0.09	0.08	0.08
20	0.18	0.17	0.17	0.16	0.15
30	0.27	0.26	0.25	0.24	0.23
40	0.35	0.34	0.33	0.32	0.30
50	0.44	0.42	0.41	0.40	0.38
100	0.88	0.84	0.82	0.79	0.75
200	1.75	1.68	1.63	1.58	1.50
300	2.62	2.52	2.44	2.36	2.24
400	3.49	3.36	3.25	3.15	2.99
500	4.36	4.20	4.06	3.94	3.73
1,000	8.72	8.40	8.12	7.87	7.46
2,000	17.43	16.79	16.23	15.74	14.92
3,000	26.14	25.18	24.34	23.60	22.37
4,000	34.85	33.57	32.45	31.47	29.83
5,000	43.56	41.96	40.56	39.33	37.28
10,000	87.12	83.91	81.12	78.66	74.56
20,000	174.23	167.82	162.23	157.32	149.12
30,000	261.34	251.73	243.34	235.97	223.68
40,000	348.45	335.64	324.45	314.63	298.23
50,000	435.56	419.54	405.57	393.29	372.79
100,000	871.11	839.08	811.13	786.57	745.58
125,000	1088.89	1048.85	1013.91	983.21	931.97
150,000	1306.67	1258.62	1216.69	1179.85	1118.36
175,000	1524.44	1468.39	1419.47	1376.49	1304.76
200,000	1742.22	1678.16	1622.25	1573.13	1491.15
225,000	1960.00	1887.92	1825.03	1769.77	1677.54
250,000	2177.77	2097.69	2027.81	1966.41	1863.94
275,000	2395.55	2307.46	2230.59	2163.05	2050.33
300,000	2613.33	2517.23	2433.37	2359.69	2236.72
325,000	2831.10	2727.00	2636.15	2556.33	2423.12
350,000	3048.88	2936.77	2838.93	2752.97	2609.51
375,000	3266.66	3146.54	3041.71	2949.61	2795.90
400,000	3484.43	3356.31	3244.49	3146.25	2982.30
425,000	3702.21	3566.07	3447.27	3342.89	3168.69
450,000	3919.99	3775.84	3650.05	3539.53	3355.08
475,000	4137.76	3985.61	3852.83	3736.17	3541.48
500,000	4355.54	4195.38	4055.61	3932.81	3727.87
525,000	4573.32	4405.15	4258.39	4129.45	3914.26
550,000	4791.10	4614.92	4461.17	4326.09	4100.66
575,000	5008.87	4824.69	4663.95	4522.73	4287.05
600,000	5226.65	5034.46	4866.73	4719.37	4473.44
625,000	5444.43	5244.23	5069.51	4916.01	4659.84
650,000	5662.20	5453.99	5272.29	5112.65	4846.23
675,000	5879.98	5663.76	5475.07	5309.29	5032.62
700,000	6097.76	5873.53	5677.85	5505.93	5219.02
725,000	6315.53	6083.30	5880.63	5702.57	5405.41
750,000	6533.31	6293.07	6083.41	5899.21	5591.80
775,000	6751.09	6502.84	6286.19	6095.85	5778.20
800,000	6968.86	6712.61	6488.97	6292.50	5964.59
825,000	7186.64	6922.38	6691.75	6489.14	6150.98
850,000	7404.42	7132.14	6894.53	6685.78	6337.38
875,000	7622.19	7341.91	7097.31	6882.42	6523.77
900,000	7839.97	7551.68	7300.09	7079.06	6710.16

Monthly Payment Loans   **6.50%**

Loan Amount	Amortization Period in Years				
	21	22	23	24	25
10	0.08	0.08	0.07	0.07	0.07
20	0.15	0.15	0.14	0.14	0.14
30	0.22	0.22	0.21	0.21	0.21
40	0.30	0.29	0.28	0.28	0.28
50	0.37	0.36	0.35	0.35	0.34
100	0.73	0.72	0.70	0.69	0.68
200	1.46	1.43	1.40	1.38	1.36
300	2.19	2.14	2.10	2.06	2.03
400	2.92	2.86	2.80	2.75	2.71
500	3.65	3.57	3.50	3.44	3.38
1,000	7.29	7.13	7.00	6.87	6.76
2,000	14.57	14.26	13.99	13.74	13.51
3,000	21.86	21.39	20.98	20.60	20.26
4,000	29.14	28.52	27.97	27.47	27.01
5,000	36.42	35.65	34.96	34.33	33.77
10,000	72.84	71.30	69.91	68.66	67.53
20,000	145.68	142.59	139.82	137.31	135.05
30,000	218.51	213.89	209.72	205.97	202.57
40,000	291.35	285.18	279.63	274.62	270.09
50,000	364.19	356.47	349.54	343.28	337.61
100,000	728.37	712.94	699.07	686.55	675.21
125,000	910.46	891.18	873.84	858.18	844.01
150,000	1092.55	1069.41	1048.60	1029.82	1012.82
175,000	1274.64	1247.65	1223.37	1201.45	1181.62
200,000	1456.73	1425.88	1398.13	1373.09	1350.42
225,000	1638.82	1604.12	1572.90	1544.73	1519.22
250,000	1820.91	1782.35	1747.67	1716.36	1688.02
275,000	2003.00	1960.59	1922.43	1888.00	1856.82
300,000	2185.09	2138.82	2097.20	2059.63	2025.63
325,000	2367.18	2317.06	2271.97	2231.27	2194.43
350,000	2549.28	2495.29	2446.73	2402.90	2363.23
375,000	2731.37	2673.53	2621.50	2574.54	2532.03
400,000	2913.46	2851.76	2796.26	2746.18	2700.83
425,000	3095.55	3030.00	2971.03	2917.81	2869.64
450,000	3277.64	3208.23	3145.80	3089.45	3038.44
475,000	3459.73	3386.47	3320.56	3261.08	3207.24
500,000	3641.82	3564.70	3495.33	3432.72	3376.04
525,000	3823.91	3742.93	3670.09	3604.35	3544.84
550,000	4006.00	3921.17	3844.86	3775.99	3713.64
575,000	4188.09	4099.40	4019.63	3947.63	3882.45
600,000	4370.18	4277.64	4194.39	4119.26	4051.25
625,000	4552.27	4455.87	4369.16	4290.90	4220.05
650,000	4734.36	4634.11	4543.93	4462.53	4388.85
675,000	4916.45	4812.34	4718.69	4634.17	4557.65
700,000	5098.55	4990.58	4893.46	4805.80	4726.46
725,000	5280.64	5168.81	5068.22	4977.44	4895.26
750,000	5462.73	5347.05	5242.99	5149.07	5064.06
775,000	5644.82	5525.28	5417.76	5320.71	5232.86
800,000	5826.91	5703.52	5592.52	5492.35	5401.66
825,000	6009.00	5881.75	5767.29	5663.98	5570.46
850,000	6191.09	6059.99	5942.05	5835.62	5739.27
875,000	6373.18	6238.22	6116.82	6007.25	5908.07
900,000	6555.27	6416.46	6291.59	6178.89	6076.87

Table 7   135

6.50%   Monthly Payment Loans

Loan Amount	26	27	28	29	30
	Amortization Period in Years				
10	0.07	0.07	0.07	0.07	0.07
20	0.14	0.14	0.13	0.13	0.13
30	0.20	0.20	0.20	0.20	0.19
40	0.27	0.27	0.26	0.26	0.26
50	0.34	0.33	0.33	0.32	0.32
100	0.67	0.66	0.65	0.64	0.64
200	1.33	1.32	1.30	1.28	1.27
300	2.00	1.97	1.95	1.92	1.90
400	2.66	2.63	2.59	2.56	2.53
500	3.33	3.28	3.24	3.20	3.17
1,000	6.65	6.56	6.48	6.40	6.33
2,000	13.30	13.12	12.95	12.79	12.65
3,000	19.95	19.67	19.42	19.18	18.97
4,000	26.60	26.23	25.89	25.57	25.29
5,000	33.25	32.78	32.36	31.97	31.61
10,000	66.50	65.56	64.71	63.93	63.21
20,000	132.99	131.12	129.41	127.85	126.42
30,000	199.48	196.67	194.11	191.77	189.63
40,000	265.97	262.23	258.81	255.69	252.83
50,000	332.46	327.78	323.51	319.61	316.04
100,000	664.92	655.56	647.02	639.22	632.07
125,000	831.15	819.45	808.78	799.02	790.09
150,000	997.38	983.34	970.53	958.82	948.11
175,000	1163.61	1147.23	1132.28	1118.63	1106.12
200,000	1329.84	1311.11	1294.04	1278.43	1264.14
225,000	1496.07	1475.00	1455.79	1438.23	1422.16
250,000	1662.30	1638.89	1617.55	1598.04	1580.18
275,000	1828.53	1802.78	1779.30	1757.84	1738.19
300,000	1994.76	1966.67	1941.05	1917.64	1896.21
325,000	2160.99	2130.56	2102.81	2077.45	2054.23
350,000	2327.22	2294.45	2264.56	2237.25	2212.24
375,000	2493.45	2458.34	2426.32	2397.05	2370.26
400,000	2659.68	2622.22	2588.07	2556.86	2528.28
425,000	2825.91	2786.11	2749.82	2716.66	2686.29
450,000	2992.14	2950.00	2911.58	2876.46	2844.31
475,000	3158.36	3113.89	3073.33	3036.27	3002.33
500,000	3324.59	3277.78	3235.09	3196.07	3160.35
525,000	3490.82	3441.67	3396.84	3355.87	3318.36
550,000	3657.05	3605.56	3558.59	3515.67	3476.38
575,000	3823.28	3769.45	3720.35	3675.48	3634.40
600,000	3989.51	3933.33	3882.10	3835.28	3792.41
625,000	4155.74	4097.22	4043.86	3995.08	3950.43
650,000	4321.97	4261.11	4205.61	4154.89	4108.45
675,000	4488.20	4425.00	4367.36	4314.69	4266.46
700,000	4654.43	4588.89	4529.12	4474.49	4424.48
725,000	4820.66	4752.78	4690.87	4634.30	4582.50
750,000	4986.89	4916.67	4852.63	4794.10	4740.52
775,000	5153.12	5080.56	5014.38	4953.90	4898.53
800,000	5319.35	5244.44	5176.13	5113.71	5056.55
825,000	5485.58	5408.33	5337.89	5273.51	5214.57
850,000	5651.81	5572.22	5499.64	5433.31	5372.58
875,000	5818.04	5736.11	5661.40	5593.12	5530.60
900,000	5984.27	5900.00	5823.15	5752.92	5688.62

Monthly Payment Loans 6.75%

Loan Amount	Amortization Period in Years				
	5	7	8	10	12
10	0.20	0.15	0.14	0.12	0.11
20	0.40	0.30	0.28	0.23	0.21
30	0.60	0.45	0.41	0.35	0.31
40	0.79	0.60	0.55	0.46	0.41
50	0.99	0.75	0.68	0.58	0.51
100	1.97	1.50	1.36	1.15	1.02
200	3.94	3.00	2.71	2.30	2.04
300	5.91	4.50	4.06	3.45	3.05
400	7.88	5.99	5.41	4.60	4.07
500	9.85	7.49	6.76	5.75	5.08
1,000	19.69	14.98	13.51	11.49	10.16
2,000	39.37	29.95	27.02	22.97	20.31
3,000	59.06	44.92	40.53	34.45	30.46
4,000	78.74	59.89	54.04	45.93	40.61
5,000	98.42	74.86	67.55	57.42	50.76
10,000	196.84	149.71	135.10	114.83	101.52
20,000	393.67	299.42	270.20	229.65	203.03
30,000	590.51	449.13	405.29	344.48	304.54
40,000	787.34	598.84	540.39	459.30	406.05
50,000	984.18	748.54	675.49	574.13	507.56
100,000	1968.35	1497.08	1350.97	1148.25	1015.11
125,000	2460.44	1871.35	1688.71	1435.31	1268.88
150,000	2952.52	2245.62	2026.45	1722.37	1522.66
175,000	3444.61	2619.89	2364.19	2009.43	1776.43
200,000	3936.70	2994.16	2701.93	2296.49	2030.21
225,000	4428.78	3368.43	3039.67	2583.55	2283.99
250,000	4920.87	3742.70	3377.42	2870.61	2537.76
275,000	5412.96	4116.96	3715.16	3157.67	2791.54
300,000	5905.04	4491.23	4052.90	3444.73	3045.31
325,000	6397.13	4865.50	4390.64	3731.79	3299.09
350,000	6889.22	5239.77	4728.38	4018.85	3552.86
375,000	7381.30	5614.04	5066.12	4305.91	3806.64
400,000	7873.39	5988.31	5403.86	4592.97	4060.42
425,000	8365.48	6362.58	5741.60	4880.03	4314.19
450,000	8857.56	6736.85	6079.34	5167.09	4567.97
475,000	9349.65	7111.12	6417.08	5454.15	4821.74
500,000	9841.74	7485.39	6754.83	5741.21	5075.52
525,000	10333.82	7859.66	7092.57	6028.27	5329.29
550,000	10825.91	8233.92	7430.31	6315.33	5583.07
575,000	11317.99	8608.19	7768.05	6602.39	5836.85
600,000	11810.08	8982.46	8105.79	6889.45	6090.62
625,000	12302.17	9356.73	8443.53	7176.51	6344.40
650,000	12794.25	9731.00	8781.27	7463.57	6598.17
675,000	13286.34	10105.27	9119.01	7750.63	6851.95
700,000	13778.43	10479.54	9456.75	8037.69	7105.72
725,000	14270.51	10853.81	9794.49	8324.75	7359.50
750,000	14762.60	11228.08	10132.24	8611.81	7613.28
775,000	15254.69	11602.35	10469.98	8898.87	7867.05
800,000	15746.77	11976.62	10807.72	9185.93	8120.83
825,000	16238.86	12350.88	11145.46	9472.99	8374.60
850,000	16730.95	12725.15	11483.20	9760.05	8628.38
875,000	17223.03	13099.42	11820.94	10047.12	8882.15
900,000	17715.12	13473.69	12158.68	10334.18	9135.93

Table 7   137

6.75%   Monthly Payment Loans

Amortization Period in Years

Loan Amount	15	16	17	18	20
10	0.09	0.09	0.09	0.09	0.08
20	0.18	0.18	0.17	0.17	0.16
30	0.27	0.26	0.25	0.25	0.23
40	0.36	0.35	0.34	0.33	0.31
50	0.45	0.43	0.42	0.41	0.39
100	0.89	0.86	0.83	0.81	0.77
200	1.77	1.71	1.66	1.61	1.53
300	2.66	2.56	2.48	2.41	2.29
400	3.54	3.42	3.31	3.21	3.05
500	4.43	4.27	4.13	4.01	3.81
1,000	8.85	8.54	8.26	8.01	7.61
2,000	17.70	17.07	16.51	16.02	15.21
3,000	26.55	25.60	24.76	24.03	22.82
4,000	35.40	34.13	33.02	32.04	30.42
5,000	44.25	42.66	41.27	40.05	38.02
10,000	88.50	85.31	82.54	80.10	76.04
20,000	176.99	170.62	165.07	160.20	152.08
30,000	265.48	255.93	247.60	240.29	228.11
40,000	353.97	341.24	330.14	320.39	304.15
50,000	442.46	426.55	412.67	400.49	380.19
100,000	884.91	853.09	825.33	800.97	760.37
125,000	1106.14	1066.36	1031.66	1001.21	950.46
150,000	1327.37	1279.63	1237.99	1201.45	1140.55
175,000	1548.60	1492.90	1444.33	1401.69	1330.64
200,000	1769.82	1706.17	1650.66	1601.93	1520.73
225,000	1991.05	1919.44	1856.99	1802.18	1710.82
250,000	2212.28	2132.71	2063.32	2002.42	1900.92
275,000	2433.51	2345.98	2269.65	2202.66	2091.01
300,000	2654.73	2559.25	2475.98	2402.90	2281.10
325,000	2875.96	2772.52	2682.32	2603.14	2471.19
350,000	3097.19	2985.79	2888.65	2803.38	2661.28
375,000	3318.42	3199.06	3094.98	3003.62	2851.37
400,000	3539.64	3412.33	3301.31	3203.86	3041.46
425,000	3760.87	3625.60	3507.64	3404.10	3231.55
450,000	3982.10	3838.87	3713.97	3604.35	3421.64
475,000	4203.32	4052.14	3920.31	3804.59	3611.73
500,000	4424.55	4265.41	4126.64	4004.83	3801.83
525,000	4645.78	4478.68	4332.97	4205.07	3991.92
550,000	4867.01	4691.95	4539.30	4405.31	4182.01
575,000	5088.23	4905.22	4745.63	4605.55	4372.10
600,000	5309.46	5118.49	4951.96	4805.79	4562.19
625,000	5530.69	5331.76	5158.30	5006.03	4752.28
650,000	5751.92	5545.03	5364.63	5206.28	4942.37
675,000	5973.14	5758.30	5570.96	5406.52	5132.46
700,000	6194.37	5971.57	5777.29	5606.76	5322.55
725,000	6415.60	6184.84	5983.62	5807.00	5512.64
750,000	6636.83	6398.11	6189.95	6007.24	5702.74
775,000	6858.05	6611.38	6396.29	6207.48	5892.83
800,000	7079.28	6824.65	6602.62	6407.72	6082.92
825,000	7300.51	7037.92	6808.95	6607.96	6273.01
850,000	7521.74	7251.19	7015.28	6808.20	6463.10
875,000	7742.96	7464.46	7221.61	7008.45	6653.19
900,000	7964.19	7677.73	7427.94	7208.69	6843.28

Monthly Payment Loans   **6.75%**

Loan Amount	Amortization Period in Years				
	21	22	23	24	25
10	0.08	0.08	0.08	0.08	0.07
20	0.15	0.15	0.15	0.15	0.14
30	0.23	0.22	0.22	0.22	0.21
40	0.30	0.30	0.29	0.29	0.28
50	0.38	0.37	0.36	0.36	0.35
100	0.75	0.73	0.72	0.71	0.70
200	1.49	1.46	1.43	1.41	1.39
300	2.24	2.19	2.15	2.11	2.08
400	2.98	2.92	2.86	2.81	2.77
500	3.72	3.65	3.58	3.52	3.46
1,000	7.44	7.29	7.15	7.03	6.91
2,000	14.87	14.57	14.29	14.05	13.82
3,000	22.31	21.85	21.44	21.07	20.73
4,000	29.74	29.13	28.58	28.09	27.64
5,000	37.17	36.41	35.73	35.11	34.55
10,000	74.34	72.82	71.45	70.21	69.10
20,000	148.67	145.63	142.89	140.42	138.19
30,000	223.01	218.44	214.33	210.63	207.28
40,000	297.34	291.25	285.77	280.83	276.37
50,000	371.68	364.06	357.21	351.04	345.46
100,000	743.35	728.11	714.42	702.08	690.92
125,000	929.18	910.14	893.02	877.59	863.64
150,000	1115.02	1092.16	1071.63	1053.11	1036.37
175,000	1300.86	1274.19	1250.23	1228.63	1209.10
200,000	1486.69	1456.22	1428.83	1404.15	1381.83
225,000	1672.53	1638.24	1607.44	1579.66	1554.56
250,000	1858.36	1820.27	1786.04	1755.18	1727.28
275,000	2044.20	2002.29	1964.64	1930.70	1900.01
300,000	2230.03	2184.32	2143.25	2106.22	2072.74
325,000	2415.87	2366.35	2321.85	2281.74	2245.47
350,000	2601.71	2548.37	2500.45	2457.25	2418.20
375,000	2787.54	2730.40	2679.06	2632.77	2590.92
400,000	2973.38	2912.43	2857.66	2808.29	2763.65
425,000	3159.21	3094.45	3036.26	2983.81	2936.38
450,000	3345.05	3276.48	3214.87	3159.32	3109.11
475,000	3530.88	3458.50	3393.47	3334.84	3281.83
500,000	3716.72	3640.53	3572.07	3510.36	3454.56
525,000	3902.56	3822.56	3750.68	3685.88	3627.29
550,000	4088.39	4004.58	3929.28	3861.40	3800.02
575,000	4274.23	4186.61	4107.88	4036.91	3972.75
600,000	4460.06	4368.64	4286.49	4212.43	4145.47
625,000	4645.90	4550.66	4465.09	4387.95	4318.20
650,000	4831.73	4732.69	4643.69	4563.47	4490.93
675,000	5017.57	4914.71	4822.30	4738.98	4663.66
700,000	5203.41	5096.74	5000.90	4914.50	4836.39
725,000	5389.24	5278.77	5179.50	5090.02	5009.11
750,000	5575.08	5460.79	5358.11	5265.54	5181.84
775,000	5760.91	5642.82	5536.71	5441.06	5354.57
800,000	5946.75	5824.85	5715.31	5616.57	5527.30
825,000	6132.59	6006.87	5893.92	5792.09	5700.03
850,000	6318.42	6188.90	6072.52	5967.61	5872.75
875,000	6504.26	6370.93	6251.12	6143.13	6045.48
900,000	6690.09	6552.95	6429.73	6318.64	6218.21

Table 7   139

6.75%   **Monthly Payment Loans**

Loan Amount	Amortization Period in Years				
	26	27	28	29	30
10	0.07	0.07	0.07	0.07	0.07
20	0.14	0.14	0.14	0.14	0.13
30	0.21	0.21	0.20	0.20	0.20
40	0.28	0.27	0.27	0.27	0.26
50	0.35	0.34	0.34	0.33	0.33
100	0.69	0.68	0.67	0.66	0.65
200	1.37	1.35	1.33	1.32	1.30
300	2.05	2.02	1.99	1.97	1.95
400	2.73	2.69	2.66	2.63	2.60
500	3.41	3.36	3.32	3.28	3.25
1,000	6.81	6.72	6.64	6.56	6.49
2,000	13.62	13.44	13.27	13.12	12.98
3,000	20.43	20.15	19.90	19.67	19.46
4,000	27.24	26.87	26.53	26.23	25.95
5,000	34.04	33.59	33.17	32.78	32.43
10,000	68.08	67.17	66.33	65.56	64.86
20,000	136.16	134.33	132.65	131.12	129.72
30,000	204.24	201.49	198.97	196.68	194.58
40,000	272.32	268.65	265.30	262.24	259.44
50,000	340.40	335.81	331.62	327.80	324.30
100,000	680.80	671.61	663.23	655.59	648.60
125,000	851.00	839.51	829.04	819.49	810.75
150,000	1021.20	1007.41	994.85	983.38	972.90
175,000	1191.40	1175.31	1160.65	1147.28	1135.05
200,000	1361.59	1343.21	1326.46	1311.17	1297.20
225,000	1531.79	1511.11	1492.27	1475.07	1459.35
250,000	1701.99	1679.01	1658.07	1638.97	1621.50
275,000	1872.19	1846.91	1823.88	1802.86	1783.65
300,000	2042.39	2014.81	1989.69	1966.76	1945.80
325,000	2212.59	2182.71	2155.49	2130.66	2107.95
350,000	2382.79	2350.61	2321.30	2294.55	2270.10
375,000	2552.98	2518.51	2487.11	2458.45	2432.25
400,000	2723.18	2686.41	2652.91	2622.34	2594.40
425,000	2893.38	2854.31	2818.72	2786.24	2756.55
450,000	3063.58	3022.21	2984.53	2950.14	2918.70
475,000	3233.78	3190.11	3150.33	3114.03	3080.85
500,000	3403.98	3358.01	3316.14	3277.93	3243.00
525,000	3574.18	3525.91	3481.95	3441.83	3405.15
550,000	3744.38	3693.81	3647.75	3605.72	3567.29
575,000	3914.57	3861.71	3813.56	3769.62	3729.44
600,000	4084.77	4029.61	3979.37	3933.51	3891.59
625,000	4254.97	4197.51	4145.17	4097.41	4053.74
650,000	4425.17	4365.41	4310.98	4261.31	4215.89
675,000	4595.37	4533.31	4476.79	4425.20	4378.04
700,000	4765.57	4701.21	4642.59	4589.10	4540.19
725,000	4935.77	4869.11	4808.40	4753.00	4702.34
750,000	5105.96	5037.01	4974.21	4916.89	4864.49
775,000	5276.16	5204.91	5140.01	5080.79	5026.64
800,000	5446.36	5372.81	5305.82	5244.68	5188.79
825,000	5616.56	5540.71	5471.63	5408.58	5350.94
850,000	5786.76	5708.61	5637.43	5572.48	5513.09
875,000	5956.96	5876.51	5803.24	5736.37	5675.24
900,000	6127.16	6044.41	5969.05	5900.27	5837.39

Monthly Payment Loans 7.00%

Loan Amount	Amortization Period in Years				
	5	7	8	10	12
10	0.20	0.16	0.14	0.12	0.11
20	0.40	0.31	0.28	0.24	0.21
30	0.60	0.46	0.41	0.35	0.31
40	0.80	0.61	0.55	0.47	0.42
50	1.00	0.76	0.69	0.59	0.52
100	1.99	1.51	1.37	1.17	1.03
200	3.97	3.02	2.73	2.33	2.06
300	5.95	4.53	4.10	3.49	3.09
400	7.93	6.04	5.46	4.65	4.12
500	9.91	7.55	6.82	5.81	5.15
1,000	19.81	15.10	13.64	11.62	10.29
2,000	39.61	30.19	27.27	23.23	20.57
3,000	59.41	45.28	40.91	34.84	30.86
4,000	79.21	60.38	54.54	46.45	41.14
5,000	99.01	75.47	68.17	58.06	51.42
10,000	198.02	150.93	136.34	116.11	102.84
20,000	396.03	301.86	272.68	232.22	205.68
30,000	594.04	452.79	409.02	348.33	308.52
40,000	792.05	603.71	545.35	464.44	411.36
50,000	990.06	754.64	681.69	580.55	514.20
100,000	1980.12	1509.27	1363.38	1161.09	1028.39
125,000	2475.15	1886.59	1704.22	1451.36	1285.48
150,000	2970.18	2263.91	2045.06	1741.63	1542.58
175,000	3465.21	2641.22	2385.91	2031.90	1799.67
200,000	3960.24	3018.54	2726.75	2322.17	2056.77
225,000	4455.27	3395.86	3067.59	2612.45	2313.86
250,000	4950.30	3773.17	3408.43	2902.72	2570.96
275,000	5445.33	4150.49	3749.28	3192.99	2828.05
300,000	5940.36	4527.81	4090.12	3483.26	3085.15
325,000	6435.39	4905.13	4430.96	3773.53	3342.24
350,000	6930.42	5282.44	4771.81	4063.80	3599.34
375,000	7425.45	5659.76	5112.65	4354.07	3856.43
400,000	7920.48	6037.08	5453.49	4644.34	4113.53
425,000	8415.51	6414.39	5794.33	4934.62	4370.62
450,000	8910.54	6791.71	6135.18	5224.89	4627.72
475,000	9405.57	7169.03	6476.02	5515.16	4884.82
500,000	9900.60	7546.34	6816.86	5805.43	5141.91
525,000	10395.63	7923.66	7157.71	6095.70	5399.01
550,000	10890.66	8300.98	7498.55	6385.97	5656.10
575,000	11385.69	8678.30	7839.39	6676.24	5913.20
600,000	11880.72	9055.61	8180.24	6966.51	6170.29
625,000	12375.75	9432.93	8521.08	7256.78	6427.39
650,000	12870.78	9810.25	8861.92	7547.06	6684.48
675,000	13365.81	10187.56	9202.76	7837.33	6941.58
700,000	13860.84	10564.88	9543.61	8127.60	7198.67
725,000	14355.87	10942.20	9884.45	8417.87	7455.77
750,000	14850.90	11319.51	10225.29	8708.14	7712.86
775,000	15345.93	11696.83	10566.14	8998.41	7969.96
800,000	15840.96	12074.15	10906.98	9288.68	8227.05
825,000	16335.99	12451.47	11247.82	9578.95	8484.15
850,000	16831.02	12828.78	11588.66	9869.23	8741.24
875,000	17326.05	13206.10	11929.51	10159.50	8998.34
900,000	17821.08	13583.42	12270.35	10449.77	9255.43

Table 7   141

7.00%   Monthly Payment Loans

Amortization Period in Years

Loan Amount	15	16	17	18	20
10	0.09	0.09	0.09	0.09	0.08
20	0.18	0.18	0.17	0.17	0.16
30	0.27	0.27	0.26	0.25	0.24
40	0.36	0.35	0.34	0.33	0.32
50	0.45	0.44	0.42	0.41	0.39
100	0.90	0.87	0.84	0.82	0.78
200	1.80	1.74	1.68	1.64	1.56
300	2.70	2.61	2.52	2.45	2.33
400	3.60	3.47	3.36	3.27	3.11
500	4.50	4.34	4.20	4.08	3.88
1,000	8.99	8.68	8.40	8.16	7.76
2,000	17.98	17.35	16.80	16.32	15.51
3,000	26.97	26.02	25.19	24.47	23.26
4,000	35.96	34.69	33.59	32.63	31.02
5,000	44.95	43.37	41.99	40.78	38.77
10,000	89.89	86.73	83.97	81.56	77.53
20,000	179.77	173.45	167.94	163.11	155.06
30,000	269.65	260.17	251.90	244.66	232.59
40,000	359.54	346.89	335.87	326.21	310.12
50,000	449.42	433.61	419.84	407.76	387.65
100,000	898.83	867.21	839.67	815.51	775.30
125,000	1123.54	1084.02	1049.58	1019.38	969.13
150,000	1348.25	1300.82	1259.50	1223.26	1162.95
175,000	1572.95	1517.62	1469.41	1427.13	1356.78
200,000	1797.66	1734.42	1679.33	1631.01	1550.60
225,000	2022.37	1951.22	1889.24	1834.88	1744.43
250,000	2247.08	2168.03	2099.16	2038.76	1938.25
275,000	2471.78	2384.83	2309.07	2242.64	2132.08
300,000	2696.49	2601.63	2518.99	2446.51	2325.90
325,000	2921.20	2818.43	2728.90	2650.39	2519.73
350,000	3145.90	3035.23	2938.82	2854.26	2713.55
375,000	3370.61	3252.04	3148.73	3058.14	2907.38
400,000	3595.32	3468.84	3358.65	3262.01	3101.20
425,000	3820.03	3685.64	3568.56	3465.89	3295.03
450,000	4044.73	3902.44	3778.48	3669.76	3488.85
475,000	4269.44	4119.24	3988.39	3873.64	3682.67
500,000	4494.15	4336.05	4198.31	4077.52	3876.50
525,000	4718.85	4552.85	4408.22	4281.39	4070.32
550,000	4943.56	4769.65	4618.14	4485.27	4264.15
575,000	5168.27	4986.45	4828.05	4689.14	4457.97
600,000	5392.97	5203.25	5037.97	4893.02	4651.80
625,000	5617.68	5420.06	5247.88	5096.89	4845.62
650,000	5842.39	5636.86	5457.80	5300.77	5039.45
675,000	6067.10	5853.66	5667.71	5504.64	5233.27
700,000	6291.80	6070.46	5877.63	5708.52	5427.10
725,000	6516.51	6287.26	6087.54	5912.40	5620.92
750,000	6741.22	6504.07	6297.46	6116.27	5814.75
775,000	6965.92	6720.87	6507.38	6320.15	6008.57
800,000	7190.63	6937.67	6717.29	6524.02	6202.40
825,000	7415.34	7154.47	6927.21	6727.90	6396.22
850,000	7640.05	7371.27	7137.12	6931.77	6590.05
875,000	7864.75	7588.08	7347.04	7135.65	6783.87
900,000	8089.46	7804.88	7556.95	7339.52	6977.70

Monthly Payment Loans 7.00%

Loan Amount	Amortization Period in Years				
	21	22	23	24	25
10	0.08	0.08	0.08	0.08	0.08
20	0.16	0.15	0.15	0.15	0.15
30	0.23	0.23	0.22	0.22	0.22
40	0.31	0.30	0.30	0.29	0.29
50	0.38	0.38	0.37	0.36	0.36
100	0.76	0.75	0.73	0.72	0.71
200	1.52	1.49	1.46	1.44	1.42
300	2.28	2.24	2.19	2.16	2.13
400	3.04	2.98	2.92	2.88	2.83
500	3.80	3.72	3.65	3.59	3.54
1,000	7.59	7.44	7.30	7.18	7.07
2,000	15.17	14.87	14.60	14.36	14.14
3,000	22.76	22.31	21.90	21.54	21.21
4,000	30.34	29.74	29.20	28.72	28.28
5,000	37.93	37.18	36.50	35.89	35.34
10,000	75.85	74.35	73.00	71.78	70.68
20,000	151.70	148.69	145.99	143.56	141.36
30,000	227.55	223.03	218.98	215.33	212.04
40,000	303.39	297.37	291.97	287.11	282.72
50,000	379.24	371.72	364.96	358.88	353.39
100,000	758.48	743.43	729.92	717.76	706.78
125,000	948.09	929.29	912.40	897.20	883.48
150,000	1137.71	1115.14	1094.88	1076.64	1060.17
175,000	1327.33	1301.00	1277.36	1256.08	1236.87
200,000	1516.95	1486.85	1459.84	1435.52	1413.56
225,000	1706.57	1672.71	1642.32	1614.96	1590.26
250,000	1896.18	1858.57	1824.80	1794.40	1766.95
275,000	2085.80	2044.42	2007.28	1973.84	1943.65
300,000	2275.42	2230.28	2189.76	2153.28	2120.34
325,000	2465.04	2416.13	2372.24	2332.72	2297.04
350,000	2654.66	2601.99	2554.72	2512.16	2473.73
375,000	2844.27	2787.85	2737.20	2691.60	2650.43
400,000	3033.89	2973.70	2919.68	2871.04	2827.12
425,000	3223.51	3159.56	3102.16	3050.48	3003.82
450,000	3413.13	3345.41	3284.64	3229.92	3180.51
475,000	3602.75	3531.27	3467.12	3409.36	3357.21
500,000	3792.36	3717.13	3649.60	3588.80	3533.90
525,000	3981.98	3902.98	3832.08	3768.24	3710.60
550,000	4171.60	4088.84	4014.56	3947.68	3887.29
575,000	4361.22	4274.69	4197.04	4127.12	4063.99
600,000	4550.84	4460.55	4379.52	4306.56	4240.68
625,000	4740.45	4646.41	4562.00	4486.00	4417.37
650,000	4930.07	4832.26	4744.48	4665.44	4594.07
675,000	5119.69	5018.12	4926.96	4844.88	4770.76
700,000	5309.31	5203.97	5109.44	5024.32	4947.46
725,000	5498.92	5389.83	5291.92	5203.76	5124.15
750,000	5688.54	5575.69	5474.40	5383.20	5300.85
775,000	5878.16	5761.54	5656.88	5562.64	5477.54
800,000	6067.78	5947.40	5839.36	5742.08	5654.24
825,000	6257.40	6133.25	6021.84	5921.52	5830.93
850,000	6447.01	6319.11	6204.32	6100.96	6007.63
875,000	6636.63	6504.97	6386.80	6280.40	6184.32
900,000	6826.25	6690.82	6569.28	6459.84	6361.02

Table 7   143

7.00%   Monthly Payment Loans

Amortization Period in Years

Loan Amount	26	27	28	29	30
10	0.07	0.07	0.07	0.07	0.07
20	0.14	0.14	0.14	0.14	0.14
30	0.21	0.21	0.21	0.21	0.20
40	0.28	0.28	0.28	0.27	0.27
50	0.35	0.35	0.34	0.34	0.34
100	0.70	0.69	0.68	0.68	0.67
200	1.40	1.38	1.36	1.35	1.34
300	2.10	2.07	2.04	2.02	2.00
400	2.79	2.76	2.72	2.69	2.67
500	3.49	3.44	3.40	3.37	3.33
1,000	6.97	6.88	6.80	6.73	6.66
2,000	13.94	13.76	13.60	13.45	13.31
3,000	20.91	20.64	20.39	20.17	19.96
4,000	27.88	27.52	27.19	26.89	26.62
5,000	34.85	34.40	33.99	33.61	33.27
10,000	69.69	68.79	67.97	67.22	66.54
20,000	139.37	137.57	135.93	134.43	133.07
30,000	209.06	206.35	203.89	201.64	199.60
40,000	278.74	275.13	271.85	268.86	266.13
50,000	348.42	343.91	339.81	336.07	332.66
100,000	696.84	687.82	679.61	672.14	665.31
125,000	871.05	859.77	849.52	840.17	831.63
150,000	1045.26	1031.73	1019.42	1008.20	997.96
175,000	1219.47	1203.68	1189.32	1176.23	1164.28
200,000	1393.68	1375.63	1359.22	1344.27	1330.61
225,000	1567.89	1547.59	1529.12	1512.30	1496.94
250,000	1742.10	1719.54	1699.03	1680.33	1663.26
275,000	1916.31	1891.50	1868.93	1848.36	1829.59
300,000	2090.52	2063.45	2038.83	2016.40	1995.91
325,000	2264.73	2235.40	2208.73	2184.43	2162.24
350,000	2438.94	2407.36	2378.64	2352.46	2328.56
375,000	2613.15	2579.31	2548.54	2520.49	2494.89
400,000	2787.36	2751.26	2718.44	2688.53	2661.21
425,000	2961.56	2923.22	2888.34	2856.56	2827.54
450,000	3135.77	3095.17	3058.24	3024.59	2993.87
475,000	3309.98	3267.13	3228.15	3192.62	3160.19
500,000	3484.19	3439.08	3398.05	3360.66	3326.52
525,000	3658.40	3611.03	3567.95	3528.69	3492.84
550,000	3832.61	3782.99	3737.85	3696.72	3659.17
575,000	4006.82	3954.94	3907.75	3864.75	3825.49
600,000	4181.03	4126.89	4077.66	4032.79	3991.82
625,000	4355.24	4298.85	4247.56	4200.82	4158.15
650,000	4529.45	4470.80	4417.46	4368.85	4324.47
675,000	4703.66	4642.76	4587.36	4536.88	4490.80
700,000	4877.87	4814.71	4757.27	4704.92	4657.12
725,000	5052.08	4986.66	4927.17	4872.95	4823.45
750,000	5226.29	5158.62	5097.07	5040.98	4989.77
775,000	5400.50	5330.57	5266.97	5209.01	5156.10
800,000	5574.71	5502.52	5436.87	5377.05	5322.42
825,000	5748.91	5674.48	5606.78	5545.08	5488.75
850,000	5923.12	5846.43	5776.68	5713.11	5655.08
875,000	6097.33	6018.39	5946.58	5881.14	5821.40
900,000	6271.54	6190.34	6116.48	6049.18	5987.73

Monthly Payment Loans   **7.25%**

Loan Amount	Amortization Period in Years				
	5	7	8	10	12
10	0.20	0.16	0.14	0.12	0.11
20	0.40	0.31	0.28	0.24	0.21
30	0.60	0.46	0.42	0.36	0.32
40	0.80	0.61	0.56	0.47	0.42
50	1.00	0.77	0.69	0.59	0.53
100	2.00	1.53	1.38	1.18	1.05
200	3.99	3.05	2.76	2.35	2.09
300	5.98	4.57	4.13	3.53	3.13
400	7.97	6.09	5.51	4.70	4.17
500	9.96	7.61	6.88	5.88	5.21
1,000	19.92	15.22	13.76	11.75	10.42
2,000	39.84	30.44	27.52	23.49	20.84
3,000	59.76	45.65	41.28	35.23	31.26
4,000	79.68	60.87	55.04	46.97	41.68
5,000	99.60	76.08	68.80	58.71	52.09
10,000	199.20	152.16	137.59	117.41	104.18
20,000	398.39	304.31	275.17	234.81	208.36
30,000	597.59	456.46	412.76	352.21	312.53
40,000	796.78	608.61	550.34	469.61	416.71
50,000	995.97	760.76	687.93	587.01	520.88
100,000	1991.94	1521.52	1375.85	1174.02	1041.76
125,000	2489.93	1901.90	1719.81	1467.52	1302.20
150,000	2987.91	2282.28	2063.77	1761.02	1562.64
175,000	3485.89	2662.66	2407.74	2054.52	1823.08
200,000	3983.88	3043.04	2751.70	2348.03	2083.52
225,000	4481.86	3423.42	3095.66	2641.53	2343.96
250,000	4979.85	3803.80	3439.62	2935.03	2604.39
275,000	5477.83	4184.18	3783.58	3228.53	2864.83
300,000	5975.81	4564.56	4127.54	3522.04	3125.27
325,000	6473.80	4944.94	4471.50	3815.54	3385.71
350,000	6971.78	5325.32	4815.47	4109.04	3646.15
375,000	7469.77	5705.70	5159.43	4402.54	3906.59
400,000	7967.75	6086.08	5503.39	4696.05	4167.03
425,000	8465.73	6466.46	5847.35	4989.55	4427.47
450,000	8963.72	6846.84	6191.31	5283.05	4687.91
475,000	9461.70	7227.22	6535.27	5576.55	4948.35
500,000	9959.69	7607.60	6879.24	5870.06	5208.78
525,000	10457.67	7987.98	7223.20	6163.56	5469.22
550,000	10955.65	8368.36	7567.16	6457.06	5729.66
575,000	11453.64	8748.74	7911.12	6750.56	5990.10
600,000	11951.62	9129.12	8255.08	7044.07	6250.54
625,000	12449.61	9509.50	8599.04	7337.57	6510.98
650,000	12947.59	9889.87	8943.00	7631.07	6771.42
675,000	13445.57	10270.25	9286.97	7924.58	7031.86
700,000	13943.56	10650.63	9630.93	8218.08	7292.30
725,000	14441.54	11031.01	9974.89	8511.58	7552.73
750,000	14939.53	11411.39	10318.85	8805.08	7813.17
775,000	15437.51	11791.77	10662.81	9098.59	8073.61
800,000	15935.49	12172.15	11006.77	9392.09	8334.05
825,000	16433.48	12552.53	11350.74	9685.59	8594.49
850,000	16931.46	12932.91	11694.70	9979.09	8854.93
875,000	17429.45	13313.29	12038.66	10272.60	9115.37
900,000	17927.43	13693.67	12382.62	10566.10	9375.81

Table 7   145

7.25%   Monthly Payment Loans

Amortization Period in Years

Loan Amount	15	16	17	18	20
10	0.10	0.09	0.09	0.09	0.08
20	0.19	0.18	0.18	0.17	0.16
30	0.28	0.27	0.26	0.25	0.24
40	0.37	0.36	0.35	0.34	0.32
50	0.46	0.45	0.43	0.42	0.40
100	0.92	0.89	0.86	0.84	0.80
200	1.83	1.77	1.71	1.67	1.59
300	2.74	2.65	2.57	2.50	2.38
400	3.66	3.53	3.42	3.33	3.17
500	4.57	4.41	4.28	4.16	3.96
1,000	9.13	8.82	8.55	8.31	7.91
2,000	18.26	17.63	17.09	16.61	15.81
3,000	27.39	26.45	25.63	24.91	23.72
4,000	36.52	35.26	34.17	33.21	31.62
5,000	45.65	44.08	42.71	41.51	39.52
10,000	91.29	88.15	85.42	83.02	79.04
20,000	182.58	176.30	170.83	166.04	158.08
30,000	273.86	264.44	256.24	249.06	237.12
40,000	365.15	352.59	341.65	332.07	316.16
50,000	456.44	440.73	427.07	415.09	395.19
100,000	912.87	881.46	854.13	830.18	790.38
125,000	1141.08	1101.83	1067.66	1037.72	987.97
150,000	1369.30	1322.19	1281.19	1245.26	1185.57
175,000	1597.52	1542.56	1494.72	1452.81	1383.16
200,000	1825.73	1762.92	1708.25	1660.35	1580.76
225,000	2053.95	1983.28	1921.78	1867.89	1778.35
250,000	2282.16	2203.65	2135.31	2075.44	1975.94
275,000	2510.38	2424.01	2348.84	2282.98	2173.54
300,000	2738.59	2644.38	2562.37	2490.52	2371.13
325,000	2966.81	2864.74	2775.90	2698.06	2568.73
350,000	3195.03	3085.11	2989.43	2905.61	2766.32
375,000	3423.24	3305.47	3202.96	3113.15	2963.91
400,000	3651.46	3525.84	3416.49	3320.69	3161.51
425,000	3879.67	3746.20	3630.02	3528.24	3359.10
450,000	4107.89	3966.56	3843.55	3735.78	3556.70
475,000	4336.10	4186.93	4057.08	3943.32	3754.29
500,000	4564.32	4407.29	4270.62	4150.87	3951.88
525,000	4792.54	4627.66	4484.15	4358.41	4149.48
550,000	5020.75	4848.02	4697.68	4565.95	4347.07
575,000	5248.97	5068.39	4911.21	4773.50	4544.67
600,000	5477.18	5288.75	5124.74	4981.04	4742.26
625,000	5705.40	5509.11	5338.27	5188.58	4939.85
650,000	5933.61	5729.48	5551.80	5396.12	5137.45
675,000	6161.83	5949.84	5765.33	5603.67	5335.04
700,000	6390.05	6170.21	5978.86	5811.21	5532.64
725,000	6618.26	6390.57	6192.39	6018.75	5730.23
750,000	6846.48	6610.94	6405.92	6226.30	5927.82
775,000	7074.69	6831.30	6619.45	6433.84	6125.42
800,000	7302.91	7051.67	6832.98	6641.38	6323.01
825,000	7531.12	7272.03	7046.51	6848.93	6520.61
850,000	7759.34	7492.39	7260.04	7056.47	6718.20
875,000	7987.56	7712.76	7473.57	7264.01	6915.79
900,000	8215.77	7933.12	7687.10	7471.55	7113.39

Monthly Payment Loans   **7.25%**

Loan Amount	Amortization Period in Years				
	21	22	23	24	25
10	0.08	0.08	0.08	0.08	0.08
20	0.16	0.16	0.15	0.15	0.15
30	0.24	0.23	0.23	0.23	0.22
40	0.31	0.31	0.30	0.30	0.29
50	0.39	0.38	0.38	0.37	0.37
100	0.78	0.76	0.75	0.74	0.73
200	1.55	1.52	1.50	1.47	1.45
300	2.33	2.28	2.24	2.21	2.17
400	3.10	3.04	2.99	2.94	2.90
500	3.87	3.80	3.73	3.67	3.62
1,000	7.74	7.59	7.46	7.34	7.23
2,000	15.48	15.18	14.92	14.68	14.46
3,000	23.22	22.77	22.37	22.01	21.69
4,000	30.95	30.36	29.83	29.35	28.92
5,000	38.69	37.95	37.28	36.69	36.15
10,000	77.38	75.89	74.56	73.37	72.29
20,000	154.75	151.78	149.12	146.73	144.57
30,000	232.13	227.67	223.68	220.09	216.85
40,000	309.50	303.56	298.24	293.45	289.13
50,000	386.88	379.45	372.79	366.81	361.41
100,000	773.75	758.90	745.58	733.61	722.81
125,000	967.19	948.62	931.98	917.01	903.51
150,000	1160.63	1138.35	1118.37	1100.41	1084.22
175,000	1354.06	1328.07	1304.77	1283.81	1264.92
200,000	1547.50	1517.79	1491.16	1467.22	1445.62
225,000	1740.94	1707.52	1677.56	1650.62	1626.32
250,000	1934.37	1897.24	1863.95	1834.02	1807.02
275,000	2127.81	2086.96	2050.35	2017.42	1987.72
300,000	2321.25	2276.69	2236.74	2200.82	2168.43
325,000	2514.68	2466.41	2423.14	2384.22	2349.13
350,000	2708.12	2656.13	2609.53	2567.62	2529.83
375,000	2901.56	2845.86	2795.93	2751.02	2710.53
400,000	3094.99	3035.58	2982.32	2934.43	2891.23
425,000	3288.43	3225.30	3168.71	3117.83	3071.93
450,000	3481.87	3415.03	3355.11	3301.23	3252.64
475,000	3675.30	3604.75	3541.50	3484.63	3433.34
500,000	3868.74	3794.47	3727.90	3668.03	3614.04
525,000	4062.18	3984.20	3914.29	3851.43	3794.74
550,000	4255.61	4173.92	4100.69	4034.83	3975.44
575,000	4449.05	4363.64	4287.08	4218.23	4156.14
600,000	4642.49	4553.37	4473.48	4401.64	4336.85
625,000	4835.92	4743.09	4659.87	4585.04	4517.55
650,000	5029.36	4932.81	4846.27	4768.44	4698.25
675,000	5222.80	5122.54	5032.66	4951.84	4878.95
700,000	5416.23	5312.26	5219.06	5135.24	5059.65
725,000	5609.67	5501.98	5405.45	5318.64	5240.35
750,000	5803.11	5691.71	5591.85	5502.04	5421.06
775,000	5996.54	5881.43	5778.24	5685.45	5601.76
800,000	6189.98	6071.15	5964.63	5868.85	5782.46
825,000	6383.42	6260.88	6151.03	6052.25	5963.16
850,000	6576.85	6450.60	6337.42	6235.65	6143.86
875,000	6770.29	6640.32	6523.82	6419.05	6324.57
900,000	6963.73	6830.05	6710.21	6602.45	6505.27

Table 7   147

7.25%　　　Monthly Payment Loans

Amortization Period in Years

Loan Amount	26	27	28	29	30
10	0.08	0.08	0.07	0.07	0.07
20	0.15	0.15	0.14	0.14	0.14
30	0.22	0.22	0.21	0.21	0.21
40	0.29	0.29	0.28	0.28	0.28
50	0.36	0.36	0.35	0.35	0.35
100	0.72	0.71	0.70	0.69	0.69
200	1.43	1.41	1.40	1.38	1.37
300	2.14	2.12	2.09	2.07	2.05
400	2.86	2.82	2.79	2.76	2.73
500	3.57	3.53	3.49	3.45	3.42
1,000	7.14	7.05	6.97	6.89	6.83
2,000	14.27	14.09	13.93	13.78	13.65
3,000	21.40	21.13	20.89	20.67	20.47
4,000	28.53	28.17	27.85	27.56	27.29
5,000	35.66	35.21	34.81	34.45	34.11
10,000	71.31	70.42	69.62	68.89	68.22
20,000	142.61	140.84	139.24	137.77	136.44
30,000	213.92	211.26	208.85	206.66	204.66
40,000	285.22	281.68	278.47	275.54	272.88
50,000	356.53	352.10	348.08	344.43	341.09
100,000	713.05	704.20	696.16	688.85	682.18
125,000	891.31	880.25	870.20	861.06	852.73
150,000	1069.57	1056.30	1044.24	1033.27	1023.27
175,000	1247.83	1232.34	1218.28	1205.48	1193.81
200,000	1426.09	1408.39	1392.32	1377.69	1364.36
225,000	1604.35	1584.44	1566.36	1549.90	1534.90
250,000	1782.61	1760.49	1740.40	1722.11	1705.45
275,000	1960.87	1936.54	1914.44	1894.32	1875.99
300,000	2139.13	2112.59	2088.48	2066.53	2046.53
325,000	2317.39	2288.64	2262.52	2238.75	2217.08
350,000	2495.66	2464.68	2436.55	2410.96	2387.62
375,000	2673.92	2640.73	2610.59	2583.17	2558.17
400,000	2852.18	2816.78	2784.63	2755.38	2728.71
425,000	3030.44	2992.83	2958.67	2927.59	2899.25
450,000	3208.70	3168.88	3132.71	3099.80	3069.80
475,000	3386.96	3344.93	3306.75	3272.01	3240.34
500,000	3565.22	3520.97	3480.79	3444.22	3410.89
525,000	3743.48	3697.02	3654.83	3616.43	3581.43
550,000	3921.74	3873.07	3828.87	3788.64	3751.97
575,000	4100.00	4049.12	4002.91	3960.85	3922.52
600,000	4278.26	4225.17	4176.95	4133.06	4093.06
625,000	4456.52	4401.22	4350.99	4305.28	4263.61
650,000	4634.78	4577.27	4525.03	4477.49	4434.15
675,000	4813.05	4753.31	4699.06	4649.70	4604.69
700,000	4991.31	4929.36	4873.10	4821.91	4775.24
725,000	5169.57	5105.41	5047.14	4994.12	4945.78
750,000	5347.83	5281.46	5221.18	5166.33	5116.33
775,000	5526.09	5457.51	5395.22	5338.54	5286.87
800,000	5704.35	5633.56	5569.26	5510.75	5457.42
825,000	5882.61	5809.61	5743.30	5682.96	5627.96
850,000	6060.87	5985.65	5917.34	5855.17	5798.50
875,000	6239.13	6161.70	6091.38	6027.38	5969.05
900,000	6417.39	6337.75	6265.42	6199.59	6139.59

Monthly Payment Loans   **7.50%**

Loan Amount	5	7	8	10	12
			Amortization Period in Years		
10	0.21	0.16	0.14	0.12	0.11
20	0.41	0.31	0.28	0.24	0.22
30	0.61	0.47	0.42	0.36	0.32
40	0.81	0.62	0.56	0.48	0.43
50	1.01	0.77	0.70	0.60	0.53
100	2.01	1.54	1.39	1.19	1.06
200	4.01	3.07	2.78	2.38	2.12
300	6.02	4.61	4.17	3.57	3.17
400	8.02	6.14	5.56	4.75	4.23
500	10.02	7.67	6.95	5.94	5.28
1,000	20.04	15.34	13.89	11.88	10.56
2,000	40.08	30.68	27.77	23.75	21.11
3,000	60.12	46.02	41.66	35.62	31.66
4,000	80.16	61.36	55.54	47.49	42.21
5,000	100.19	76.70	69.42	59.36	52.77
10,000	200.38	153.39	138.84	118.71	105.53
20,000	400.76	306.77	277.68	237.41	211.05
30,000	601.14	460.15	416.52	356.11	316.57
40,000	801.52	613.54	555.36	474.81	422.10
50,000	1001.90	766.92	694.20	593.51	527.62
100,000	2003.80	1533.83	1388.39	1187.02	1055.23
125,000	2504.75	1917.29	1735.49	1483.78	1319.04
150,000	3005.70	2300.75	2082.59	1780.53	1582.84
175,000	3506.65	2684.20	2429.68	2077.29	1846.65
200,000	4007.59	3067.66	2776.78	2374.04	2110.46
225,000	4508.54	3451.12	3123.88	2670.79	2374.26
250,000	5009.49	3834.57	3470.97	2967.55	2638.07
275,000	5510.44	4218.03	3318.07	3264.30	2901.88
300,000	6011.39	4601.49	4165.17	3561.06	3165.68
325,000	6512.34	4984.94	4512.26	3857.81	3429.49
350,000	7013.29	5368.40	4859.36	4154.57	3693.30
375,000	7514.24	5751.86	5206.46	4451.32	3957.10
400,000	8015.10	6135.32	5553.55	4748.08	4220.91
425,000	8516.13	6518.77	5900.65	5044.83	4484.72
450,000	9017.08	6902.23	6247.75	5341.58	4748.52
475,000	9518.03	7285.69	6594.84	5638.34	5012.33
500,000	10018.98	7669.14	6941.94	5935.09	5276.14
525,000	10519.93	8052.60	7289.04	6231.85	5539.94
550,000	11020.88	8436.06	7636.13	6528.60	5803.75
575,000	11521.83	8819.51	7983.23	6825.36	6067.56
600,000	12022.77	9202.97	8330.33	7122.11	6331.36
625,000	12523.72	9586.43	8677.42	7418.87	6595.17
650,000	13024.67	9969.88	9024.52	7715.62	6858.98
675,000	13525.62	10353.34	9371.62	8012.37	7122.78
700,000	14026.57	10736.80	9718.71	8309.13	7386.59
725,000	14527.52	11120.25	10065.81	8605.88	7650.40
750,000	15028.47	11503.71	10412.91	8902.64	7914.20
775,000	15529.42	11887.17	10760.00	9199.39	8178.01
800,000	16030.36	12270.63	11107.10	9496.15	8441.82
825,000	16531.31	12654.08	11454.20	9792.90	8705.62
850,000	17032.26	13037.54	11801.29	10009.66	8969.43
875,000	17533.21	13421.00	12148.39	10386.41	9233.24
900,000	18034.16	13804.45	12495.49	10683.16	9497.04

Table 7   149

7.50%   Monthly Payment Loans

Loan Amount	15	16	17	18	20
10	0.10	0.09	0.09	0.09	0.09
20	0.19	0.18	0.18	0.17	0.17
30	0.28	0.27	0.27	0.26	0.25
40	0.38	0.36	0.35	0.34	0.33
50	0.47	0.45	0.44	0.43	0.41
100	0.93	0.90	0.87	0.85	0.81
200	1.86	1.80	1.74	1.69	1.62
300	2.79	2.69	2.61	2.54	2.42
400	3.71	3.59	3.48	3.38	3.23
500	4.64	4.48	4.35	4.23	4.03
1,000	9.28	8.96	8.69	8.45	8.06
2,000	18.55	17.92	17.38	16.90	16.12
3,000	27.82	26.88	26.07	25.35	24.17
4,000	37.09	35.84	34.75	33.80	32.23
5,000	46.36	44.80	43.44	42.25	40.28
10,000	92.71	89.59	86.88	84.50	80.56
20,000	185.41	179.17	173.75	169.00	161.12
30,000	278.11	268.75	260.62	253.50	241.68
40,000	370.81	358.34	347.49	337.99	322.24
50,000	463.51	447.92	434.36	422.49	402.80
100,000	927.02	895.83	868.71	844.98	805.60
125,000	1158.77	1119.79	1085.89	1056.22	1007.00
150,000	1390.52	1343.75	1303.07	1267.46	1208.39
175,000	1622.28	1567.70	1520.25	1478.71	1409.79
200,000	1854.03	1791.66	1737.42	1689.95	1611.19
225,000	2085.78	2015.62	1954.60	1901.19	1812.59
250,000	2317.54	2239.57	2171.78	2112.44	2013.99
275,000	2549.29	2463.53	2388.96	2323.68	2215.39
300,000	2781.04	2687.49	2606.13	2534.92	2416.78
325,000	3012.80	2911.44	2823.31	2746.17	2618.18
350,000	3244.55	3135.40	3040.49	2957.41	2819.58
375,000	3476.30	3359.36	3257.67	3168.65	3020.98
400,000	3708.05	3583.32	3474.84	3379.90	3222.38
425,000	3939.81	3807.27	3692.02	3591.14	3423.78
450,000	4171.56	4031.23	3909.20	3802.38	3625.17
475,000	4403.31	4255.19	4126.37	4013.63	3826.57
500,000	4635.07	4479.14	4343.55	4224.87	4027.97
525,000	4866.82	4703.10	4560.73	4436.11	4229.37
550,000	5098.57	4927.06	4777.91	4647.36	4430.77
575,000	5330.33	5151.01	4995.08	4858.60	4632.17
600,000	5562.08	5374.97	5212.26	5069.84	4833.56
625,000	5793.83	5598.93	5429.44	5281.09	5034.96
650,000	6025.59	5822.88	5646.62	5492.33	5236.36
675,000	6257.34	6046.84	5863.79	5703.57	5437.76
700,000	6489.09	6270.80	6080.97	5914.82	5639.16
725,000	6720.84	6494.76	6298.15	6126.06	5840.56
750,000	6952.60	6718.71	6515.33	6337.30	6041.95
775,000	7184.35	6942.67	6732.50	6548.55	6243.35
800,000	7416.10	7166.63	6949.68	6759.79	6444.75
825,000	7647.86	7390.58	7166.86	6971.03	6646.15
850,000	7879.61	7614.54	7384.03	7182.28	6847.55
875,000	8111.36	7838.50	7601.21	7393.52	7048.95
900,000	8343.12	8062.45	7818.39	7604.76	7250.34

Monthly Payment Loans   7.50%

Loan Amount	Amortization Period in Years				
	21	22	23	24	25
10	0.08	0.08	0.08	0.08	0.08
20	0.16	0.16	0.16	0.15	0.15
30	0.24	0.24	0.23	0.23	0.23
40	0.32	0.31	0.31	0.30	0.30
50	0.40	0.39	0.39	0.38	0.37
100	0.79	0.78	0.77	0.75	0.74
200	1.58	1.55	1.53	1.50	1.48
300	2.37	2.33	2.29	2.25	2.22
400	3.16	3.10	3.05	3.00	2.96
500	3.95	3.88	3.81	3.75	3.70
1,000	7.90	7.75	7.62	7.50	7.39
2,000	15.79	15.50	15.23	15.00	14.78
3,000	23.68	23.24	22.85	22.49	22.17
4,000	31.57	30.99	30.46	29.99	29.56
5,000	39.46	38.73	38.07	37.49	36.95
10,000	78.92	77.46	76.14	74.97	73.90
20,000	157.84	154.91	152.28	149.93	147.80
30,000	236.75	232.36	228.42	224.89	221.70
40,000	315.67	309.81	304.56	299.85	295.60
50,000	394.59	387.26	380.70	374.81	369.50
100,000	789.17	774.52	761.39	749.61	739.00
125,000	986.46	968.14	951.74	937.01	923.74
150,000	1183.75	1161.77	1142.09	1124.41	1108.49
175,000	1381.05	1355.40	1332.44	1311.81	1293.24
200,000	1578.34	1549.03	1522.78	1499.21	1477.99
225,000	1775.63	1742.65	1713.13	1686.62	1662.74
250,000	1972.92	1936.28	1903.48	1874.02	1847.48
275,000	2170.21	2129.91	2093.83	2061.42	2032.23
300,000	2367.50	2323.54	2284.17	2248.82	2216.98
325,000	2564.79	2517.16	2474.52	2436.22	2401.73
350,000	2762.09	2710.79	2664.87	2623.62	2586.47
375,000	2959.38	2904.42	2855.21	2811.02	2771.22
400,000	3156.67	3098.05	3045.56	2998.42	2955.97
425,000	3353.96	3291.67	3235.91	3185.83	3140.72
450,000	3551.25	3485.30	3426.26	3373.23	3325.47
475,000	3748.54	3678.93	3616.60	3560.63	3510.21
500,000	3945.84	3872.56	3806.95	3748.03	3694.96
525,000	4143.13	4066.18	3997.30	3935.43	3879.71
550,000	4340.42	4259.81	4187.65	4122.83	4064.46
575,000	4537.71	4453.44	4377.99	4310.23	4249.20
600,000	4735.00	4647.07	4568.34	4497.63	4433.95
625,000	4932.29	4840.69	4758.69	4685.04	4618.70
650,000	5129.58	5034.32	4949.04	4872.44	4803.45
675,000	5326.88	5227.95	5139.38	5059.84	4988.20
700,000	5524.17	5421.58	5329.73	5247.24	5172.94
725,000	5721.46	5615.21	5520.08	5434.64	5357.69
750,000	5918.75	5808.83	5710.42	5622.04	5542.44
775,000	6116.04	6002.46	5900.77	5809.44	5727.19
800,000	6313.33	6196.09	6091.12	5996.84	5911.93
825,000	6510.62	6389.72	6281.47	6184.25	6096.68
850,000	6707.92	6583.34	6471.81	6371.65	6281.43
875,000	6905.21	6776.97	6662.16	6559.05	6466.18
900,000	7102.50	6970.60	6852.51	6746.45	6650.93

Table 7   151

7.50%   Monthly Payment Loans

Loan Amount	26	27	28	29	30
10	0.08	0.08	0.08	0.08	0.07
20	0.15	0.15	0.15	0.15	0.14
30	0.22	0.22	0.22	0.22	0.21
40	0.30	0.29	0.29	0.29	0.28
50	0.37	0.37	0.36	0.36	0.35
100	0.73	0.73	0.72	0.71	0.70
200	1.46	1.45	1.43	1.42	1.40
300	2.19	2.17	2.14	2.12	2.10
400	2.92	2.89	2.86	2.83	2.80
500	3.65	3.61	3.57	3.53	3.50
1,000	7.30	7.21	7.13	7.06	7.00
2,000	14.59	14.42	14.26	14.12	13.99
3,000	21.89	21.63	21.39	21.18	20.98
4,000	29.18	28.83	28.52	28.23	27.97
5,000	36.48	36.04	35.65	35.29	34.97
10,000	72.95	72.08	71.29	70.58	69.93
20,000	145.89	144.15	142.58	141.15	139.85
30,000	218.83	216.23	213.87	211.72	209.77
40,000	291.77	288.30	285.15	282.29	279.69
50,000	364.71	360.37	356.44	352.87	349.61
100,000	729.41	720.74	712.87	705.73	699.22
125,000	911.76	900.92	891.09	882.16	874.02
150,000	1094.12	1081.11	1069.31	1058.59	1048.83
175,000	1276.47	1261.29	1247.52	1235.02	1223.63
200,000	1458.82	1441.47	1425.74	1411.45	1398.43
225,000	1641.17	1621.66	1603.96	1587.88	1573.24
250,000	1823.52	1801.84	1782.17	1764.31	1748.04
275,000	2005.88	1982.02	1960.39	1940.74	1922.84
300,000	2188.23	2162.21	2138.61	2117.17	2097.65
325,000	2370.58	2342.39	2316.82	2293.60	2272.45
350,000	2552.93	2522.57	2495.04	2470.03	2447.26
375,000	2735.28	2702.76	2673.26	2646.46	2622.06
400,000	2917.63	2882.94	2851.48	2822.89	2796.86
425,000	3099.99	3063.12	3029.69	2999.32	2971.67
450,000	3282.34	3243.31	3207.91	3175.75	3146.47
475,000	3464.69	3423.49	3386.13	3352.18	3321.27
500,000	3647.04	3603.67	3564.34	3528.61	3496.08
525,000	3829.39	3783.86	3742.56	3705.04	3670.88
550,000	4011.75	3964.04	3920.78	3881.47	3845.68
575,000	4194.10	4144.22	4098.99	4057.90	4020.49
600,000	4376.45	4324.41	4277.21	4234.33	4195.29
625,000	4558.80	4504.59	4455.43	4410.76	4370.10
650,000	4741.15	4684.77	4633.64	4587.19	4544.90
675,000	4923.51	4864.96	4811.86	4763.62	4719.70
700,000	5105.86	5045.14	4990.08	4940.05	4894.51
725,000	5288.21	5225.33	5168.29	5116.48	5069.31
750,000	5470.56	5405.51	5346.51	5292.91	5244.11
775,000	5652.91	5585.69	5524.73	5469.34	5418.92
800,000	5835.26	5765.88	5702.95	5645.77	5593.72
825,000	6017.62	5946.06	5881.16	5822.20	5768.52
850,000	6199.97	6126.24	6059.38	5998.63	5943.33
875,000	6382.32	6306.43	6237.60	6175.06	6118.13
900,000	6564.67	6486.61	6415.61	6351.49	6292.94

Monthly Payment Loans 7.75%

Loan Amount	Amortization Period in Years				
	5	7	8	10	12
10	0.21	0.16	0.15	0.13	0.11
20	0.41	0.31	0.29	0.25	0.22
30	0.61	0.47	0.43	0.37	0.33
40	0.81	0.62	0.57	0.49	0.43
50	1.01	0.78	0.71	0.61	0.54
100	2.02	1.55	1.41	1.21	1.07
200	4.04	3.10	2.81	2.41	2.14
300	6.05	4.64	4.21	3.61	3.21
400	8.07	6.19	5.61	4.81	4.28
500	10.08	7.74	7.01	6.01	5.35
1,000	20.16	15.47	14.01	12.01	10.69
2,000	40.32	30.93	28.02	24.01	21.38
3,000	60.48	46.39	42.03	36.01	32.07
4,000	80.63	61.85	56.04	48.01	42.76
5,000	100.79	77.31	70.05	60.01	53.44
10,000	201.57	154.62	140.10	120.02	106.88
20,000	403.14	309.24	280.20	240.03	213.76
30,000	604.71	463.86	420.30	360.04	320.64
40,000	806.28	618.48	560.40	480.05	427.52
50,000	1007.85	773.10	700.50	600.06	534.40
100,000	2015.70	1546.20	1401.00	1200.11	1068.80
125,000	2519.62	1932.75	1751.25	1500.14	1336.00
150,000	3023.55	2319.30	2101.50	1800.16	1603.19
175,000	3527.47	2705.85	2451.75	2100.19	1870.39
200,000	4031.40	3092.40	2801.99	2400.22	2137.59
225,000	4535.32	3478.94	3152.24	2700.24	2404.79
250,000	5039.24	3865.49	3502.49	3000.27	2671.99
275,000	5543.17	4252.04	3852.74	3300.30	2939.18
300,000	6047.09	4638.59	4202.99	3600.32	3206.38
325,000	6551.02	5025.14	4553.24	3900.35	3473.58
350,000	7054.94	5411.69	4903.49	4200.38	3740.78
375,000	7558.86	5798.24	5253.73	4500.40	4007.98
400,000	8062.79	6184.79	5603.98	4800.43	4275.17
425,000	8566.71	6571.33	5954.23	5100.46	4542.37
450,000	9070.64	6957.88	6304.48	5400.48	4809.57
475,000	9574.56	7344.43	6654.73	5700.51	5076.77
500,000	10078.48	7730.98	7004.98	6000.54	5343.97
525,000	10582.41	8117.53	7355.23	6300.56	5611.16
550,000	11086.33	8504.08	7705.47	6600.59	5878.36
575,000	11590.26	8890.63	8055.72	6900.62	6145.56
600,000	12094.18	9277.18	8405.97	7200.64	6412.76
625,000	12598.10	9663.73	8756.22	7500.67	6679.96
650,000	13102.03	10050.27	9106.47	7800.70	6947.15
675,000	13605.95	10436.82	9456.72	8100.72	7214.35
700,000	14109.88	10823.37	9806.97	8400.75	7481.55
725,000	14613.80	11209.92	10157.21	8700.78	7748.75
750,000	15117.72	11596.47	10507.46	9000.80	8015.95
775,000	15621.65	11983.02	10857.71	9300.83	8283.14
800,000	16125.57	12369.57	11207.96	9600.86	8550.34
825,000	16629.50	12756.12	11558.21	9900.88	8817.54
850,000	17133.42	13142.66	11908.46	10200.91	9084.74
875,000	17637.34	13529.21	12258.71	10500.94	9351.94
900,000	18141.27	13915.76	12608.95	10800.96	9619.13

Table 7   153

7.75%   **Monthly Payment Loans**

Amortization Period in Years

Loan Amount	15	16	17	18	20
10	0.10	0.10	0.09	0.09	0.09
20	0.19	0.19	0.18	0.18	0.17
30	0.29	0.28	0.27	0.26	0.25
40	0.38	0.37	0.36	0.35	0.33
50	0.48	0.46	0.45	0.43	0.42
100	0.95	0.92	0.89	0.86	0.83
200	1.89	1.83	1.77	1.72	1.65
300	2.83	2.74	2.66	2.58	2.47
400	3.77	3.65	3.54	3.44	3.29
500	4.71	4.56	4.42	4.30	4.11
1,000	9.42	9.11	8.84	8.60	8.21
2,000	18.83	18.21	17.67	17.20	16.42
3,000	28.24	27.31	26.51	25.80	24.63
4,000	37.66	36.42	35.34	34.40	32.84
5,000	47.07	45.52	44.18	43.00	41.05
10,000	94.13	91.04	88.35	86.00	82.10
20,000	188.26	182.07	176.69	171.99	164.19
30,000	282.39	273.10	265.03	257.98	246.29
40,000	376.52	364.13	353.37	343.97	328.38
50,000	470.64	455.16	441.72	429.96	410.48
100,000	941.28	910.32	883.43	859.91	820.95
125,000	1176.60	1137.90	1104.28	1074.88	1026.19
150,000	1411.92	1365.48	1325.14	1289.86	1231.43
175,000	1647.24	1593.06	1545.99	1504.84	1436.66
200,000	1882.56	1820.64	1766.85	1719.81	1641.90
225,000	2117.88	2048.22	1987.70	1934.79	1847.14
250,000	2353.19	2275.80	2208.56	2149.76	2052.38
275,000	2588.51	2503.38	2429.41	2364.74	2257.61
300,000	2823.83	2730.96	2650.27	2579.72	2462.85
325,000	3059.15	2958.54	2871.12	2794.69	2668.09
350,000	3294.47	3186.12	3091.98	3009.67	2873.32
375,000	3529.79	3413.69	3312.84	3224.64	3078.56
400,000	3765.11	3641.27	3533.69	3439.62	3283.80
425,000	4000.43	3868.85	3754.55	3654.60	3489.04
450,000	4235.75	4096.43	3975.40	3869.57	3694.27
475,000	4471.06	4324.01	4195.26	4084.55	3899.51
500,000	4706.38	4551.59	4417.11	4299.52	4104.75
525,000	4941.70	4779.17	4637.97	4514.50	4309.98
550,000	5177.02	5006.75	4858.82	4729.48	4515.22
575,000	5412.34	5234.33	5079.68	4944.45	4720.46
600,000	5647.66	5461.91	5300.53	5159.43	4925.70
625,000	5882.98	5689.49	5521.39	5374.40	5130.93
650,000	6118.30	5917.07	5742.24	5589.38	5336.17
675,000	6353.62	6144.65	5963.10	5804.36	5541.41
700,000	6588.94	6372.23	6183.96	6019.33	5746.64
725,000	6824.25	6599.80	6404.81	6234.31	5951.88
750,000	7059.57	6827.38	6625.67	6449.28	6157.12
775,000	7294.89	7054.96	6846.52	6664.26	6362.36
800,000	7530.21	7282.54	7067.38	6879.24	6567.59
825,000	7765.53	7510.12	7288.23	7094.21	6772.83
850,000	8000.85	7737.70	7509.09	7309.19	6978.07
875,000	8236.17	7965.28	7729.94	7524.16	7183.30
900,000	8471.49	8192.86	7950.80	7739.14	7388.54

Monthly Payment Loans   7.75%

Loan Amount	\multicolumn{5}{c}{Amortization Period in Years}
	21	22	23	24	25
10	0.09	0.08	0.08	0.08	0.08
20	0.17	0.16	0.16	0.16	0.16
30	0.25	0.24	0.24	0.23	0.23
40	0.33	0.32	0.32	0.31	0.31
50	0.41	0.40	0.39	0.39	0.38
100	0.81	0.80	0.78	0.77	0.76
200	1.61	1.59	1.56	1.54	1.52
300	2.42	2.38	2.34	2.30	2.27
400	3.22	3.17	3.11	3.07	3.03
500	4.03	3.96	3.89	3.83	3.78
1,000	8.05	7.91	7.78	7.66	7.56
2,000	16.10	15.81	15.55	15.32	15.11
3,000	24.15	23.71	23.33	22.98	22.66
4,000	32.19	31.62	31.10	30.64	30.22
5,000	40.24	39.52	38.87	38.29	37.77
10,000	80.48	79.03	77.74	76.58	75.54
20,000	160.95	158.06	155.47	153.16	151.07
30,000	241.42	237.09	233.21	229.73	226.60
40,000	321.90	316.11	310.94	306.31	302.14
50,000	402.37	395.14	388.68	382.88	377.67
100,000	804.73	790.28	777.35	765.76	755.33
125,000	1005.91	987.85	971.69	957.20	944.17
150,000	1207.10	1185.41	1166.03	1148.64	1133.00
175,000	1408.28	1382.98	1360.36	1340.08	1321.83
200,000	1609.46	1580.55	1554.70	1531.52	1510.66
225,000	1810.64	1778.12	1749.04	1722.96	1699.49
250,000	2011.82	1975.69	1943.38	1914.39	1888.33
275,000	2213.00	2173.26	2137.71	2105.83	2077.16
300,000	2414.19	2370.82	2332.05	2297.27	2265.99
325,000	2615.37	2568.39	2526.39	2488.71	2454.82
350,000	2816.55	2765.96	2720.72	2680.15	2643.66
375,000	3017.73	2963.53	2915.06	2871.59	2832.49
400,000	3218.91	3161.10	3109.40	3063.03	3021.32
425,000	3420.10	3358.66	3303.73	3254.47	3210.15
450,000	3621.28	3556.23	3498.07	3445.91	3398.98
475,000	3822.46	3753.80	3692.41	3637.34	3587.82
500,000	4023.64	3951.37	3886.75	3828.78	3776.65
525,000	4224.82	4148.94	4081.08	4020.22	3965.48
550,000	4426.00	4346.51	4275.42	4211.66	4154.31
575,000	4627.19	4544.07	4469.76	4403.10	4343.15
600,000	4828.37	4741.64	4664.09	4594.54	4531.98
625,000	5029.55	4939.21	4858.43	4785.98	4720.81
650,000	5230.73	5136.78	5052.77	4977.42	4909.64
675,000	5431.91	5334.35	5247.11	5168.86	5098.47
700,000	5633.10	5531.91	5441.44	5360.29	5287.31
725,000	5834.28	5729.48	5635.78	5551.73	5476.14
750,000	6035.46	5927.05	5830.12	5743.17	5664.97
775,000	6236.64	6124.62	6024.45	5934.61	5853.80
800,000	6437.82	6322.19	6218.79	6126.05	6042.64
825,000	6639.00	6519.76	6413.13	6317.49	6231.47
850,000	6840.19	6717.32	6607.46	6508.93	6420.30
875,000	7041.37	6914.89	6801.80	6700.37	6609.13
900,000	7242.55	7112.46	6996.14	6891.81	6797.96

Table 7   155

7.75%   Monthly Payment Loans

Amortization Period in Years

Loan Amount	26	27	28	29	30
10	0.08	0.08	0.08	0.08	0.08
20	0.15	0.15	0.15	0.15	0.15
30	0.23	0.23	0.22	0.22	0.22
40	0.30	0.30	0.30	0.29	0.29
50	0.38	0.37	0.37	0.37	0.36
100	0.75	0.74	0.73	0.73	0.72
200	1.50	1.48	1.46	1.45	1.44
300	2.24	2.22	2.19	2.17	2.15
400	2.99	2.95	2.92	2.90	2.87
500	3.73	3.69	3.65	3.62	3.59
1,000	7.46	7.38	7.30	7.23	7.17
2,000	14.92	14.75	14.60	14.46	14.33
3,000	22.38	22.13	21.90	21.69	21.50
4,000	29.84	29.50	29.19	28.92	28.66
5,000	37.30	36.88	36.49	36.14	35.83
10,000	74.60	73.75	72.98	72.28	71.65
20,000	149.19	147.49	145.95	144.56	143.29
30,000	223.78	221.23	218.93	216.83	214.93
40,000	298.38	294.98	291.90	289.11	286.57
50,000	372.97	368.72	364.87	361.38	358.21
100,000	745.93	737.44	729.74	722.76	716.42
125,000	932.41	921.79	912.18	903.45	895.52
150,000	1118.90	1106.15	1094.61	1084.14	1074.62
175,000	1305.38	1290.51	1277.04	1264.83	1253.73
200,000	1491.86	1474.87	1459.48	1445.52	1432.83
225,000	1678.34	1659.22	1641.91	1626.21	1611.93
250,000	1864.82	1843.58	1824.35	1806.89	1791.04
275,000	2051.30	2027.94	2006.78	1987.58	1970.14
300,000	2237.79	2212.30	2189.21	2168.27	2149.24
325,000	2424.27	2396.65	2371.65	2348.96	2328.34
350,000	2610.75	2581.01	2554.08	2529.65	2507.45
375,000	2797.23	2765.37	2736.52	2710.34	2686.55
400,000	2983.71	2949.73	2918.95	2891.03	2865.65
425,000	3170.19	3134.08	3101.38	3071.72	3044.76
450,000	3356.68	3318.44	3283.82	3252.41	3223.86
475,000	3543.16	3502.80	3466.25	3433.09	3402.96
500,000	3729.64	3687.16	3648.69	3613.78	3582.07
525,000	3916.12	3871.51	3831.12	3794.47	3761.17
550,000	4102.60	4055.87	4013.55	3975.16	3940.27
575,000	4289.09	4240.23	4195.99	4155.85	4119.38
600,000	4475.57	4424.59	4378.42	4336.54	4298.48
625,000	4662.05	4608.95	4560.86	4517.23	4477.58
650,000	4848.53	4793.30	4743.29	4697.92	4656.68
675,000	5035.01	4977.66	4925.72	4878.61	4835.79
700,000	5221.49	5162.02	5108.16	5059.30	5014.89
725,000	5407.98	5346.38	5290.59	5239.98	5193.99
750,000	5594.46	5530.73	5473.03	5420.67	5373.10
775,000	5780.94	5715.09	5655.46	5601.36	5552.20
800,000	5967.42	5899.45	5837.90	5782.05	5731.30
825,000	6153.90	6083.81	6020.33	5962.74	5910.41
850,000	6340.38	6268.16	6202.76	6143.43	6089.51
875,000	6526.87	6452.52	6385.20	6324.12	6268.61
900,000	6713.35	6636.88	6567.63	6504.81	6447.72

Monthly Payment Loans   **8.00%**

Loan Amount	Amortization Period in Years				
	5	7	8	10	12
10	0.21	0.16	0.15	0.13	0.11
20	0.41	0.32	0.29	0.25	0.22
30	0.61	0.47	0.43	0.37	0.33
40	0.82	0.63	0.57	0.49	0.44
50	1.02	0.78	0.71	0.61	0.55
100	2.03	1.56	1.42	1.22	1.09
200	4.06	3.12	2.83	2.43	2.17
300	6.09	4.68	4.25	3.64	3.25
400	8.12	6.24	5.66	4.86	4.33
500	10.14	7.80	7.07	6.07	5.42
1,000	20.28	15.59	14.14	12.14	10.83
2,000	40.56	31.18	28.28	24.27	21.65
3,000	60.83	46.76	42.42	36.40	32.48
4,000	81.11	62.35	56.55	48.54	43.30
5,000	101.39	77.94	70.69	60.67	54.13
10,000	202.77	155.87	141.37	121.33	108.25
20,000	405.53	311.73	282.74	242.66	216.50
30,000	608.30	467.59	424.11	363.99	324.74
40,000	811.06	623.45	565.47	485.32	432.99
50,000	1013.82	779.32	706.84	606.64	541.23
100,000	2027.64	1558.63	1413.67	1213.28	1082.46
125,000	2534.55	1948.28	1767.09	1516.60	1353.07
150,000	3041.46	2337.94	2120.51	1819.92	1623.68
175,000	3548.37	2727.59	2473.92	2123.24	1894.30
200,000	4055.28	3117.25	2827.34	2426.56	2164.91
225,000	4562.19	3506.90	3180.76	2729.88	2435.52
250,000	5069.10	3896.56	3534.17	3033.19	2706.14
275,000	5576.01	4286.21	3887.59	3336.51	2976.75
300,000	6082.92	4675.87	4241.01	3639.83	3247.36
325,000	6589.83	5065.52	4594.43	3943.15	3517.98
350,000	7096.74	5455.18	4947.84	4246.47	3788.59
375,000	7603.65	5844.84	5301.26	4549.79	4059.20
400,000	8110.56	6234.49	5654.68	4853.11	4329.82
425,000	8617.47	6624.15	6008.09	5156.43	4600.43
450,000	9124.38	7013.80	6361.51	5459.75	4871.04
475,000	9631.29	7403.46	6714.93	5763.07	5141.65
500,000	10138.20	7793.11	7068.34	6066.38	5412.27
525,000	10645.11	8182.77	7421.76	6369.70	5682.88
550,000	11152.02	8572.42	7775.18	6673.02	5953.49
575,000	11658.93	8962.08	8128.60	6976.34	6224.11
600,000	12165.84	9351.73	8482.01	7279.66	6494.72
625,000	12672.75	9741.39	8835.43	7582.98	6765.33
650,000	13179.66	10131.04	9188.85	7886.30	7035.95
675,000	13686.57	10520.70	9542.26	8189.62	7306.56
700,000	14193.48	10910.36	9895.68	8492.94	7577.17
725,000	14700.39	11300.01	10249.10	8796.26	7847.79
750,000	15207.30	11689.67	10602.51	9099.57	8118.40
775,000	15714.21	12079.32	10955.93	9402.89	8389.01
800,000	16221.12	12468.98	11309.35	9706.21	8659.63
825,000	16728.03	12858.63	11662.77	10009.53	8930.24
850,000	17234.94	13248.29	12016.18	10312.85	9200.85
875,000	17741.85	13637.94	12369.60	10616.17	9471.47
900,000	18248.76	14027.60	12723.02	10919.49	9742.08

Table 7   157

8.00% Monthly Payment Loans

Loan Amount	Amortization Period in Years				
	15	16	17	18	20
10	0.10	0.10	0.09	0.09	0.09
20	0.20	0.19	0.18	0.18	0.17
30	0.29	0.28	0.27	0.27	0.26
40	0.39	0.37	0.36	0.35	0.34
50	0.48	0.47	0.45	0.44	0.42
100	0.96	0.93	0.90	0.88	0.84
200	1.92	1.85	1.80	1.75	1.68
300	2.87	2.78	2.70	2.63	2.51
400	3.83	3.70	3.60	3.50	3.35
500	4.78	4.63	4.50	4.38	4.19
1,000	9.56	9.25	8.99	8.75	8.37
2,000	19.12	18.50	17.97	17.50	16.73
3,000	28.67	27.75	26.95	26.25	25.10
4,000	38.23	37.00	35.94	35.00	33.46
5,000	47.79	46.25	44.92	43.75	41.83
10,000	95.57	92.50	89.83	87.50	83.65
20,000	191.14	184.99	179.66	175.00	167.29
30,000	286.70	277.48	269.48	262.49	250.94
40,000	382.27	369.98	359.31	349.99	334.58
50,000	477.83	462.47	449.13	437.49	418.23
100,000	955.66	924.93	898.26	874.97	836.45
125,000	1194.57	1156.16	1122.83	1093.71	1045.56
150,000	1433.48	1387.39	1347.39	1312.45	1254.67
175,000	1672.40	1618.62	1571.95	1531.19	1463.78
200,000	1911.31	1849.86	1796.52	1749.93	1672.89
225,000	2150.22	2081.09	2021.08	1968.67	1882.00
250,000	2389.14	2312.32	2245.65	2187.41	2091.11
275,000	2628.05	2543.55	2470.21	2406.15	2300.22
300,000	2866.96	2774.78	2694.78	2624.89	2509.33
325,000	3105.87	3006.01	2919.34	2843.63	2718.44
350,000	3344.79	3237.24	3143.90	3062.37	2927.55
375,000	3583.70	3468.47	3368.47	3281.11	3136.66
400,000	3822.61	3699.71	3593.03	3499.86	3345.77
425,000	4061.53	3930.94	3817.60	3718.60	3554.88
450,000	4300.44	4162.17	4042.16	3937.34	3763.99
475,000	4539.35	4393.40	4266.73	4156.08	3973.10
500,000	4778.27	4624.63	4491.29	4374.82	4182.21
525,000	5017.18	4855.86	4715.85	4593.56	4391.32
550,000	5256.09	5087.09	4940.42	4812.30	4600.43
575,000	5495.00	5318.32	5164.98	5031.04	4809.54
600,000	5733.92	5549.56	5389.55	5249.78	5018.65
625,000	5972.83	5780.79	5614.11	5468.52	5227.76
650,000	6211.74	6012.02	5838.67	5687.26	5436.87
675,000	6450.66	6243.25	6063.24	5906.00	5645.98
700,000	6689.57	6474.48	6287.80	6124.74	5855.09
725,000	6928.48	6705.71	6512.37	6343.48	6064.20
750,000	7167.40	6936.94	6736.93	6562.22	6273.31
775,000	7406.31	7168.17	6961.50	6780.97	6482.42
800,000	7645.22	7399.41	7186.06	6999.71	6691.53
825,000	7884.13	7630.64	7410.62	7218.45	6900.64
850,000	8123.05	7861.87	7635.19	7437.19	7109.75
875,000	8361.96	8093.10	7859.75	7655.93	7318.86
900,000	8600.87	8324.33	8084.32	7874.67	7527.97

Monthly Payment Loans   **8.00%**

Loan Amount	\multicolumn{5}{c}{Amortization Period in Years}
	21	22	23	24	25
10	0.09	0.09	0.08	0.08	0.08
20	0.17	0.17	0.16	0.16	0.16
30	0.25	0.25	0.24	0.24	0.24
40	0.33	0.33	0.32	0.32	0.31
50	0.42	0.41	0.40	0.40	0.39
100	0.83	0.81	0.80	0.79	0.78
200	1.65	1.62	1.59	1.57	1.55
300	2.47	2.42	2.39	2.35	2.32
400	3.29	3.23	3.18	3.13	3.09
500	4.11	4.04	3.97	3.92	3.86
1,000	8.21	8.07	7.94	7.83	7.72
2,000	16.41	16.13	15.87	15.65	15.44
3,000	24.62	24.19	23.81	23.47	23.16
4,000	32.82	32.25	31.74	31.29	30.88
5,000	41.03	40.31	39.68	39.11	38.60
10,000	82.05	80.62	79.35	78.21	77.19
20,000	164.09	161.24	158.70	156.42	154.37
30,000	246.13	241.86	238.04	234.62	231.55
40,000	328.18	322.48	317.39	312.83	308.73
50,000	410.22	403.09	396.73	391.03	385.91
100,000	820.43	806.18	793.46	782.06	771.82
125,000	1025.54	1007.73	991.82	977.57	964.78
150,000	1230.65	1209.27	1190.18	1173.09	1157.73
175,000	1435.75	1410.82	1388.55	1368.60	1350.68
200,000	1640.86	1612.36	1586.91	1564.11	1543.64
225,000	1845.97	1813.91	1785.27	1759.63	1736.59
250,000	2051.07	2015.45	1983.64	1955.14	1929.55
275,000	2256.18	2216.99	2182.00	2150.65	2122.50
300,000	2461.29	2418.54	2380.36	2346.17	2315.45
325,000	2666.40	2620.08	2578.73	2541.68	2508.41
350,000	2871.50	2821.63	2777.09	2737.19	2701.36
375,000	3076.61	3023.17	2975.45	2932.71	2894.32
400,000	3281.72	3224.72	3173.82	3128.22	3087.27
425,000	3486.82	3426.26	3372.18	3323.74	3280.22
450,000	3691.93	3627.81	3570.54	3519.25	3473.18
475,000	3897.04	3829.35	3768.90	3714.76	3666.13
500,000	4102.14	4030.89	3967.27	3910.28	3859.09
525,000	4307.25	4232.44	4165.63	4105.79	4052.04
550,000	4512.36	4433.98	4363.99	4301.30	4244.99
575,000	4717.47	4635.53	4562.36	4496.82	4437.95
600,000	4922.57	4837.07	4760.72	4692.33	4630.90
625,000	5127.68	5038.62	4959.08	4887.84	4823.86
650,000	5332.79	5240.16	5157.45	5083.36	5016.81
675,000	5537.89	5441.71	5355.81	5278.87	5209.76
700,000	5743.00	5643.25	5554.17	5474.38	5402.72
725,000	5948.11	5844.79	5752.54	5669.90	5595.67
750,000	6153.21	6046.34	5950.90	5865.41	5788.63
775,000	6358.32	6247.88	6149.26	6060.92	5981.58
800,000	6563.43	6449.43	6347.63	6256.44	6174.53
825,000	6768.54	6650.97	6545.99	6451.95	6367.49
850,000	6973.64	6852.52	6744.35	6647.47	6560.44
875,000	7178.75	7054.06	6942.72	6842.98	6753.40
900,000	7383.86	7255.61	7141.08	7038.49	6946.35

Table 7   159

Monthly Payment Loans

Loan Amount	Amortization Period in Years				
	26	27	28	29	30
10	0.08	0.08	0.08	0.08	0.08
20	0.16	0.16	0.15	0.15	0.15
30	0.23	0.23	0.23	0.23	0.23
40	0.31	0.31	0.30	0.30	0.30
50	0.39	0.38	0.38	0.37	0.37
100	0.77	0.76	0.75	0.74	0.74
200	1.53	1.51	1.50	1.48	1.47
300	2.29	2.27	2.25	2.22	2.21
400	3.06	3.02	2.99	2.96	2.94
500	3.82	3.78	3.74	3.70	3.67
1,000	7.63	7.55	7.47	7.40	7.34
2,000	15.26	15.09	14.94	14.80	14.68
3,000	22.88	22.63	22.41	22.20	22.02
4,000	30.51	30.18	29.88	29.60	29.36
5,000	38.13	37.72	37.34	37.00	36.69
10,000	76.26	75.43	74.68	74.00	73.38
20,000	152.52	150.86	149.36	147.99	146.76
30,000	228.78	226.29	224.03	221.99	220.13
40,000	305.04	301.72	298.71	295.98	293.51
50,000	381.30	377.14	373.38	369.98	366.89
100,000	762.60	754.28	746.76	739.95	733.77
125,000	953.25	942.85	933.45	924.94	917.21
150,000	1143.90	1131.42	1120.14	1109.92	1100.65
175,000	1334.55	1319.99	1306.83	1294.91	1284.09
200,000	1525.20	1508.56	1493.52	1479.90	1467.53
225,000	1715.85	1697.13	1680.21	1664.88	1650.98
250,000	1906.50	1885.70	1866.90	1849.87	1834.42
275,000	2097.15	2074.27	2053.59	2034.86	2017.86
300,000	2287.80	2262.84	2240.28	2219.84	2201.30
325,000	2478.45	2451.41	2426.97	2404.83	2384.74
350,000	2669.10	2639.98	2613.66	2589.82	2568.18
375,000	2859.75	2828.55	2800.35	2774.80	2751.62
400,000	3050.40	3017.12	2987.04	2959.79	2935.06
425,000	3241.05	3205.69	3173.73	3144.77	3118.50
450,000	3431.70	3394.26	3360.42	3329.76	3301.95
475,000	3622.35	3582.83	3547.11	3514.75	3485.39
500,000	3813.00	3771.40	3733.80	3699.73	3668.83
525,000	4003.65	3959.97	3920.49	3884.72	3852.27
550,000	4194.29	4148.54	4107.18	4069.71	4035.71
575,000	4384.94	4337.11	4293.87	4254.69	4219.15
600,000	4575.59	4525.68	4480.56	4439.68	4402.59
625,000	4766.24	4714.25	4667.25	4624.67	4586.03
650,000	4956.89	4902.82	4853.94	4809.65	4769.47
675,000	5147.54	5091.39	5040.63	4994.64	4952.92
700,000	5338.19	5279.96	5227.32	5179.63	5136.36
725,000	5528.84	5468.53	5414.01	5364.61	5319.80
750,000	5719.49	5657.10	5600.69	5549.60	5503.24
775,000	5910.14	5845.67	5787.38	5734.59	5686.68
800,000	6100.79	6034.24	5974.07	5919.57	5870.12
825,000	6291.44	6222.81	6160.76	6104.56	6053.56
850,000	6482.09	6411.38	6347.45	6289.54	6237.00
875,000	6672.74	6599.95	6534.14	6474.53	6420.45
900,000	6863.39	6788.52	6720.83	6659.52	6603.89

Monthly Payment Loans   **8.25%**

Loan Amount	Amortization Period in Years				
	5	7	8	10	12
10	0.21	0.16	0.15	0.13	0.11
20	0.41	0.32	0.29	0.25	0.22
30	0.62	0.48	0.43	0.37	0.33
40	0.82	0.63	0.58	0.50	0.44
50	1.02	0.79	0.72	0.62	0.55
100	2.04	1.58	1.43	1.23	1.10
200	4.08	3.15	2.86	2.46	2.20
300	6.12	4.72	4.28	3.68	3.29
400	8.16	6.29	5.71	4.91	4.39
500	10.20	7.86	7.14	6.14	5.49
1,000	20.40	15.72	14.27	12.27	10.97
2,000	40.80	31.43	28.53	24.54	21.93
3,000	61.19	47.14	42.80	36.80	32.89
4,000	81.59	62.85	57.06	49.07	43.85
5,000	101.99	78.56	71.33	61.33	54.82
10,000	203.97	157.12	142.65	122.66	109.63
20,000	407.93	314.23	285.29	245.31	219.25
30,000	611.89	471.34	427.93	367.96	328.87
40,000	815.86	628.45	570.57	490.62	438.49
50,000	1019.82	785.56	713.21	613.27	548.11
100,000	2039.63	1571.11	1426.41	1226.53	1096.21
125,000	2549.54	1963.89	1783.01	1533.16	1370.26
150,000	3059.44	2356.66	2139.62	1839.79	1644.32
175,000	3569.35	2749.44	2496.22	2146.43	1918.37
200,000	4079.26	3142.22	2852.82	2453.06	2192.42
225,000	4589.16	3534.99	3209.42	2759.69	2466.47
250,000	5099.07	3927.77	3566.02	3066.32	2740.52
275,000	5608.97	4320.55	3922.63	3372.95	3014.57
300,000	6118.88	4713.32	4279.23	3679.58	3288.63
325,000	6628.79	5106.10	4635.83	3986.22	3562.68
350,000	7138.69	5498.88	4992.43	4292.85	3836.73
375,000	7648.60	5891.65	5349.03	4599.48	4110.78
400,000	8158.51	6284.43	5705.63	4906.11	4384.83
425,000	8668.41	6677.21	6062.24	5212.74	4658.89
450,000	9178.32	7069.98	6418.84	5519.37	4932.94
475,000	9688.22	7462.76	6775.44	5826.00	5206.99
500,000	10198.13	7855.53	7132.04	6132.64	5481.04
525,000	10708.04	8248.31	7488.64	6439.27	5755.09
550,000	11217.94	8641.09	7845.25	6745.90	6029.14
575,000	11727.85	9033.86	8201.85	7052.53	6303.20
600,000	12237.76	9426.64	8558.45	7359.16	6577.25
625,000	12747.66	9819.42	8915.05	7665.79	6851.30
650,000	13257.57	10212.19	9271.65	7972.43	7125.35
675,000	13767.47	10604.97	9628.26	8279.06	7399.40
700,000	14277.38	10997.75	9984.86	8585.69	7673.46
725,000	14787.29	11390.52	10341.46	8892.32	7947.51
750,000	15297.19	11783.30	10698.06	9198.95	8221.56
775,000	15807.10	12176.08	11054.66	9505.58	8495.61
800,000	16317.01	12568.85	11411.26	9812.22	8769.66
825,000	16826.91	12961.63	11767.87	10118.85	9043.71
850,000	17336.82	13354.41	12124.47	10425.48	9317.77
875,000	17846.73	13747.18	12481.07	10732.11	9591.82
900,000	18356.63	14139.96	12837.67	11038.74	9865.87

Table 7   161

Monthly Payment Loans

Amortization Period in Years

Loan Amount	15	16	17	18	20
10	0.10	0.10	0.10	0.09	0.09
20	0.20	0.19	0.19	0.18	0.18
30	0.30	0.29	0.28	0.27	0.26
40	0.39	0.38	0.37	0.36	0.35
50	0.49	0.47	0.46	0.45	0.43
100	0.98	0.94	0.92	0.90	0.86
200	1.95	1.88	1.83	1.79	1.71
300	2.92	2.82	2.74	2.68	2.56
400	3.89	3.76	3.66	3.57	3.41
500	4.86	4.70	4.57	4.46	4.27
1,000	9.71	9.40	9.14	8.91	8.53
2,000	19.41	18.80	18.27	17.81	17.05
3,000	29.11	28.19	27.40	26.71	22.57
4,000	38.81	37.59	36.53	35.61	34.09
5,000	48.51	46.99	45.67	44.51	42.61
10,000	97.02	93.97	91.33	89.02	85.21
20,000	194.03	187.94	182.65	178.03	170.42
30,000	291.05	281.90	273.97	267.05	255.62
40,000	388.06	375.87	365.29	356.06	340.83
50,000	485.08	469.83	456.61	445.08	426.04
100,000	970.15	939.66	913.22	890.15	852.07
125,000	1212.68	1174.57	1141.52	1112.69	1065.09
150,000	1455.22	1409.48	1369.83	1335.23	1278.10
175,000	1697.75	1644.39	1598.13	1557.76	1491.12
200,000	1940.29	1879.31	1826.43	1780.30	1704.14
225,000	2182.82	2114.22	2054.74	2002.84	1917.15
250,000	2425.36	2349.13	2283.04	2225.37	2130.17
275,000	2667.89	2584.04	2511.34	2447.91	2343.19
300,000	2910.43	2818.96	2739.65	2670.45	2556.20
325,000	3152.96	3053.87	2967.95	2892.98	2769.22
350,000	3395.50	3288.78	3196.25	3115.52	2982.23
375,000	3638.03	3523.69	3424.56	3338.06	3195.25
400,000	3880.57	3758.61	3652.86	3560.60	3408.27
425,000	4123.10	3993.52	3881.17	3783.13	3621.28
450,000	4365.64	4228.43	4109.47	4005.67	3834.30
475,000	4608.17	4463.34	4337.77	4228.21	4047.32
500,000	4850.71	4698.26	4566.08	4450.74	4260.33
525,000	5093.24	4933.17	4794.38	4673.28	4473.35
550,000	5335.78	5168.08	5022.68	4895.82	4686.37
575,000	5578.31	5402.99	5250.99	5118.35	4899.38
600,000	5820.85	5637.91	5479.29	5340.89	5112.40
625,000	6063.38	5872.82	5707.59	5563.43	5325.42
650,000	6305.92	6107.73	5935.90	5785.96	5538.43
675,000	6548.45	6342.64	6164.20	6008.50	5751.45
700,000	6790.99	6577.56	6392.50	6231.04	5964.46
725,000	7033.52	6812.47	6620.81	6453.58	6177.48
750,000	7276.06	7047.38	6849.11	6676.11	6390.50
775,000	7518.59	7282.29	7077.41	6898.65	6603.51
800,000	7761.13	7517.21	7305.72	7121.19	6816.53
825,000	8003.66	7752.12	7534.02	7343.72	7029.55
850,000	8246.20	7987.03	7762.33	7566.26	7242.56
875,000	8488.73	8221.94	7990.63	7788.80	7455.58
900,000	8731.27	8456.86	8218.93	8011.33	7668.60

Monthly Payment Loans   8.25%

Loan Amount	\multicolumn{5}{c}{Amortization Period in Years}
	21	22	23	24	25
10	0.09	0.09	0.09	0.08	0.08
20	0.17	0.17	0.17	0.16	0.16
30	0.26	0.25	0.25	0.24	0.24
40	0.34	0.33	0.33	0.32	0.32
50	0.42	0.42	0.41	0.40	0.40
100	0.84	0.83	0.81	0.80	0.79
200	1.68	1.65	1.62	1.60	1.58
300	2.51	2.47	2.43	2.40	2.37
400	3.35	3.29	3.24	3.20	3.16
500	4.19	4.12	4.05	4.00	3.95
1,000	8.37	8.23	8.10	7.99	7.89
2,000	16.73	16.45	16.20	15.97	15.77
3,000	25.09	24.67	24.30	23.96	23.66
4,000	33.46	32.89	32.39	31.94	31.54
5,000	41.82	41.12	40.49	39.93	39.43
10,000	83.63	82.23	80.97	79.85	78.85
20,000	167.26	164.45	161.94	159.70	157.70
30,000	250.88	246.67	242.91	239.55	236.54
40,000	334.51	328.89	323.88	319.40	315.39
50,000	418.14	411.12	404.85	399.25	394.23
100,000	836.27	822.23	809.70	798.50	788.46
125,000	1045.34	1027.78	1012.13	998.13	985.57
150,000	1254.40	1233.34	1214.55	1197.75	1182.68
175,000	1463.47	1438.90	1416.98	1397.38	1379.79
200,000	1672.54	1644.45	1619.40	1597.00	1576.91
225,000	1881.60	1850.01	1821.83	1796.62	1774.02
250,000	2090.67	2055.56	2024.25	1996.25	1971.13
275,000	2299.74	2261.12	2226.68	2195.87	2168.24
300,000	2508.80	2466.67	2429.10	2395.50	2365.36
325,000	2717.87	2672.23	2631.53	2595.12	2562.47
350,000	2926.94	2877.79	2833.95	2794.75	2759.58
375,000	3136.00	3083.34	3036.38	2994.37	2956.69
400,000	3345.07	3288.90	3238.80	3193.99	3153.81
425,000	3554.14	3494.45	3441.23	3393.62	3350.92
450,000	3763.20	3700.01	3643.65	3593.24	3548.03
475,000	3972.27	3905.57	3846.08	3792.87	3745.14
500,000	4181.34	4111.12	4048.50	3992.49	3942.26
525,000	4390.40	4316.68	4250.93	4192.12	4139.37
550,000	4599.47	4522.23	4453.35	4391.74	4336.48
575,000	4808.53	4727.79	4655.78	4591.37	4533.59
600,000	5017.60	4933.34	4858.20	4790.99	4730.71
625,000	5226.67	5138.90	5060.63	4990.61	4927.82
650,000	5435.73	5344.46	5263.05	5190.24	5124.93
675,000	5644.80	5550.01	5465.48	5389.86	5322.04
700,000	5853.87	5755.57	5667.90	5589.49	5519.16
725,000	6062.93	5961.12	5870.33	5789.11	5716.27
750,000	6272.00	6166.68	6072.75	5988.74	5913.38
775,000	6481.07	6372.24	6275.18	6188.36	6110.49
800,000	6690.13	6577.79	6477.60	6387.98	6307.61
825,000	6899.20	6783.35	6680.03	6587.61	6504.72
850,000	7108.27	6988.90	6882.45	6787.23	6701.83
875,000	7317.33	7194.46	7084.88	6986.86	6898.94
900,000	7526.40	7400.01	7287.30	7186.48	7096.06

Table 7   163

8.25% Monthly Payment Loans

Loan Amount	Amortization Period in Years				
	26	27	28	29	30
10	0.08	0.08	0.08	0.08	0.08
20	0.16	0.16	0.16	0.16	0.16
30	0.24	0.24	0.23	0.23	0.23
40	0.32	0.31	0.31	0.31	0.31
50	0.39	0.39	0.39	0.38	0.38
100	0.78	0.78	0.77	0.76	0.76
200	1.56	1.55	1.53	1.52	1.51
300	2.34	2.32	2.30	2.28	2.26
400	3.12	3.09	3.06	3.03	3.01
500	3.90	3.86	3.82	3.79	3.76
1,000	7.80	7.72	7.64	7.58	7.52
2,000	15.59	15.43	15.28	15.15	15.03
3,000	23.39	23.14	22.92	22.72	22.54
4,000	31.18	30.86	30.56	30.30	30.06
5,000	38.98	38.57	38.20	37.87	37.57
10,000	77.95	77.13	76.40	75.73	75.13
20,000	155.89	154.26	152.79	151.46	150.26
30,000	233.83	231.39	229.18	227.19	225.38
40,000	311.77	308.52	305.58	302.92	300.51
50,000	389.71	385.64	381.97	378.65	375.64
100,000	779.42	771.28	763.94	757.29	751.27
125,000	974.28	964.10	954.92	946.61	939.09
150,000	1169.13	1156.92	1145.90	1135.93	1126.90
175,000	1363.98	1349.74	1336.88	1325.25	1314.72
200,000	1558.84	1542.56	1527.87	1514.58	1502.54
225,000	1753.69	1735.38	1718.85	1703.90	1690.35
250,000	1948.55	1928.20	1909.83	1893.22	1878.17
275,000	2143.40	2121.02	2100.81	2082.54	2065.99
300,000	2338.26	2313.84	2291.80	2271.86	2253.80
325,000	2533.11	2506.66	2482.78	2461.18	2441.62
350,000	2727.96	2699.48	2673.76	2650.50	2629.44
375,000	2922.82	2892.30	2864.74	2839.83	2817.25
400,000	3117.67	3085.12	3055.73	3029.15	3005.07
425,000	3312.53	3277.94	3246.71	3218.47	3192.89
450,000	3507.38	3470.76	3437.69	3407.79	3380.70
475,000	3702.24	3663.58	3628.67	3597.11	3568.52
500,000	3897.09	3856.40	3819.66	3786.43	3756.34
525,000	4091.94	4049.21	4010.64	3975.75	3944.15
550,000	4286.80	4242.03	4201.62	4165.08	4131.97
575,000	4481.65	4434.85	4392.61	4354.40	4319.79
600,000	4676.51	4627.67	4583.59	4543.72	4507.60
625,000	4871.36	4820.49	4774.57	4733.04	4695.42
650,000	5066.22	5013.31	4965.55	4922.36	4883.24
675,000	5261.07	5206.13	5156.54	5111.68	5071.05
700,000	5455.92	5398.95	5347.52	5301.00	5258.87
725,000	5650.78	5591.77	5538.50	5490.33	5446.69
750,000	5845.63	5784.59	5729.48	5679.65	5634.50
775,000	6040.49	5977.41	5920.47	5868.97	5822.32
800,000	6235.34	6170.23	6111.45	6058.29	6010.14
825,000	6430.20	6363.05	6302.43	6247.61	6197.95
850,000	6625.05	6555.87	6493.41	6436.93	6385.77
875,000	6819.90	6748.69	6684.40	6626.25	6573.59
900,000	7014.76	6941.51	6875.38	6815.58	6761.40

Monthly Payment Loans   **8.50%**

Loan Amount	Amortization Period in Years				
	5	7	8	10	12
10	0.21	0.16	0.15	0.13	0.12
20	0.42	0.32	0.29	0.25	0.23
30	0.62	0.48	0.44	0.38	0.34
40	0.83	0.64	0.58	0.50	0.45
50	1.03	0.80	0.72	0.62	0.56
100	2.06	1.59	1.44	1.24	1.12
200	4.11	3.17	2.88	2.48	2.23
300	6.16	4.76	4.32	3.72	3.34
400	8.21	6.34	5.76	4.96	4.45
500	10.26	7.92	7.20	6.20	5.56
1,000	20.52	15.84	14.40	12.40	11.11
2,000	41.04	31.68	28.79	24.80	22.21
3,000	61.55	47.51	43.18	37.20	33.31
4,000	82.07	63.35	57.57	49.60	44.41
5,000	102.59	79.19	71.97	62.00	55.51
10,000	205.17	158.37	143.93	123.99	111.01
20,000	410.34	316.73	287.85	247.98	222.02
30,000	615.50	475.10	431.77	371.96	333.02
40,000	820.67	633.46	575.69	495.95	444.03
50,000	1025.83	791.83	719.61	619.93	555.03
100,000	2051.66	1583.65	1439.22	1239.86	1110.06
125,000	2564.57	1979.57	1799.02	1549.83	1387.57
150,000	3077.48	2375.48	2158.82	1859.79	1665.09
175,000	3590.40	2771.39	2518.63	2169.75	1942.60
200,000	4103.31	3167.30	2878.43	2479.72	2220.12
225,000	4616.22	3563.21	3238.23	2789.68	2497.63
250,000	5129.14	3959.13	3598.04	3099.65	2775.14
275,000	5642.05	4355.04	3957.84	3409.61	3052.66
300,000	6154.96	4750.95	4317.64	3719.58	3330.17
325,000	6667.88	5146.86	4677.45	4029.54	3607.69
350,000	7180.79	5542.77	5037.25	4339.50	3885.20
375,000	7693.70	5938.69	5397.05	4649.47	4162.71
400,000	8206.62	6334.60	5756.86	4959.43	4440.23
425,000	8719.53	6730.51	6116.66	5269.40	4717.74
450,000	9232.44	7126.42	6476.46	5579.36	4995.26
475,000	9745.36	7522.34	6836.27	5889.33	5272.77
500,000	10258.27	7918.25	7196.07	6199.29	5550.28
525,000	10771.18	8314.16	7555.87	6509.25	5827.80
550,000	11284.10	8710.07	7915.68	6819.22	6105.31
575,000	11797.01	9105.98	8275.48	7129.18	6382.82
600,000	12309.92	9501.90	8635.28	7439.15	6660.34
625,000	12822.84	9897.81	8995.09	7749.11	6937.85
650,000	13335.75	10293.72	9354.89	8059.07	7215.37
675,000	13848.66	10689.63	9714.69	8369.04	7492.88
700,000	14361.58	11085.54	10074.50	8679.00	7770.39
725,000	14874.49	11481.46	10434.30	8988.97	8047.91
750,000	15387.40	11877.37	10794.10	9298.93	8325.42
775,000	15900.32	12273.28	11153.90	9608.90	8602.94
800,000	16413.23	12669.19	11513.71	9918.86	8880.45
825,000	16926.14	13065.11	11873.51	10228.82	9157.96
850,000	17439.06	13461.02	12233.31	10538.79	9435.48
875,000	17951.97	13856.93	12593.12	10848.75	9712.99
900,000	18464.88	14252.84	12952.92	11158.72	9990.51

Table 7   165

8.50%   Monthly Payment Loans

Amortization Period in Years

Loan Amount	15	16	17	18	20
10	0.10	0.10	0.10	0.10	0.09
20	0.20	0.20	0.19	0.19	0.18
30	0.30	0.29	0.28	0.28	0.27
40	0.40	0.39	0.38	0.37	0.35
50	0.50	0.48	0.47	0.46	0.44
100	0.99	0.96	0.93	0.91	0.87
200	1.97	1.91	1.86	1.82	1.74
300	2.96	2.87	2.79	2.72	2.61
400	3.94	3.82	3.72	3.63	3.48
500	4.93	4.78	4.65	4.53	4.34
1,000	9.85	9.55	9.29	9.06	8.68
2,000	19.70	19.09	18.57	18.11	17.36
3,000	29.55	28.64	27.85	27.17	26.04
4,000	39.39	38.18	37.14	36.22	34.72
5,000	49.24	47.73	46.42	45.28	43.40
10,000	98.48	95.45	92.83	90.55	86.79
20,000	196.95	190.90	185.66	181.10	173.57
30,000	295.43	286.35	278.49	271.64	260.35
40,000	393.90	381.80	371.32	362.19	347.13
50,000	492.37	477.25	464.15	452.73	433.92
100,000	984.74	954.50	928.30	905.46	867.83
125,000	1230.93	1193.12	1160.37	1131.83	1084.78
150,000	1477.11	1431.74	1392.44	1358.19	1301.74
175,000	1723.30	1670.36	1624.52	1584.56	1518.70
200,000	1969.48	1908.99	1856.59	1810.92	1735.65
225,000	2215.67	2147.61	2088.66	2037.28	1952.61
250,000	2461.85	2386.23	2320.74	2263.65	2169.56
275,000	2708.04	2624.86	2552.81	2490.01	2386.52
300,000	2954.22	2863.48	2784.88	2716.38	2603.47
325,000	3200.41	3102.10	3016.95	2942.74	2820.43
350,000	3446.59	3340.72	3249.03	3169.11	3037.39
375,000	3692.78	3579.35	3481.10	3395.47	3254.34
400,000	3938.96	3817.97	3713.17	3621.83	3471.30
425,000	4185.15	4056.59	3945.25	3848.20	3688.25
450,000	4431.33	4295.21	4177.32	4074.56	3905.21
475,000	4677.52	4533.84	4409.39	4300.93	4122.17
500,000	4923.70	4772.46	4641.47	4527.29	4339.12
525,000	5169.89	5011.08	4873.54	4753.66	4556.08
550,000	5416.07	5249.71	5105.61	4980.02	4773.03
575,000	5662.26	5488.33	5337.68	5206.39	4989.99
600,000	5908.44	5726.95	5569.76	5432.75	5206.94
625,000	6154.63	5965.57	5801.83	5659.11	5423.90
650,000	6400.81	6204.20	6033.90	5885.48	5640.86
675,000	6647.00	6442.82	6265.98	6111.84	5857.81
700,000	6893.18	6681.44	6498.05	6338.21	6074.77
725,000	7139.37	6920.06	6730.12	6564.57	6291.72
750,000	7385.55	7158.69	6962.20	6790.94	6508.68
775,000	7631.74	7397.31	7194.27	7017.30	6725.64
800,000	7877.92	7635.93	7426.34	7243.66	6942.59
825,000	8124.11	7874.56	7658.41	7470.03	7159.55
850,000	8370.29	8113.18	7890.49	7696.39	7376.50
875,000	8616.48	8351.80	8122.56	7922.76	7593.46
900,000	8862.66	8590.42	8354.63	8149.12	7810.41

166   Table 7

Monthly Payment Loans   8.50%

Loan Amount		Amortization Period in Years			
	21	22	23	24	25
10	0.09	0.09	0.09	0.09	0.09
20	0.18	0.17	0.17	0.17	0.17
30	0.26	0.26	0.25	0.25	0.25
40	0.35	0.34	0.34	0.33	0.33
50	0.43	0.42	0.42	0.41	0.41
100	0.86	0.84	0.83	0.82	0.81
200	1.71	1.68	1.66	1.64	1.62
300	2.56	2.52	2.48	2.45	2.42
400	3.41	3.36	3.31	3.27	3.23
500	4.27	4.20	4.14	4.08	4.03
1,000	8.53	8.39	8.27	8.16	8.06
2,000	17.05	16.77	16.53	16.31	16.11
3,000	25.57	25.16	24.79	24.46	24.16
4,000	34.09	33.54	33.05	32.61	32.21
5,000	42.62	41.93	41.31	40.76	40.27
10,000	85.23	83.85	82.61	81.51	80.53
20,000	170.45	167.69	165.22	163.02	161.05
30,000	255.68	251.53	247.83	244.53	241.57
40,000	340.90	335.37	330.44	326.04	322.10
50,000	426.12	419.21	413.05	407.55	402.62
100,000	852.24	838.41	826.09	815.09	805.23
125,000	1065.30	1048.01	1032.61	1018.86	1006.54
150,000	1278.36	1257.61	1239.13	1222.63	1207.85
175,000	1491.42	1467.22	1445.66	1426.40	1409.15
200,000	1704.48	1676.82	1652.18	1630.17	1610.46
225,000	1917.54	1886.42	1858.70	1833.94	1811.77
250,000	2130.60	2096.02	2065.22	2037.71	2013.07
275,000	2343.66	2305.62	2271.74	2241.48	2214.38
300,000	2556.72	2515.22	2478.26	2445.25	2415.69
325,000	2769.78	2724.83	2684.79	2649.02	2616.99
350,000	2982.84	2934.43	2891.31	2852.79	2818.30
375,000	3195.90	3144.03	3097.83	3056.56	3019.61
400,000	3408.96	3353.63	3304.35	3260.33	3220.91
425,000	3622.02	3563.23	3510.87	3464.10	3422.22
450,000	3835.08	3772.83	3717.39	3667.88	3623.53
475,000	4048.14	3982.43	3923.92	3871.65	3824.83
500,000	4261.20	4192.04	4130.44	4075.42	4026.14
525,000	4474.26	4401.64	4336.96	4279.19	4227.45
550,000	4687.32	4611.24	4543.48	4482.96	4428.75
575,000	4900.38	4820.84	4750.00	4686.73	4630.06
600,000	5113.44	5030.44	4956.52	4890.50	4831.37
625,000	5326.50	5240.04	5163.05	5094.27	5032.67
650,000	5539.56	5449.65	5369.57	5298.04	5233.98
675,000	5752.62	5659.25	5576.09	5501.81	5435.29
700,000	5965.68	5868.85	5782.61	5705.58	5636.59
725,000	6178.74	6078.45	5989.13	5909.35	5837.90
750,000	6391.80	6288.05	6195.65	6113.12	6039.21
775,000	6604.86	6497.65	6402.18	6316.89	6240.51
800,000	6817.92	6707.25	6608.70	6520.66	6441.82
825,000	7030.98	6916.86	6815.22	6724.43	6643.13
850,000	7244.04	7126.46	7021.74	6928.20	6844.44
875,000	7457.10	7336.06	7228.26	7131.98	7045.74
900,000	7670.16	7545.66	7434.78	7335.75	7247.05

Table 7   167

8.50%   Monthly Payment Loans

Amortization Period in Years

Loan Amount	26	27	28	29	30
10	0.08	0.08	0.08	0.08	0.08
20	0.16	0.16	0.16	0.16	0.16
30	0.24	0.24	0.24	0.24	0.24
40	0.32	0.32	0.32	0.31	0.31
50	0.40	0.40	0.40	0.39	0.39
100	0.80	0.79	0.79	0.78	0.77
200	1.60	1.58	1.57	1.55	1.54
300	2.39	2.37	2.35	2.33	2.31
400	3.19	3.16	3.13	3.10	3.08
500	3.99	3.95	3.91	3.88	3.85
1,000	7.97	7.89	7.82	7.75	7.69
2,000	15.93	15.77	15.63	15.50	15.38
3,000	23.90	23.66	23.44	23.25	23.07
4,000	31.86	31.54	31.25	31.00	30.76
5,000	39.82	39.43	39.07	38.74	38.45
10,000	79.64	78.85	78.13	77.48	76.90
20,000	159.28	157.69	156.25	154.96	153.79
30,000	238.92	236.53	234.38	232.44	230.68
40,000	318.56	315.37	312.50	309.91	307.57
50,000	398.19	394.22	390.63	387.39	384.46
100,000	796.38	788.43	781.25	774.78	768.92
125,000	995.48	985.53	976.56	968.47	961.15
150,000	1194.57	1182.64	1171.88	1162.16	1153.38
175,000	1393.67	1379.74	1367.19	1355.85	1345.60
200,000	1592.76	1576.85	1562.50	1549.55	1537.83
225,000	1791.86	1773.95	1757.81	1743.24	1730.06
250,000	1990.95	1971.06	1953.12	1936.93	1922.29
275,000	2190.05	2168.16	2148.44	2130.62	2114.52
300,000	2389.14	2365.27	2343.75	2324.32	2306.75
325,000	2588.24	2562.37	2539.06	2518.01	2498.97
350,000	2787.33	2759.48	2734.37	2711.70	2691.20
375,000	2986.43	2956.58	2929.68	2905.39	2883.43
400,000	3185.52	3153.69	3124.99	3099.09	3075.66
425,000	3384.62	3350.79	3320.31	3292.78	3267.89
450,000	3583.71	3547.90	3515.62	3486.47	3460.12
475,000	3782.81	3745.00	3710.93	3680.16	3652.34
500,000	3981.90	3942.11	3906.24	3873.86	3844.57
525,000	4181.00	4139.22	4101.55	4067.55	4036.80
550,000	4380.09	4336.32	4296.87	4261.24	4229.03
575,000	4579.19	4533.43	4492.18	4454.94	4421.26
600,000	4778.28	4730.53	4687.49	4648.63	4613.49
625,000	4977.38	4927.64	4882.80	4842.32	4805.71
650,000	5176.47	5124.74	5078.11	5036.01	4997.94
675,000	5375.57	5321.85	5273.42	5229.71	5190.17
700,000	5574.66	5518.95	5468.74	5423.40	5382.40
725,000	5773.76	5716.06	5664.05	5617.09	5574.63
750,000	5972.85	5913.16	5859.36	5810.78	5766.86
775,000	6171.95	6110.27	6054.67	6004.48	5959.08
800,000	6371.04	6307.37	6249.98	6198.17	6151.31
825,000	6570.14	6504.48	6445.30	6391.86	6343.54
850,000	6769.23	6701.58	6640.61	6585.55	6535.77
875,000	6968.33	6898.69	6835.92	6779.25	6728.00
900,000	7167.42	7095.79	7031.23	6972.94	6920.23

Monthly Payment Loans   **8.75%**

Loan Amount	Amortization Period in Years				
	5	7	8	10	12
10	0.21	0.16	0.15	0.13	0.12
20	0.42	0.32	0.30	0.26	0.23
30	0.62	0.48	0.44	0.38	0.34
40	0.83	0.64	0.59	0.51	0.45
50	1.04	0.80	0.73	0.63	0.57
100	2.07	1.60	1.46	1.26	1.13
200	4.13	3.20	2.91	2.51	2.25
300	6.20	4.79	4.36	3.76	3.38
400	8.26	6.39	5.81	5.02	4.50
500	10.32	7.99	7.27	6.27	5.62
1,000	20.64	15.97	14.53	12.54	11.24
2,000	41.28	31.93	29.05	25.07	22.48
3,000	61.92	47.89	43.57	37.60	33.72
4,000	82.55	63.85	58.09	50.14	44.96
5,000	103.19	79.82	72.61	62.67	56.20
10,000	206.38	159.63	145.21	125.33	112.40
20,000	412.75	319.25	290.42	250.66	224.80
30,000	619.12	478.88	435.63	375.99	337.20
40,000	825.49	638.50	580.84	501.31	449.60
50,000	1031.87	798.13	726.05	626.64	562.00
100,000	2063.73	1596.25	1452.09	1253.27	1124.00
125,000	2579.66	1995.32	1815.11	1566.59	1405.00
150,000	3095.59	2394.38	2178.13	1879.91	1686.00
175,000	3611.52	2793.44	2541.15	2193.22	1967.00
200,000	4127.45	3192.50	2904.17	2506.54	2248.00
225,000	4643.38	3591.57	3267.19	2819.86	2529.00
250,000	5159.31	3990.63	3630.21	3133.17	2810.00
275,000	5675.24	4389.69	3993.24	3446.49	3091.00
300,000	6191.17	4788.75	4356.26	3759.81	3372.00
325,000	6707.11	5187.82	4719.28	4073.12	3652.99
350,000	7223.04	5586.88	5082.30	4386.44	3933.99
375,000	7738.97	5985.94	5445.32	4699.76	4214.99
400,000	8254.90	6385.00	5808.34	5013.08	4495.99
425,000	8770.83	6784.06	6171.36	5326.39	4776.99
450,000	9286.76	7183.13	6534.38	5639.71	5057.99
475,000	9802.69	7582.19	6897.40	5953.03	5338.99
500,000	10318.62	7981.25	7260.42	6266.34	5619.99
525,000	10834.55	8380.31	7623.45	6579.66	5900.99
550,000	11350.48	8779.38	7986.47	6892.98	6181.99
575,000	11866.41	9178.44	8349.49	7206.29	6462.99
600,000	12382.34	9577.50	8712.51	7519.61	6743.99
625,000	12898.28	9976.56	9075.53	7832.93	7024.99
650,000	13414.21	10375.63	9438.55	8146.24	7305.98
675,000	13930.14	10774.69	9801.57	8459.56	7586.98
700,000	14446.07	11173.75	10164.59	8772.88	7867.98
725,000	14962.00	11572.81	10527.61	9086.19	8148.98
750,000	15477.93	11971.87	10890.63	9399.51	8429.98
775,000	15993.86	12370.94	11253.66	9712.83	8710.98
800,000	16509.79	12770.00	11616.68	10026.15	8991.98
825,000	17025.72	13169.06	11979.70	10339.46	9272.98
850,000	17541.65	13568.12	12342.72	10652.78	9553.98
875,000	18057.58	13967.19	12705.74	10966.10	9834.98
900,000	18573.51	14366.25	13068.76	11279.41	10115.98

Table 7   169

Monthly Payment Loans

Amortization Period in Years

Loan Amount	15	16	17	18	20
10	0.10	0.10	0.10	0.10	0.09
20	0.20	0.20	0.19	0.19	0.18
30	0.30	0.30	0.29	0.28	0.27
40	0.40	0.39	0.38	0.37	0.36
50	0.50	0.49	0.48	0.47	0.45
100	1.00	0.97	0.95	0.93	0.89
200	2.00	1.94	1.89	1.85	1.77
300	3.00	2.91	2.84	2.77	2.66
400	4.00	3.88	3.78	3.69	3.54
500	5.00	4.85	4.72	4.61	4.42
1,000	10.00	9.70	9.44	9.21	8.84
2,000	19.99	19.39	18.87	18.42	17.68
3,000	29.99	29.09	28.31	27.63	26.52
4,000	39.98	38.78	37.74	36.84	35.35
5,000	49.98	48.48	47.18	46.05	44.19
10,000	99.95	96.95	94.35	92.09	88.38
20,000	199.89	193.89	188.70	184.18	176.75
30,000	299.84	290.84	283.05	276.27	265.12
40,000	399.78	387.78	377.40	368.36	353.49
50,000	499.73	484.73	471.75	460.45	441.86
100,000	999.45	969.45	943.49	920.90	883.72
125,000	1249.32	1211.81	1179.37	1151.12	1104.64
150,000	1499.18	1454.18	1415.24	1381.34	1325.57
175,000	1749.04	1696.54	1651.11	1611.56	1546.50
200,000	1998.90	1938.90	1886.98	1841.79	1767.43
225,000	2248.76	2181.26	2122.86	2072.01	1988.35
250,000	2498.63	2423.62	2358.73	2302.23	2209.28
275,000	2748.49	2665.98	2594.60	2532.45	2430.21
300,000	2998.35	2908.35	2830.47	2762.68	2651.14
325,000	3248.21	3150.71	3066.34	2992.90	2872.06
350,000	3498.08	3393.07	3302.22	3223.12	3092.99
375,000	3747.94	3635.43	3538.09	3453.34	3313.92
400,000	3997.80	3877.79	3773.96	3683.57	3534.85
425,000	4247.66	4120.15	4009.83	3913.79	3755.78
450,000	4497.52	4362.52	4245.71	4144.01	3976.70
475,000	4747.39	4604.88	4481.58	4374.23	4197.63
500,000	4997.25	4847.24	4717.45	4604.46	4418.56
525,000	5247.11	5089.60	4953.32	4834.68	4639.49
550,000	5496.97	5331.96	5189.20	5064.90	4860.41
575,000	5746.83	5574.32	5425.07	5295.12	5081.34
600,000	5996.70	5816.69	5660.94	5525.35	5302.27
625,000	6246.56	6059.05	5896.81	5755.57	5523.20
650,000	6496.42	6301.41	6132.68	5985.79	5744.12
675,000	6746.28	6543.77	6368.56	6216.02	5965.05
700,000	6996.15	6786.13	6604.43	6446.24	6185.98
725,000	7246.01	7028.49	6840.30	6676.46	6406.91
750,000	7495.87	7270.86	7076.17	6906.68	6627.84
775,000	7745.73	7513.22	7312.05	7136.91	6848.76
800,000	7995.59	7755.58	7547.92	7367.13	7069.69
825,000	8245.46	7997.94	7783.79	7597.35	7290.62
850,000	8495.32	8240.30	8019.66	7827.57	7511.55
875,000	8745.18	8482.66	8255.54	8057.80	7732.47
900,000	8995.04	8725.03	8491.41	8288.02	7953.40

Monthly Payment Loans   **8.75%**

Loan Amount	Amortization Period in Years				
	21	22	23	24	25
10	0.09	0.09	0.09	0.09	0.09
20	0.18	0.18	0.17	0.17	0.17
30	0.27	0.26	0.26	0.25	0.25
40	0.35	0.35	0.34	0.34	0.33
50	0.44	0.43	0.43	0.42	0.42
100	0.87	0.86	0.85	0.84	0.83
200	1.74	1.71	1.69	1.67	1.65
300	2.61	2.57	2.53	2.50	2.47
400	3.48	3.42	3.38	3.33	3.29
500	4.35	4.28	4.22	4.16	4.12
1,000	8.69	8.55	8.43	8.32	8.23
2,000	17.37	17.10	16.86	16.64	16.45
3,000	26.06	25.65	25.28	24.96	24.67
4,000	34.74	34.19	33.71	33.28	32.89
5,000	43.42	42.74	42.14	41.60	41.11
10,000	86.84	85.48	84.27	83.19	82.22
20,000	173.67	170.95	168.53	166.37	164.43
30,000	260.51	256.42	252.79	249.55	246.65
40,000	347.34	341.89	337.05	332.73	328.86
50,000	434.18	427.37	421.31	415.91	411.08
100,000	868.35	854.73	842.62	831.81	822.15
125,000	1085.44	1068.41	1053.27	1039.76	1027.68
150,000	1302.52	1282.09	1263.92	1247.71	1233.22
175,000	1519.61	1495.77	1474.57	1455.66	1438.76
200,000	1736.69	1709.45	1685.23	1663.62	1644.29
225,000	1953.78	1923.13	1895.88	1871.57	1849.83
250,000	2170.87	2136.82	2106.53	2079.52	2055.36
275,000	2387.95	2350.50	2317.18	2287.47	2260.90
300,000	2605.04	2564.18	2527.84	2495.42	2466.44
325,000	2822.13	2777.86	2738.49	2703.37	2671.97
350,000	3039.21	2991.54	2949.14	2911.32	2877.51
375,000	3256.30	3205.22	3159.79	3119.28	3083.04
400,000	3473.38	3418.90	3370.45	3327.23	3288.58
425,000	3690.47	3632.58	3581.10	3535.18	3494.12
450,000	3907.56	3846.26	3791.75	3743.13	3699.65
475,000	4124.64	4059.94	4002.40	3951.08	3905.19
500,000	4341.73	4273.63	4213.06	4159.03	4110.72
525,000	4558.82	4487.31	4423.71	4366.98	4316.26
550,000	4775.90	4700.99	4634.36	4574.94	4521.79
575,000	4992.99	4914.67	4845.01	4782.89	4727.33
600,000	5210.07	5128.35	5055.67	4990.84	4932.87
625,000	5427.16	5342.03	5266.32	5198.79	5138.40
650,000	5644.25	5555.71	5476.97	5406.74	5343.94
675,000	5861.33	5769.39	5687.62	5614.69	5549.47
700,000	6078.42	5983.07	5898.28	5822.64	5755.01
725,000	6295.51	6196.75	6108.93	6030.60	5960.55
750,000	6512.59	6410.44	6319.58	6238.55	6166.08
775,000	6729.68	6624.12	6530.24	6446.50	6371.62
800,000	6946.76	6837.80	6740.89	6654.45	6577.15
825,000	7163.85	7051.48	6951.54	6862.40	6782.69
850,000	7380.94	7265.16	7162.19	7070.35	6988.23
875,000	7598.02	7478.84	7372.85	7278.30	7193.76
900,000	7815.11	7692.52	7583.50	7486.26	7399.30

Table 7   171

Monthly Payment Loans

Loan Amount	Amortization Period in Years				
	26	27	28	29	30
10	0.09	0.09	0.08	0.08	0.08
20	0.17	0.17	0.16	0.16	0.16
30	0.25	0.25	0.24	0.24	0.24
40	0.33	0.33	0.32	0.32	0.32
50	0.41	0.41	0.40	0.40	0.40
100	0.82	0.81	0.80	0.80	0.79
200	1.63	1.62	1.60	1.59	1.58
300	2.45	2.42	2.40	2.38	2.37
400	3.26	3.23	3.20	3.17	3.15
500	4.07	4.03	4.00	3.97	3.94
1,000	8.14	8.06	7.99	7.93	7.87
2,000	16.27	16.12	15.98	15.85	15.74
3,000	24.41	24.18	23.97	23.78	23.61
4,000	32.54	32.23	31.95	31.70	31.47
5,000	40.68	40.29	39.94	39.62	39.34
10,000	81.35	80.58	79.88	79.24	78.68
20,000	162.70	161.15	159.75	158.48	157.35
30,000	244.05	241.72	239.62	237.72	236.02
40,000	325.40	322.29	319.49	316.96	314.69
50,000	406.75	402.86	399.36	396.20	393.36
100,000	813.49	805.71	798.71	792.40	786.71
125,000	1016.86	1007.14	998.39	990.50	983.38
150,000	1220.23	1208.56	1198.06	1188.60	1180.06
175,000	1423.60	1409.99	1397.74	1386.70	1376.73
200,000	1626.97	1611.41	1597.42	1584.80	1573.41
225,000	1830.34	1812.84	1797.09	1782.90	1770.08
250,000	2033.71	2014.27	1996.77	1980.99	1966.76
275,000	2237.08	2215.69	2196.44	2179.09	2163.43
300,000	2440.46	2417.12	2396.12	2377.19	2360.11
325,000	2643.83	2618.55	2595.80	2575.29	2556.78
350,000	2847.20	2819.97	2795.47	2773.39	2753.46
375,000	3050.57	3021.40	2995.15	2971.49	2950.13
400,000	3253.94	3222.82	3194.83	3169.59	3146.81
425,000	3457.31	3424.25	3394.50	3367.69	3343.48
450,000	3660.68	3625.68	3594.18	3565.79	3540.16
475,000	3864.05	3827.10	3793.85	3763.89	3736.83
500,000	4067.42	4028.53	3993.53	3961.98	3933.51
525,000	4270.79	4229.96	4193.21	4160.08	4130.18
550,000	4474.16	4431.38	4392.88	4358.18	4326.86
575,000	4677.53	4632.81	4592.56	4556.28	4523.53
600,000	4880.91	4834.23	4792.24	4754.38	4720.21
625,000	5084.28	5035.66	4991.91	4952.48	4916.88
650,000	5287.65	5237.09	5191.59	5150.58	5113.56
675,000	5491.02	5438.51	5391.27	5348.68	5310.23
700,000	5694.39	5639.94	5590.94	5546.78	5506.91
725,000	5897.76	5841.36	5790.62	5744.88	5703.58
750,000	6101.13	6042.79	5990.29	5942.97	5900.26
775,000	6304.50	6244.22	6189.97	6141.07	6096.93
800,000	6507.87	6445.64	6389.65	6339.17	6293.61
825,000	6711.24	6647.07	6589.32	6537.27	6490.28
850,000	6914.61	6848.50	6789.00	6735.37	6686.96
875,000	7117.98	7049.92	6988.68	6933.47	6883.63
900,000	7321.36	7251.35	7188.35	7131.57	7080.31

Monthly Payment Loans   9.00%

Loan Amount	Amortization Period in Years				
	5	7	8	10	12
10	0.21	0.17	0.15	0.13	0.12
20	0.42	0.33	0.30	0.26	0.23
30	0.63	0.49	0.44	0.39	0.35
40	0.84	0.65	0.59	0.51	0.46
50	1.04	0.81	0.74	0.64	0.57
100	2.08	1.61	1.47	1.27	1.14
200	4.16	3.22	2.94	2.54	2.28
300	6.23	4.83	4.40	3.81	3.42
400	8.31	6.44	5.87	5.07	4.56
500	10.38	8.05	7.33	6.34	5.70
1,000	20.76	16.09	14.66	12.67	11.39
2,000	41.52	32.18	29.31	25.34	22.77
3,000	62.28	48.27	43.96	38.01	34.15
4,000	83.04	64.36	58.61	50.68	45.53
5,000	103.80	80.45	73.26	63.34	56.91
10,000	207.59	160.90	146.51	126.68	113.81
20,000	415.17	321.79	293.01	253.36	227.61
30,000	622.76	482.68	439.51	380.03	341.41
40,000	830.34	643.57	586.01	506.71	455.22
50,000	1037.92	804.46	732.52	633.38	569.02
100,000	2075.84	1608.91	1465.03	1266.76	1138.04
125,000	2594.80	2011.14	1831.28	1583.45	1422.54
150,000	3113.76	2413.37	2197.54	1900.14	1707.05
175,000	3632.72	2815.59	2563.79	2216.83	1991.56
200,000	4151.68	3217.82	2930.05	2533.52	2276.07
225,000	4670.63	3620.05	3296.30	2850.21	2560.57
250,000	5189.59	4022.27	3662.56	3166.90	2845.08
275,000	5708.55	4424.50	4028.81	3483.59	3129.59
300,000	6227.51	4826.73	4395.07	3800.28	3414.10
325,000	6746.47	5228.96	4761.32	4116.97	3698.60
350,000	7265.43	5631.18	5127.58	4433.66	3983.11
375,000	7784.39	6033.41	5493.83	4750.35	4267.62
400,000	8303.35	6435.64	5860.09	5067.04	4552.13
425,000	8822.31	6837.86	6226.34	5383.73	4836.64
450,000	9341.26	7240.09	6592.60	5700.41	5121.14
475,000	9860.22	7642.32	6958.85	6017.10	5405.65
500,000	10379.18	8044.54	7325.11	6333.79	5690.16
525,000	10898.14	8446.77	7691.36	6650.48	5974.67
550,000	11417.10	8849.00	8057.62	6967.17	6259.17
575,000	11936.06	9251.22	8423.87	7283.86	6543.68
600,000	12455.02	9653.45	8790.13	7600.55	6828.19
625,000	12973.98	10055.68	9156.38	7917.24	7112.70
650,000	13492.94	10457.91	9522.64	8233.93	7397.20
675,000	14011.89	10860.13	9888.89	8550.62	7681.71
700,000	14530.85	11262.36	10255.15	8867.31	7966.22
725,000	15049.81	11664.59	10621.40	9184.00	8250.73
750,000	15568.77	12066.81	10987.66	9500.69	8535.24
775,000	16087.73	12469.04	11353.91	9817.38	8819.74
800,000	16606.69	12871.27	11720.17	10134.07	9104.25
825,000	17125.65	13273.49	12086.42	10450.76	9388.76
850,000	17644.61	13675.72	12452.68	10767.45	9673.27
875,000	18163.57	14077.95	12818.93	11084.14	9957.77
900,000	18682.52	14480.18	13185.19	11400.82	10242.28

Table 7   173

9.00%　　　Monthly Payment Loans

Loan Amount	\multicolumn{5}{c}{Amortization Period in Years}				
	15	16	17	18	20
10	0.11	0.10	0.10	0.10	0.09
20	0.21	0.20	0.20	0.19	0.18
30	0.31	0.30	0.29	0.29	0.27
40	0.41	0.40	0.39	0.38	0.36
50	0.51	0.50	0.48	0.47	0.45
100	1.02	0.99	0.96	0.94	0.90
200	2.03	1.97	1.92	1.88	1.80
300	3.05	2.96	2.88	2.81	2.70
400	4.06	3.94	3.84	3.75	3.60
500	5.08	4.93	4.80	4.69	4.50
1,000	10.15	9.85	9.59	9.37	9.00
2,000	20.29	19.70	19.18	18.73	18.00
3,000	30.43	29.54	28.77	28.10	27.00
4,000	40.58	39.39	38.36	37.46	35.99
5,000	50.72	49.23	47.95	46.83	44.99
10,000	101.43	98.46	95.89	93.65	89.98
20,000	202.86	196.91	191.77	187.29	179.95
30,000	304.28	295.36	287.65	280.94	269.92
40,000	405.71	393.81	383.53	374.58	359.90
50,000	507.14	492.26	479.41	468.23	449.87
100,000	1014.27	984.52	958.81	936.45	899.73
125,000	1267.84	1230.65	1198.51	1170.56	1124.66
150,000	1521.40	1476.78	1438.21	1404.67	1349.59
175,000	1774.97	1722.91	1677.91	1638.78	1574.53
200,000	2028.54	1969.04	1917.61	1872.89	1799.46
225,000	2282.10	2215.17	2157.31	2107.01	2024.39
250,000	2535.67	2461.29	2397.01	2341.12	2249.32
275,000	2789.24	2707.42	2636.72	2575.23	2474.25
300,000	3042.80	2953.55	2876.42	2809.34	2699.18
325,000	3296.37	3199.68	3116.12	3043.45	2924.11
350,000	3549.94	3445.81	3355.82	3277.56	3149.05
375,000	3803.50	3691.94	3595.52	3511.67	3373.98
400,000	4057.07	3938.07	3835.22	3745.78	3598.91
425,000	4310.64	4184.20	4074.92	3979.90	3823.84
450,000	4564.20	4430.33	4314.62	4214.01	4048.77
475,000	4817.77	4676.46	4554.32	4448.12	4273.70
500,000	5071.34	4922.58	4794.02	4682.23	4498.63
525,000	5324.90	5168.71	5033.73	4916.34	4723.57
550,000	5578.47	5414.84	5273.43	5150.45	4948.50
575,000	5832.04	5660.97	5513.13	5384.56	5173.43
600,000	6085.60	5907.10	5752.83	5618.67	5398.36
625,000	6339.17	6153.23	5992.53	5852.79	5623.29
650,000	6592.74	6399.36	6232.23	6086.90	5848.22
675,000	6846.30	6645.49	6471.93	6321.01	6073.16
700,000	7099.87	6891.62	6711.63	6555.12	6298.09
725,000	7353.44	7137.74	6951.33	6789.23	6523.02
750,000	7607.00	7383.87	7191.03	7023.34	6747.95
775,000	7860.57	7630.00	7430.74	7257.45	6972.88
800,000	8114.14	7876.13	7670.44	7491.56	7197.81
825,000	8367.70	8122.26	7910.14	7725.67	7422.74
850,000	8621.27	8368.39	8149.84	7959.79	7647.68
875,000	8874.84	8614.52	8389.54	8193.90	7872.61
900,000	9128.40	8860.65	8629.24	8428.01	8097.54

Monthly Payment Loans   **9.00%**

Loan Amount	Amortization Period in Years				
	21	22	23	24	25
10	0.09	0.09	0.09	0.09	0.09
20	0.18	0.18	0.18	0.17	0.17
30	0.27	0.27	0.26	0.26	0.26
40	0.36	0.35	0.35	0.34	0.34
50	0.45	0.44	0.43	0.43	0.42
100	0.89	0.88	0.86	0.85	0.84
200	1.77	1.75	1.72	1.70	1.68
300	2.66	2.62	2.58	2.55	2.52
400	3.54	3.49	3.44	3.40	3.36
500	4.43	4.36	4.30	4.25	4.20
1,000	8.85	8.72	8.60	8.49	8.40
2,000	17.70	17.43	17.19	16.98	16.79
3,000	26.54	26.14	25.78	25.46	25.18
4,000	35.39	34.85	34.38	33.95	33.57
5,000	44.23	43.56	42.97	42.44	41.96
10,000	88.46	87.12	85.93	84.87	83.92
20,000	176.92	174.24	171.86	169.74	167.84
30,000	265.38	261.36	257.79	254.60	251.76
40,000	353.84	348.47	343.71	339.47	335.68
50,000	442.30	435.59	429.64	424.34	419.60
100,000	884.59	871.18	859.27	848.67	839.20
125,000	1105.73	1088.97	1074.09	1060.84	1049.00
150,000	1326.88	1306.77	1288.91	1273.00	1258.80
175,000	1548.02	1524.56	1503.72	1485.17	1468.60
200,000	1769.17	1742.35	1718.54	1697.33	1678.40
225,000	1990.31	1960.15	1933.36	1909.50	1888.20
250,000	2211.46	2177.94	2148.18	2121.67	2098.00
275,000	2432.60	2395.73	2362.99	2333.83	2307.79
300,000	2653.75	2613.53	2577.81	2546.00	2517.59
325,000	2874.89	2831.32	2792.63	2758.16	2727.39
350,000	3096.04	3049.12	3007.44	2970.33	2937.19
375,000	3317.18	3266.91	3222.26	3182.50	3146.99
400,000	3538.33	3484.70	3437.08	3394.66	3356.79
425,000	3759.47	3702.50	3651.89	3606.83	3566.59
450,000	3980.62	3920.29	3866.71	3818.99	3776.39
475,000	4201.76	4138.08	4081.53	4031.16	3986.19
500,000	4422.91	4355.88	4296.35	4243.33	4195.99
525,000	4644.06	4573.67	4511.16	4455.49	4405.79
550,000	4865.20	4791.46	4725.98	4667.66	4615.58
575,000	5086.35	5009.26	4940.80	4879.82	4825.38
600,000	5307.49	5227.05	5155.61	5091.99	5035.18
625,000	5528.64	5444.84	5370.43	5304.16	5244.98
650,000	5749.78	5662.64	5585.25	5516.32	5454.78
675,000	5970.93	5880.43	5800.07	5728.49	5664.58
700,000	6192.07	6098.23	6014.88	5940.66	5874.38
725,000	6413.22	6316.02	6229.70	6152.82	6084.18
750,000	6634.36	6533.81	6444.52	6364.99	6293.98
775,000	6855.51	6751.61	6659.33	6577.15	6503.78
800,000	7076.65	6969.40	6874.15	6789.32	6713.58
825,000	7297.80	7187.19	7088.97	7001.49	6923.37
850,000	7518.94	7404.99	7303.78	7213.65	7133.17
875,000	7740.09	7622.78	7518.60	7425.82	7342.97
900,000	7961.23	7840.57	7733.42	7637.98	7552.77

Table 7   175

9.00%

Monthly Payment Loans

Loan Amount	Amortization Period in Years				
	26	27	28	29	30
10	0.09	0.09	0.09	0.09	0.09
20	0.17	0.17	0.17	0.17	0.17
30	0.25	0.25	0.25	0.25	0.25
40	0.34	0.33	0.33	0.33	0.33
50	0.42	0.42	0.41	0.41	0.41
100	0.84	0.83	0.82	0.82	0.81
200	1.67	1.65	1.64	1.63	1.61
300	2.50	2.47	2.45	2.44	2.42
400	3.33	3.30	3.27	3.25	3.22
500	4.16	4.12	4.09	4.06	4.03
1,000	8.31	8.24	8.17	8.11	8.05
2,000	16.62	16.47	16.33	16.21	16.10
3,000	24.93	24.70	24.49	24.31	24.14
4,000	33.23	32.93	32.66	32.41	32.19
5,000	41.54	41.16	40.82	40.51	40.24
10,000	83.08	82.32	81.63	81.02	80.47
20,000	166.15	164.63	163.26	162.04	160.93
30,000	249.22	246.94	244.89	243.05	241.39
40,000	332.29	329.26	326.52	324.07	321.85
50,000	415.37	411.57	408.15	405.08	402.32
100,000	830.73	823.13	816.30	810.16	804.63
125,000	1038.41	1028.91	1020.38	1012.70	1005.78
150,000	1246.09	1234.69	1224.45	1215.24	1206.94
175,000	1453.77	1440.47	1428.53	1417.78	1408.09
200,000	1661.45	1646.26	1632.60	1620.32	1609.25
225,000	1869.13	1852.04	1836.68	1822.86	1810.41
250,000	2076.81	2057.82	2040.75	2025.40	2011.56
275,000	2284.49	2263.60	2244.83	2227.94	2212.72
300,000	2492.18	2469.38	2448.90	2430.48	2413.87
325,000	2699.86	2675.16	2652.98	2633.02	2615.03
350,000	2907.54	2880.94	2857.05	2835.56	2816.18
375,000	3115.22	3086.73	3061.13	3038.10	3017.34
400,000	3322.90	3292.51	3265.20	3240.64	3218.50
425,000	3530.58	3498.29	3469.28	3443.17	3419.65
450,000	3738.26	3704.07	3673.35	3645.71	3620.81
475,000	3945.94	3909.85	3877.43	3848.25	3821.96
500,000	4153.62	4115.63	4081.50	4050.79	4023.12
525,000	4361.30	4321.41	4285.58	4253.33	4224.27
550,000	4568.98	4527.19	4489.65	4455.87	4425.43
575,000	4776.66	4732.98	4693.73	4658.41	4626.59
600,000	4984.35	4938.76	4897.80	4860.95	4827.74
625,000	5192.03	5144.54	5101.88	5063.49	5028.90
650,000	5399.71	5350.32	5305.95	5266.03	5230.05
675,000	5607.39	5556.10	5510.03	5468.57	5431.21
700,000	5815.07	5761.88	5714.10	5671.11	5632.36
725,000	6022.75	5967.66	5918.18	5873.65	5833.52
750,000	6230.43	6173.45	6122.25	6076.19	6034.67
775,000	6438.11	6379.23	6326.33	6278.73	6235.83
800,000	6645.79	6585.01	6530.40	6481.27	6436.99
825,000	6853.47	6790.79	6734.48	6683.81	6638.14
850,000	7061.15	6996.57	6938.55	6886.34	6839.30
875,000	7268.83	7202.35	7142.63	7088.88	7040.45
900,000	7476.52	7408.13	7346.70	7291.42	7241.61

Monthly Payment Loans   **9.25%**

Loan Amount	\multicolumn{5}{c}{Amortization Period in Years}				
	5	7	8	10	12
10	0.21	0.17	0.15	0.13	0.12
20	0.42	0.33	0.30	0.26	0.24
30	0.63	0.49	0.45	0.39	0.35
40	0.84	0.65	0.60	0.52	0.47
50	1.05	0.82	0.74	0.65	0.58
100	2.09	1.63	1.48	1.29	1.16
200	4.18	3.25	2.96	2.57	2.31
300	6.27	4.87	4.44	3.85	3.46
400	8.36	6.49	5.92	5.13	4.61
500	10.44	8.11	7.40	6.41	5.77
1,000	20.88	16.22	14.79	12.81	11.53
2,000	41.76	32.44	29.57	25.61	23.05
3,000	62.64	48.65	44.35	38.41	34.57
4,000	83.52	64.87	59.13	51.22	46.09
5,000	104.40	81.09	73.91	64.02	57.61
10,000	208.80	162.17	147.81	128.04	115.22
20,000	417.60	324.33	295.61	256.07	230.44
30,000	626.40	486.49	443.41	384.10	345.65
40,000	835.20	648.65	591.21	512.14	460.87
50,000	1044.00	810.82	739.02	640.17	576.08
100,000	2087.99	1621.63	1478.03	1280.33	1152.16
125,000	2609.99	2027.04	1847.53	1600.41	1440.20
150,000	3131.99	2432.44	2217.04	1920.50	1728.24
175,000	3653.99	2837.85	2586.54	2240.58	2016.28
200,000	4175.98	3243.25	2956.05	2560.66	2304.32
225,000	4697.98	3648.66	3325.55	2880.74	2592.36
250,000	5219.98	4054.07	3695.06	3200.82	2880.40
275,000	5741.98	4459.47	4064.57	3520.90	3168.43
300,000	6263.97	4864.88	4434.07	3840.99	3456.47
325,000	6785.97	5270.28	4803.58	4161.07	3744.51
350,000	7307.97	5675.69	5173.08	4481.15	4032.55
375,000	7829.97	6081.10	5542.59	4801.23	4320.59
400,000	8351.96	6486.50	5912.09	5121.31	4608.63
425,000	8873.96	6891.91	6281.60	5441.40	4896.67
450,000	9395.96	7297.31	6651.10	5761.48	5184.71
475,000	9917.96	7702.72	7020.61	6081.56	5472.75
500,000	10439.95	8108.13	7390.12	6401.64	5760.79
525,000	10961.95	8513.53	7759.62	6721.72	6048.83
550,000	11483.95	8918.94	8129.13	7041.80	6336.86
575,000	12005.95	9324.34	8498.63	7361.89	6624.90
600,000	12527.94	9729.75	8868.14	7681.97	6912.94
625,000	13049.94	10135.16	9237.64	8002.05	7200.98
650,000	13571.94	10540.56	9607.15	8322.13	7489.02
675,000	14093.94	10945.97	9976.65	8642.21	7777.06
700,000	14615.93	11351.37	10346.16	8962.30	8065.10
725,000	15137.93	11756.78	10715.66	9282.38	8353.14
750,000	15659.93	12162.19	11085.17	9602.46	8641.18
775,000	16181.93	12567.59	11454.68	9922.54	8929.22
800,000	16703.92	12973.00	11824.18	10242.62	9217.26
825,000	17225.92	13378.40	12193.69	10562.70	9505.29
850,000	17747.92	13783.81	12563.19	10882.79	9793.33
875,000	18269.92	14189.22	12932.70	11202.87	10081.37
900,000	18791.91	14594.62	13302.20	11522.95	10369.41

Table 7   177

9.25% Monthly Payment Loans

Amortization Period in Years

Loan Amount	15	16	17	18	20
10	0.11	0.10	0.10	0.10	0.10
20	0.21	0.20	0.20	0.20	0.19
30	0.31	0.30	0.30	0.29	0.28
40	0.42	0.40	0.39	0.39	0.37
50	0.52	0.50	0.49	0.48	0.46
100	1.03	1.00	0.98	0.96	0.92
200	2.06	2.00	1.95	1.91	1.84
300	3.09	3.00	2.93	2.86	2.75
400	4.12	4.00	3.90	3.81	3.67
500	5.15	5.00	4.88	4.77	4.58
1,000	10.30	10.00	9.75	9.53	9.16
2,000	20.59	20.00	19.49	19.05	18.32
3,000	30.88	30.00	29.23	28.57	27.48
4,000	41.17	39.99	38.97	38.09	36.64
5,000	51.46	49.99	48.72	47.61	45.80
10,000	102.92	99.97	97.43	95.22	91.59
20,000	205.84	199.94	194.85	190.43	183.18
30,000	308.76	299.91	292.28	285.64	274.77
40,000	411.68	399.88	389.70	380.85	366.35
50,000	514.60	499.85	487.12	476.06	457.94
100,000	1029.20	999.70	974.24	952.12	915.87
125,000	1286.50	1249.63	1217.80	1190.15	1144.84
150,000	1543.79	1499.55	1461.36	1428.18	1373.81
175,000	1801.09	1749.48	1704.92	1666.21	1602.77
200,000	2058.39	1999.40	1948.47	1904.24	1831.74
225,000	2315.69	2249.32	2192.03	2142.27	2060.71
250,000	2572.99	2499.25	2435.59	2380.30	2289.67
275,000	2830.28	2749.17	2679.15	2618.33	2518.64
300,000	3087.58	2999.10	2922.71	2856.36	2747.61
325,000	3344.88	3249.02	3166.27	3094.39	2976.57
350,000	3602.18	3498.95	3409.83	3332.42	3205.54
375,000	3859.48	3748.87	3653.39	3570.45	3434.51
400,000	4116.77	3998.79	3896.94	3808.48	3663.47
425,000	4374.07	4248.72	4140.50	4046.51	3892.44
450,000	4631.37	4498.64	4384.06	4284.54	4121.41
475,000	4888.67	4748.57	4627.62	4522.57	4350.37
500,000	5145.97	4998.49	4871.18	4760.60	4579.34
525,000	5403.26	5248.42	5114.74	4998.63	4808.31
550,000	5660.56	5498.34	5358.30	5236.66	5037.27
575,000	5917.86	5748.26	5601.86	5474.69	5266.24
600,000	6175.16	5998.19	5845.41	5712.72	5495.21
625,000	6432.46	6248.11	6088.97	5950.75	5724.17
650,000	6689.75	6498.04	6332.53	6188.78	5953.14
675,000	6947.05	6747.96	6576.09	6426.81	6182.11
700,000	7204.35	6997.89	6819.65	6664.84	6411.07
725,000	7461.65	7247.81	7063.21	6902.87	6640.04
750,000	7718.95	7497.73	7306.77	7140.90	6869.01
775,000	7976.25	7747.66	7550.33	7378.93	7097.97
800,000	8233.54	7997.58	7793.88	7616.96	7326.94
825,000	8490.84	8247.51	8037.44	7854.99	7555.91
850,000	8748.14	8497.43	8281.00	8093.02	7784.87
875,000	9005.44	8747.36	8524.56	8331.05	8013.84
900,000	9262.74	8997.28	8768.12	8569.08	8242.81

Monthly Payment Loans   9.25%

Loan Amount	Amortization Period in Years				
	21	22	23	24	25
10	0.10	0.09	0.09	0.09	0.09
20	0.19	0.18	0.18	0.18	0.18
30	0.28	0.27	0.27	0.26	0.26
40	0.37	0.36	0.36	0.35	0.35
50	0.46	0.45	0.44	0.44	0.43
100	0.91	0.89	0.88	0.87	0.86
200	1.81	1.78	1.76	1.74	1.72
300	2.71	2.67	2.63	2.60	2.57
400	3.61	3.56	3.51	3.47	3.43
500	4.51	4.44	4.39	4.33	4.29
1,000	9.01	8.88	8.77	8.66	8.57
2,000	18.02	17.76	17.53	17.32	17.13
3,000	27.03	26.64	26.29	25.97	25.70
4,000	36.04	35.52	35.05	34.63	34.26
5,000	45.05	44.39	43.81	43.29	42.82
10,000	90.10	88.78	87.61	86.57	85.64
20,000	180.19	177.56	175.22	173.14	171.28
30,000	270.29	266.33	262.82	259.70	256.92
40,000	360.38	355.11	350.43	346.27	342.56
50,000	450.48	443.88	438.03	432.83	428.20
100,000	900.95	887.76	876.06	865.66	856.39
125,000	1126.19	1109.70	1095.08	1082.07	1070.48
150,000	1351.42	1331.64	1314.09	1298.49	1284.58
175,000	1576.66	1553.58	1533.10	1514.90	1498.67
200,000	1801.89	1775.51	1752.12	1731.32	1712.77
225,000	2027.13	1997.45	1971.13	1947.73	1926.86
250,000	2252.37	2219.39	2190.15	2164.14	2140.96
275,000	2477.60	2441.33	2409.16	2380.56	2355.06
300,000	2702.84	2663.27	2628.18	2596.97	2569.15
325,000	2928.08	2885.21	2847.19	2813.38	2783.25
350,000	3153.31	3107.15	3066.20	3029.80	2997.34
375,000	3378.55	3329.08	3285.22	3246.21	3211.44
400,000	3603.78	3551.02	3504.23	3462.63	3425.53
425,000	3829.02	3772.96	3723.25	3679.04	3639.63
450,000	4054.26	3994.90	3942.26	3895.45	3853.72
475,000	4279.49	4216.84	4161.28	4111.87	4067.82
500,000	4504.73	4438.78	4380.29	4328.28	4281.91
525,000	4729.97	4660.72	4599.30	4544.69	4496.01
550,000	4955.20	4882.65	4818.32	4761.11	4710.11
575,000	5180.44	5104.59	5037.33	4977.52	4924.20
600,000	5405.67	5326.53	5256.35	5193.94	5138.30
625,000	5630.91	5548.47	5475.36	5410.35	5352.39
650,000	5856.15	5770.41	5694.38	5626.76	5566.49
675,000	6081.38	5992.35	5913.39	5843.18	5780.58
700,000	6306.62	6214.29	6132.40	6059.59	5994.68
725,000	6531.86	6436.22	6351.42	6276.00	6208.77
750,000	6757.09	6658.16	6570.43	6492.42	6422.87
775,000	6982.33	6880.10	6789.45	6708.83	6636.96
800,000	7207.56	7102.04	7008.46	6925.25	6851.06
825,000	7432.80	7323.98	7227.48	7141.66	7065.16
850,000	7658.04	7545.92	7446.49	7358.07	7279.25
875,000	7883.27	7767.86	7665.50	7574.49	7493.35
900,000	8108.51	7989.79	7884.52	7790.90	7707.44

Table 7   179

9.25% Monthly Payment Loans

Amortization Period in Years

Loan Amount	26	27	28	29	30
10	0.09	0.09	0.09	0.09	0.09
20	0.17	0.17	0.17	0.17	0.17
30	0.26	0.26	0.26	0.25	0.25
40	0.34	0.34	0.34	0.34	0.33
50	0.43	0.43	0.42	0.42	0.42
100	0.85	0.85	0.84	0.83	0.83
200	1.70	1.69	1.67	1.66	1.65
300	2.55	2.53	2.51	2.49	2.47
400	3.40	3.37	3.34	3.32	3.30
500	4.25	4.21	4.18	4.15	4.12
1,000	8.49	8.41	8.35	8.29	8.23
2,000	16.97	16.82	16.69	16.57	16.46
3,000	25.45	25.23	25.03	24.85	24.69
4,000	33.93	33.63	33.37	33.13	32.91
5,000	42.41	42.04	41.71	41.41	41.14
10,000	84.81	84.07	83.41	82.81	82.27
20,000	169.62	168.14	166.81	165.62	164.54
30,000	254.43	252.21	250.21	248.42	246.81
40,000	339.24	336.28	333.62	331.23	329.08
50,000	424.05	420.34	417.02	414.03	411.34
100,000	848.10	840.68	834.03	828.06	822.68
125,000	1060.13	1050.85	1042.54	1035.07	1028.35
150,000	1272.15	1261.02	1251.04	1242.08	1234.02
175,000	1484.17	1471.19	1459.55	1449.09	1439.69
200,000	1696.20	1681.36	1668.06	1656.11	1645.36
225,000	1908.22	1891.53	1876.56	1863.12	1851.02
250,000	2120.25	2101.70	2085.07	2070.13	2056.69
275,000	2332.27	2311.87	2293.58	2277.14	2262.36
300,000	2544.29	2522.04	2502.08	2484.16	2468.03
325,000	2756.32	2732.21	2710.59	2691.17	2673.70
350,000	2963.34	2942.38	2919.10	2898.18	2879.37
375,000	3180.37	3152.55	3127.60	3105.20	3085.04
400,000	3392.39	3362.72	3336.11	3312.21	3290.71
425,000	3604.41	3572.89	3544.62	3519.22	3496.38
450,000	3816.44	3783.06	3753.12	3726.23	3702.04
475,000	4028.46	3993.23	3961.63	3933.25	3907.71
500,000	4240.49	4203.40	4170.14	4140.26	4113.38
525,000	4452.51	4413.57	4378.64	4347.27	4319.05
550,000	4664.54	4623.74	4587.15	4554.28	4524.72
575,000	4876.56	4833.91	4795.66	4761.30	4730.39
600,000	5088.58	5044.08	5004.16	4968.31	4936.06
625,000	5300.61	5254.25	5212.67	5175.32	5141.73
650,000	5512.63	5464.42	5421.18	5382.34	5347.40
675,000	5724.66	5674.59	5629.68	5589.35	5553.06
700,000	5936.68	5884.76	5838.19	5796.36	5758.73
725,000	6148.70	6094.93	6046.70	6003.37	5964.40
750,000	6360.73	6305.10	6255.20	6210.39	6170.07
775,000	6572.75	6515.27	6463.71	6417.40	6375.74
800,000	6784.78	6725.44	6672.22	6624.41	6581.41
825,000	6996.80	6935.61	6880.72	6831.42	6787.08
850,000	7208.82	7145.78	7089.23	7038.44	6992.75
875,000	7420.85	7355.95	7297.74	7245.45	7198.41
900,000	7632.87	7566.11	7506.24	7452.46	7404.08

Monthly Payment Loans 9.50%

Loan Amount	Amortization Period in Years				
	5	7	8	10	12
10	0.22	0.17	0.15	0.13	0.12
20	0.43	0.33	0.30	0.26	0.24
30	0.64	0.50	0.45	0.39	0.35
40	0.85	0.66	0.60	0.52	0.47
50	1.06	0.82	0.75	0.65	0.59
100	2.11	1.64	1.50	1.30	1.17
200	4.21	3.27	2.99	2.59	2.34
300	6.31	4.91	4.48	3.89	3.50
400	8.41	6.54	5.97	5.18	4.67
500	10.51	8.18	7.46	6.47	5.84
1,000	21.01	16.35	14.92	12.94	11.67
2,000	42.01	32.69	29.83	25.88	23.33
3,000	63.01	49.04	44.74	38.82	35.00
4,000	84.01	65.38	59.65	51.76	46.66
5,000	105.01	81.72	74.56	64.70	58.32
10,000	210.02	163.44	149.11	129.40	116.64
20,000	420.04	326.88	298.22	258.80	233.28
30,000	630.06	490.32	447.33	388.20	349.92
40,000	840.08	653.76	596.44	517.60	466.55
50,000	1050.10	817.20	745.55	646.99	583.19
100,000	2100.19	1634.40	1491.09	1293.98	1166.38
125,000	2625.24	2043.00	1863.87	1617.47	1457.97
150,000	3150.28	2451.60	2236.64	1940.97	1749.56
175,000	3675.33	2860.20	2609.41	2264.46	2041.16
200,000	4200.38	3268.80	2982.18	2587.96	2332.75
225,000	4725.42	3677.40	3354.95	2911.45	2624.34
250,000	5250.47	4086.00	3727.73	3234.94	2915.94
275,000	5775.52	4494.60	4100.50	3558.44	3207.53
300,000	6300.56	4903.20	4473.27	3881.93	3499.12
325,000	6825.61	5311.80	4846.04	4205.43	3790.72
350,000	7350.66	5720.40	5218.82	4528.92	4082.31
375,000	7875.70	6129.00	5591.59	4852.41	4373.90
400,000	8400.75	6537.60	5964.36	5175.91	4665.50
425,000	8925.80	6946.20	6337.13	5499.40	4957.09
450,000	9450.84	7354.80	6709.90	5822.90	5248.68
475,000	9975.89	7763.40	7082.68	6146.39	5540.28
500,000	10500.94	8172.00	7455.45	6469.88	5831.87
525,000	11025.98	8580.60	7828.22	6793.38	6123.46
550,000	11551.03	8989.19	8200.99	7116.87	6415.06
575,000	12076.08	9397.79	8573.77	7440.36	6706.65
600,000	12601.12	9806.39	8946.54	7763.86	6998.24
625,000	13126.17	10214.99	9319.31	8087.35	7289.84
650,000	13651.21	10623.59	9692.08	8410.85	7581.43
675,000	14176.26	11032.19	10064.85	8734.34	7873.02
700,000	14701.31	11440.79	10437.63	9057.83	8164.62
725,000	15226.35	11849.39	10810.40	9381.33	8456.21
750,000	15751.40	12257.99	11183.17	9704.82	8747.80
775,000	16276.45	12666.59	11555.94	10028.32	9039.40
800,000	16801.49	13075.19	11928.71	10351.81	9330.99
825,000	17326.54	13483.79	12301.49	10675.30	9622.58
850,000	17851.59	13892.39	12674.26	10998.80	9914.18
875,000	18376.63	14300.99	13047.03	11322.29	10205.77
900,000	18901.68	14709.59	13419.80	11645.79	10497.36

Table 7   181

9.50%   Monthly Payment Loans

Amortization Period in Years

Loan Amount	15	16	17	18	20
10	0.11	0.11	0.10	0.10	0.10
20	0.21	0.21	0.20	0.20	0.19
30	0.32	0.31	0.30	0.30	0.28
40	0.42	0.41	0.40	0.39	0.38
50	0.53	0.51	0.50	0.49	0.47
100	1.05	1.02	0.99	0.97	0.94
200	2.09	2.03	1.98	1.94	1.87
300	3.14	3.05	2.97	2.91	2.80
400	4.18	4.06	3.96	3.88	3.73
500	5.23	5.08	4.95	4.84	4.67
1,000	10.45	10.15	9.90	9.68	9.33
2,000	20.89	20.30	19.80	19.36	18.65
3,000	31.33	30.45	29.70	29.04	27.97
4,000	41.77	40.60	39.60	38.72	37.29
5,000	52.22	50.75	49.49	48.40	46.61
10,000	104.43	101.50	98.98	96.80	93.22
20,000	208.85	203.00	197.96	193.59	186.43
30,000	313.27	304.50	296.94	290.38	279.64
40,000	417.69	406.00	395.92	387.17	372.86
50,000	522.12	507.50	494.90	483.96	466.07
100,000	1044.23	1014.99	989.79	967.92	932.14
125,000	1305.29	1268.74	1237.23	1209.89	1165.17
150,000	1566.34	1522.49	1484.68	1451.87	1398.20
175,000	1827.40	1776.24	1732.12	1693.85	1631.23
200,000	2088.45	2029.98	1979.57	1935.83	1864.27
225,000	2349.51	2283.73	2227.01	2177.81	2097.30
250,000	2610.57	2537.48	2474.46	2419.78	2330.33
275,000	2871.62	2791.23	2721.90	2661.76	2563.37
300,000	3132.68	3044.97	2969.35	2903.74	2796.40
325,000	3393.74	3298.72	3216.79	3145.72	3029.43
350,000	3654.79	3552.47	3464.24	3387.70	3262.46
375,000	3915.85	3806.22	3711.68	3629.67	3495.50
400,000	4176.90	4059.96	3959.13	3871.65	3728.53
425,000	4437.96	4313.71	4206.57	4113.63	3961.56
450,000	4699.02	4567.46	4454.02	4355.61	4194.60
475,000	4960.07	4821.21	4701.46	4597.58	4427.63
500,000	5221.13	5074.95	4948.91	4839.56	4660.66
525,000	5482.18	5328.70	5196.35	5081.54	4893.69
550,000	5743.24	5582.45	5443.80	5323.52	5126.73
575,000	6004.30	5836.20	5691.24	5565.50	5359.76
600,000	6265.35	6089.94	5938.69	5807.47	5592.79
625,000	6526.41	6343.69	6186.13	6049.45	5825.82
650,000	6787.47	6597.44	6433.58	6291.43	6058.86
675,000	7048.52	6851.18	6681.02	6533.41	6291.89
700,000	7309.58	7104.93	6928.47	6775.39	6524.92
725,000	7570.63	7358.68	7175.91	7017.36	6757.96
750,000	7831.69	7612.43	7423.36	7259.34	6990.99
775,000	8092.75	7866.17	7670.81	7501.32	7224.02
800,000	8353.80	8119.92	7918.25	7743.30	7457.05
825,000	8614.86	8373.67	8165.70	7985.27	7690.09
850,000	8875.91	8627.42	8413.14	8227.25	7923.12
875,000	9136.97	8881.16	8660.59	8469.23	8156.15
900,000	9398.03	9134.91	8908.03	8711.21	8389.19

Monthly Payment Loans   **9.50%**

Loan Amount	\multicolumn{5}{c}{Amortization Period in Years}
	21	22	23	24	25
10	0.10	0.10	0.09	0.09	0.09
20	0.19	0.19	0.18	0.18	0.18
30	0.28	0.28	0.27	0.27	0.27
40	0.37	0.37	0.36	0.36	0.35
50	0.46	0.46	0.45	0.45	0.44
100	0.92	0.91	0.90	0.89	0.88
200	1.84	1.81	1.79	1.77	1.75
300	2.76	2.72	2.68	2.65	2.63
400	3.67	3.62	3.58	3.54	3.50
500	4.59	4.53	4.47	4.42	4.37
1,000	9.18	9.05	8.93	8.83	8.74
2,000	18.35	18.09	17.86	17.66	17.48
3,000	27.53	27.14	26.79	26.49	26.22
4,000	36.70	36.18	35.72	35.32	34.95
5,000	45.88	45.23	44.65	44.14	43.69
10,000	91.75	90.45	89.30	88.28	87.37
20,000	183.49	180.90	178.60	176.56	174.74
30,000	275.24	271.34	267.90	264.84	262.11
40,000	366.98	361.79	357.19	353.11	349.48
50,000	458.72	452.24	446.49	441.39	436.85
100,000	917.44	904.47	892.98	882.78	873.70
125,000	1146.80	1130.58	1116.22	1103.47	1092.13
150,000	1376.16	1356.70	1339.47	1324.17	1310.55
175,000	1605.52	1582.81	1562.71	1544.86	1528.97
200,000	1834.87	1808.93	1785.95	1765.55	1747.40
225,000	2064.23	2035.04	2009.20	1986.25	1965.82
250,000	2293.59	2261.16	2232.44	2206.94	2184.25
275,000	2522.95	2487.27	2455.68	2427.64	2402.67
300,000	2752.31	2713.39	2678.93	2648.33	2621.09
325,000	2981.67	2939.50	2902.17	2869.02	2839.52
350,000	3211.03	3165.62	3125.41	3089.72	3057.94
375,000	3440.38	3391.74	3348.66	3310.41	3276.37
400,000	3669.74	3617.85	3571.90	3531.10	3494.79
425,000	3899.10	3843.97	3795.15	3751.80	3713.22
450,000	4128.46	4070.08	4018.39	3972.49	3931.64
475,000	4357.82	4296.20	4241.63	4193.19	4150.06
500,000	4587.18	4522.31	4464.88	4413.88	4368.49
525,000	4816.54	4748.43	4688.12	4634.57	4586.91
550,000	5045.89	4974.54	4911.36	4855.27	4805.34
575,000	5275.25	5200.66	5134.61	5075.96	5023.76
600,000	5504.61	5426.77	5357.85	5296.65	5242.18
625,000	5733.97	5652.89	5581.09	5517.35	5460.61
650,000	5963.33	5879.00	5804.34	5738.04	5679.03
675,000	6192.69	6105.12	6027.58	5958.74	5897.46
700,000	6422.05	6331.23	6250.82	6179.43	6115.88
725,000	6651.40	6557.35	6474.07	6400.12	6334.31
750,000	6880.76	6783.47	6697.31	6620.82	6552.73
775,000	7110.12	7009.58	6920.56	6841.51	6771.15
800,000	7339.48	7235.70	7143.80	7062.20	6989.58
825,000	7568.84	7461.81	7367.04	7282.90	7208.00
850,000	7798.20	7687.93	7590.29	7503.59	7426.43
875,000	8027.56	7914.04	7813.53	7724.29	7644.85
900,000	8256.91	8140.16	8036.77	7944.98	7863.27

Table 7   183

9.50%   Monthly Payment Loans

Amortization Period in Years

Loan Amount	26	27	28	29	30
10	0.09	0.09	0.09	0.09	0.09
20	0.18	0.18	0.18	0.17	0.17
30	0.26	0.26	0.26	0.26	0.26
40	0.35	0.35	0.35	0.34	0.34
50	0.44	0.43	0.43	0.43	0.43
100	0.87	0.86	0.86	0.85	0.85
200	1.74	1.72	1.71	1.70	1.69
300	2.60	2.58	2.56	2.54	2.53
400	3.47	3.44	3.41	3.39	3.37
500	4.33	4.30	4.26	4.24	4.21
1,000	8.66	8.59	8.52	8.47	8.41
2,000	17.32	17.17	17.04	16.93	16.82
3,000	25.97	25.76	25.56	25.39	25.23
4,000	34.63	34.34	34.08	33.85	33.64
5,000	43.28	42.92	42.60	42.31	42.05
10,000	86.56	85.84	85.19	84.61	84.09
20,000	173.12	171.68	170.38	169.22	168.18
30,000	259.68	257.51	255.57	253.83	252.26
40,000	346.24	343.35	340.76	338.43	336.35
50,000	432.80	429.19	425.95	423.04	420.43
100,000	865.60	858.37	851.89	846.08	840.86
125,000	1082.00	1072.96	1064.86	1057.59	1051.07
150,000	1298.40	1287.55	1277.83	1269.11	1261.29
175,000	1514.80	1502.14	1490.80	1480.63	1471.50
200,000	1731.20	1716.73	1703.77	1692.15	1681.71
225,000	1947.60	1931.32	1916.74	1903.67	1891.93
250,000	2164.00	2145.91	2129.71	2115.18	2102.14
275,000	2380.40	2360.50	2342.68	2326.70	2312.35
300,000	2596.80	2575.09	2555.65	2538.22	2522.57
325,000	2813.20	2789.68	2768.62	2749.74	2732.78
350,000	3029.60	3004.27	2981.59	2961.26	2942.99
375,000	3246.00	3218.86	3194.56	3172.77	3153.21
400,000	3462.40	3433.45	3407.53	3384.29	3363.42
425,000	3678.80	3648.04	3620.50	3595.81	3573.64
450,000	3895.20	3862.63	3833.47	3807.33	3783.85
475,000	4111.60	4077.22	4046.44	4018.84	3994.06
500,000	4328.00	4291.81	4259.41	4230.36	4204.28
525,000	4544.40	4506.40	4472.38	4441.88	4414.49
550,000	4760.80	4720.99	4685.35	4653.40	4624.70
575,000	4977.20	4935.58	4898.32	4864.92	4834.92
600,000	5193.60	5150.17	5111.30	5076.43	5045.13
625,000	5410.00	5364.76	5324.27	5287.95	5255.34
650,000	5626.40	5579.35	5537.24	5499.47	5465.56
675,000	5842.80	5793.94	5750.21	5710.99	5675.77
700,000	6059.20	6008.53	5963.18	5922.51	5885.98
725,000	6275.60	6223.12	6176.15	6134.02	6096.20
750,000	6492.00	6437.72	6389.12	6345.54	6306.41
775,000	6708.40	6652.31	6602.09	6557.06	6516.63
800,000	6924.80	6866.90	6815.06	6768.58	6726.84
825,000	7141.19	7081.49	7028.03	6980.09	6937.05
850,000	7357.59	7296.08	7241.00	7191.61	7147.27
875,000	7573.99	7510.67	7453.97	7403.13	7357.48
900,000	7790.39	7725.26	7666.94	7614.65	7567.69

Monthly Payment Loans   9.75%

Loan Amount	Amortization Period in Years				
	5	7	8	10	12
10	0.22	0.17	0.16	0.14	0.12
20	0.43	0.33	0.31	0.27	0.24
30	0.64	0.50	0.46	0.40	0.36
40	0.85	0.66	0.61	0.53	0.48
50	1.06	0.83	0.76	0.66	0.60
100	2.12	1.65	1.51	1.31	1.19
200	4.23	3.30	3.01	2.62	2.37
300	6.34	4.95	4.52	3.93	3.55
400	8.45	6.59	6.02	5.24	4.73
500	10.57	8.24	7.53	6.54	5.91
1,000	21.13	16.48	15.05	13.08	11.81
2,000	42.25	32.95	30.09	26.16	23.62
3,000	63.38	49.42	45.13	39.24	35.43
4,000	84.50	65.89	60.17	52.31	47.23
5,000	105.63	82.37	75.22	65.39	59.04
10,000	211.25	164.73	150.43	130.78	118.07
20,000	422.49	329.45	300.85	261.55	236.14
30,000	633.73	494.17	451.27	392.32	354.21
40,000	844.97	658.90	601.69	523.09	472.28
50,000	1056.22	823.62	752.12	653.86	590.35
100,000	2112.43	1647.23	1504.23	1307.71	1180.69
125,000	2640.54	2059.04	1880.28	1634.63	1475.86
150,000	3168.64	2470.85	2256.34	1961.56	1771.03
175,000	3696.75	2882.66	2632.39	2288.48	2066.20
200,000	4224.85	3294.46	3008.45	2615.41	2361.37
225,000	4752.96	3706.27	3384.50	2942.34	2656.54
250,000	5281.07	4118.08	3760.56	3269.26	2951.71
275,000	5809.17	4529.89	4136.61	3596.19	3246.88
300,000	6337.28	4941.69	4512.67	3923.11	3542.05
325,000	6865.38	5353.50	4888.72	4250.04	3837.22
350,000	7393.49	5765.31	5264.78	4576.96	4132.39
375,000	7921.60	6177.12	5640.83	4903.89	4427.56
400,000	8449.70	6588.92	6016.89	5230.81	4722.73
425,000	8977.81	7000.73	6392.94	5557.74	5017.90
450,000	9505.91	7412.54	6769.00	5884.67	5313.07
475,000	10034.02	7824.35	7145.05	6211.59	5608.24
500,000	10562.13	8236.15	7521.11	6538.52	5903.41
525,000	11090.23	8647.96	7897.16	6865.44	6198.58
550,000	11618.34	9059.77	8273.22	7192.37	6493.75
575,000	12146.45	9471.58	8649.27	7519.29	6788.92
600,000	12674.55	9883.38	9025.33	7846.22	7084.09
625,000	13202.66	10295.19	9401.38	8173.15	7379.26
650,000	13730.76	10707.00	9777.44	8500.07	7674.43
675,000	14258.87	11118.80	10153.49	8827.00	7969.60
700,000	14786.98	11530.61	10529.55	9153.92	8264.77
725,000	15315.08	11942.42	10905.60	9480.85	8559.94
750,000	15843.19	12354.23	11281.66	9807.77	8855.11
775,000	16371.29	12766.03	11657.71	10134.70	9150.28
800,000	16899.40	13177.84	12033.77	10461.62	9445.45
825,000	17427.51	13589.65	12409.82	10788.55	9740.62
850,000	17955.61	14001.46	12785.88	11115.48	10035.79
875,000	18483.72	14413.26	13161.93	11442.40	10330.96
900,000	19011.82	14825.07	13537.99	11769.33	10626.13

Table 7   185

9.75%   Monthly Payment Loans

Amortization Period in Years

Loan Amount	15	16	17	18	20
10	0.11	0.11	0.11	0.10	0.10
20	0.22	0.21	0.21	0.20	0.19
30	0.32	0.31	0.31	0.30	0.29
40	0.43	0.42	0.41	0.40	0.38
50	0.53	0.52	0.51	0.50	0.48
100	1.06	1.04	1.01	0.99	0.95
200	2.12	2.07	2.02	1.97	1.90
300	3.18	3.10	3.02	2.96	2.85
400	4.24	4.13	4.03	3.94	3.80
500	5.30	5.16	5.03	4.92	4.75
1,000	10.60	10.31	10.06	9.84	9.49
2,000	21.19	20.61	20.11	19.68	18.98
3,000	31.79	30.92	30.17	29.52	28.46
4,000	42.38	41.22	40.22	39.36	37.95
5,000	52.97	51.52	50.28	49.20	47.43
10,000	105.94	103.04	100.55	98.39	94.86
20,000	211.88	206.08	201.09	196.77	189.71
30,000	317.81	309.12	301.64	295.15	284.56
40,000	423.75	412.16	402.18	393.53	379.41
50,000	529.69	515.20	502.72	491.92	474.26
100,000	1059.37	1030.40	1005.44	983.83	948.52
125,000	1324.21	1287.99	1256.80	1229.78	1185.65
150,000	1589.05	1545.59	1508.16	1475.74	1422.78
175,000	1853.89	1803.19	1759.52	1721.69	1659.91
200,000	2118.73	2060.79	2010.88	1967.65	1897.04
225,000	2383.57	2318.39	2262.24	2213.60	2134.17
250,000	2648.41	2575.98	2513.60	2459.56	2371.30
275,000	2913.26	2833.58	2764.96	2705.51	2608.43
300,000	3178.09	3091.18	3016.32	2951.47	2845.56
325,000	3442.93	3348.78	3267.68	3197.42	3082.68
350,000	3707.77	3606.38	3519.04	3443.38	3319.81
375,000	3972.61	3863.97	3770.40	3689.33	3556.94
400,000	4237.46	4121.57	4021.76	3935.29	3794.07
425,000	4502.30	4379.17	4273.12	4181.24	4031.20
450,000	4767.14	4636.77	4524.48	4427.20	4268.33
475,000	5031.98	4894.36	4775.84	4673.15	4505.46
500,000	5296.82	5151.96	5027.20	4919.11	4742.59
525,000	5561.66	5409.56	5278.56	5165.06	4979.72
550,000	5826.50	5667.16	5529.92	5411.02	5216.85
575,000	6091.34	5924.76	5781.28	5656.97	5453.98
600,000	6356.18	6182.35	6032.64	5902.93	5691.11
625,000	6621.02	6439.95	6284.00	6148.88	5928.24
650,000	6885.86	6697.55	6535.36	6394.84	6165.36
675,000	7150.70	6955.15	6786.72	6640.79	6402.49
700,000	7415.54	7212.75	7038.08	6886.75	6639.62
725,000	7680.38	7470.34	7289.44	7132.70	6876.75
750,000	7945.22	7727.94	7540.80	7378.66	7113.88
775,000	8210.07	7985.54	7792.16	7624.61	7351.01
800,000	8474.91	8243.14	8043.52	7870.57	7588.14
825,000	8739.75	8500.74	8294.88	8116.52	7825.27
850,000	9004.59	8758.33	8546.24	8362.48	8062.40
875,000	9269.43	9015.93	8797.60	8608.43	8299.53
900,000	9534.27	9273.53	9048.96	8854.39	8536.66

Monthly Payment Loans   **9.75%**

Loan Amount	Amortization Period in Years				
	21	22	23	24	25
10	0.10	0.10	0.10	0.10	0.09
20	0.19	0.19	0.19	0.19	0.18
30	0.29	0.28	0.28	0.28	0.27
40	0.38	0.37	0.37	0.37	0.36
50	0.47	0.47	0.46	0.46	0.45
100	0.94	0.93	0.92	0.91	0.90
200	1.87	1.85	1.83	1.81	1.79
300	2.81	2.77	2.74	2.71	2.68
400	3.74	3.69	3.65	3.61	3.57
500	4.68	4.61	4.56	4.51	4.46
1,000	9.35	9.22	9.11	9.01	8.92
2,000	18.69	18.43	18.21	18.01	17.83
3,000	28.03	27.64	27.31	27.01	26.74
4,000	37.37	36.86	36.41	36.01	35.65
5,000	46.71	46.07	45.51	45.01	44.56
10,000	93.41	92.13	91.01	90.01	89.12
20,000	186.81	184.26	182.01	180.01	178.23
30,000	280.22	276.39	273.01	270.01	267.35
40,000	373.62	368.52	364.01	360.01	356.46
50,000	467.03	460.65	455.01	450.02	445.57
100,000	934.05	921.30	910.02	900.03	891.14
125,000	1167.56	1151.62	1137.53	1125.03	1113.93
150,000	1401.08	1381.94	1365.03	1350.04	1336.71
175,000	1634.59	1612.27	1592.53	1575.04	1559.50
200,000	1868.10	1842.59	1820.04	1800.05	1782.28
225,000	2101.61	2072.91	2047.54	2025.05	2005.06
250,000	2335.12	2303.24	2275.05	2250.06	2227.85
275,000	2568.63	2533.56	2502.55	2475.06	2450.63
300,000	2802.15	2763.88	2730.06	2700.07	2673.42
325,000	3035.66	2994.21	2957.56	2925.07	2896.20
350,000	3269.17	3224.53	3185.06	3150.08	3118.99
375,000	3502.68	3454.85	3412.57	3375.08	3341.77
400,000	3736.19	3685.18	3640.07	3600.09	3564.55
425,000	3969.70	3915.50	3867.58	3825.09	3787.34
450,000	4203.22	4145.82	4095.08	4050.10	4010.12
475,000	4436.73	4376.15	4322.58	4275.10	4232.91
500,000	4670.24	4606.47	4550.09	4500.11	4455.69
525,000	4903.75	4836.79	4777.59	4725.11	4678.48
550,000	5137.26	5067.12	5005.10	4950.12	4901.26
575,000	5370.77	5297.44	5232.60	5175.12	5124.05
600,000	5604.29	5527.76	5460.11	5400.13	5346.83
625,000	5837.80	5758.08	5687.61	5625.13	5569.61
650,000	6071.31	5988.41	5915.11	5850.14	5792.40
675,000	6304.82	6218.73	6142.62	6075.14	6015.18
700,000	6538.33	6449.05	6370.12	6300.15	6237.97
725,000	6771.84	6679.38	6597.63	6525.15	6460.75
750,000	7005.36	6909.70	6825.13	6750.16	6683.54
775,000	7238.87	7140.02	7052.63	6975.16	6906.32
800,000	7472.38	7370.35	7280.14	7200.17	7129.10
825,000	7705.89	7600.67	7507.64	7425.17	7351.89
850,000	7939.40	7830.99	7735.15	7650.18	7574.67
875,000	8172.91	8061.32	7962.65	7875.18	7797.46
900,000	8406.43	8291.64	8190.16	8100.19	8020.24

Table 7   187

9.75%   Monthly Payment Loans

Loan Amount	26	27	28	29	30
10	0.09	0.09	0.09	0.09	0.09
20	0.18	0.18	0.18	0.18	0.18
30	0.27	0.27	0.27	0.26	0.26
40	0.36	0.36	0.35	0.35	0.35
50	0.45	0.44	0.44	0.44	0.43
100	0.89	0.88	0.87	0.87	0.86
200	1.77	1.76	1.74	1.73	1.72
300	2.65	2.63	2.61	2.60	2.58
400	3.54	3.51	3.48	3.46	3.44
500	4.42	4.39	4.35	4.33	4.30
1,000	8.84	8.77	8.70	8.65	8.60
2,000	17.67	17.53	17.40	17.29	17.19
3,000	26.50	26.29	26.10	25.93	25.78
4,000	35.33	35.05	34.80	34.57	34.37
5,000	44.17	43.81	43.50	43.22	42.96
10,000	88.33	87.62	86.99	86.43	85.92
20,000	176.65	175.24	173.98	172.85	171.84
30,000	264.97	262.86	260.96	259.27	257.75
40,000	353.30	350.47	347.95	345.69	343.67
50,000	441.62	438.09	434.94	432.11	429.58
100,000	883.23	876.17	869.87	864.22	859.16
125,000	1104.04	1095.22	1087.33	1080.27	1073.95
150,000	1324.85	1314.26	1304.80	1296.33	1288.74
175,000	1545.65	1533.30	1522.26	1512.38	1503.53
200,000	1766.46	1752.34	1739.73	1728.43	1718.31
225,000	1987.27	1971.38	1957.19	1944.49	1933.10
250,000	2208.07	2190.43	2174.66	2160.54	2147.89
275,000	2428.88	2409.47	2392.12	2376.60	2362.68
300,000	2649.69	2628.51	2609.59	2592.65	2577.47
325,000	2870.49	2847.55	2827.05	2808.70	2792.26
350,000	3091.30	3066.60	3044.52	3024.76	3007.05
375,000	3312.11	3285.64	3261.98	3240.81	3221.83
400,000	3532.91	3504.68	3479.45	3456.86	3436.62
425,000	3753.72	3723.72	3696.91	3672.92	3651.41
450,000	3974.53	3942.76	3914.38	3888.97	3866.20
475,000	4195.33	4161.81	4131.84	4105.03	4080.99
500,000	4416.14	4380.85	4349.31	4321.08	4295.78
525,000	4636.95	4599.89	4566.78	4537.13	4510.57
550,000	4857.75	4818.93	4784.24	4753.19	4725.35
575,000	5078.56	5037.98	5001.71	4969.24	4940.14
600,000	5299.37	5257.02	5219.17	5185.29	5154.93
625,000	5520.17	5476.06	5436.64	5401.35	5369.72
650,000	5740.98	5695.10	5654.10	5617.40	5584.51
675,000	5961.79	5914.14	5871.57	5833.46	5799.30
700,000	6182.59	6133.19	6089.03	6049.51	6014.09
725,000	6403.40	6352.23	6306.50	6265.56	6228.87
750,000	6624.21	6571.27	6523.96	6481.62	6443.66
775,000	6845.01	6790.31	6741.43	6697.67	6658.45
800,000	7065.82	7009.36	6958.89	6913.72	6873.24
825,000	7286.63	7228.40	7176.36	7129.78	7088.03
850,000	7507.43	7447.44	7393.82	7345.83	7302.82
875,000	7728.24	7666.48	7611.29	7561.89	7517.61
900,000	7949.05	7885.52	7828.75	7777.94	7732.39

Monthly Payment Loans   **10.00%**

Loan Amount	Amortization Period in Years				
	5	7	8	10	12
10	0.22	0.17	0.16	0.14	0.12
20	0.43	0.34	0.31	0.27	0.24
30	0.64	0.50	0.46	0.40	0.36
40	0.85	0.67	0.61	0.53	0.48
50	1.07	0.84	0.76	0.67	0.60
100	2.13	1.67	1.52	1.33	1.20
200	4.25	3.33	3.04	2.65	2.40
300	6.38	4.99	4.56	3.97	3.59
400	8.50	6.65	6.07	5.29	4.79
500	10.63	8.31	7.59	6.61	5.98
1,000	21.25	16.61	15.18	13.22	11.96
2,000	42.50	33.21	30.35	26.44	23.91
3,000	63.75	49.81	45.53	39.65	35.86
4,000	84.99	66.41	60.70	52.87	47.81
5,000	106.24	83.01	75.88	66.08	59.76
10,000	212.48	166.02	151.75	132.16	119.51
20,000	424.95	332.03	303.49	264.31	239.02
30,000	637.42	498.04	455.23	396.46	358.53
40,000	849.89	664.05	606.97	528.61	478.04
50,000	1062.36	830.06	758.71	660.76	597.54
100,000	2124.71	1660.12	1517.42	1321.51	1195.08
125,000	2655.89	2075.15	1896.78	1651.89	1493.85
150,000	3187.06	2490.18	2276.13	1982.27	1792.62
175,000	3718.24	2905.21	2655.48	2312.64	2091.39
200,000	4249.41	3320.24	3034.84	2643.02	2390.16
225,000	4780.59	3735.27	3414.19	2973.40	2688.93
250,000	5311.77	4150.30	3793.55	3303.77	2987.70
275,000	5842.94	4565.33	4172.90	3634.15	3286.47
300,000	6374.12	4980.36	4552.25	3964.53	3585.24
325,000	6905.29	5395.39	4931.61	4294.90	3884.01
350,000	7436.47	5810.42	5310.96	4625.28	4182.78
375,000	7967.65	6225.45	5690.32	4955.66	4481.55
400,000	8498.82	6640.48	6069.67	5286.03	4780.32
425,000	9030.00	7055.51	6449.02	5616.41	5079.09
450,000	9561.18	7470.54	6828.38	5946.79	5377.86
475,000	10092.35	7885.57	7207.73	6277.17	5676.63
500,000	10623.53	8300.60	7587.09	6607.54	5975.40
525,000	11154.70	8715.63	7966.44	6937.92	6274.17
550,000	11685.88	9130.66	8345.80	7268.30	6572.94
575,000	12217.06	9545.69	8725.15	7598.67	6871.71
600,000	12748.23	9960.72	9104.50	7929.05	7170.47
625,000	13279.41	10375.75	9483.86	8259.43	7469.24
650,000	13810.58	10790.77	9863.21	8589.80	7768.01
675,000	14341.76	11205.80	10242.57	8920.18	8066.78
700,000	14872.94	11620.83	10621.92	9250.56	8365.55
725,000	15404.11	12035.86	11001.27	9580.93	8664.32
750,000	15935.29	12450.89	11380.63	9911.31	8963.09
775,000	16466.46	12865.92	11759.98	10241.69	9261.86
800,000	16997.64	13280.95	12139.34	10572.06	9560.63
825,000	17528.82	13695.98	12518.69	10902.44	9859.40
850,000	18059.99	14111.01	12898.04	11232.82	10158.17
875,000	18591.17	14526.04	13277.40	11563.19	10456.94
900,000	19122.35	14941.07	13656.75	11893.57	10755.71

Table 7   189

10.00%   Monthly Payment Loans

Amortization Period in Years

Loan Amount	15	16	17	18	20
10	0.11	0.11	0.11	0.10	0.10
20	0.22	0.21	0.21	0.20	0.20
30	0.33	0.32	0.31	0.30	0.29
40	0.43	0.42	0.41	0.40	0.39
50	0.54	0.53	0.52	0.50	0.49
100	1.08	1.05	1.03	1.00	0.97
200	2.15	2.10	2.05	2.00	1.94
300	3.23	3.14	3.07	3.00	2.90
400	4.30	4.19	4.09	4.00	3.87
500	5.38	5.23	5.11	5.00	4.83
1,000	10.75	10.46	10.22	10.00	9.66
2,000	21.50	20.92	20.43	20.00	19.31
3,000	32.24	31.38	30.64	30.00	28.96
4,000	42.99	41.84	40.85	40.00	38.61
5,000	53.74	52.30	51.07	50.00	48.26
10,000	107.47	104.60	102.13	99.99	96.51
20,000	214.93	209.19	204.25	199.97	193.01
30,000	322.39	313.78	306.37	299.96	289.51
40,000	429.85	418.37	408.49	399.94	386.01
50,000	537.31	522.96	510.61	499.93	482.52
100,000	1074.61	1045.91	1021.22	999.85	965.03
125,000	1343.26	1307.38	1276.52	1249.81	1206.28
150,000	1611.91	1568.86	1531.82	1499.77	1447.54
175,000	1880.56	1830.33	1787.12	1749.73	1688.79
200,000	2149.22	2091.81	2042.43	1999.69	1930.05
225,000	2417.87	2353.28	2297.73	2249.65	2171.30
250,000	2686.52	2614.76	2553.03	2499.61	2412.56
275,000	2955.17	2876.24	2808.33	2749.58	2653.81
300,000	3223.82	3137.71	3063.64	2999.54	2895.07
325,000	3492.47	3399.19	3318.94	3249.50	3136.33
350,000	3761.12	3660.66	3574.24	3499.46	3377.58
375,000	4029.77	3922.14	3829.54	3749.42	3618.84
400,000	4298.43	4183.61	4084.85	3999.38	3860.09
425,000	4567.08	4445.09	4340.15	4249.34	4101.35
450,000	4835.73	4706.56	4595.45	4499.30	4342.60
475,000	5104.38	4968.04	4850.75	4749.26	4583.86
500,000	5373.03	5229.51	5106.06	4999.22	4825.11
525,000	5641.68	5490.99	5361.36	5249.18	5066.37
550,000	5910.33	5752.47	5616.66	5499.15	5307.62
575,000	6178.98	6013.94	5871.97	5749.11	5548.88
600,000	6447.64	6275.42	6127.27	5999.07	5790.13
625,000	6716.29	6536.89	6382.57	6249.03	6031.39
650,000	6984.94	6798.37	6637.87	6498.99	6272.65
675,000	7253.59	7059.84	6893.18	6748.95	6513.90
700,000	7522.24	7321.32	7148.48	6998.91	6755.16
725,000	7790.89	7582.79	7403.78	7248.87	6996.41
750,000	8059.54	7844.27	7659.08	7498.83	7237.67
775,000	8328.19	8105.74	7914.39	7748.79	7478.92
800,000	8596.85	8367.22	8169.69	7998.75	7720.18
825,000	8865.50	8628.70	8424.99	8248.72	7961.43
850,000	9134.15	8890.17	8680.29	8498.68	8202.69
875,000	9402.80	9151.65	8935.60	8748.64	8443.94
900,000	9671.45	9413.12	9190.90	8998.60	8685.20

Monthly Payment Loans   **10.00%**

Loan Amount	21	22	23	24	25
	Amortization Period in Years				
10	0.10	0.10	0.10	0.10	0.10
20	0.20	0.19	0.19	0.19	0.19
30	0.29	0.29	0.28	0.28	0.28
40	0.39	0.38	0.38	0.37	0.37
50	0.48	0.47	0.47	0.46	0.46
100	0.96	0.94	0.93	0.92	0.91
200	1.91	1.88	1.86	1.84	1.82
300	2.86	2.82	2.79	2.76	2.73
400	3.81	3.76	3.71	3.67	3.64
500	4.76	4.70	4.64	4.59	4.55
1,000	9.51	9.39	9.28	9.18	9.09
2,000	19.02	18.77	18.55	18.35	18.18
3,000	28.53	28.15	27.82	27.53	27.27
4,000	38.04	37.53	37.09	36.70	36.35
5,000	47.54	46.92	46.36	45.87	45.44
10,000	95.08	93.83	92.72	91.74	90.88
20,000	190.16	187.65	185.44	183.48	181.75
30,000	285.24	281.48	278.16	275.22	272.62
40,000	380.32	375.30	370.88	366.96	363.49
50,000	475.40	469.13	463.60	458.70	454.36
100,000	950.79	938.25	927.19	917.39	908.71
125,000	1188.48	1172.81	1158.98	1146.74	1135.88
150,000	1426.18	1407.37	1390.78	1376.09	1363.06
175,000	1663.87	1641.94	1622.57	1605.44	1590.23
200,000	1901.57	1876.50	1854.37	1834.78	1817.41
225,000	2139.26	2111.06	2086.16	2064.13	2044.58
250,000	2376.96	2345.62	2317.96	2293.48	2271.76
275,000	2614.65	2580.18	2549.75	2522.82	2498.93
300,000	2852.35	2814.74	2781.55	2752.17	2726.11
325,000	3090.04	3049.30	3013.35	2981.52	2953.28
350,000	3327.74	3283.87	3245.14	3210.87	3180.46
375,000	3565.43	3518.43	3476.94	3440.21	3407.63
400,000	3803.13	3752.99	3708.73	3669.56	3634.81
425,000	4040.82	3987.55	3940.53	3898.91	3861.98
450,000	4278.52	4222.11	4172.32	4128.25	4089.16
475,000	4516.21	4456.67	4404.12	4357.60	4316.33
500,000	4753.91	4691.23	4635.91	4586.95	4543.51
525,000	4991.60	4925.80	4867.71	4816.30	4770.68
550,000	5229.30	5160.36	5099.50	5045.64	4997.86
575,000	5466.99	5394.92	5331.30	5274.99	5225.03
600,000	5704.69	5629.48	5563.09	5504.34	5452.21
625,000	5942.38	5864.04	5794.89	5733.68	5679.38
650,000	6180.08	6098.60	6026.69	5963.03	5906.56
675,000	6417.77	6333.17	6258.48	6192.38	6133.74
700,000	6655.47	6567.73	6490.28	6421.73	6360.91
725,000	6893.16	6802.29	6722.07	6651.07	6588.09
750,000	7130.86	7036.85	6953.87	6880.42	6815.26
775,000	7368.55	7271.41	7185.66	7109.77	7042.44
800,000	7606.25	7505.97	7417.46	7339.11	7269.61
825,000	7843.94	7740.53	7649.25	7568.46	7496.79
850,000	8081.64	7975.10	7881.05	7797.81	7723.96
875,000	8319.33	8209.66	8112.84	8027.16	7951.14
900,000	8557.03	8444.22	8344.64	8256.50	8178.31

Table 7   191

Monthly Payment Loans

Amortization Period in Years

Loan Amount	26	27	28	29	30
10	0.10	0.09	0.09	0.09	0.09
20	0.19	0.18	0.18	0.18	0.18
30	0.28	0.27	0.27	0.27	0.27
40	0.37	0.36	0.36	0.36	0.36
50	0.46	0.45	0.45	0.45	0.44
100	0.91	0.90	0.89	0.89	0.88
200	1.81	1.79	1.78	1.77	1.76
300	2.71	2.69	2.67	2.65	2.64
400	3.61	3.58	3.56	3.53	3.52
500	4.51	4.48	4.44	4.42	4.39
1,000	9.01	8.95	8.88	8.83	8.78
2,000	18.02	17.89	17.76	17.65	17.56
3,000	27.03	26.83	26.64	26.48	26.33
4,000	36.04	35.77	35.52	35.30	35.11
5,000	45.05	44.71	44.40	44.13	43.88
10,000	90.10	89.41	88.80	88.25	87.76
20,000	180.20	178.82	177.60	176.50	175.52
30,000	270.30	268.23	266.39	264.75	263.28
40,000	360.40	357.64	355.19	353.00	351.03
50,000	450.49	447.05	443.99	441.24	438.79
100,000	900.98	894.10	887.97	882.48	877.58
125,000	1126.23	1117.63	1109.96	1103.10	1096.97
150,000	1351.47	1341.15	1331.95	1323.72	1316.36
175,000	1576.71	1564.68	1553.94	1544.34	1535.76
200,000	1801.96	1788.20	1775.93	1764.96	1755.15
225,000	2027.20	2011.72	1997.92	1985.58	1974.54
250,000	2252.45	2235.25	2219.91	2206.20	2193.93
275,000	2477.69	2458.77	2441.90	2426.82	2413.33
300,000	2702.94	2682.30	2663.89	2647.44	2632.72
325,000	2928.18	2905.82	2885.88	2868.06	2852.11
350,000	3153.42	3129.35	3107.87	3088.67	3071.51
375,000	3378.67	3352.87	3329.86	3309.29	3290.90
400,000	3603.91	3576.40	3551.85	3529.91	3510.29
425,000	3829.16	3799.92	3773.84	3750.53	3729.68
450,000	4054.40	4023.44	3995.83	3971.15	3949.08
475,000	4279.65	4246.97	4217.82	4191.77	4168.47
500,000	4504.89	4470.49	4439.81	4412.39	4387.86
525,000	4730.13	4694.02	4661.80	4633.01	4607.26
550,000	4955.38	4917.54	4883.79	4853.63	4826.65
575,000	5180.62	5141.07	5105.78	5074.25	5046.04
600,000	5405.87	5364.59	5327.77	5294.87	5265.43
625,000	5631.11	5588.12	5549.76	5515.49	5484.83
650,000	5856.36	5811.64	5771.75	5736.11	5704.22
675,000	6081.60	6035.16	5993.74	5956.73	5923.61
700,000	6306.84	6258.69	6215.73	6177.34	6143.01
725,000	6532.09	6482.21	6437.72	6397.96	6362.40
750,000	6757.33	6705.74	6659.71	6618.58	6581.79
775,000	6982.58	6929.26	6881.70	6839.20	6801.18
800,000	7207.82	7152.79	7103.69	7059.82	7020.58
825,000	7433.06	7376.31	7325.68	7280.44	7239.97
850,000	7658.31	7599.84	7547.67	7501.06	7459.36
875,000	7883.55	7823.36	7769.66	7721.68	7678.76
900,000	8108.80	8046.88	7991.65	7942.30	7898.15

Monthly Payment Loans   **10.25%**

Loan Amount	Amortization Period in Years				
	5	7	8	10	12
10	0.22	0.17	0.16	0.14	0.13
20	0.43	0.34	0.31	0.27	0.25
30	0.65	0.51	0.46	0.41	0.37
40	0.86	0.67	0.62	0.54	0.49
50	1.07	0.84	0.77	0.67	0.61
100	2.14	1.68	1.54	1.34	1.21
200	4.28	3.35	3.07	2.68	2.42
300	6.42	5.02	4.60	4.01	3.63
400	8.55	6.70	6.13	5.35	4.84
500	10.69	8.37	7.66	6.68	6.05
1,000	21.38	16.74	15.31	13.36	12.10
2,000	42.75	33.47	30.62	26.71	24.20
3,000	64.12	50.20	45.93	40.07	36.29
4,000	85.49	66.93	61.23	53.42	48.39
5,000	106.86	83.66	76.54	66.77	60.48
10,000	213.71	167.31	153.07	133.54	120.96
20,000	427.41	334.62	306.14	267.08	241.92
30,000	641.11	501.92	459.21	400.62	362.87
40,000	854.82	669.23	612.28	534.16	483.83
50,000	1068.52	836.54	765.34	667.70	604.79
100,000	2137.03	1673.07	1530.68	1335.40	1209.57
125,000	2671.29	2091.34	1913.35	1669.24	1511.96
150,000	3205.54	2509.60	2296.02	2003.09	1814.35
175,000	3739.80	2927.87	2678.69	2336.94	2116.74
200,000	4274.06	3346.13	3061.36	2670.79	2419.14
225,000	4808.31	3764.40	3444.03	3004.63	2721.53
250,000	5342.57	4182.67	3826.70	3338.48	3023.92
275,000	5876.83	4600.93	4209.37	3672.33	3326.31
300,000	6411.08	5019.20	4592.04	4006.18	3628.70
325,000	6945.34	5437.46	4974.71	4340.02	3931.09
350,000	7479.60	5855.73	5357.37	4673.87	4233.48
375,000	8013.85	6274.00	5740.04	5007.72	4535.87
400,000	8548.11	6692.26	6122.71	5341.57	4838.27
425,000	9082.37	7110.53	6505.38	5675.41	5140.66
450,000	9616.62	7528.79	6888.05	6009.26	5443.05
475,000	10150.88	7947.06	7270.72	6343.11	5745.44
500,000	10685.14	8365.33	7653.39	6676.96	6047.83
525,000	11219.39	8783.59	8036.06	7010.80	6350.22
550,000	11753.65	9201.86	8418.73	7344.65	6652.61
575,000	12287.91	9620.13	8801.40	7678.50	6955.00
600,000	12822.16	10038.39	9184.07	8012.35	7257.40
625,000	13356.42	10456.66	9566.74	8346.19	7559.79
650,000	13890.68	10874.92	9949.41	8680.04	7862.18
675,000	14424.93	11293.19	10332.07	9013.89	8164.57
700,000	14959.19	11711.46	10714.74	9347.74	8466.96
725,000	15493.45	12129.72	11097.41	9681.58	8769.35
750,000	16027.70	12547.99	11480.08	10015.43	9071.74
775,000	16561.96	12966.25	11862.75	10349.28	9374.13
800,000	17096.22	13384.52	12245.42	10683.13	9676.53
825,000	17630.47	13802.79	12628.09	11016.97	9978.92
850,000	18164.73	14221.05	13010.76	11350.82	10281.31
875,000	18698.99	14639.32	13393.43	11684.67	10583.70
900,000	19233.24	15057.58	13776.10	12018.52	10886.09

Table 7   193

10.25%　　Monthly Payment Loans

Amortization Period in Years

Loan Amount	15	16	17	18	20
10	0.11	0.11	0.11	0.11	0.10
20	0.22	0.22	0.21	0.21	0.20
30	0.33	0.32	0.32	0.31	0.30
40	0.44	0.43	0.42	0.41	0.40
50	0.55	0.54	0.52	0.51	0.50
100	1.09	1.07	1.04	1.02	0.99
200	2.18	2.13	2.08	2.04	1.97
300	3.27	3.19	3.12	3.05	2.95
400	4.36	4.25	4.15	4.07	3.93
500	5.45	5.31	5.19	5.08	4.91
1,000	10.90	10.62	10.38	10.16	9.82
2,000	21.80	21.24	20.75	20.32	19.64
3,000	32.70	31.85	31.12	30.48	29.45
4,000	43.60	42.47	41.49	40.64	39.27
5,000	54.50	53.08	51.86	50.80	49.09
10,000	109.00	106.16	103.71	101.60	98.17
20,000	218.00	212.31	207.42	203.20	196.33
30,000	326.99	318.46	311.13	304.80	294.50
40,000	435.99	424.61	414.84	406.40	392.66
50,000	544.98	530.76	518.55	508.00	490.83
100,000	1089.96	1061.52	1037.10	1015.99	981.65
125,000	1362.44	1326.90	1296.37	1269.98	1227.06
150,000	1634.93	1592.28	1555.64	1523.98	1472.47
175,000	1907.42	1857.66	1814.92	1777.97	1717.88
200,000	2179.91	2123.04	2074.19	2031.97	1963.29
225,000	2452.39	2388.42	2333.46	2285.96	2208.70
250,000	2724.88	2653.80	2592.73	2539.96	2454.11
275,000	2997.37	2919.18	2852.01	2793.95	2699.52
300,000	3269.86	3184.56	3111.28	3047.95	2944.94
325,000	3542.35	3449.94	3370.55	3301.94	3190.35
350,000	3814.83	3715.32	3629.83	3555.94	3435.76
375,000	4087.32	3980.70	3889.10	3809.93	3681.17
400,000	4359.81	4246.08	4148.37	4063.93	3926.58
425,000	4632.30	4511.46	4407.64	4317.92	4171.99
450,000	4904.78	4776.84	4666.92	4571.92	4417.40
475,000	5177.27	5042.22	4926.19	4825.91	4662.81
500,000	5449.76	5307.60	5185.46	5079.91	4908.22
525,000	5722.25	5572.98	5444.74	5333.90	5153.63
550,000	5994.74	5838.36	5704.01	5587.90	5399.04
575,000	6267.22	6103.74	5963.28	5841.89	5644.45
600,000	6539.71	6369.12	6222.55	6095.89	5889.87
625,000	6812.20	6634.50	6481.83	6349.88	6135.28
650,000	7084.69	6899.88	6741.10	6603.88	6380.69
675,000	7357.17	7165.26	7000.37	6857.87	6626.10
700,000	7629.66	7430.64	7259.65	7111.87	6871.51
725,000	7902.15	7696.02	7518.92	7365.86	7116.92
750,000	8174.64	7961.40	7778.19	7619.86	7362.33
775,000	8447.12	8226.78	8037.46	7873.85	7607.74
800,000	8719.61	8492.16	8296.74	8127.85	7853.15
825,000	8992.10	8757.54	8556.01	8381.84	8098.56
850,000	9264.59	9022.92	8815.28	8635.84	8343.97
875,000	9537.08	9288.30	9074.56	8889.83	8589.38
900,000	9809.56	9553.68	9333.83	9143.83	8834.80

Monthly Payment Loans   **10.25%**

Loan Amount	Amortization Period in Years				
	21	22	23	24	25
10	0.10	0.10	0.10	0.10	0.10
20	0.20	0.20	0.19	0.19	0.19
30	0.30	0.29	0.29	0.29	0.28
40	0.39	0.39	0.38	0.38	0.38
50	0.49	0.48	0.48	0.47	0.47
100	0.97	0.96	0.95	0.94	0.93
200	1.94	1.92	1.89	1.87	1.86
300	2.91	2.87	2.84	2.81	2.78
400	3.88	3.83	3.78	3.74	3.71
500	4.84	4.78	4.73	4.68	4.64
1,000	9.68	9.56	9.45	9.35	9.27
2,000	19.36	19.11	18.89	18.70	18.53
3,000	29.03	28.66	28.34	28.05	27.80
4,000	38.71	38.22	37.78	37.40	37.06
5,000	48.39	47.77	47.23	46.75	46.32
10,000	96.77	95.54	94.45	93.49	92.64
20,000	193.53	191.07	188.90	186.98	185.28
30,000	290.29	286.60	283.34	280.47	277.92
40,000	387.06	382.13	377.79	373.96	370.56
50,000	483.82	477.66	472.24	467.44	463.20
100,000	967.64	955.32	944.47	934.88	926.39
125,000	1209.54	1194.15	1180.59	1168.60	1157.98
150,000	1451.45	1432.98	1416.70	1402.32	1389.58
175,000	1693.36	1671.81	1652.82	1636.04	1621.18
200,000	1935.27	1910.64	1888.94	1869.76	1852.77
225,000	2177.18	2149.47	2125.05	2103.48	2084.37
250,000	2419.08	2388.30	2361.17	2337.20	2315.96
275,000	2660.99	2627.13	2597.29	2570.92	2547.56
300,000	2902.90	2865.96	2833.40	2804.63	2779.15
325,000	3144.81	3104.79	3069.52	3038.35	3010.75
350,000	3386.71	3343.62	3305.64	3272.07	3242.35
375,000	3628.62	3582.45	3541.75	3505.79	3473.94
400,000	3870.53	3821.28	3777.87	3739.51	3705.54
425,000	4112.44	4060.11	4013.99	3973.23	3937.13
450,000	4354.35	4298.94	4250.10	4206.95	4168.73
475,000	4596.25	4537.77	4486.22	4440.67	4400.33
500,000	4838.16	4776.60	4722.34	4674.39	4631.92
525,000	5080.07	5015.43	4958.45	4908.11	4863.52
550,000	5321.98	5254.26	5194.57	5141.83	5095.11
575,000	5563.89	5493.09	5430.69	5375.55	5326.71
600,000	5805.79	5731.91	5666.80	5609.26	5558.30
625,000	6047.70	5970.74	5902.92	5842.98	5789.90
650,000	6289.61	6209.57	6139.03	6076.70	6021.50
675,000	6531.52	6448.40	6375.15	6310.42	6253.09
700,000	6773.42	6687.23	6611.27	6544.14	6484.69
725,000	7015.33	6926.06	6847.38	6777.86	6716.28
750,000	7257.24	7164.89	7083.50	7011.58	6947.88
775,000	7499.15	7403.72	7319.62	7245.30	7179.48
800,000	7741.06	7642.55	7555.73	7479.02	7411.07
825,000	7982.96	7881.38	7791.85	7712.74	7642.67
850,000	8224.87	8120.21	8027.97	7946.46	7874.26
875,000	8466.78	8359.04	8264.08	8180.18	8105.86
900,000	8708.69	8597.87	8500.20	8413.89	8337.45

Table 7   195

10.25%　　Monthly Payment Loans

Loan Amount	26	27	28	29	30
10	0.10	0.10	0.10	0.10	0.09
20	0.19	0.19	0.19	0.19	0.18
30	0.28	0.28	0.28	0.28	0.27
40	0.37	0.37	0.37	0.37	0.36
50	0.46	0.46	0.46	0.46	0.45
100	0.92	0.92	0.91	0.91	0.90
200	1.84	1.83	1.82	1.81	1.80
300	2.76	2.74	2.72	2.71	2.69
400	3.68	3.65	3.63	3.61	3.59
500	4.60	4.57	4.54	4.51	4.49
1,000	9.19	9.13	9.07	9.01	8.97
2,000	18.38	18.25	18.13	18.02	17.93
3,000	27.57	27.37	27.19	27.03	26.89
4,000	36.76	36.49	36.25	36.04	35.85
5,000	45.95	45.61	45.31	45.05	44.81
10,000	91.89	91.22	90.62	90.09	89.62
20,000	183.77	182.43	181.24	180.18	179.23
30,000	275.66	273.65	271.86	270.26	268.84
40,000	367.54	364.86	362.48	360.35	358.45
50,000	459.43	456.08	453.09	450.43	448.06
100,000	918.85	912.15	906.18	900.86	896.11
125,000	1148.56	1140.18	1132.72	1126.07	1120.13
150,000	1378.27	1368.22	1359.27	1351.29	1344.16
175,000	1607.98	1596.26	1585.81	1576.50	1568.18
200,000	1837.70	1824.29	1812.36	1801.71	1792.21
225,000	2067.41	2052.33	2038.90	2026.93	2016.23
250,000	2297.12	2280.36	2265.44	2252.14	2240.26
275,000	2526.83	2508.40	2491.99	2477.35	2464.28
300,000	2756.54	2736.44	2718.53	2702.57	2688.31
325,000	2986.25	2964.47	2945.08	2927.78	2912.33
350,000	3215.96	3192.51	3171.62	3152.99	3136.36
375,000	3445.68	3420.54	3398.16	3378.21	3360.38
400,000	3675.39	3648.58	3624.71	3603.42	3584.41
425,000	3905.10	3876.62	3851.25	3828.63	3808.44
450,000	4134.81	4104.65	4077.80	4053.85	4032.46
475,000	4364.52	4332.69	4304.34	4279.06	4256.49
500,000	4594.23	4560.72	4530.88	4504.27	4480.51
525,000	4823.94	4788.76	4757.43	4729.49	4704.54
550,000	5053.66	5016.80	4983.97	4954.70	4928.56
575,000	5283.37	5244.83	5210.52	5179.91	5152.59
600,000	5513.08	5472.87	5437.06	5405.13	5376.61
625,000	5742.79	5700.90	5663.60	5630.34	5600.64
650,000	5972.50	5928.94	5890.15	5855.55	5824.66
675,000	6202.21	6156.98	6116.69	6080.77	6048.69
700,000	6431.92	6385.01	6343.24	6305.98	6272.71
725,000	6661.64	6613.05	6569.78	6531.19	6496.74
750,000	6891.35	6841.08	6796.32	6756.41	6720.76
775,000	7121.06	7069.12	7022.87	6981.62	6944.79
800,000	7350.77	7297.16	7249.41	7206.83	7168.82
825,000	7580.48	7525.19	7475.96	7432.05	7392.84
850,000	7810.19	7753.23	7702.50	7657.26	7616.87
875,000	8039.90	7981.26	7929.04	7882.47	7840.89
900,000	8269.62	8209.30	8155.59	8107.69	8064.92

Monthly Payment Loans   <u>10.50%</u>

Loan Amount	Amortization Period in Years				
	5	7	8	10	12
10	0.22	0.17	0.16	0.14	0.13
20	0.43	0.34	0.31	0.27	0.25
30	0.65	0.51	0.47	0.41	0.37
40	0.86	0.68	0.62	0.54	0.49
50	1.08	0.85	0.78	0.68	0.62
100	2.15	1.69	1.55	1.35	1.23
200	4.30	3.38	3.09	2.70	2.45
300	6.45	5.06	4.64	4.05	3.68
400	8.60	6.75	6.18	5.40	4.90
500	10.75	8.44	7.73	6.75	6.13
1,000	21.50	16.87	15.45	13.50	12.25
2,000	42.99	33.73	30.89	26.99	24.49
3,000	64.49	50.59	46.33	40.49	36.73
4,000	85.98	67.45	61.77	53.98	48.97
5,000	107.47	84.31	77.21	67.47	61.21
10,000	214.94	168.61	154.41	134.94	122.42
20,000	429.88	337.22	308.81	269.87	244.83
30,000	644.82	505.83	463.21	404.81	367.25
40,000	859.76	674.43	617.61	539.74	489.66
50,000	1074.70	843.04	772.01	674.68	612.08
100,000	2149.40	1686.07	1544.01	1349.35	1224.15
125,000	2686.74	2107.59	1930.01	1686.69	1530.18
150,000	3224.09	2529.11	2316.01	2024.03	1836.22
175,000	3761.44	2950.62	2702.01	2361.37	2142.25
200,000	4298.79	3372.14	3088.01	2698.70	2448.29
225,000	4836.13	3793.66	3474.01	3036.04	2754.32
250,000	5373.48	4215.17	3860.01	3373.38	3060.36
275,000	5910.83	4636.69	4246.01	3710.72	3366.39
300,000	6448.18	5058.21	4632.01	4048.05	3672.43
325,000	6985.52	5479.72	5018.01	4385.39	3978.46
350,000	7522.87	5901.24	5404.01	4722.73	4284.50
375,000	8060.22	6322.76	5790.01	5060.07	4590.53
400,000	8597.57	6744.27	6176.01	5397.40	4896.57
425,000	9134.91	7165.79	6562.01	5734.74	5202.60
450,000	9672.26	7587.31	6948.01	6072.08	5508.64
475,000	10209.61	8008.82	7334.01	6409.42	5814.67
500,000	10746.96	8430.34	7720.01	6746.75	6120.71
525,000	11284.30	8851.86	8106.01	7084.09	6426.74
550,000	11821.65	9273.38	8492.01	7421.43	6732.78
575,000	12359.00	9694.89	8878.01	7758.77	7038.81
600,000	12896.35	10116.41	9264.01	8096.10	7344.85
625,000	13433.69	10537.93	9650.02	8433.44	7650.88
650,000	13971.04	10959.44	10036.02	8770.78	7956.92
675,000	14508.39	11380.96	10422.02	9108.12	8262.95
700,000	15045.74	11802.48	10808.02	9445.45	8568.99
725,000	15583.08	12223.99	11194.02	9782.79	8875.02
750,000	16120.43	12645.51	11580.02	10120.13	9181.06
775,000	16657.78	13067.03	11966.02	10457.47	9487.10
800,000	17195.13	13488.54	12352.02	10794.80	9793.13
825,000	17732.47	13910.06	12738.02	11132.14	10099.17
850,000	18269.82	14331.58	13124.02	11469.48	10405.20
875,000	18807.17	14753.09	13510.02	11806.82	10711.24
900,000	19344.52	15174.61	13896.02	12144.15	11017.27

Table 7   197

10.50%   Monthly Payment Loans

Amortization Period in Years

Loan Amount	15	16	17	18	20
10	0.12	0.11	0.11	0.11	0.10
20	0.23	0.22	0.22	0.21	0.20
30	0.34	0.33	0.32	0.31	0.30
40	0.45	0.44	0.43	0.42	0.40
50	0.56	0.54	0.53	0.52	0.50
100	1.11	1.08	1.06	1.04	1.00
200	2.22	2.16	2.11	2.07	2.00
300	3.32	3.24	3.16	3.10	3.00
400	4.43	4.31	4.22	4.13	4.00
500	5.53	5.39	5.27	5.17	5.00
1,000	11.06	10.78	10.54	10.33	9.99
2,000	22.11	21.55	21.07	20.65	19.97
3,000	33.17	32.32	31.60	30.97	29.96
4,000	44.22	43.09	42.13	41.29	39.94
5,000	55.27	53.87	52.66	51.62	49.92
10,000	110.54	107.73	105.31	103.23	99.84
20,000	221.08	215.45	210.62	206.45	199.68
30,000	331.62	323.18	315.93	309.67	299.52
40,000	442.16	430.90	421.24	412.90	399.36
50,000	552.70	538.63	526.55	516.12	499.19
100,000	1105.40	1077.25	1053.09	1032.23	998.38
125,000	1381.75	1346.56	1316.36	1290.29	1247.98
150,000	1658.10	1615.87	1579.63	1548.35	1497.57
175,000	1934.45	1885.18	1842.90	1806.40	1747.17
200,000	2210.80	2154.49	2106.17	2064.46	1996.76
225,000	2487.15	2423.80	2369.44	2322.52	2246.36
250,000	2763.50	2693.11	2632.71	2580.57	2495.95
275,000	3039.85	2962.42	2895.98	2838.63	2745.55
300,000	3316.20	3231.73	3159.25	3096.69	2995.14
325,000	3592.55	3501.04	3422.52	3354.75	3244.74
350,000	3868.90	3770.35	3685.79	3612.80	3494.33
375,000	4145.25	4039.66	3949.06	3870.86	3743.93
400,000	4421.60	4308.97	4212.33	4128.92	3993.52
425,000	4697.95	4578.29	4475.60	4386.97	4243.12
450,000	4974.30	4847.60	4738.87	4645.03	4492.71
475,000	5250.65	5116.91	5002.14	4903.09	4742.31
500,000	5527.00	5386.22	5265.41	5161.14	4991.90
525,000	5803.35	5655.53	5528.68	5419.20	5241.50
550,000	6079.70	5924.84	5791.95	5677.26	5491.09
575,000	6356.05	6194.15	6055.22	5935.31	5740.69
600,000	6632.40	6463.46	6318.49	6193.37	5990.28
625,000	6908.75	6732.77	6581.76	6451.43	6239.88
650,000	7185.10	7002.08	6845.03	6709.49	6489.47
675,000	7461.45	7271.39	7108.30	6967.54	6739.07
700,000	7737.80	7540.70	7371.57	7225.60	6988.66
725,000	8014.15	7810.01	7634.84	7483.66	7238.26
750,000	8290.50	8079.32	7898.11	7741.71	7487.85
775,000	8566.85	8348.63	8161.38	7999.77	7737.45
800,000	8843.20	8617.94	8424.65	8257.83	7987.04
825,000	9119.55	8887.26	8687.93	8515.88	8236.64
850,000	9395.90	9156.57	8951.20	8773.94	8486.23
875,000	9672.25	9425.88	9214.47	9032.00	8735.83
900,000	9948.60	9695.19	9477.74	9290.05	8985.42

Monthly Payment Loans   **10.50%**

Loan Amount	21	22	23	24	25
			Amortization Period in Years		
10	0.10	0.10	0.10	0.10	0.10
20	0.20	0.20	0.20	0.20	0.19
30	0.30	0.30	0.29	0.29	0.29
40	0.40	0.39	0.39	0.39	0.38
50	0.50	0.49	0.49	0.48	0.48
100	0.99	0.98	0.97	0.96	0.95
200	1.97	1.95	1.93	1.91	1.89
300	2.96	2.92	2.89	2.86	2.84
400	3.94	3.90	3.85	3.81	3.78
500	4.93	4.87	4.81	4.77	4.73
1,000	9.85	9.73	9.62	9.53	9.45
2,000	19.70	19.46	19.24	19.05	18.89
3,000	29.54	29.18	28.86	28.58	28.33
4,000	39.39	38.91	38.48	38.10	37.77
5,000	49.23	48.63	48.10	47.63	47.21
10,000	98.46	97.26	96.19	95.25	94.42
20,000	196.92	194.51	192.38	190.50	188.84
30,000	295.38	291.76	288.57	285.75	283.26
40,000	393.84	389.01	384.75	381.00	377.68
50,000	492.30	486.26	480.94	476.25	472.10
100,000	984.60	972.51	961.87	952.49	944.19
125,000	1230.75	1215.64	1202.34	1190.61	1180.23
150,000	1476.90	1458.77	1442.81	1428.73	1416.28
175,000	1723.05	1701.89	1683.27	1666.85	1652.32
200,000	1969.20	1945.02	1923.74	1904.97	1888.37
225,000	2215.35	2188.15	2164.21	2143.09	2124.41
250,000	2461.50	2431.27	2404.67	2381.21	2360.46
275,000	2707.65	2674.40	2645.14	2619.33	2596.50
300,000	2953.80	2917.53	2885.61	2857.45	2832.55
325,000	3199.95	3160.65	3126.07	3095.57	3068.60
350,000	3446.10	3403.78	3366.54	3333.69	3304.64
375,000	3692.25	3646.91	3607.01	3571.81	3540.69
400,000	3938.40	3890.03	3847.47	3809.93	3776.73
425,000	4184.55	4133.16	4087.94	4048.05	4012.78
450,000	4430.70	4376.29	4328.41	4286.17	4248.82
475,000	4676.85	4619.41	4568.87	4524.29	4484.87
500,000	4923.00	4862.54	4809.34	4762.41	4720.91
525,000	5169.15	5105.67	5049.81	5000.53	4956.96
550,000	5415.30	5348.79	5290.27	5238.65	5193.00
575,000	5661.45	5591.92	5530.74	5476.77	5429.05
600,000	5907.60	5835.05	5771.21	5714.89	5665.10
625,000	6153.75	6078.17	6011.68	5953.01	5901.14
650,000	6399.90	6321.30	6252.14	6191.13	6137.19
675,000	6646.05	6564.43	6492.61	6429.25	6373.23
700,000	6892.20	6807.55	6733.08	6667.37	6609.28
725,000	7138.35	7050.68	6973.54	6905.49	6845.32
750,000	7384.49	7293.81	7214.01	7143.61	7081.37
775,000	7630.64	7536.93	7454.48	7381.73	7317.41
800,000	7876.79	7780.06	7694.94	7619.85	7553.46
825,000	8122.94	8023.19	7935.41	7857.97	7789.50
850,000	8369.09	8266.32	8175.88	8096.09	8025.55
875,000	8615.24	8509.44	8416.34	8334.21	8261.59
900,000	8861.39	8752.57	8656.81	8572.33	8497.64

Table 7   199

10.50% Monthly Payment Loans

Loan Amount	26	27	28	29	30
		Amortization Period in Years			
10	0.10	0.10	0.10	0.10	0.10
20	0.19	0.19	0.19	0.19	0.19
30	0.29	0.28	0.28	0.28	0.28
40	0.38	0.38	0.37	0.37	0.37
50	0.47	0.47	0.47	0.46	0.46
100	0.94	0.94	0.93	0.92	0.92
200	1.88	1.87	1.85	1.84	1.83
300	2.82	2.80	2.78	2.76	2.75
400	3.75	3.73	3.70	3.68	3.66
500	4.69	4.66	4.63	4.60	4.58
1,000	9.37	9.31	9.25	9.20	9.15
2,000	18.74	18.61	18.50	18.39	18.30
3,000	28.11	27.91	27.74	27.59	27.45
4,000	37.48	37.22	36.99	36.78	36.59
5,000	46.85	46.52	46.23	45.97	45.74
10,000	93.69	93.04	92.46	91.94	91.48
20,000	187.37	186.07	184.91	183.87	182.95
30,000	281.05	279.10	277.36	275.81	274.43
40,000	374.74	372.13	369.81	367.74	365.90
50,000	468.42	465.16	462.26	459.68	457.37
100,000	936.83	930.31	924.51	919.35	914.74
125,000	1171.04	1162.88	1155.63	1149.18	1143.43
150,000	1405.25	1395.46	1386.76	1379.02	1372.11
175,000	1639.46	1628.04	1617.89	1608.85	1600.80
200,000	1873.66	1860.61	1849.01	1838.69	1829.48
225,000	2107.87	2093.19	2080.14	2068.52	2058.17
250,000	2342.08	2325.76	2311.26	2298.36	2286.85
275,000	2576.29	2558.34	2542.39	2528.19	2515.54
300,000	2810.49	2790.92	2773.52	2758.03	2744.22
325,000	3044.70	3023.49	3004.64	2987.86	2972.91
350,000	3278.91	3256.07	3235.77	3217.70	3201.59
375,000	3513.11	3488.64	3466.89	3447.53	3430.28
400,000	3747.32	3721.22	3698.02	3677.37	3658.96
425,000	3981.53	3953.80	3929.15	3907.20	3887.65
450,000	4215.74	4186.37	4160.27	4137.04	4116.33
475,000	4449.94	4418.95	4391.40	4366.87	4345.02
500,000	4684.15	4651.52	4622.52	4596.71	4573.70
525,000	4918.36	4884.10	4853.65	4826.54	4802.39
550,000	5152.57	5116.68	5084.77	5056.38	5031.07
575,000	5386.77	5349.25	5315.90	5286.21	5259.76
600,000	5620.98	5581.83	5547.03	5516.05	5488.44
625,000	5855.19	5814.40	5778.15	5745.88	5717.13
650,000	6089.39	6046.98	6009.28	5975.72	5945.81
675,000	6323.60	6279.56	6240.40	6205.55	6174.50
700,000	6557.81	6512.13	6471.53	6435.39	6403.18
725,000	6792.02	6744.71	6702.66	6665.22	6631.86
750,000	7026.22	6977.28	6933.78	6895.06	6860.55
775,000	7260.43	7209.86	7164.91	7124.89	7089.23
800,000	7494.64	7442.44	7396.03	7354.73	7317.92
825,000	7728.85	7675.01	7627.16	7584.57	7546.60
850,000	7963.05	7907.59	7858.29	7814.40	7775.29
875,000	8197.26	8140.16	8089.41	8044.24	8003.97
900,000	8431.47	8372.74	8320.54	8274.07	8232.66

Monthly Payment Loans <u>10.75%</u>

Loan Amount	Amortization Period in Years				
	5	7	8	10	12
10	0.22	0.17	0.16	0.14	0.13
20	0.44	0.34	0.32	0.28	0.25
30	0.65	0.51	0.47	0.41	0.38
40	0.87	0.68	0.63	0.55	0.50
50	1.09	0.85	0.78	0.69	0.62
100	2.17	1.70	1.56	1.37	1.24
200	4.33	3.40	3.12	2.73	2.48
300	6.49	5.10	4.68	4.10	3.72
400	8.65	6.80	6.23	5.46	4.96
500	10.81	8.50	7.79	6.82	6.20
1,000	21.62	17.00	15.58	13.64	12.39
2,000	43.24	33.99	31.15	27.27	24.78
3,000	64.86	50.98	46.73	40.91	37.17
4,000	86.48	67.97	62.30	54.54	49.56
5,000	108.09	84.96	77.87	68.17	61.95
10,000	216.18	169.92	155.74	136.34	123.89
20,000	432.36	339.83	311.48	272.68	247.77
30,000	648.54	509.74	467.22	409.02	371.65
40,000	864.72	679.66	622.96	545.36	495.53
50,000	1080.90	849.57	778.70	681.70	619.41
100,000	2161.80	1699.13	1557.40	1363.39	1238.81
125,000	2702.25	2123.91	1946.74	1704.24	1548.51
150,000	3242.70	2548.70	2336.09	2045.09	1858.21
175,000	3783.15	2973.48	2725.44	2385.93	2167.91
200,000	4323.60	3398.26	3114.79	2726.78	2477.61
225,000	4864.04	3823.04	3504.13	3067.63	2787.31
250,000	5404.49	4247.82	3893.48	3408.47	3097.02
275,000	5944.94	4672.60	4282.83	3749.32	3406.72
300,000	6485.39	5097.39	4672.18	4090.17	3716.42
325,000	7025.84	5522.17	5061.52	4431.01	4026.12
350,000	7566.29	5946.95	5450.87	4771.86	4335.82
375,000	8106.74	6371.73	5840.22	5112.71	4645.52
400,000	8647.19	6796.51	6229.57	5453.55	4955.22
425,000	9187.64	7221.30	6618.91	5794.40	5264.92
450,000	9728.08	7646.08	7008.26	6135.25	5574.62
475,000	10268.53	8070.86	7397.61	6476.09	5884.33
500,000	10808.98	8495.64	7786.96	6816.94	6194.03
525,000	11349.43	8920.42	8176.30	7157.79	6503.73
550,000	11889.88	9345.20	8565.65	7498.63	6813.43
575,000	12430.33	9769.99	8955.00	7839.48	7123.13
600,000	12970.78	10194.77	9344.35	8180.33	7432.83
625,000	13511.23	10619.55	9733.69	8521.17	7742.53
650,000	14051.67	11044.33	10123.04	8862.02	8052.23
675,000	14592.12	11469.11	10512.39	9202.87	8361.93
700,000	15132.57	11893.89	10901.74	9543.71	8671.63
725,000	15673.02	12318.68	11291.08	9884.56	8981.34
750,000	16213.47	12743.46	11680.43	10225.41	9291.04
775,000	16753.92	13168.24	12069.78	10566.25	9600.74
800,000	17294.37	13593.02	12459.13	10907.10	9910.44
825,000	17834.82	14017.80	12848.47	11247.95	10220.14
850,000	18375.27	14442.59	13237.82	11588.79	10529.84
875,000	18915.71	14867.37	13627.17	11929.64	10839.54
900,000	19456.16	15292.15	14016.52	12270.49	11149.24

Table 7   201

10.75%   Monthly Payment Loans

Amortization Period in Years

Loan Amount	15	16	17	18	20
10	0.12	0.11	0.11	0.11	0.11
20	0.23	0.22	0.22	0.21	0.21
30	0.34	0.33	0.33	0.32	0.31
40	0.45	0.44	0.43	0.42	0.41
50	0.57	0.55	0.54	0.53	0.51
100	1.13	1.10	1.07	1.05	1.02
200	2.25	2.19	2.14	2.10	2.04
300	3.37	3.28	3.21	3.15	3.05
400	4.49	4.38	4.28	4.20	4.07
500	5.61	5.47	5.35	5.25	5.08
1,000	11.21	10.94	10.70	10.49	10.16
2,000	22.42	21.87	21.39	20.98	20.31
3,000	33.63	32.80	32.08	31.46	30.46
4,000	44.84	43.73	42.77	41.95	40.61
5,000	56.05	54.66	53.46	52.43	50.77
10,000	112.10	109.31	106.92	104.86	101.53
20,000	224.19	218.62	213.84	209.72	203.05
30,000	336.29	327.93	320.76	314.58	304.57
40,000	448.38	437.23	427.68	419.44	406.10
50,000	560.48	546.54	534.59	524.30	507.62
100,000	1120.95	1093.07	1069.18	1048.59	1015.23
125,000	1401.19	1366.34	1336.48	1310.74	1269.04
150,000	1681.43	1639.61	1603.77	1572.88	1522.85
175,000	1961.66	1912.88	1871.07	1835.03	1776.66
200,000	2241.90	2186.14	2138.36	2097.17	2030.46
225,000	2522.14	2459.41	2405.66	2359.32	2284.27
250,000	2802.37	2732.68	2672.95	2621.47	2538.08
275,000	3082.61	3005.95	2940.24	2883.61	2791.88
300,000	3362.85	3279.21	3207.54	3145.76	3045.69
325,000	3643.09	3552.48	3474.83	3407.91	3299.50
350,000	3923.32	3825.75	3742.13	3670.05	3553.31
375,000	4203.56	4099.02	4009.42	3932.20	3807.11
400,000	4483.80	4372.28	4276.72	4194.34	4060.92
425,000	4764.03	4645.55	4544.01	4456.49	4314.73
450,000	5044.27	4918.82	4811.31	4718.64	4568.54
475,000	5324.51	5192.09	5078.60	4980.78	4822.34
500,000	5604.74	5465.35	5345.90	5242.93	5076.15
525,000	5884.98	5738.62	5613.19	5505.08	5329.96
550,000	6165.22	6011.89	5880.48	5767.22	5583.76
575,000	6445.46	6285.16	6147.78	6029.37	5837.57
600,000	6725.69	6558.42	6415.07	6291.51	6091.38
625,000	7005.93	6831.69	6682.37	6553.66	6345.19
650,000	7286.17	7104.96	6949.66	6815.81	6598.99
675,000	7566.40	7378.23	7216.96	7077.95	6852.80
700,000	7846.64	7651.49	7484.25	7340.10	7106.61
725,000	8126.88	7924.76	7751.55	7602.25	7360.41
750,000	8407.11	8198.03	8018.84	7864.39	7614.22
775,000	8687.35	8471.30	8286.14	8126.54	7868.03
800,000	8967.59	8744.56	8553.43	8388.68	8121.84
825,000	9247.83	9017.83	8820.72	8650.83	8375.64
850,000	9528.06	9291.10	9088.02	8912.98	8629.45
875,000	9808.30	9564.37	9355.31	9175.12	8883.26
900,000	10088.54	9837.63	9622.61	9437.27	9137.07

Monthly Payment Loans   10.75%

Loan Amount	\multicolumn{5}{c}{Amortization Period in Years}
	21	22	23	24	25
10	0.11	0.10	0.10	0.10	0.10
20	0.21	0.20	0.20	0.20	0.20
30	0.31	0.30	0.30	0.30	0.29
40	0.41	0.40	0.40	0.39	0.39
50	0.51	0.50	0.49	0.49	0.49
100	1.01	0.99	0.98	0.98	0.97
200	2.01	1.98	1.96	1.95	1.93
300	3.01	2.97	2.94	2.92	2.89
400	4.01	3.96	3.92	3.89	3.85
500	5.01	4.95	4.90	4.86	4.82
1,000	10.02	9.90	9.80	9.71	9.63
2,000	20.04	19.80	19.59	19.41	19.25
3,000	30.06	29.70	29.39	29.11	28.87
4,000	40.07	39.60	39.18	38.81	38.49
5,000	50.09	49.50	48.97	48.51	48.11
10,000	100.17	98.99	97.94	97.02	96.21
20,000	200.34	197.97	195.88	194.04	192.42
30,000	300.51	296.95	293.82	291.06	288.63
40,000	400.68	395.93	391.76	388.08	384.84
50,000	500.84	494.91	489.70	485.10	481.05
100,000	1001.68	989.81	979.39	970.20	962.10
125,000	1252.10	1237.27	1224.23	1212.75	1202.62
150,000	1502.52	1484.72	1469.08	1455.30	1443.14
175,000	1752.94	1732.17	1713.92	1697.85	1683.67
200,000	2003.36	1979.62	1958.77	1940.40	1924.19
225,000	2253.78	2227.08	2203.61	2182.95	2164.71
250,000	2504.20	2474.53	2448.46	2425.50	2405.24
275,000	2754.62	2721.98	2693.31	2668.05	2645.76
300,000	3005.04	2969.43	2938.15	2910.60	2886.28
325,000	3255.46	3216.89	3183.00	3153.15	3126.81
350,000	3505.88	3464.34	3427.84	3395.70	3367.33
375,000	3756.30	3711.79	3672.69	3638.25	3607.85
400,000	4006.72	3959.24	3917.53	3880.80	3848.38
425,000	4257.14	4206.70	4162.38	4123.35	4088.90
450,000	4507.56	4454.15	4407.22	4365.90	4329.42
475,000	4757.98	4701.60	4652.07	4608.45	4569.95
500,000	5008.40	4949.05	4896.92	4851.00	4810.47
525,000	5258.82	5196.51	5141.76	5093.55	5050.99
550,000	5509.24	5443.96	5386.61	5336.10	5291.51
575,000	5759.66	5691.41	5631.45	5578.65	5532.04
600,000	6010.08	5938.86	5876.30	5821.20	5772.56
625,000	6260.50	6186.32	6121.14	6063.75	6013.08
650,000	6510.92	6433.77	6365.99	6306.30	6253.61
675,000	6761.34	6681.22	6610.83	6548.85	6494.13
700,000	7011.76	6928.67	6855.68	6791.39	6734.65
725,000	7262.18	7176.13	7100.53	7033.94	6975.18
750,000	7512.60	7423.58	7345.37	7276.49	7215.70
775,000	7763.02	7671.03	7590.22	7519.04	7456.22
800,000	8013.44	7918.48	7835.06	7761.59	7696.75
825,000	8263.86	8165.93	8079.91	8004.14	7937.27
850,000	8514.28	8413.39	8324.75	8246.69	8177.79
875,000	8764.70	8660.84	8569.60	8489.24	8418.32
900,000	9015.12	8908.29	8814.44	8731.79	8658.84

Table 7   203

10.75%   Monthly Payment Loans

Loan Amount	Amortization Period in Years				
	26	27	28	29	30
10	0.10	0.10	0.10	0.10	0.10
20	0.20	0.19	0.19	0.19	0.19
30	0.29	0.29	0.29	0.29	0.29
40	0.39	0.38	0.38	0.38	0.38
50	0.48	0.48	0.48	0.47	0.47
100	0.96	0.95	0.95	0.94	0.94
200	1.91	1.90	1.89	1.88	1.87
300	2.87	2.85	2.83	2.82	2.81
400	3.82	3.80	3.78	3.76	3.74
500	4.78	4.75	4.72	4.69	4.67
1,000	9.55	9.49	9.43	9.38	9.34
2,000	19.10	18.98	18.86	18.76	18.67
3,000	28.65	28.46	28.29	28.14	28.01
4,000	38.20	37.95	37.72	37.52	37.34
5,000	47.75	47.43	47.15	46.90	46.68
10,000	95.50	94.86	94.30	93.80	93.35
20,000	190.99	189.72	188.59	187.59	186.70
30,000	286.48	284.58	282.89	281.39	280.05
40,000	381.97	379.43	377.18	375.18	373.40
50,000	477.47	474.29	471.47	468.97	466.75
100,000	954.93	948.58	942.94	937.94	933.49
125,000	1193.66	1185.72	1178.68	1172.42	1166.86
150,000	1432.39	1422.87	1414.41	1406.91	1400.23
175,000	1671.12	1660.01	1650.15	1641.39	1633.60
200,000	1909.85	1897.15	1885.88	1875.87	1866.97
225,000	2148.58	2134.30	2121.62	2110.36	2100.34
250,000	2387.32	2371.44	2357.35	2344.84	2333.71
275,000	2626.05	2608.58	2593.09	2579.32	2567.06
300,000	2864.78	2845.73	2828.82	2813.81	2800.45
325,000	3103.51	3082.87	3064.56	3048.29	3033.82
350,000	3342.24	3320.01	3300.29	3282.77	3267.19
375,000	3580.97	3557.16	3536.03	3517.26	3500.56
400,000	3819.70	3794.30	3771.76	3751.74	3733.93
425,000	4058.43	4031.44	4007.50	3986.22	3967.30
450,000	4297.16	4268.59	4243.23	4220.71	4200.67
475,000	4535.90	4505.73	4478.97	4455.19	4434.04
500,000	4774.63	4742.87	4714.70	4689.67	4667.41
525,000	5013.36	4980.02	4950.44	4924.16	4900.78
550,000	5252.09	5217.16	5186.17	5158.64	5134.15
575,000	5490.82	5454.30	5421.91	5393.12	5367.52
600,000	5729.55	5691.45	5657.64	5627.61	5600.89
625,000	5968.28	5928.59	5893.38	5862.09	5834.26
650,000	6207.01	6165.73	6129.11	6096.58	6067.63
675,000	6445.74	6402.88	6364.85	6331.06	6301.00
700,000	6684.47	6640.02	6600.58	6565.54	6534.37
725,000	6923.21	6877.17	6836.32	6800.03	6767.74
750,000	7161.94	7114.31	7072.05	7034.51	7001.12
775,000	7400.67	7351.45	7307.79	7268.99	7234.49
800,000	7639.40	7588.60	7543.52	7503.48	7467.86
825,000	7878.13	7825.74	7779.26	7737.96	7701.23
850,000	8116.86	8062.88	8014.99	7972.44	7934.60
875,000	8355.59	8300.03	8250.73	8206.93	8167.97
900,000	8594.32	8537.17	8486.46	8441.41	8401.34

Monthly Payment Loans   **11.00%**

Loan Amount	Amortization Period in Years				
	5	7	8	10	12
10	0.22	0.18	0.16	0.14	0.13
20	0.44	0.35	0.32	0.28	0.26
30	0.66	0.52	0.48	0.42	0.38
40	0.87	0.69	0.63	0.56	0.51
50	1.09	0.86	0.79	0.69	0.63
100	2.18	1.72	1.58	1.38	1.26
200	4.35	3.43	3.15	2.76	2.51
300	6.53	5.14	4.72	4.14	3.77
400	8.70	6.85	6.29	5.52	5.02
500	10.88	8.57	7.86	6.89	6.27
1,000	21.75	17.13	15.71	13.78	12.54
2,000	43.49	34.25	31.42	27.56	25.08
3,000	65.23	51.37	47.13	41.33	37.61
4,000	86.97	68.49	62.84	55.11	50.15
5,000	108.72	85.62	78.55	68.88	62.68
10,000	217.43	171.23	157.09	137.76	125.36
20,000	434.85	342.45	314.17	275.51	250.72
30,000	652.28	513.68	471.26	413.26	376.07
40,000	869.70	684.90	628.34	551.01	501.43
50,000	1087.13	856.13	785.43	688.76	626.78
100,000	2174.25	1712.25	1570.85	1377.51	1253.56
125,000	2717.81	2140.31	1963.56	1721.88	1566.95
150,000	3261.37	2568.37	2356.27	2066.26	1880.34
175,000	3804.93	2996.43	2748.98	2410.63	2193.73
200,000	4348.49	3424.49	3141.69	2755.01	2507.12
225,000	4892.05	3852.55	3534.40	3099.38	2820.50
250,000	5435.61	4280.61	3927.11	3443.76	3133.89
275,000	5979.17	4708.68	4319.82	3788.13	3447.28
300,000	6522.73	5136.74	4712.53	4132.51	3760.67
325,000	7066.29	5564.80	5105.24	4476.88	4074.06
350,000	7609.85	5992.86	5497.95	4821.26	4387.45
375,000	8153.41	6420.92	5890.66	5165.63	4700.84
400,000	8696.97	6848.98	6283.38	5510.01	5014.23
425,000	9240.53	7277.04	6676.09	5854.38	5327.61
450,000	9784.10	7705.10	7068.80	6198.76	5641.00
475,000	10327.66	8133.16	7461.51	6543.13	5954.39
500,000	10871.22	8561.22	7854.22	6887.51	6267.78
525,000	11414.78	8989.28	8246.93	7231.88	6581.17
550,000	11958.34	9417.35	8639.64	7576.26	6894.56
575,000	12501.90	9845.41	9032.35	7920.63	7207.95
600,000	13045.46	10273.47	9425.06	8265.01	7521.34
625,000	13589.02	10701.53	9817.77	8609.38	7834.73
650,000	14132.58	11129.59	10210.48	8953.76	8148.11
675,000	14676.14	11557.65	10603.19	9298.13	8461.50
700,000	15219.70	11985.71	10995.90	9642.51	8774.89
725,000	15763.26	12413.77	11388.61	9986.88	9088.28
750,000	16306.82	12841.83	11781.32	10331.26	9401.67
775,000	16850.38	13269.89	12174.03	10675.63	9715.06
800,000	17393.94	13697.95	12566.75	11020.01	10028.45
825,000	17937.50	14126.02	12959.46	11364.38	10341.84
850,000	18481.06	14554.08	13352.17	11708.76	10655.22
875,000	19024.63	14982.14	13744.88	12053.13	10968.61
900,000	19568.19	15410.20	14137.59	12397.51	11282.00

Table 7   205

11.00%   Monthly Payment Loans

Amortization Period in Years

Loan Amount	15	16	17	18	20
10	0.12	0.12	0.11	0.11	0.11
20	0.23	0.23	0.22	0.22	0.21
30	0.35	0.34	0.33	0.32	0.31
40	0.46	0.45	0.44	0.43	0.42
50	0.57	0.56	0.55	0.54	0.52
100	1.14	1.11	1.09	1.07	1.04
200	2.28	2.22	2.18	2.14	2.07
300	3.41	3.33	3.26	3.20	3.10
400	4.55	4.44	4.35	4.27	4.13
500	5.69	5.55	5.43	5.33	5.17
1,000	11.37	11.10	10.86	10.66	10.33
2,000	22.74	22.19	21.71	21.31	20.65
3,000	34.10	33.28	32.57	31.96	30.97
4,000	45.47	44.37	43.42	42.61	41.29
5,000	56.83	55.46	54.27	53.26	51.61
10,000	113.66	110.91	108.54	106.51	103.22
20,000	227.32	221.81	217.08	213.01	206.44
30,000	340.98	332.71	325.62	319.52	309.66
40,000	454.64	443.61	434.16	426.02	412.88
50,000	568.30	554.51	542.70	532.53	516.10
100,000	1136.60	1109.01	1085.39	1065.05	1032.19
125,000	1420.75	1386.26	1356.73	1331.32	1290.24
150,000	1704.90	1663.51	1628.08	1597.58	1548.29
175,000	1989.05	1940.76	1899.42	1863.84	1806.33
200,000	2273.20	2218.01	2170.77	2130.10	2064.38
225,000	2557.35	2495.26	2442.11	2396.37	2322.43
250,000	2841.50	2772.51	2713.46	2662.63	2580.48
275,000	3125.65	3049.76	2984.80	2928.89	2838.52
300,000	3409.80	3327.01	3256.15	3195.15	3096.57
325,000	3693.95	3604.26	3527.49	3461.42	3354.62
350,000	3978.09	3881.51	3798.84	3727.68	3612.66
375,000	4262.24	4158.76	4070.18	3993.94	3870.71
400,000	4546.39	4436.01	4341.53	4260.20	4128.76
425,000	4830.54	4713.26	4612.87	4526.47	4386.81
450,000	5114.69	4990.51	4884.22	4792.73	4644.85
475,000	5398.84	5267.76	5155.56	5058.99	4902.90
500,000	5682.99	5545.01	5426.91	5325.25	5160.95
525,000	5967.14	5822.26	5698.25	5591.52	5418.99
550,000	6251.29	6099.51	5969.60	5857.78	5677.04
575,000	6535.44	6376.76	6240.94	6124.04	5935.09
600,000	6819.59	6654.01	6512.29	6390.30	6193.14
625,000	7103.74	6931.26	6783.63	6656.57	6451.18
650,000	7387.89	7208.51	7054.98	6922.83	6709.23
675,000	7672.03	7485.76	7326.32	7189.09	6967.28
700,000	7956.18	7763.01	7597.67	7455.35	7225.32
725,000	8240.33	8040.26	7869.01	7721.61	7483.37
750,000	8524.48	8317.51	8140.36	7987.88	7741.42
775,000	8808.63	8594.76	8411.70	8254.14	7999.47
800,000	9092.78	8872.01	8683.05	8520.40	8257.51
825,000	9376.93	9149.26	8954.40	8786.66	8515.56
850,000	9661.08	9426.51	9225.74	9052.93	8773.61
875,000	9945.23	9703.76	9497.09	9319.19	9031.65
900,000	10229.38	9981.01	9768.43	9585.45	9289.70

Monthly Payment Loans   **11.00%**

Loan Amount	Amortization Period in Years				
	21	22	23	24	25
10	0.11	0.11	0.10	0.10	0.10
20	0.21	0.21	0.20	0.20	0.20
30	0.31	0.31	0.30	0.30	0.30
40	0.41	0.41	0.40	0.40	0.40
50	0.51	0.51	0.50	0.50	0.50
100	1.02	1.01	1.00	0.99	0.99
200	2.04	2.02	2.00	1.98	1.97
300	3.06	3.03	3.00	2.97	2.95
400	4.08	4.03	3.99	3.96	3.93
500	5.10	5.04	4.99	4.95	4.91
1,000	10.19	10.08	9.98	9.89	9.81
2,000	20.38	20.15	19.95	19.77	19.61
3,000	30.57	30.22	29.92	29.65	29.41
4,000	40.76	40.29	39.89	39.53	39.21
5,000	50.95	50.37	49.86	49.41	49.01
10,000	101.89	100.73	99.71	98.81	98.02
20,000	203.78	201.45	199.41	197.61	196.03
30,000	305.67	302.17	299.11	296.41	294.04
40,000	407.55	402.89	398.81	395.22	392.05
50,000	509.44	503.62	498.51	494.02	490.06
100,000	1018.88	1007.23	997.01	988.03	980.12
125,000	1273.59	1259.03	1246.27	1235.04	1225.15
150,000	1528.31	1510.84	1495.52	1482.04	1470.17
175,000	1783.03	1762.65	1744.77	1729.05	1715.20
200,000	2037.75	2014.45	1994.02	1976.06	1960.23
225,000	2292.46	2266.26	2243.27	2223.06	2205.26
250,000	2547.18	2518.06	2492.53	2470.07	2450.29
275,000	2801.90	2769.87	2741.78	2717.08	2695.32
300,000	3056.62	3021.68	2991.03	2964.08	2940.34
325,000	3311.34	3273.48	3240.28	3211.09	3185.37
350,000	3566.05	3525.29	3489.53	3458.10	3430.40
375,000	3820.77	3777.09	3738.79	3705.10	3675.43
400,000	4075.49	4028.90	3988.04	3952.11	3920.46
425,000	4330.21	4280.70	4237.29	4199.12	4165.49
450,000	4584.92	4532.51	4486.54	4446.12	4410.51
475,000	4839.64	4784.32	4735.79	4693.13	4655.54
500,000	5094.36	5036.12	4985.05	4940.14	4900.57
525,000	5349.08	5287.93	5234.30	5187.14	5145.60
550,000	5603.80	5539.73	5483.55	5434.15	5390.63
575,000	5858.51	5791.54	5732.80	5681.16	5635.66
600,000	6113.23	6043.35	5982.05	5928.16	5880.68
625,000	6367.95	6295.15	6231.31	6175.17	6125.71
650,000	6622.67	6546.96	6480.56	6422.18	6370.74
675,000	6877.38	6798.76	6729.81	6669.18	6615.77
700,000	7132.10	7050.57	6979.06	6916.19	6860.80
725,000	7386.82	7302.38	7228.31	7163.20	7105.82
750,000	7641.54	7554.18	7477.57	7410.20	7350.85
775,000	7896.25	7805.99	7726.82	7657.21	7595.88
800,000	8150.97	8057.79	7976.07	7904.22	7840.91
825,000	8405.69	8309.60	8225.32	8151.22	8085.94
850,000	8660.41	8561.40	8474.57	8398.23	8330.97
875,000	8915.13	8813.21	8723.83	8645.24	8575.99
900,000	9169.84	9065.02	8973.08	8892.24	8821.02

Table 7   207

11.00%   Monthly Payment Loans

Loan Amount	Amortization Period in Years				
	26	27	28	29	30
10	0.10	0.10	0.10	0.10	0.10
20	0.20	0.20	0.20	0.20	0.20
30	0.30	0.30	0.29	0.29	0.29
40	0.39	0.39	0.39	0.39	0.39
50	0.49	0.49	0.49	0.48	0.48
100	0.98	0.97	0.97	0.96	0.96
200	1.95	1.94	1.93	1.92	1.91
300	2.92	2.91	2.89	2.87	2.86
400	3.90	3.87	3.85	3.83	3.81
500	4.87	4.84	4.81	4.79	4.77
1,000	9.74	9.67	9.62	9.57	9.53
2,000	19.47	19.34	19.23	19.14	19.05
3,000	29.20	29.01	28.85	28.70	28.57
4,000	38.93	38.68	38.46	38.27	38.10
5,000	48.66	48.35	48.08	47.84	47.62
10,000	97.32	96.70	96.15	95.67	95.24
20,000	194.63	193.40	192.30	191.33	190.47
30,000	291.94	290.09	288.45	286.99	285.70
40,000	389.26	386.79	384.60	382.66	380.93
50,000	486.57	483.48	480.74	478.32	476.17
100,000	973.13	966.96	961.48	956.63	952.33
125,000	1216.41	1208.69	1201.85	1195.79	1190.41
150,000	1459.70	1450.43	1442.22	1434.95	1428.49
175,000	1702.98	1692.17	1682.59	1674.11	1666.57
200,000	1946.26	1933.91	1922.96	1913.26	1904.65
225,000	2189.54	2175.64	2163.33	2152.42	2142.73
250,000	2432.82	2417.38	2403.70	2391.58	2380.81
275,000	2676.11	2659.12	2644.07	2630.74	2618.89
300,000	2919.39	2900.86	2884.44	2869.89	2856.98
325,000	3162.67	3142.59	3124.81	3109.05	3095.06
350,000	3405.95	3384.33	3365.18	3348.21	3333.14
375,000	3649.23	3626.07	3605.55	3587.37	3571.22
400,000	3892.51	3867.81	3845.92	3826.52	3809.30
425,000	4135.80	4109.54	4086.29	4065.68	4047.38
450,000	4379.08	4351.28	4326.66	4304.84	4285.46
475,000	4622.36	4593.02	4567.03	4543.99	4523.54
500,000	4865.64	4834.76	4807.40	4783.15	4761.62
525,000	5108.92	5076.49	5047.77	5022.31	4999.70
550,000	5352.21	5318.23	5288.14	5261.47	5237.78
575,000	5595.49	5559.97	5528.51	5500.62	5475.86
600,000	5838.77	5801.71	5768.88	5739.78	5713.95
625,000	6082.05	6043.44	6009.25	5978.94	5952.03
650,000	6325.33	6285.18	6249.62	6218.10	6190.11
675,000	6568.61	6526.92	6489.99	6457.25	6428.19
700,000	6811.90	6768.66	6730.36	6696.41	6666.27
725,000	7055.18	7010.39	6970.73	6935.57	6904.35
750,000	7298.46	7252.13	7211.10	7174.73	7142.43
775,000	7541.74	7493.87	7451.47	7413.88	7380.51
800,000	7785.02	7735.61	7691.84	7653.04	7618.59
825,000	8028.31	7977.34	7932.21	7892.20	7856.67
850,000	8271.59	8219.08	8172.58	8131.36	8094.75
875,000	8514.87	8460.82	8412.95	8370.51	8332.83
900,000	8758.15	8702.56	8653.32	8609.67	8570.92

Monthly Payment Loans **11.25%**

Loan Amount	Amortization Period in Years				
	5	7	8	10	12
10	0.22	0.18	0.16	0.14	0.13
20	0.44	0.35	0.32	0.28	0.26
30	0.66	0.52	0.48	0.42	0.39
40	0.88	0.70	0.64	0.56	0.51
50	1.10	0.87	0.80	0.70	0.64
100	2.19	1.73	1.59	1.40	1.27
200	4.38	3.46	3.17	2.79	2.54
300	6.57	5.18	4.76	4.18	3.81
400	8.75	6.91	6.34	5.57	5.08
500	10.94	8.63	7.93	6.96	6.35
1,000	21.87	17.26	15.85	13.92	12.69
2,000	43.74	34.51	31.69	27.84	25.37
3,000	65.61	51.77	47.54	41.76	38.06
4,000	87.47	69.02	63.38	55.67	50.74
5,000	109.34	86.28	79.22	69.59	63.42
10,000	218.68	172.55	158.44	139.17	126.84
20,000	437.35	345.09	316.88	278.34	253.68
30,000	656.02	517.63	475.31	417.51	380.52
40,000	874.70	690.17	633.75	556.68	507.36
50,000	1093.37	862.71	792.18	695.85	634.20
100,000	2186.74	1725.42	1584.36	1391.69	1268.40
125,000	2733.42	2156.78	1980.45	1739.62	1585.50
150,000	3280.10	2588.13	2376.54	2087.54	1902.59
175,000	3826.78	3019.48	2772.63	2435.46	2219.69
200,000	4373.47	3450.84	3168.72	2783.38	2536.79
225,000	4920.15	3882.19	3564.81	3131.31	2853.89
250,000	5466.83	4313.55	3960.90	3479.23	3170.99
275,000	6013.51	4744.90	4356.99	3827.15	3488.09
300,000	6560.20	5176.26	4753.08	4175.07	3805.18
325,000	7106.88	5607.61	5149.17	4523.00	4122.28
350,000	7653.56	6038.96	5545.26	4870.92	4439.38
375,000	8200.25	6470.32	5941.35	5218.84	4756.48
400,000	8746.93	6901.67	6337.44	5566.76	5073.58
425,000	9293.61	7333.03	6733.53	5914.69	5390.67
450,000	9840.29	7764.38	7129.62	6262.61	5707.77
475,000	10386.98	8195.73	7525.71	6610.53	6024.87
500,000	10933.66	8627.09	7921.80	6958.45	6341.97
525,000	11480.34	9058.44	8317.89	7306.37	6659.07
550,000	12027.02	9489.80	8713.98	7654.30	6976.17
575,000	12573.71	9921.15	9110.07	8002.22	7293.26
600,000	13120.39	10352.51	9506.16	8350.14	7610.36
625,000	13667.07	10783.86	9902.24	8698.06	7927.46
650,000	14213.76	11215.21	10298.33	9045.99	8244.56
675,000	14760.44	11646.57	10694.42	9393.91	8561.66
700,000	15307.12	12077.92	11090.51	9741.83	8878.76
725,000	15853.80	12509.28	11486.60	10089.75	9195.85
750,000	16400.49	12940.63	11882.69	10437.68	9512.95
775,000	16947.17	13371.98	12278.78	10785.60	9830.05
800,000	17493.85	13803.34	12674.87	11133.52	10147.15
825,000	18040.53	14234.69	13070.96	11481.44	10464.25
850,000	18587.22	14666.05	13467.05	11829.37	10781.34
875,000	19133.90	15097.40	13863.14	12177.29	11098.44
900,000	19680.58	15528.76	14259.23	12525.21	11415.54

Table 7   209

11.25%   Monthly Payment Loans

Amortization Period in Years

Loan Amount	15	16	17	18	20
10	0.12	0.12	0.12	0.11	0.11
20	0.24	0.23	0.23	0.22	0.21
30	0.35	0.34	0.34	0.33	0.32
40	0.47	0.46	0.45	0.44	0.42
50	0.58	0.57	0.56	0.55	0.53
100	1.16	1.13	1.11	1.09	1.05
200	2.31	2.26	2.21	2.17	2.10
300	3.46	3.38	3.31	3.25	3.15
400	4.61	4.51	4.41	4.33	4.20
500	5.77	5.63	5.51	5.41	5.25
1,000	11.53	11.26	11.02	10.82	10.50
2,000	23.05	22.51	22.04	21.64	20.99
3,000	34.58	33.76	33.06	32.45	31.48
4,000	46.10	45.01	44.07	43.27	41.98
5,000	57.62	56.26	55.09	54.09	52.47
10,000	115.24	112.51	110.17	108.17	104.93
20,000	230.47	225.01	220.34	216.33	209.86
30,000	345.71	337.51	330.51	324.49	314.78
40,000	460.94	450.02	440.68	432.65	419.71
50,000	576.18	562.52	550.85	540.82	524.63
100,000	1152.35	1125.04	1101.69	1081.63	1049.26
125,000	1440.44	1406.30	1377.11	1352.03	1311.58
150,000	1728.52	1687.55	1652.54	1622.44	1573.89
175,000	2016.61	1968.81	1927.96	1892.84	1836.20
200,000	2304.69	2250.07	2203.38	2163.25	2098.52
225,000	2592.78	2531.33	2478.80	2433.65	2360.83
250,000	2880.87	2812.59	2754.22	2704.06	2623.15
275,000	3168.95	3093.84	3029.64	2974.46	2885.46
300,000	3457.04	3375.10	3305.07	3244.87	3147.77
325,000	3745.12	3656.36	3580.49	3515.27	3410.09
350,000	4033.21	3937.62	3855.91	3785.68	3672.40
375,000	4321.30	4218.88	4131.33	4056.08	3934.72
400,000	4609.38	4500.14	4406.75	4326.49	4197.03
425,000	4897.47	4781.39	4682.18	4596.89	4459.34
450,000	5185.56	5062.65	4957.60	4867.30	4721.66
475,000	5473.64	5343.91	5233.02	5137.70	4983.97
500,000	5761.73	5625.17	5508.44	5408.11	5246.29
525,000	6049.81	5906.43	5783.86	5678.51	5508.60
550,000	6337.90	6187.68	6059.28	5948.92	5770.91
575,000	6625.99	6468.94	6334.71	6219.32	6033.23
600,000	6914.07	6750.20	6610.13	6489.73	6295.54
625,000	7202.16	7031.46	6885.55	6760.13	6557.86
650,000	7490.24	7312.72	7160.97	7030.54	6820.17
675,000	7778.33	7593.97	7436.39	7300.94	7082.48
700,000	8066.42	7875.23	7711.82	7571.35	7344.80
725,000	8354.50	8156.49	7987.24	7841.75	7607.11
750,000	8642.59	8437.75	8262.66	8112.16	7869.43
775,000	8930.68	8719.01	8538.08	8382.56	8131.74
800,000	9218.76	9000.27	8813.50	8652.97	8394.05
825,000	9506.85	9281.52	9088.92	8923.37	8656.37
850,000	9794.93	9562.78	9364.35	9193.78	8918.68
875,000	10083.02	9844.04	9639.77	9464.18	9181.00
900,000	10371.11	10125.30	9915.19	9734.59	9443.31

Monthly Payment Loans   **11.25%**

Loan Amount	Amortization Period in Years				
	21	22	23	24	25
10	0.11	0.11	0.11	0.11	0.10
20	0.21	0.21	0.21	0.21	0.20
30	0.32	0.31	0.31	0.31	0.30
40	0.42	0.41	0.41	0.41	0.40
50	0.52	0.52	0.51	0.51	0.50
100	1.04	1.03	1.02	1.01	1.00
200	2.08	2.05	2.03	2.02	2.00
300	3.11	3.08	3.05	3.02	3.00
400	4.15	4.10	4.06	4.03	4.00
500	5.19	5.13	5.08	5.03	5.00
1,000	10.37	10.25	10.15	10.06	9.99
2,000	20.73	20.50	20.30	20.12	19.97
3,000	31.09	30.75	30.45	30.18	29.95
4,000	41.45	40.99	40.59	40.24	39.93
5,000	51.81	51.24	50.74	50.30	49.92
10,000	103.62	102.48	101.48	100.60	99.83
20,000	207.24	204.95	202.95	201.20	199.65
30,000	310.86	307.43	304.43	301.79	299.48
40,000	414.47	409.90	405.90	402.39	399.30
50,000	518.09	512.38	507.38	502.99	499.12
100,000	1036.18	1024.75	1014.75	1005.97	998.24
125,000	1295.22	1280.94	1268.43	1257.46	1247.80
150,000	1554.26	1537.12	1522.12	1508.95	1497.36
175,000	1813.30	1793.31	1775.80	1760.44	1746.92
200,000	2072.35	2049.50	2029.49	2011.93	1996.48
225,000	2331.39	2305.68	2283.17	2263.42	2246.04
250,000	2590.43	2561.87	2536.86	2514.91	2495.60
275,000	2849.48	2818.06	2790.55	2766.40	2745.16
300,000	3108.52	3074.24	3044.23	3017.89	2994.72
325,000	3367.56	3330.43	3297.92	3269.38	3244.28
350,000	3626.60	3586.62	3551.60	3520.87	3493.84
375,000	3885.65	3842.80	3805.29	3772.36	3743.40
400,000	4144.69	4098.99	4058.97	4023.85	3992.96
425,000	4403.73	4355.17	4312.66	4275.34	4242.52
450,000	4662.78	4611.36	4566.34	4526.83	4492.08
475,000	4921.82	4867.55	4820.03	4778.32	4741.64
500,000	5180.86	5123.73	5073.71	5029.81	4991.20
525,000	5439.90	5379.92	5327.40	5281.30	5240.76
550,000	5698.95	5636.11	5581.09	5532.80	5490.32
575,000	5957.99	5892.29	5834.77	5784.29	5739.88
600,000	6217.03	6148.48	6088.46	6035.78	5989.44
625,000	6476.08	6404.67	6342.14	6287.27	6239.00
650,000	6735.12	6660.85	6595.83	6538.76	6488.56
675,000	6994.16	6917.04	6849.51	6790.25	6738.12
700,000	7253.20	7173.23	7103.20	7041.74	6987.68
725,000	7512.25	7429.41	7356.88	7293.23	7237.24
750,000	7771.29	7685.60	7610.57	7544.72	7486.80
775,000	8030.33	7941.78	7864.26	7796.21	7736.36
800,000	8289.37	8197.97	8117.94	8047.70	7985.92
825,000	8548.42	8454.16	8371.63	8299.19	8235.48
850,000	8807.46	8710.34	8625.31	8550.68	8485.04
875,000	9066.50	8966.53	8879.00	8802.17	8734.60
900,000	9325.55	9222.72	9132.68	9053.66	8984.16

Table 7   211

11.25%   Monthly Payment Loans

Amortization Period in Years

Loan Amount	26	27	28	29	30
10	0.10	0.10	0.10	0.10	0.10
20	0.20	0.20	0.20	0.20	0.20
30	0.30	0.30	0.30	0.30	0.30
40	0.40	0.40	0.40	0.40	0.39
50	0.50	0.50	0.50	0.49	0.49
100	1.00	0.99	0.99	0.98	0.98
200	1.99	1.98	1.97	1.96	1.95
300	2.98	2.96	2.95	2.93	2.92
400	3.97	3.95	3.93	3.91	3.89
500	4.96	4.93	4.91	4.88	4.86
1,000	9.92	9.86	9.81	9.76	9.72
2,000	19.83	19.71	19.61	19.51	19.43
3,000	29.75	29.57	29.41	29.27	29.14
4,000	39.66	39.42	39.21	39.02	38.86
5,000	49.58	49.28	49.01	48.78	48.57
10,000	99.15	98.55	98.02	97.55	97.13
20,000	198.29	197.09	196.03	195.09	194.26
30,000	297.44	295.63	294.04	292.63	291.38
40,000	396.58	394.18	392.05	390.17	388.51
50,000	495.72	492.72	490.07	487.72	485.64
100,000	991.44	985.43	980.13	975.43	971.27
125,000	1239.30	1231.79	1225.16	1219.28	1214.08
150,000	1487.16	1478.15	1470.19	1463.14	1456.90
175,000	1735.02	1724.51	1715.22	1707.00	1699.71
200,000	1982.87	1970.86	1960.25	1950.85	1942.53
225,000	2230.73	2217.22	2205.28	2194.71	2185.34
250,000	2478.59	2463.58	2450.31	2438.56	2428.16
275,000	2726.45	2709.94	2695.34	2682.42	2670.97
300,000	2974.31	2956.29	2940.37	2926.28	2913.79
325,000	3222.17	3202.65	3185.40	3170.13	3156.60
350,000	3470.03	3449.01	3430.43	3413.99	3399.42
375,000	3717.89	3695.36	3675.46	3657.84	3642.24
400,000	3965.74	3941.72	3920.49	3901.70	3885.05
425,000	4213.60	4188.08	4165.52	4145.55	4127.87
450,000	4461.46	4434.44	4410.55	4389.41	4370.68
475,000	4709.32	4680.79	4655.58	4633.27	4613.50
500,000	4957.18	4927.15	4900.61	4877.12	4856.31
525,000	5205.04	5173.51	5145.64	5120.98	5099.13
550,000	5452.90	5419.87	5390.67	5364.83	5341.94
575,000	5700.76	5666.22	5635.70	5608.69	5584.76
600,000	5948.61	5912.58	5880.73	5852.55	5827.57
625,000	6196.47	6158.94	6125.76	6096.40	6070.39
650,000	6444.33	6405.30	6370.79	6340.26	6313.20
675,000	6692.19	6651.65	6615.82	6584.11	6556.02
700,000	6940.05	6898.01	6860.85	6827.97	6798.83
725,000	7187.91	7144.37	7105.88	7071.83	7041.65
750,000	7435.77	7390.72	7350.91	7315.68	7284.47
775,000	7683.63	7637.08	7595.94	7559.54	7527.28
800,000	7931.48	7883.44	7840.97	7803.39	7770.10
825,000	8179.34	8129.80	8086.00	8047.25	8012.91
850,000	8427.20	8376.15	8331.03	8291.10	8255.73
875,000	8675.06	8622.51	8576.06	8534.96	8498.54
900,000	8922.92	8868.87	8821.10	8778.82	8741.36

Monthly Payment Loans   11.50%

Loan Amount	Amortization Period in Years				
	5	7	8	10	12
10	0.22	0.18	0.16	0.15	0.13
20	0.44	0.35	0.32	0.29	0.26
30	0.66	0.53	0.48	0.43	0.39
40	0.88	0.70	0.64	0.57	0.52
50	1.10	0.87	0.80	0.71	0.65
100	2.20	1.74	1.60	1.41	1.29
200	4.40	3.48	3.20	2.82	2.57
300	6.60	5.22	4.80	4.22	3.85
400	8.80	6.96	6.40	5.63	5.14
500	11.00	8.70	7.99	7.03	6.42
1,000	22.00	17.39	15.98	14.06	12.84
2,000	43.99	34.78	31.96	28.12	25.67
3,000	65.98	52.16	47.94	42.18	38.50
4,000	87.98	69.55	63.92	56.24	51.34
5,000	109.97	86.94	79.90	70.30	64.17
10,000	219.93	173.87	159.80	140.60	128.34
20,000	439.86	347.73	319.59	281.20	256.67
30,000	659.78	521.60	479.39	421.79	385.00
40,000	879.71	695.46	639.18	562.39	513.33
50,000	1099.64	869.33	798.97	702.98	641.66
100,000	2199.27	1738.65	1597.94	1405.96	1283.32
125,000	2749.08	2173.31	1997.43	1757.45	1604.15
150,000	3298.90	2607.97	2396.91	2108.94	1924.98
175,000	3848.71	3042.64	2796.40	2460.43	2245.81
200,000	4398.53	3477.30	3195.88	2811.91	2566.64
225,000	4948.34	3911.96	3595.36	3163.40	2887.47
250,000	5498.16	4346.62	3994.85	3514.89	3208.30
275,000	6047.97	4781.28	4394.33	3866.38	3529.13
300,000	6597.79	5215.94	4793.82	4217.87	3849.95
325,000	7147.60	5650.60	5193.30	4569.36	4170.78
350,000	7697.42	6085.27	5592.79	4920.85	4491.61
375,000	8247.23	6519.93	5992.27	5272.33	4812.44
400,000	8797.05	6954.59	6391.75	5623.82	5133.27
425,000	9346.86	7389.25	6791.24	5975.31	5454.10
450,000	9896.68	7823.91	7190.72	6326.80	5774.93
475,000	10446.49	8258.57	7590.21	6678.29	6095.76
500,000	10996.31	8693.24	7989.69	7029.78	6416.59
525,000	11546.12	9127.90	8389.18	7381.27	6737.42
550,000	12095.94	9562.56	8788.66	7732.75	7058.25
575,000	12645.75	9997.22	9188.14	8084.24	7379.08
600,000	13195.57	10431.88	9587.63	8435.73	7699.90
625,000	13745.38	10866.54	9987.11	8787.22	8020.73
650,000	14295.20	11301.20	10386.60	9138.71	8341.56
675,000	14845.01	11735.87	10786.08	9490.20	8662.39
700,000	15394.83	12170.53	11185.57	9841.69	8983.22
725,000	15944.65	12605.19	11585.05	10193.17	9304.05
750,000	16494.46	13039.85	11984.54	10544.66	9624.88
775,000	17044.28	13474.51	12384.02	10896.15	9945.71
800,000	17594.09	13909.17	12783.50	11247.64	10266.54
825,000	18143.91	14343.84	13182.99	11599.13	10587.37
850,000	18693.72	14778.50	13582.47	11950.62	10908.20
875,000	19243.54	15213.16	13981.96	12302.11	11229.03
900,000	19793.35	15647.82	14381.44	12653.59	11549.85

Table 7   213

11.50%   Monthly Payment Loans

Loan Amount	15	16	17	18	20
		Amortization Period in Years			
10	0.12	0.12	0.12	0.11	0.11
20	0.24	0.23	0.23	0.22	0.22
30	0.36	0.35	0.34	0.33	0.32
40	0.47	0.46	0.45	0.44	0.43
50	0.59	0.58	0.56	0.55	0.54
100	1.17	1.15	1.12	1.10	1.07
200	2.34	2.29	2.24	2.20	2.14
300	3.51	3.43	3.36	3.30	3.20
400	4.68	4.57	4.48	4.40	4.27
500	5.85	5.71	5.60	5.50	5.34
1,000	11.69	11.42	11.19	10.99	10.67
2,000	23.37	22.83	22.37	21.97	21.33
3,000	35.05	34.24	33.55	32.95	32.00
4,000	46.73	45.65	44.73	43.94	42.66
5,000	58.41	57.06	55.91	54.92	53.33
10,000	116.82	114.12	111.81	109.83	106.65
20,000	233.64	228.24	223.62	219.66	213.29
30,000	350.46	342.35	335.43	329.49	319.93
40,000	467.28	456.47	447.24	439.32	426.58
50,000	584.10	570.59	559.05	549.15	533.22
100,000	1168.19	1141.17	1118.10	1098.30	1066.43
125,000	1460.24	1426.46	1397.63	1372.87	1333.04
150,000	1752.29	1711.75	1677.15	1647.45	1599.65
175,000	2044.34	1997.04	1956.67	1922.02	1866.26
200,000	2336.38	2282.33	2236.20	2196.60	2132.86
225,000	2628.43	2567.63	2515.72	2471.17	2399.47
250,000	2920.48	2852.92	2795.25	2745.74	2666.08
275,000	3212.53	3138.21	3074.77	3020.32	2932.69
300,000	3504.57	3423.50	3354.29	3294.89	3199.29
325,000	3796.62	3708.79	3633.82	3569.46	3465.90
350,000	4088.67	3994.08	3913.34	3844.04	3732.51
375,000	4380.72	4279.37	4192.87	4118.61	3999.12
400,000	4672.76	4564.66	4472.39	4393.19	4265.72
425,000	4964.81	4849.96	4751.91	4667.76	4532.33
450,000	5256.86	5135.25	5031.44	4942.33	4798.94
475,000	5548.91	5420.54	5310.96	5216.91	5065.55
500,000	5840.95	5705.83	5590.49	5491.48	5332.15
525,000	6133.00	5991.12	5870.01	5766.06	5598.76
550,000	6425.05	6276.41	6149.53	6040.63	5865.37
575,000	6717.10	6561.70	6429.06	6315.20	6131.98
600,000	7009.14	6846.99	6708.58	6589.78	6398.58
625,000	7301.19	7132.29	6988.11	6864.35	6665.19
650,000	7593.24	7417.58	7267.63	7138.92	6931.80
675,000	7885.29	7702.87	7547.15	7413.50	7198.41
700,000	8177.33	7988.16	7826.68	7688.07	7465.01
725,000	8469.38	8273.45	8106.20	7962.65	7731.62
750,000	8761.43	8558.74	8385.73	8237.22	7998.23
775,000	9053.48	8844.03	8665.25	8511.79	8264.83
800,000	9345.52	9129.32	8944.78	8786.37	8531.44
825,000	9637.57	9414.62	9224.30	9060.94	8798.05
850,000	9929.62	9699.91	9503.82	9335.51	9064.66
875,000	10221.67	9985.20	9783.35	9610.09	9331.26
900,000	10513.71	10270.49	10062.87	9884.66	9597.87

Monthly Payment Loans   **11.50%**

Loan Amount	Amortization Period in Years				
	21	22	23	24	25
10	0.11	0.11	0.11	0.11	0.11
20	0.22	0.21	0.21	0.21	0.21
30	0.32	0.32	0.31	0.31	0.31
40	0.43	0.42	0.42	0.41	0.41
50	0.53	0.53	0.52	0.52	0.51
100	1.06	1.05	1.04	1.03	1.02
200	2.11	2.09	2.07	2.05	2.04
300	3.17	3.13	3.10	3.08	3.05
400	4.22	4.17	4.14	4.10	4.07
500	5.27	5.22	5.17	5.13	5.09
1,000	10.54	10.43	10.33	10.25	10.17
2,000	21.08	20.85	20.66	20.49	20.33
3,000	31.61	31.28	30.98	30.73	30.50
4,000	42.15	41.70	41.31	40.97	40.66
5,000	52.68	52.12	51.63	51.21	50.83
10,000	105.36	104.24	103.26	102.41	101.65
20,000	210.72	208.48	206.52	204.81	203.30
30,000	316.08	312.72	309.78	307.21	304.95
40,000	421.44	416.95	413.04	409.61	406.59
50,000	526.79	521.19	516.30	512.01	508.24
100,000	1053.58	1042.38	1032.59	1024.01	1016.47
125,000	1316.98	1302.97	1290.73	1280.01	1270.59
150,000	1580.37	1563.57	1548.88	1536.01	1524.71
175,000	1843.77	1824.16	1807.02	1792.01	1778.83
200,000	2107.16	2084.75	2065.17	2048.01	2032.94
225,000	2370.55	2345.35	2323.31	2304.01	2287.06
250,000	2633.95	2605.94	2581.46	2560.01	2541.18
275,000	2897.34	2866.53	2839.60	2816.01	2795.29
300,000	3160.74	3127.13	3097.75	3072.01	3049.41
325,000	3424.13	3387.72	3355.89	3328.01	3303.53
350,000	3687.53	3648.31	3614.04	3584.01	3557.65
375,000	3950.92	3908.91	3872.18	3840.01	3811.76
400,000	4214.32	4169.50	4130.33	4096.01	4065.88
425,000	4477.71	4430.10	4388.48	4352.01	4320.00
450,000	4741.10	4690.69	4646.62	4608.01	4574.12
475,000	5004.50	4951.28	4904.77	4864.01	4828.23
500,000	5267.89	5211.88	5162.91	5120.01	5082.35
525,000	5531.29	5472.47	5421.06	5376.01	5336.47
550,000	5794.68	5733.06	5679.20	5632.01	5590.58
575,000	6058.08	5993.66	5937.35	5888.01	5844.70
600,000	6321.47	6254.25	6195.49	6144.01	6098.82
625,000	6584.87	6514.84	6453.64	6400.01	6352.94
650,000	6848.26	6775.44	6711.78	6656.01	6607.05
675,000	7111.65	7036.03	6969.93	6912.02	6861.17
700,000	7375.05	7296.62	7228.07	7168.02	7115.29
725,000	7638.44	7557.22	7486.22	7424.02	7369.40
750,000	7901.84	7817.81	7744.36	7680.02	7623.52
775,000	8165.23	8078.40	8002.51	7936.02	7877.64
800,000	8428.63	8339.00	8260.66	8192.02	8131.76
825,000	8692.02	8599.59	8518.80	8448.02	8385.87
850,000	8955.42	8860.19	8776.95	8704.02	8639.99
875,000	9218.81	9120.78	9035.09	8960.02	8894.11
900,000	9482.20	9381.37	9293.24	9216.02	9148.23

Table 7   215

11.50%   Monthly Payment Loans

Loan Amount	Amortization Period in Years				
	26	27	28	29	30
10	0.11	0.11	0.10	0.10	0.10
20	0.21	0.21	0.20	0.20	0.20
30	0.31	0.31	0.30	0.30	0.30
40	0.41	0.41	0.40	0.40	0.40
50	0.51	0.51	0.50	0.50	0.50
100	1.01	1.01	1.00	1.00	1.00
200	2.02	2.01	2.00	1.99	1.99
300	3.03	3.02	3.00	2.99	2.98
400	4.04	4.02	4.00	3.98	3.97
500	5.05	5.03	5.00	4.98	4.96
1,000	10.10	10.05	9.99	9.95	9.91
2,000	20.20	20.09	19.98	19.89	19.81
3,000	30.30	30.13	29.97	29.83	29.71
4,000	40.40	40.17	39.96	39.78	39.62
5,000	50.50	50.21	49.95	49.72	49.52
10,000	100.99	100.41	99.89	99.44	99.03
20,000	201.97	200.81	199.78	198.87	198.06
30,000	302.96	301.21	299.66	298.30	297.09
40,000	403.94	401.61	399.55	397.73	396.12
50,000	504.93	502.01	499.43	497.16	495.15
100,000	1009.85	1004.01	998.86	994.32	990.30
125,000	1262.31	1255.01	1248.58	1242.90	1237.87
150,000	1514.77	1506.02	1498.29	1491.47	1485.44
175,000	1767.23	1757.02	1748.01	1740.05	1733.02
200,000	2019.69	2008.02	1997.72	1988.63	1980.59
225,000	2272.15	2259.02	2247.44	2237.21	2228.16
250,000	2524.61	2510.02	2497.15	2485.79	2475.73
275,000	2777.08	2761.03	2746.87	2734.36	2723.31
300,000	3029.54	3012.03	2996.58	2982.94	2970.88
325,000	3282.00	3263.03	3246.30	3231.52	3218.45
350,000	3534.46	3514.03	3496.01	3480.10	3466.03
375,000	3786.92	3765.03	3745.73	3728.68	3713.60
400,000	4039.38	4016.04	3995.44	3977.25	3961.17
425,000	4291.84	4267.04	4245.16	4225.83	4208.74
450,000	4544.30	4518.04	4494.87	4474.41	4456.32
475,000	4796.76	4769.04	4744.59	4722.99	4703.89
500,000	5049.22	5020.04	4994.30	4971.57	4951.46
525,000	5301.69	5271.05	5244.02	5220.14	5199.04
550,000	5554.15	5522.05	5493.73	5468.72	5446.61
575,000	5806.61	5773.05	5743.45	5717.30	5694.18
600,000	6059.07	6024.05	5993.16	5965.88	5941.75
625,000	6311.53	6275.05	6242.88	6214.46	6189.33
650,000	6563.99	6526.06	6492.59	6463.03	6436.90
675,000	6816.45	6777.06	6742.31	6711.61	6684.47
700,000	7068.91	7028.06	6992.02	6960.19	6932.05
725,000	7321.37	7279.06	7241.74	7208.77	7179.62
750,000	7573.83	7530.06	7491.45	7457.35	7427.19
775,000	7826.30	7781.07	7741.17	7705.92	7674.76
800,000	8078.76	8032.07	7990.88	7954.50	7922.34
825,000	8331.22	8283.07	8240.60	8203.08	8169.91
850,000	8583.68	8534.07	8490.31	8451.66	8417.48
875,000	8836.14	8785.07	8740.02	8700.24	8665.06
900,000	9088.60	9036.07	8989.74	8948.81	8912.63

Monthly Payment Loans   **11.75%**

Loan Amount	Amortization Period in Years				
	5	7	8	10	12
10	0.23	0.18	0.17	0.15	0.13
20	0.45	0.36	0.33	0.29	0.26
30	0.67	0.53	0.49	0.43	0.39
40	0.89	0.71	0.65	0.57	0.52
50	1.11	0.88	0.81	0.72	0.65
100	2.22	1.76	1.62	1.43	1.30
200	4.43	3.51	3.23	2.85	2.60
300	6.64	5.26	4.84	4.27	3.90
400	8.85	7.01	6.45	5.69	5.20
500	11.06	8.76	8.06	7.11	6.50
1,000	22.12	17.52	16.12	14.21	12.99
2,000	44.24	35.04	32.24	28.41	25.97
3,000	66.36	52.56	48.35	42.61	38.95
4,000	88.48	70.08	64.47	56.82	51.94
5,000	110.60	87.60	80.58	71.02	64.92
10,000	221.19	175.20	161.16	142.03	129.84
20,000	442.37	350.39	322.32	284.06	259.67
30,000	663.55	525.58	483.48	426.09	389.50
40,000	884.74	700.78	644.64	568.12	519.34
50,000	1105.92	875.97	805.79	710.15	649.17
100,000	2211.84	1751.94	1611.58	1420.30	1298.33
125,000	2764.80	2189.92	2014.48	1775.37	1622.91
150,000	3317.75	2627.90	2417.37	2130.45	1947.49
175,000	3870.71	3065.89	2820.27	2485.52	2272.07
200,000	4423.67	3503.87	3223.16	2840.59	2596.66
225,000	4976.63	3941.85	3626.06	3195.67	2921.24
250,000	5529.59	4379.83	4028.95	3550.74	3245.82
275,000	6082.54	4817.82	4431.85	3905.82	3570.40
300,000	6635.50	5255.80	4834.74	4260.89	3894.98
325,000	7188.46	5693.78	5237.64	4615.96	4219.56
350,000	7741.42	6131.77	5640.53	4971.04	4544.14
375,000	8294.38	6569.75	6043.43	5326.11	4868.73
400,000	8847.33	7007.73	6446.32	5681.18	5193.31
425,000	9400.29	7445.71	6849.22	6036.26	5517.89
450,000	9953.25	7883.70	7252.11	6391.33	5842.47
475,000	10506.21	8321.68	7655.01	6746.40	6167.05
500,000	11059.17	8759.66	8057.90	7101.48	6491.63
525,000	11612.12	9197.65	8460.80	7456.55	6816.21
550,000	12165.08	9635.63	8863.69	7811.63	7140.80
575,000	12718.04	10073.61	9266.59	8166.70	7465.38
600,000	13271.00	10511.60	9669.48	8521.77	7789.96
625,000	13823.96	10949.58	10072.38	8876.85	8114.54
650,000	14376.91	11387.56	10475.27	9231.92	8439.12
675,000	14929.87	11825.54	10878.17	9586.99	8763.70
700,000	15482.83	12263.53	11281.06	9942.07	9088.28
725,000	16035.79	12701.51	11683.96	10297.14	9412.87
750,000	16588.75	13139.49	12086.85	10652.21	9737.45
775,000	17141.70	13577.48	12489.75	11007.29	10062.03
800,000	17694.66	14015.46	12892.64	11362.36	10386.61
825,000	18247.62	14453.44	13295.53	11717.44	10711.19
850,000	18800.58	14891.42	13698.43	12072.51	11035.77
875,000	19353.54	15329.41	14101.32	12427.58	11360.35
900,000	19906.49	15767.39	14504.22	12782.66	11684.94

Table 7   217

11.75%   Monthly Payment Loans

Amortization Period in Years

Loan Amount	15	16	17	18	20
10	0.12	0.12	0.12	0.12	0.11
20	0.24	0.24	0.23	0.23	0.22
30	0.36	0.35	0.35	0.34	0.33
40	0.48	0.47	0.46	0.45	0.44
50	0.60	0.58	0.57	0.56	0.55
100	1.19	1.16	1.14	1.12	1.09
200	2.37	2.32	2.27	2.24	2.17
300	3.56	3.48	3.41	3.35	3.26
400	4.74	4.63	4.54	4.47	4.34
500	5.93	5.79	5.68	5.58	5.42
1,000	11.85	11.58	11.35	11.16	10.84
2,000	23.69	23.15	22.70	22.31	21.68
3,000	35.53	34.73	34.04	33.46	32.52
4,000	47.37	46.30	45.39	44.61	43.35
5,000	59.21	57.87	56.74	55.76	54.19
10,000	118.42	115.74	113.47	111.51	108.38
20,000	236.83	231.48	226.93	223.02	216.75
30,000	355.24	347.22	340.39	334.53	325.12
40,000	473.66	462.96	453.85	446.03	433.49
50,000	592.07	578.70	567.31	557.54	541.86
100,000	1184.14	1157.40	1134.61	1115.08	1083.71
125,000	1480.17	1446.75	1418.26	1393.85	1354.64
150,000	1776.20	1736.10	1701.91	1672.61	1625.57
175,000	2072.23	2025.45	1985.57	1951.38	1896.49
200,000	2368.27	2314.80	2269.22	2230.15	2167.42
225,000	2664.30	2604.15	2552.87	2508.92	2438.35
250,000	2960.33	2893.50	2836.52	2787.69	2709.27
275,000	3256.37	3182.84	3120.17	3066.45	2980.20
300,000	3552.40	3472.19	3403.82	3345.22	3251.13
325,000	3848.43	3761.54	3687.48	3623.99	3522.05
350,000	4144.46	4050.89	3971.13	3902.76	3792.98
375,000	4440.50	4340.24	4254.78	4181.53	4063.91
400,000	4736.53	4629.59	4538.43	4460.30	4334.83
425,000	5032.56	4918.94	4822.08	4739.06	4605.76
450,000	5328.60	5208.29	5105.73	5017.83	4876.69
475,000	5624.63	5497.64	5389.38	5296.60	5147.61
500,000	5920.66	5786.99	5673.04	5575.37	5418.54
525,000	6216.69	6076.34	5956.69	5854.14	5689.47
550,000	6512.73	6365.68	6240.34	6132.90	5960.39
575,000	6808.76	6655.03	6523.99	6411.67	6231.32
600,000	7104.79	6944.38	6807.64	6690.44	6502.25
625,000	7400.83	7233.73	7091.29	6969.21	6773.17
650,000	7696.86	7523.08	7374.95	7247.98	7044.10
675,000	7992.89	7812.43	7658.60	7526.74	7315.03
700,000	8288.92	8101.78	7942.25	7805.51	7585.95
725,000	8584.96	8391.13	8225.90	8084.28	7856.88
750,000	8880.99	8680.48	8509.55	8363.05	8127.81
775,000	9177.02	8969.83	8793.20	8641.82	8398.73
800,000	9473.06	9259.18	9076.85	8920.59	8669.66
825,000	9769.09	9548.52	9360.51	9199.35	8940.59
850,000	10065.12	9837.87	9644.16	9478.12	9211.52
875,000	10361.15	10127.22	9927.81	9756.89	9482.44
900,000	10657.19	10416.57	10211.46	10035.66	9753.37

Monthly Payment Loans **11.75%**

Loan Amount	Amortization Period in Years				
	21	22	23	24	25
10	0.11	0.11	0.11	0.11	0.11
20	0.22	0.22	0.22	0.21	0.21
30	0.33	0.32	0.32	0.32	0.32
40	0.43	0.43	0.43	0.42	0.42
50	0.54	0.54	0.53	0.53	0.52
100	1.08	1.07	1.06	1.05	1.04
200	2.15	2.13	2.11	2.09	2.07
300	3.22	3.19	3.16	3.13	3.11
400	4.29	4.25	4.21	4.17	4.14
500	5.36	5.31	5.26	5.22	5.18
1,000	10.72	10.61	10.51	10.43	10.35
2,000	21.43	21.21	21.02	20.85	20.70
3,000	32.14	31.81	31.52	31.27	31.05
4,000	42.85	42.41	42.03	41.69	41.40
5,000	53.56	53.01	52.53	52.11	51.74
10,000	107.11	106.02	105.06	104.22	103.48
20,000	214.22	212.03	210.11	208.43	206.96
30,000	321.33	318.04	315.16	312.65	310.44
40,000	428.44	424.05	420.21	416.86	413.92
50,000	535.55	530.06	525.27	521.08	517.40
100,000	1071.09	1060.11	1050.53	1042.15	1034.80
125,000	1338.86	1325.14	1313.16	1302.68	1293.50
150,000	1606.64	1590.16	1575.79	1563.22	1552.20
175,000	1874.41	1855.19	1838.42	1823.75	1810.90
200,000	2142.18	2120.22	2101.05	2084.29	2069.60
225,000	2409.95	2385.24	2363.68	2344.83	2328.30
250,000	2677.72	2650.27	2626.31	2605.36	2587.00
275,000	2945.50	2915.30	2888.94	2865.90	2845.70
300,000	3213.27	3180.32	3151.57	3126.43	3104.40
325,000	3481.04	3445.35	3414.21	3386.97	3363.10
350,000	3748.81	3710.38	3676.84	3647.50	3621.80
375,000	4016.58	3975.40	3939.47	3908.04	3880.50
400,000	4284.36	4240.43	4202.10	4168.57	4139.20
425,000	4552.13	4505.45	4464.73	4429.11	4397.90
450,000	4819.90	4770.48	4727.36	4689.65	4656.60
475,000	5087.67	5035.51	4989.99	4950.18	4915.30
500,000	5355.44	5300.53	5252.62	5210.72	5174.00
525,000	5623.22	5565.56	5515.25	5471.25	5432.70
550,000	5890.99	5830.59	5777.88	5731.79	5691.40
575,000	6158.76	6095.61	6040.51	5992.32	5950.09
600,000	6426.53	6360.64	6303.14	6252.86	6208.79
625,000	6694.30	6625.67	6565.77	6513.40	6467.49
650,000	6962.08	6890.69	6828.41	6773.93	6726.19
675,000	7229.85	7155.72	7091.04	7034.47	6984.89
700,000	7497.62	7420.75	7353.67	7295.00	7243.59
725,000	7765.39	7685.77	7616.30	7555.54	7502.29
750,000	8033.16	7950.80	7878.93	7816.07	7760.99
775,000	8300.94	8215.83	8141.56	8076.61	8019.69
800,000	8568.71	8480.85	8404.19	8337.14	8278.39
825,000	8836.48	8745.88	8666.82	8597.68	8537.09
850,000	9104.25	9010.90	8929.45	8858.22	8795.79
875,000	9372.02	9275.93	9192.08	9118.75	9054.49
900,000	9639.80	9540.96	9454.71	9379.29	9313.19

Table 7   219

11.75%   Monthly Payment Loans

Amortization Period in Years

Loan Amount	26	27	28	29	30
10	0.11	0.11	0.11	0.11	0.11
20	0.21	0.21	0.21	0.21	0.21
30	0.31	0.31	0.31	0.31	0.31
40	0.42	0.41	0.41	0.41	0.41
50	0.52	0.52	0.51	0.51	0.51
100	1.03	1.03	1.02	1.02	1.01
200	2.06	2.05	2.04	2.03	2.02
300	3.09	3.07	3.06	3.04	3.03
400	4.12	4.10	4.08	4.06	4.04
500	5.15	5.12	5.09	5.07	5.05
1,000	10.29	10.23	10.18	10.14	10.10
2,000	20.57	20.46	20.36	20.27	20.19
3,000	30.86	30.69	30.54	30.40	30.29
4,000	41.14	40.91	40.71	40.54	40.38
5,000	51.42	51.14	50.89	50.67	50.48
10,000	102.84	102.27	101.77	101.33	100.95
20,000	205.68	204.54	203.54	202.66	201.89
30,000	308.51	306.61	305.31	303.99	302.83
40,000	411.35	409.08	407.08	405.32	403.77
50,000	514.18	511.35	508.85	506.65	504.71
100,000	1028.36	1022.69	1017.70	1013.30	1009.41
125,000	1285.44	1278.36	1272.12	1266.62	1261.77
150,000	1542.53	1534.03	1526.54	1519.94	1514.12
175,000	1799.62	1789.70	1780.96	1773.27	1766.47
200,000	2056.71	2045.37	2035.39	2026.59	2018.82
225,000	2313.79	2301.04	2289.81	2279.91	2271.18
250,000	2570.88	2556.71	2544.23	2533.23	2523.53
275,000	2827.97	2812.38	2798.66	2786.56	2775.88
300,000	3085.06	3068.05	3053.08	3039.68	3028.23
325,000	3342.15	3323.72	3307.50	3293.20	3280.59
350,000	3599.23	3579.39	3561.92	3546.53	3532.94
375,000	3856.32	3835.06	3816.35	3799.85	3785.29
400,000	4113.41	4090.73	4070.77	4053.17	4037.64
425,000	4370.50	4346.40	4325.19	4306.50	4290.00
450,000	4627.58	4602.07	4579.62	4559.82	4542.35
475,000	4884.67	4857.74	4834.04	4813.14	4794.70
500,000	5141.76	5113.42	5088.46	5066.46	5047.05
525,000	5398.85	5369.09	5342.88	5319.79	5299.41
550,000	5655.93	5624.76	5597.31	5573.11	5551.76
575,000	5913.02	5880.43	5851.73	5826.43	5804.11
600,000	6170.11	6136.10	6106.15	6079.76	6056.46
625,000	6427.20	6391.77	6360.57	6333.08	6308.82
650,000	6684.29	6647.44	6615.00	6586.40	6561.17
675,000	6941.37	6903.11	6869.42	6839.72	6813.52
700,000	7198.46	7158.78	7123.84	7093.05	7065.87
725,000	7455.55	7414.45	7378.27	7346.37	7318.23
750,000	7712.64	7670.12	7632.69	7599.69	7570.58
775,000	7969.72	7925.79	7887.11	7853.02	7822.93
800,000	8226.81	8181.46	8141.53	8106.34	8075.28
825,000	8483.90	8437.13	8395.96	8359.66	8327.64
850,000	8740.99	8692.80	8650.38	8612.99	8579.99
875,000	8998.07	8948.47	8904.80	8866.31	8832.34
900,000	9255.16	9204.14	9159.23	9119.63	9084.69

Monthly Payment Loans   **12.00%**

Loan Amount	Amortization Period in Years				
	5	7	8	10	12
10	0.23	0.18	0.17	0.15	0.14
20	0.45	0.36	0.33	0.29	0.27
30	0.67	0.53	0.49	0.44	0.40
40	0.89	0.71	0.66	0.58	0.53
50	1.12	0.89	0.82	0.72	0.66
100	2.23	1.77	1.63	1.44	1.32
200	4.45	3.54	3.26	2.87	2.63
300	6.68	5.30	4.88	4.31	3.95
400	8.90	7.07	6.51	5.74	5.26
500	11.13	8.83	8.13	7.18	6.57
1,000	22.25	17.66	16.26	14.35	13.14
2,000	44.49	35.31	32.51	28.70	26.27
3,000	66.74	52.96	48.76	43.05	39.41
4,000	88.98	70.62	65.02	57.39	52.54
5,000	111.23	88.27	81.27	71.74	65.68
10,000	222.45	176.53	162.53	143.48	131.35
20,000	444.89	353.06	325.06	286.95	262.69
30,000	667.34	529.59	487.59	430.42	394.03
40,000	889.76	706.11	650.12	573.89	525.37
50,000	1112.23	882.64	812.65	717.36	656.71
100,000	2224.45	1765.28	1625.29	1434.71	1313.42
125,000	2780.56	2206.60	2031.61	1793.39	1641.78
150,000	3336.67	2647.91	2437.93	2152.07	1970.13
175,000	3892.78	3089.23	2844.25	2510.75	2298.49
200,000	4448.89	3530.55	3250.57	2869.42	2626.84
225,000	5005.01	3971.87	3656.89	3228.10	2955.20
250,000	5561.12	4413.19	4063.22	3586.78	3283.55
275,000	6117.23	4854.51	4469.54	3945.46	3611.91
300,000	6673.34	5295.82	4875.86	4304.13	3940.26
325,000	7229.45	5737.14	5282.18	4662.81	4268.62
350,000	7785.56	6178.46	5688.50	5021.49	4596.97
375,000	8341.67	6619.78	6094.82	5380.17	4925.33
400,000	8897.78	7061.10	6501.14	5738.84	5253.68
425,000	9453.90	7502.42	6907.46	6097.52	5582.04
450,000	10010.01	7943.73	7313.78	6456.20	5910.39
475,000	10566.12	8385.05	7720.10	6814.88	6238.75
500,000	11122.23	8826.37	8126.43	7173.55	6567.10
525,000	11678.34	9267.69	8532.75	7532.23	6895.46
550,000	12234.45	9709.01	8939.07	7890.91	7223.81
575,000	12790.56	10150.33	9345.39	8249.58	7552.17
600,000	13346.67	10591.64	9751.71	8608.26	7880.52
625,000	13902.78	11032.96	10158.03	8966.94	8208.87
650,000	14458.90	11474.28	10564.35	9325.62	8537.23
675,000	15015.01	11915.60	10970.67	9684.29	8865.58
700,000	15571.12	12356.92	11376.99	10042.97	9193.94
725,000	16127.23	12798.24	11783.32	10401.65	9522.29
750,000	16683.34	13239.55	12189.64	10760.33	9850.65
775,000	17239.45	13680.87	12595.96	11119.00	10179.00
800,000	17795.56	14122.19	13002.28	11477.68	10507.36
825,000	18351.67	14563.51	13408.60	11836.36	10835.71
850,000	18907.79	15004.83	13814.92	12195.04	11164.07
875,000	19463.90	15446.15	14221.24	12553.71	11492.42
900,000	20020.01	15887.46	14627.56	12912.39	11820.78

Table 7   221

12.00%   Monthly Payment Loans

Amortization Period in Years

Loan Amount	15	16	17	18	20
10	0.13	0.12	0.12	0.12	0.12
20	0.25	0.24	0.24	0.23	0.23
30	0.37	0.36	0.35	0.34	0.34
40	0.49	0.47	0.47	0.46	0.45
50	0.61	0.59	0.58	0.57	0.56
100	1.21	1.18	1.16	1.14	1.11
200	2.41	2.35	2.31	2.27	2.21
300	3.61	3.53	3.46	3.40	3.31
400	4.81	4.70	4.61	4.53	4.41
500	6.01	5.87	5.76	5.66	5.51
1,000	12.01	11.74	11.52	11.32	11.02
2,000	24.01	23.48	23.03	22.64	22.03
3,000	36.01	35.22	34.54	33.96	33.04
4,000	48.01	46.95	46.05	45.28	44.05
5,000	60.01	58.69	57.57	56.60	55.06
10,000	120.02	117.38	115.13	113.20	110.11
20,000	240.04	234.75	230.25	226.40	220.22
30,000	360.06	352.12	345.37	339.59	330.33
40,000	480.07	469.50	460.49	452.79	440.44
50,000	600.09	586.87	575.61	565.98	550.55
100,000	1200.17	1173.73	1151.22	1131.96	1101.09
125,000	1500.22	1467.16	1439.02	1414.94	1376.36
150,000	1800.26	1760.59	1726.83	1697.93	1651.63
175,000	2100.30	2054.02	2014.63	1980.92	1926.91
200,000	2400.34	2347.46	2302.44	2263.91	2202.18
225,000	2700.38	2640.89	2590.24	2546.89	2477.45
250,000	3000.43	2934.32	2878.04	2829.88	2752.72
275,000	3300.47	3227.75	3165.85	3112.87	3027.99
300,000	3600.51	3521.18	3453.65	3395.86	3303.26
325,000	3900.55	3814.61	3741.46	3678.84	3578.53
350,000	4200.59	4108.04	4029.26	3961.83	3853.81
375,000	4500.64	4401.47	4317.06	4244.82	4129.08
400,000	4800.68	4694.91	4604.87	4527.81	4404.35
425,000	5100.72	4988.34	4892.67	4810.79	4679.62
450,000	5400.76	5281.77	5180.47	5093.78	4954.89
475,000	5700.80	5575.20	5468.28	5376.77	5230.16
500,000	6000.85	5868.63	5756.08	5659.76	5505.44
525,000	6300.89	6162.06	6043.89	5942.74	5780.71
550,000	6600.93	6455.49	6331.69	6225.73	6055.98
575,000	6900.97	6748.92	6619.49	6508.72	6331.25
600,000	7201.01	7042.36	6907.30	6791.71	6606.52
625,000	7501.06	7335.79	7195.10	7074.69	6881.79
650,000	7801.10	7629.22	7482.91	7357.68	7157.06
675,000	8101.14	7922.65	7770.71	7640.67	7432.34
700,000	8401.18	8216.08	8058.51	7923.66	7707.61
725,000	8701.22	8509.51	8346.32	8206.65	7982.88
750,000	9001.27	8802.94	8634.12	8489.63	8258.15
775,000	9301.31	9096.37	8921.93	8772.62	8533.42
800,000	9601.35	9389.81	9209.73	9055.61	8808.69
825,000	9901.39	9683.24	9497.53	9338.60	9083.97
850,000	10201.43	9976.67	9785.34	9621.58	9359.24
875,000	10501.48	10270.10	10073.14	9904.57	9634.51
900,000	10801.52	10563.53	10360.94	10187.56	9909.78

Monthly Payment Loans — 12.00%

Loan Amount	Amortization Period in Years				
	21	22	23	24	25
10	0.11	0.11	0.11	0.11	0.11
20	0.22	0.22	0.22	0.22	0.22
30	0.33	0.33	0.33	0.32	0.32
40	0.44	0.44	0.43	0.43	0.43
50	0.55	0.54	0.54	0.54	0.53
100	1.09	1.08	1.07	1.07	1.06
200	2.18	2.16	2.14	2.13	2.11
300	3.27	3.24	3.21	3.19	3.16
400	4.36	4.32	4.28	4.25	4.22
500	5.45	5.39	5.35	5.31	5.27
1,000	10.89	10.78	10.69	10.61	10.54
2,000	21.78	21.56	21.38	21.21	21.07
3,000	32.67	32.34	32.06	31.82	31.60
4,000	43.55	43.12	42.75	42.42	42.13
5,000	54.44	53.90	53.43	53.02	52.67
10,000	108.87	107.80	106.86	106.04	105.33
20,000	217.74	215.59	213.72	212.08	210.65
30,000	326.61	323.39	320.57	318.12	315.97
40,000	435.48	431.18	427.43	424.16	421.29
50,000	544.35	538.97	534.29	530.20	526.62
100,000	1088.70	1077.94	1068.57	1060.39	1053.23
125,000	1360.88	1347.43	1335.71	1325.48	1316.54
150,000	1633.05	1616.91	1602.85	1590.58	1579.84
175,000	1905.23	1886.40	1869.99	1855.67	1843.15
200,000	2177.40	2155.88	2137.13	2120.77	2106.45
225,000	2449.58	2425.37	2404.28	2385.86	2369.76
250,000	2721.75	2694.85	2671.42	2650.96	2633.07
275,000	2993.93	2964.34	2938.56	2916.06	2896.37
300,000	3266.10	3233.82	3205.70	3181.15	3159.68
325,000	3538.28	3503.30	3472.84	3446.25	3422.98
350,000	3810.45	3772.79	3739.98	3711.34	3686.29
375,000	4082.63	4042.27	4007.12	3976.44	3949.60
400,000	4354.80	4311.76	4274.26	4241.53	4212.90
425,000	4626.98	4581.24	4541.41	4506.63	4476.21
450,000	4899.15	4850.73	4808.55	4771.72	4739.51
475,000	5171.33	5120.21	5075.69	5036.82	5002.62
500,000	5443.50	5389.70	5342.83	5301.91	5266.13
525,000	5715.68	5659.18	5609.97	5567.01	5529.43
550,000	5987.85	5928.67	5877.11	5832.11	5792.74
575,000	6260.03	6198.15	6144.25	6097.20	6056.04
600,000	6532.20	6467.64	6411.39	6362.30	6319.35
625,000	6804.38	6737.12	6678.54	6627.39	6582.66
650,000	7076.55	7006.60	6945.68	6892.49	6845.96
675,000	7348.73	7276.09	7212.82	7157.58	7109.27
700,000	7620.90	7545.57	7479.96	7422.68	7372.57
725,000	7893.08	7815.06	7747.10	7687.77	7635.88
750,000	8165.25	8084.54	8014.24	7952.87	7899.19
775,000	8437.43	8354.03	8281.38	8217.96	8162.49
800,000	8709.60	8623.51	8548.52	8483.06	8425.80
825,000	8981.78	8893.00	8815.67	8748.16	8689.10
850,000	9253.95	9162.48	9082.81	9013.25	8952.41
875,000	9526.13	9431.97	9349.95	9278.35	9215.72
900,000	9798.30	9701.45	9617.09	9543.44	9479.02

Table 7   223

12.00%   Monthly Payment Loans

Loan Amount	\multicolumn{5}{c}{Amortization Period in Years}
	26	27	28	29	30
10	0.11	0.11	0.11	0.11	0.11
20	0.21	0.21	0.21	0.21	0.21
30	0.32	0.32	0.32	0.31	0.31
40	0.42	0.42	0.42	0.42	0.42
50	0.53	0.53	0.52	0.52	0.52
100	1.05	1.05	1.04	1.04	1.03
200	2.10	2.09	2.08	2.07	2.06
300	3.15	3.13	3.11	3.10	3.09
400	4.19	4.17	4.15	4.13	4.12
500	5.24	5.21	5.19	5.17	5.15
1,000	10.47	10.42	10.37	10.33	10.29
2,000	20.94	20.83	20.74	20.65	20.58
3,000	31.41	31.25	31.10	30.98	30.86
4,000	41.88	41.66	41.47	41.30	41.15
5,000	52.35	52.08	51.84	51.62	51.44
10,000	104.70	104.15	103.67	103.24	102.87
20,000	209.40	208.29	207.33	206.48	205.73
30,000	314.09	312.44	310.99	309.71	308.59
40,000	418.79	416.58	414.65	412.95	411.45
50,000	523.48	520.73	518.31	516.18	514.31
100,000	1046.96	1041.45	1036.62	1032.36	1028.62
125,000	1308.70	1301.82	1295.77	1290.45	1285.77
150,000	1570.43	1562.18	1554.92	1548.54	1542.92
175,000	1832.17	1822.54	1814.08	1806.63	1800.08
200,000	2093.91	2082.90	2073.23	2064.72	2057.23
225,000	2355.65	2343.26	2332.36	2322.81	2314.38
250,000	2617.39	2603.63	2591.54	2580.90	2571.54
275,000	2879.12	2863.99	2850.69	2838.99	2828.69
300,000	3140.86	3124.35	3109.84	3097.08	3085.84
325,000	3402.60	3384.71	3369.00	3355.17	3343.00
350,000	3664.34	3645.08	3628.15	3613.26	3600.15
375,000	3926.08	3905.44	3887.30	3871.35	3857.30
400,000	4187.81	4165.80	4146.46	4129.44	4114.46
425,000	4449.55	4426.16	4405.61	4387.53	4371.61
450,000	4711.29	4686.52	4664.76	4645.62	4628.76
475,000	4973.03	4946.89	4923.92	4903.71	4885.91
500,000	5234.77	5207.25	5183.07	5161.60	5143.07
525,000	5496.51	5467.61	5442.22	5419.89	5400.22
550,000	5758.24	5727.97	5701.38	5677.98	5657.37
575,000	6019.98	5988.34	5960.53	5936.07	5914.53
600,000	6281.72	6248.70	6219.68	6194.16	6171.68
625,000	6543.46	6509.06	6476.84	6452.25	6428.83
650,000	6805.20	6769.42	6737.99	6710.34	6685.99
675,000	7066.93	7029.78	6997.14	6968.43	6943.14
700,000	7328.67	7290.15	7256.30	7226.52	7200.29
725,000	7590.41	7550.51	7515.45	7484.61	7457.45
750,000	7852.15	7810.87	7774.60	7742.70	7714.60
775,000	8113.69	8071.23	8033.76	8000.79	7971.75
800,000	8375.62	8331.60	8292.91	8258.88	8228.91
825,000	8637.36	8591.96	8552.06	8516.97	8486.06
850,000	8899.10	8852.32	8811.22	8775.05	8743.21
875,000	9160.84	9112.68	9070.37	9033.14	9000.37
900,000	9422.58	9373.04	9329.52	9291.23	9257.52

Monthly Payment Loans   **12.25%**

Loan Amount	Amortization Period in Years				
	5	7	8	10	12
10	0.23	0.18	0.17	0.15	0.14
20	0.45	0.36	0.33	0.29	0.27
30	0.68	0.54	0.50	0.44	0.40
40	0.90	0.72	0.66	0.58	0.54
50	1.12	0.89	0.82	0.73	0.67
100	2.24	1.78	1.64	1.45	1.33
200	4.48	3.56	3.28	2.90	2.66
300	6.72	5.34	4.92	4.35	3.99
400	8.95	7.12	6.56	5.80	5.32
500	11.19	8.90	8.20	7.25	6.65
1,000	22.38	17.79	16.40	14.50	13.29
2,000	44.75	35.58	32.79	28.99	26.58
3,000	67.12	53.37	49.18	43.48	39.86
4,000	89.49	71.15	65.57	57.97	53.15
5,000	111.86	88.94	81.96	72.46	66.43
10,000	223.71	177.87	163.91	144.92	132.86
20,000	447.42	355.74	327.82	289.84	265.72
30,000	671.13	533.61	491.72	434.76	398.58
40,000	894.84	711.47	655.63	579.68	531.44
50,000	1118.55	889.34	819.53	724.60	664.30
100,000	2237.10	1778.68	1639.06	1449.20	1328.60
125,000	2796.38	2223.34	2048.82	1811.50	1660.75
150,000	3355.65	2668.01	2458.58	2173.80	1992.90
175,000	3914.93	3112.68	2868.34	2536.10	2325.05
200,000	4474.20	3557.35	3278.11	2898.40	2657.20
225,000	5033.48	4002.01	3687.87	3260.70	2989.35
250,000	5592.75	4446.68	4097.63	3623.00	3321.50
275,000	6152.03	4891.35	4507.40	3985.30	3653.65
300,000	6711.30	5336.02	4917.16	4347.60	3985.79
325,000	7270.58	5780.68	5326.92	4709.90	4317.94
350,000	7829.85	6225.35	5736.68	5072.20	4650.09
375,000	8389.13	6670.02	6146.45	5434.50	4982.24
400,000	8948.40	7114.69	6556.21	5796.80	5314.39
425,000	9507.67	7559.36	6965.97	6159.10	5646.54
450,000	10066.95	8004.02	7375.74	6521.40	5978.69
475,000	10626.22	8448.69	7785.50	6883.70	6310.84
500,000	11185.50	8893.36	8195.26	7246.00	6642.99
525,000	11744.77	9338.03	8605.02	7608.30	6975.14
550,000	12304.05	9782.69	9014.79	7970.60	7307.29
575,000	12863.32	10227.36	9424.55	8332.90	7639.44
600,000	13422.60	10672.03	9834.31	8695.20	7971.58
625,000	13981.87	11116.70	10244.08	9057.50	8303.73
650,000	14541.15	11561.36	10653.84	9419.80	8635.88
675,000	15100.42	12006.03	11063.60	9782.10	8968.03
700,000	15659.70	12450.70	11473.36	10144.40	9300.18
725,000	16218.97	12895.37	11883.13	10506.70	9632.33
750,000	16778.25	13340.04	12292.89	10868.99	9964.48
775,000	17337.52	13784.70	12702.65	11231.29	10296.63
800,000	17896.79	14229.37	13112.42	11593.59	10628.78
825,000	18456.07	14674.04	13522.18	11955.89	10960.93
850,000	19015.34	15118.71	13931.94	12318.19	11293.08
875,000	19574.62	15563.37	14341.70	12680.49	11625.23
900,000	20133.89	16008.04	14751.47	13042.79	11957.37

Table 7   225

12.25%   Monthly Payment Loans

Amortization Period in Years

Loan Amount	15	16	17	18	20
10	0.13	0.12	0.12	0.12	0.12
20	0.25	0.24	0.24	0.23	0.23
30	0.37	0.36	0.36	0.35	0.34
40	0.49	0.48	0.47	0.46	0.45
50	0.61	0.60	0.59	0.58	0.56
100	1.22	1.20	1.17	1.15	1.12
200	2.44	2.39	2.34	2.30	2.24
300	3.65	3.58	3.51	3.45	3.36
400	4.87	4.77	4.68	4.60	4.48
500	6.09	5.96	5.84	5.75	5.60
1,000	12.17	11.91	11.68	11.49	11.19
2,000	24.33	23.81	23.36	22.98	22.38
3,000	36.49	35.71	35.04	34.47	33.56
4,000	48.66	47.61	46.72	45.96	44.75
5,000	60.82	59.51	58.40	57.45	55.93
10,000	121.63	119.02	116.80	114.90	111.86
20,000	243.26	238.04	233.59	229.79	223.72
30,000	364.89	357.05	350.38	344.68	335.57
40,000	486.52	476.07	467.17	459.58	447.43
50,000	608.15	595.08	583.97	574.47	559.29
100,000	1216.30	1190.16	1167.93	1148.93	1118.57
125,000	1520.38	1487.69	1459.91	1436.16	1398.21
150,000	1824.45	1785.23	1751.89	1723.40	1677.85
175,000	2128.53	2082.77	2043.87	2010.63	1957.49
200,000	2432.60	2380.31	2335.85	2297.86	2237.13
225,000	2736.68	2677.84	2627.83	2585.09	2516.76
250,000	3040.75	2975.38	2919.81	2872.32	2796.42
275,000	3344.83	3272.92	3211.79	3159.55	3076.06
300,000	3648.90	3570.46	3503.77	3446.79	3355.70
325,000	3952.98	3867.99	3795.75	3734.02	3635.34
350,000	4257.05	4165.53	4087.73	4021.25	3914.98
375,000	4561.13	4463.07	4379.71	4308.48	4194.62
400,000	4865.20	4760.61	4671.70	4595.71	4474.26
425,000	5169.27	5058.14	4963.68	4882.95	4753.90
450,000	5473.35	5355.68	5255.66	5170.18	5033.55
475,000	5777.42	5653.22	5547.64	5457.41	5313.19
500,000	6081.50	5950.76	5839.62	5744.64	5592.83
525,000	6385.57	6248.29	6131.60	6031.87	5872.47
550,000	6689.65	6545.83	6423.58	6319.10	6152.11
575,000	6993.72	6843.37	6715.56	6606.34	6431.75
600,000	7297.80	7140.91	7007.54	6893.57	6711.39
625,000	7601.87	7438.44	7299.52	7180.80	6991.03
650,000	7905.95	7735.98	7591.50	7468.03	7270.68
675,000	8210.02	8033.52	7883.48	7755.26	7550.32
700,000	8514.10	8331.06	8175.46	8042.49	7829.96
725,000	8818.17	8628.59	8467.44	8329.73	8109.60
750,000	9122.25	8926.13	8759.42	8616.96	8389.24
775,000	9426.32	9223.67	9051.40	8904.19	8668.88
800,000	9730.39	9521.21	9343.39	9191.42	8948.52
825,000	10034.47	9818.74	9635.37	9478.65	9228.16
850,000	10338.54	10116.28	9927.35	9765.89	9507.80
875,000	10642.62	10413.82	10219.33	10053.12	9787.45
900,000	10946.69	10711.36	10511.31	10340.35	10067.09

Monthly Payment Loans   **12.25%**

Loan Amount	Amortization Period in Years				
	21	22	23	24	25
10	0.12	0.11	0.11	0.11	0.11
20	0.23	0.22	0.22	0.22	0.22
30	0.34	0.33	0.33	0.33	0.33
40	0.45	0.44	0.44	0.44	0.43
50	0.56	0.55	0.55	0.54	0.54
100	1.11	1.10	1.09	1.08	1.08
200	2.22	2.20	2.18	2.16	2.15
300	3.32	3.29	3.27	3.24	3.22
400	4.43	4.39	4.35	4.32	4.29
500	5.54	5.48	5.44	5.40	5.36
1,000	11.07	10.96	10.87	10.79	10.72
2,000	22.13	21.92	21.74	21.58	21.44
3,000	33.20	32.88	32.61	32.37	32.16
4,000	44.26	43.84	43.47	43.15	42.87
5,000	55.33	54.80	54.34	53.94	53.59
10,000	110.65	109.59	108.68	107.88	107.18
20,000	221.29	219.18	217.35	215.75	214.35
30,000	331.93	328.77	326.02	323.62	321.53
40,000	442.57	438.35	434.69	431.49	428.70
50,000	553.21	547.94	543.36	539.36	535.88
100,000	1106.42	1095.87	1086.71	1078.72	1071.75
125,000	1383.02	1369.84	1358.38	1348.40	1339.68
150,000	1659.62	1643.81	1630.06	1618.08	1607.62
175,000	1936.22	1917.78	1901.74	1887.76	1875.56
200,000	2212.83	2191.74	2173.41	2157.44	2143.49
225,000	2489.43	2465.71	2445.09	2427.12	2411.43
250,000	2766.03	2739.68	2716.76	2696.80	2679.36
275,000	3042.63	3013.65	2988.44	2966.48	2947.30
300,000	3319.24	3287.61	3260.12	3236.16	3215.24
325,000	3595.84	3561.58	3531.79	3505.83	3483.17
350,000	3872.44	3835.55	3803.47	3775.51	3751.11
375,000	4149.04	4109.51	4075.14	4045.19	4019.04
400,000	4425.65	4383.48	4346.82	4314.87	4286.98
425,000	4702.25	4657.45	4618.50	4584.55	4554.92
450,000	4978.85	4931.42	4890.17	4854.23	4822.85
475,000	5255.45	5205.38	5161.85	5123.91	5090.79
500,000	5532.06	5479.35	5433.52	5393.59	5358.72
525,000	5808.66	5753.32	5705.20	5663.27	5626.66
550,000	6085.26	6027.29	5976.88	5932.95	5894.60
575,000	6361.87	6301.25	6248.55	6202.63	6162.53
600,000	6638.47	6575.22	6520.23	6472.31	6430.47
625,000	6915.07	6849.19	6791.90	6741.99	6698.40
650,000	7191.67	7123.15	7063.58	7011.66	6966.34
675,000	7468.28	7397.12	7335.25	7281.34	7234.28
700,000	7744.88	7671.09	7606.93	7551.02	7502.21
725,000	8021.48	7945.06	7878.61	7820.70	7770.15
750,000	8298.08	8219.02	8150.28	8090.38	8038.08
775,000	8574.69	8492.99	8421.96	8360.06	8306.02
800,000	8851.29	8766.96	8693.63	8629.74	8573.96
825,000	9127.89	9040.93	8965.31	8899.42	8841.89
850,000	9404.49	9314.89	9236.99	9169.10	9109.83
875,000	9681.10	9588.86	9508.66	9438.78	9377.76
900,000	9957.70	9862.83	9780.34	9708.46	9645.70

Table 7   227

12.25%   Monthly Payment Loans

Amortization Period in Years

Loan Amount	26	27	28	29	30
10	0.11	0.11	0.11	0.11	0.11
20	0.22	0.22	0.22	0.22	0.21
30	0.32	0.32	0.32	0.32	0.32
40	0.43	0.43	0.43	0.43	0.42
50	0.54	0.54	0.53	0.53	0.53
100	1.07	1.07	1.06	1.06	1.05
200	2.14	2.13	2.12	2.11	2.10
300	3.20	3.19	3.17	3.16	3.15
400	4.27	4.25	4.23	4.21	4.20
500	5.33	5.31	5.28	5.26	5.24
1,000	10.66	10.61	10.56	10.52	10.48
2,000	21.32	21.21	21.12	21.04	20.96
3,000	31.97	31.81	31.67	31.55	31.44
4,000	42.63	42.42	42.23	42.07	41.92
5,000	53.29	53.02	52.79	52.58	52.40
10,000	106.57	106.04	105.57	105.16	104.79
20,000	213.13	212.07	211.13	210.31	209.58
30,000	319.70	318.10	316.69	315.46	314.37
40,000	426.26	424.13	422.25	420.61	419.16
50,000	532.83	530.16	527.82	525.76	523.95
100,000	1065.65	1060.31	1055.63	1051.51	1047.90
125,000	1332.06	1325.39	1319.53	1314.39	1309.88
150,000	1598.47	1590.46	1583.44	1577.27	1571.85
175,000	1864.88	1855.54	1847.34	1840.15	1833.82
200,000	2131.30	2120.61	2111.25	2103.02	2095.80
225,000	2397.71	2385.69	2375.15	2365.90	2357.77
250,000	2664.12	2650.77	2639.06	2628.78	2619.75
275,000	2930.53	2915.84	2902.96	2891.66	2881.72
300,000	3196.94	3180.92	3166.67	3154.53	3143.69
325,000	3463.35	3446.00	3430.77	3417.41	3405.67
350,000	3729.76	3711.07	3694.68	3680.29	3667.64
375,000	3996.18	3976.15	3958.59	3943.17	3929.62
400,000	4262.59	4241.22	4222.49	4206.04	4191.59
425,000	4529.00	4506.30	4486.40	4468.92	4453.56
450,000	4795.41	4771.38	4750.30	4731.80	4715.54
475,000	5061.82	5036.45	5014.21	4994.68	4977.51
500,000	5328.23	5301.53	5278.11	5257.55	5239.49
525,000	5594.64	5566.61	5542.02	5520.43	5501.46
550,000	5861.06	5831.68	5805.92	5783.31	5763.44
575,000	6127.47	6096.76	6069.83	6046.19	6025.41
600,000	6393.88	6361.83	6333.73	6309.06	6287.38
625,000	6660.29	6626.91	6597.64	6571.94	6549.36
650,000	6926.70	6891.99	6861.54	6834.82	6811.33
675,000	7193.11	7157.06	7125.45	7097.70	7073.31
700,000	7459.52	7422.14	7389.35	7360.57	7335.28
725,000	7725.94	7687.22	7653.26	7623.45	7597.25
750,000	7992.35	7952.29	7917.17	7886.33	7859.23
775,000	8258.76	8217.37	8181.07	8149.21	8121.20
800,000	8525.17	8482.44	8444.98	8412.08	8383.18
825,000	8791.58	8747.52	8708.88	8674.96	8645.15
850,000	9057.99	9012.60	8972.79	8937.84	8907.12
875,000	9324.40	9277.67	9236.69	9200.71	9169.10
900,000	9590.82	9542.75	9500.60	9463.59	9431.07

Monthly Payment Loans   **12.50%**

Loan Amount	\multicolumn{5}{c}{Amortization Period in Years}
	5	7	8	10	12
10	0.23	0.18	0.17	0.15	0.14
20	0.45	0.36	0.34	0.30	0.27
30	0.68	0.54	0.50	0.44	0.41
40	0.90	0.72	0.67	0.59	0.54
50	1.13	0.90	0.83	0.74	0.68
100	2.25	1.80	1.66	1.47	1.35
200	4.50	3.59	3.31	2.93	2.69
300	6.75	5.38	4.96	4.40	4.04
400	9.00	7.17	6.62	5.86	5.38
500	11.25	8.97	8.27	7.32	6.72
1,000	22.50	17.93	16.53	14.64	13.44
2,000	45.00	35.85	33.06	29.28	26.88
3,000	67.50	53.77	49.59	43.92	40.32
4,000	90.00	71.69	66.12	58.56	53.76
5,000	112.49	89.61	82.65	73.19	67.20
10,000	224.98	179.22	165.29	146.38	134.39
20,000	449.96	358.43	330.58	292.76	268.78
30,000	674.94	537.64	495.87	439.13	403.16
40,000	899.92	716.85	661.16	585.51	537.55
50,000	1124.90	896.07	826.45	731.89	671.93
100,000	2249.80	1792.13	1652.89	1463.77	1343.86
125,000	2812.25	2240.16	2066.11	1829.71	1679.83
150,000	3374.70	2688.19	2479.33	2195.65	2015.79
175,000	3937.14	3136.22	2892.55	2561.59	2351.76
200,000	4499.59	3584.25	3305.77	2927.53	2687.72
225,000	5062.04	4032.28	3718.99	3293.47	3023.68
250,000	5624.49	4480.31	4132.21	3659.41	3359.65
275,000	6186.94	4928.35	4545.43	4025.35	3695.61
300,000	6749.39	5376.38	4958.65	4391.29	4031.58
325,000	7311.83	5824.41	5371.87	4757.23	4367.54
350,000	7874.28	6272.44	5785.09	5123.17	4703.51
375,000	8436.73	6720.47	6198.31	5489.11	5039.47
400,000	8999.18	7168.50	6611.53	5855.05	5375.43
425,000	9561.63	7616.53	7024.75	6220.99	5711.40
450,000	10124.08	8064.56	7437.97	6586.93	6047.36
475,000	10686.53	8512.59	7851.19	6952.87	6383.33
500,000	11248.97	8960.62	8264.41	7318.81	6719.29
525,000	11811.42	9408.66	8677.63	7684.75	7055.26
550,000	12373.87	9856.69	9090.85	8050.69	7391.22
575,000	12936.32	10304.72	9504.07	8416.63	7727.18
600,000	13498.77	10752.75	9917.29	8782.58	8063.15
625,000	14061.22	11200.78	10330.51	9148.52	8399.11
650,000	14623.66	11648.81	10743.73	9514.46	8735.08
675,000	15186.11	12096.84	11156.95	9880.40	9071.04
700,000	15748.56	12544.87	11570.17	10246.34	9407.01
725,000	16311.01	12992.90	11983.39	10612.28	9742.97
750,000	16873.46	13440.93	12396.61	10978.22	10078.93
775,000	17435.91	13888.96	12809.83	11344.16	10414.90
800,000	17998.36	14337.00	13223.05	11710.10	10750.86
825,000	18560.80	14785.03	13636.27	12076.04	11086.83
850,000	19123.25	15233.06	14049.49	12441.98	11422.79
875,000	19685.70	15681.09	14462.71	12807.92	11758.76
900,000	20248.15	16129.12	14875.93	13173.86	12094.72

Table 7   229

12.50%   Monthly Payment Loans

Loan Amount	Amortization Period in Years				
	15	16	17	18	20
10	0.13	0.13	0.12	0.12	0.12
20	0.25	0.25	0.24	0.24	0.23
30	0.37	0.37	0.36	0.35	0.35
40	0.50	0.49	0.48	0.47	0.46
50	0.62	0.61	0.60	0.59	0.57
100	1.24	1.21	1.19	1.17	1.14
200	2.47	2.42	2.37	2.34	2.28
300	3.70	3.63	3.56	3.50	3.41
400	4.94	4.83	4.74	4.67	4.55
500	6.17	6.04	5.93	5.84	5.69
1,000	12.33	12.07	11.85	11.67	11.37
2,000	24.66	24.14	23.70	23.33	22.73
3,000	36.98	36.21	35.55	34.99	34.09
4,000	49.31	48.27	47.39	46.65	45.45
5,000	61.63	60.34	59.24	58.31	56.81
10,000	123.26	120.67	118.48	116.61	113.62
20,000	246.51	241.34	236.95	233.21	227.23
30,000	369.76	362.01	355.42	349.81	340.85
40,000	493.01	482.67	473.90	466.41	454.46
50,000	616.27	603.34	592.37	583.01	568.08
100,000	1232.53	1206.67	1184.73	1166.01	1136.15
125,000	1540.66	1508.34	1480.91	1457.51	1420.18
150,000	1848.79	1810.01	1777.09	1749.01	1704.22
175,000	2156.92	2111.68	2073.28	2040.51	1988.25
200,000	2465.05	2413.34	2369.46	2332.01	2272.29
225,000	2773.18	2715.01	2665.64	2623.51	2556.32
250,000	3081.31	3016.68	2961.82	2915.01	2840.36
275,000	3389.44	3318.35	3258.00	3206.51	3124.39
300,000	3697.57	3620.01	3554.18	3498.01	3408.43
325,000	4005.70	3921.68	3850.36	3789.51	3692.46
350,000	4313.83	4223.35	4146.55	4081.01	3976.50
375,000	4621.96	4525.02	4442.73	4372.51	4260.53
400,000	4930.09	4826.68	4738.91	4664.01	4544.57
425,000	5238.22	5128.35	5035.09	4955.51	4828.60
450,000	5546.35	5430.02	5331.27	5247.01	5112.64
475,000	5854.48	5731.69	5627.45	5538.51	5396.67
500,000	6162.62	6033.35	5923.63	5830.01	5680.71
525,000	6470.75	6335.02	6219.82	6121.51	5964.74
550,000	6778.88	6636.69	6516.00	6413.01	6248.78
575,000	7087.01	6938.36	6812.18	6704.51	6532.81
600,000	7395.14	7240.02	7108.36	6996.01	6816.85
625,000	7703.27	7541.69	7404.54	7287.51	7100.88
650,000	8011.40	7843.36	7700.72	7579.01	7384.92
675,000	8319.53	8145.03	7996.90	7870.51	7668.95
700,000	8627.66	8446.69	8293.09	8162.01	7952.99
725,000	8935.79	8748.36	8589.27	8453.51	8237.02
750,000	9243.92	9050.03	8885.45	8745.01	8521.06
775,000	9552.05	9351.70	9181.63	9036.51	8805.09
800,000	9860.18	9653.36	9477.81	9328.01	9089.13
825,000	10168.31	9955.03	9773.99	9619.51	9373.16
850,000	10476.44	10256.70	10070.17	9911.01	9657.20
875,000	10784.57	10558.37	10366.36	10202.51	9941.23
900,000	11092.70	10860.03	10662.54	10494.01	10225.27

Monthly Payment Loans   12.50%

Loan Amount	21	22	23	24	25
			Amortization Period in Years		
10	0.12	0.12	0.12	0.11	0.11
20	0.23	0.23	0.23	0.22	0.22
30	0.34	0.34	0.34	0.33	0.33
40	0.45	0.45	0.45	0.44	0.44
50	0.57	0.56	0.56	0.55	0.55
100	1.13	1.12	1.11	1.10	1.10
200	2.25	2.23	2.21	2.20	2.19
300	3.38	3.35	3.32	3.30	3.28
400	4.50	4.46	4.42	4.39	4.37
500	5.63	5.57	5.53	5.49	5.46
1,000	11.25	11.14	11.05	10.98	10.91
2,000	22.49	22.28	22.10	21.95	21.81
3,000	33.73	33.42	33.15	32.92	32.72
4,000	44.97	44.56	44.20	43.89	43.62
5,000	56.22	55.70	55.25	54.86	54.52
10,000	112.43	111.39	110.50	109.72	109.04
20,000	224.85	222.78	220.99	219.43	218.08
30,000	337.27	334.17	331.49	329.15	327.11
40,000	449.69	445.56	441.98	438.86	436.15
50,000	562.11	556.95	552.47	548.58	545.18
100,000	1124.22	1113.90	1104.94	1097.15	1090.36
125,000	1405.28	1392.37	1381.18	1371.44	1362.95
150,000	1686.33	1670.85	1657.41	1645.72	1635.54
175,000	1967.39	1949.32	1933.64	1920.01	1900.12
200,000	2248.44	2227.80	2209.88	2194.29	2180.71
225,000	2529.50	2506.27	2486.11	2468.58	2453.30
250,000	2810.55	2784.74	2762.35	2742.87	2725.89
275,000	3091.60	3063.22	3038.58	3017.15	2998.48
300,000	3372.66	3341.69	3314.82	3291.44	3271.07
325,000	3653.71	3620.17	3591.05	3565.72	3543.66
350,000	3934.77	3898.64	3867.28	3840.01	3816.24
375,000	4215.82	4177.11	4143.52	4114.30	4088.83
400,000	4496.88	4455.59	4419.75	4388.58	4361.42
425,000	4777.93	4734.06	4695.99	4662.87	4634.01
450,000	5058.99	5012.54	4972.22	4937.16	4906.60
475,000	5340.04	5291.01	5248.46	5211.44	5179.19
500,000	5621.10	5569.48	5524.69	5485.73	5451.78
525,000	5902.15	5847.96	5800.92	5760.01	5724.36
550,000	6183.20	6126.43	6077.16	6034.30	5996.95
575,000	6464.26	6404.91	6353.39	6308.59	6269.54
600,000	6745.31	6683.38	6629.63	6582.87	6542.13
625,000	7026.37	6961.85	6905.86	6857.16	6814.72
650,000	7307.42	7240.33	7182.09	7131.44	7087.31
675,000	7588.48	7518.80	7458.33	7405.73	7359.90
700,000	7869.53	7797.28	7734.56	7680.02	7632.48
725,000	8150.59	8075.75	8010.80	7954.30	7905.07
750,000	8431.64	8354.22	8287.03	8228.59	8177.66
775,000	8712.69	8632.70	8563.27	8502.87	8450.25
800,000	8993.75	8911.17	8839.50	8777.16	8722.84
825,000	9274.80	9189.65	9115.73	9051.45	8995.43
850,000	9555.86	9468.12	9391.97	9325.73	9268.02
875,000	9836.91	9746.59	9668.20	9600.02	9540.60
900,000	10117.97	10025.07	9944.44	9874.31	9813.19

Table 7   231

12.50%   Monthly Payment Loans

Loan Amount	Amortization Period in Years				
	26	27	28	29	30
10	0.11	0.11	0.11	0.11	0.11
20	0.22	0.22	0.22	0.22	0.22
30	0.33	0.33	0.33	0.33	0.33
40	0.44	0.44	0.43	0.43	0.43
50	0.55	0.54	0.54	0.54	0.54
100	1.09	1.08	1.08	1.08	1.07
200	2.17	2.16	2.15	2.15	2.14
300	3.26	3.24	3.23	3.22	3.21
400	4.34	4.32	4.30	4.29	4.27
500	5.43	5.40	5.38	5.36	5.34
1,000	10.85	10.80	10.75	10.71	10.68
2,000	21.69	21.59	21.50	21.42	21.35
3,000	32.54	32.38	32.25	32.13	32.02
4,000	43.38	43.17	42.99	42.83	42.70
5,000	54.23	53.97	53.74	53.54	53.37
10,000	108.45	107.93	107.48	107.08	106.73
20,000	216.89	215.85	214.95	214.15	213.46
30,000	325.33	323.78	322.42	321.23	320.18
40,000	433.78	431.70	429.89	428.30	426.91
50,000	542.22	539.63	537.36	535.38	533.63
100,000	1084.43	1079.25	1074.72	1070.75	1067.26
125,000	1355.54	1349.06	1343.40	1338.43	1334.08
150,000	1626.65	1618.88	1612.07	1606.12	1600.89
175,000	1897.75	1888.69	1880.75	1873.80	1867.71
200,000	2168.86	2158.50	2149.43	2141.49	2134.52
225,000	2439.97	2428.31	2418.11	2409.17	2401.33
250,000	2711.07	2698.12	2686.79	2676.86	2668.13
275,000	2982.18	2967.93	2955.47	2944.54	2934.96
300,000	3253.29	3237.75	3224.14	3212.23	3201.78
325,000	3524.39	3507.56	3492.82	3479.91	3468.59
350,000	3795.50	3777.37	3761.50	3747.60	3735.41
375,000	4066.61	4047.18	4030.18	4015.28	4002.22
400,000	4337.71	4316.99	4298.86	4282.97	4269.04
425,000	4608.82	4586.80	4567.54	4550.65	4535.85
450,000	4879.93	4856.62	4836.21	4818.34	4802.66
475,000	5151.03	5126.43	5104.89	5086.02	5069.48
500,000	5422.14	5396.24	5373.57	5353.71	5336.29
525,000	5693.25	5666.05	5642.25	5621.40	5603.11
550,000	5964.36	5935.86	5910.93	5889.08	5869.92
575,000	6235.46	6205.67	6179.61	6156.77	6136.74
600,000	6506.57	6475.49	6448.28	6424.45	6403.55
625,000	6777.68	6745.30	6716.96	6692.14	6670.37
650,000	7048.78	7015.11	6985.64	6959.82	6937.18
675,000	7319.89	7284.92	7254.32	7227.51	7203.99
700,000	7591.00	7554.73	7523.00	7495.19	7470.81
725,000	7862.10	7824.54	7791.67	7762.88	7737.62
750,000	8133.21	8094.36	8060.35	8030.56	8004.44
775,000	8404.32	8364.17	8329.03	8298.25	8271.25
800,000	8675.42	8633.98	8597.71	8565.93	8538.07
825,000	8946.53	8903.79	8866.39	8833.62	8804.88
850,000	9217.64	9173.60	9135.07	9101.30	9071.70
875,000	9488.74	9443.41	9403.74	9368.99	9338.51
900,000	9759.85	9713.23	9672.42	9636.67	9605.32

Monthly Payment Loans   **12.75%**

Loan Amount	Amortization Period in Years				
	5	7	8	10	12
10	0.23	0.19	0.17	0.15	0.14
20	0.46	0.37	0.34	0.30	0.28
30	0.68	0.55	0.51	0.45	0.41
40	0.91	0.73	0.67	0.60	0.55
50	1.14	0.91	0.84	0.74	0.68
100	2.27	1.81	1.67	1.48	1.36
200	4.53	3.62	3.34	2.96	2.72
300	6.79	5.42	5.01	4.44	4.08
400	9.06	7.23	6.67	5.92	5.44
500	11.32	9.03	8.34	7.40	6.80
1,000	22.63	18.06	16.67	14.79	13.60
2,000	45.26	36.12	33.34	29.57	27.19
3,000	67.88	54.17	50.01	44.36	40.70
4,000	90.51	72.23	66.68	59.14	54.37
5,000	113.13	90.29	83.34	73.92	67.97
10,000	226.26	180.57	166.68	147.84	135.93
20,000	452.51	361.13	333.36	295.68	271.85
30,000	678.76	541.69	500.04	443.52	407.77
40,000	905.02	722.26	666.71	591.36	543.69
50,000	1131.27	902.82	833.39	739.20	679.61
100,000	2262.54	1805.64	1666.78	1478.40	1359.21
125,000	2828.17	2257.05	2083.47	1848.00	1699.01
150,000	3393.80	2708.45	2500.16	2217.60	2038.81
175,000	3959.43	3159.86	2916.86	2587.20	2378.61
200,000	4525.07	3611.27	3333.55	2956.80	2718.41
225,000	5090.70	4062.68	3750.24	3326.40	3058.21
250,000	5656.33	4514.09	4166.94	3696.00	3398.01
275,000	6221.96	4965.49	4583.63	4065.60	3737.81
300,000	6787.60	5416.90	5000.32	4435.20	4077.61
325,000	7353.23	5868.31	5417.02	4804.80	4417.41
350,000	7918.86	6319.72	5833.71	5174.40	4757.21
375,000	8484.49	6771.13	6250.40	5544.00	5097.01
400,000	9050.13	7222.53	6667.09	5913.60	5436.81
425,000	9615.76	7673.94	7083.79	6283.20	5776.61
450,000	10181.39	8125.35	7500.48	6652.80	6116.41
475,000	10747.02	8576.76	7917.17	7022.40	6456.21
500,000	11312.66	9028.17	8333.87	7392.00	6796.01
525,000	11878.29	9479.58	8750.56	7761.59	7135.81
550,000	12443.92	9930.98	9167.25	8131.19	7475.61
575,000	13009.55	10382.39	9583.95	8500.79	7815.41
600,000	13575.19	10833.80	10000.64	8870.39	8155.21
625,000	14140.82	11285.21	10417.33	9239.99	8495.01
650,000	14706.45	11736.62	10834.03	9609.59	8834.81
675,000	15272.08	12188.02	11250.72	9979.19	9174.61
700,000	15837.72	12639.43	11667.41	10348.79	9514.41
725,000	16403.35	13090.84	12084.10	10718.39	9854.21
750,000	16968.98	13542.25	12500.80	11087.99	10194.01
775,000	17534.61	13993.66	12917.49	11457.59	10533.81
800,000	18100.25	14445.06	13334.18	11827.19	10873.61
825,000	18665.88	14896.47	13750.88	12196.79	11213.41
850,000	19231.51	15347.88	14167.57	12566.39	11553.21
875,000	19797.14	15799.29	14584.26	12935.99	11893.01
900,000	20362.78	16250.70	15000.96	13305.59	12232.81

Table 7   233

12.75% Monthly Payment Loans

Amortization Period in Years

Loan Amount	15	16	17	18	20
10	0.13	0.13	0.13	0.12	0.12
20	0.25	0.25	0.25	0.24	0.24
30	0.38	0.37	0.37	0.36	0.35
40	0.50	0.49	0.49	0.48	0.47
50	0.63	0.62	0.61	0.60	0.58
100	1.25	1.23	1.21	1.19	1.16
200	2.50	2.45	2.41	2.37	2.31
300	3.75	3.67	3.61	3.55	3.47
400	5.00	4.90	4.81	4.74	4.62
500	6.25	6.12	6.01	5.92	5.77
1,000	12.49	12.24	12.02	11.84	11.54
2,000	24.98	24.47	24.04	23.67	23.08
3,000	37.47	36.70	36.05	35.50	34.62
4,000	49.96	48.94	48.07	47.33	46.16
5,000	62.45	61.17	60.09	59.16	57.70
10,000	124.89	122.33	120.17	118.32	115.39
20,000	249.77	244.66	240.33	236.64	230.77
30,000	374.66	366.99	360.49	354.96	346.15
40,000	499.54	489.32	480.65	473.27	461.53
50,000	624.42	611.65	600.82	591.59	576.91
100,000	1248.84	1223.29	1201.63	1183.17	1153.82
125,000	1561.05	1529.11	1502.03	1478.97	1442.27
150,000	1873.26	1834.93	1802.44	1774.76	1730.72
175,000	2185.47	2140.75	2102.85	2070.55	2019.18
200,000	2497.68	2446.57	2403.25	2366.34	2307.63
225,000	2809.89	2752.39	2703.66	2662.14	2596.08
250,000	3122.10	3058.21	3004.06	2957.93	2884.53
275,000	3434.31	3364.03	3304.47	3253.72	3172.99
300,000	3746.52	3669.85	3604.88	3549.51	3461.44
325,000	4058.73	3975.67	3905.28	3845.31	3749.89
350,000	4370.93	4281.49	4205.69	4141.10	4038.35
375,000	4683.14	4587.32	4506.09	4436.89	4326.80
400,000	4995.35	4893.14	4806.50	4732.68	4615.25
425,000	5307.56	5198.96	5106.91	5028.48	4903.70
450,000	5619.77	5504.78	5407.31	5324.27	5192.16
475,000	5931.98	5810.60	5707.72	5620.06	5480.61
500,000	6244.19	6116.42	6008.12	5915.85	5769.06
525,000	6556.40	6422.24	6308.53	6211.65	6057.52
550,000	6868.61	6728.06	6608.93	6507.44	6345.97
575,000	7180.82	7033.88	6909.34	6803.23	6634.42
600,000	7493.03	7339.70	7209.75	7099.02	6922.87
625,000	7805.24	7645.52	7510.15	7394.82	7211.33
650,000	8117.45	7951.34	7810.56	7690.61	7499.78
675,000	8429.65	8257.16	8110.96	7986.40	7788.23
700,000	8741.86	8562.98	8411.37	8282.19	8076.69
725,000	9054.07	8868.81	8711.78	8577.99	8365.14
750,000	9366.28	9174.63	9012.18	8873.78	8653.59
775,000	9678.49	9480.45	9312.59	9169.57	8942.04
800,000	9990.70	9786.27	9612.99	9465.36	9230.50
825,000	10302.91	10092.09	9913.40	9761.16	9518.95
850,000	10615.12	10397.91	10213.81	10056.95	9807.40
875,000	10927.33	10703.73	10514.21	10352.74	10095.86
900,000	11239.54	11009.55	10814.62	10648.53	10384.31

Monthly Payment Loans   **12.75%**

Loan Amount	Amortization Period in Years				
	21	22	23	24	25
10	0.12	0.12	0.12	0.12	0.12
20	0.23	0.23	0.23	0.23	0.23
30	0.35	0.34	0.34	0.34	0.34
40	0.46	0.46	0.45	0.45	0.45
50	0.58	0.57	0.57	0.56	0.56
100	1.15	1.14	1.13	1.12	1.11
200	2.29	2.27	2.25	2.24	2.22
300	3.43	3.40	3.37	3.35	3.33
400	4.57	4.53	4.50	4.47	4.44
500	5.72	5.67	5.62	5.58	5.55
1,000	11.43	11.33	11.24	11.16	11.10
2,000	22.85	22.65	22.47	22.32	22.19
3,000	34.27	33.97	33.70	33.47	33.28
4,000	45.69	45.29	44.94	44.63	44.37
5,000	57.11	56.61	56.17	55.79	55.46
10,000	114.22	113.21	112.33	111.57	110.91
20,000	228.43	226.41	224.66	223.14	221.82
30,000	342.64	339.61	336.98	334.70	332.72
40,000	456.85	452.81	449.31	446.27	443.63
50,000	571.07	566.01	561.64	557.84	554.53
100,000	1142.13	1132.02	1123.27	1115.67	1109.06
125,000	1427.66	1415.02	1404.08	1394.58	1386.32
150,000	1713.19	1698.03	1684.90	1673.50	1663.58
175,000	1998.72	1981.03	1965.71	1952.41	1940.85
200,000	2284.25	2264.04	2246.53	2231.33	2218.11
225,000	2569.78	2547.04	2527.34	2510.24	2495.37
250,000	2855.31	2830.04	2808.16	2789.16	2772.64
275,000	3140.84	3113.05	3088.97	3068.08	3049.90
300,000	3426.37	3396.05	3369.79	3346.99	3327.16
325,000	3711.90	3679.06	3650.61	3625.91	3604.42
350,000	3997.43	3962.06	3931.42	3904.82	3881.69
375,000	4282.96	4245.06	4212.24	4183.74	4158.95
400,000	4568.49	4528.07	4493.05	4462.65	4436.21
425,000	4854.02	4811.07	4773.87	4741.57	4713.48
450,000	5139.55	5094.08	5054.68	5020.48	4990.74
475,000	5425.08	5377.08	5335.50	5299.40	5268.00
500,000	5710.61	5660.08	5616.31	5578.32	5545.27
525,000	5996.14	5943.09	5897.13	5857.23	5822.53
550,000	6281.67	6226.09	6177.94	6136.15	6099.79
575,000	6567.20	6509.09	6458.76	6415.06	6377.06
600,000	6852.73	6792.10	6739.58	6693.98	6654.32
625,000	7138.26	7075.10	7020.39	6972.89	6931.58
650,000	7423.79	7358.11	7301.21	7251.81	7208.84
675,000	7709.32	7641.11	7582.02	7530.72	7486.11
700,000	7994.85	7924.11	7862.84	7809.64	7763.37
725,000	8280.38	8207.12	8143.65	8088.56	8040.63
750,000	8565.91	8490.12	8424.47	8367.47	8317.90
775,000	8851.44	8773.13	8705.28	8646.39	8595.16
800,000	9136.97	9056.13	8986.10	8925.30	8872.42
825,000	9422.50	9339.13	9266.91	9204.22	9149.69
850,000	9708.03	9622.14	9547.73	9483.13	9426.95
875,000	9993.56	9905.14	9828.55	9762.05	9704.21
900,000	10279.09	10188.15	10109.36	10040.96	9981.48

Table 7   235

12.75% Monthly Payment Loans

Loan Amount	Amortization Period in Years				
	26	27	28	29	30
10	0.12	0.11	0.11	0.11	0.11
20	0.23	0.22	0.22	0.22	0.22
30	0.34	0.33	0.33	0.33	0.33
40	0.45	0.44	0.44	0.44	0.44
50	0.56	0.55	0.55	0.55	0.55
100	1.11	1.10	1.10	1.10	1.09
200	2.21	2.20	2.19	2.19	2.18
300	3.31	3.30	3.29	3.28	3.27
400	4.42	4.40	4.38	4.37	4.35
500	5.52	5.50	5.47	5.46	5.44
1,000	11.04	10.99	10.94	10.91	10.87
2,000	22.07	21.97	21.88	21.81	21.74
3,000	33.10	32.95	32.82	32.71	32.61
4,000	44.14	43.94	43.76	43.61	43.47
5,000	55.17	54.92	54.70	54.51	54.34
10,000	110.33	109.83	109.39	109.01	108.67
20,000	220.66	219.66	218.78	218.01	217.34
30,000	330.99	329.49	328.17	327.02	326.01
40,000	441.32	439.31	437.56	436.02	434.68
50,000	551.65	549.14	546.95	545.03	543.35
100,000	1103.30	1098.28	1093.89	1090.05	1086.70
125,000	1379.12	1372.84	1367.36	1362.57	1358.37
150,000	1654.95	1647.41	1640.83	1635.08	1630.04
175,000	1930.77	1921.98	1914.30	1907.59	1901.72
200,000	2206.59	2196.55	2187.77	2180.10	2173.39
225,000	2482.42	2471.12	2461.25	2452.62	2445.06
250,000	2758.24	2745.68	2734.72	2725.13	2716.74
275,000	3034.06	3020.25	3008.19	2997.64	2988.41
300,000	3309.89	3294.82	3281.66	3270.15	3260.08
325,000	3585.71	3569.39	3555.13	3542.67	3531.76
350,000	3861.54	3843.96	3828.60	3815.18	3803.43
375,000	4137.36	4118.52	4102.07	4087.69	4075.10
400,000	4413.18	4393.09	4375.54	4360.20	4346.78
425,000	4689.01	4667.66	4649.02	4632.72	4618.45
450,000	4964.83	4942.23	4922.49	4905.23	4890.12
475,000	5240.65	5216.79	5195.96	5177.74	5161.80
500,000	5516.48	5491.36	5469.43	5450.25	5433.47
525,000	5792.30	5765.93	5742.90	5722.76	5705.14
550,000	6068.12	6040.50	6016.37	5995.28	5976.82
575,000	6343.95	6315.07	6289.84	6267.79	6248.49
600,000	6619.77	6589.63	6563.31	6540.30	6520.16
625,000	6895.59	6864.20	6836.78	6812.81	6791.84
650,000	7171.42	7138.77	7110.26	7085.33	7063.51
675,000	7447.24	7413.34	7383.73	7357.84	7335.18
700,000	7723.07	7687.91	7657.20	7630.35	7606.86
725,000	7998.89	7962.47	7930.67	7902.86	7878.53
750,000	8274.71	8237.04	8204.14	8175.38	8150.20
775,000	8550.54	8511.61	8477.61	8447.89	8421.88
800,000	8826.36	8786.18	8751.08	8720.40	8693.55
825,000	9102.18	9060.75	9024.55	8992.91	8965.22
850,000	9378.01	9335.31	9298.03	9265.43	9236.90
875,000	9653.83	9609.88	9571.50	9537.94	9508.57
900,000	9929.65	9884.45	9844.97	9810.45	9780.24

Monthly Payment Loans   **13.00%**

Loan Amount	Amortization Period in Years				
	5	7	8	10	12
10	0.23	0.19	0.17	0.15	0.14
20	0.46	0.37	0.34	0.30	0.28
30	0.69	0.55	0.51	0.45	0.42
40	0.92	0.73	0.68	0.60	0.55
50	1.14	0.91	0.85	0.75	0.69
100	2.28	1.82	1.69	1.50	1.38
200	4.56	3.64	3.37	2.99	2.75
300	6.83	5.46	5.05	4.48	4.13
400	9.11	7.28	6.73	5.98	5.50
500	11.38	9.10	8.41	7.47	6.88
1,000	22.76	18.20	16.81	14.94	13.75
2,000	45.51	36.39	33.62	29.87	27.50
3,000	68.26	54.58	50.43	44.80	41.24
4,000	91.02	72.77	67.23	59.73	54.99
5,000	113.77	90.96	84.04	74.66	68.74
10,000	227.54	181.92	168.08	149.32	137.47
20,000	455.07	363.84	336.15	298.63	274.93
30,000	682.60	545.76	504.22	447.94	412.39
40,000	910.13	727.68	672.30	597.25	549.86
50,000	1137.66	909.60	840.37	746.56	687.32
100,000	2275.31	1819.20	1680.73	1493.11	1374.63
125,000	2844.14	2274.00	2100.91	1866.39	1718.29
150,000	3412.97	2728.80	2521.09	2239.67	2061.94
175,000	3981.79	3183.60	2941.27	2612.94	2405.60
200,000	4550.62	3638.40	3361.46	2986.22	2749.26
225,000	5119.45	4093.20	3781.64	3359.50	3092.91
250,000	5688.27	4548.00	4201.82	3732.77	3436.57
275,000	6257.10	5002.79	4622.00	4106.05	3780.22
300,000	6825.93	5457.59	5042.18	4479.33	4123.88
325,000	7394.75	5912.39	5462.36	4852.60	4467.54
350,000	7963.58	6367.19	5882.54	5225.88	4811.19
375,000	8532.41	6821.99	6302.73	5599.16	5154.85
400,000	9101.23	7276.79	6722.91	5972.43	5498.51
425,000	9670.06	7731.59	7143.09	6345.71	5842.16
450,000	10238.89	8186.39	7563.27	6718.99	6185.82
475,000	10807.71	8641.19	7983.45	7092.27	6529.47
500,000	11376.54	9095.99	8403.63	7465.54	6873.13
525,000	11945.37	9550.79	8823.81	7838.82	7216.79
550,000	12514.20	10005.58	9244.00	8212.10	7560.44
575,000	13083.02	10460.38	9664.18	8585.37	7904.10
600,000	13651.85	10915.18	10084.36	8958.65	8247.76
625,000	14220.68	11369.98	10504.54	9331.93	8591.41
650,000	14789.50	11824.78	10924.72	9705.20	8935.07
675,000	15358.33	12279.58	11344.90	10078.48	9278.73
700,000	15927.16	12734.38	11765.08	10451.76	9622.38
725,000	16495.98	13189.18	12185.26	10825.03	9966.04
750,000	17064.81	13643.98	12605.45	11198.31	10309.69
775,000	17633.64	14098.78	13025.63	11571.59	10653.35
800,000	18202.46	14553.58	13445.81	11944.86	10997.01
825,000	18771.29	15008.37	13865.99	12318.14	11340.66
850,000	19340.12	15463.17	14286.17	12691.42	11684.32
875,000	19908.94	15917.97	14706.35	13064.69	12027.98
900,000	20477.77	16372.77	15126.53	13437.97	12371.63

Table 7   237

13.00%   Monthly Payment Loans

Loan Amount	Amortization Period in Years				
	15	16	17	18	20
10	0.13	0.13	0.13	0.13	0.12
20	0.26	0.25	0.25	0.25	0.24
30	0.38	0.38	0.37	0.37	0.36
40	0.51	0.50	0.49	0.49	0.47
50	0.64	0.62	0.61	0.61	0.59
100	1.27	1.24	1.22	1.21	1.18
200	2.54	2.48	2.44	2.41	2.35
300	3.80	3.72	3.66	3.61	3.52
400	5.07	4.96	4.88	4.81	4.69
500	6.33	6.20	6.10	6.01	5.86
1,000	12.66	12.40	12.19	12.01	11.72
2,000	25.31	24.80	24.38	24.01	23.44
3,000	37.96	37.20	36.56	36.02	35.15
4,000	50.61	49.60	48.75	48.02	46.87
5,000	63.27	62.00	60.94	60.03	58.58
10,000	126.53	124.00	121.87	120.05	117.16
20,000	253.05	248.00	243.73	240.09	234.32
30,000	379.58	372.00	365.59	360.13	351.48
40,000	506.10	496.00	487.45	480.18	468.64
50,000	632.63	620.00	609.31	600.22	585.79
100,000	1265.25	1239.99	1218.62	1200.44	1171.58
125,000	1581.56	1549.99	1523.27	1500.55	1464.47
150,000	1897.87	1859.99	1827.93	1800.65	1757.37
175,000	2214.18	2169.98	2132.58	2100.76	2050.26
200,000	2530.49	2479.98	2437.23	2400.87	2343.16
225,000	2846.80	2789.98	2741.89	2700.98	2636.05
250,000	3163.11	3099.97	3046.54	3001.09	2928.94
275,000	3479.42	3409.97	3351.19	3301.19	3221.84
300,000	3795.73	3719.97	3655.85	3601.30	3514.73
325,000	4112.04	4029.97	3960.50	3901.41	3807.63
350,000	4428.35	4339.96	4265.16	4201.52	4100.52
375,000	4744.66	4649.96	4569.81	4501.63	4393.41
400,000	5060.97	4959.96	4874.46	4801.74	4686.31
425,000	5377.28	5269.95	5179.12	5101.84	4979.20
450,000	5693.59	5579.95	5483.77	5401.95	5272.10
475,000	6009.91	5889.95	5788.42	5702.06	5564.99
500,000	6326.22	6199.94	6093.08	6002.17	5857.88
525,000	6642.53	6509.94	6397.73	6302.28	6150.78
550,000	6958.84	6819.94	6702.38	6602.38	6443.67
575,000	7275.15	7129.94	7007.04	6902.49	6736.57
600,000	7591.46	7439.93	7311.69	7202.60	7029.46
625,000	7907.77	7749.93	7616.35	7502.71	7322.35
650,000	8224.08	8059.93	7921.00	7802.82	7615.25
675,000	8540.39	8369.92	8225.65	8102.92	7908.14
700,000	8856.70	8679.92	8530.31	8403.03	8201.03
725,000	9173.01	8989.92	8834.96	8703.14	8493.93
750,000	9489.32	9299.91	9139.61	9003.25	8786.82
775,000	9805.63	9609.91	9444.27	9303.36	9079.72
800,000	10121.94	9919.91	9748.92	9603.47	9372.61
825,000	10438.25	10229.90	10053.57	9903.57	9665.50
850,000	10754.56	10539.90	10358.23	10203.68	9958.40
875,000	11070.87	10849.90	10662.88	10503.79	10251.29
900,000	11387.18	11159.90	10967.53	10803.90	10544.19

Monthly Payment Loans   **13.00%**

Loan Amount	Amortization Period in Years				
	21	22	23	24	25
10	0.12	0.12	0.12	0.12	0.12
20	0.24	0.24	0.23	0.23	0.23
30	0.35	0.35	0.35	0.35	0.34
40	0.47	0.47	0.46	0.46	0.46
50	0.59	0.58	0.58	0.57	0.57
100	1.17	1.16	1.15	1.14	1.13
200	2.33	2.31	2.29	2.27	2.26
300	3.49	3.46	3.43	3.41	3.39
400	4.65	4.61	4.57	4.54	4.52
500	5.81	5.76	5.71	5.68	5.64
1,000	11.61	11.51	11.42	11.35	11.28
2,000	23.21	23.01	22.84	22.69	22.56
3,000	34.81	34.51	34.26	34.03	33.84
4,000	46.41	46.01	45.67	45.38	45.12
5,000	58.01	57.52	57.09	56.72	56.40
10,000	116.02	115.03	114.17	113.43	112.79
20,000	232.03	230.05	228.34	226.86	225.57
30,000	348.04	345.07	342.51	340.29	338.36
40,000	464.05	460.10	456.68	453.71	451.14
50,000	580.06	575.12	570.84	567.14	563.92
100,000	1160.12	1150.23	1141.68	1134.27	1127.84
125,000	1450.15	1437.79	1427.10	1417.84	1409.80
150,000	1740.18	1725.34	1712.52	1701.41	1691.76
175,000	2030.20	2012.90	1997.94	1984.97	1973.72
200,000	2320.23	2300.46	2283.36	2268.54	2255.68
225,000	2610.26	2588.01	2568.78	2552.11	2537.63
250,000	2900.29	2875.57	2854.19	2835.67	2819.59
275,000	3190.32	3163.13	3139.61	3119.24	3101.55
300,000	3480.35	3450.68	3425.03	3402.81	3383.51
325,000	3770.38	3738.24	3710.45	3686.37	3665.47
350,000	4060.40	4025.80	3995.87	3969.94	3947.43
375,000	4350.43	4313.35	4281.29	4253.51	4229.39
400,000	4640.46	4600.91	4566.71	4537.07	4511.35
425,000	4930.49	4888.47	4852.13	4820.64	4793.31
450,000	5220.52	5176.02	5137.55	5104.21	5075.26
475,000	5510.55	5463.58	5422.97	5387.77	5357.22
500,000	5800.58	5751.14	5708.38	5671.34	5639.18
525,000	6090.60	6038.69	5993.80	5954.91	5921.14
550,000	6380.63	6326.25	6279.22	6238.47	6203.10
575,000	6670.66	6613.81	6564.64	6522.04	6485.06
600,000	6960.69	6901.36	6850.06	6805.61	6767.02
625,000	7250.72	7188.92	7135.48	7089.17	7048.98
650,000	7540.75	7476.48	7420.90	7372.74	7330.93
675,000	7830.78	7764.03	7706.32	7656.31	7612.89
700,000	8120.80	8051.59	7991.74	7939.87	7894.85
725,000	8410.83	8339.15	8277.16	8223.44	8176.81
750,000	8700.86	8626.70	8562.57	8507.01	8458.77
775,000	8990.89	8914.26	8847.99	8790.57	8740.73
800,000	9280.92	9201.82	9133.41	9074.14	9022.69
825,000	9570.95	9489.37	9418.83	9357.71	9304.65
850,000	9860.98	9776.93	9704.25	9641.27	9586.61
875,000	10151.00	10064.49	9989.67	9924.84	9868.56
900,000	10441.03	10352.04	10275.09	10208.41	10150.52

Table 7   239

13.00%   Monthly Payment Loans

Loan Amount	Amortization Period in Years				
	26	27	28	29	30
10	0.12	0.12	0.12	0.12	0.12
20	0.23	0.23	0.23	0.23	0.23
30	0.34	0.34	0.34	0.34	0.34
40	0.45	0.45	0.45	0.45	0.45
50	0.57	0.56	0.56	0.56	0.56
100	1.13	1.12	1.12	1.11	1.11
200	2.25	2.24	2.23	2.22	2.22
300	3.37	3.36	3.34	3.33	3.32
400	4.49	4.47	4.46	4.44	4.43
500	5.62	5.59	5.57	5.55	5.54
1,000	11.23	11.18	11.14	11.10	11.07
2,000	22.45	22.35	22.27	22.19	22.13
3,000	33.67	33.53	33.40	33.29	33.19
4,000	44.89	44.70	44.53	44.38	44.25
5,000	56.12	55.87	55.66	55.48	55.31
10,000	112.23	111.74	111.32	110.95	110.62
20,000	224.45	223.48	222.63	221.89	221.24
30,000	336.68	335.22	333.95	332.83	331.86
40,000	448.90	446.96	445.26	443.78	442.48
50,000	561.13	558.69	556.57	554.72	553.10
100,000	1122.25	1117.38	1113.14	1109.44	1106.20
125,000	1402.81	1396.73	1391.42	1386.79	1382.75
150,000	1683.37	1676.07	1669.71	1664.15	1659.30
175,000	1963.93	1955.41	1947.99	1941.51	1935.85
200,000	2244.49	2234.76	2226.27	2218.87	2212.40
225,000	2525.05	2514.10	2504.56	2496.23	2488.95
250,000	2805.61	2793.45	2782.84	2773.58	2765.50
275,000	3086.18	3072.79	3061.12	3050.94	3042.05
300,000	3366.74	3352.13	3339.41	3328.30	3318.60
325,000	3647.30	3631.48	3617.69	3605.66	3595.15
350,000	3927.86	3910.82	3895.97	3883.02	3871.70
375,000	4208.42	4190.17	4174.26	4160.37	4148.25
400,000	4488.98	4469.51	4452.54	4437.73	4424.80
425,000	4769.54	4748.85	4730.82	4715.09	4701.35
450,000	5050.10	5028.20	5009.11	4992.45	4977.90
475,000	5330.66	5307.54	5287.39	5269.81	5254.45
500,000	5611.22	5586.89	5565.67	5547.16	5531.00
525,000	5891.78	5866.23	5843.96	5824.52	5807.55
550,000	6172.35	6145.57	6122.24	6101.88	6084.10
575,000	6452.91	6424.92	6400.52	6379.24	6360.65
600,000	6733.47	6704.26	6678.81	6656.60	6637.20
625,000	7014.03	6983.61	6957.09	6933.95	6913.75
650,000	7294.59	7262.95	7235.37	7211.31	7190.30
675,000	7575.15	7542.29	7513.66	7488.67	7466.85
700,000	7855.71	7821.64	7791.94	7766.03	7743.40
725,000	8136.27	8100.98	8070.22	8043.39	8019.95
750,000	8416.83	8380.33	8348.51	8320.74	8296.50
775,000	8697.39	8659.67	8626.79	8598.10	8573.05
800,000	8977.96	8939.01	8905.07	8875.46	8849.60
825,000	9258.52	9218.36	9183.36	9152.82	9126.15
850,000	9539.08	9497.70	9461.64	9430.18	9402.70
875,000	9819.64	9777.05	9739.92	9707.53	9679.25
900,000	10100.20	10056.39	10018.21	9984.89	9955.80

Monthly Payment Loans <u>13.25%</u>

Loan Amount	Amortization Period in Years				
	5	7	8	10	12
10	0.23	0.19	0.17	0.16	0.14
20	0.46	0.37	0.34	0.31	0.28
30	0.69	0.55	0.51	0.46	0.42
40	0.92	0.74	0.68	0.61	0.56
50	1.15	0.92	0.85	0.76	0.70
100	2.29	1.84	1.70	1.51	1.40
200	4.58	3.67	3.39	3.02	2.79
300	6.87	5.50	5.09	4.53	4.18
400	9.16	7.34	6.78	6.04	5.57
500	11.45	9.17	8.48	7.54	6.96
1,000	22.89	18.33	16.95	15.08	13.91
2,000	45.77	36.66	33.90	30.16	27.81
3,000	68.65	54.99	50.85	45.24	41.71
4,000	91.53	73.32	67.79	60.32	55.61
5,000	114.41	91.65	84.74	75.40	69.51
10,000	228.82	183.29	169.48	150.79	139.02
20,000	457.63	366.57	338.95	301.58	278.03
30,000	686.44	549.85	508.43	452.37	417.04
40,000	915.26	733.13	677.90	603.16	556.06
50,000	1144.07	916.41	847.38	753.95	695.07
100,000	2288.13	1832.82	1694.75	1507.89	1390.14
125,000	2860.16	2291.02	2118.43	1884.87	1737.67
150,000	3432.19	2749.23	2542.12	2261.84	2085.20
175,000	4004.22	3207.43	2965.80	2638.81	2432.73
200,000	4576.26	3665.64	3389.49	3015.78	2780.27
225,000	5148.29	4123.84	3813.17	3392.76	3127.80
250,000	5720.32	4582.04	4236.86	3769.73	3475.33
275,000	6292.35	5040.25	4660.54	4146.70	3822.87
300,000	6864.38	5498.45	5084.23	4523.67	4170.40
325,000	7436.41	5956.65	5507.91	4900.64	4517.93
350,000	8008.44	6414.86	5931.60	5277.62	4865.46
375,000	8580.48	6873.06	6355.28	5654.59	5213.00
400,000	9152.51	7331.27	6778.97	6031.56	5560.53
425,000	9724.54	7789.47	7202.65	6408.53	5908.06
450,000	10296.57	8247.67	7626.34	6785.51	6255.59
475,000	10868.60	8705.88	8050.02	7162.48	6603.13
500,000	11440.63	9164.08	8473.71	7539.45	6950.66
525,000	12012.66	9622.29	8897.39	7916.42	7298.19
550,000	12584.70	10080.49	9321.08	8293.40	7645.73
575,000	13156.73	10538.69	9744.76	8670.37	7993.26
600,000	13728.76	10996.90	10168.45	9047.34	8340.79
625,000	14300.79	11455.10	10592.13	9424.31	8688.32
650,000	14872.82	11913.30	11015.82	9801.28	9035.86
675,000	15444.85	12371.51	11439.50	10178.26	9383.39
700,000	16016.88	12829.71	11863.19	10555.23	9730.92
725,000	16588.91	13287.92	12286.87	10932.20	10078.46
750,000	17160.95	13746.12	12710.56	11309.17	10425.99
775,000	17732.98	14204.32	13134.24	11686.15	10773.52
800,000	18305.01	14662.53	13557.93	12063.12	11121.05
825,000	18877.04	15120.73	13981.61	12440.09	11468.59
850,000	19449.07	15578.94	14405.30	12817.06	11816.12
875,000	20021.10	16037.14	14828.98	13194.04	12163.65
900,000	20593.13	16495.34	15252.67	13571.01	12511.18

Table 7   241

13.25%   Monthly Payment Loans

Amortization Period in Years

Loan Amount	15	16	17	18	20
10	0.13	0.13	0.13	0.13	0.12
20	0.26	0.26	0.25	0.25	0.24
30	0.39	0.38	0.38	0.37	0.36
40	0.52	0.51	0.50	0.49	0.48
50	0.65	0.63	0.62	0.61	0.60
100	1.29	1.26	1.24	1.22	1.19
200	2.57	2.52	2.48	2.44	2.38
300	3.85	3.78	3.71	3.66	3.57
400	5.13	5.03	4.95	4.88	4.76
500	6.41	6.29	6.18	6.09	5.95
1,000	12.82	12.57	12.36	12.18	11.90
2,000	25.64	25.14	24.72	24.36	23.79
3,000	38.46	37.71	37.08	36.54	35.69
4,000	51.27	50.28	49.43	48.72	47.58
5,000	64.09	62.84	61.79	60.89	59.48
10,000	128.18	125.68	123.57	121.78	118.95
20,000	256.35	251.36	247.14	243.56	237.89
30,000	384.53	377.04	370.71	365.34	356.83
40,000	512.70	502.72	494.28	487.12	475.78
50,000	640.87	628.40	617.85	608.90	594.72
100,000	1281.74	1256.79	1235.70	1217.79	1189.44
125,000	1602.18	1570.98	1544.63	1522.24	1486.79
150,000	1922.61	1885.18	1853.55	1826.69	1784.15
175,000	2243.04	2199.38	2162.47	2131.13	2081.51
200,000	2563.48	2513.57	2471.40	2435.58	2378.87
225,000	2883.91	2827.77	2780.32	2740.03	2676.22
250,000	3204.35	3141.96	3089.25	3044.47	2973.58
275,000	3524.78	3456.16	3398.17	3348.92	3270.94
300,000	3845.21	3770.36	3707.10	3653.37	3568.30
325,000	4165.65	4084.55	4016.02	3957.81	3865.65
350,000	4486.08	4398.75	4324.94	4262.26	4163.01
375,000	4806.52	4712.94	4633.87	4566.71	4460.37
400,000	5126.95	5027.14	4942.79	4871.15	4757.73
425,000	5447.38	5341.33	5251.72	5175.60	5055.09
450,000	5767.82	5655.53	5560.64	5480.05	5352.44
475,000	6088.25	5969.73	5869.56	5784.49	5649.80
500,000	6408.69	6283.92	6178.49	6088.94	5947.16
525,000	6729.12	6598.12	6487.41	6393.39	6244.52
550,000	7049.56	6912.31	6796.34	6897.83	6541.87
575,000	7369.99	7226.51	7105.26	7002.28	6839.23
600,000	7690.42	7540.71	7414.19	7306.73	7136.59
625,000	8010.86	7854.90	7723.11	7611.17	7433.95
650,000	8331.29	8169.10	8032.03	7915.62	7731.30
675,000	8651.73	8483.29	8340.96	8220.07	8028.66
700,000	8972.16	8797.49	8649.88	8524.51	8326.02
725,000	9292.59	9111.68	8958.81	8828.96	8623.38
750,000	9613.03	9425.88	9267.73	9133.41	8920.74
775,000	9933.46	9740.08	9576.65	9437.85	9218.09
800,000	10253.90	10054.27	9885.58	9742.30	9515.45
825,000	10574.33	10368.47	10194.50	10046.75	9812.81
850,000	10894.76	10682.66	10503.43	10351.19	10110.17
875,000	11215.20	10996.86	10812.35	10655.64	10407.52
900,000	11535.63	11311.06	11121.28	10960.09	10704.88

Monthly Payment Loans 13.25%

Loan Amount	Amortization Period in Years				
	21	22	23	24	25
10	0.12	0.12	0.12	0.12	0.12
20	0.24	0.24	0.24	0.24	0.23
30	0.36	0.36	0.35	0.35	0.35
40	0.48	0.47	0.47	0.47	0.46
50	0.59	0.59	0.59	0.58	0.58
100	1.18	1.17	1.17	1.16	1.15
200	2.36	2.34	2.33	2.31	2.30
300	3.54	3.51	3.49	3.46	3.45
400	4.72	4.68	4.65	4.62	4.59
500	5.90	5.85	5.81	5.77	5.74
1,000	11.79	11.69	11.61	11.53	11.47
2,000	23.57	23.38	23.21	23.06	22.94
3,000	35.35	35.06	34.81	34.59	34.41
4,000	47.13	46.75	46.41	46.12	45.87
5,000	58.91	58.43	58.01	57.65	57.34
10,000	117.82	116.86	116.02	115.30	114.68
20,000	235.64	233.71	232.04	230.60	229.35
30,000	353.46	350.56	348.06	345.89	344.02
40,000	471.28	467.42	464.08	461.19	458.69
50,000	589.10	584.27	580.09	576.48	573.36
100,000	1178.20	1168.53	1160.18	1152.96	1146.71
125,000	1472.75	1460.66	1450.23	1441.20	1433.38
150,000	1767.30	1752.79	1740.27	1729.44	1720.06
175,000	2061.85	2044.92	2030.31	2017.68	2006.73
200,000	2356.40	2337.06	2320.36	2305.92	2293.41
225,000	2650.95	2629.19	2610.40	2594.16	2580.08
250,000	2945.50	2921.32	2900.45	2882.40	2866.76
275,000	3240.05	3213.45	3190.49	3170.63	3153.43
300,000	3534.60	3505.58	3480.53	3458.87	3440.11
325,000	3829.15	3797.71	3770.58	3747.11	3726.78
350,000	4123.70	4089.84	4060.62	4035.35	4013.46
375,000	4418.25	4381.98	4350.67	4323.59	4300.13
400,000	4712.80	4674.11	4640.71	4611.83	4586.81
425,000	5007.35	4966.24	4930.76	4900.07	4873.48
450,000	5301.90	5258.37	5220.80	5188.31	5160.16
475,000	5596.45	5550.50	5510.84	5476.55	5446.83
500,000	5891.00	5842.63	5800.89	5764.79	5733.51
525,000	6185.55	6134.76	6090.93	6053.02	6020.18
550,000	6480.10	6426.90	6380.98	6341.26	6306.86
575,000	6774.64	6719.03	6671.02	6629.50	6593.53
600,000	7069.19	7011.16	6961.06	6917.74	6880.21
625,000	7363.74	7303.29	7251.11	7205.98	7166.88
650,000	7658.29	7595.42	7541.15	7494.22	7453.56
675,000	7952.84	7887.55	7831.20	7782.46	7740.23
700,000	8247.39	8179.68	8121.24	8070.70	8026.91
725,000	8541.94	8471.81	8411.29	8358.94	8313.58
750,000	8836.49	8763.95	8701.33	8647.18	8600.26
775,000	9131.04	9056.08	8991.37	8935.41	8886.93
800,000	9425.59	9348.21	9281.42	9223.65	9173.61
825,000	9720.14	9640.34	9571.46	9511.89	9460.28
850,000	10014.69	9932.47	9861.51	9800.13	9746.96
875,000	10309.24	10224.60	10151.55	10088.37	10033.63
900,000	10603.79	10516.73	10441.59	10376.61	10320.31

Table 7   243

13.25%   Monthly Payment Loans

Amortization Period in Years

Loan Amount	26	27	28	29	30
10	0.12	0.12	0.12	0.12	0.12
20	0.23	0.23	0.23	0.23	0.23
30	0.35	0.35	0.34	0.34	0.34
40	0.46	0.46	0.46	0.46	0.46
50	0.58	0.57	0.57	0.57	0.57
100	1.15	1.14	1.14	1.13	1.13
200	2.29	2.28	2.27	2.26	2.26
300	3.43	3.41	3.40	3.39	3.38
400	4.57	4.55	4.53	4.52	4.51
500	5.71	5.69	5.67	5.65	5.63
1,000	11.42	11.37	11.33	11.29	11.26
2,000	22.83	22.74	22.65	22.58	22.52
3,000	34.24	34.10	33.98	33.87	33.78
4,000	45.66	45.47	45.30	45.16	45.04
5,000	57.07	56.83	56.63	56.45	56.29
10,000	114.13	113.66	113.25	112.89	112.58
20,000	228.26	227.32	226.50	225.78	225.16
30,000	342.39	340.97	339.74	338.67	337.74
40,000	456.51	454.63	452.99	451.56	450.31
50,000	570.64	568.28	566.23	564.45	562.89
100,000	1141.28	1136.56	1132.46	1128.89	1125.78
125,000	1426.60	1420.70	1415.57	1411.11	1407.22
150,000	1711.91	1704.84	1698.69	1693.33	1688.67
175,000	1997.23	1988.98	1981.80	1975.55	1970.11
200,000	2282.55	2273.12	2264.92	2257.77	2251.55
225,000	2567.87	2557.26	2548.03	2540.00	2533.00
250,000	2853.19	2841.40	2831.14	2822.22	2814.44
275,000	3138.50	3125.54	3114.26	3104.44	3095.88
300,000	3423.82	3409.68	3397.37	3386.66	3377.33
325,000	3709.14	3693.82	3680.49	3668.88	3658.77
350,000	3994.46	3977.96	3963.60	3951.10	3940.21
375,000	4279.78	4262.09	4246.71	4233.32	4221.66
400,000	4565.10	4546.23	4529.83	4515.54	4503.10
425,000	4850.41	4830.37	4812.94	4797.77	4784.54
450,000	5135.73	5114.51	5096.06	5079.99	5065.99
475,000	5421.05	5398.65	5379.17	5362.21	5347.43
500,000	5706.37	5682.79	5662.28	5644.43	5628.87
525,000	5991.69	5966.93	5945.40	5926.65	5910.32
550,000	6277.00	6251.07	6228.51	6208.87	6191.76
575,000	6562.32	6535.21	6511.63	6491.09	6473.20
600,000	6847.64	6819.35	6794.74	6773.31	6754.65
625,000	7132.96	7103.49	7077.85	7055.54	7036.09
650,000	7418.28	7387.63	7360.97	7337.76	7317.53
675,000	7703.60	7671.77	7644.08	7619.98	7598.98
700,000	7988.91	7955.91	7927.20	7902.20	7880.42
725,000	8274.23	8240.04	8210.31	8184.42	8161.86
750,000	8559.55	8524.18	8493.42	8466.64	8443.31
775,000	8844.87	8808.32	8776.54	8748.86	8724.75
800,000	9130.19	9092.46	9059.65	9031.08	9006.19
825,000	9415.50	9376.60	9342.77	9313.31	9287.64
850,000	9700.82	9660.74	9625.88	9595.53	9569.08
875,000	9986.14	9944.88	9908.99	9877.75	9850.52
900,000	10271.46	10229.02	10192.11	10159.97	10131.97

Monthly Payment Loans   **13.50%**

Loan Amount	5	7	8	10	12
10	0.24	0.19	0.18	0.16	0.15
20	0.47	0.37	0.35	0.31	0.29
30	0.70	0.56	0.52	0.46	0.43
40	0.93	0.74	0.69	0.61	0.57
50	1.16	0.93	0.86	0.77	0.71
100	2.31	1.85	1.71	1.53	1.41
200	4.61	3.70	3.42	3.05	2.82
300	6.91	5.54	5.13	4.57	4.22
400	9.21	7.39	6.84	6.10	5.63
500	11.51	9.24	8.55	7.62	7.03
1,000	23.01	18.47	17.09	15.23	14.06
2,000	46.02	36.93	34.18	30.46	28.12
3,000	69.03	55.40	51.27	45.69	42.18
4,000	92.04	73.86	68.36	60.91	56.23
5,000	115.05	92.33	85.45	76.14	70.29
10,000	230.10	184.65	170.89	152.28	140.58
20,000	460.20	369.30	341.77	304.55	281.15
30,000	690.30	553.95	512.65	456.83	421.72
40,000	920.40	738.60	683.53	609.10	562.29
50,000	1150.50	923.25	854.41	761.38	702.86
100,000	2300.99	1846.49	1708.82	1522.75	1405.72
125,000	2876.24	2308.12	2136.02	1903.43	1757.15
150,000	3451.48	2769.74	2563.23	2284.12	2108.58
175,000	4026.73	3231.36	2990.43	2664.81	2460.01
200,000	4601.97	3692.98	3417.64	3045.49	2811.44
225,000	5177.22	4154.61	3844.84	3426.18	3162.87
250,000	5752.47	4616.23	4272.04	3806.86	3514.30
275,000	6327.71	5077.85	4699.25	4187.55	3865.73
300,000	6902.96	5539.47	5126.45	4568.23	4217.16
325,000	7478.20	6001.10	5553.66	4948.92	4568.59
350,000	8053.45	6462.72	5980.86	5329.61	4920.02
375,000	8628.70	6924.34	6408.06	5710.29	5271.44
400,000	9203.94	7385.96	6835.27	6090.98	5622.87
425,000	9779.19	7847.58	7262.47	6471.66	5974.30
450,000	10354.44	8309.21	7689.68	6852.35	6325.73
475,000	10929.68	8770.83	8116.88	7233.03	6677.16
500,000	11504.93	9232.45	8544.08	7613.72	7028.59
525,000	12080.17	9694.07	8971.29	7994.41	7380.02
550,000	12655.42	10155.70	9398.49	8375.09	7731.45
575,000	13230.67	10617.32	9825.70	8755.78	8082.88
600,000	13805.91	11078.94	10252.90	9136.46	8434.31
625,000	14381.16	11540.56	10680.10	9517.15	8785.74
650,000	14956.40	12002.19	11107.31	9897.83	9137.17
675,000	15531.65	12463.81	11534.51	10278.52	9488.60
700,000	16106.90	12925.43	11961.72	10659.21	9840.03
725,000	16682.14	13387.05	12388.92	11039.89	10191.45
750,000	17257.39	13848.67	12816.12	11420.58	10542.88
775,000	17832.64	14310.30	13243.33	11801.26	10894.31
800,000	18407.88	14771.92	13670.53	12181.95	11245.74
825,000	18983.13	15233.54	14097.74	12562.63	11597.17
850,000	19558.37	15695.16	14524.94	12943.32	11948.60
875,000	20133.62	16156.79	14952.14	13324.01	12300.03
900,000	20708.87	16618.41	15379.35	13704.69	12651.46

Table 7   245

13.50%   Monthly Payment Loans

Amortization Period in Years

Loan Amount	15	16	17	18	20
10	0.13	0.13	0.13	0.13	0.13
20	0.26	0.26	0.26	0.25	0.25
30	0.39	0.39	0.38	0.38	0.37
40	0.52	0.51	0.51	0.50	0.49
50	0.65	0.64	0.63	0.62	0.61
100	1.30	1.28	1.26	1.24	1.21
200	2.60	2.55	2.51	2.48	2.42
300	3.90	3.83	3.76	3.71	3.63
400	5.20	5.10	5.02	4.95	4.83
500	6.50	6.37	6.27	6.18	6.04
1,000	12.99	12.74	12.53	12.36	12.08
2,000	25.97	25.48	25.06	24.71	24.15
3,000	38.95	38.22	37.59	37.06	36.23
4,000	51.94	50.95	50.12	49.41	48.30
5,000	64.92	63.69	62.65	61.77	60.37
10,000	129.84	127.37	125.29	123.53	120.74
20,000	259.67	254.74	250.58	247.05	241.48
30,000	389.50	382.11	375.87	370.57	362.22
40,000	519.33	509.47	501.15	494.10	482.95
50,000	649.16	636.84	626.44	617.62	603.69
100,000	1298.32	1273.67	1252.87	1235.24	1207.38
125,000	1622.90	1592.09	1566.09	1544.04	1509.22
150,000	1947.48	1910.51	1879.31	1852.85	1811.07
175,000	2272.06	2228.92	2192.53	2161.66	2112.91
200,000	2596.64	2547.34	2505.74	2470.47	2414.75
225,000	2921.22	2865.76	2818.96	2779.28	2716.60
250,000	3245.80	3184.18	3132.18	3088.08	3018.44
275,000	3570.38	3502.59	3445.39	3396.89	3320.29
300,000	3894.96	3821.01	3758.61	3705.70	3622.13
325,000	4219.54	4139.43	4071.83	4014.51	3923.97
350,000	4544.12	4457.84	4385.05	4323.31	4225.82
375,000	4868.70	4776.26	4698.26	4632.12	4527.66
400,000	5193.28	5094.68	5011.48	4940.93	4829.50
425,000	5517.86	5413.09	5324.70	5249.74	5131.35
450,000	5842.44	5731.51	5637.91	5558.55	5433.19
475,000	6167.02	6049.93	5951.13	5867.35	5735.03
500,000	6491.60	6368.35	6264.35	6176.16	6036.88
525,000	6816.18	6686.76	6577.57	6484.97	6338.72
550,000	7140.76	7005.18	6890.78	6793.78	6640.57
575,000	7465.34	7323.60	7204.00	7102.58	6942.41
600,000	7789.92	7642.01	7517.22	7411.39	7244.25
625,000	8114.50	7960.43	7830.43	7720.20	7546.10
650,000	8439.08	8278.85	8143.65	8029.01	7847.94
675,000	8763.66	8597.26	8456.67	8337.82	8149.78
700,000	9088.23	8915.68	8770.09	8646.62	8451.63
725,000	9412.81	9234.10	9083.30	8955.43	8753.47
750,000	9737.39	9552.52	9396.52	9264.24	9055.32
775,000	10061.97	9870.93	9709.74	9573.05	9357.16
800,000	10386.55	10189.35	10022.96	9881.86	9659.00
825,000	10711.13	10507.77	10336.17	10190.66	9960.85
850,000	11035.71	10826.18	10649.39	10499.47	10262.69
875,000	11360.29	11144.60	10962.61	10808.28	10564.53
900,000	11684.87	11463.02	11275.82	11117.09	10866.38

Monthly Payment Loans   **13.50%**

Loan Amount	\multicolumn{5}{c}{Amortization Period in Years}				
	21	22	23	24	25
10	0.12	0.12	0.12	0.12	0.12
20	0.24	0.24	0.24	0.24	0.24
30	0.36	0.36	0.36	0.36	0.35
40	0.48	0.48	0.48	0.47	0.47
50	0.60	0.60	0.59	0.59	0.59
100	1.20	1.19	1.18	1.18	1.17
200	2.40	2.38	2.36	2.35	2.34
300	3.59	3.57	3.54	3.52	3.50
400	4.79	4.75	4.72	4.69	4.67
500	5.99	5.94	5.90	5.86	5.83
1,000	11.97	11.87	11.79	11.72	11.66
2,000	23.93	23.74	23.58	23.44	23.32
3,000	35.90	35.61	35.37	35.16	34.97
4,000	47.86	47.48	47.16	46.87	46.63
5,000	59.82	59.35	58.94	58.59	58.29
10,000	119.64	118.70	117.88	117.18	116.57
20,000	239.28	237.39	235.76	234.35	233.13
30,000	358.92	356.08	353.63	351.52	349.70
40,000	478.55	474.77	471.51	468.70	466.26
50,000	598.19	593.46	589.39	585.87	582.83
100,000	1196.37	1186.92	1178.77	1171.73	1165.65
125,000	1495.47	1483.64	1473.46	1464.66	1457.06
150,000	1794.56	1780.37	1768.15	1757.60	1748.47
175,000	2093.65	2077.10	2062.84	2050.53	2039.88
200,000	2392.74	2373.83	2357.53	2343.46	2331.29
225,000	2691.84	2670.55	2652.22	2636.39	2622.71
250,000	2990.93	2967.28	2946.91	2929.32	2914.12
275,000	3290.02	3264.01	3241.60	3222.25	3205.53
300,000	3589.11	3560.74	3536.29	3515.19	3496.94
325,000	3888.21	3857.46	3830.98	3808.12	3788.35
350,000	4187.30	4154.19	4125.67	4101.05	4079.76
375,000	4486.39	4450.92	4420.36	4393.98	4371.17
400,000	4785.48	4747.65	4715.05	4686.91	4662.58
425,000	5084.58	5044.37	5009.74	4979.85	4954.00
450,000	5383.67	5341.10	5304.43	5272.78	5245.41
475,000	5682.76	5637.83	5599.12	5565.71	5536.82
500,000	5981.85	5934.56	5893.81	5858.64	5828.23
525,000	6280.95	6231.29	6188.50	6151.57	6119.64
550,000	6580.04	6528.01	6483.19	6444.50	6411.05
575,000	6879.13	6824.74	6777.88	6737.44	6702.46
600,000	7178.22	7121.47	7072.57	7030.37	6993.87
625,000	7477.32	7418.20	7367.26	7323.30	7285.29
650,000	7776.41	7714.92	7661.95	7616.23	7576.70
675,000	8075.50	8011.65	7956.64	7909.16	7868.11
700,000	8374.59	8308.38	8251.33	8202.09	8159.52
725,000	8673.69	8605.11	8546.02	8495.03	8450.93
750,000	8972.78	8901.83	8840.72	8787.96	8742.34
775,000	9271.87	9198.56	9135.41	9080.89	9033.75
800,000	9570.96	9495.29	9430.10	9373.82	9325.16
825,000	9870.06	9792.02	9724.79	9666.75	9616.58
850,000	10169.15	10088.74	10019.48	9959.69	9907.99
875,000	10468.24	10385.47	10314.17	10252.62	10199.40
900,000	10767.33	10682.20	10608.86	10545.55	10490.81

Table 7   247

13.50% Monthly Payment Loans

Amortization Period in Years

Loan Amount	26	27	28	29	30
10	0.12	0.12	0.12	0.12	0.12
20	0.24	0.24	0.24	0.23	0.23
30	0.35	0.35	0.35	0.35	0.35
40	0.47	0.47	0.47	0.46	0.46
50	0.59	0.58	0.58	0.58	0.58
100	1.17	1.16	1.16	1.15	1.15
200	2.33	2.32	2.31	2.30	2.30
300	3.49	3.47	3.46	3.45	3.44
400	4.65	4.63	4.61	4.60	4.59
500	5.81	5.78	5.76	5.75	5.73
1,000	11.61	11.56	11.52	11.49	11.46
2,000	23.21	23.12	23.04	22.97	22.91
3,000	34.82	34.68	34.56	34.46	34.37
4,000	46.42	46.24	46.08	45.94	45.82
5,000	58.02	57.80	57.60	57.43	57.28
10,000	116.04	115.59	115.19	114.85	114.55
20,000	232.08	231.17	230.37	229.69	229.09
30,000	348.12	346.75	345.56	344.53	343.63
40,000	464.16	462.33	460.74	459.37	458.17
50,000	580.19	577.91	575.93	574.21	572.71
100,000	1160.38	1155.82	1151.85	1148.41	1145.42
125,000	1450.48	1444.77	1439.82	1435.51	1431.77
150,000	1740.57	1733.72	1727.78	1722.61	1718.12
175,000	2030.67	2022.68	2015.74	2009.72	2004.48
200,000	2320.76	2311.63	2303.70	2296.82	2290.83
225,000	2610.86	2600.58	2591.67	2583.92	2577.18
250,000	2900.95	2889.54	2879.63	2871.02	2863.54
275,000	3191.05	3178.49	3167.59	3158.12	3149.89
300,000	3481.14	3467.44	3455.55	3445.22	3436.24
325,000	3771.23	3756.39	3743.51	3732.32	3722.59
350,000	4061.33	4045.35	4031.48	4019.43	4008.95
375,000	4351.42	4334.30	4319.44	4306.53	4295.30
400,000	4641.52	4623.25	4607.40	4593.63	4581.65
425,000	4931.61	4912.21	4895.36	4880.73	4868.01
450,000	5221.71	5201.16	5183.33	5167.83	5154.36
475,000	5511.80	5490.11	5471.29	5454.93	5440.71
500,000	5801.90	5779.07	5759.25	5742.03	5727.07
525,000	6091.99	6068.02	6047.21	6029.14	6013.42
550,000	6382.09	6356.97	6335.17	6316.24	6299.77
575,000	6672.18	6645.92	6623.14	6603.34	6586.13
600,000	6962.27	6934.88	6911.10	6890.44	6872.48
625,000	7252.37	7223.83	7199.06	7177.54	7158.83
650,000	7542.46	7512.78	7487.02	7464.64	7445.18
675,000	7832.56	7801.74	7774.99	7751.74	7731.54
700,000	8122.65	8090.69	8062.95	8038.85	8017.89
725,000	8412.75	8379.64	8350.91	8325.95	8304.24
750,000	8702.84	8668.60	8638.87	8613.05	8590.60
775,000	8992.94	8957.55	8926.83	8900.15	8876.95
800,000	9283.03	9246.50	9214.80	9187.25	9163.30
825,000	9573.13	9535.46	9502.76	9474.35	9449.66
850,000	9863.22	9824.41	9790.72	9761.46	9736.01
875,000	10153.32	10113.36	10078.68	10048.56	10022.36
900,000	10443.41	10402.31	10366.65	10335.66	10308.71

Monthly Payment Loans   13.75%

Loan Amount	Amortization Period in Years				
	5	7	8	10	12
10	0.24	0.19	0.18	0.16	0.15
20	0.47	0.38	0.35	0.31	0.29
30	0.70	0.56	0.52	0.47	0.43
40	0.93	0.75	0.69	0.62	0.57
50	1.16	0.94	0.87	0.77	0.72
100	2.32	1.87	1.73	1.54	1.43
200	4.63	3.73	3.45	3.08	2.85
300	6.95	5.59	5.17	4.62	4.27
400	9.26	7.45	6.90	6.16	5.69
500	11.57	9.31	8.62	7.69	7.11
1,000	23.14	18.61	17.23	15.38	14.22
2,000	46.28	37.21	34.46	30.76	28.43
3,000	69.42	55.81	51.69	46.14	42.65
4,000	92.56	74.41	68.92	61.51	56.86
5,000	115.70	93.02	86.15	76.89	71.07
10,000	231.39	186.03	172.30	153.77	142.14
20,000	462.78	372.05	344.60	307.54	284.28
30,000	694.17	558.07	516.89	461.31	426.42
40,000	925.56	744.09	689.19	615.07	568.56
50,000	1156.95	930.11	861.48	768.84	710.70
100,000	2313.89	1860.22	1722.96	1537.67	1421.39
125,000	2892.36	2325.28	2153.70	1922.09	1776.73
150,000	3470.83	2790.33	2584.43	2306.51	2132.08
175,000	4049.30	3255.39	3015.17	2690.92	2487.42
200,000	4627.77	3720.44	3445.91	3075.34	2842.77
225,000	5206.25	4185.50	3876.65	3459.76	3198.12
250,000	5784.72	4650.55	4307.39	3844.18	3553.46
275,000	6363.19	5115.60	4738.12	4228.59	3908.81
300,000	6941.66	5580.66	5168.86	4613.01	4264.15
325,000	7520.13	6045.71	5599.60	4997.43	4619.50
350,000	8098.60	6510.77	6030.34	5381.84	4974.84
375,000	8677.07	6975.82	6461.08	5766.26	5330.19
400,000	9255.54	7440.88	6891.82	6150.68	5685.54
425,000	9834.01	7905.93	7322.55	6535.09	6040.88
450,000	10412.49	8370.99	7753.29	6919.51	6396.23
475,000	10990.96	8836.04	8184.03	7303.93	6751.57
500,000	11569.43	9301.09	8614.77	7688.35	7106.92
525,000	12147.90	9766.15	9045.51	8072.76	7462.26
550,000	12726.37	10231.20	9476.24	8457.18	7817.61
575,000	13304.84	10696.26	9906.98	8841.60	8172.96
600,000	13883.31	11161.31	10337.72	9226.01	8528.30
625,000	14461.78	11626.37	10768.46	9610.43	8883.65
650,000	15040.25	12091.42	11199.20	9994.85	9238.99
675,000	15618.73	12556.48	11629.94	10379.26	9594.34
700,000	16197.20	13021.53	12060.67	10763.68	9949.68
725,000	16775.67	13486.59	12491.41	11148.10	10305.03
750,000	17354.14	13951.64	12922.15	11532.52	10660.38
775,000	17932.61	14416.69	13352.89	11916.93	11015.72
800,000	18511.08	14881.75	13783.63	12301.35	11371.07
825,000	19089.55	15346.80	14214.36	12685.77	11726.41
850,000	19668.03	15811.86	14645.10	13070.18	12081.76
875,000	20246.49	16276.91	15075.84	13454.60	12437.10
900,000	20824.97	16741.97	15506.58	13839.02	12792.45

Table 7   249

13.75%   Monthly Payment Loans

Loan Amount	15	16	17	18	20
10	0.14	0.13	0.13	0.13	0.13
20	0.27	0.26	0.26	0.26	0.25
30	0.40	0.39	0.39	0.38	0.37
40	0.53	0.52	0.51	0.51	0.50
50	0.66	0.65	0.64	0.63	0.62
100	1.32	1.30	1.28	1.26	1.23
200	2.63	2.59	2.55	2.51	2.46
300	3.95	3.88	3.82	3.76	3.68
400	5.26	5.17	5.09	5.02	4.91
500	6.58	6.46	6.36	6.27	6.13
1,000	13.15	12.91	12.71	12.53	12.26
2,000	26.30	25.82	25.41	25.06	24.51
3,000	39.45	38.72	38.11	37.59	36.77
4,000	52.60	51.63	50.81	50.12	49.02
5,000	65.75	64.54	63.51	62.64	61.28
10,000	131.50	129.07	127.02	125.28	122.55
20,000	263.00	258.13	254.03	250.56	245.09
30,000	394.50	387.20	381.04	375.83	367.63
40,000	526.00	516.26	508.06	501.11	490.17
50,000	657.50	645.33	635.07	626.39	612.71
100,000	1314.99	1290.65	1270.13	1252.77	1225.41
125,000	1643.74	1613.31	1587.67	1565.96	1531.76
150,000	1972.49	1935.97	1905.20	1879.15	1838.11
175,000	2301.23	2258.63	2222.73	2192.34	2144.46
200,000	2629.98	2581.29	2540.26	2505.53	2450.82
225,000	2958.73	2903.95	2857.80	2818.72	2757.17
250,000	3287.47	3226.61	3175.33	3131.91	3063.52
275,000	3616.22	3549.27	3492.86	3445.11	3369.87
300,000	3944.97	3871.93	3810.39	3758.30	3676.22
325,000	4273.71	4194.59	4127.92	4071.49	3982.57
350,000	4602.46	4517.25	4445.46	4384.68	4288.92
375,000	4931.21	4839.91	4762.99	4697.87	4595.28
400,000	5259.95	5162.57	5080.52	5011.06	4901.63
425,000	5588.70	5485.23	5398.05	5324.25	5207.98
450,000	5917.45	5807.89	5715.59	5637.44	5514.33
475,000	6246.19	6130.55	6033.12	5950.63	5820.68
500,000	6574.94	6453.21	6350.65	6263.82	6127.03
525,000	6903.69	6775.87	6668.18	6577.02	6433.38
550,000	7232.43	7098.53	6985.72	6890.21	6739.73
575,000	7561.18	7421.19	7303.25	7203.40	7046.09
600,000	7889.93	7743.85	7620.78	7516.59	7352.44
625,000	8218.68	8066.51	7938.31	7829.78	7658.79
650,000	8547.42	8389.17	8255.84	8142.97	7965.14
675,000	8876.17	8711.83	8573.38	8456.16	8271.49
700,000	9204.92	9034.49	8890.91	8769.35	8577.84
725,000	9533.66	9357.15	9208.44	9082.54	8884.19
750,000	9862.41	9679.81	9525.97	9395.73	9190.55
775,000	10191.16	10002.47	9843.51	9708.93	9496.90
800,000	10519.90	10325.13	10161.04	10022.12	9803.25
825,000	10848.65	10647.79	10478.57	10335.31	10109.60
850,000	11177.40	10970.45	10796.10	10648.50	10415.95
875,000	11506.14	11293.11	11113.64	10961.69	10722.30
900,000	11834.89	11615.77	11431.17	11274.88	11028.65

Monthly Payment Loans   **13.75%**

Loan Amount	Amortization Period in Years				
	21	22	23	24	25
10	0.13	0.13	0.12	0.12	0.12
20	0.25	0.25	0.24	0.24	0.24
30	0.37	0.37	0.36	0.36	0.36
40	0.49	0.49	0.48	0.48	0.48
50	0.61	0.61	0.60	0.60	0.60
100	1.22	1.21	1.20	1.20	1.19
200	2.43	2.42	2.40	2.39	2.37
300	3.65	3.62	3.60	3.58	3.56
400	4.86	4.83	4.79	4.77	4.74
500	6.08	6.03	5.99	5.96	5.93
1,000	12.15	12.06	11.98	11.91	11.85
2,000	24.30	24.11	23.95	23.82	23.70
3,000	36.44	36.17	35.93	35.72	35.54
4,000	48.59	48.22	47.90	47.63	47.39
5,000	60.74	60.27	59.88	59.53	59.24
10,000	121.47	120.54	119.75	119.06	118.47
20,000	242.93	241.08	239.49	238.12	236.94
30,000	364.39	361.62	359.23	357.18	355.40
40,000	485.86	482.16	478.98	476.24	473.87
50,000	607.32	602.69	598.72	595.29	592.34
100,000	1214.63	1205.38	1197.43	1190.58	1184.67
125,000	1518.29	1506.73	1496.79	1488.23	1480.84
150,000	1821.95	1808.07	1796.15	1785.87	1777.00
175,000	2125.60	2109.42	2095.50	2083.52	2073.17
200,000	2429.26	2410.76	2394.86	2381.16	2369.34
225,000	2732.92	2712.11	2694.22	2678.80	2665.50
250,000	3036.57	3013.45	2993.57	2976.45	2961.67
275,000	3340.23	3314.80	3292.93	3274.09	3257.84
300,000	3643.89	3616.14	3592.29	3571.74	3554.00
325,000	3947.54	3917.49	3891.64	3869.38	3850.17
350,000	4251.20	4218.83	4191.00	4167.03	4146.34
375,000	4554.86	4520.18	4490.36	4464.67	4442.50
400,000	4858.51	4821.52	4789.72	4762.31	4738.67
425,000	5162.17	5122.87	5089.07	5059.96	5034.84
450,000	5465.83	5424.21	5388.43	5357.60	5331.00
475,000	5769.48	5725.56	5687.79	5655.25	5627.17
500,000	6073.14	6026.90	5987.14	5952.89	5923.33
525,000	6376.80	6328.25	6286.50	6250.54	6219.50
550,000	6680.45	6629.59	6585.86	6548.18	6515.67
575,000	6984.11	6930.94	6885.21	6845.82	6811.83
600,000	7287.77	7232.28	7184.57	7143.47	7108.00
625,000	7591.42	7533.63	7483.93	7441.11	7404.17
650,000	7895.08	7834.97	7783.28	7738.76	7700.33
675,000	8198.74	8136.32	8082.64	8036.40	7996.50
700,000	8502.39	8437.66	8382.00	8334.05	8292.67
725,000	8806.05	8739.01	8681.36	8631.69	8588.83
750,000	9109.71	9040.35	8980.71	8929.33	8885.00
775,000	9413.36	9341.69	9280.07	9226.98	9181.17
800,000	9717.02	9643.04	9579.43	9524.62	9477.33
825,000	10020.68	9944.38	9878.78	9822.27	9773.50
850,000	10324.33	10245.73	10178.14	10119.91	10069.67
875,000	10627.99	10547.07	10477.50	10417.56	10365.83
900,000	10931.65	10848.42	10776.85	10715.20	10662.00

Table 7   251

13.75%   **Monthly Payment Loans**

Loan Amount	Amortization Period in Years				
	26	27	28	29	30
10	0.12	0.12	0.12	0.12	0.12
20	0.24	0.24	0.24	0.24	0.24
30	0.36	0.36	0.36	0.36	0.35
40	0.48	0.48	0.47	0.47	0.47
50	0.59	0.59	0.59	0.59	0.59
100	1.18	1.18	1.18	1.17	1.17
200	2.36	2.36	2.35	2.34	2.34
300	3.54	3.53	3.52	3.51	3.50
400	4.72	4.71	4.69	4.68	4.67
500	5.90	5.88	5.86	5.84	5.83
1,000	11.80	11.76	11.72	11.68	11.66
2,000	23.60	23.51	23.43	23.36	23.31
3,000	35.39	35.26	35.14	35.04	34.96
4,000	47.19	47.01	46.86	46.72	46.61
5,000	58.98	58.76	58.57	58.40	58.26
10,000	117.96	117.52	117.14	116.80	116.52
20,000	235.92	235.03	234.27	233.60	233.03
30,000	353.87	352.55	351.40	350.40	349.54
40,000	471.83	470.06	468.53	467.20	466.05
50,000	589.78	587.57	585.66	584.00	582.56
100,000	1179.56	1175.14	1171.32	1168.00	1165.12
125,000	1474.45	1468.93	1464.14	1459.99	1456.40
150,000	1769.34	1762.71	1756.97	1751.99	1747.67
175,000	2064.23	2056.50	2049.80	2043.99	2038.95
200,000	2359.12	2350.28	2342.63	2335.99	2330.23
225,000	2654.01	2644.07	2635.45	2627.99	2621.51
250,000	2948.90	2937.85	2928.28	2919.98	2912.79
275,000	3243.79	3231.63	3221.11	3211.98	3204.06
300,000	3538.68	3525.42	3513.94	3503.98	3495.34
325,000	3833.57	3819.20	3806.76	3795.98	3786.62
350,000	4128.46	4112.99	4099.59	4087.98	4077.90
375,000	4423.35	4406.77	4392.42	4379.97	4369.18
400,000	4718.24	4700.56	4685.25	4671.97	4660.46
425,000	5013.13	4994.34	4978.07	4963.97	4951.73
450,000	5308.01	5288.13	5270.90	5255.97	5243.01
475,000	5602.90	5581.91	5563.73	5547.97	5534.29
500,000	5897.79	5875.70	5856.56	5839.96	5825.57
525,000	6192.68	6169.48	6149.38	6131.96	6116.85
550,000	6487.57	6463.26	6442.21	6423.96	6408.12
575,000	6782.46	6757.05	6735.04	6715.96	6699.40
600,000	7077.35	7050.83	7027.87	7007.95	6990.68
625,000	7372.24	7344.62	7320.69	7299.95	7281.96
650,000	7667.13	7638.40	7613.52	7591.95	7573.24
675,000	7962.02	7932.19	7906.35	7883.95	7864.51
700,000	8256.91	8225.97	8199.18	8175.95	8155.79
725,000	8551.80	8519.76	8492.00	8467.94	8447.07
750,000	8846.69	8813.54	8784.83	8759.94	8738.35
775,000	9141.58	9107.33	9077.66	9051.94	9029.63
800,000	9436.47	9401.11	9370.49	9343.94	9320.91
825,000	9731.36	9694.89	9663.31	9635.94	9612.18
850,000	10026.25	9988.68	9956.14	9927.93	9903.46
875,000	10321.14	10282.46	10248.97	10219.93	10194.74
900,000	10616.02	10576.25	10541.80	10511.93	10486.02

Monthly Payment Loans   **14.00%**

Loan Amount	Amortization Period in Years				
	5	7	8	10	12
10	0.24	0.19	0.18	0.16	0.15
20	0.47	0.38	0.35	0.32	0.29
30	0.70	0.57	0.53	0.47	0.44
40	0.94	0.75	0.70	0.63	0.58
50	1.17	0.94	0.87	0.78	0.72
100	2.33	1.88	1.74	1.56	1.44
200	4.66	3.75	3.48	3.11	2.88
300	6.99	5.63	5.22	4.66	4.32
400	9.31	7.50	6.95	6.22	5.75
500	11.64	9.38	8.69	7.77	7.19
1,000	23.27	18.75	17.38	15.53	14.38
2,000	46.54	37.49	34.75	31.06	28.75
3,000	69.81	56.23	52.12	46.58	43.12
4,000	93.08	74.97	69.49	62.11	57.49
5,000	116.35	93.71	86.86	77.64	71.86
10,000	232.69	187.41	173.72	155.27	143.72
20,000	465.37	374.81	347.44	310.54	287.43
30,000	698.05	562.21	521.15	465.80	431.14
40,000	930.74	749.61	694.87	621.07	574.86
50,000	1163.42	937.01	868.58	776.34	718.57
100,000	2326.83	1874.01	1737.16	1552.67	1437.13
125,000	2908.54	2342.51	2171.44	1940.84	1796.41
150,000	3490.24	2811.01	2605.73	2329.00	2155.70
175,000	4071.95	3279.51	3040.02	2717.17	2514.98
200,000	4653.66	3748.01	3474.31	3105.33	2874.26
225,000	5235.36	4216.51	3908.59	3493.50	3233.54
250,000	5817.07	4685.01	4342.88	3881.67	3592.82
275,000	6398.77	5153.51	4777.17	4269.83	3952.10
300,000	6980.48	5622.01	5211.46	4658.00	4311.39
325,000	7562.19	6090.51	5645.74	5046.16	4670.67
350,000	8143.89	6559.01	6080.03	5434.33	5029.95
375,000	8725.60	7027.51	6514.32	5822.50	5389.23
400,000	9307.31	7496.01	6948.61	6210.66	5748.51
425,000	9889.01	7964.51	7382.89	6598.83	6107.80
450,000	10470.72	8433.01	7817.18	6986.99	6467.08
475,000	11052.42	8901.51	8251.47	7375.16	6826.36
500,000	11634.13	9370.01	8685.76	7763.33	7185.64
525,000	12215.84	9838.51	9120.04	8151.49	7544.92
550,000	12797.54	10307.01	9554.33	8539.66	7904.20
575,000	13379.25	10775.51	9988.62	8927.83	8263.49
600,000	13960.96	11244.01	10422.91	9315.99	8622.77
625,000	14542.66	11712.51	10857.19	9704.16	8982.05
650,000	15124.37	12181.01	11291.48	10092.32	9341.33
675,000	15706.07	12649.51	11725.77	10480.49	9700.61
700,000	16287.78	13118.01	12160.06	10868.66	10059.89
725,000	16869.49	13586.51	12594.34	11256.82	10419.18
750,000	17451.19	14055.01	13028.63	11644.99	10778.46
775,000	18032.90	14523.51	13462.92	12033.15	11137.74
800,000	18614.61	14992.01	13897.21	12421.32	11497.02
825,000	19196.31	15460.51	14331.49	12809.49	11856.30
850,000	19778.02	15929.01	14765.78	13197.65	12215.59
875,000	20359.72	16397.52	15200.07	13585.82	12574.87
900,000	20941.43	16866.02	15634.36	13973.98	12934.15

Table 7   253

14.00%   Monthly Payment Loans

Loan Amount	Amortization Period in Years				
	15	16	17	18	20
10	0.14	0.14	0.13	0.13	0.13
20	0.27	0.27	0.26	0.26	0.25
30	0.40	0.40	0.39	0.39	0.38
40	0.54	0.53	0.52	0.51	0.50
50	0.67	0.66	0.65	0.64	0.63
100	1.34	1.31	1.29	1.28	1.25
200	2.67	2.62	2.58	2.55	2.49
300	4.00	3.93	3.87	3.82	3.74
400	5.33	5.24	5.15	5.09	4.98
500	6.66	6.54	6.44	6.36	6.22
1,000	13.32	13.08	12.88	12.71	12.44
2,000	26.64	26.16	25.75	25.41	24.88
3,000	39.96	39.24	38.63	38.12	37.31
4,000	53.27	52.31	51.50	50.82	49.75
5,000	66.59	65.39	64.38	63.52	62.18
10,000	133.18	130.77	128.75	127.04	124.36
20,000	266.35	261.54	257.50	254.08	248.71
30,000	399.53	392.31	386.25	381.12	373.06
40,000	532.70	523.08	515.00	508.16	497.41
50,000	665.88	653.85	643.74	635.20	621.77
100,000	1331.75	1307.70	1287.48	1270.39	1243.53
125,000	1664.68	1634.63	1609.35	1587.98	1554.41
150,000	1997.62	1961.55	1931.22	1905.58	1865.29
175,000	2330.55	2288.48	2253.09	2223.18	2176.17
200,000	2663.49	2615.40	2574.96	2540.77	2487.05
225,000	2996.42	2942.33	2896.83	2858.37	2797.93
250,000	3329.36	3269.25	3218.70	3175.96	3108.81
275,000	3662.29	3596.18	3540.56	3493.56	3419.69
300,000	3995.23	3923.10	3862.43	3811.15	3730.57
325,000	4328.16	4250.03	4184.30	4128.75	4041.45
350,000	4661.10	4576.95	4506.17	4446.35	4352.33
375,000	4994.04	4903.88	4828.04	4763.94	4663.21
400,000	5326.97	5230.80	5149.91	5081.54	4974.09
425,000	5659.91	5557.73	5471.78	5399.13	5284.97
450,000	5992.84	5884.65	5793.65	5716.73	5595.85
475,000	6325.78	6211.58	6115.52	6034.32	5906.73
500,000	6658.71	6538.50	6437.39	6351.92	6217.61
525,000	6991.65	6865.43	6759.26	6669.52	6528.49
550,000	7324.58	7192.35	7081.12	6987.11	6839.37
575,000	7657.52	7519.28	7402.99	7304.71	7150.25
600,000	7990.45	7846.20	7724.86	7622.30	7461.13
625,000	8323.39	8173.12	8046.73	7939.90	7772.01
650,000	8656.32	8500.05	8368.60	8257.50	8082.89
675,000	8989.26	8826.97	8690.47	8575.09	8393.77
700,000	9322.19	9153.90	9012.34	8892.69	8704.65
725,000	9655.13	9480.82	9334.21	9210.28	9015.53
750,000	9988.07	9807.75	9656.08	9527.88	9326.41
775,000	10321.00	10134.67	9977.95	9845.47	9637.29
800,000	10653.94	10461.60	10299.81	10163.07	9948.17
825,000	10986.87	10788.52	10621.68	10480.67	10259.05
850,000	11319.81	11115.45	10943.55	10798.26	10569.93
875,000	11652.74	11442.37	11265.42	11115.86	10880.81
900,000	11985.68	11769.30	11587.29	11433.45	11191.69

Monthly Payment Loans   **14.00%**

Loan Amount	\multicolumn{5}{c}{Amortization Period in Years}
	21	22	23	24	25
10	0.13	0.13	0.13	0.13	0.13
20	0.25	0.25	0.25	0.25	0.25
30	0.37	0.37	0.37	0.37	0.37
40	0.50	0.49	0.49	0.49	0.49
50	0.62	0.62	0.61	0.61	0.61
100	1.24	1.23	1.22	1.21	1.21
200	2.47	2.45	2.44	2.42	2.41
300	3.70	3.68	3.65	3.63	3.62
400	4.94	4.90	4.87	4.84	4.82
500	6.17	6.12	6.09	6.05	6.02
1,000	12.33	12.24	12.17	12.10	12.04
2,000	24.66	24.48	24.33	24.20	24.08
3,000	36.99	36.72	36.49	36.29	36.12
4,000	49.32	48.96	48.65	48.39	48.16
5,000	61.65	61.20	60.81	60.48	60.19
10,000	123.30	122.40	121.62	120.96	120.38
20,000	246.60	244.79	243.24	241.91	240.76
30,000	369.90	367.18	364.86	362.86	361.13
40,000	493.19	489.58	486.47	483.81	481.51
50,000	616.49	611.97	608.09	604.76	601.89
100,000	1232.97	1223.93	1216.18	1209.51	1203.77
125,000	1541.21	1529.92	1520.22	1511.89	1504.71
150,000	1849.46	1835.90	1824.26	1814.26	1805.65
175,000	2157.70	2141.88	2128.31	2116.64	2106.59
200,000	2465.94	2447.86	2432.35	2419.01	2407.53
225,000	2774.18	2753.85	2736.39	2721.39	2708.47
250,000	3082.42	3059.83	3040.44	3023.77	3009.41
275,000	3390.66	3365.81	3344.48	3326.14	3310.35
300,000	3698.91	3671.79	3648.52	3628.52	3611.29
325,000	4007.15	3977.78	3952.57	3930.89	3912.23
350,000	4315.39	4283.76	4256.61	4233.27	4213.17
375,000	4623.63	4589.74	4560.65	4535.65	4514.11
400,000	4931.87	4895.72	4864.70	4838.02	4815.05
425,000	5240.12	5201.70	5168.74	5140.40	5115.99
450,000	5548.36	5507.69	5472.78	5442.77	5416.93
475,000	5856.60	5813.67	5776.83	5745.15	5717.87
500,000	6164.84	6119.65	6080.87	6047.53	6018.81
525,000	6473.08	6425.63	6384.91	6349.90	6319.75
550,000	6781.32	6731.62	6688.96	6652.28	6620.69
575,000	7089.57	7037.60	6993.00	6954.65	6921.63
600,000	7397.81	7343.58	7297.04	7257.03	7222.57
625,000	7706.05	7649.56	7601.09	7559.41	7523.51
650,000	8014.29	7955.55	7905.13	7861.78	7824.45
675,000	8322.53	8261.53	8209.17	8164.16	8125.39
700,000	8630.77	8567.51	8513.22	8466.53	8426.33
725,000	8939.02	8873.49	8817.26	8768.91	8727.27
750,000	9247.26	9179.48	9121.30	9071.29	9028.21
775,000	9555.50	9485.46	9425.35	9373.66	9329.15
800,000	9863.74	9791.44	9729.39	9676.04	9630.09
825,000	10171.98	10097.42	10033.43	9978.41	9931.03
850,000	10480.23	10403.40	10337.48	10280.79	10231.97
875,000	10788.47	10709.39	10641.52	10583.17	10532.91
900,000	11096.71	11015.37	10945.56	10885.54	10833.85

Table 7   255

14.00%

Monthly Payment Loans

Amortization Period in Years

Loan Amount	26	27	28	29	30
10	0.12	0.12	0.12	0.12	0.12
20	0.24	0.24	0.24	0.24	0.24
30	0.36	0.36	0.36	0.36	0.36
40	0.48	0.48	0.48	0.48	0.48
50	0.60	0.60	0.60	0.60	0.60
100	1.20	1.20	1.20	1.19	1.19
200	2.40	2.39	2.39	2.38	2.37
300	3.60	3.59	3.58	3.57	3.56
400	4.80	4.78	4.77	4.76	4.74
500	6.00	5.98	5.96	5.94	5.93
1,000	11.99	11.95	11.91	11.88	11.85
2,000	23.98	23.90	23.82	23.76	23.70
3,000	35.97	35.84	35.73	35.63	35.55
4,000	47.96	47.79	47.64	47.51	47.40
5,000	59.95	59.73	59.55	59.39	59.25
10,000	119.89	119.46	119.09	118.77	118.49
20,000	239.77	238.91	238.17	237.53	236.98
30,000	359.65	358.36	357.26	356.30	355.47
40,000	479.53	477.82	476.34	475.06	473.95
50,000	599.41	597.27	595.42	593.82	592.44
100,000	1198.81	1194.54	1190.84	1187.64	1184.88
125,000	1498.52	1493.17	1488.55	1484.55	1481.09
150,000	1798.22	1791.80	1786.26	1781.46	1777.31
175,000	2097.92	2090.44	2083.97	2078.37	2073.53
200,000	2397.62	2389.07	2381.68	2375.28	2369.75
225,000	2697.32	2687.70	2679.39	2672.19	2665.97
250,000	2997.03	2986.34	2977.10	2969.10	2962.18
275,000	3296.73	3284.97	3274.81	3266.01	3258.40
300,000	3596.43	3583.60	3572.51	3562.92	3554.62
325,000	3896.13	3882.23	3870.22	3859.83	3850.84
350,000	4195.83	4180.87	4167.93	4156.74	4147.06
375,000	4495.54	4479.50	4465.64	4453.65	4443.27
400,000	4795.24	4778.13	4763.35	4750.56	4739.49
425,000	5094.94	5076.77	5061.06	5047.47	5035.71
450,000	5394.64	5375.40	5358.77	5344.38	5331.93
475,000	5694.34	5674.03	5656.48	5641.29	5628.15
500,000	5994.05	5972.67	5954.19	5938.20	5924.36
525,000	6293.75	6271.30	6251.90	6235.11	6220.58
550,000	6593.45	6569.93	6549.61	6532.02	6516.80
575,000	6893.15	6868.57	6847.31	6828.93	6813.02
600,000	7192.85	7167.20	7145.02	7125.84	7109.24
625,000	7492.56	7465.83	7442.73	7422.75	7405.45
650,000	7792.26	7764.46	7740.44	7719.66	7701.67
675,000	8091.96	8063.10	8038.15	8016.57	7997.89
700,000	8391.66	8361.73	8335.86	8313.48	8294.11
725,000	8691.37	8660.36	8633.57	8610.39	8590.33
750,000	8991.07	8959.00	8931.28	8907.30	8886.54
775,000	9290.77	9257.63	9228.99	9204.21	9182.76
800,000	9590.47	9556.26	9526.70	9501.12	9478.98
825,000	9890.17	9854.90	9824.41	9798.03	9775.20
850,000	10189.88	10153.53	10122.11	10094.94	10071.41
875,000	10489.58	10452.16	10419.82	10391.85	10367.63
900,000	10789.28	10750.79	10717.53	10688.76	10663.85

Monthly Payment Loans **14.25%**

Loan Amount	Amortization Period in Years				
	5	7	8	10	12
10	0.24	0.19	0.18	0.16	0.15
20	0.47	0.38	0.36	0.32	0.30
30	0.71	0.57	0.53	0.48	0.44
40	0.94	0.76	0.71	0.63	0.59
50	1.17	0.95	0.88	0.79	0.73
100	2.34	1.89	1.76	1.57	1.46
200	4.68	3.78	3.51	3.14	2.91
300	7.02	5.67	5.26	4.71	4.36
400	9.36	7.56	7.01	6.28	5.82
500	11.70	9.44	8.76	7.84	7.27
1,000	23.40	18.88	17.52	15.68	14.53
2,000	46.80	37.76	35.03	31.36	29.06
3,000	70.20	56.64	52.55	47.04	43.59
4,000	93.60	75.52	70.06	62.71	58.12
5,000	117.00	94.40	87.58	78.39	72.65
10,000	233.99	188.79	175.15	156.78	145.30
20,000	467.97	377.57	350.29	313.55	290.59
30,000	701.95	566.36	525.43	470.32	435.89
40,000	935.93	755.14	700.57	627.10	581.18
50,000	1169.91	943.92	875.71	783.87	726.48
100,000	2339.81	1887.84	1751.41	1567.74	1452.95
125,000	2924.76	2359.80	2189.26	1959.67	1816.19
150,000	3509.71	2831.76	2627.12	2351.60	2179.43
175,000	4094.67	3303.72	3064.97	2743.53	2542.67
200,000	4679.62	3775.68	3502.82	3135.47	2905.90
225,000	5264.57	4247.64	3940.67	3527.40	3269.14
250,000	5849.52	4719.60	4378.52	3919.33	3632.38
275,000	6434.47	5191.56	4816.38	4311.27	3995.62
300,000	7019.42	5663.52	5254.23	4703.20	4358.85
325,000	7604.38	6135.48	5692.08	5095.13	4722.09
350,000	8189.33	6607.44	6129.93	5487.06	5085.33
375,000	8774.28	7079.40	6567.78	5879.00	5448.57
400,000	9359.23	7551.36	7005.64	6270.93	5811.80
425,000	9944.18	8023.32	7443.49	6662.86	6175.04
450,000	10529.13	8495.28	7881.34	7054.79	6538.28
475,000	11114.09	8967.24	8319.19	7446.73	6901.51
500,000	11699.04	9439.20	8757.04	7838.66	7264.75
525,000	12283.99	9911.16	9194.90	8230.59	7627.99
550,000	12868.94	10383.12	9632.75	8622.53	7991.23
575,000	13453.89	10855.08	10070.60	9014.46	8354.46
600,000	14038.84	11327.04	10508.45	9406.39	8717.70
625,000	14623.79	11799.00	10946.30	9798.32	9080.94
650,000	15208.75	12270.96	11384.16	10190.26	9444.18
675,000	15793.70	12742.92	11822.01	10582.19	9807.41
700,000	16378.65	13214.88	12259.86	10974.12	10170.65
725,000	16963.60	13686.84	12697.71	11366.06	10533.89
750,000	17548.55	14158.80	13135.56	11757.99	10897.13
775,000	18133.50	14630.76	13573.42	12149.92	11260.36
800,000	18718.46	15102.71	14011.27	12541.85	11623.60
825,000	19303.41	15574.67	14449.12	12933.79	11986.84
850,000	19888.36	16046.63	14886.97	13325.72	12350.08
875,000	20473.31	16518.59	15324.82	13717.65	12713.31
900,000	21058.26	16990.55	15762.68	14109.58	13076.55

Table 7 257

14.25%   Monthly Payment Loans

Amortization Period in Years

Loan Amount	15	16	17	18	20
10	0.14	0.14	0.14	0.13	0.13
20	0.27	0.27	0.27	0.26	0.26
30	0.41	0.40	0.40	0.39	0.38
40	0.54	0.53	0.53	0.52	0.51
50	0.68	0.67	0.66	0.65	0.64
100	1.35	1.33	1.31	1.29	1.27
200	2.70	2.65	2.61	2.58	2.53
300	4.05	3.98	3.92	3.87	3.79
400	5.40	5.30	5.22	5.16	5.05
500	6.75	6.63	6.53	6.45	6.31
1,000	13.49	13.25	13.05	12.89	12.62
2,000	26.98	26.50	26.10	25.77	25.24
3,000	40.46	39.75	39.15	38.65	37.86
4,000	53.95	53.00	52.20	51.53	50.47
5,000	67.43	66.25	65.25	64.41	63.09
10,000	134.86	132.49	130.50	128.81	126.18
20,000	269.72	264.97	260.99	257.62	252.35
30,000	404.58	397.46	391.48	386.43	378.52
40,000	539.44	529.94	521.97	515.24	504.69
50,000	674.29	662.43	652.46	644.05	630.86
100,000	1348.58	1324.85	1304.91	1288.09	1261.72
125,000	1685.73	1656.06	1631.14	1610.11	1577.15
150,000	2022.87	1987.27	1957.37	1932.14	1892.58
175,000	2360.02	2318.48	2283.59	2254.16	2208.01
200,000	2697.16	2649.69	2609.82	2576.18	2523.44
225,000	3034.31	2980.90	2936.05	2898.20	2838.87
250,000	3371.45	3312.11	3262.28	3220.22	3154.30
275,000	3708.60	3643.32	3588.50	3542.24	3469.73
300,000	4045.74	3974.53	3914.73	3864.27	3785.16
325,000	4382.89	4305.74	4240.96	4186.29	4100.59
350,000	4720.03	4636.96	4567.18	4508.31	4416.02
375,000	5057.18	4968.17	4893.41	4830.33	4731.45
400,000	5394.32	5299.38	5219.64	5152.35	5046.88
425,000	5731.47	5630.59	5545.87	5474.38	5362.31
450,000	6068.61	5961.80	5872.09	5796.40	5677.74
475,000	6405.76	6293.01	6198.32	6118.42	5993.17
500,000	6742.90	6624.22	6524.55	6440.44	6308.60
525,000	7080.05	6955.43	6850.77	6762.46	6624.03
550,000	7417.19	7286.64	7177.00	7084.48	6939.46
575,000	7754.34	7617.85	7503.23	7406.51	7254.89
600,000	8091.48	7949.06	7829.46	7728.53	7570.32
625,000	8428.63	8280.27	8155.68	8050.55	7885.75
650,000	8765.77	8611.48	8481.91	8372.57	8201.18
675,000	9102.92	8942.69	8808.14	8694.59	8516.61
700,000	9440.06	9273.91	9134.36	9016.61	8832.04
725,000	9777.21	9605.12	9460.59	9338.64	9147.47
750,000	10114.35	9936.33	9786.82	9660.66	9462.90
775,000	10451.50	10267.54	10113.05	9982.68	9778.33
800,000	10788.64	10598.75	10439.27	10304.70	10093.76
825,000	11125.79	10929.96	10765.50	10626.72	10409.19
850,000	11462.93	11261.17	11091.73	10948.75	10724.62
875,000	11800.08	11592.38	11417.95	11270.77	11040.05
900,000	12137.22	11923.59	11744.18	11592.79	11355.48

258   Table 7

Monthly Payment Loans ## 14.25%

Loan Amount	\multicolumn{5}{c}{Amortization Period in Years}				
	21	22	23	24	25
10	0.13	0.13	0.13	0.13	0.13
20	0.26	0.25	0.25	0.25	0.25
30	0.38	0.38	0.38	0.37	0.37
40	0.51	0.50	0.50	0.50	0.49
50	0.63	0.63	0.62	0.62	0.62
100	1.26	1.25	1.24	1.23	1.23
200	2.51	2.49	2.47	2.46	2.45
300	3.76	3.73	3.71	3.69	3.67
400	5.01	4.98	4.94	4.92	4.90
500	6.26	6.22	6.18	6.15	6.12
1,000	12.52	12.43	12.35	12.29	12.23
2,000	25.03	24.86	24.70	24.58	24.46
3,000	37.55	37.28	37.05	36.86	36.69
4,000	50.06	49.71	49.40	49.15	48.92
5,000	62.57	62.13	61.75	61.43	61.15
10,000	125.14	124.26	123.50	122.86	122.30
20,000	250.28	248.52	247.00	245.71	244.59
30,000	375.42	372.77	370.50	368.56	366.88
40,000	500.56	497.03	494.00	491.41	489.18
50,000	625.70	621.28	617.50	614.26	611.47
100,000	1251.39	1242.56	1235.00	1228.51	1222.93
125,000	1564.24	1553.20	1543.75	1535.64	1528.66
150,000	1877.09	1863.84	1852.50	1842.76	1834.40
175,000	2189.93	2174.48	2161.25	2149.89	2140.13
200,000	2502.78	2485.12	2470.00	2457.02	2445.86
225,000	2815.63	2795.76	2778.74	2764.14	2751.59
250,000	3128.48	3106.40	3087.49	3071.27	3057.32
275,000	3441.32	3417.04	3396.24	3378.39	3363.06
300,000	3754.17	3727.68	3704.99	3685.52	3668.79
325,000	4067.02	4038.32	4013.74	3992.65	3974.52
350,000	4379.86	4348.96	4322.49	4299.77	4280.25
375,000	4692.71	4659.60	4631.24	4606.90	4585.98
400,000	5005.56	4970.24	4939.99	4914.03	4891.72
425,000	5318.41	5280.88	5248.73	5221.15	5197.45
450,000	5631.25	5591.52	5557.48	5528.28	5503.18
475,000	5944.10	5902.16	5866.23	5835.40	5808.91
500,000	6256.95	6212.80	6174.98	6142.53	6114.64
525,000	6569.79	6523.44	6483.73	6449.66	6420.37
550,000	6882.64	6834.08	6792.48	6756.78	6726.11
575,000	7195.49	7144.72	7101.23	7063.91	7031.84
600,000	7508.34	7455.36	7409.98	7371.04	7337.57
625,000	7821.18	7766.00	7718.73	7678.16	7643.30
650,000	8134.03	8076.64	8027.47	7985.29	7949.03
675,000	8446.88	8387.27	8336.22	8292.42	8254.77
700,000	8759.72	8697.91	8644.97	8599.54	8560.50
725,000	9072.57	9008.55	8953.72	8906.67	8866.23
750,000	9385.42	9319.19	9262.47	9213.79	9171.96
775,000	9698.26	9629.83	9571.22	9520.92	9477.69
800,000	10011.11	9940.47	9879.97	9828.05	9783.43
825,000	10323.96	10251.11	10188.72	10135.17	10089.16
850,000	10636.81	10561.75	10497.46	10442.30	10394.89
875,000	10949.65	10872.39	10806.21	10749.43	10700.62
900,000	11262.50	11183.03	11114.96	11056.55	11006.35

Table 7   259

14.25%   Monthly Payment Loans

Loan Amount	26	27	28	29	30
10	0.13	0.13	0.13	0.13	0.13
20	0.25	0.25	0.25	0.25	0.25
30	0.37	0.37	0.37	0.37	0.37
40	0.49	0.49	0.49	0.49	0.49
50	0.61	0.61	0.61	0.61	0.61
100	1.22	1.22	1.22	1.21	1.21
200	2.44	2.43	2.43	2.42	2.41
300	3.66	3.65	3.64	3.63	3.62
400	4.88	4.86	4.85	4.83	4.82
500	6.10	6.07	6.06	6.04	6.03
1,000	12.19	12.14	12.11	12.08	12.05
2,000	24.37	24.28	24.21	24.15	24.10
3,000	36.55	36.42	36.32	36.23	36.15
4,000	48.73	48.56	48.42	48.30	48.19
5,000	60.91	60.70	60.53	60.37	60.24
10,000	121.82	121.40	121.05	120.74	120.47
20,000	243.63	242.80	242.09	241.47	240.94
30,000	365.44	364.20	363.13	362.21	361.41
40,000	487.26	485.60	484.18	482.94	481.88
50,000	609.07	607.00	605.22	603.68	602.35
100,000	1218.13	1214.00	1210.43	1207.35	1204.69
125,000	1522.66	1517.49	1513.04	1509.19	1505.86
150,000	1827.20	1820.99	1815.64	1811.02	1807.04
175,000	2131.73	2124.49	2118.25	2112.86	2108.21
200,000	2436.26	2427.99	2420.86	2414.70	2409.38
225,000	2740.79	2731.49	2723.46	2716.53	2710.55
250,000	3045.32	3034.98	3026.07	3018.37	3011.72
275,000	3349.86	3338.48	3328.67	3320.21	3312.89
300,000	3654.39	3641.98	3631.28	3622.04	3614.07
325,000	3958.92	3945.48	3933.89	3923.88	3915.24
350,000	4263.45	4248.98	4236.49	4225.72	4216.41
375,000	4567.98	4552.47	4539.10	4527.55	4517.58
400,000	4872.51	4855.97	4841.71	4829.39	4818.75
425,000	5177.05	5159.47	5144.31	5131.23	5119.93
450,000	5481.58	5462.97	5446.92	5433.06	5421.10
475,000	5786.11	5766.47	5749.52	5734.90	5722.27
500,000	6090.64	6069.96	6052.13	6036.74	6023.44
525,000	6395.17	6373.46	6354.74	6338.57	6324.61
550,000	6699.71	6676.96	6657.34	6640.41	6625.78
575,000	7004.24	6980.46	6959.95	6942.25	6926.96
600,000	7308.77	7283.96	7262.56	7244.08	7228.13
625,000	7613.30	7587.45	7565.16	7545.92	7529.30
650,000	7917.83	7890.95	7867.77	7847.76	7830.47
675,000	8222.37	8194.45	8170.37	8149.59	8131.64
700,000	8526.90	8497.95	8472.98	8451.43	8432.81
725,000	8831.43	8801.45	8775.59	8753.27	8733.99
750,000	9135.96	9104.94	9078.19	9055.10	9035.16
775,000	9440.49	9408.44	9380.80	9356.94	9336.33
800,000	9745.02	9711.94	9683.41	9658.78	9637.50
825,000	10049.56	10015.44	9986.01	9960.61	9938.67
850,000	10354.09	10318.94	10288.62	10262.45	10239.85
875,000	10658.62	10622.43	10591.22	10564.29	10541.02
900,000	10963.15	10925.93	10893.83	10866.12	10842.19

Monthly Payment Loans   14.50%

Loan Amount	\multicolumn{5}{c}{Amortization Period in Years}				
	5	7	8	10	12
10	0.24	0.20	0.18	0.16	0.15
20	0.48	0.39	0.36	0.32	0.30
30	0.71	0.58	0.53	0.48	0.45
40	0.95	0.77	0.71	0.64	0.59
50	1.18	0.96	0.89	0.80	0.74
100	2.36	1.91	1.77	1.59	1.47
200	4.71	3.81	3.54	3.17	2.94
300	7.06	5.71	5.30	4.75	4.41
400	9.42	7.61	7.07	6.34	5.88
500	11.77	9.51	8.83	7.92	7.35
1,000	23.53	19.02	17.66	15.83	14.69
2,000	47.06	38.04	35.32	31.66	29.38
3,000	70.59	57.06	52.98	47.49	44.07
4,000	94.12	76.07	70.63	63.32	58.76
5,000	117.65	95.09	88.29	79.15	73.45
10,000	235.29	190.18	176.58	158.29	146.89
20,000	470.57	380.35	353.15	316.58	293.77
30,000	705.85	570.52	529.72	474.87	440.66
40,000	941.14	760.70	706.30	633.15	587.54
50,000	1176.42	950.87	882.87	791.44	734.43
100,000	2352.83	1901.74	1765.73	1582.87	1468.85
125,000	2941.04	2377.17	2207.16	1978.59	1836.07
150,000	3529.25	2852.60	2648.59	2374.31	2203.28
175,000	4117.45	3328.03	3090.02	2770.02	2570.49
200,000	4705.66	3803.47	3531.46	3165.74	2937.70
225,000	5293.87	4278.90	3972.89	3561.46	3304.92
250,000	5882.08	4754.33	4414.32	3957.17	3672.13
275,000	6470.28	5229.76	4855.75	4352.89	4039.34
300,000	7058.49	5705.20	5297.18	4748.61	4406.55
325,000	7646.70	6180.63	5730.61	5144.33	4773.76
350,000	8234.90	6656.06	6180.04	5540.04	5140.98
375,000	8823.11	7131.49	6621.48	5935.76	5508.19
400,000	9411.32	7606.93	7062.91	6331.48	5875.40
425,000	9999.52	8082.36	7504.34	6727.19	6242.61
450,000	10587.73	8557.79	7945.77	7122.91	6609.83
475,000	11175.94	9033.22	8387.20	7518.63	6977.04
500,000	11764.15	9508.66	8828.63	7914.34	7344.25
525,000	12352.35	9984.09	9270.06	8310.06	7711.46
550,000	12940.56	10459.52	9711.50	8705.78	8078.67
575,000	13528.77	10934.95	10152.93	9101.50	8445.89
600,000	14116.97	11410.39	10594.36	9497.21	8813.10
625,000	14705.18	11885.82	11035.79	9892.93	9180.31
650,000	15293.39	12361.25	11477.22	10288.65	9547.52
675,000	15881.59	12836.69	11918.65	10684.36	9914.74
700,000	16469.80	13312.12	12360.08	11080.08	10281.95
725,000	17058.01	13787.55	12801.52	11475.80	10649.16
750,000	17646.22	14262.98	13242.95	11871.51	11016.37
775,000	18234.42	14738.42	13684.38	12267.23	11383.58
800,000	18822.63	15213.85	14125.81	12662.95	11750.80
825,000	19410.84	15689.28	14567.24	13058.67	12118.01
850,000	19999.04	16164.71	15008.67	13454.38	12485.22
875,000	20587.25	16640.15	15450.10	13850.10	12852.43
900,000	21175.46	17115.58	15891.54	14245.82	13219.65

Table 7   261

14.50% Monthly Payment Loans

Amortization Period in Years

Loan Amount	15	16	17	18	20
10	0.14	0.14	0.14	0.14	0.13
20	0.28	0.27	0.27	0.27	0.26
30	0.41	0.41	0.40	0.40	0.39
40	0.55	0.54	0.53	0.53	0.52
50	0.69	0.68	0.67	0.66	0.64
100	1.37	1.35	1.33	1.31	1.28
200	2.74	2.69	2.65	2.62	2.56
300	4.10	4.03	3.97	3.92	3.84
400	5.47	5.37	5.29	5.23	5.12
500	6.83	6.72	6.62	6.53	6.40
1,000	13.66	13.43	13.23	13.06	12.80
2,000	27.32	26.85	26.45	26.12	25.60
3,000	40.97	40.27	39.68	39.18	38.40
4,000	54.63	53.69	52.90	52.24	51.20
5,000	68.28	67.11	66.13	65.30	64.00
10,000	136.56	134.21	132.25	130.59	128.00
20,000	273.11	268.42	264.49	261.18	256.00
30,000	409.66	402.63	396.73	391.77	384.00
40,000	546.21	536.83	528.97	522.35	512.00
50,000	682.76	671.04	661.22	652.94	640.00
100,000	1365.51	1342.08	1322.43	1305.88	1280.00
125,000	1706.88	1677.59	1653.04	1632.35	1600.00
150,000	2048.26	2013.11	1983.64	1958.82	1920.00
175,000	2389.63	2348.63	2314.25	2285.28	2240.00
200,000	2731.01	2684.15	2644.85	2611.75	2560.00
225,000	3072.38	3019.66	2975.46	2938.22	2880.00
250,000	3413.76	3355.18	3306.07	3264.69	3200.00
275,000	3755.13	3690.70	3636.67	3591.16	3520.00
300,000	4096.51	4026.22	3967.28	3917.63	3840.00
325,000	4437.88	4361.73	4297.88	4244.10	4160.00
350,000	4779.26	4697.25	4628.49	4570.56	4480.00
375,000	5120.63	5032.77	4959.10	4897.03	4800.00
400,000	5462.01	5368.29	5289.70	5223.50	5120.00
425,000	5803.38	5703.80	5620.31	5549.97	5440.00
450,000	6144.76	6039.32	5950.91	5876.44	5759.99
475,000	6486.13	6374.84	6281.52	6202.91	6079.99
500,000	6827.51	6710.36	6612.13	6529.38	6399.99
525,000	7168.88	7045.87	6942.73	6855.84	6719.99
550,000	7510.26	7381.39	7273.34	7182.31	7039.99
575,000	7851.63	7716.91	7603.94	7508.78	7359.99
600,000	8193.01	8052.43	7934.55	7835.25	7679.99
625,000	8534.39	8387.94	8265.16	8161.72	7999.99
650,000	8875.76	8723.46	8595.76	8488.19	8319.99
675,000	9217.14	9058.98	8926.37	8814.66	8639.99
700,000	9558.51	9394.50	9256.97	9141.12	8959.99
725,000	9899.89	9730.01	9587.58	9467.59	9279.99
750,000	10241.26	10065.53	9918.19	9794.06	9599.99
775,000	10582.64	10401.05	10248.79	10120.53	9919.99
800,000	10924.01	10736.57	10579.40	10447.00	10239.99
825,000	11265.39	11072.08	10910.01	10773.47	10559.99
850,000	11606.76	11407.60	11240.61	11099.94	10879.99
875,000	11948.14	11743.12	11571.22	11426.40	11199.99
900,000	12289.51	12078.64	11901.82	11752.87	11519.98

Monthly Payment Loans   **14.50%**

Loan Amount	Amortization Period in Years				
	21	22	23	24	25
10	0.13	0.13	0.13	0.13	0.13
20	0.26	0.26	0.26	0.25	0.25
30	0.39	0.38	0.38	0.38	0.38
40	0.51	0.51	0.51	0.50	0.50
50	0.64	0.64	0.63	0.63	0.63
100	1.27	1.27	1.26	1.25	1.25
200	2.54	2.53	2.51	2.50	2.49
300	3.81	3.79	3.77	3.75	3.73
400	5.08	5.05	5.02	5.00	4.97
500	6.35	6.31	6.27	6.24	6.22
1,000	12.70	12.62	12.54	12.48	12.43
2,000	25.40	25.23	25.08	24.96	24.85
3,000	38.10	37.84	37.62	37.43	37.27
4,000	50.80	50.46	50.16	49.91	49.69
5,000	63.50	63.07	62.70	62.38	62.11
10,000	126.99	126.13	125.39	124.76	124.22
20,000	253.98	252.26	250.78	249.52	248.44
30,000	380.97	378.38	376.17	374.28	372.65
40,000	507.96	504.51	501.56	499.04	496.87
50,000	634.95	630.64	626.95	623.79	621.09
100,000	1269.89	1261.27	1253.90	1247.58	1242.17
125,000	1587.37	1576.59	1567.37	1559.48	1552.71
150,000	1904.84	1891.90	1880.84	1871.37	1863.25
175,000	2222.31	2207.22	2194.32	2183.27	2173.79
200,000	2539.78	2522.53	2507.79	2495.16	2484.33
225,000	2857.25	2837.85	2821.26	2807.06	2794.87
250,000	3174.73	3153.17	3134.73	3118.95	3105.41
275,000	3492.20	3468.48	3448.21	3430.84	3415.95
300,000	3809.67	3783.80	3761.68	3742.74	3726.49
325,000	4127.14	4099.11	4075.15	4054.63	4037.03
350,000	4444.61	4414.43	4388.63	4366.53	4347.58
375,000	4762.09	4729.75	4702.10	4678.42	4658.12
400,000	5079.56	5045.06	5015.57	4990.32	4968.66
425,000	5397.03	5360.38	5329.04	5302.21	5279.20
450,000	5714.50	5675.69	5642.52	5614.11	5589.74
475,000	6031.98	5991.01	5955.99	5926.00	5900.28
500,000	6349.45	6306.33	6269.46	6237.90	6210.82
525,000	6666.92	6621.64	6582.94	6549.79	6521.36
550,000	6984.39	6936.96	6896.41	6861.68	6831.90
575,000	7301.86	7252.27	7209.88	7173.58	7142.44
600,000	7619.34	7567.59	7523.36	7485.47	7452.98
625,000	7936.81	7882.91	7836.83	7797.37	7763.52
650,000	8254.28	8198.22	8150.30	8109.26	8074.06
675,000	8571.75	8513.54	8463.77	8421.16	8384.60
700,000	8889.22	8828.86	8777.25	8733.05	8695.15
725,000	9206.70	9144.17	9090.72	9044.95	9005.69
750,000	9524.17	9459.49	9404.19	9356.84	9316.23
775,000	9841.64	9774.80	9717.67	9668.73	9626.77
800,000	10159.11	10090.12	10031.14	9980.63	9937.31
825,000	10476.59	10405.44	10344.61	10292.52	10247.85
850,000	10794.06	10720.75	10658.08	10604.42	10558.39
875,000	11111.53	11036.07	10971.56	10916.31	10868.93
900,000	11429.00	11351.38	11285.03	11228.21	11179.47

Table 7   263

14.50%   Monthly Payment Loans

Amortization Period in Years

Loan Amount	26	27	28	29	30
10	0.13	0.13	0.13	0.13	0.13
20	0.25	0.25	0.25	0.25	0.25
30	0.38	0.38	0.37	0.37	0.37
40	0.50	0.50	0.50	0.50	0.49
50	0.62	0.62	0.62	0.62	0.62
100	1.24	1.24	1.24	1.23	1.23
200	2.48	2.47	2.47	2.46	2.45
300	3.72	3.71	3.70	3.69	3.68
400	4.96	4.94	4.93	4.91	4.90
500	6.19	6.17	6.16	6.14	6.13
1,000	12.38	12.34	12.31	12.28	12.25
2,000	24.76	24.68	24.61	24.55	24.50
3,000	37.13	37.01	36.91	36.82	36.74
4,000	49.51	49.35	49.21	49.09	48.99
5,000	61.88	61.68	61.51	61.36	61.23
10,000	123.76	123.36	123.01	122.72	122.46
20,000	247.51	246.71	246.02	245.43	244.92
30,000	371.26	370.06	369.03	368.14	367.37
40,000	495.01	493.41	492.03	490.85	489.83
50,000	618.76	616.76	615.04	613.56	612.28
100,000	1237.52	1233.52	1230.08	1227.12	1224.56
125,000	1546.90	1541.90	1537.60	1533.89	1530.70
150,000	1856.27	1850.28	1845.12	1840.67	1836.84
175,000	2165.65	2158.65	2152.63	2147.45	2142.98
200,000	2475.03	2467.03	2460.15	2454.23	2449.12
225,000	2784.41	2775.41	2767.67	2761.00	2755.26
250,000	3093.79	3083.79	3075.19	3067.78	3061.39
275,000	3403.16	3392.17	3382.71	3374.56	3367.53
300,000	3712.54	3700.55	3690.23	3681.34	3673.67
325,000	4021.92	4008.93	3997.74	3988.11	3979.81
350,000	4331.30	4317.30	4305.26	4294.89	4285.95
375,000	4640.68	4625.68	4612.78	4601.67	4592.09
400,000	4950.05	4934.06	4920.30	4908.45	4898.23
425,000	5259.43	5242.44	5227.82	5215.22	5204.37
450,000	5568.81	5550.82	5535.34	5522.00	5510.51
475,000	5878.19	5859.20	5842.85	5828.78	5816.65
500,000	6187.57	6167.58	6150.37	6135.56	6122.78
525,000	6496.95	6475.95	6457.89	6442.33	6428.92
550,000	6806.32	6784.33	6765.41	6749.11	6735.06
575,000	7115.70	7092.71	7072.93	7055.89	7041.20
600,000	7425.08	7401.09	7380.45	7362.67	7347.34
625,000	7734.46	7709.47	7687.96	7669.44	7653.48
650,000	8043.84	8017.85	7995.48	7976.22	7959.62
675,000	8353.21	8326.23	8303.00	8283.00	8265.76
700,000	8662.59	8634.60	8610.52	8589.78	8571.90
725,000	8971.97	8942.98	8918.04	8896.55	8878.04
750,000	9281.35	9251.36	9225.56	9203.33	9184.17
775,000	9590.73	9559.74	9533.07	9510.11	9490.31
800,000	9900.10	9868.12	9840.59	9816.89	9796.45
825,000	10209.48	10176.50	10148.11	10123.66	10102.59
850,000	10518.86	10484.88	10455.63	10430.44	10408.73
875,000	10828.24	10793.25	10763.15	10737.22	10714.87
900,000	11137.62	11101.63	11070.67	11044.00	11021.01

Monthly Payment Loans 14.75%

Loan Amount	\multicolumn{5}{c}{Amortization Period in Years}				
	5	7	8	10	12
10	0.24	0.20	0.18	0.16	0.15
20	0.48	0.39	0.36	0.32	0.30
30	0.71	0.58	0.54	0.48	0.45
40	0.95	0.77	0.72	0.64	0.60
50	1.19	0.96	0.90	0.80	0.75
100	2.37	1.92	1.79	1.60	1.49
200	4.74	3.84	3.57	3.20	2.97
300	7.10	5.75	5.35	4.80	4.46
400	9.47	7.67	7.13	6.40	5.94
500	11.83	9.58	8.91	8.00	7.43
1,000	23.66	19.16	17.81	15.99	14.85
2,000	47.32	38.32	35.61	31.97	29.70
3,000	70.98	57.48	53.41	47.95	44.55
4,000	94.64	76.63	71.21	63.93	59.40
5,000	118.30	95.79	89.01	79.91	74.25
10,000	236.59	191.57	178.02	159.81	148.49
20,000	473.18	383.14	356.03	319.62	296.97
30,000	709.77	574.71	534.04	479.43	445.45
40,000	946.36	766.28	712.05	639.23	593.94
50,000	1182.95	957.84	890.06	799.04	742.42
100,000	2365.90	1915.68	1780.11	1598.08	1484.83
125,000	2957.37	2394.60	2225.13	1997.60	1856.04
150,000	3548.84	2873.52	2670.16	2397.12	2227.24
175,000	4140.31	3352.44	3115.19	2796.63	2598.45
200,000	4731.79	3831.36	3560.21	3196.15	2969.66
225,000	5323.26	4310.28	4005.24	3595.67	3340.86
250,000	5914.73	4789.20	4450.26	3995.19	3712.07
275,000	6506.20	5268.11	4895.29	4394.71	4083.27
300,000	7097.68	5747.03	5340.32	4794.23	4454.48
325,000	7689.15	6225.95	5785.34	5193.75	4825.69
350,000	8280.62	6704.87	6230.37	5593.26	5196.89
375,000	8872.09	7183.79	6675.39	5992.78	5560.10
400,000	9463.57	7662.71	7120.42	6392.30	5939.31
425,000	10055.04	8141.63	7565.44	6791.82	6310.51
450,000	10646.51	8620.55	8010.47	7191.34	6681.72
475,000	11237.98	9099.47	8455.50	7590.86	7052.92
500,000	11829.46	9578.39	8900.52	7990.38	7424.13
525,000	12420.93	10057.30	9345.55	8389.89	7795.34
550,000	13012.40	10536.22	9790.57	8789.41	8166.54
575,000	13603.87	11015.14	10235.60	9188.93	8537.75
600,000	14195.35	11494.06	10680.63	9588.45	8908.96
625,000	14786.82	11972.98	11125.65	9987.97	9280.16
650,000	15378.29	12451.90	11570.68	10387.49	9651.37
675,000	15969.76	12930.82	12015.70	10787.01	10022.57
700,000	16561.24	13409.74	12460.73	11186.52	10393.78
725,000	17152.71	13888.66	12905.75	11586.04	10764.99
750,000	17744.18	14367.58	13350.78	11985.56	11136.19
775,000	18335.66	14846.49	13795.81	12385.08	11507.40
800,000	18927.13	15325.41	14240.83	12784.60	11878.61
825,000	19518.60	15804.33	14685.86	13184.12	12249.81
850,000	20110.07	16283.25	15130.88	13583.64	12621.02
875,000	20701.55	16762.17	15575.91	13983.15	12992.22
900,000	21293.02	17241.09	16020.94	14382.67	13363.43

Table 7   265

14.75%   Monthly Payment Loans

Amortization Period in Years

Loan Amount	15	16	17	18	20
10	0.14	0.14	0.14	0.14	0.13
20	0.28	0.28	0.27	0.27	0.26
30	0.42	0.41	0.41	0.40	0.39
40	0.56	0.55	0.54	0.53	0.52
50	0.70	0.68	0.68	0.67	0.65
100	1.39	1.36	1.35	1.33	1.30
200	2.77	2.72	2.69	2.65	2.60
300	4.15	4.08	4.03	3.98	3.90
400	5.54	5.44	5.37	5.30	5.20
500	6.92	6.80	6.71	6.62	6.50
1,000	13.83	13.60	13.41	13.24	12.99
2,000	27.66	27.19	26.81	26.48	25.97
3,000	41.48	40.79	40.21	39.72	38.96
4,000	55.31	54.38	53.61	52.95	51.94
5,000	69.13	67.97	67.01	66.19	64.92
10,000	138.26	135.94	134.01	132.38	129.84
20,000	276.51	271.88	268.01	264.75	259.68
30,000	414.76	407.82	402.01	397.13	389.51
40,000	553.01	543.76	536.01	529.50	519.35
50,000	691.26	679.69	670.02	661.88	649.18
100,000	1382.51	1359.38	1340.03	1323.75	1298.36
125,000	1728.13	1699.23	1675.03	1654.68	1622.95
150,000	2073.76	2039.07	2010.04	1985.62	1947.54
175,000	2419.39	2378.92	2345.04	2316.55	2272.13
200,000	2765.01	2718.76	2680.05	2647.49	2596.72
225,000	3110.64	3058.61	3015.05	2978.43	2921.30
250,000	3456.26	3398.45	3350.06	3309.36	3245.89
275,000	3801.89	3738.30	3685.07	3640.30	3570.48
300,000	4147.52	4078.14	4020.07	3971.23	3895.07
325,000	4493.14	4417.99	4355.08	4302.17	4219.66
350,000	4838.77	4757.83	4690.08	4633.10	4544.25
375,000	5184.39	5097.68	5025.09	4964.04	4868.84
400,000	5530.02	5437.52	5360.09	5294.98	5193.43
425,000	5875.65	5777.37	5695.10	5625.91	5518.02
450,000	6221.27	6117.21	6030.10	5956.85	5842.60
475,000	6566.90	6457.06	6365.11	6287.78	6167.19
500,000	6912.52	6796.90	6700.12	6618.72	6491.78
525,000	7258.15	7136.75	7035.12	6949.65	6816.37
550,000	7603.78	7476.59	7370.13	7280.59	7140.96
575,000	7949.40	7816.44	7705.13	7611.52	7465.55
600,000	8295.03	8156.28	8040.14	7942.46	7790.14
625,000	8640.65	8496.13	8375.14	8273.40	8114.73
650,000	8986.28	8835.97	8710.15	8604.33	8439.31
675,000	9331.91	9175.82	9045.15	8935.27	8763.90
700,000	9677.53	9515.66	9380.16	9266.20	9088.49
725,000	10023.16	9855.51	9715.17	9597.14	9413.08
750,000	10368.78	10195.35	10050.17	9928.07	9737.67
775,000	10714.41	10535.20	10385.18	10259.01	10062.26
800,000	11060.04	10875.04	10720.18	10589.95	10386.85
825,000	11405.66	11214.89	11055.19	10920.88	10711.44
850,000	11751.29	11554.73	11390.19	11251.82	11036.03
875,000	12096.91	11894.58	11725.20	11582.75	11360.61
900,000	12442.54	12234.42	12060.20	11913.69	11685.20

266   Table 7

Monthly Payment Loans   **14.75%**

Loan Amount	Amortization Period in Years				
	21	22	23	24	25
10	0.13	0.13	0.13	0.13	0.13
20	0.26	0.26	0.26	0.26	0.26
30	0.39	0.39	0.39	0.39	0.38
40	0.52	0.52	0.51	0.51	0.51
50	0.65	0.65	0.64	0.64	0.64
100	1.29	1.29	1.28	1.27	1.27
200	2.58	2.57	2.55	2.54	2.53
300	3.87	3.85	3.82	3.81	3.79
400	5.16	5.13	5.10	5.07	5.05
500	6.45	6.41	6.37	6.34	6.31
1,000	12.89	12.81	12.73	12.67	12.62
2,000	25.77	25.61	25.46	25.34	25.23
3,000	38.66	38.41	38.19	38.01	37.85
4,000	51.54	51.21	50.92	50.67	50.46
5,000	64.43	64.01	63.65	63.34	63.08
10,000	128.85	128.01	127.29	126.68	126.15
20,000	257.70	256.01	254.58	253.35	252.30
30,000	386.54	384.02	381.86	380.02	378.44
40,000	515.39	512.02	509.15	506.69	504.59
50,000	644.24	640.03	636.44	633.37	630.74
100,000	1288.47	1280.05	1272.87	1266.73	1261.47
125,000	1610.59	1600.06	1591.08	1583.41	1576.84
150,000	1932.70	1920.07	1909.30	1900.09	1892.20
175,000	2254.82	2240.08	2227.51	2216.77	2207.57
200,000	2576.94	2560.09	2545.73	2533.45	2522.93
225,000	2899.05	2880.11	2863.94	2850.13	2838.30
250,000	3221.17	3200.12	3182.16	3166.81	3153.67
275,000	3543.29	3520.13	3500.37	3483.49	3469.03
300,000	3865.40	3840.14	3818.59	3800.17	3784.40
325,000	4187.52	4160.15	4136.80	4116.85	4099.77
350,000	4509.63	4480.16	4455.02	4433.53	4415.13
375,000	4831.75	4800.17	4773.23	4750.21	4730.50
400,000	5153.87	5120.18	5091.45	5066.89	5045.86
425,000	5475.98	5440.20	5409.66	5383.57	5361.23
450,000	5798.10	5760.21	5727.88	5700.25	5676.60
475,000	6120.22	6080.22	6046.09	6016.93	5991.96
500,000	6442.33	6400.23	6364.31	6333.61	6307.33
525,000	6764.45	6720.24	6682.52	6650.29	6622.69
550,000	7086.57	7040.25	7000.74	6966.97	6938.06
575,000	7408.68	7360.26	7318.95	7283.65	7253.43
600,000	7730.80	7680.27	7637.17	7600.33	7568.79
625,000	8052.91	8000.28	7955.38	7917.01	7884.16
650,000	8375.03	8320.30	8273.60	8233.69	8199.53
675,000	8697.15	8640.31	8591.81	8550.37	8514.89
700,000	9019.26	8960.32	8910.03	8867.05	8830.26
725,000	9341.38	9280.33	9228.24	9183.73	9145.62
750,000	9663.50	9600.34	9546.46	9500.41	9460.99
775,000	9985.61	9920.35	9864.67	9817.09	9776.36
800,000	10307.73	10240.36	10182.89	10133.77	10091.72
825,000	10629.85	10560.37	10501.10	10450.45	10407.09
850,000	10951.96	10880.39	10819.32	10767.13	10722.46
875,000	11274.08	11200.40	11137.53	11083.81	11037.82
900,000	11596.19	11520.41	11455.75	11400.49	11353.19

Table 7   267

Monthly Payment Loans

Amortization Period in Years

Loan Amount	26	27	28	29	30
10	0.13	0.13	0.13	0.13	0.13
20	0.26	0.26	0.25	0.25	0.25
30	0.38	0.38	0.38	0.38	0.38
40	0.51	0.51	0.50	0.50	0.50
50	0.63	0.63	0.63	0.63	0.63
100	1.26	1.26	1.25	1.25	1.25
200	2.52	2.51	2.50	2.50	2.49
300	3.78	3.76	3.75	3.75	3.74
400	5.03	5.02	5.00	4.99	4.98
500	6.29	6.27	6.25	6.24	6.23
1,000	12.57	12.54	12.50	12.47	12.45
2,000	25.14	25.07	25.00	24.94	24.89
3,000	37.71	37.60	37.50	37.41	37.34
4,000	50.28	50.13	50.00	49.88	49.78
5,000	62.85	62.66	62.49	62.35	62.23
10,000	125.70	125.31	124.98	124.70	124.45
20,000	251.40	250.62	249.96	249.39	248.90
30,000	377.09	375.93	374.94	374.08	373.35
40,000	502.79	501.24	499.92	498.78	497.80
50,000	628.49	626.55	624.89	623.47	622.24
100,000	1256.97	1253.10	1249.78	1246.93	1244.48
125,000	1571.21	1566.38	1562.23	1558.66	1555.60
150,000	1885.45	1879.65	1874.67	1870.40	1866.72
175,000	2199.69	2192.92	2187.12	2182.13	2177.84
200,000	2513.93	2506.20	2499.56	2493.86	2488.96
225,000	2828.17	2819.47	2812.01	2805.59	2800.08
250,000	3142.41	3132.73	3124.45	3117.32	3111.19
275,000	3456.65	3446.02	3436.90	3429.06	3422.31
300,000	3770.89	3759.30	3749.34	3740.79	3733.43
325,000	4085.13	4072.57	4061.79	4052.52	4044.55
350,000	4399.37	4385.84	4374.23	4364.25	4355.67
375,000	4713.61	4699.12	4686.68	4675.98	4666.79
400,000	5027.85	5012.39	4999.12	4987.72	4977.91
425,000	5342.09	5325.67	5311.57	5299.45	5289.03
450,000	5656.33	5638.94	5624.01	5611.18	5600.15
475,000	5970.57	5952.22	5936.46	5922.91	5911.26
500,000	6284.81	6265.49	6248.90	6234.64	6222.38
525,000	6599.05	6578.76	6561.35	6546.38	6533.50
550,000	6913.29	6892.04	6873.79	6858.11	6844.62
575,000	7227.53	7205.31	7186.24	7169.84	7155.74
600,000	7541.77	7518.59	7498.68	7481.57	7466.86
625,000	7856.01	7831.86	7811.12	7793.30	7777.98
650,000	8170.25	8145.14	8123.57	8105.04	8089.10
675,000	8484.49	8458.41	8436.01	8416.77	8400.22
700,000	8798.73	8771.68	8748.46	8728.50	8711.34
725,000	9112.97	9084.96	9060.90	9040.23	9022.45
750,000	9427.21	9398.23	9373.35	9351.96	9333.57
775,000	9741.45	9711.51	9685.79	9663.70	9644.69
800,000	10055.69	10024.78	9998.24	9975.43	9955.81
825,000	10369.93	10338.06	10310.68	10287.16	10266.93
850,000	10684.17	10651.33	10623.13	10598.89	10578.05
875,000	10998.41	10964.60	10935.57	10910.62	10889.17
900,000	11312.65	11277.88	11248.02	11222.36	11200.29

Monthly Payment Loans   **15.00%**

Loan Amount	\multicolumn{5}{c}{Amortization Period in Years}				
	5	7	8	10	12
10	0.24	0.20	0.18	0.17	0.16
20	0.48	0.39	0.36	0.33	0.31
30	0.72	0.58	0.54	0.49	0.46
40	0.96	0.78	0.72	0.65	0.61
50	1.19	0.97	0.90	0.81	0.76
100	2.38	1.93	1.80	1.62	1.51
200	4.76	3.86	3.59	3.23	3.01
300	7.14	5.79	5.39	4.85	4.51
400	9.52	7.72	7.18	6.46	6.01
500	11.90	9.65	8.98	8.07	7.51
1,000	23.79	19.30	17.95	16.14	15.01
2,000	47.58	38.60	35.90	32.27	30.02
3,000	71.37	57.90	53.84	48.41	45.03
4,000	95.16	77.19	71.79	64.54	60.04
5,000	118.95	96.49	89.73	80.67	75.05
10,000	237.90	192.97	179.46	161.34	150.09
20,000	475.80	385.94	358.91	322.67	300.18
30,000	713.70	578.91	538.37	484.01	450.27
40,000	951.60	771.88	717.82	645.34	600.36
50,000	1189.50	964.84	897.28	806.68	750.44
100,000	2379.00	1929.68	1794.55	1613.35	1500.88
125,000	2973.75	2412.10	2243.18	2016.69	1876.10
150,000	3568.49	2894.52	2691.82	2420.03	2251.32
175,000	4163.24	3376.94	3140.45	2823.37	2626.54
200,000	4757.99	3859.36	3589.09	3226.70	3001.76
225,000	5352.74	4341.77	4037.72	3630.04	3376.98
250,000	5947.49	4824.19	4486.36	4033.38	3752.20
275,000	6542.24	5306.61	4934.99	4436.72	4127.42
300,000	7136.98	5789.03	5383.63	4840.05	4502.64
325,000	7731.73	6271.45	5832.26	5243.39	4877.85
350,000	8326.48	6753.87	6280.90	5646.73	5253.07
375,000	8921.23	7236.29	6729.53	6050.07	5628.29
400,000	9515.98	7718.71	7178.17	6453.40	6003.51
425,000	10110.73	8201.13	7626.80	6856.74	6378.73
450,000	10705.47	8683.54	8075.44	7260.08	6753.95
475,000	11300.22	9165.96	8524.07	7663.42	7129.17
500,000	11894.97	9648.38	8972.71	8066.75	7504.39
525,000	12489.72	10130.80	9421.34	8470.09	7879.61
550,000	13084.47	10613.22	9869.98	8873.43	8254.83
575,000	13679.21	11095.64	10318.61	9276.77	8630.05
600,000	14273.96	11578.06	10767.25	9680.10	9005.27
625,000	14868.71	12060.48	11215.88	10083.44	9380.48
650,000	15463.46	12542.90	11664.52	10486.78	9755.70
675,000	16058.21	13025.31	12113.15	10890.11	10130.92
700,000	16652.96	13507.73	12561.79	11293.45	10506.14
725,000	17247.70	13990.15	13010.42	11696.79	10881.36
750,000	17842.45	14472.57	13459.06	12100.13	11256.58
775,000	18437.20	14954.99	13907.69	12503.46	11631.80
800,000	19031.95	15437.41	14356.33	12906.80	12007.02
825,000	19626.70	15919.83	14804.96	13310.14	12382.24
850,000	20221.45	16402.25	15253.60	13713.48	12757.46
875,000	20816.19	16884.67	15702.23	14116.81	13132.68
900,000	21410.94	17367.08	16150.87	14520.15	13507.90

Table 7   269

15.00%   Monthly Payment Loans

Amortization Period in Years

Loan Amount	15	16	17	18	20
10	0.14	0.14	0.14	0.14	0.14
20	0.28	0.28	0.28	0.27	0.27
30	0.42	0.42	0.41	0.41	0.40
40	0.56	0.56	0.55	0.54	0.53
50	0.70	0.69	0.68	0.68	0.66
100	1.40	1.38	1.36	1.35	1.32
200	2.80	2.76	2.72	2.69	2.64
300	4.20	4.14	4.08	4.03	3.96
400	5.60	5.51	5.44	5.37	5.27
500	7.00	6.89	6.79	6.71	6.59
1,000	14.00	13.77	13.58	13.42	13.17
2,000	28.00	27.54	27.16	26.84	26.34
3,000	41.99	41.31	40.74	40.26	39.51
4,000	55.99	55.08	54.31	53.67	52.68
5,000	69.98	68.84	67.89	67.09	65.84
10,000	139.96	137.68	135.78	134.17	131.68
20,000	279.92	275.36	271.55	268.34	263.36
30,000	419.88	413.04	407.32	402.51	395.04
40,000	559.84	550.71	543.09	536.68	526.72
50,000	699.80	688.39	678.86	670.85	658.40
100,000	1399.59	1376.77	1357.71	1341.70	1316.79
125,000	1749.49	1720.97	1697.13	1677.12	1645.99
150,000	2099.39	2065.16	2036.56	2012.54	1975.19
175,000	2449.28	2409.35	2375.98	2347.96	2304.39
200,000	2799.18	2753.54	2715.41	2683.39	2633.58
225,000	3149.08	3097.74	3054.83	3018.81	2962.78
250,000	3498.97	3441.93	3394.26	3354.23	3291.98
275,000	3848.87	3786.12	3733.68	3689.65	3621.18
300,000	4198.77	4130.31	4073.11	4025.08	3950.37
325,000	4548.66	4474.51	4412.53	4360.50	4279.57
350,000	4898.56	4818.70	4751.96	4695.92	4608.77
375,000	5248.46	5162.89	5091.38	5031.35	4937.97
400,000	5598.35	5507.08	5430.81	5366.77	5267.16
425,000	5948.25	5851.28	5770.23	5702.19	5596.36
450,000	6298.15	6195.47	6109.66	6037.61	5925.56
475,000	6648.04	6539.66	6449.08	6373.04	6254.76
500,000	6997.94	6883.85	6788.51	6708.46	6583.95
525,000	7347.84	7228.05	7127.93	7043.88	6913.15
550,000	7697.73	7572.24	7467.36	7379.30	7242.35
575,000	8047.63	7916.43	7806.78	7714.73	7571.55
600,000	8397.53	8260.62	8146.21	8050.15	7900.74
625,000	8747.42	8604.82	8485.63	8385.57	8229.94
650,000	9097.32	8949.01	8825.06	8720.99	8559.14
675,000	9447.22	9293.20	9164.48	9056.42	8888.33
700,000	9797.11	9637.39	9503.91	9391.84	9217.53
725,000	10147.01	9981.58	9843.33	9727.26	9546.73
750,000	10496.91	10325.78	10182.76	10062.69	9875.93
775,000	10846.81	10669.97	10522.18	10398.11	10205.12
800,000	11196.70	11014.16	10861.61	10733.53	10534.32
825,000	11546.60	11358.35	11201.03	11068.95	10863.52
850,000	11896.50	11702.55	11540.46	11404.38	11192.72
875,000	12246.39	12046.74	11879.88	11739.80	11521.91
900,000	12596.29	12390.93	12219.31	12075.22	11851.11

Monthly Payment Loans   15.00%

Loan Amount	\multicolumn{5}{c}{Amortization Period in Years}				
	21	22	23	24	25
10	0.14	0.13	0.13	0.13	0.13
20	0.27	0.26	0.26	0.26	0.26
30	0.40	0.39	0.39	0.39	0.39
40	0.53	0.52	0.52	0.52	0.52
50	0.66	0.65	0.65	0.65	0.65
100	1.31	1.30	1.30	1.29	1.29
200	2.62	2.60	2.59	2.58	2.57
300	3.93	3.90	3.88	3.86	3.85
400	5.23	5.20	5.17	5.15	5.13
500	6.54	6.50	6.46	6.43	6.41
1,000	13.08	12.99	12.92	12.86	12.81
2,000	26.15	25.98	25.84	25.72	25.62
3,000	39.22	38.97	38.76	38.58	38.43
4,000	52.29	51.96	51.68	51.44	51.24
5,000	65.36	64.95	64.60	64.30	64.05
10,000	130.72	129.89	129.19	128.60	128.09
20,000	261.43	259.78	258.38	257.19	256.17
30,000	392.14	389.67	387.57	385.78	384.25
40,000	522.85	519.56	516.76	514.38	512.34
50,000	653.56	649.45	645.95	642.97	640.42
100,000	1307.12	1298.90	1291.90	1285.93	1280.84
125,000	1633.90	1623.63	1614.88	1607.42	1601.04
150,000	1960.68	1948.35	1937.85	1928.90	1921.25
175,000	2287.46	2273.08	2260.83	2250.38	2241.46
200,000	2614.24	2597.80	2583.80	2571.86	2561.67
225,000	2941.02	2922.52	2906.78	2893.35	2881.87
250,000	3267.80	3247.25	3229.75	3214.83	3202.08
275,000	3594.58	3571.97	3552.73	3536.31	3522.29
300,000	3921.36	3896.69	3875.70	3857.79	3842.50
325,000	4248.14	4221.42	4198.68	4179.27	4162.70
350,000	4574.92	4546.15	4521.65	4500.76	4482.91
375,000	4901.69	4870.87	4844.62	4822.24	4803.12
400,000	5228.47	5195.59	5167.60	5143.72	5123.33
425,000	5555.25	5520.32	5490.57	5465.20	5443.54
450,000	5882.03	5845.04	5813.55	5786.69	5763.74
475,000	6208.81	6169.77	6136.52	6108.17	6083.95
500,000	6535.59	6494.49	6459.50	6429.65	6404.16
525,000	6862.37	6819.22	6782.47	6751.13	6724.37
550,000	7189.15	7143.94	7105.45	7072.62	7044.57
575,000	7515.93	7468.67	7428.42	7394.10	7364.78
600,000	7842.71	7793.39	7751.40	7715.58	7684.99
625,000	8169.49	8118.11	8074.37	8037.06	8005.20
650,000	8496.27	8442.84	8397.35	8358.54	8325.40
675,000	8823.05	8767.56	8720.32	8680.03	8645.61
700,000	9149.83	9092.29	9043.30	9001.51	8965.82
725,000	9476.60	9417.01	9366.27	9322.99	9286.03
750,000	9803.38	9741.74	9689.24	9644.47	9606.23
775,000	10130.16	10066.46	10012.22	9965.96	9926.44
800,000	10456.94	10391.18	10335.19	10287.44	10246.65
825,000	10783.72	10715.91	10658.17	10608.92	10566.86
850,000	11110.50	11040.63	10981.14	10930.40	10887.07
875,000	11437.28	11365.36	11304.12	11251.89	11207.27
900,000	11764.06	11690.08	11627.09	11573.37	11527.48

Table 7   271

15.00% Monthly Payment Loans

Loan Amount	Amortization Period in Years				
	26	27	28	29	30
10	0.13	0.13	0.13	0.13	0.13
20	0.26	0.26	0.26	0.26	0.26
30	0.39	0.39	0.39	0.39	0.38
40	0.52	0.51	0.51	0.51	0.51
50	0.64	0.64	0.64	0.64	0.64
100	1.28	1.28	1.27	1.27	1.27
200	2.56	2.55	2.54	2.54	2.53
300	3.83	3.82	3.81	3.81	3.80
400	5.11	5.10	5.08	5.07	5.06
500	6.39	6.37	6.35	6.34	6.33
1,000	12.77	12.73	12.70	12.67	12.65
2,000	25.53	25.46	25.40	25.34	25.29
3,000	38.30	38.19	38.09	38.01	37.94
4,000	51.06	50.91	50.79	50.68	50.58
5,000	63.83	63.64	63.48	63.34	63.23
10,000	127.65	127.28	126.96	126.68	126.45
20,000	255.30	254.55	253.91	253.36	252.89
30,000	382.95	381.83	380.87	380.04	379.34
40,000	510.59	509.10	507.82	506.72	505.78
50,000	638.24	636.37	634.77	633.40	632.23
100,000	1276.48	1272.74	1269.54	1266.80	1264.45
125,000	1595.59	1590.93	1586.93	1583.50	1580.56
150,000	1914.71	1909.11	1904.31	1900.20	1896.67
175,000	2233.83	2227.30	2221.70	2216.90	2212.78
200,000	2552.95	2545.48	2539.08	2533.60	2528.89
225,000	2872.06	2863.67	2856.47	2850.30	2845.00
250,000	3191.18	3181.85	3173.85	3167.00	3161.12
275,000	3510.30	3500.03	3491.24	3483.70	3477.23
300,000	3829.42	3818.22	3808.62	3800.40	3793.34
325,000	4148.53	4136.40	4126.01	4117.10	4109.45
350,000	4467.65	4454.59	4443.39	4433.80	4425.56
375,000	4786.77	4772.77	4760.78	4750.49	4741.67
400,000	5105.89	5090.96	5078.16	5067.19	5057.78
425,000	5425.00	5409.14	5395.55	5383.89	5373.89
450,000	5744.12	5727.33	5712.93	5700.59	5690.00
475,000	6063.24	6045.51	6030.32	6017.29	6006.11
500,000	6382.36	6363.69	6347.70	6333.99	6322.23
525,000	6701.47	6681.88	6665.09	6650.69	6638.34
550,000	7020.59	7000.06	6982.47	6967.39	6954.45
575,000	7339.71	7318.25	7299.86	7284.09	7270.56
600,000	7658.83	7636.43	7617.24	7600.79	7586.67
625,000	7977.95	7954.62	7934.63	7917.49	7902.78
650,000	8297.06	8272.80	8252.01	8234.19	8218.89
675,000	8616.18	8590.99	8569.40	8550.89	8535.00
700,000	8935.30	8909.17	8886.78	8867.59	8851.11
725,000	9254.42	9227.35	9204.17	9184.28	9167.22
750,000	9573.53	9545.54	9521.55	9500.98	9483.34
775,000	9892.65	9863.72	9838.94	9817.68	9799.45
800,000	10211.77	10181.91	10156.32	10134.38	10115.56
825,000	10530.89	10500.09	10473.71	10451.08	10431.67
850,000	10850.00	10818.28	10791.09	10767.78	10747.78
875,000	11169.12	11136.46	11108.48	11084.48	11063.89
900,000	11488.24	11454.65	11425.86	11401.18	11380.00

Monthly Payment Loans   15.25%

Loan Amount	Amortization Period in Years				
	5	7	8	10	12
10	0.24	0.20	0.19	0.17	0.16
20	0.48	0.39	0.37	0.33	0.31
30	0.72	0.59	0.55	0.49	0.46
40	0.96	0.78	0.73	0.66	0.61
50	1.20	0.98	0.91	0.82	0.76
100	2.40	1.95	1.81	1.63	1.52
200	4.79	3.89	3.62	3.26	3.04
300	7.18	5.84	5.43	4.89	4.56
400	9.57	7.78	7.24	6.52	6.07
500	11.97	9.72	9.05	8.15	7.59
1,000	23.93	19.44	18.10	16.29	15.18
2,000	47.85	38.88	36.19	32.58	30.35
3,000	71.77	58.32	54.28	48.87	45.52
4,000	95.69	77.75	72.37	65.15	60.69
5,000	119.61	97.19	90.46	81.44	75.86
10,000	239.22	194.38	180.91	162.87	151.71
20,000	478.43	388.75	361.81	325.74	303.41
30,000	717.65	583.12	542.72	488.61	455.11
40,000	956.86	777.50	723.62	651.48	606.81
50,000	1196.07	971.87	904.52	814.35	758.51
100,000	2392.14	1943.73	1809.04	1628.70	1517.01
125,000	2990.17	2429.67	2261.30	2035.87	1896.26
150,000	3588.21	2915.60	2713.56	2443.05	2275.51
175,000	4186.24	3401.53	3165.82	2850.22	2654.76
200,000	4784.28	3887.46	3618.08	3257.39	3034.01
225,000	5382.31	4373.39	4070.34	3664.57	3413.26
250,000	5980.34	4859.33	4522.60	4071.74	3792.51
275,000	6578.38	5345.26	4974.86	4478.91	4171.76
300,000	7176.41	5831.19	5427.12	4886.09	4551.02
325,000	7774.45	6317.12	5879.38	5293.26	4930.27
350,000	8372.48	6803.05	6331.63	5700.43	5309.52
375,000	8970.51	7288.99	6783.89	6107.61	5688.77
400,000	9568.55	7774.92	7236.15	6514.78	6068.02
425,000	10166.58	8260.85	7688.41	6921.95	6447.27
450,000	10764.62	8746.78	8140.67	7329.13	6826.52
475,000	11362.65	9232.71	8592.93	7736.30	7205.77
500,000	11960.68	9718.65	9045.19	8143.47	7585.02
525,000	12558.72	10204.58	9497.45	8550.65	7964.27
550,000	13156.75	10690.51	9949.71	8957.82	8343.52
575,000	13754.79	11176.44	10401.97	9364.99	8722.77
600,000	14352.82	11662.38	10854.23	9772.17	9102.03
625,000	14950.85	12148.31	11306.49	10179.34	9481.28
650,000	15548.89	12634.24	11758.75	10586.51	9860.53
675,000	16146.92	13120.17	12211.00	10993.69	10239.78
700,000	16744.96	13606.10	12663.26	11400.86	10619.03
725,000	17342.99	14092.04	13115.52	11808.03	10998.28
750,000	17941.02	14577.97	13567.78	12215.21	11377.53
775,000	18539.06	15063.90	14020.04	12622.38	11756.78
800,000	19137.09	15549.83	14472.30	13029.55	12136.03
825,000	19735.13	16035.76	14924.56	13436.73	12515.28
850,000	20333.16	16521.70	15376.82	13843.90	12894.53
875,000	20931.19	17007.63	15829.08	14251.07	13273.79
900,000	21529.23	17493.56	16281.34	14658.25	13653.04

Table 7   273

15.25% Monthly Payment Loans

Amortization Period in Years

Loan Amount	15	16	17	18	20
10	0.15	0.14	0.14	0.14	0.14
20	0.29	0.28	0.28	0.28	0.27
30	0.43	0.42	0.42	0.41	0.41
40	0.57	0.56	0.56	0.55	0.54
50	0.71	0.70	0.69	0.68	0.67
100	1.42	1.40	1.38	1.36	1.34
200	2.84	2.79	2.76	2.72	2.68
300	4.26	4.19	4.13	4.08	4.01
400	5.67	5.58	5.51	5.44	5.35
500	7.09	6.98	6.88	6.80	6.68
1,000	14.17	13.95	13.76	13.60	13.36
2,000	28.34	27.89	27.51	27.20	26.71
3,000	42.51	41.83	41.27	40.80	40.06
4,000	56.67	55.77	55.02	54.39	53.42
5,000	70.84	69.72	68.78	67.99	66.77
10,000	141.68	139.43	137.55	135.98	133.53
20,000	283.35	278.85	275.10	271.95	267.06
30,000	425.03	418.28	412.64	407.92	400.59
40,000	566.70	557.70	550.19	543.89	534.12
50,000	708.38	697.12	687.73	679.86	667.65
100,000	1416.75	1394.24	1375.46	1359.72	1335.30
125,000	1770.94	1742.80	1719.33	1699.65	1669.13
150,000	2125.13	2091.36	2063.19	2039.58	2002.95
175,000	2479.32	2439.92	2407.06	2379.51	2336.78
200,000	2833.50	2788.48	2750.92	2719.44	2670.60
225,000	3187.69	3137.04	3094.78	3059.37	3004.43
250,000	3541.88	3485.60	3438.65	3399.30	3338.25
275,000	3896.07	3834.16	3782.51	3739.23	3672.08
300,000	4250.25	4182.72	4126.38	4079.16	4005.90
325,000	4604.44	4531.28	4470.24	4419.09	4339.73
350,000	4958.63	4879.84	4814.11	4759.01	4673.55
375,000	5312.82	5228.40	5157.97	5098.94	5007.38
400,000	5667.00	5576.96	5501.84	5438.87	5341.20
425,000	6021.19	5925.52	5845.70	5778.80	5675.02
450,000	6375.38	6274.08	6189.56	6118.73	6008.85
475,000	6729.57	6622.64	6533.43	6458.66	6342.67
500,000	7083.75	6971.20	6877.29	6798.59	6676.50
525,000	7437.94	7319.76	7221.16	7138.52	7010.32
550,000	7792.13	7668.32	7565.02	7478.45	7344.15
575,000	8146.32	8016.88	7908.89	7818.38	7677.97
600,000	8500.50	8365.44	8252.75	8158.31	8011.80
625,000	8854.69	8714.00	8596.62	8498.24	8345.62
650,000	9208.88	9062.56	8940.48	8838.17	8679.45
675,000	9563.07	9411.12	9284.34	9178.09	9013.27
700,000	9917.25	9759.68	9628.21	9518.02	9347.10
725,000	10271.44	10108.24	9972.07	9857.95	9680.92
750,000	10625.63	10456.80	10315.94	10197.88	10014.75
775,000	10979.82	10805.36	10659.80	10537.81	10348.57
800,000	11334.00	11153.92	11003.67	10877.74	10682.39
825,000	11688.19	11502.48	11347.53	11217.67	11016.22
850,000	12042.38	11851.04	11691.40	11557.60	11350.04
875,000	12396.57	12199.60	12035.26	11897.53	11683.87
900,000	12750.75	12548.16	12379.12	12237.46	12017.69

Monthly Payment Loans   15.25%

Loan Amount	Amortization Period in Years				
	21	22	23	24	25
10	0.14	0.14	0.14	0.14	0.14
20	0.27	0.27	0.27	0.27	0.27
30	0.40	0.40	0.40	0.40	0.40
40	0.54	0.53	0.53	0.53	0.53
50	0.67	0.66	0.66	0.66	0.66
100	1.33	1.32	1.32	1.31	1.31
200	2.66	2.64	2.63	2.62	2.61
300	3.98	3.96	3.94	3.92	3.91
400	5.31	5.28	5.25	5.23	5.21
500	6.63	6.59	6.56	6.53	6.51
1,000	13.26	13.18	13.12	13.06	13.01
2,000	26.52	26.36	26.23	26.11	26.01
3,000	39.78	39.54	39.34	39.16	39.01
4,000	53.04	52.72	52.45	52.21	52.02
5,000	66.30	65.90	65.56	65.27	65.02
10,000	132.59	131.79	131.11	130.53	130.03
20,000	265.17	263.57	262.21	261.05	260.06
30,000	397.76	395.35	393.31	391.57	390.08
40,000	530.34	527.13	524.41	522.09	520.11
50,000	662.93	658.92	655.51	652.61	650.13
100,000	1325.85	1317.83	1311.01	1305.21	1300.26
125,000	1657.31	1647.28	1638.76	1631.51	1625.33
150,000	1988.77	1976.74	1966.51	1957.81	1950.39
175,000	2320.23	2306.19	2294.26	2284.11	2275.46
200,000	2651.69	2635.65	2622.01	2610.41	2600.52
225,000	2983.15	2965.10	2949.77	2936.71	2925.59
250,000	3314.61	3294.56	3277.52	3263.01	3250.65
275,000	3646.07	3624.01	3605.27	3589.31	3575.72
300,000	3977.53	3953.47	3933.02	3915.61	3900.78
325,000	4308.99	4282.92	4260.77	4241.91	4225.84
350,000	4640.45	4612.38	4588.52	4568.22	4550.91
375,000	4971.91	4941.83	4916.27	4894.52	4875.97
400,000	5303.37	5271.29	5244.02	5220.82	5201.04
425,000	5634.83	5600.74	5571.77	5547.12	5526.10
450,000	5966.29	5930.20	5899.53	5873.42	5851.17
475,000	6297.75	6259.65	6227.28	6199.72	6176.23
500,000	6629.21	6589.11	6555.03	6526.02	6501.30
525,000	6960.67	6918.56	6882.78	6852.32	6826.36
550,000	7292.13	7248.02	7210.53	7178.62	7151.43
575,000	7623.59	7577.47	7538.28	7504.92	7476.49
600,000	7955.05	7906.93	7866.03	7831.22	7801.55
625,000	8286.51	8236.38	8193.78	8157.52	8126.62
650,000	8617.97	8565.84	8521.53	8483.82	8451.68
675,000	8949.43	8895.29	8849.29	8810.13	8776.75
700,000	9280.90	9224.75	9177.04	9136.43	9101.81
725,000	9612.36	9554.20	9504.79	9462.73	9426.88
750,000	9943.82	9883.66	9832.54	9789.03	9751.94
775,000	10275.28	10213.11	10160.29	10115.33	10077.01
800,000	10606.74	10542.57	10488.04	10441.63	10402.07
825,000	10930.20	10872.02	10815.79	10767.93	10727.14
850,000	11269.66	11201.48	11143.54	11094.23	11052.20
875,000	11601.12	11530.93	11471.29	11420.53	11377.26
900,000	11932.58	11860.39	11799.05	11746.83	11702.33

Table 7   275

Monthly Payment Loans

Loan Amount	Amortization Period in Years				
	26	27	28	29	30
10	0.13	0.13	0.13	0.13	0.13
20	0.26	0.26	0.26	0.26	0.26
30	0.39	0.39	0.39	0.39	0.39
40	0.52	0.52	0.52	0.52	0.52
50	0.65	0.65	0.65	0.65	0.65
100	1.30	1.30	1.29	1.29	1.29
200	2.60	2.59	2.58	2.58	2.57
300	3.89	3.88	3.87	3.87	3.86
400	5.19	5.17	5.16	5.15	5.14
500	6.49	6.47	6.45	6.44	6.43
1,000	12.97	12.93	12.90	12.87	12.85
2,000	25.93	25.85	25.79	25.74	25.69
3,000	38.89	38.78	38.69	38.61	38.54
4,000	51.85	51.70	51.58	51.47	51.38
5,000	64.81	64.63	64.47	64.34	64.23
10,000	129.61	129.25	128.94	128.68	128.45
20,000	259.21	258.49	257.88	257.35	256.90
30,000	388.82	387.74	386.81	386.02	385.34
40,000	518.42	516.98	515.75	514.69	513.79
50,000	648.02	646.22	644.68	643.36	642.23
100,000	1296.04	1292.44	1289.36	1286.72	1284.46
125,000	1620.05	1615.55	1611.70	1608.40	1605.58
150,000	1944.06	1938.66	1934.03	1930.08	1926.69
175,000	2268.07	2261.76	2256.37	2251.76	2247.81
200,000	2592.08	2584.87	2578.71	2573.44	2568.92
225,000	2916.09	2907.98	2901.05	2895.12	2890.04
250,000	3240.10	3231.09	3223.39	3216.79	3211.15
275,000	3564.11	3554.20	3545.72	3538.47	3532.27
300,000	3888.12	3877.31	3868.06	3860.15	3853.38
325,000	4212.13	4200.42	4190.40	4181.83	4174.50
350,000	4536.14	4523.52	4512.74	4503.51	4495.61
375,000	4860.15	4846.63	4835.08	4825.19	4816.72
400,000	5184.16	5169.74	5157.41	5146.87	5137.84
425,000	5508.17	5492.85	5479.75	5468.55	5458.95
450,000	5832.18	5815.96	5802.09	5790.23	5780.07
475,000	6156.19	6139.07	6124.43	6111.90	6101.18
500,000	6480.20	6462.18	6446.77	6433.58	6422.30
525,000	6804.21	6785.28	6769.11	6755.26	6743.41
550,000	7128.22	7108.39	7091.44	7076.94	7064.53
575,000	7452.23	7431.50	7413.78	7398.62	7385.64
600,000	7776.24	7754.61	7736.12	7720.30	7706.76
625,000	8100.25	8077.72	8058.46	8041.98	8027.87
650,000	8424.26	8400.83	8380.80	8363.66	8348.99
675,000	8748.27	8723.93	8703.13	8685.34	8670.10
700,000	9072.27	9047.04	9025.47	9007.02	8991.21
725,000	9396.28	9370.15	9347.81	9328.69	9312.33
750,000	9720.29	9693.26	9670.15	9650.37	9633.44
775,000	10044.30	10016.37	9992.49	9972.05	9954.56
800,000	10368.31	10339.48	10314.82	10293.73	10275.67
825,000	10692.32	10662.59	10637.16	10615.41	10596.79
850,000	11016.33	10985.69	10959.50	10937.09	10917.90
875,000	11340.34	11308.80	11281.84	11258.77	11239.02
900,000	11664.35	11631.91	11604.18	11580.45	11560.13

Monthly Payment Loans   **15.50%**

Loan Amount	Amortization Period in Years				
	5	7	8	10	12
10	0.25	0.20	0.19	0.17	0.16
20	0.49	0.40	0.37	0.33	0.31
30	0.73	0.59	0.55	0.50	0.46
40	0.97	0.79	0.73	0.66	0.62
50	1.21	0.98	0.92	0.83	0.77
100	2.41	1.96	1.83	1.65	1.54
200	4.82	3.92	3.65	3.29	3.07
300	7.22	5.88	5.48	4.94	4.60
400	9.63	7.84	7.30	6.58	6.14
500	12.03	9.79	9.12	8.23	7.67
1,000	24.06	19.58	18.24	16.45	15.34
2,000	48.11	39.16	36.48	32.89	30.67
3,000	72.16	58.74	54.71	49.33	46.00
4,000	96.22	78.32	72.95	65.77	61.33
5,000	120.27	97.90	91.18	82.21	76.67
10,000	240.54	195.79	182.36	164.42	153.33
20,000	481.07	391.57	364.72	328.83	306.65
30,000	721.60	587.36	547.08	493.24	459.97
40,000	962.13	783.14	729.44	657.65	613.29
50,000	1202.66	978.92	911.80	822.06	766.61
100,000	2405.32	1957.84	1823.60	1644.11	1533.21
125,000	3006.65	2447.30	2279.50	2055.14	1916.51
150,000	3607.98	2936.76	2735.39	2466.16	2299.81
175,000	4209.31	3426.22	3191.29	2877.19	2683.11
200,000	4810.64	3915.67	3647.19	3288.22	3066.41
225,000	5411.97	4405.13	4103.09	3699.24	3449.71
250,000	6013.30	4894.59	4558.99	4110.27	3833.02
275,000	6614.63	5384.05	5014.88	4521.29	4216.32
300,000	7215.96	5873.51	5470.78	4932.32	4599.62
325,000	7817.29	6362.97	5926.68	5343.35	4982.92
350,000	8418.62	6852.43	6382.58	5754.37	5366.22
375,000	9019.95	7341.89	6838.48	6165.40	5749.52
400,000	9621.28	7831.34	7294.37	6576.43	6132.82
425,000	10222.61	8320.80	7750.27	6987.45	6516.12
450,000	10823.94	8810.26	8206.17	7398.48	6899.42
475,000	11425.27	9299.72	8662.07	7809.51	7282.73
500,000	12026.60	9789.18	9117.97	8220.53	7666.03
525,000	12627.93	10278.64	9573.86	8631.56	8049.33
550,000	13229.26	10768.10	10029.76	9042.58	8432.63
575,000	13830.59	11257.55	10485.66	9453.61	8815.93
600,000	14431.92	11747.01	10941.56	9864.64	9199.23
625,000	15033.25	12236.47	11397.46	10275.66	9582.53
650,000	15634.58	12725.93	11853.35	10686.69	9965.83
675,000	16235.91	13215.39	12309.25	11097.72	10349.13
700,000	16837.24	13704.85	12765.15	11508.74	10732.43
725,000	17438.57	14194.31	13221.05	11919.77	11115.74
750,000	18039.90	14683.77	13676.95	12330.80	11499.04
775,000	18641.23	15173.22	14132.85	12741.82	11882.34
800,000	19242.56	15662.68	14588.74	13152.85	12265.64
825,000	19843.89	16152.14	15044.64	13563.87	12648.94
850,000	20445.22	16641.60	15500.54	13974.90	13032.24
875,000	21046.55	17131.06	15956.44	14385.93	13415.54
900,000	21647.88	17620.52	16412.34	14796.95	13798.84

Table 7   277

15.50%   Monthly Payment Loans

Loan Amount	\multicolumn{5}{c}{Amortization Period in Years}
	15	16	17	18	20
10	0.15	0.15	0.14	0.14	0.14
20	0.29	0.29	0.28	0.28	0.28
30	0.44	0.43	0.42	0.42	0.41
40	0.58	0.57	0.56	0.56	0.55
50	0.72	0.71	0.70	0.69	0.68
100	1.44	1.42	1.40	1.38	1.36
200	2.87	2.83	2.79	2.76	2.71
300	4.31	4.24	4.18	4.14	4.07
400	5.74	5.65	5.58	5.52	5.42
500	7.17	7.06	6.97	6.89	6.77
1,000	14.34	14.12	13.94	13.78	13.54
2,000	28.68	28.24	27.87	27.56	27.08
3,000	43.02	42.36	41.80	41.34	40.62
4,000	57.36	56.48	55.74	55.12	54.16
5,000	71.70	70.59	69.67	68.90	67.70
10,000	143.40	141.18	139.33	137.79	135.39
20,000	286.80	282.36	278.66	275.57	270.78
30,000	430.20	423.54	417.99	413.35	406.17
40,000	573.60	564.72	557.32	551.13	541.56
50,000	717.00	705.90	696.65	688.91	676.95
100,000	1434.00	1411.79	1393.30	1377.82	1353.89
125,000	1792.49	1764.74	1741.62	1722.28	1692.36
150,000	2150.99	2117.69	2089.94	2066.73	2030.83
175,000	2509.49	2470.63	2438.27	2411.19	2369.30
200,000	2867.99	2823.58	2786.59	2755.64	2707.77
225,000	3226.48	3176.53	3134.91	3100.10	3046.24
250,000	3584.98	3529.47	3483.24	3444.55	3384.71
275,000	3943.48	3882.42	3831.56	3789.01	3723.18
300,000	4301.98	4235.37	4179.88	4133.46	4061.65
325,000	4660.47	4588.31	4528.21	4477.92	4400.12
350,000	5018.97	4941.26	4876.53	4822.37	4738.59
375,000	5377.47	5294.21	5224.85	5166.83	5077.06
400,000	5735.97	5647.15	5573.17	5511.28	5415.53
425,000	6094.46	6000.10	5921.50	5855.74	5754.00
450,000	6452.96	6353.05	6269.82	6200.19	6092.47
475,000	6811.46	6705.99	6618.14	6544.65	6430.94
500,000	7169.96	7058.94	6966.47	6889.10	6769.41
525,000	7528.45	7411.89	7314.79	7233.56	7107.88
550,000	7886.95	7764.83	7663.11	7578.01	7446.35
575,000	8245.45	8117.78	8011.44	7922.47	7784.82
600,000	8603.95	8470.73	8359.76	8266.92	8123.29
625,000	8962.44	8823.67	8708.08	8611.38	8461.76
650,000	9320.94	9176.62	9056.41	8955.83	8800.23
675,000	9679.44	9529.57	9404.73	9300.29	9138.70
700,000	10037.94	9882.51	9753.05	9644.74	9477.17
725,000	10396.43	10235.46	10101.38	9989.20	9815.64
750,000	10754.93	10588.41	10449.70	10333.65	10154.11
775,000	11113.43	10941.35	10798.02	10678.11	10492.58
800,000	11471.93	11294.30	11146.34	11022.56	10831.05
825,000	11830.43	11647.25	11494.67	11367.02	11169.52
850,000	12188.92	12000.19	11842.99	11711.47	11507.99
875,000	12547.42	12353.14	12191.31	12055.93	11846.46
900,000	12905.92	12706.09	12539.64	12400.38	12184.93

Monthly Payment Loans   15.50%

Loan Amount	Amortization Period in Years				
	21	22	23	24	25
10	0.14	0.14	0.14	0.14	0.14
20	0.27	0.27	0.27	0.27	0.27
30	0.41	0.41	0.40	0.40	0.40
40	0.54	0.54	0.54	0.53	0.53
50	0.68	0.67	0.67	0.67	0.66
100	1.35	1.34	1.34	1.33	1.32
200	2.69	2.68	2.67	2.65	2.64
300	4.04	4.02	4.00	3.98	3.96
400	5.38	5.35	5.33	5.30	5.28
500	6.73	6.69	6.66	6.63	6.60
1,000	13.45	13.37	13.31	13.25	13.20
2,000	26.90	26.74	26.61	26.50	26.40
3,000	40.34	40.11	39.91	39.74	39.60
4,000	53.79	53.48	53.21	52.99	52.79
5,000	67.24	66.85	66.51	66.23	65.99
10,000	134.47	133.69	133.02	132.46	131.98
20,000	268.93	267.37	266.04	264.91	263.95
30,000	403.40	401.05	399.06	397.37	395.93
40,000	537.86	534.73	532.08	529.82	527.90
50,000	672.32	668.41	665.09	662.27	659.88
100,000	1344.64	1336.82	1330.18	1324.54	1319.75
125,000	1680.80	1671.02	1662.72	1655.68	1649.69
150,000	2016.96	2005.22	1995.27	1986.81	1979.62
175,000	2353.12	2339.43	2327.81	2317.95	2309.56
200,000	2689.28	2673.63	2660.36	2649.08	2639.50
225,000	3025.44	3007.83	2992.90	2980.22	2969.43
250,000	3361.60	3342.03	3325.44	3311.35	3299.37
275,000	3697.76	3676.24	3657.99	3642.49	3629.30
300,000	4033.91	4010.44	3990.53	3973.62	3959.24
325,000	4370.07	4344.64	4323.08	4304.76	4289.18
350,000	4706.23	4678.85	4655.62	4635.89	4619.11
375,000	5042.39	5013.05	4988.16	4967.03	4949.05
400,000	5378.55	5347.25	5320.71	5298.16	5278.99
425,000	5714.71	5681.45	5653.25	5629.30	5608.92
450,000	6050.87	6015.66	5985.80	5960.43	5938.86
475,000	6387.03	6349.86	6318.34	6291.57	6268.79
500,000	6723.19	6684.06	6650.88	6622.70	6598.73
525,000	7059.35	7018.27	6983.43	6953.84	6928.67
550,000	7395.51	7352.47	7315.97	7284.97	7258.60
575,000	7731.66	7686.67	7648.52	7616.11	7588.54
600,000	8067.82	8020.87	7981.06	7947.24	7918.48
625,000	8403.98	8355.08	8313.60	8278.38	8248.41
650,000	8740.14	8689.28	8646.15	8609.51	8578.35
675,000	9076.30	9023.48	8978.69	8940.65	8908.29
700,000	9412.46	9357.69	9311.24	9271.78	9238.22
725,000	9748.62	9691.89	9643.78	9602.91	9568.16
750,000	10084.78	10026.09	9976.32	9934.05	9898.09
775,000	10420.94	10360.29	10308.87	10265.18	10228.03
800,000	10757.10	10694.50	10641.41	10596.32	10557.97
825,000	11093.26	11028.70	10973.95	10927.45	10887.90
850,000	11429.41	11362.90	11306.50	11258.59	11217.84
875,000	11765.57	11697.11	11639.04	11589.72	11547.78
900,000	12101.73	12031.31	11971.59	11920.86	11877.71

Table 7   279

15.50% Monthly Payment Loans

Loan Amount	Amortization Period in Years				
	26	27	28	29	30
10	0.14	0.14	0.14	0.14	0.14
20	0.27	0.27	0.27	0.27	0.27
30	0.40	0.40	0.40	0.40	0.40
40	0.53	0.53	0.53	0.53	0.53
50	0.66	0.66	0.66	0.66	0.66
100	1.32	1.32	1.31	1.31	1.31
200	2.64	2.63	2.62	2.62	2.61
300	3.95	3.94	3.93	3.93	3.92
400	5.27	5.25	5.24	5.23	5.22
500	6.58	6.57	6.55	6.54	6.53
1,000	13.16	13.13	13.10	13.07	13.05
2,000	26.32	26.25	26.19	26.14	26.10
3,000	39.47	39.37	39.28	39.21	39.14
4,000	52.63	52.49	52.37	52.27	52.19
5,000	65.79	65.61	65.47	65.34	65.23
10,000	131.57	131.22	130.93	130.67	130.46
20,000	263.14	262.44	261.85	261.34	260.91
30,000	394.70	393.66	392.77	392.01	391.36
40,000	526.27	524.88	523.69	522.68	521.81
50,000	657.84	656.10	654.61	653.35	652.26
100,000	1315.67	1312.19	1309.22	1306.69	1304.52
125,000	1644.58	1640.23	1636.52	1633.36	1630.65
150,000	1973.50	1968.28	1963.83	1960.03	1956.78
175,000	2302.42	2296.33	2291.13	2286.70	2282.91
200,000	2631.33	2624.37	2618.44	2613.37	2609.04
225,000	2960.25	2952.42	2945.74	2940.04	2935.17
250,000	3289.16	3280.46	3273.04	3266.71	3261.30
275,000	3618.08	3608.51	3600.35	3593.38	3587.43
300,000	3946.99	3936.56	3927.65	3920.05	3913.56
325,000	4275.91	4264.60	4254.95	4246.72	4239.68
350,000	4604.83	4592.65	4582.26	4573.39	4565.81
375,000	4933.74	4920.69	4909.56	4900.06	4891.94
400,000	5262.66	5248.74	5236.87	5226.73	5218.07
425,000	5591.57	5576.78	5564.17	5553.40	5544.20
450,000	5920.49	5904.83	5891.47	5880.07	5870.33
475,000	6249.40	6232.88	6218.78	6206.74	6196.46
500,000	6578.32	6560.92	6546.08	6533.41	6522.59
525,000	6907.24	6888.97	6873.39	6860.08	6848.72
550,000	7236.15	7217.01	7200.69	7186.75	7174.85
575,000	7565.07	7545.06	7527.99	7513.42	7500.98
600,000	7893.98	7873.11	7855.30	7840.09	7827.11
625,000	8222.90	8201.15	8182.60	8166.76	8153.24
650,000	8551.81	8529.20	8509.90	8493.43	8479.36
675,000	8880.73	8857.24	8837.21	8820.10	8805.49
700,000	9209.65	9185.29	9164.51	9146.77	9131.62
725,000	9538.56	9513.34	9491.82	9473.44	9457.75
750,000	9867.48	9841.38	9819.12	9800.12	9783.88
775,000	10196.39	10169.43	10146.42	10126.79	10110.01
800,000	10525.31	10497.47	10473.73	10453.46	10436.14
825,000	10854.22	10825.52	10801.03	10780.13	10762.27
850,000	11183.14	11153.56	11128.33	11106.80	11088.40
875,000	11512.06	11481.61	11455.64	11433.47	11414.53
900,000	11840.97	11809.66	11782.94	11760.14	11740.66

Monthly Payment Loans   15.75%

Loan Amount	Amortization Period in Years				
	5	7	8	10	12
10	0.25	0.20	0.19	0.17	0.16
20	0.49	0.40	0.37	0.34	0.31
30	0.73	0.60	0.56	0.50	0.47
40	0.97	0.79	0.74	0.67	0.62
50	1.21	0.99	0.92	0.83	0.78
100	2.42	1.98	1.84	1.66	1.55
200	4.84	3.95	3.68	3.32	3.10
300	7.26	5.92	5.52	4.98	4.65
400	9.68	7.89	7.36	6.64	6.20
500	12.10	9.86	9.20	8.30	7.75
1,000	24.19	19.72	18.39	16.60	15.50
2,000	48.38	39.44	36.77	33.20	30.99
3,000	72.56	59.16	55.15	49.79	46.49
4,000	96.75	78.88	73.53	66.39	61.98
5,000	120.93	98.60	91.92	82.98	77.48
10,000	241.86	197.20	183.83	165.96	154.95
20,000	483.71	394.40	367.65	331.92	309.90
30,000	725.57	591.60	551.47	497.88	464.85
40,000	967.42	788.80	735.29	663.84	619.80
50,000	1209.28	986.00	919.11	829.80	774.74
100,000	2418.55	1972.00	1838.21	1659.59	1549.48
125,000	3023.18	2465.00	2297.76	2074.49	1936.85
150,000	3627.82	2958.00	2757.31	2489.38	2324.22
175,000	4232.45	3450.99	3216.87	2904.28	2711.59
200,000	4837.09	3943.99	3676.42	3319.17	3098.96
225,000	5441.73	4436.99	4135.97	3734.07	3486.33
250,000	6046.36	4929.99	4595.52	4148.97	3873.70
275,000	6651.00	5422.99	5055.07	4563.86	4261.07
300,000	7255.63	5915.99	5514.62	4978.76	4648.44
325,000	7860.27	6408.99	5974.18	5393.66	5035.81
350,000	8464.90	6901.98	6433.73	5808.55	5423.18
375,000	9069.54	7394.98	6893.28	6223.45	5810.55
400,000	9674.17	7887.98	7352.83	6638.34	6197.92
425,000	10278.81	8380.98	7812.38	7053.24	6585.29
450,000	10883.45	8873.98	8271.93	7468.14	6972.66
475,000	11488.08	9366.98	8731.48	7883.03	7360.03
500,000	12092.72	9859.98	9191.04	8297.93	7747.40
525,000	12697.35	10352.97	9650.59	8712.83	8134.77
550,000	13301.99	10845.97	10110.14	9127.72	8522.14
575,000	13906.62	11338.97	10569.69	9542.62	8909.51
600,000	14511.26	11831.97	11029.24	9957.51	9296.88
625,000	15115.89	12324.97	11488.79	10372.41	9684.25
650,000	15720.53	12817.97	11948.35	10787.31	10071.62
675,000	16325.17	13310.97	12407.90	11202.20	10458.98
700,000	16929.80	13803.96	12867.45	11617.10	10846.35
725,000	17534.44	14296.96	13327.00	12031.99	11233.72
750,000	18139.07	14789.96	13786.55	12446.89	11621.09
775,000	18743.71	15282.96	14246.10	12861.79	12008.46
800,000	19348.34	15775.96	14705.66	13276.68	12395.83
825,000	19952.98	16268.96	15165.21	13691.58	12783.20
850,000	20557.62	16761.95	15624.76	14106.48	13170.57
875,000	21162.25	17254.95	16084.31	14521.37	13557.94
900,000	21766.89	17747.95	16543.86	14936.27	13945.31

Table 7   281

15.75%   Monthly Payment Loans

Loan Amount	Amortization Period in Years				
	15	16	17	18	20
10	0.15	0.15	0.15	0.14	0.14
20	0.30	0.29	0.29	0.28	0.28
30	0.44	0.43	0.43	0.42	0.42
40	0.59	0.58	0.57	0.56	0.55
50	0.73	0.72	0.71	0.70	0.69
100	1.46	1.43	1.42	1.40	1.38
200	2.91	2.86	2.83	2.80	2.75
300	4.36	4.29	4.24	4.19	4.12
400	5.81	5.72	5.65	5.59	5.50
500	7.26	7.15	7.06	6.98	6.87
1,000	14.52	14.30	14.12	13.96	13.73
2,000	29.03	28.59	28.23	27.92	27.46
3,000	43.54	42.89	42.34	41.88	41.18
4,000	58.06	57.18	56.45	55.84	54.91
5,000	72.57	71.48	70.57	69.80	68.63
10,000	145.14	142.95	141.13	139.60	137.26
20,000	290.27	285.89	282.25	279.20	274.51
30,000	435.40	428.83	423.37	418.80	411.77
40,000	580.53	571.77	564.49	558.40	549.02
50,000	725.66	714.71	705.61	698.00	686.27
100,000	1451.31	1429.42	1411.21	1396.00	1372.54
125,000	1814.14	1786.77	1764.01	1745.00	1715.67
150,000	2176.97	2144.12	2116.81	2094.00	2058.81
175,000	2539.79	2501.47	2469.61	2443.00	2401.94
200,000	2902.62	2858.83	2822.41	2792.00	2745.07
225,000	3265.45	3216.18	3175.21	3141.00	3088.21
250,000	3628.27	3573.53	3528.01	3490.00	3431.34
275,000	3991.10	3930.88	3880.81	3839.00	3774.47
300,000	4353.93	4288.24	4233.61	4188.00	4117.61
325,000	4716.76	4645.59	4586.42	4536.99	4460.74
350,000	5079.58	5002.94	4939.22	4885.99	4803.87
375,000	5442.41	5360.30	5292.02	5234.99	5147.01
400,000	5805.24	5717.65	5644.82	5583.99	5490.14
425,000	6168.06	6075.00	5997.62	5932.99	5833.27
450,000	6530.89	6432.35	6350.42	6281.99	6176.41
475,000	6893.72	6789.71	6703.22	6630.99	6519.54
500,000	7256.54	7147.06	7056.02	6979.99	6862.67
525,000	7619.37	7504.41	7408.82	7328.99	7205.81
550,000	7982.20	7861.76	7761.62	7677.99	7548.94
575,000	8345.02	8219.12	8114.42	8026.99	7892.07
600,000	8707.85	8576.47	8467.22	8375.99	8235.21
625,000	9070.68	8933.82	8820.02	8724.98	8578.34
650,000	9433.51	9291.18	9172.83	9073.98	8921.47
675,000	9796.33	9648.53	9525.63	9422.98	9264.61
700,000	10159.16	10005.88	9878.43	9771.98	9607.74
725,000	10521.99	10363.23	10231.23	10120.98	9950.87
750,000	10884.81	10720.59	10584.03	10469.98	10294.01
775,000	11247.64	11077.94	10936.83	10818.98	10637.14
800,000	11610.47	11435.29	11289.63	11167.98	10980.27
825,000	11973.29	11792.64	11642.43	11516.98	11323.41
850,000	12336.12	12150.00	11995.23	11865.98	11666.54
875,000	12698.95	12507.35	12348.03	12214.98	12009.68
900,000	13061.77	12864.70	12700.83	12563.98	12352.81

Monthly Payment Loans   15.75%

Loan Amount	Amortization Period in Years				
	21	22	23	24	25
10	0.14	0.14	0.14	0.14	0.14
20	0.28	0.28	0.27	0.27	0.27
30	0.41	0.41	0.41	0.41	0.41
40	0.55	0.55	0.54	0.54	0.54
50	0.69	0.68	0.68	0.68	0.67
100	1.37	1.36	1.35	1.35	1.34
200	2.73	2.72	2.70	2.69	2.68
300	4.10	4.07	4.05	4.04	4.02
400	5.46	5.43	5.40	5.38	5.36
500	6.82	6.78	6.75	6.72	6.70
1,000	13.64	13.56	13.50	13.44	13.40
2,000	27.28	27.12	26.99	26.88	26.79
3,000	40.91	40.68	40.49	40.32	40.18
4,000	54.55	54.24	53.98	53.76	53.58
5,000	68.18	67.80	67.48	67.20	66.97
10,000	136.36	135.59	134.95	134.40	133.93
20,000	272.71	271.18	269.89	268.79	267.86
30,000	409.06	406.77	404.83	403.19	401.79
40,000	545.41	542.35	539.77	537.58	535.72
50,000	681.76	677.94	674.71	671.97	669.65
100,000	1363.51	1355.87	1349.42	1343.94	1339.29
125,000	1704.38	1694.84	1686.77	1679.92	1674.12
150,000	2045.26	2033.81	2024.12	2015.91	2008.94
175,000	2386.13	2372.78	2361.47	2351.89	2343.76
200,000	2727.01	2711.74	2698.83	2687.88	2678.58
225,000	3067.88	3050.71	3036.18	3023.86	3013.41
250,000	3408.76	3389.68	3373.53	3359.84	3348.23
275,000	3749.63	3728.64	3710.88	3695.83	3683.05
300,000	4090.51	4067.61	4048.24	4031.81	4017.87
325,000	4431.38	4406.58	4385.59	4367.80	4352.70
350,000	4772.26	4745.55	4722.94	4703.78	4687.52
375,000	5113.13	5084.51	5060.29	5039.76	5022.34
400,000	5454.01	5423.48	5397.65	5375.75	5357.16
425,000	5794.88	5762.45	5735.00	5711.73	5691.99
450,000	6135.76	6101.41	6072.35	6047.72	6026.81
475,000	6476.63	6440.38	6409.70	6383.70	6361.63
500,000	6817.51	6779.35	6747.06	6719.68	6696.45
525,000	7158.38	7118.32	7084.41	7055.67	7031.27
550,000	7499.26	7457.28	7421.76	7391.65	7366.10
575,000	7840.13	7796.25	7759.11	7727.64	7700.92
600,000	8181.01	8135.22	8096.47	8063.62	8035.74
625,000	8521.88	8474.18	8433.82	8399.60	8370.56
650,000	8862.76	8813.15	8771.17	8735.59	8705.39
675,000	9203.63	9152.12	9108.52	9071.57	9040.21
700,000	9544.51	9491.09	9445.88	9407.56	9375.03
725,000	9885.38	9830.05	9783.23	9743.54	9709.85
750,000	10226.26	10169.02	10120.58	10079.52	10044.68
775,000	10567.13	10507.99	10457.93	10415.51	10379.50
800,000	10908.01	10846.96	10795.29	10751.49	10714.32
825,000	11248.88	11185.92	11132.64	11087.48	11049.14
850,000	11589.76	11524.89	11469.99	11423.46	11383.97
875,000	11930.63	11863.86	11807.34	11759.44	11718.79
900,000	12271.51	12202.82	12144.70	12095.43	12053.61

Table 7   283

15.75%   **Monthly Payment Loans**

Loan Amount	Amortization Period in Years				
	26	27	28	29	30
10	0.14	0.14	0.14	0.14	0.14
20	0.27	0.27	0.27	0.27	0.27
30	0.41	0.40	0.40	0.40	0.40
40	0.54	0.54	0.54	0.54	0.53
50	0.67	0.67	0.67	0.67	0.67
100	1.34	1.34	1.33	1.33	1.33
200	2.68	2.67	2.66	2.66	2.65
300	4.01	4.00	3.99	3.99	3.98
400	5.35	5.33	5.32	5.31	5.30
500	6.68	6.66	6.65	6.64	6.63
1,000	13.36	13.32	13.30	13.27	13.25
2,000	26.71	26.64	26.59	26.54	26.50
3,000	40.07	39.96	39.88	39.81	39.74
4,000	53.42	53.28	53.17	53.07	52.99
5,000	66.77	66.60	66.46	66.34	66.24
10,000	133.54	133.20	132.92	132.67	132.47
20,000	267.07	266.40	265.83	265.34	264.93
30,000	400.61	399.60	398.74	398.01	397.39
40,000	534.14	532.80	531.66	530.68	529.85
50,000	667.68	666.00	664.57	663.35	662.31
100,000	1335.35	1331.99	1329.13	1326.70	1324.62
125,000	1669.18	1664.98	1661.41	1658.37	1655.78
150,000	2003.02	1997.98	1993.69	1990.04	1986.93
175,000	2336.85	2330.98	2325.98	2321.72	2318.08
200,000	2670.69	2663.97	2658.26	2653.39	2649.24
225,000	3004.52	2996.97	2990.54	2985.06	2980.39
250,000	3338.36	3329.96	3322.82	3316.73	3311.55
275,000	3672.19	3662.96	3655.10	3648.41	3642.70
300,000	4006.03	3995.96	3987.38	3980.08	3973.86
325,000	4339.87	4328.95	4319.66	4311.75	4305.01
350,000	4673.70	4661.95	4651.95	4643.43	4636.16
375,000	5007.54	4994.94	4984.23	4975.10	4967.32
400,000	5341.37	5327.94	5316.51	5306.77	5298.47
425,000	5675.21	5660.94	5648.79	5638.44	5629.63
450,000	6009.04	5993.93	5981.07	5970.12	5960.78
475,000	6342.88	6326.93	6313.35	6301.79	6291.94
500,000	6676.71	6659.92	6645.63	6633.46	6623.09
525,000	7010.55	6992.92	6977.92	6965.14	6954.24
550,000	7344.38	7325.92	7310.20	7296.81	7285.40
575,000	7678.22	7658.91	7642.48	7628.48	7616.55
600,000	8012.05	7991.91	7974.76	7960.16	7947.71
625,000	8345.89	8324.90	8307.04	8291.83	8278.86
650,000	8679.73	8657.90	8639.32	8623.50	8610.02
675,000	9013.56	8990.90	8971.61	8955.17	8941.17
700,000	9347.40	9323.89	9303.89	9286.85	9272.32
725,000	9681.23	9656.89	9636.17	9618.52	9603.48
750,000	10015.07	9989.88	9968.45	9950.19	9934.63
775,000	10348.90	10322.88	10300.73	10281.87	10265.79
800,000	10682.74	10655.88	10633.01	10613.54	10596.94
825,000	11016.57	10988.87	10965.29	10945.21	10928.10
850,000	11350.41	11321.87	11297.58	11276.88	11259.25
875,000	11684.24	11654.86	11629.86	11608.56	11590.40
900,000	12018.08	11987.86	11962.14	11940.23	11921.56

284   Table 7

Monthly Payment Loans   **16.00%**

Loan Amount	\multicolumn{5}{c}{Amortization Period in Years}				
	5	7	8	10	12
10	0.25	0.20	0.19	0.17	0.16
20	0.49	0.40	0.38	0.34	0.32
30	0.73	0.60	0.56	0.51	0.47
40	0.98	0.80	0.75	0.68	0.63
50	1.22	1.00	0.93	0.84	0.79
100	2.44	1.99	1.86	1.68	1.57
200	4.87	3.98	3.71	3.36	3.14
300	7.30	5.96	5.56	5.03	4.70
400	9.73	7.95	7.42	6.71	6.27
500	12.16	9.94	9.27	8.38	7.83
1,000	24.32	19.87	18.53	16.76	15.66
2,000	48.64	39.73	37.06	33.51	31.32
3,000	72.96	59.59	55.59	50.26	46.98
4,000	97.28	79.45	74.12	67.01	62.64
5,000	121.60	99.32	92.65	83.76	78.30
10,000	243.19	198.63	185.29	167.52	156.59
20,000	486.37	397.25	370.58	335.03	313.17
30,000	729.55	595.87	555.87	502.54	469.75
40,000	972.73	794.49	741.16	670.06	626.34
50,000	1215.91	993.11	926.44	837.57	782.92
100,000	2431.81	1986.21	1852.88	1675.14	1565.83
125,000	3039.76	2482.76	2316.10	2093.92	1957.29
150,000	3647.71	2979.31	2779.32	2512.70	2348.74
175,000	4255.66	3475.87	3242.54	2931.48	2740.20
200,000	4863.62	3972.42	3705.76	3350.27	3131.66
225,000	5471.57	4468.97	4168.98	3769.05	3523.11
250,000	6079.52	4965.52	4632.20	4187.83	3914.57
275,000	6687.47	5462.07	5095.42	4606.62	4306.02
300,000	7295.42	5958.62	5558.64	5025.40	4697.48
325,000	7903.37	6455.18	6021.86	5444.18	5088.94
350,000	8511.32	6951.73	6485.08	5862.96	5480.39
375,000	9119.28	7448.28	6948.30	6281.75	5871.85
400,000	9727.23	7944.83	7411.52	6700.53	6263.31
425,000	10335.18	8441.38	7874.74	7119.31	6654.76
450,000	10943.13	8937.93	8337.96	7538.10	7046.22
475,000	11551.08	9434.49	8801.18	7956.88	7437.68
500,000	12159.03	9931.04	9264.40	8375.66	7829.13
525,000	12766.98	10427.59	9727.62	8794.44	8220.59
550,000	13374.94	10924.14	10190.84	9213.23	8612.04
575,000	13982.89	11420.69	10654.06	9632.01	9003.50
600,000	14590.84	11917.24	11117.28	10050.79	9394.96
625,000	15198.79	12413.79	11580.50	10469.58	9786.41
650,000	15806.74	12910.35	12043.72	10888.36	10177.87
675,000	16414.69	13406.90	12506.94	11307.14	10569.33
700,000	17022.64	13903.45	12970.16	11725.92	10960.78
725,000	17630.60	14400.00	13433.37	12144.71	11352.24
750,000	18238.55	14896.55	13896.59	12563.49	11743.69
775,000	18846.50	15393.10	14359.81	12982.27	12135.15
800,000	19454.45	15889.66	14823.03	13401.05	12526.61
825,000	20062.40	16386.21	15286.25	13819.84	12918.06
850,000	20670.35	16882.76	15749.47	14238.62	13309.52
875,000	21278.30	17379.31	16212.69	14657.40	13700.98
900,000	21886.26	17875.86	16675.91	15076.19	14092.43

Table 7   285

16.00%   Monthly Payment Loans

Amortization Period in Years

Loan Amount	15	16	17	18	20
10	0.15	0.15	0.15	0.15	0.14
20	0.30	0.29	0.29	0.29	0.28
30	0.45	0.44	0.43	0.43	0.42
40	0.59	0.58	0.58	0.57	0.56
50	0.74	0.73	0.72	0.71	0.70
100	1.47	1.45	1.43	1.42	1.40
200	2.94	2.90	2.86	2.83	2.79
300	4.41	4.35	4.29	4.25	4.18
400	5.88	5.79	5.72	5.66	5.57
500	7.35	7.24	7.15	7.08	6.96
1,000	14.69	14.48	14.30	14.15	13.92
2,000	29.38	28.95	28.59	28.29	27.83
3,000	44.07	43.42	42.88	42.43	41.74
4,000	58.75	57.89	57.17	56.57	55.66
5,000	73.44	72.36	71.46	70.72	69.57
10,000	146.88	144.72	142.92	141.43	139.13
20,000	293.75	289.43	285.84	282.85	278.26
30,000	440.62	434.14	428.76	424.28	417.38
40,000	587.49	578.85	571.68	565.70	556.51
50,000	734.36	723.56	714.60	707.13	695.63
100,000	1468.71	1447.12	1429.19	1414.25	1391.26
125,000	1835.88	1808.89	1786.49	1767.81	1739.07
150,000	2203.06	2170.67	2143.79	2121.38	2086.89
175,000	2570.23	2532.45	2501.08	2474.94	2434.70
200,000	2937.41	2894.23	2858.38	2828.50	2782.52
225,000	3304.58	3256.00	3215.68	3182.06	3130.33
250,000	3671.76	3617.78	3572.98	3535.62	3478.14
275,000	4038.93	3979.56	3930.27	3889.18	3825.96
300,000	4406.11	4341.34	4287.57	4242.75	4173.77
325,000	4773.28	4703.11	4644.87	4596.31	4521.59
350,000	5140.46	5064.89	5002.16	4949.87	4869.40
375,000	5507.63	5426.67	5359.46	5303.43	5217.21
400,000	5874.81	5788.45	5716.76	5656.99	5565.03
425,000	6241.98	6150.22	6074.06	6010.56	5912.84
450,000	6609.16	6512.00	6431.35	6364.12	6260.66
475,000	6976.33	6873.78	6788.65	6717.68	6608.47
500,000	7343.51	7235.56	7145.95	7071.24	6956.28
525,000	7710.68	7597.33	7503.24	7424.80	7304.10
550,000	8077.86	7959.11	7860.54	7778.36	7651.91
575,000	8445.03	8320.89	8217.84	8131.93	7999.73
600,000	8812.21	8682.67	8575.13	8485.49	8347.54
625,000	9179.38	9044.44	8932.43	8839.05	8695.35
650,000	9546.56	9406.22	9289.73	9192.61	9043.17
675,000	9913.74	9768.00	9647.03	9546.17	9390.98
700,000	10280.91	10129.78	10004.32	9899.73	9738.80
725,000	10648.09	10491.55	10361.62	10253.30	10086.61
750,000	11015.26	10853.33	10718.92	10606.86	10434.42
775,000	11382.44	11215.11	11076.21	10960.42	10782.24
800,000	11749.61	11576.89	11433.51	11313.98	11130.05
825,000	12116.79	11938.67	11790.81	11667.54	11477.87
850,000	12483.96	12300.44	12148.11	12021.11	11825.68
875,000	12851.14	12662.22	12505.40	12374.67	12173.49
900,000	13218.31	13024.00	12862.70	12728.23	12521.31

Monthly Payment Loans   <u>16.00%</u>

Loan Amount	Amortization Period in Years				
	21	22	23	24	25
10	0.14	0.14	0.14	0.14	0.14
20	0.28	0.28	0.28	0.28	0.28
30	0.42	0.42	0.42	0.41	0.41
40	0.56	0.55	0.55	0.55	0.55
50	0.70	0.69	0.69	0.69	0.68
100	1.39	1.38	1.37	1.37	1.36
200	2.77	2.75	2.74	2.73	2.72
300	4.15	4.13	4.11	4.10	4.08
400	5.53	5.50	5.48	5.46	5.44
500	6.92	6.88	6.85	6.82	6.80
1,000	13.83	13.75	13.69	13.64	13.59
2,000	27.65	27.50	27.38	27.27	27.18
3,000	41.48	41.25	41.07	40.91	40.77
4,000	55.30	55.00	54.75	54.54	54.36
5,000	69.13	68.75	68.44	68.17	67.95
10,000	138.25	137.50	136.88	136.34	135.89
20,000	276.49	275.00	273.75	272.68	271.78
30,000	414.73	412.50	410.62	409.02	407.67
40,000	552.98	550.00	547.49	545.36	543.56
50,000	691.22	687.50	684.36	681.70	679.45
100,000	1382.44	1375.00	1368.71	1363.40	1358.89
125,000	1728.04	1718.74	1710.89	1704.24	1698.62
150,000	2073.65	2062.49	2053.06	2045.09	2038.34
175,000	2419.26	2406.24	2395.24	2385.94	2378.06
200,000	2764.87	2749.99	2737.42	2726.79	2717.78
225,000	3110.47	3093.73	3079.59	3067.63	3057.50
250,000	3456.08	3437.48	3421.77	3408.48	3397.23
275,000	3801.69	3781.23	3763.95	3749.33	3736.95
300,000	4147.30	4124.98	4106.12	4090.18	4076.67
325,000	4492.90	4468.72	4448.30	4431.02	4416.39
350,000	4838.51	4812.47	4790.48	4771.87	4756.12
375,000	5184.12	5156.22	5132.65	5112.72	5095.84
400,000	5529.73	5499.97	5474.83	5453.57	5435.56
425,000	5875.33	5843.71	5817.01	5794.42	5775.28
450,000	6220.94	6187.46	6159.18	6135.26	6115.00
475,000	6566.55	6531.21	6501.36	6476.11	6454.73
500,000	6912.16	6874.96	6843.53	6816.96	6794.45
525,000	7257.77	7218.70	7185.71	7157.81	7134.17
550,000	7603.37	7562.45	7527.89	7498.65	7473.89
575,000	7948.98	7906.20	7870.06	7839.50	7813.62
600,000	8294.59	8249.95	8212.24	8180.35	8153.34
625,000	8640.20	8593.69	8554.42	8521.20	8493.06
650,000	8985.80	8937.44	8896.59	8862.04	8832.78
675,000	9331.41	9281.19	9238.77	9202.89	9172.50
700,000	9677.02	9624.94	9580.95	9543.74	9512.23
725,000	10022.63	9968.68	9923.12	9884.59	9851.95
750,000	10368.23	10312.43	10265.30	10225.43	10191.67
775,000	10713.84	10656.18	10607.48	10566.28	10531.39
800,000	11059.45	10999.93	10949.65	10907.13	10871.12
825,000	11405.06	11343.67	11291.83	11247.98	11210.84
850,000	11750.66	11687.42	11634.01	11588.83	11550.56
875,000	12096.27	12031.17	11976.18	11929.67	11890.28
900,000	12441.88	12374.92	12318.36	12270.52	12230.00

Table 7   287

16.00%   Monthly Payment Loans

Loan Amount	Amortization Period in Years				
	26	27	28	29	30
10	0.14	0.14	0.14	0.14	0.14
20	0.28	0.28	0.27	0.27	0.27
30	0.41	0.41	0.41	0.41	0.41
40	0.55	0.55	0.54	0.54	0.54
50	0.68	0.68	0.68	0.68	0.68
100	1.36	1.36	1.35	1.35	1.35
200	2.72	2.71	2.70	2.70	2.69
300	4.07	4.06	4.05	4.05	4.04
400	5.43	5.41	5.40	5.39	5.38
500	6.78	6.76	6.75	6.74	6.73
1,000	13.56	13.52	13.50	13.47	13.45
2,000	27.11	27.04	26.99	26.94	26.90
3,000	40.66	40.56	40.48	40.41	40.35
4,000	54.21	54.08	53.97	53.87	53.80
5,000	67.76	67.60	67.46	67.34	67.24
10,000	135.51	135.19	134.91	134.68	134.48
20,000	271.02	270.37	269.82	269.35	268.96
30,000	406.53	405.55	404.73	404.03	403.43
40,000	542.03	540.74	539.64	538.70	537.91
50,000	677.54	675.92	674.55	673.38	672.38
100,000	1355.08	1351.84	1349.09	1346.75	1344.76
125,000	1693.85	1689.80	1686.36	1683.44	1680.95
150,000	2032.61	2027.75	2023.63	2020.12	2017.14
175,000	2371.38	2365.71	2360.90	2356.81	2353.33
200,000	2710.15	2703.67	2698.17	2693.49	2689.52
225,000	3048.92	3041.63	3035.44	3030.18	3025.71
250,000	3387.69	3379.59	3372.71	3366.87	3361.90
275,000	3726.45	3717.55	3709.98	3703.55	3698.09
300,000	4065.22	4055.50	4047.25	4040.24	4034.28
325,000	4403.99	4393.46	4384.52	4376.93	4370.47
350,000	4742.76	4731.42	4721.79	4713.61	4706.65
375,000	5081.53	5069.38	5059.06	5050.30	5042.84
400,000	5420.29	5407.34	5396.33	5386.98	5379.03
425,000	5759.06	5745.30	5733.61	5723.67	5715.22
450,000	6097.83	6083.25	6070.88	6060.36	6051.41
475,000	6436.60	6421.21	6408.15	6397.04	6387.60
500,000	6775.37	6759.17	6745.42	6733.73	6723.79
525,000	7114.13	7097.13	7082.69	7070.41	7059.98
550,000	7452.90	7435.09	7419.96	7407.10	7396.17
575,000	7791.67	7773.05	7757.23	7743.79	7732.36
600,000	8130.44	8111.00	8094.50	8080.47	8068.55
625,000	8469.21	8448.96	8431.77	8417.16	8404.74
650,000	8807.97	8786.92	8769.04	8753.85	8740.93
675,000	9146.74	9124.88	9106.31	9090.53	9077.11
700,000	9485.51	9462.84	9443.58	9427.22	9413.30
725,000	9824.28	9800.80	9780.85	9763.90	9749.49
750,000	10163.05	10138.75	10118.12	10100.59	10085.68
775,000	10501.81	10476.71	10455.39	10437.28	10421.87
800,000	10840.58	10814.67	10792.66	10773.96	10758.06
825,000	11179.35	11152.63	11129.94	11110.65	11094.25
850,000	11518.12	11490.59	11467.21	11447.34	11430.44
875,000	11856.89	11828.55	11804.48	11784.02	11766.63
900,000	12195.65	12166.50	12141.75	12120.71	12102.82

Monthly Payment Loans   **16.25%**

Loan Amount	Amortization Period in Years				
	5	7	8	10	12
10	0.25	0.21	0.19	0.17	0.16
20	0.49	0.41	0.38	0.34	0.32
30	0.74	0.61	0.57	0.51	0.48
40	0.98	0.81	0.75	0.68	0.64
50	1.23	1.01	0.94	0.85	0.80
100	2.45	2.01	1.87	1.70	1.59
200	4.90	4.01	3.74	3.39	3.17
300	7.34	6.01	5.61	5.08	4.75
400	9.79	8.01	7.48	6.77	6.33
500	12.23	10.01	9.34	8.46	7.92
1,000	24.46	20.01	18.68	16.91	15.83
2,000	48.91	40.01	37.36	33.82	31.65
3,000	73.36	60.02	56.03	50.73	47.47
4,000	97.81	80.02	74.71	67.63	63.29
5,000	122.26	100.03	93.39	84.54	79.12
10,000	244.52	200.05	186.77	169.08	158.23
20,000	489.03	400.10	373.53	338.15	316.45
30,000	733.54	600.15	560.29	507.23	474.68
40,000	978.05	800.19	747.05	676.30	632.90
50,000	1222.56	1000.24	933.81	845.38	791.13
100,000	2445.11	2000.48	1867.61	1690.75	1582.25
125,000	3056.39	2500.59	2334.52	2113.44	1977.81
150,000	3667.67	3000.71	2801.42	2536.12	2373.37
175,000	4278.95	3500.83	3268.32	2958.81	2768.93
200,000	4890.22	4000.95	3735.22	3381.49	3164.49
225,000	5501.50	4501.07	4202.13	3804.18	3560.05
250,000	6112.78	5001.18	4669.03	4226.87	3955.61
275,000	6724.05	5501.30	5135.93	4649.55	4351.18
300,000	7335.33	6001.42	5602.83	5072.24	4746.74
325,000	7946.61	6501.54	6069.73	5494.92	5142.30
350,000	8557.89	7001.65	6536.64	5917.61	5537.86
375,000	9169.16	7501.77	7003.54	6340.30	5933.42
400,000	9780.44	8001.89	7470.44	6762.98	6328.98
425,000	10391.72	8502.01	7937.34	7185.67	6724.54
450,000	11003.00	9002.13	8404.25	7608.35	7120.10
475,000	11614.27	9502.24	8871.15	8031.04	7515.66
500,000	12225.55	10002.36	9338.05	8453.73	7911.22
525,000	12836.83	10502.48	9804.95	8876.41	8306.79
550,000	13448.10	11002.60	10271.85	9299.10	8702.35
575,000	14059.38	11502.72	10738.76	9721.78	9097.91
600,000	14670.66	12002.83	11205.66	10144.47	9493.47
625,000	15281.94	12502.95	11672.56	10567.16	9889.03
650,000	15893.21	13003.07	12139.46	10989.84	10284.59
675,000	16504.49	13503.19	12606.37	11412.53	10680.15
700,000	17115.77	14003.30	13073.27	11835.21	11075.71
725,000	17727.05	14503.42	13540.17	12257.90	11471.27
750,000	18338.32	15003.54	14007.07	12680.59	11866.83
775,000	18949.60	15503.66	14473.97	13103.27	12262.40
800,000	19560.88	16003.78	14940.88	13525.96	12657.96
825,000	20172.15	16503.89	15407.78	13948.64	13053.52
850,000	20783.43	17004.01	15874.68	14371.33	13449.08
875,000	21394.71	17504.13	16341.58	14794.02	13844.64
900,000	22005.99	18004.25	16808.49	15216.70	14240.20

Table 7   289

16.25% Monthly Payment Loans

Loan Amount	Amortization Period in Years				
	15	16	17	18	20
10	0.15	0.15	0.15	0.15	0.15
20	0.30	0.30	0.29	0.29	0.29
30	0.45	0.44	0.44	0.43	0.43
40	0.60	0.59	0.58	0.58	0.57
50	0.75	0.74	0.73	0.72	0.71
100	1.49	1.47	1.45	1.44	1.42
200	2.98	2.93	2.90	2.87	2.83
300	4.46	4.40	4.35	4.30	4.24
400	5.95	5.86	5.79	5.74	5.65
500	7.44	7.33	7.24	7.17	7.06
1,000	14.87	14.65	14.48	14.33	14.11
2,000	29.73	29.30	28.95	28.66	28.21
3,000	44.59	43.95	43.42	42.98	42.31
4,000	59.45	58.60	57.89	57.31	56.41
5,000	74.31	73.25	72.37	71.63	70.51
10,000	148.62	146.49	144.73	143.26	141.01
20,000	297.24	292.98	289.45	286.52	282.01
30,000	445.86	439.47	434.18	429.78	423.02
40,000	594.47	585.96	578.90	573.03	564.02
50,000	743.09	732.45	723.63	716.29	705.03
100,000	1486.17	1464.89	1447.25	1432.57	1410.05
125,000	1857.72	1831.11	1809.06	1790.72	1762.56
150,000	2229.26	2197.33	2170.87	2148.86	2115.07
175,000	2600.80	2563.55	2532.69	2507.00	2467.58
200,000	2972.34	2929.77	2894.50	2865.14	2820.10
225,000	3343.88	3295.99	3256.31	3223.28	3172.61
250,000	3715.43	3662.21	3618.12	3581.43	3525.12
275,000	4086.97	4028.44	3979.93	3939.57	3877.63
300,000	4458.51	4394.66	4341.74	4297.71	4230.14
325,000	4830.05	4760.88	4703.56	4655.85	4582.65
350,000	5201.59	5127.10	5065.37	5014.00	4935.16
375,000	5573.14	5493.32	5427.18	5372.14	5287.68
400,000	5944.68	5859.54	5788.99	5730.28	5640.19
425,000	6316.22	6225.76	6150.80	6088.42	5992.70
450,000	6687.76	6591.98	6512.61	6446.56	6345.21
475,000	7059.30	6958.20	6874.42	6804.71	6697.72
500,000	7430.85	7324.42	7236.24	7162.85	7050.23
525,000	7802.39	7690.64	7598.05	7520.99	7402.74
550,000	8173.93	8056.87	7959.86	7879.13	7755.26
575,000	8545.47	8423.09	8321.67	8237.28	8107.77
600,000	8917.01	8789.31	8683.48	8595.42	8460.28
625,000	9288.56	9155.53	9045.29	8953.56	8812.79
650,000	9660.10	9521.75	9407.11	9311.70	9165.30
675,000	10031.64	9887.97	9768.92	9669.84	9517.81
700,000	10403.18	10254.19	10130.73	10027.99	9870.32
725,000	10774.72	10620.41	10492.54	10386.13	10222.83
750,000	11146.27	10986.63	10854.35	10744.27	10575.35
775,000	11517.81	11352.85	11216.16	11102.41	10927.86
800,000	11889.35	11719.07	11577.98	11460.56	11280.37
825,000	12260.89	12085.30	11939.79	11818.70	11632.88
850,000	12632.43	12451.52	12301.60	12176.84	11985.39
875,000	13003.98	12817.74	12663.41	12534.98	12337.90
900,000	13375.52	13183.96	13025.22	12893.12	12690.41

Monthly Payment Loans   16.25%

Loan Amount	\multicolumn{5}{c}{Amortization Period in Years}				
	21	22	23	24	25
10	0.15	0.14	0.14	0.14	0.14
20	0.29	0.28	0.28	0.28	0.28
30	0.43	0.42	0.42	0.42	0.42
40	0.57	0.56	0.56	0.56	0.56
50	0.71	0.70	0.70	0.70	0.69
100	1.41	1.40	1.39	1.39	1.38
200	2.81	2.79	2.78	2.77	2.76
300	4.21	4.19	4.17	4.15	4.14
400	5.61	5.58	5.56	5.54	5.52
500	7.01	6.98	6.95	6.92	6.90
1,000	14.02	13.95	13.89	13.83	13.79
2,000	28.03	27.89	27.77	27.66	27.58
3,000	42.05	41.83	41.65	41.49	41.36
4,000	56.06	55.77	55.53	55.32	55.15
5,000	70.08	69.71	69.41	69.15	68.93
10,000	140.15	139.42	138.81	138.30	137.86
20,000	280.29	278.84	277.62	276.59	275.71
30,000	420.43	418.26	416.42	414.88	413.57
40,000	560.58	557.67	555.23	553.17	551.42
50,000	700.72	697.09	694.04	691.46	689.28
100,000	1401.43	1394.18	1388.07	1382.91	1378.55
125,000	1751.79	1742.72	1735.08	1728.63	1723.18
150,000	2102.14	2091.27	2082.10	2074.36	2067.82
175,000	2452.50	2439.81	2429.11	2420.08	2412.45
200,000	2802.86	2788.35	2776.13	2765.81	2757.09
225,000	3153.21	3136.90	3123.14	3111.53	3101.72
250,000	3503.57	3485.44	3470.16	3457.26	3446.36
275,000	3853.93	3833.98	3817.17	3802.98	3790.99
300,000	4204.28	4182.53	4164.19	4148.71	4135.63
325,000	4554.64	4531.07	4511.20	4494.43	4480.26
350,000	4905.00	4879.61	4858.22	4840.16	4824.90
375,000	5255.35	5228.16	5205.23	5185.89	5169.53
400,000	5605.71	5576.70	5552.25	5531.61	5514.17
425,000	5956.06	5925.24	5899.26	5877.34	5858.81
450,000	6306.42	6273.79	6246.28	6223.06	6203.44
475,000	6656.78	6622.33	6593.29	6568.79	6548.08
500,000	7007.13	6970.87	6940.31	6914.51	6892.71
525,000	7357.49	7319.42	7287.32	7260.24	7237.35
550,000	7707.85	7667.96	7634.34	7605.96	7581.98
575,000	8058.20	8016.50	7981.35	7951.69	7926.62
600,000	8408.56	8365.05	8328.37	8297.41	8271.25
625,000	8758.92	8713.59	8675.39	8643.14	8615.89
650,000	9109.27	9062.13	9022.40	8988.86	8960.52
675,000	9459.63	9410.68	9369.42	9334.59	9305.16
700,000	9809.99	9759.22	9716.43	9680.32	9649.79
725,000	10160.34	10107.76	10063.45	10026.04	9994.43
750,000	10510.70	10456.31	10410.46	10371.77	10339.06
775,000	10861.05	10804.85	10757.48	10717.49	10683.70
800,000	11211.41	11153.39	11104.49	11063.22	11028.34
825,000	11561.77	11501.94	11451.51	11408.94	11372.97
850,000	11912.12	11850.48	11798.52	11754.67	11717.61
875,000	12262.48	12199.02	12145.54	12100.39	12062.24
900,000	12612.84	12547.57	12492.55	12446.12	12406.88

Table 7   291

16.25%   Monthly Payment Loans

Amortization Period in Years

Loan Amount	26	27	28	29	30
10	0.14	0.14	0.14	0.14	0.14
20	0.28	0.28	0.28	0.28	0.28
30	0.42	0.42	0.42	0.42	0.41
40	0.55	0.55	0.55	0.55	0.55
50	0.69	0.69	0.69	0.69	0.69
100	1.38	1.38	1.37	1.37	1.37
200	2.75	2.75	2.74	2.74	2.73
300	4.13	4.12	4.11	4.11	4.10
400	5.50	5.49	5.48	5.47	5.46
500	6.88	6.86	6.85	6.84	6.83
1,000	13.75	13.72	13.70	13.67	13.65
2,000	27.50	27.44	27.39	27.34	27.30
3,000	41.25	41.16	41.08	41.01	40.95
4,000	55.00	54.87	54.77	54.68	54.60
5,000	68.75	68.59	68.46	68.35	68.25
10,000	137.49	137.18	136.91	136.69	136.50
20,000	274.98	274.35	273.82	273.37	272.99
30,000	412.46	411.52	410.73	410.06	409.49
40,000	549.95	548.70	547.64	546.74	545.98
50,000	687.43	685.87	684.55	683.42	682.47
100,000	1374.86	1371.73	1369.09	1366.84	1364.94
125,000	1718.57	1714.67	1711.36	1708.55	1706.17
150,000	2062.28	2057.60	2053.63	2050.26	2047.41
175,000	2406.00	2400.53	2395.90	2391.97	2388.64
200,000	2749.71	2743.46	2738.17	2733.68	2729.87
225,000	3093.42	3086.40	3080.44	3075.39	3071.11
250,000	3437.14	3429.33	3422.71	3417.10	3412.34
275,000	3780.85	3772.26	3764.98	3758.81	3753.58
300,000	4124.56	4115.19	4107.25	4100.52	4094.81
325,000	4468.28	4458.12	4449.52	4442.23	4436.04
350,000	4811.99	4801.06	4791.79	4783.94	4777.28
375,000	5155.70	5143.99	5134.06	5125.65	5118.51
400,000	5499.42	5486.92	5476.34	5467.36	5459.74
425,000	5843.13	5829.85	5818.61	5809.07	5800.98
450,000	6186.84	6172.79	6160.88	6150.78	6142.21
475,000	6530.55	6515.72	6503.15	6492.49	6483.44
500,000	6874.27	6858.65	6845.42	6834.20	6824.68
525,000	7217.98	7201.58	7187.69	7175.91	7165.91
550,000	7561.69	7544.52	7529.96	7517.62	7507.15
575,000	7905.41	7887.45	7872.23	7859.33	7848.38
600,000	8249.12	8230.38	8214.50	8201.04	8189.61
625,000	8592.83	8573.31	8556.77	8542.75	8530.85
650,000	8936.55	8916.24	8899.04	8884.45	8872.08
675,000	9280.26	9259.18	9241.31	9226.16	9213.31
700,000	9623.97	9602.11	9683.58	9567.87	9554.55
725,000	9967.69	9945.04	9925.85	9909.58	9895.78
750,000	10311.40	10287.97	10268.12	10251.29	10237.01
775,000	10655.11	10630.91	10610.39	10593.00	10578.25
800,000	10998.83	10973.84	10952.67	10934.71	10919.48
825,000	11342.54	11316.77	11294.94	11276.42	11260.72
850,000	11686.25	11659.70	11637.21	11618.13	11601.95
875,000	12029.97	12002.64	11979.48	11959.84	11943.18
900,000	12373.68	12345.57	12321.75	12301.55	12284.42

Monthly Payment Loans 16.50%

Loan Amount	Amortization Period in Years				
	5	7	8	10	12
10	0.25	0.21	0.19	0.18	0.16
20	0.50	0.41	0.38	0.35	0.32
30	0.74	0.61	0.57	0.52	0.48
40	0.99	0.81	0.76	0.69	0.64
50	1.23	1.01	0.95	0.86	0.80
100	2.46	2.02	1.89	1.71	1.60
200	4.92	4.03	3.77	3.42	3.20
300	7.38	6.05	5.65	5.12	4.80
400	9.84	8.06	7.53	6.83	6.40
500	12.30	10.08	9.42	8.54	8.00
1,000	24.59	20.15	18.83	17.07	15.99
2,000	49.17	40.30	37.65	34.13	31.98
3,000	73.76	60.45	56.48	51.20	47.97
4,000	98.34	80.60	75.30	68.26	63.95
5,000	122.93	100.74	94.12	85.33	79.94
10,000	245.85	201.48	188.24	170.65	159.88
20,000	491.70	402.96	376.48	341.29	319.75
30,000	737.54	604.44	564.72	511.93	479.63
40,000	983.39	805.92	752.96	682.57	639.50
50,000	1229.23	1007.40	941.20	853.22	799.37
100,000	2458.46	2014.79	1882.40	1706.43	1598.74
125,000	3073.07	2518.49	2353.00	2133.03	1998.42
150,000	3687.68	3022.19	2823.60	2559.64	2398.11
175,000	4302.30	3525.89	3294.20	2986.25	2797.79
200,000	4916.91	4029.58	3764.80	3412.85	3197.47
225,000	5531.52	4533.28	4235.40	3839.46	3597.16
250,000	6146.14	5036.98	4706.00	4266.06	3996.84
275,000	6760.75	5540.67	5176.60	4692.67	4396.52
300,000	7375.36	6044.37	5647.20	5119.27	4796.21
325,000	7989.97	6548.07	6117.80	5545.88	5195.89
350,000	8604.59	7051.77	6588.39	5972.49	5595.57
375,000	9219.20	7555.46	7058.99	6399.09	5995.26
400,000	9833.81	8059.16	7529.59	6825.70	6394.94
425,000	10448.43	8562.86	8000.19	7252.30	6794.62
450,000	11063.04	9066.56	8470.79	7678.91	7194.31
475,000	11677.65	9570.25	8941.39	8105.51	7593.99
500,000	12292.27	10073.95	9411.99	8532.12	7993.67
525,000	12906.88	10577.65	9882.59	8958.73	8393.36
550,000	13521.49	11081.34	10353.19	9385.33	8793.04
575,000	14136.10	11585.04	10823.79	9811.94	9192.72
600,000	14750.72	12088.74	11294.39	10238.54	9592.41
625,000	15365.33	12592.44	11764.99	10665.15	9992.09
650,000	15979.94	13096.13	12235.59	11091.75	10391.77
675,000	16594.56	13599.83	12706.19	11518.36	10791.46
700,000	17209.17	14103.53	13176.78	11944.97	11191.14
725,000	17823.78	14607.22	13647.38	12371.57	11590.82
750,000	18438.40	15110.92	14117.98	12798.18	11990.51
775,000	19053.01	15614.62	14588.58	13224.78	12390.19
800,000	19667.62	16118.32	15059.18	13651.39	12789.87
825,000	20282.23	16622.01	15529.78	14077.99	13189.56
850,000	20896.85	17125.71	16000.38	14504.60	13589.24
875,000	21511.46	17629.41	16470.98	14931.21	13988.92
900,000	22126.07	18133.11	16941.58	15357.81	14388.61

Table 7   293

16.50%   Monthly Payment Loans

Amortization Period in Years

Loan Amount	15	16	17	18	20
10	0.16	0.15	0.15	0.15	0.15
20	0.31	0.30	0.30	0.30	0.29
30	0.46	0.45	0.44	0.44	0.43
40	0.61	0.60	0.59	0.59	0.58
50	0.76	0.75	0.74	0.73	0.72
100	1.51	1.49	1.47	1.46	1.43
200	3.01	2.97	2.94	2.91	2.86
300	4.52	4.45	4.40	4.36	4.29
400	6.02	5.94	5.87	5.81	5.72
500	7.52	7.42	7.33	7.26	7.15
1,000	15.04	14.83	14.66	14.51	14.29
2,000	30.08	29.66	29.31	29.02	28.58
3,000	45.12	44.49	43.97	43.53	42.87
4,000	60.15	59.31	58.62	58.04	57.16
5,000	75.19	74.14	73.27	72.55	71.45
10,000	150.38	148.28	146.54	145.10	142.90
20,000	300.75	296.55	293.08	290.20	285.79
30,000	451.12	444.82	439.62	435.29	428.68
40,000	601.49	593.10	586.16	580.39	571.57
50,000	751.86	741.37	732.69	725.49	714.46
100,000	1503.71	1482.73	1465.38	1450.97	1428.91
125,000	1879.64	1853.42	1831.72	1813.71	1786.13
150,000	2255.57	2224.10	2198.07	2176.45	2143.36
175,000	2631.50	2594.78	2564.41	2539.19	2500.58
200,000	3007.42	2965.46	2930.76	2901.93	2857.81
225,000	3383.35	3336.15	3297.10	3264.67	3215.03
250,000	3759.28	3706.83	3663.44	3627.41	3572.26
275,000	4135.20	4077.51	4029.79	3990.15	3929.48
300,000	4511.13	4448.19	4396.13	4352.89	4286.71
325,000	4887.06	4818.88	4762.48	4715.63	4643.93
350,000	5262.99	5189.56	5128.82	5078.37	5001.16
375,000	5638.91	5560.24	5495.16	5441.11	5358.38
400,000	6014.84	5930.92	5861.51	5803.85	5715.61
425,000	6390.77	6301.61	6227.85	6166.59	6072.83
450,000	6766.69	6672.29	6594.20	6529.33	6430.06
475,000	7142.62	7042.97	6960.54	6892.07	6787.28
500,000	7518.55	7413.65	7326.88	7254.81	7144.51
525,000	7894.48	7784.34	7693.23	7617.55	7501.73
550,000	8270.40	8155.02	8059.57	7980.29	7858.96
575,000	8646.33	8525.70	8425.92	8343.03	8216.18
600,000	9022.26	8896.38	8792.26	8705.77	8573.41
625,000	9398.18	9267.07	9158.60	9068.51	8930.63
650,000	9774.11	9637.75	9524.95	9431.25	9287.86
675,000	10150.04	10008.43	9891.29	9793.99	9645.08
700,000	10525.97	10379.11	10257.64	10156.73	10002.31
725,000	10901.89	10749.80	10623.98	10519.47	10359.53
750,000	11277.82	11120.48	10990.32	10882.21	10716.76
775,000	11653.75	11491.16	11356.67	11244.95	11073.98
800,000	12029.67	11861.84	11723.01	11607.69	11431.21
825,000	12405.60	12232.53	12089.36	11970.43	11788.44
850,000	12781.53	12603.21	12455.70	12333.17	12145.66
875,000	13157.46	12973.89	12822.04	12695.91	12502.89
900,000	13533.38	13344.57	13188.39	13058.65	12860.11

Monthly Payment Loans   **16.50%**

Loan Amount	Amortization Period in Years				
	21	22	23	24	25
10	0.15	0.15	0.15	0.15	0.14
20	0.29	0.29	0.29	0.29	0.28
30	0.43	0.43	0.43	0.43	0.42
40	0.57	0.57	0.57	0.57	0.56
50	0.72	0.71	0.71	0.71	0.70
100	1.43	1.42	1.41	1.41	1.40
200	2.85	2.83	2.82	2.81	2.80
300	4.27	4.25	4.23	4.21	4.20
400	5.69	5.66	5.63	5.61	5.60
500	7.11	7.07	7.04	7.02	7.00
1,000	14.21	14.14	14.08	14.03	13.99
2,000	28.41	28.27	28.15	28.05	27.97
3,000	42.62	42.41	42.23	42.08	41.95
4,000	56.82	56.54	56.30	56.10	55.93
5,000	71.03	70.68	70.38	70.13	69.92
10,000	142.05	141.35	140.75	140.25	139.83
20,000	284.10	282.69	281.50	280.50	279.65
30,000	426.15	424.03	422.25	420.74	419.48
40,000	568.20	565.37	562.99	560.99	559.30
50,000	710.25	706.71	703.74	701.24	699.13
100,000	1420.49	1413.42	1407.48	1402.47	1398.25
125,000	1775.61	1766.78	1759.35	1753.09	1747.81
150,000	2130.73	2120.13	2111.21	2103.70	2097.37
175,000	2485.85	2473.48	2463.08	2454.32	2446.93
200,000	2840.97	2826.84	2814.95	2804.94	2796.49
225,000	3196.09	3180.19	3166.82	3155.55	3146.06
250,000	3551.21	3533.55	3518.69	3506.17	3495.62
275,000	3906.34	3886.90	3870.56	3856.79	3845.18
300,000	4261.46	4240.26	4222.42	4207.40	4194.74
325,000	4616.58	4593.61	4574.29	4558.02	4544.30
350,000	4971.70	4946.96	4926.16	4908.64	4893.86
375,000	5326.82	5300.32	5278.03	5259.25	5243.42
400,000	5681.94	5653.67	5629.90	5609.87	5592.98
425,000	6037.06	6007.03	5981.76	5960.49	5942.54
450,000	6392.18	6360.38	6333.63	6311.10	6292.11
475,000	6747.30	6713.73	6685.50	6661.72	6641.67
500,000	7102.42	7067.09	7037.37	7012.34	6991.23
525,000	7457.55	7420.44	7389.24	7362.95	7340.79
550,000	7812.67	7773.80	7741.11	7713.57	7690.35
575,000	8167.79	8127.15	8092.97	8064.19	8039.91
600,000	8522.91	8480.51	8444.84	8414.80	8389.47
625,000	8878.03	8833.86	8796.71	8765.42	8739.03
650,000	9233.15	9187.21	9148.58	9116.04	9088.60
675,000	9588.27	9540.57	9500.45	9466.65	9438.16
700,000	9943.39	9893.92	9852.32	9817.27	9787.72
725,000	10298.51	10247.28	10204.18	10167.89	10137.28
750,000	10653.63	10600.63	10556.05	10518.50	10486.84
775,000	11008.76	10953.99	10907.92	10869.12	10836.40
800,000	11363.88	11307.34	11259.79	11219.74	11185.96
825,000	11719.00	11660.69	11611.66	11570.35	11535.52
850,000	12074.12	12014.05	11963.52	11920.97	11885.08
875,000	12429.24	12367.40	12315.39	12271.59	12234.65
900,000	12784.36	12720.76	12667.26	12622.20	12584.21

Table 7   295

16.50%   Monthly Payment Loans

Loan	Amortization Period in Years				
Amount	26	27	28	29	30
10	0.14	0.14	0.14	0.14	0.14
20	0.28	0.28	0.28	0.28	0.28
30	0.42	0.42	0.42	0.42	0.42
40	0.56	0.56	0.56	0.56	0.56
50	0.70	0.70	0.70	0.70	0.70
100	1.40	1.40	1.39	1.39	1.39
200	2.79	2.79	2.78	2.78	2.78
300	4.19	4.18	4.17	4.17	4.16
400	5.58	5.57	5.56	5.55	5.55
500	6.98	6.96	6.95	6.94	6.93
1,000	13.95	13.92	13.90	13.87	13.86
2,000	27.90	27.84	27.79	27.74	27.71
3,000	41.85	41.76	41.68	41.61	41.56
4,000	55.79	55.67	55.57	55.48	55.41
5,000	69.74	69.59	69.46	69.35	69.26
10,000	139.47	139.17	138.92	138.70	138.52
20,000	278.94	278.34	277.83	277.40	277.03
30,000	418.41	417.51	416.74	416.10	415.55
40,000	557.88	556.67	555.65	554.79	554.06
50,000	697.35	695.84	694.57	693.49	692.58
100,000	1394.69	1391.67	1389.13	1386.98	1385.15
125,000	1743.36	1739.59	1736.41	1733.72	1731.44
150,000	2092.03	2087.51	2083.69	2080.46	2077.73
175,000	2440.70	2435.43	2430.97	2427.20	2424.01
200,000	2789.37	2783.34	2778.25	2773.95	2770.30
225,000	3138.04	3131.26	3125.53	3120.69	3116.59
250,000	3486.71	3479.18	3472.82	3467.43	3462.88
275,000	3835.38	3827.10	3820.10	3814.17	3809.16
300,000	4184.05	4175.01	4167.38	4160.92	4155.45
325,000	4532.72	4522.93	4514.66	4507.66	4501.74
350,000	4881.39	4870.85	4861.94	4854.40	4848.02
375,000	5230.06	5218.77	5209.22	5201.15	5194.31
400,000	5578.73	5566.68	5556.50	5547.89	5540.60
425,000	5927.40	5914.60	5903.78	5894.63	5886.88
450,000	6276.07	6262.52	6251.06	6241.37	6233.17
475,000	6624.74	6610.44	6598.35	6588.12	6579.46
500,000	6973.41	6958.35	6945.63	6934.86	6925.75
525,000	7322.08	7306.27	7292.91	7281.60	7272.03
550,000	7670.75	7654.19	7640.19	7628.34	7618.32
575,000	8019.42	8002.11	7987.47	7975.09	7964.61
600,000	8368.09	8350.02	8334.75	8321.83	8310.89
625,000	8716.76	8697.94	8682.03	8668.57	8657.18
650,000	9065.43	9045.86	9029.31	9015.32	9003.47
675,000	9414.10	9393.78	9376.59	9362.06	9349.75
700,000	9762.77	9741.69	9723.88	9708.80	9696.04
725,000	10111.44	10089.61	10071.16	10055.54	10042.33
750,000	10460.11	10437.53	10418.44	10402.29	10388.62
775,000	10808.78	10785.45	10765.72	10749.03	10734.90
800,000	11157.45	11133.36	11113.00	11095.77	11081.19
825,000	11506.12	11481.28	11460.28	11442.51	11427.48
850,000	11854.79	11829.20	11807.56	11789.20	11773.76
875,000	12203.46	12177.12	12154.84	12136.00	12120.05
900,000	12552.13	12525.03	12502.12	12482.74	12466.34

Monthly Payment Loans　　16.75%

Loan Amount	Amortization Period in Years				
	5	7	8	10	12
10	0.25	0.21	0.19	0.18	0.17
20	0.50	0.41	0.38	0.35	0.33
30	0.75	0.61	0.57	0.52	0.49
40	0.99	0.82	0.76	0.69	0.65
50	1.24	1.02	0.95	0.87	0.81
100	2.48	2.03	1.90	1.73	1.62
200	4.95	4.06	3.80	3.45	3.24
300	7.42	6.09	5.70	5.17	4.85
400	9.89	8.12	7.59	6.89	6.47
500	12.36	10.15	9.49	8.62	8.08
1,000	24.72	20.30	18.98	17.23	16.16
2,000	49.44	40.59	37.95	34.45	32.31
3,000	74.16	60.88	56.92	51.67	48.46
4,000	98.88	81.17	75.89	68.89	64.62
5,000	123.60	101.46	94.87	86.11	80.77
10,000	247.19	202.92	189.73	172.22	161.53
20,000	494.37	405.84	379.45	344.44	323.06
30,000	741.56	608.75	569.18	516.66	484.59
40,000	988.74	811.67	758.90	688.87	646.12
50,000	1235.92	1014.58	948.63	861.09	807.65
100,000	2471.84	2029.16	1897.25	1722.17	1615.30
125,000	3089.80	2536.45	2371.56	2152.71	2019.12
150,000	3707.76	3043.74	2845.87	2583.26	2422.95
175,000	4325.72	3551.03	3320.18	3013.80	2826.77
200,000	4943.68	4058.32	3794.49	3444.34	3230.59
225,000	5561.63	4565.61	4268.80	3874.88	3634.42
250,000	6179.59	5072.90	4743.11	4305.42	4038.24
275,000	6797.55	5580.19	5217.42	4735.97	4442.06
300,000	7415.51	6087.48	5691.73	5166.51	4845.89
325,000	8033.47	6594.77	6166.04	5597.05	5249.71
350,000	8651.43	7102.06	6640.35	6027.59	5653.53
375,000	9269.39	7609.35	7114.67	6458.13	6057.36
400,000	9887.35	8116.64	7588.98	6888.67	6461.18
425,000	10505.30	8623.93	8063.29	7319.22	6865.00
450,000	11123.26	9131.22	8537.60	7749.76	7268.83
475,000	11741.22	9638.51	9011.91	8180.30	7672.65
500,000	12359.18	10145.80	9486.22	8610.84	8076.47
525,000	12977.14	10653.09	9960.53	9041.38	8480.30
550,000	13595.10	11160.38	10434.84	9471.93	8884.12
575,000	14213.06	11667.67	10909.15	9902.47	9287.94
600,000	14831.02	12174.96	11383.46	10333.01	9691.77
625,000	15448.97	12682.25	11857.77	10763.55	10095.59
650,000	16066.93	13189.54	12332.08	11194.09	10499.41
675,000	16684.89	13696.83	12806.39	11624.63	10903.24
700,000	17302.85	14204.12	13280.70	12055.18	11307.06
725,000	17920.81	14711.41	13755.01	12485.72	11710.88
750,000	18538.77	15218.70	14229.33	12916.26	12114.71
775,000	19156.73	15725.98	14703.64	13346.80	12518.53
800,000	19774.69	16233.27	15177.95	13777.34	12922.35
825,000	20392.64	16740.56	15652.26	14207.89	13326.18
850,000	21010.60	17247.85	16126.57	14638.43	13730.00
875,000	21628.56	17755.14	16600.88	15068.97	14133.82
900,000	22246.52	18262.43	17075.19	15499.51	14537.65

Table 7　297

16.75%   Monthly Payment Loans

Amortization Period in Years

Loan Amount	15	16	17	18	20
10	0.16	0.16	0.15	0.15	0.15
20	0.31	0.31	0.30	0.30	0.29
30	0.46	0.46	0.45	0.45	0.44
40	0.61	0.61	0.60	0.59	0.58
50	0.77	0.76	0.75	0.74	0.73
100	1.53	1.51	1.49	1.47	1.45
200	3.05	3.01	2.97	2.94	2.90
300	4.57	4.51	4.46	4.41	4.35
400	6.09	6.01	5.94	5.88	5.80
500	7.61	7.51	7.42	7.35	7.24
1,000	15.22	15.01	14.84	14.70	14.48
2,000	30.43	30.02	29.68	29.39	28.96
3,000	45.64	45.02	44.51	44.09	43.44
4,000	60.86	60.03	59.35	58.78	57.92
5,000	76.07	75.04	74.18	73.48	72.40
10,000	152.14	150.07	148.36	146.95	144.79
20,000	304.27	300.13	296.72	293.89	289.57
30,000	456.40	450.20	445.08	440.83	434.35
40,000	608.53	600.26	593.44	587.77	579.13
50,000	760.67	750.33	741.79	734.72	723.91
100,000	1521.33	1500.65	1483.58	1469.43	1447.82
125,000	1901.66	1875.81	1854.47	1836.78	1809.78
150,000	2281.99	2250.98	2225.37	2204.14	2171.73
175,000	2662.32	2626.14	2596.26	2571.49	2533.69
200,000	3042.65	3001.30	2967.16	2938.85	2895.64
225,000	3422.98	3376.46	3338.05	3306.20	3257.60
250,000	3803.31	3751.62	3708.94	3673.56	3619.55
275,000	4183.64	4126.78	4079.84	4040.91	3981.51
300,000	4563.97	4501.95	4450.73	4408.27	4343.46
325,000	4944.30	4877.11	4821.62	4775.62	4705.42
350,000	5324.63	5252.27	5192.52	5142.98	5067.37
375,000	5704.96	5627.43	5563.41	5510.33	5429.33
400,000	6085.29	6002.59	5934.31	5877.69	5791.28
425,000	6465.62	6377.75	6305.20	6245.04	6153.24
450,000	6845.95	6752.92	6676.09	6612.40	6515.19
475,000	7226.28	7128.08	7046.99	6979.75	6877.15
500,000	7606.61	7503.24	7417.88	7347.11	7239.10
525,000	7986.94	7878.40	7788.78	7714.46	7601.06
550,000	8367.27	8253.56	8159.67	8081.82	7963.01
575,000	8747.60	8628.72	8530.56	8449.17	8324.97
600,000	9127.93	9003.89	8901.46	8816.53	8686.92
625,000	9508.26	9379.05	9272.35	9183.88	9048.88
650,000	9888.59	9754.21	9643.24	9551.24	9410.83
675,000	10268.92	10129.37	10014.14	9918.59	9772.79
700,000	10649.25	10504.53	10385.03	10285.95	10134.74
725,000	11029.58	10879.70	10755.93	10653.30	10496.70
750,000	11409.91	11254.86	11126.82	11020.66	10858.65
775,000	11790.24	11630.02	11497.71	11388.01	11220.61
800,000	12170.57	12005.18	11868.61	11755.37	11582.56
825,000	12550.90	12380.34	12239.50	12122.72	11944.52
850,000	12931.23	12755.50	12610.40	12490.08	12306.47
875,000	13311.56	13130.67	12981.29	12857.44	12668.43
900,000	13691.89	13505.83	13352.18	13224.79	13030.38

Monthly Payment Loans   **16.75%**

Loan Amount	Amortization Period in Years				
	21	22	23	24	25
10	0.15	0.15	0.15	0.15	0.15
20	0.29	0.29	0.29	0.29	0.29
30	0.44	0.43	0.43	0.43	0.43
40	0.58	0.58	0.58	0.57	0.57
50	0.72	0.72	0.72	0.72	0.71
100	1.44	1.44	1.43	1.43	1.42
200	2.88	2.87	2.86	2.85	2.84
300	4.32	4.30	4.29	4.27	4.26
400	5.76	5.74	5.71	5.69	5.68
500	7.20	7.17	7.14	7.12	7.09
1,000	14.40	14.33	14.27	14.23	14.18
2,000	28.80	28.66	28.54	28.45	28.36
3,000	43.19	42.99	42.81	42.67	42.54
4,000	57.59	57.31	57.08	56.89	56.72
5,000	71.99	71.64	71.35	71.11	70.90
10,000	143.97	143.28	142.70	142.21	141.80
20,000	287.93	286.55	285.39	284.42	283.60
30,000	431.89	429.82	428.09	426.63	425.40
40,000	575.85	573.09	570.78	568.84	567.20
50,000	719.81	716.36	713.48	711.05	709.00
100,000	1439.61	1432.72	1426.95	1422.09	1418.00
125,000	1799.51	1790.90	1783.68	1777.61	1772.50
150,000	2159.41	2149.08	2140.42	2133.13	2127.00
175,000	2519.31	2507.26	2497.15	2488.65	2481.50
200,000	2879.21	2865.44	2853.89	2844.17	2836.00
225,000	3239.11	3223.62	3210.62	3199.69	3190.50
250,000	3599.01	3581.80	3567.36	3555.21	3545.00
275,000	3958.91	3939.98	3924.09	3910.73	3899.50
300,000	4318.81	4298.16	4280.83	4266.26	4254.00
325,000	4678.72	4656.34	4637.56	4621.78	4608.50
350,000	5038.62	5014.52	4994.30	4977.30	4962.99
375,000	5398.52	5372.70	5351.03	5332.82	5317.49
400,000	5758.42	5730.88	5707.77	5688.34	5671.99
425,000	6118.32	6089.06	6064.50	6043.86	6026.49
450,000	6478.22	6447.24	6421.24	6399.38	6380.99
475,000	6838.12	6805.42	6777.97	6754.90	6735.49
500,000	7198.02	7163.60	7134.71	7110.42	7089.99
525,000	7557.92	7521.78	7491.44	7465.94	7444.49
550,000	7917.82	7879.96	7848.18	7821.46	7798.99
575,000	8277.72	8238.14	8204.91	8176.99	8153.49
600,000	8637.62	8596.32	8561.65	8532.51	8507.99
625,000	8997.53	8954.50	8918.38	8888.03	8862.49
650,000	9357.43	9312.68	9275.12	9243.55	9216.99
675,000	9717.33	9670.86	9631.85	9599.07	9571.49
700,000	10077.23	10029.03	9988.59	9954.59	9925.98
725,000	10437.13	10387.21	10345.32	10310.11	10280.48
750,000	10797.03	10745.39	10702.06	10665.63	10634.98
775,000	11156.93	11103.57	11058.79	11021.15	10989.48
800,000	11516.83	11461.75	11415.53	11376.67	11343.98
825,000	11876.73	11819.93	11772.26	11732.19	11698.48
850,000	12236.63	12178.11	12129.00	12087.72	12052.98
875,000	12596.53	12536.29	12485.73	12443.24	12407.48
900,000	12956.43	12894.47	12842.47	12798.76	12761.98

Table 7   299

16.75%

Monthly Payment Loans

Loan Amount	Amortization Period in Years				
	26	27	28	29	30
10	0.15	0.15	0.15	0.15	0.15
20	0.29	0.29	0.29	0.29	0.29
30	0.43	0.43	0.43	0.43	0.43
40	0.57	0.57	0.57	0.57	0.57
50	0.71	0.71	0.71	0.71	0.71
100	1.42	1.42	1.41	1.41	1.41
200	2.83	2.83	2.82	2.82	2.82
300	4.25	4.24	4.23	4.23	4.22
400	5.66	5.65	5.64	5.63	5.63
500	7.08	7.06	7.05	7.04	7.03
1,000	14.15	14.12	14.10	14.08	14.06
2,000	28.30	28.24	28.19	28.15	28.11
3,000	42.44	42.35	42.28	42.22	42.17
4,000	56.59	56.47	56.37	56.29	56.22
5,000	70.73	70.59	70.47	70.36	70.27
10,000	141.46	141.17	140.93	140.72	140.54
20,000	282.92	282.34	281.85	281.43	281.08
30,000	424.37	423.50	422.77	422.15	421.62
40,000	565.83	564.67	563.69	562.86	562.16
50,000	707.28	705.83	704.61	703.58	702.70
100,000	1414.56	1411.66	1409.21	1407.15	1405.40
125,000	1768.20	1764.57	1761.51	1758.93	1756.75
150,000	2121.84	2117.49	2113.81	2110.72	2108.10
175,000	2475.48	2470.40	2466.12	2462.50	2459.45
200,000	2829.12	2823.31	2818.42	2814.29	2810.80
225,000	3182.75	3176.23	3170.72	3166.07	3162.15
250,000	3536.39	3529.14	3523.02	3517.86	3513.49
275,000	3890.03	3882.05	3875.32	3869.64	3864.84
300,000	4243.67	4234.97	4227.62	4221.43	4216.19
325,000	4597.31	4587.88	4579.92	4573.21	4567.54
350,000	4950.95	4940.79	4932.23	4925.00	4918.89
375,000	5304.59	5293.71	5284.53	5276.78	5270.24
400,000	5658.23	5646.62	5636.83	5628.57	5621.59
425,000	6011.86	5999.53	5989.13	5980.35	5972.94
450,000	6365.50	6352.45	6341.43	6332.14	6324.29
475,000	6719.14	6705.36	6693.73	6683.92	6675.63
500,000	7072.78	7058.27	7046.03	7035.71	7026.98
525,000	7426.42	7411.19	7398.34	7387.49	7378.33
550,000	7780.06	7764.10	7750.64	7739.28	7729.68
575,000	8133.70	8117.01	8102.94	8091.06	8081.03
600,000	8487.34	8469.93	8455.24	8442.85	8432.38
625,000	8840.97	8822.84	8807.54	8794.63	8783.73
650,000	9194.61	9175.75	9159.84	9146.42	9135.08
675,000	9548.25	9528.67	9512.15	9498.20	9486.43
700,000	9901.89	9881.58	9864.45	9849.99	9837.77
725,000	10255.53	10234.49	10216.75	10201.77	10189.12
750,000	10609.17	10587.41	10569.05	10553.56	10540.47
775,000	10962.81	10940.32	10921.35	10905.34	10891.82
800,000	11316.45	11293.23	11273.65	11257.13	11243.17
825,000	11670.08	11646.15	11625.95	11608.91	11594.52
850,000	12023.72	11999.06	11978.26	11960.70	11945.87
875,000	12377.36	12351.97	12330.56	12312.48	12297.22
900,000	12731.00	12704.89	12682.86	12664.27	12648.57

Monthly Payment Loans   **17.00%**

Loan Amount	\multicolumn{5}{c}{Amortization Period in Years}				
	5	7	8	10	12
10	0.25	0.21	0.20	0.18	0.17
20	0.50	0.41	0.39	0.35	0.33
30	0.75	0.62	0.58	0.53	0.49
40	1.00	0.82	0.77	0.70	0.66
50	1.25	1.03	0.96	0.87	0.82
100	2.49	2.05	1.92	1.74	1.64
200	4.98	4.09	3.83	3.48	3.27
300	7.46	6.14	5.74	5.22	4.90
400	9.95	8.18	7.65	6.96	6.53
500	12.43	10.22	9.57	8.69	8.16
1,000	24.86	20.44	19.13	17.38	16.32
2,000	49.71	40.88	38.25	34.76	32.64
3,000	74.56	61.31	57.37	52.14	48.96
4,000	99.42	81.75	76.49	69.52	65.28
5,000	124.27	102.18	95.61	86.90	81.60
10,000	248.53	204.36	191.22	173.80	163.20
20,000	497.06	408.72	382.43	347.60	326.39
30,000	745.58	613.08	573.65	521.40	489.58
40,000	994.11	817.44	764.86	695.20	652.77
50,000	1242.63	1021.80	956.08	868.99	815.97
100,000	2485.26	2043.59	1912.15	1737.98	1631.93
125,000	3106.58	2554.48	2390.19	2177.48	2039.91
150,000	3727.89	3065.38	2868.22	2606.97	2447.89
175,000	4349.21	3576.27	3346.26	3041.46	2855.87
200,000	4970.52	4087.17	3824.30	3475.96	3263.85
225,000	5591.83	4598.06	4302.33	3910.45	3671.83
250,000	6213.15	5108.96	4780.37	4344.95	4079.81
275,000	6834.46	5619.85	5258.40	4779.44	4487.79
300,000	7455.78	6130.75	5736.44	5213.93	4895.77
325,000	8077.09	6641.64	6214.48	5648.43	5303.75
350,000	8698.41	7152.54	6692.51	6082.92	5711.74
375,000	9319.72	7663.43	7170.55	6517.42	6119.72
400,000	9941.04	8174.33	7648.59	6951.91	6527.70
425,000	10562.35	8685.22	8126.62	7386.41	6935.68
450,000	11183.66	9196.12	8604.66	7820.90	7343.66
475,000	11804.98	9707.01	9082.70	8255.39	7751.64
500,000	12426.29	10217.91	9560.73	8689.89	8159.62
525,000	13047.61	10728.80	10038.77	9124.38	8567.60
550,000	13668.92	11239.70	10516.80	9558.88	8975.58
575,000	14290.24	11750.59	10994.84	9993.37	9383.56
600,000	14911.55	12261.49	11472.88	10427.86	9791.54
625,000	15532.86	12772.38	11950.91	10862.36	10199.52
650,000	16154.18	13283.28	12428.95	11296.85	10607.50
675,000	16775.49	13794.17	12906.99	11731.35	11015.48
700,000	17396.81	14305.07	13385.02	12165.84	11423.47
725,000	18018.12	14815.96	13863.06	12600.33	11831.45
750,000	18639.44	15326.86	14341.10	13034.83	12239.43
775,000	19260.75	15837.75	14819.13	13469.32	12647.41
800,000	19882.07	16348.65	15297.17	13903.82	13055.39
825,000	20503.38	16859.54	15775.20	14338.31	13463.37
850,000	21124.69	17370.44	16253.24	14772.81	13871.35
875,000	21746.01	17881.33	16731.28	15207.30	14279.33
900,000	22367.32	18392.23	17209.31	15641.79	14687.31

Table 7   301

17.00% Monthly Payment Loans

Loan Amount	Amortization Period in Years				
	15	16	17	18	20
10	0.16	0.16	0.16	0.15	0.15
20	0.31	0.31	0.31	0.30	0.30
30	0.47	0.46	0.46	0.45	0.45
40	0.62	0.61	0.61	0.60	0.59
50	0.77	0.76	0.76	0.75	0.74
100	1.54	1.52	1.51	1.49	1.47
200	3.08	3.04	3.01	2.98	2.94
300	4.62	4.56	4.51	4.47	4.41
400	6.16	6.08	6.01	5.96	5.87
500	7.70	7.60	7.51	7.44	7.34
1,000	15.40	15.19	15.02	14.88	14.67
2,000	30.79	30.38	30.04	29.76	29.34
3,000	46.18	45.56	45.06	44.64	44.01
4,000	61.57	60.75	60.08	59.52	58.68
5,000	76.96	75.94	75.10	74.40	73.35
10,000	153.91	151.87	150.19	148.80	146.69
20,000	307.81	303.73	300.37	297.59	293.37
30,000	461.71	455.60	450.56	446.39	440.05
40,000	615.61	607.46	600.74	595.18	586.73
50,000	769.51	759.32	750.93	743.98	733.41
100,000	1539.01	1518.64	1501.85	1487.95	1466.81
125,000	1923.76	1898.30	1877.31	1859.94	1833.51
150,000	2308.51	2277.96	2252.77	2231.93	2200.21
175,000	2693.26	2657.61	2628.23	2603.91	2566.91
200,000	3078.01	3037.27	3003.69	2975.90	2933.61
225,000	3462.76	3416.93	3379.15	3347.89	3300.31
250,000	3847.52	3796.59	3754.61	3719.87	3667.01
275,000	4232.27	4176.25	4130.07	4091.86	4033.71
300,000	4617.02	4555.91	4505.54	4463.85	4400.41
325,000	5001.77	4935.57	4881.00	4835.83	4767.11
350,000	5386.52	5315.22	5256.46	5207.82	5133.81
375,000	5771.27	5694.88	5631.92	5579.81	5500.51
400,000	6156.02	6074.54	6007.38	5951.79	5867.21
425,000	6540.77	6454.20	6382.84	6323.78	6233.91
450,000	6925.52	6833.86	6758.30	6695.77	6600.61
475,000	7310.28	7213.52	7133.76	7067.75	6967.31
500,000	7695.03	7593.18	7509.22	7439.74	7334.01
525,000	8079.78	7972.83	7884.68	7811.73	7700.71
550,000	8464.53	8352.49	8260.14	8183.72	8067.41
575,000	8849.28	8732.15	8635.60	8555.70	8434.11
600,000	9234.03	9111.81	9011.07	8927.69	8800.81
625,000	9618.78	9491.47	9386.53	9299.68	9167.51
650,000	10003.53	9871.13	9761.99	9671.66	9534.21
675,000	10388.28	10250.78	10137.45	10043.65	9900.91
700,000	10773.04	10630.44	10512.91	10415.64	10267.61
725,000	11157.79	11010.10	10888.37	10787.62	10634.31
750,000	11542.54	11389.76	11263.83	11159.61	11001.01
775,000	11927.29	11769.42	11639.29	11531.60	11367.71
800,000	12312.04	12149.08	12014.75	11903.58	11734.41
825,000	12696.79	12528.74	12390.21	12275.57	12101.11
850,000	13081.54	12908.39	12765.67	12647.56	12467.81
875,000	13466.29	13288.05	13141.13	13019.54	12834.51
900,000	13851.04	13667.71	13516.60	13391.53	13201.21

Monthly Payment Loans 17.00%

Loan Amount	21	22	23	24	25
	\multicolumn{5}{c}{Amortization Period in Years}				
10	0.15	0.15	0.15	0.15	0.15
20	0.30	0.30	0.29	0.29	0.29
30	0.44	0.44	0.44	0.44	0.44
40	0.59	0.59	0.58	0.58	0.58
50	0.73	0.73	0.73	0.73	0.72
100	1.46	1.46	1.45	1.45	1.44
200	2.92	2.91	2.90	2.89	2.88
300	4.38	4.36	4.34	4.33	4.32
400	5.84	5.81	5.79	5.77	5.76
500	7.30	7.27	7.24	7.21	7.19
1,000	14.59	14.53	14.47	14.42	14.38
2,000	29.18	29.05	28.93	28.84	28.76
3,000	43.77	43.57	43.40	43.26	43.14
4,000	58.36	58.09	57.86	57.68	57.52
5,000	72.94	72.61	72.33	72.09	71.89
10,000	145.88	145.21	144.65	144.18	143.78
20,000	291.76	290.42	289.30	288.36	287.56
30,000	437.64	435.63	433.94	432.53	431.34
40,000	583.52	580.84	578.59	576.71	575.12
50,000	729.40	726.04	723.24	720.88	718.90
100,000	1458.79	1452.08	1446.47	1441.76	1437.80
125,000	1823.48	1815.10	1808.08	1802.19	1797.25
150,000	2188.18	2178.12	2169.70	2162.63	2156.70
175,000	2552.87	2541.14	2531.31	2523.07	2516.15
200,000	2917.57	2904.16	2892.93	2883.51	2875.60
225,000	3282.26	3267.18	3254.54	3243.94	3235.05
250,000	3646.96	3630.20	3616.16	3604.38	3594.50
275,000	4011.66	3993.22	3977.77	3964.82	3953.95
300,000	4376.35	4356.23	4339.39	4325.26	4313.39
325,000	4741.05	4719.25	4701.00	4685.70	4672.84
350,000	5105.74	5082.27	5062.62	5046.13	5032.29
375,000	5470.44	5445.29	5424.23	5406.57	5391.74
400,000	5835.13	5808.31	5785.85	5767.01	5751.19
425,000	6199.83	6171.33	6147.46	6127.45	6110.64
450,000	6564.52	6534.35	6509.08	6487.88	6470.09
475,000	6929.22	6897.37	6870.69	6848.32	6829.54
500,000	7293.91	7260.39	7232.31	7208.76	7188.99
525,000	7658.61	7623.41	7593.92	7569.20	7548.44
550,000	8023.31	7986.43	7955.54	7929.64	7907.89
575,000	8388.00	8349.45	8317.15	8290.07	8267.34
600,000	8752.70	8712.46	8678.77	8650.51	8626.78
625,000	9117.39	9075.48	9040.39	9010.95	8986.23
650,000	9482.09	9438.50	9402.00	9371.39	9345.68
675,000	9846.78	9801.52	9763.62	9731.82	9705.13
700,000	10211.48	10164.54	10125.23	10092.26	10064.58
725,000	10576.17	10527.56	10486.85	10452.70	10424.03
750,000	10940.87	10890.58	10848.46	10813.14	10783.48
775,000	11305.56	11253.60	11210.08	11173.58	11142.93
800,000	11670.26	11616.62	11571.69	11534.01	11502.38
825,000	12034.96	11979.64	11933.31	11894.45	11861.83
850,000	12399.65	12342.66	12294.92	12254.89	12221.28
875,000	12764.35	12705.68	12656.54	12615.33	12580.73
900,000	13129.04	13068.69	13018.15	12975.76	12940.17

Table 7   303

17.00%   Monthly Payment Loans

Loan Amount	Amortization Period in Years				
	26	27	28	29	30
10	0.15	0.15	0.15	0.15	0.15
20	0.29	0.29	0.29	0.29	0.29
30	0.44	0.43	0.43	0.43	0.43
40	0.58	0.58	0.58	0.58	0.58
50	0.72	0.72	0.72	0.72	0.72
100	1.44	1.44	1.43	1.43	1.43
200	2.87	2.87	2.86	2.86	2.86
300	4.31	4.30	4.29	4.29	4.28
400	5.74	5.73	5.72	5.71	5.71
500	7.18	7.16	7.15	7.14	7.13
1,000	14.35	14.32	14.30	14.28	14.26
2,000	28.69	28.64	28.59	28.55	28.52
3,000	43.04	42.96	42.88	42.83	42.78
4,000	57.38	57.27	57.18	57.10	57.03
5,000	71.73	71.59	71.47	71.37	71.29
10,000	143.45	143.17	142.94	142.74	142.57
20,000	286.90	286.34	285.87	285.47	285.14
30,000	430.35	429.51	428.80	428.21	427.71
40,000	573.79	572.68	571.74	570.94	570.28
50,000	717.24	715.84	714.67	713.68	712.84
100,000	1434.48	1431.68	1429.33	1427.35	1425.68
125,000	1793.10	1789.60	1786.66	1784.19	1782.10
150,000	2151.71	2147.52	2143.99	2141.02	2138.52
175,000	2510.33	2505.44	2501.32	2497.86	2494.94
200,000	2868.95	2863.36	2858.66	2854.69	2851.36
225,000	3227.57	3221.28	3215.99	3211.53	3207.77
250,000	3586.19	3579.20	3573.32	3568.37	3564.19
275,000	3944.81	3937.12	3930.65	3925.20	3920.61
300,000	4303.42	4295.04	4287.98	4282.04	4277.03
325,000	4662.04	4652.96	4645.31	4638.87	4633.45
350,000	5020.66	5010.88	5002.64	4995.71	4989.87
375,000	5379.28	5368.80	5359.98	5352.55	5346.29
400,000	5737.90	5726.72	5717.31	5709.38	5702.71
425,000	6096.52	6084.64	6074.64	6066.22	6059.13
450,000	6455.13	6442.56	6431.97	6423.06	6415.54
475,000	6813.75	6800.48	6789.30	6779.89	6771.96
500,000	7172.37	7158.40	7146.63	7136.73	7128.38
525,000	7530.99	7516.31	7503.96	7493.56	7484.80
550,000	7889.61	7874.23	7861.30	7850.40	7841.22
575,000	8248.23	8232.15	8218.63	8207.24	8197.64
600,000	8606.84	8590.07	8575.96	8564.07	8554.06
625,000	8965.46	8947.99	8933.29	8920.91	8910.48
650,000	9324.08	9305.91	9290.62	9277.74	9266.89
675,000	9682.70	9663.83	9647.95	9634.58	9623.31
700,000	10041.32	10021.75	10005.28	9991.42	9979.73
725,000	10399.94	10379.67	10362.62	10348.25	10336.15
750,000	10758.55	10737.59	10719.93	10705.09	10692.57
775,000	11117.17	11095.51	11077.28	11061.92	11048.99
800,000	11475.79	11453.43	11434.61	11418.76	11405.41
825,000	11834.41	11811.35	11791.94	11775.60	11761.83
850,000	12193.03	12169.27	12149.27	12132.43	12118.25
875,000	12551.65	12527.19	12506.60	12489.27	12474.66
900,000	12910.26	12885.11	12863.93	12846.11	12831.08

Monthly Payment Loans   17.25%

Loan Amount	Amortization Period in Years				
	5	7	8	10	12
10	0.25	0.21	0.20	0.18	0.17
20	0.50	0.42	0.39	0.36	0.33
30	0.75	0.62	0.58	0.53	0.50
40	1.00	0.83	0.78	0.71	0.66
50	1.25	1.03	0.97	0.88	0.83
100	2.50	2.06	1.93	1.76	1.65
200	5.00	4.12	3.86	3.51	3.30
300	7.50	6.18	5.79	5.27	4.95
400	10.00	8.24	7.71	7.02	6.60
500	12.50	10.30	9.64	8.77	8.25
1,000	24.99	20.59	19.28	17.54	16.49
2,000	49.98	41.17	38.55	35.08	32.98
3,000	74.97	61.75	57.82	52.62	49.46
4,000	99.95	82.33	77.09	70.16	65.95
5,000	124.94	102.91	96.36	87.70	82.44
10,000	249.88	205.81	192.72	175.39	164.87
20,000	499.75	411.62	385.43	350.78	329.73
30,000	749.62	617.42	578.14	526.16	494.59
40,000	999.49	823.23	770.85	701.55	659.45
50,000	1249.36	1029.03	963.56	876.93	824.32
100,000	2498.72	2058.06	1927.11	1753.86	1648.63
125,000	3123.40	2572.57	2408.89	2192.32	2060.78
150,000	3748.08	3087.09	2890.66	2630.78	2472.94
175,000	4372.76	3601.60	3372.44	3069.24	2885.09
200,000	4997.44	4116.11	3854.21	3507.71	3297.25
225,000	5622.12	4630.63	4335.99	3946.17	3709.40
250,000	6246.80	5145.14	4817.77	4384.63	4121.56
275,000	6871.48	5659.65	5299.54	4823.09	4533.71
300,000	7496.16	6174.17	5781.32	5261.56	4945.87
325,000	8120.84	6688.68	6263.10	5700.02	5358.02
350,000	8745.52	7203.19	6744.87	6138.48	5770.18
375,000	9370.20	7717.71	7226.65	6576.94	6182.33
400,000	9994.88	8232.22	7708.42	7015.41	6594.49
425,000	10619.56	8746.74	8190.20	7453.87	7006.64
450,000	11244.24	9261.25	8671.98	7892.33	7418.80
475,000	11868.92	9775.76	9153.75	8330.79	7830.95
500,000	12493.60	10290.28	9635.53	8769.26	8243.11
525,000	13118.28	10804.79	10117.31	9207.72	8655.27
550,000	13742.96	11319.30	10599.08	9646.18	9067.42
575,000	14367.64	11833.82	11080.86	10084.64	9479.58
600,000	14992.32	12348.33	11562.63	10523.11	9891.73
625,000	15617.00	12862.84	12044.41	10961.57	10303.89
650,000	16241.68	13377.36	12526.19	11400.03	10716.04
675,000	16866.36	13891.87	13007.96	11838.49	11128.20
700,000	17491.04	14406.38	13489.74	12276.96	11540.35
725,000	18115.72	14920.90	13971.52	12715.42	11952.51
750,000	18740.40	15435.41	14453.29	13153.88	12364.66
775,000	19365.08	15949.92	14935.07	13592.34	12776.82
800,000	19989.76	16464.44	15416.84	14030.81	13188.97
825,000	20614.44	16978.95	15898.62	14469.27	13601.13
850,000	21239.12	17493.47	16380.40	14907.73	14013.28
875,000	21863.80	18007.98	16862.17	15346.19	14425.44
900,000	22488.48	18522.49	17343.95	15784.66	14837.59

Table 7   305

17.25%   Monthly Payment Loans

Loan Amount	15	16	17	18	20
10	0.16	0.16	0.16	0.16	0.15
20	0.32	0.31	0.31	0.31	0.30
30	0.47	0.47	0.46	0.46	0.45
40	0.63	0.62	0.61	0.61	0.60
50	0.78	0.77	0.77	0.76	0.75
100	1.56	1.54	1.53	1.51	1.49
200	3.12	3.08	3.05	3.02	2.98
300	4.68	4.62	4.57	4.52	4.46
400	6.23	6.15	6.09	6.03	5.95
500	7.79	7.69	7.61	7.54	7.43
1,000	15.57	15.37	15.21	15.07	14.86
2,000	31.14	30.74	30.41	30.14	29.72
3,000	46.71	46.11	45.61	45.20	44.58
4,000	62.28	61.47	60.81	60.27	59.44
5,000	77.84	76.84	76.01	75.33	74.30
10,000	155.68	153.67	152.02	150.66	148.59
20,000	311.36	307.34	304.04	301.31	297.17
30,000	467.03	461.01	456.06	451.97	445.76
40,000	622.71	614.68	608.08	602.62	594.34
50,000	778.38	768.35	760.09	753.27	742.93
100,000	1556.76	1536.69	1520.18	1506.54	1485.85
125,000	1945.95	1920.87	1900.23	1883.18	1857.31
150,000	2335.14	2305.04	2280.27	2259.81	2228.77
175,000	2724.33	2689.21	2660.32	2636.45	2600.23
200,000	3113.52	3073.38	3040.36	3013.08	2971.69
225,000	3502.71	3457.56	3420.41	3389.72	3343.15
250,000	3891.90	3841.73	3800.45	3766.35	3714.61
275,000	4281.09	4225.90	4180.50	4142.99	4086.07
300,000	4670.28	4610.07	4560.54	4519.62	4457.53
325,000	5059.47	4994.25	4940.59	4896.26	4828.99
350,000	5448.65	5378.42	5320.63	5272.89	5200.45
375,000	5837.84	5762.59	5700.67	5649.53	5571.91
400,000	6227.03	6146.76	6080.72	6026.16	5943.37
425,000	6616.22	6530.94	6460.76	6402.80	6314.83
450,000	7005.41	6915.11	6840.81	6779.43	6686.29
475,000	7394.60	7299.28	7220.85	7156.07	7057.75
500,000	7783.79	7683.45	7600.90	7532.70	7429.21
525,000	8172.98	8067.63	7980.94	7909.34	7800.67
550,000	8562.17	8451.80	8360.99	8285.97	8172.14
575,000	8951.36	8835.97	8741.03	8662.61	8543.60
600,000	9340.55	9220.14	9121.08	9039.24	8915.06
625,000	9729.74	9604.32	9501.12	9415.88	9286.52
650,000	10118.93	9988.49	9881.17	9792.51	9657.98
675,000	10508.12	10372.66	10261.21	10169.15	10029.44
700,000	10897.30	10756.83	10641.26	10545.78	10400.90
725,000	11286.49	11141.01	11021.30	10922.41	10772.36
750,000	11675.68	11525.18	11401.34	11299.05	11143.82
775,000	12064.87	11909.35	11781.39	11675.68	11515.28
800,000	12454.06	12293.52	12161.43	12052.32	11886.74
825,000	12843.25	12677.70	12541.48	12428.95	12258.20
850,000	13232.44	13061.87	12921.52	12805.59	12629.66
875,000	13621.63	13446.04	13301.57	13182.22	13001.12
900,000	14010.82	13830.21	13681.61	13558.86	13372.58

Monthly Payment Loans   17.25%

Loan Amount	Amortization Period in Years				
	21	22	23	24	25
10	0.15	0.15	0.15	0.15	0.15
20	0.30	0.30	0.30	0.30	0.30
30	0.45	0.45	0.44	0.44	0.44
40	0.60	0.59	0.59	0.59	0.59
50	0.74	0.74	0.74	0.74	0.73
100	1.48	1.48	1.47	1.47	1.46
200	2.96	2.95	2.94	2.93	2.92
300	4.44	4.42	4.40	4.39	4.38
400	5.92	5.89	5.87	5.85	5.84
500	7.40	7.36	7.34	7.31	7.29
1,000	14.79	14.72	14.67	14.62	14.58
2,000	29.57	29.43	29.33	29.23	29.16
3,000	44.35	44.15	43.99	43.85	43.73
4,000	59.13	58.86	58.65	58.46	58.31
5,000	73.91	73.58	73.31	73.08	72.89
10,000	147.81	147.15	146.61	146.15	145.77
20,000	295.61	294.30	293.21	292.30	291.53
30,000	443.41	441.45	439.81	438.45	437.30
40,000	591.21	588.60	586.42	584.59	583.06
50,000	739.01	735.75	733.02	730.74	728.83
100,000	1478.02	1471.49	1466.04	1461.47	1457.65
125,000	1847.53	1839.37	1832.55	1826.84	1822.06
150,000	2217.03	2207.24	2199.05	2192.21	2186.47
175,000	2586.54	2575.11	2565.56	2557.57	2550.88
200,000	2956.04	2942.98	2932.07	2922.94	2915.29
225,000	3325.55	3310.86	3298.58	3288.31	3279.70
250,000	3695.05	3678.73	3665.09	3653.67	3644.11
275,000	4064.55	4046.60	4031.60	4019.04	4008.52
300,000	4434.06	4414.47	4398.10	4384.41	4372.93
325,000	4803.56	4782.35	4764.61	4749.77	4737.34
350,000	5173.07	5150.22	5131.12	5115.14	5101.75
375,000	5542.57	5518.09	5497.63	5480.51	5466.16
400,000	5912.08	5885.96	5864.14	5845.87	5830.57
425,000	6281.58	6253.83	6230.65	6211.24	6194.98
450,000	6651.09	6621.71	6597.15	6576.61	6559.39
475,000	7020.59	6989.58	6963.66	6941.97	6923.80
500,000	7390.10	7357.45	7330.17	7307.34	7288.21
525,000	7759.60	7725.32	7696.68	7672.71	7652.62
550,000	8129.10	8093.20	8063.19	8038.07	8017.03
575,000	8498.61	8461.07	8429.69	8403.44	8381.44
600,000	8868.11	8828.94	8796.20	8768.81	8745.85
625,000	9237.62	9196.81	9162.71	9134.17	9110.26
650,000	9607.12	9564.69	9529.22	9499.54	9474.67
675,000	9976.63	9932.56	9895.73	9864.91	9839.08
700,000	10346.13	10300.43	10262.24	10230.27	10203.49
725,000	10715.64	10668.30	10628.74	10595.64	10567.91
750,000	11085.14	11036.18	10995.25	10961.01	10932.32
775,000	11454.64	11404.05	11361.76	11326.37	11296.73
800,000	11824.15	11771.92	11728.27	11691.74	11661.14
825,000	12193.65	12139.79	12094.78	12057.11	12025.55
850,000	12563.16	12507.66	12461.29	12422.47	12389.96
875,000	12932.66	12875.54	12827.79	12787.84	12754.37
900,000	13302.17	13243.41	13194.30	13153.21	13118.78

Table 7   307

17.25%   Monthly Payment Loans

Loan Amount	\multicolumn{5}{c}{Amortization Period in Years}				
	26	27	28	29	30
10	0.15	0.15	0.15	0.15	0.15
20	0.30	0.30	0.29	0.29	0.29
30	0.44	0.44	0.44	0.44	0.44
40	0.59	0.59	0.58	0.58	0.58
50	0.73	0.73	0.73	0.73	0.73
100	1.46	1.46	1.45	1.45	1.45
200	2.91	2.91	2.90	2.90	2.90
300	4.37	4.36	4.35	4.35	4.34
400	5.82	5.81	5.80	5.80	5.79
500	7.28	7.26	7.25	7.24	7.23
1,000	14.55	14.52	14.50	14.48	14.46
2,000	29.09	29.04	28.99	28.96	28.92
3,000	43.64	43.56	43.49	43.43	43.38
4,000	58.18	58.07	57.98	57.91	57.84
5,000	72.73	72.59	72.48	72.38	72.30
10,000	145.45	145.18	144.95	144.76	144.60
20,000	290.89	290.35	289.90	289.52	289.20
30,000	436.34	435.53	434.85	434.28	433.80
40,000	581.78	580.70	579.80	579.04	578.40
50,000	727.22	725.88	724.75	723.80	723.00
100,000	1454.44	1451.75	1449.49	1447.59	1445.99
125,000	1818.05	1814.68	1811.86	1809.48	1807.49
150,000	2181.66	2177.62	2174.23	2171.38	2168.98
175,000	2545.26	2540.55	2536.60	2533.27	2530.48
200,000	2908.87	2903.49	2898.97	2895.17	2891.98
225,000	3272.48	3266.42	3261.34	3257.06	3253.47
250,000	3636.09	3629.36	3623.71	3618.96	3614.97
275,000	3999.70	3992.29	3986.08	3980.86	3976.47
300,000	4363.31	4355.23	4348.45	4342.75	4337.96
325,000	4726.91	4718.17	4710.82	4704.65	4699.46
350,000	5090.52	5081.10	5073.19	5066.54	5060.96
375,000	5454.13	5444.04	5435.56	5428.44	5422.45
400,000	5817.74	5806.97	5797.93	5790.33	5783.95
425,000	6181.35	6169.91	6160.30	6152.23	6145.44
450,000	6544.96	6532.84	6522.67	6514.12	6506.94
475,000	6908.56	6895.78	6885.04	6876.02	6868.44
500,000	7272.17	7258.71	7247.41	7237.92	7229.93
525,000	7635.78	7621.65	7609.78	7599.81	7591.43
550,000	7999.39	7984.58	7972.15	7961.71	7952.93
575,000	8363.00	8347.52	8334.52	8323.60	8314.42
600,000	8726.61	8710.46	8696.89	8685.50	8675.92
625,000	9090.22	9073.39	9059.26	9047.39	9037.42
650,000	9453.82	9436.33	9421.63	9409.29	9398.91
675,000	9817.43	9799.26	9784.00	9771.18	9760.41
700,000	10181.04	10162.20	10146.37	10133.08	10121.91
725,000	10544.65	10525.13	10508.74	10494.98	10483.40
750,000	10908.26	10888.07	10871.11	10856.87	10844.90
775,000	11271.87	11251.00	11233.49	11218.77	11206.39
800,000	11635.47	11613.94	11595.86	11580.66	11567.89
825,000	11999.08	11976.87	11958.23	11942.56	11929.39
850,000	12362.69	12339.81	12320.60	12304.45	12290.88
875,000	12726.30	12702.75	12682.97	12666.35	12652.38
900,000	13089.91	13065.68	13045.34	13028.24	13013.88

Monthly Payment Loans   **17.50%**

Loan Amount	Amortization Period in Years				
	5	7	8	10	12
10	0.26	0.21	0.20	0.18	0.17
20	0.51	0.42	0.39	0.36	0.34
30	0.76	0.63	0.59	0.54	0.50
40	1.01	0.83	0.78	0.71	0.67
50	1.26	1.04	0.98	0.89	0.84
100	2.52	2.08	1.95	1.77	1.67
200	5.03	4.15	3.89	3.54	3.34
300	7.54	6.22	5.83	5.31	5.00
400	10.05	8.30	7.77	7.08	6.67
500	12.57	10.37	9.72	8.85	8.33
1,000	25.13	20.73	19.43	17.70	16.66
2,000	50.25	41.46	38.85	35.40	33.31
3,000	75.37	62.18	58.27	53.10	49.97
4,000	100.49	82.91	77.69	70.80	66.62
5,000	125.62	103.63	97.11	88.49	83.27
10,000	251.23	207.26	194.22	176.98	166.54
20,000	502.45	414.52	388.43	353.96	333.08
30,000	753.67	621.78	582.64	530.94	499.62
40,000	1004.89	829.04	776.85	707.92	666.16
50,000	1256.12	1036.29	971.07	884.90	832.70
100,000	2512.23	2072.58	1942.13	1769.79	1665.39
125,000	3140.28	2590.73	2427.66	2212.24	2081.74
150,000	3768.34	3108.87	2913.19	2654.69	2498.09
175,000	4396.39	3627.02	3398.72	3097.13	2914.43
200,000	5024.45	4145.16	3884.25	3539.58	3330.78
225,000	5652.50	4663.31	4369.78	3982.03	3747.13
250,000	6280.56	5181.45	4855.31	4424.47	4163.47
275,000	6908.61	5699.60	5340.84	4866.92	4579.82
300,000	7536.67	6217.74	5826.37	5309.37	4996.17
325,000	8164.72	6735.89	6311.90	5751.81	5412.51
350,000	8792.78	7254.03	6797.43	6194.26	5828.86
375,000	9420.84	7772.18	7282.96	6636.71	6245.21
400,000	10048.89	8290.32	7768.49	7079.16	6661.55
425,000	10676.95	8808.47	8254.02	7521.60	7077.90
450,000	11305.00	9326.61	8739.55	7964.05	7494.25
475,000	11933.06	9844.76	9225.08	8406.50	7910.59
500,000	12561.11	10362.90	9710.61	8848.94	8326.94
525,000	13189.17	10881.05	10196.14	9291.39	8743.29
550,000	13817.22	11399.19	10681.67	9733.84	9159.63
575,000	14445.28	11917.34	11167.20	10176.28	9575.98
600,000	15073.33	12435.48	11652.73	10618.73	9992.33
625,000	15701.39	12953.63	12138.26	11061.18	10408.67
650,000	16329.44	13471.77	12623.79	11503.62	10825.02
675,000	16957.50	13989.92	13109.32	11946.07	11241.37
700,000	17585.55	14508.06	13594.85	12388.52	11657.71
725,000	18213.61	15026.21	14080.38	12830.97	12074.06
750,000	18841.67	15544.35	14565.91	13273.41	12490.41
775,000	19469.72	16062.50	15051.44	13715.86	12906.75
800,000	20097.78	16580.64	15536.97	14158.31	13323.10
825,000	20725.83	17098.78	16022.50	14600.75	13739.45
850,000	21353.89	17616.93	16508.03	15043.20	14155.79
875,000	21981.94	18135.07	16993.56	15485.65	14572.14
900,000	22610.00	18653.22	17479.09	15928.09	14988.49

Table 7   309

17.50%   Monthly Payment Loans

Loan Amount	\multicolumn{5}{c}{Amortization Period in Years}
	15	16	17	18	20
10	0.16	0.16	0.16	0.16	0.16
20	0.32	0.32	0.31	0.31	0.31
30	0.48	0.47	0.47	0.46	0.46
40	0.63	0.63	0.62	0.62	0.61
50	0.79	0.78	0.77	0.77	0.76
100	1.58	1.56	1.54	1.53	1.51
200	3.15	3.11	3.08	3.06	3.01
300	4.73	4.67	4.62	4.58	4.52
400	6.30	6.22	6.16	6.11	6.02
500	7.88	7.78	7.70	7.63	7.53
1,000	15.75	15.55	15.39	15.26	15.05
2,000	31.50	31.10	30.78	30.51	30.10
3,000	47.24	46.65	46.16	45.76	45.15
4,000	62.99	62.20	61.55	61.01	60.20
5,000	78.73	77.75	76.93	76.26	75.25
10,000	157.46	155.49	153.86	152.52	150.50
20,000	314.92	310.97	307.72	305.04	300.99
30,000	472.38	466.45	461.58	457.56	451.49
40,000	629.84	621.93	615.44	610.08	601.98
50,000	787.29	777.41	769.29	762.60	752.48
100,000	1574.58	1554.82	1538.58	1525.20	1504.95
125,000	1968.23	1943.52	1923.23	1906.50	1881.18
150,000	2361.87	2332.22	2307.87	2287.80	2257.42
175,000	2755.52	2720.93	2692.52	2669.10	2633.65
200,000	3149.16	3109.63	3077.16	3050.39	3009.89
225,000	3542.81	3498.33	3461.81	3431.69	3386.12
250,000	3936.45	3887.04	3846.45	3812.99	3762.36
275,000	4330.10	4275.74	4231.10	4194.29	4138.60
300,000	4723.74	4664.44	4615.74	4575.59	4514.83
325,000	5117.38	5053.15	5000.39	4956.89	4891.07
350,000	5511.03	5441.85	5385.03	5338.19	5267.30
375,000	5904.67	5830.55	5769.68	5719.49	5643.54
400,000	6298.32	6219.26	6154.32	6100.78	6019.77
425,000	6691.96	6607.96	6538.97	6482.08	6396.01
450,000	7085.61	6996.66	6923.61	6863.38	6772.24
475,000	7479.25	7385.37	7308.26	7244.68	7148.48
500,000	7872.90	7774.07	7692.90	7625.98	7524.71
525,000	8266.54	8162.77	8077.55	8007.28	7900.95
550,000	8660.19	8551.48	8462.19	8388.58	8277.19
575,000	9053.83	8940.18	8846.84	8769.88	8653.42
600,000	9447.47	9328.88	9231.48	9151.17	9029.66
625,000	9841.12	9717.59	9616.13	9532.47	9405.89
650,000	10234.76	10106.29	10000.77	9913.77	9782.13
675,000	10628.41	10494.99	10385.42	10295.07	10158.36
700,000	11022.05	10883.69	10770.06	10676.37	10534.60
725,000	11415.70	11272.40	11154.71	11057.67	10910.83
750,000	11809.34	11661.10	11539.35	11438.97	11287.07
775,000	12202.99	12049.80	11924.00	11820.27	11663.30
800,000	12596.63	12438.51	12308.64	12201.56	12039.54
825,000	12990.28	12827.21	12693.29	12582.86	12415.78
850,000	13383.92	13215.91	13077.93	12964.16	12792.01
875,000	13777.56	13604.62	13462.58	13345.46	13168.25
900,000	14171.21	13993.32	13847.22	13726.76	13544.48

Monthly Payment Loans   **17.50%**

Loan Amount	21	22	23	24	25
	Amortization Period in Years				
10	0.15	0.15	0.15	0.15	0.15
20	0.30	0.30	0.30	0.30	0.30
30	0.45	0.45	0.45	0.45	0.45
40	0.60	0.60	0.60	0.60	0.60
50	0.75	0.75	0.75	0.75	0.74
100	1.50	1.50	1.49	1.49	1.48
200	3.00	2.99	2.98	2.97	2.96
300	4.50	4.48	4.46	4.45	4.44
400	5.99	5.97	5.95	5.93	5.92
500	7.49	7.46	7.43	7.41	7.39
1,000	14.98	14.91	14.86	14.82	14.78
2,000	29.95	29.82	29.72	29.63	29.56
3,000	44.92	44.73	44.57	44.44	44.33
4,000	59.90	59.64	59.43	59.25	59.11
5,000	74.87	74.55	74.29	74.07	73.88
10,000	149.74	149.10	148.57	148.13	147.76
20,000	299.47	298.20	297.14	296.25	295.51
30,000	449.20	447.29	445.70	444.37	443.26
40,000	598.93	596.39	594.27	592.50	591.02
50,000	748.66	745.48	742.83	740.62	738.77
100,000	1497.32	1490.96	1485.66	1481.23	1477.53
125,000	1871.64	1863.70	1857.07	1851.54	1846.92
150,000	2245.97	2236.44	2228.49	2221.85	2216.30
175,000	2620.30	2609.18	2599.90	2592.16	2585.68
200,000	2994.63	2981.91	2971.31	2962.46	2955.06
225,000	3368.95	3354.65	3342.73	3332.77	3324.45
250,000	3743.28	3727.39	3714.14	3703.08	3693.83
275,000	4117.61	4100.13	4085.56	4073.39	4063.21
300,000	4491.94	4472.87	4456.97	4443.69	4432.59
325,000	4866.26	4845.61	4828.38	4814.00	4801.98
350,000	5240.59	5218.35	5199.80	5184.31	5171.36
375,000	5614.92	5591.09	5571.21	5554.61	5540.74
400,000	5989.25	5963.82	5942.62	5924.92	5910.12
425,000	6363.57	6336.56	6314.04	6295.23	6279.51
450,000	6737.90	6709.30	6685.45	6665.54	6648.89
475,000	7112.23	7082.04	7056.87	7035.84	7018.27
500,000	7486.56	7454.78	7428.28	7406.15	7387.65
525,000	7860.88	7827.52	7799.69	7776.46	7757.04
550,000	8235.21	8200.26	8171.11	8146.77	8126.42
575,000	8609.54	8573.00	8542.52	8517.07	8495.80
600,000	8983.87	8945.73	8913.93	8887.38	8865.18
625,000	9358.19	9318.47	9285.35	9257.69	9234.57
650,000	9732.52	9691.21	9656.76	9628.00	9603.95
675,000	10106.85	10063.95	10028.18	9998.30	9973.33
700,000	10481.18	10436.69	10399.59	10368.61	10342.71
725,000	10855.50	10809.43	10771.00	10738.92	10712.10
750,000	11229.83	11182.17	11142.42	11109.22	11081.48
775,000	11604.16	11554.91	11513.83	11479.53	11450.86
800,000	11978.49	11927.64	11885.24	11849.84	11820.24
825,000	12352.81	12300.38	12256.66	12220.15	12189.63
850,000	12727.14	12673.12	12628.07	12590.45	12559.01
875,000	13101.47	13045.86	12999.49	12960.76	12928.39
900,000	13475.80	13418.60	13370.90	13331.07	13297.77

Table 7   311

17.50% Monthly Payment Loans

Loan Amount	Amortization Period in Years				
	26	27	28	29	30
10	0.15	0.15	0.15	0.15	0.15
20	0.30	0.30	0.30	0.30	0.30
30	0.45	0.45	0.45	0.45	0.44
40	0.59	0.59	0.59	0.59	0.59
50	0.74	0.74	0.74	0.74	0.74
100	1.48	1.48	1.47	1.47	1.47
200	2.95	2.95	2.94	2.94	2.94
300	4.43	4.42	4.41	4.41	4.40
400	5.90	5.89	5.88	5.88	5.87
500	7.38	7.36	7.35	7.34	7.34
1,000	14.75	14.72	14.70	14.68	14.67
2,000	29.49	29.44	29.40	29.36	29.33
3,000	44.24	44.16	44.10	44.04	43.99
4,000	58.98	58.88	58.79	58.72	58.66
5,000	73.73	73.60	73.49	73.40	73.32
10,000	147.45	147.19	146.97	146.79	146.64
20,000	294.89	294.37	293.94	293.58	293.27
30,000	442.34	441.56	440.91	440.36	439.90
40,000	589.78	588.74	587.87	587.15	586.54
50,000	737.22	735.93	734.84	733.93	733.17
100,000	1474.44	1471.85	1469.68	1467.86	1466.33
125,000	1843.05	1839.81	1837.09	1834.82	1832.91
150,000	2211.66	2207.77	2204.51	2201.78	2199.49
175,000	2580.27	2575.73	2571.93	2568.75	2566.07
200,000	2948.87	2943.69	2939.35	2935.71	2932.66
225,000	3317.48	3311.65	3306.77	3302.67	3299.24
250,000	3686.09	3679.61	3674.18	3669.63	3665.82
275,000	4054.70	4047.57	4041.60	4036.60	4032.40
300,000	4423.31	4415.53	4409.02	4403.56	4398.98
325,000	4791.92	4783.49	4776.44	4770.52	4765.56
350,000	5160.53	5151.45	5143.86	5137.49	5132.14
375,000	5529.13	5519.42	5511.27	5504.45	5498.72
400,000	5897.74	5887.38	5878.69	5871.41	5865.31
425,000	6266.35	6255.34	6246.11	6238.37	6231.89
450,000	6634.96	6623.30	6613.53	6605.34	6598.47
475,000	7003.57	6991.26	6980.94	6972.30	6965.05
500,000	7372.18	7359.22	7348.36	7339.26	7331.63
525,000	7740.79	7727.18	7715.78	7706.23	7698.21
550,000	8109.39	8095.14	8083.20	8073.19	8064.79
575,000	8478.00	8463.10	8450.62	8440.15	8431.38
600,000	8846.61	8831.06	8818.03	8807.11	8797.96
625,000	9215.22	9199.02	9185.45	9174.08	9164.54
650,000	9583.83	9566.98	9552.87	9541.04	9531.12
675,000	9952.44	9934.94	9920.29	9908.00	9897.70
700,000	10321.05	10302.90	10287.71	10274.97	10264.28
725,000	10689.65	10670.87	10655.12	10641.93	10630.86
750,000	11058.26	11038.83	11022.54	11008.89	10997.44
775,000	11426.87	11406.79	11389.96	11375.85	11364.03
800,000	11795.48	11774.75	11757.38	11742.82	11730.61
825,000	12164.09	12142.71	12124.80	12109.78	12097.19
850,000	12532.70	12510.67	12492.21	12476.74	12463.77
875,000	12901.31	12878.63	12859.63	12843.71	12830.35
900,000	13269.91	13246.59	13227.05	13210.67	13196.93

Monthly Payment Loans 17.75%

Loan Amount	Amortization Period in Years				
	5	7	8	10	12
10	0.26	0.21	0.20	0.18	0.17
20	0.51	0.42	0.40	0.36	0.34
30	0.76	0.63	0.59	0.54	0.51
40	1.02	0.84	0.79	0.72	0.68
50	1.27	1.05	0.98	0.90	0.85
100	2.53	2.09	1.96	1.79	1.69
200	5.06	4.18	3.92	3.58	3.37
300	7.58	6.27	5.88	5.36	5.05
400	10.11	8.35	7.83	7.15	6.73
500	12.63	10.44	9.79	8.93	8.42
1,000	25.26	20.88	19.58	17.86	16.83
2,000	50.52	41.75	39.15	35.72	33.65
3,000	75.78	62.62	58.72	53.58	50.47
4,000	101.04	83.49	78.29	71.44	67.29
5,000	126.29	104.36	97.86	89.29	84.12
10,000	252.58	208.72	195.72	178.58	168.23
20,000	505.16	417.44	391.44	357.16	336.45
30,000	757.73	626.15	587.16	535.74	504.67
40,000	1010.31	834.87	782.88	714.32	672.89
50,000	1262.89	1043.58	978.60	892.90	841.12
100,000	2525.77	2087.16	1957.20	1785.79	1682.23
125,000	3157.21	2608.95	2446.50	2232.24	2102.78
150,000	3788.65	3130.74	2935.79	2678.69	2523.34
175,000	4420.09	3652.53	3425.09	3125.13	2943.89
200,000	5051.53	4174.32	3914.39	3571.58	3364.45
225,000	5682.97	4696.11	4403.69	4018.03	3785.00
250,000	6314.41	5217.90	4892.99	4464.48	4205.56
275,000	6945.85	5739.68	5382.29	4910.92	4626.11
300,000	7577.29	6261.47	5871.58	5357.37	5046.67
325,000	8208.73	6783.26	6360.88	5803.82	5467.22
350,000	8840.17	7305.05	6850.18	6250.26	5887.78
375,000	9471.61	7826.84	7339.48	6696.71	6308.33
400,000	10103.05	8348.63	7828.78	7143.16	6728.89
425,000	10734.50	8870.42	8318.08	7589.61	7149.44
450,000	11365.94	9392.21	8807.37	8036.05	7570.00
475,000	11997.38	9914.00	9296.67	8482.50	7990.55
500,000	12628.82	10435.79	9785.97	8928.95	8411.11
525,000	13260.26	10957.57	10275.27	9375.39	8831.66
550,000	13891.70	11479.36	10764.57	9821.84	9252.22
575,000	14523.14	12001.15	11253.87	10268.29	9672.77
600,000	15154.58	12522.94	11743.16	10714.74	10093.33
625,000	15786.02	13044.73	12232.46	11161.18	10513.88
650,000	16417.46	13566.52	12721.76	11607.63	10934.44
675,000	17048.90	14088.31	13211.06	12054.08	11354.99
700,000	17680.34	14610.10	13700.36	12500.52	11775.55
725,000	18311.78	15131.89	14189.66	12946.97	12196.10
750,000	18943.22	15653.68	14678.95	13393.42	12616.66
775,000	19574.66	16175.46	15168.25	13839.87	13037.21
800,000	20206.10	16697.25	15657.55	14286.31	13457.77
825,000	20837.54	17219.04	16146.85	14732.76	13878.32
850,000	21468.99	17740.83	16636.15	15179.21	14298.88
875,000	22100.43	18262.62	17125.45	15625.65	14719.43
900,000	22731.87	18784.41	17614.74	16072.10	15139.99

Table 7   313

17.75% Monthly Payment Loans

Loan Amount	15	16	17	18	20
10	0.16	0.16	0.16	0.16	0.16
20	0.32	0.32	0.32	0.31	0.31
30	0.48	0.48	0.47	0.47	0.46
40	0.64	0.63	0.63	0.62	0.61
50	0.80	0.79	0.78	0.78	0.77
100	1.60	1.58	1.56	1.55	1.53
200	3.19	3.15	3.12	3.09	3.05
300	4.78	4.72	4.68	4.64	4.58
400	6.37	6.30	6.23	6.18	6.10
500	7.97	7.87	7.79	7.72	7.63
1,000	15.93	15.74	15.58	15.44	15.25
2,000	31.85	31.47	31.15	30.88	30.49
3,000	47.78	47.20	46.72	46.32	45.73
4,000	63.70	62.93	62.29	61.76	60.97
5,000	79.63	78.66	77.86	77.20	76.21
10,000	159.25	157.31	155.71	154.40	152.41
20,000	318.50	314.61	311.41	308.79	304.82
30,000	477.74	471.91	467.12	463.18	457.23
40,000	636.99	629.21	622.82	617.57	609.64
50,000	796.24	786.51	778.53	771.96	762.05
100,000	1592.47	1573.01	1557.05	1543.92	1524.10
125,000	1990.59	1966.26	1946.31	1929.90	1905.13
150,000	2388.70	2359.51	2335.57	2315.87	2286.15
175,000	2786.82	2752.76	2724.83	2701.85	2667.18
200,000	3184.94	3146.01	3114.09	3087.83	3048.20
225,000	3583.05	3539.26	3503.36	3473.81	3429.23
250,000	3981.17	3932.51	3892.62	3859.79	3810.25
275,000	4379.29	4325.76	4281.88	4245.77	4191.28
300,000	4777.40	4719.01	4671.14	4631.74	4572.30
325,000	5175.52	5112.26	5060.40	5017.72	4953.33
350,000	5573.64	5505.51	5449.66	5403.70	5334.35
375,000	5971.75	5898.76	5838.92	5789.68	5715.38
400,000	6369.87	6292.01	6228.18	6175.66	6096.40
425,000	6767.99	6685.26	6617.45	6561.63	6477.43
450,000	7166.10	7078.51	7006.71	6947.61	6858.45
475,000	7564.22	7471.76	7395.97	7333.59	7239.48
500,000	7962.34	7865.01	7785.23	7719.57	7620.50
525,000	8360.45	8258.26	8174.49	8105.55	8001.52
550,000	8758.57	8651.52	8563.75	8491.53	8382.55
575,000	9156.69	9044.77	8953.01	8877.50	8763.57
600,000	9554.80	9438.02	9342.27	9263.48	9144.60
625,000	9952.92	9831.27	9731.53	9649.46	9525.62
650,000	10351.04	10224.52	10120.80	10035.44	9906.65
675,000	10749.15	10617.77	10510.06	10421.42	10287.67
700,000	11147.27	11011.02	10899.32	10807.39	10668.70
725,000	11545.39	11404.27	11288.58	11193.37	11049.72
750,000	11943.50	11797.52	11677.84	11579.35	11430.75
775,000	12341.62	12190.77	12067.10	11965.33	11811.77
800,000	12739.74	12584.02	12456.36	12351.31	12192.80
825,000	13137.85	12977.27	12845.62	12737.29	12573.82
850,000	13535.97	13370.52	13234.89	13123.26	12954.85
875,000	13934.09	13763.77	13624.15	13509.24	13335.87
900,000	14332.20	14157.02	14013.41	13895.22	13716.90

Monthly Payment Loans   17.75%

Loan Amount	Amortization Period in Years				
	21	22	23	24	25
10	0.16	0.16	0.16	0.16	0.15
20	0.31	0.31	0.31	0.31	0.30
30	0.46	0.46	0.46	0.46	0.45
40	0.61	0.61	0.61	0.61	0.60
50	0.76	0.76	0.76	0.76	0.75
100	1.52	1.52	1.51	1.51	1.50
200	3.04	3.03	3.02	3.01	3.00
300	4.55	4.54	4.52	4.51	4.50
400	6.07	6.05	6.03	6.01	5.99
500	7.59	7.56	7.53	7.51	7.49
1,000	15.17	15.11	15.06	15.02	14.98
2,000	30.34	30.21	30.11	30.03	29.95
3,000	45.50	45.32	45.16	45.04	44.93
4,000	60.67	60.42	60.22	60.05	59.90
5,000	75.84	75.53	75.27	75.06	74.88
10,000	151.67	151.05	150.54	150.11	149.75
20,000	303.34	302.10	301.07	300.21	299.50
30,000	455.00	453.15	451.60	450.32	449.24
40,000	606.67	604.19	602.13	600.42	598.99
50,000	758.33	755.24	752.67	750.52	748.73
100,000	1516.66	1510.48	1505.33	1501.04	1497.46
125,000	1895.83	1888.09	1881.66	1876.30	1871.83
150,000	2274.99	2265.71	2257.99	2251.56	2246.19
175,000	2654.15	2643.33	2634.32	2626.82	2620.56
200,000	3033.32	3020.95	3010.65	3002.08	2994.92
225,000	3412.48	3398.57	3386.99	3377.34	3369.29
250,000	3791.65	3776.18	3763.32	3752.60	3743.65
275,000	4170.81	4153.80	4139.65	4127.86	4118.02
300,000	4549.97	4531.42	4515.98	4503.11	4492.38
325,000	4929.14	4909.04	4892.31	4878.37	4866.75
350,000	5308.30	5286.66	5268.64	5253.63	5241.11
375,000	5687.47	5664.27	5644.97	5628.89	5615.48
400,000	6066.63	6041.89	6021.30	6004.15	5989.04
425,000	6445.79	6419.51	6397.64	6379.41	6364.21
450,000	6824.96	6797.13	6773.97	6754.67	6738.57
475,000	7204.12	7174.75	7150.30	7129.93	7112.94
500,000	7583.29	7552.36	7526.63	7505.19	7487.30
525,000	7962.45	7929.98	7902.96	7880.45	7861.67
550,000	8341.61	8307.60	8279.29	8255.71	8236.03
575,000	8720.78	8685.22	8655.62	8630.97	8610.40
600,000	9099.94	9062.83	9031.95	9006.22	8984.76
625,000	9479.11	9440.45	9408.29	9381.48	9359.13
650,000	9858.27	9818.07	9784.62	9756.74	9733.49
675,000	10237.43	10195.69	10160.95	10132.00	10107.86
700,000	10616.60	10573.31	10537.28	10507.26	10482.22
725,000	10995.76	10950.92	10913.61	10882.52	10856.59
750,000	11374.93	11328.54	11289.94	11257.78	11230.95
775,000	11754.09	11706.16	11666.27	11633.04	11605.32
800,000	12133.25	12083.78	12042.60	12008.30	11979.68
825,000	12512.42	12461.40	12418.94	12383.56	12354.05
850,000	12891.58	12839.01	12795.27	12758.82	12728.41
875,000	13270.75	13216.63	13171.60	13134.07	13102.78
900,000	13649.91	13594.25	13547.93	13509.33	13477.14

Table 7   315

17.75% Monthly Payment Loans

Amortization Period in Years

Loan Amount	26	27	28	29	30
10	0.15	0.15	0.15	0.15	0.15
20	0.30	0.30	0.30	0.30	0.30
30	0.45	0.45	0.45	0.45	0.45
40	0.60	0.60	0.60	0.60	0.60
50	0.75	0.75	0.75	0.75	0.75
100	1.50	1.50	1.49	1.49	1.49
200	2.99	2.99	2.98	2.98	2.98
300	4.49	4.48	4.47	4.47	4.47
400	5.98	5.97	5.96	5.96	5.95
500	7.48	7.46	7.45	7.45	7.44
1,000	14.95	14.92	14.90	14.89	14.87
2,000	29.89	29.84	29.80	29.77	29.74
3,000	44.84	44.76	44.70	44.65	44.61
4,000	59.78	59.68	59.60	59.53	59.47
5,000	74.73	74.60	74.50	74.41	74.34
10,000	149.45	149.20	148.99	148.82	148.67
20,000	298.90	298.40	297.98	297.64	297.34
30,000	448.35	447.60	446.97	446.45	446.01
40,000	597.79	596.80	595.96	595.27	594.68
50,000	747.24	745.99	744.95	744.08	743.35
100,000	1494.48	1491.98	1489.90	1488.16	1486.70
125,000	1868.10	1864.98	1862.37	1860.19	1858.37
150,000	2241.72	2237.97	2234.85	2232.23	2230.04
175,000	2615.33	2610.97	2607.32	2604.27	2601.72
200,000	2988.95	2983.96	2979.79	2976.31	2973.39
225,000	3362.57	3356.96	3352.27	3348.34	3345.06
250,000	3736.19	3729.95	3724.74	3720.38	3716.74
275,000	4109.81	4102.95	4097.22	4092.42	4088.41
300,000	4483.43	4475.94	4469.69	4464.46	4460.08
325,000	4857.05	4848.94	4842.16	4836.50	4831.75
350,000	5230.66	5221.93	5214.64	5208.53	5203.43
375,000	5604.28	5594.93	5587.11	5580.57	5575.10
400,000	5977.90	5967.92	5959.58	5952.61	5946.77
425,000	6351.52	6340.92	6332.06	6324.65	6318.45
450,000	6725.14	6713.91	6704.53	6696.68	6690.12
475,000	7098.76	7086.91	7077.00	7068.72	7061.79
500,000	7472.37	7459.90	7449.48	7440.76	7433.47
525,000	7845.99	7832.90	7821.95	7812.80	7805.14
550,000	8219.61	8205.89	8194.43	8184.84	8176.81
575,000	8593.23	8578.89	8566.90	8556.87	8548.49
600,000	8966.85	8951.88	8939.37	8928.91	8920.16
625,000	9340.47	9324.88	9311.85	9300.95	9291.83
650,000	9714.09	9697.87	9684.32	9672.99	9663.50
675,000	10087.70	10070.87	10056.79	10045.02	10035.18
700,000	10461.32	10443.86	10429.27	10417.06	10406.85
725,000	10834.94	10816.86	10801.74	10789.10	10778.52
750,000	11208.56	11189.85	11174.22	11161.14	11150.20
775,000	11582.18	11562.85	11546.69	11533.18	11521.87
800,000	11955.80	11935.84	11919.16	11905.21	11893.54
825,000	12329.42	12308.84	12291.64	12277.25	12265.22
850,000	12703.03	12681.83	12664.11	12649.29	12636.89
875,000	13076.65	13054.83	13036.58	13021.33	13008.56
900,000	13450.27	13427.82	13409.06	13393.36	13380.24

Monthly Payment Loans   **18.00%**

Loan Amount	Amortization Period in Years				
	5	7	8	10	12
10	0.26	0.22	0.20	0.19	0.17
20	0.51	0.43	0.40	0.37	0.34
30	0.77	0.64	0.60	0.55	0.51
40	1.02	0.85	0.79	0.73	0.68
50	1.27	1.06	0.99	0.91	0.85
100	2.54	2.11	1.98	1.81	1.70
200	5.08	4.21	3.95	3.61	3.40
300	7.62	6.31	5.92	5.41	5.10
400	10.16	8.41	7.89	7.21	6.80
500	12.70	10.51	9.87	9.01	8.50
1,000	25.40	21.02	19.73	18.02	17.00
2,000	50.79	42.04	39.45	36.04	33.99
3,000	76.19	63.06	59.17	54.06	50.98
4,000	101.58	84.08	78.90	72.08	67.97
5,000	126.97	105.09	98.62	90.10	84.96
10,000	253.94	210.18	197.24	180.19	169.92
20,000	507.87	420.36	394.47	360.38	339.83
30,000	761.81	630.54	591.70	540.56	509.74
40,000	1015.74	840.72	788.93	720.75	679.65
50,000	1269.68	1050.90	986.17	900.93	849.56
100,000	2539.35	2101.79	1972.33	1801.86	1699.12
125,000	3174.18	2627.23	2465.41	2252.32	2123.90
150,000	3809.02	3152.68	2958.49	2702.78	2548.68
175,000	4443.85	3678.13	3451.57	3153.25	2973.46
200,000	5078.69	4203.57	3944.65	3603.71	3398.24
225,000	5713.53	4729.02	4437.73	4054.17	3823.02
250,000	6348.36	5254.46	4930.81	4504.63	4247.80
275,000	6983.20	5779.91	5423.89	4955.10	4672.58
300,000	7618.03	6305.36	5916.97	5405.56	5097.36
325,000	8252.87	6830.80	6410.05	5856.02	5522.14
350,000	8887.70	7356.25	6903.13	6306.49	5946.92
375,000	9522.54	7881.69	7396.21	6756.95	6371.70
400,000	10157.38	8407.14	7889.29	7207.41	6796.48
425,000	10792.21	8932.59	8382.37	7657.88	7221.26
450,000	11427.05	9458.03	8875.45	8108.34	7646.04
475,000	12061.88	9983.48	9368.53	8558.80	8070.82
500,000	12696.72	10508.92	9861.61	9009.26	8495.60
525,000	13331.55	11034.37	10354.69	9459.73	8920.38
550,000	13966.39	11559.82	10847.77	9910.19	9345.16
575,000	14601.23	12085.26	11340.85	10360.65	9769.94
600,000	15236.06	12610.71	11833.93	10811.12	10194.72
625,000	15870.90	13136.15	12327.01	11261.58	10619.50
650,000	16505.73	13661.60	12820.09	11712.04	11044.28
675,000	17140.57	14187.05	13313.17	12162.51	11469.06
700,000	17775.40	14712.49	13806.25	12612.97	11893.84
725,000	18410.24	15237.94	14299.34	13063.43	12318.62
750,000	19045.08	15763.38	14792.42	13513.89	12743.40
775,000	19679.91	16288.83	15285.50	13964.36	13168.18
800,000	20314.75	16814.28	15778.58	14414.82	13592.96
825,000	20949.58	17339.72	16271.66	14865.28	14017.74
850,000	21584.42	17865.17	16764.74	15315.75	14442.52
875,000	22219.25	18390.61	17257.82	15766.21	14867.30
900,000	22854.09	18916.06	17750.90	16216.67	15292.08

Table 7   317

18.00% Monthly Payment Loans

Loan Amount	Amortization Period in Years				
	15	16	17	18	20
10	0.17	0.16	0.16	0.16	0.16
20	0.33	0.32	0.32	0.32	0.31
30	0.49	0.48	0.48	0.47	0.47
40	0.65	0.64	0.64	0.63	0.62
50	0.81	0.80	0.79	0.79	0.78
100	1.62	1.60	1.58	1.57	1.55
200	3.23	3.19	3.16	3.13	3.09
300	4.84	4.78	4.73	4.69	4.63
400	6.45	6.37	6.31	6.26	6.18
500	8.06	7.96	7.88	7.82	7.72
1,000	16.11	15.92	15.76	15.63	15.44
2,000	32.21	31.83	31.52	31.26	30.87
3,000	48.32	47.74	47.27	46.89	46.30
4,000	64.42	63.66	63.03	62.51	61.74
5,000	80.53	79.57	78.78	78.14	77.17
10,000	161.05	159.13	157.56	156.27	154.34
20,000	322.09	318.26	315.12	312.54	308.67
30,000	483.13	477.38	472.68	468.81	463.00
40,000	644.17	636.51	630.23	625.08	617.33
50,000	805.22	795.63	787.79	781.35	771.66
100,000	1610.43	1591.26	1575.58	1562.70	1543.32
125,000	2013.03	1989.07	1969.47	1953.37	1929.14
150,000	2415.64	2386.89	2363.36	2344.04	2314.97
175,000	2818.24	2784.70	2757.26	2734.71	2700.80
200,000	3220.85	3182.52	3151.15	3125.39	3086.63
225,000	3623.45	3580.33	3545.04	3516.06	3472.46
250,000	4026.06	3978.14	3938.94	3906.73	3858.28
275,000	4428.66	4375.96	4332.83	4297.41	4244.11
300,000	4831.27	4773.77	4726.72	4688.08	4629.94
325,000	5233.87	5171.59	5120.62	5078.75	5015.77
350,000	5636.48	5569.40	5514.51	5469.42	5401.60
375,000	6039.08	5967.21	5908.40	5860.10	5787.42
400,000	6441.69	6365.03	6302.30	6250.77	6173.25
425,000	6844.29	6762.84	6696.19	6641.44	6559.08
450,000	7246.90	7160.66	7090.08	7032.12	6944.91
475,000	7649.50	7558.47	7483.98	7422.79	7330.73
500,000	8052.11	7956.28	7877.87	7813.46	7716.56
525,000	8454.72	8354.10	8271.76	8204.13	8102.39
550,000	8857.32	8751.91	8665.66	8594.81	8488.22
575,000	9259.93	9149.73	9059.55	8985.48	8874.05
600,000	9662.53	9547.54	9453.44	9376.15	9259.87
625,000	10065.14	9945.35	9847.34	9766.83	9645.70
650,000	10467.74	10343.17	10241.23	10157.50	10031.53
675,000	10870.35	10740.98	10635.12	10548.17	10417.36
700,000	11272.95	11138.79	11029.02	10938.84	10803.19
725,000	11675.56	11536.61	11422.91	11329.52	11189.01
750,000	12078.16	11934.42	11816.80	11720.19	11574.84
775,000	12480.77	12332.24	12210.69	12110.86	11960.67
800,000	12883.37	12730.05	12604.59	12501.54	12346.50
825,000	13285.98	13127.86	12998.48	12892.21	12732.33
850,000	13688.58	13525.68	13392.37	13282.88	13118.15
875,000	14091.19	13923.49	13786.27	13673.55	13503.98
900,000	14493.79	14321.31	14180.16	14064.23	13889.81

Monthly Payment Loans $\underline{18.00\%}$

Loan Amount	Amortization Period in Years				
	21	22	23	24	25
10	0.16	0.16	0.16	0.16	0.16
20	0.31	0.31	0.31	0.31	0.31
30	0.47	0.46	0.46	0.46	0.46
40	0.62	0.62	0.62	0.61	0.61
50	0.77	0.77	0.77	0.77	0.76
100	1.54	1.54	1.53	1.53	1.52
200	3.08	3.07	3.06	3.05	3.04
300	4.61	4.60	4.58	4.57	4.56
400	6.15	6.13	6.11	6.09	6.07
500	7.69	7.66	7.63	7.61	7.59
1,000	15.37	15.31	15.26	15.21	15.18
2,000	30.73	30.61	30.51	30.42	30.35
3,000	46.09	45.91	45.76	45.63	45.53
4,000	61.45	61.21	61.01	60.84	60.70
5,000	76.81	76.51	76.26	76.05	75.88
10,000	153.61	153.01	152.51	152.09	151.75
20,000	307.22	306.01	305.01	304.18	303.49
30,000	460.82	459.02	457.52	456.27	455.23
40,000	614.43	612.02	610.02	608.36	606.98
50,000	768.03	765.02	762.53	760.45	758.72
100,000	1536.06	1530.04	1525.05	1520.89	1517.43
125,000	1920.07	1912.55	1906.31	1901.11	1896.79
150,000	2304.09	2295.06	2287.57	2281.34	2276.15
175,000	2688.10	2677.57	2668.83	2661.56	2655.51
200,000	3072.11	3060.08	3050.09	3041.78	3034.86
225,000	3456.13	3442.59	3431.35	3422.00	3414.22
250,000	3840.14	3825.10	3812.61	3802.22	3793.58
275,000	4224.16	4207.61	4193.87	4182.44	4172.94
300,000	4608.17	4590.12	4575.13	4562.67	4552.29
325,000	4992.18	4972.63	4956.39	4942.89	4931.65
350,000	5376.20	5355.14	5337.65	5323.11	5311.01
375,000	5760.21	5737.65	5718.91	5703.33	5690.37
400,000	6144.22	6120.16	6100.17	6083.55	6069.72
425,000	6528.24	6502.67	6481.43	6463.77	6449.08
450,000	6912.25	6885.17	6862.69	6844.00	6828.44
475,000	7296.27	7267.68	7243.95	7224.22	7207.80
500,000	7680.28	7650.19	7625.21	7604.44	7587.15
525,000	8064.29	8032.70	8006.47	7984.66	7966.51
550,000	8448.31	8415.21	8387.73	8364.88	8345.87
575,000	8832.32	8797.72	8768.99	8745.11	8725.23
600,000	9216.33	9180.23	9150.25	9125.33	9104.58
625,000	9600.35	9562.74	9531.51	9505.55	9483.94
650,000	9984.36	9945.25	9912.77	9885.77	9863.30
675,000	10368.38	10327.76	10294.03	10265.99	10242.66
700,000	10752.39	10710.27	10675.29	10646.21	10622.01
725,000	11136.40	11092.78	11056.55	11026.44	11001.37
750,000	11520.42	11475.29	11437.81	11406.66	11380.73
775,000	11904.43	11857.80	11819.07	11786.88	11760.09
800,000	12288.44	12240.31	12200.33	12167.10	12139.44
825,000	12672.46	12622.82	12581.59	12547.32	12518.80
850,000	13056.47	13005.33	12962.85	12927.54	12898.16
875,000	13440.49	13387.84	13344.11	13307.77	13277.52
900,000	13824.50	13770.34	13725.38	13687.99	13656.87

Table 7   319

18.00% Monthly Payment Loans

Loan Amount	Amortization Period in Years				
	26	27	28	29	30
10	0.16	0.16	0.16	0.16	0.16
20	0.31	0.31	0.31	0.31	0.31
30	0.46	0.46	0.46	0.46	0.46
40	0.61	0.61	0.61	0.61	0.61
50	0.76	0.76	0.76	0.76	0.76
100	1.52	1.52	1.52	1.51	1.51
200	3.03	3.03	3.03	3.02	3.02
300	4.55	4.54	4.54	4.53	4.53
400	6.06	6.05	6.05	6.04	6.03
500	7.58	7.57	7.56	7.55	7.54
1,000	15.15	15.13	15.11	15.09	15.08
2,000	30.30	30.25	30.21	30.17	30.15
3,000	45.44	45.37	45.31	45.26	45.22
4,000	60.59	60.49	60.41	60.34	60.29
5,000	75.73	75.61	75.51	75.43	75.36
10,000	151.46	151.22	151.02	150.85	150.71
20,000	302.92	302.44	302.03	301.70	301.42
30,000	454.37	453.65	453.05	452.55	452.13
40,000	605.83	604.87	604.06	603.40	602.84
50,000	757.28	756.08	755.08	754.24	753.55
100,000	1514.56	1512.16	1510.15	1508.48	1507.09
125,000	1893.19	1890.19	1887.69	1885.60	1883.86
150,000	2271.83	2268.23	2265.23	2262.72	2260.63
175,000	2650.47	2646.27	2642.77	2639.84	2637.40
200,000	3029.11	3024.31	3020.30	3016.96	3014.18
225,000	3407.74	3402.34	3397.84	3394.08	3390.95
250,000	3786.38	3780.38	3775.38	3771.20	3767.72
275,000	4165.02	4158.42	4152.92	4148.32	4144.49
300,000	4543.66	4536.46	4530.45	4525.44	4521.26
325,000	4922.29	4914.49	4907.99	4902.56	4898.03
350,000	5300.93	5292.53	5285.53	5279.68	5274.80
375,000	5679.57	5670.57	5663.06	5656.80	5651.58
400,000	6058.21	6048.61	6040.60	6033.92	6028.35
425,000	6436.84	6426.65	6418.14	6411.04	6405.12
450,000	6815.48	6804.68	6795.68	6788.16	6781.89
475,000	7194.12	7182.72	7173.21	7165.28	7158.66
500,000	7572.76	7560.76	7550.75	7542.40	7535.43
525,000	7951.40	7938.80	7928.29	7919.52	7912.20
550,000	8330.03	8316.83	8305.83	8296.64	8288.97
575,000	8708.67	8694.87	8683.36	8673.76	8665.75
600,000	9087.31	9072.91	9060.90	9050.88	9042.52
625,000	9465.95	9450.95	9438.44	9428.00	9419.29
650,000	9844.58	9828.98	9815.97	9805.12	9796.06
675,000	10223.22	10207.02	10193.51	10182.24	10172.83
700,000	10601.86	10585.06	10571.05	10559.36	10549.60
725,000	10980.50	10963.10	10948.59	10936.48	10926.37
750,000	11359.13	11341.13	11326.12	11313.60	11303.15
775,000	11737.77	11719.17	11703.66	11690.72	11679.92
800,000	12116.41	12097.21	12081.20	12067.84	12056.69
825,000	12495.05	12475.25	12458.74	12444.96	12433.46
850,000	12873.68	12853.29	12836.27	12822.08	12810.23
875,000	13252.32	13231.32	13213.81	13199.20	13187.00
900,000	13630.96	13609.36	13591.35	13576.32	13563.77

Glossary

adjustable rate mortgage (ARM)—loan with an interest rate that varies according to an index

amortization—reduction of a loan amount by principal payments at regular intervals

amortization period—time required to pay a loan entirely through periodic payments

Annual Percentage Rate (APR)—yield to maturity to a lender from interest, points, and certain fees

appraisal—estimate of the present value of real estate prepared according to formal regulations

balloon—loan clause making the entire balance due before the end of the amortization period

balloon payment—entire remaining balance of a loan required as a single payment

closing costs—charges related to a sale or loan, such as legal fees, transfer taxes, title insurance

commitment—agreement binding a lender to lend on given terms, if closing is within a stated time

debt service—payments required on a loan for both principal and interest

discount—reduction in the proceeds loaned to a borrower to increase the yield of a lender

equity—share of sale price or property value held by the owner, as opposed to debt held by the lender

escrow—process of closing a sale or loan through the efforts of a neutral third party

escrow payment—monthly deposit with a lender to cover future real estate taxes and insurance

guarantor—third party who agrees to be responsible for repayment of a loan

interest—payment for the use of money for a term

loan-to-value ratio—percentage of appraised value or sales price that a lender will agree to lend

maturity—date on which a loan is due in full

mortgage—document binding title to real estate until a loan is repaid; **mortgage note,** written evidence of a debt and the terms of its repayment

PMI—private mortgage insurance

point—one percent of a loan; same as **discount point**, a sum paid to increase a lender's yield

prepayment—payment of a loan in full or in part before the time required by the loan documents

principal—amount of a debt as of a given time

service fee—fee by the lender to cover costs, as opposed to discount points which increase its yield

term—period of time until a loan must be repaid to a lender or leased realty returned to a landlord

variable rate mortgage—adjustable rate mortgage